ASSESSING CULTURAL ANTHROPOLOGY

ASSESSING CULTURAL ANTHROPOLOGY

EDITED BY

Robert Borofsky

HAWAII PACIFIC UNIVERSITY

McGRAW-HILL, INC.

New York   St. Louis   San Francisco   Auckland   Bogotá   Caracas

Lisbon   London   Madrid   Mexico City   Milan   Montreal   New Delhi

San Juan   Singapore   Sydney   Tokyo   Toronto

7 8 9 0 AGM AGM 9 0 9 8 7

ISBN 0-07-006578-0

This book was set in Bembo by Pat McCarney.
The editors were Sylvia Shepard and Sylvia Warren;
the production supervisor was Denise L. Puryear.
The cover was designed by John Hite.
Arcata Graphics/Martinsburg was printer and binder.

Library of Congress Cataloging-in-Publication Data is available: LC Card #93-5323.

To Three Generations of Women:
to Ruth, to Nancy, and to Amelia and Robyn,
with Much Love

CONTENTS

SECTION THREE
Rethinking Past Perspectives 145

SECTION FOUR
Rethinking the Cultural 243

This volume had its origin in an all-day session organized for the 1989 American Anthropological Association's annual meeting entitled "Assessing Developments in Anthropology." With the encouragement of editors at McGraw-Hill and the book's reviewers, further contributors were added to provide a more international character to the volume and/or to cover topics not previously included. It has been impossible, practically speaking, to include everyone and every view that should be associated with a volume such as this. But it is reasonable to hope that others will be stimulated by what is written here and carry on the dialogue with those in the volume—filling in missing blanks, suggesting new possibilities.

Assessing Cultural Anthropology addresses a number of audiences. It is a book for upper-level undergraduate and graduate students. And it is a book for the profession as a whole. One of the volume's hopes is to bring this collectivity—anthropologists and anthropologists in the making—into a common dialogue regarding the discipline.

For those who find stimulus and vitality in the argument and counterargument of various positions—the push and pull of debate—the volume's papers offer much excitement. They sketch out a variety of provocative positions; they offer a range of thoughtful possibilities. As editor, I have tried to balance this diverse set of perspectives with statements, in the editorial material, regarding the shared heritage and concerns of the discipline. In the overlap and tension between these different ways of looking at the discipline—what I refer to as "centrifugal" and "centripetal" tendencies in the Introduction—one perceives the intellectual dynamics of anthropology as a field of study.

This volume does not depict anthropology's future. The future has not yet arrived, at least not for anthropology. But what I think *Assessing Cultural Anthropology* does well is to provide a *platform*, a foundation, upon which anthropologists and anthropologists in the making can together build this future. In a time of fragmentation, it presents intriguing overlaps that help clarify where we are intellectually. And it offers a basis for anthropologists, working with anthropologists in the making, to establish clearer lines of continuity among the discipline's past, present, and future. My hope is that those who read this volume will consider it with both care and daring. With care, because the future needs to be built on the present and past concerns of the discipline. But also with daring, because there is much potential in the volume's contributions. The book is meant to encourage innovation and change. If *Assessing Cultural Anthropology* stimulates further dialogue about the discipline's future, if it helps ignite new insights, new analyses, that draw us forward as a discipline, then it will have served its purpose well.

Conceptually, the book is divided into two parts: the contributions themselves (which are organized into six sections) and a set of editorial materials which place the contributions in context. A statement regarding an author's "intellectual roots" follows each chapter. These statements emphasize that anthropology is not being reinvented every generation. Despite the discipline's present fragmentation, real continuity exists from one generation of scholars to the next as teachers mentor students, as senior professors influence junior colleagues. One can see in the statements, moreover, a framing of key disciplinary issues. They provide a personal, close-up perspective on anthropology and its concerns.

ACKNOWLEDGMENTS

Many people assisted with *Assessing Cultural Anthropology*. Let me formally acknowledge them as a small token of my appreciation. I owe an important debt to the volume's contributors. It was through their help and support that this volume was completed. In their roles as representatives of the American Anthropological Association (or its affiliated units), I would like to express my thanks to the following 1989 program chairs who sponsored the A.A.A. session that led to this volume: Harriet Klein, Jim Peacock, and Dorothy Holland. At Hawaii Pacific University (and especially the Hawaii Loa campus, formerly Hawaii Loa College), the following provided important assistance: Marvin and Eda Anderson, Chatt Wright, Jim Hochberg, John Fleckles, Ruby Okano, Leslie Rodrigues, Janice Uyeda, Greg Molfino, Lynette Cruz, Kalani English, Andy St. Onge, Barbara Ideta, Melodee Deutsch, Beata Gierasinski-Iragui, and Jerry Feldman. Greg Molfino, in particular, through countless checkings and recheckings of material as well as numerous suggestions provided invaluable help. At McGraw-Hill, I would like to acknowledge the assistance of: Sylvia Shepard, Phil Butcher, Conrad Kottak, Sylvia Warren, Lori Pearson, Melissa Mashburn, and Yanett Pena. Sylvia Shepard and Conrad Kottak, in particular, provided much help. Sylvia offered many important editorial suggestions and insights; Conrad first suggested the idea of this volume.

More generally, I wish to thank a number of people who helped in a variety of ways: Fred and Ann Schildt, David Friedman, Iris Wiley, George and Jean Campbell, Mimi Fox, Rachel Davis-Green, Ted Green, Helena Morrison, Dave Hanlon, Abigail Lipson, Karen Peacock, Susan Murata, Jim Bauman, White/Eisenstein, Stan Bowers, and Jerry and Richie Borofsky. This project was begun while I was Fellow of the East-West Center's Institute of Communication and Culture, and I would like to particularly thank Mary Bitterman for her support. I also wish to thank for their assistance, while at the East-West Center: Victor Lee, Meg White, Geoff White, Vimal Dissanayake, David Wu, and Helen Palmore. The reviewers of this volume deserve an extra debt of gratitude for their unflagging assistance, insights, and suggestions: Don Brenneis, Elizabeth Colson, Virginia Dominguez, Janet Keller, Conrad Kottak, and Mary Jo Schneider. They, together with Sylvia Shepard, proved critical in the book's development.

The volume is dedicated to three generations of women who played important roles in my intellectual development: my mother, Ruth; my wife, Nancy; and my two daughters, Amelia and Robyn. To all those who assisted, but especially my mother, wife, and daughters, thank you.

ROBERT BOROFSKY
KAILUA, O'AHU
HAWAI'I

A PERSONAL NOTE
TO UNDERGRADUATES

Today numerous people voice opinions about the state of undergraduate education. To quote from L. Lewis (1992:44-46) in a recent review of *How College Affects Students*:

Many Americans have a keen interest in what, if anything, students learn in college. Parents and taxpayers want to know what they are getting for their money. Students want to know what they are getting for their time. Academic administrators and faculty are uncertain about what programmatic changes might work and how to make undergraduate education work better.

It might interest you to know, as an undergraduate, that one theme I hear often from many professional colleagues is that the intellectual standards of colleges seem to be declining. Not as much is being demanded of students as in the past, and today grade inflation is common.

The reasons for this decline in academic standards remain unclear. Some blame you, as students. A new generation, raised on television, it is said, is more interested in "sound bites" and superficial analyses than an in-depth reading of complex books. But attributing the problem mainly to students ignores a critical point, I believe. The composition of the undergraduate student body at American colleges and universities has significantly changed in recent decades. It now includes a far more diverse group of people in terms of backgrounds and ages. While encouraging the enrollment of these new students, colleges and their faculties have not always adapted their curriculum, learning-skills programs, and teaching styles to fit these students' needs and concerns. The result is that today students and faculty often come into classrooms not sharing important understandings regarding what needs to be learned and/or how one is to learn it.

Consequently, despite all the time, energy, and money you spend at college, you may not be developing important cognitive skills, may not be learning important intellectual material. The slippage of standards and lack of shared understandings regarding learning, in other words, directly affect you as a student—in terms of your personal development, future horizons, and job potential. Listen to what Ernest Boyer (1987:281), in the Carnegie Foundation report *College: The Undergraduate Experience in America*, recently observed:

After visiting dozens of colleges and speaking with hundreds of faculty members and students, we are forced to conclude that a dangerous parochialism pervades many higher learning institutions. While some students have a global perspective, the vast majority, although vaguely concerned, are inadequately informed about the interdependent world in which they live. They lack historical understanding and have little knowledge of significant social trends that will consequently shape their lives.

How are you going to succeed in life with such limited knowledge, especially in today's global economy? Business as usual, just getting by, will not do. With today's declining academic standards, a college education may now not, in and of itself, open doors of opportunity that were available in the past—especially if you have not learned to handle demanding intellectual challenges, especially if you have not learned to read and critically evaluate the complex materials that help widen your intellectual horizons.

RISING TO A CHALLENGE

Assessing Cultural Anthropology is not necessarily an easy book for undergraduates to read—especially if you expect everything to be stated simply. *Assessing Cultural Anthropology* is a book in which contributors struggle to conceptualize key issues in the field. This is not a book with all the answers formally laid out. It is a book where the answers are waiting to be discovered—by you and by others. Reading it, you can see anthropology in the making.

My sense is that many students like to be challenged in this way. Contrary to what some suggest, I find most undergraduates full of intellectual determination and curiosity. What some may lack, however, are the specific reading skills that allow them to successfully face up to certain academic challenges.

Let me state my point in a different way. To make *Assessing Cultural Anthropology* more accessible to undergraduates, some colleagues suggested I might include definitions at the end of each chapter. That way, I was told, students would be able to more easily follow the material. In exploring this possibility, I wondered what words needed defining. I asked someone else, more knowledgeable about the problem, to select a list of words. She started off enthusiastically highlighting a range of terms. But within hours, she gave up. It became clear to her, as it became clear to me, one could go on endlessly finding new words to define until the defined words outnumbered the undefined ones, until one had brought the undefined text down to an eighth-grade reading level. Better to give students the tools to read effectively and be able to discover meanings on their own, she suggested, than to bring the level of the book down.

Assessing Cultural Anthropology is written in the spirit that students should be challenged, that they should read critically and reflect deeply about certain ideas. But *Assessing Cultural Anthropology* is also written with the appreciation that some students may need to review certain skills to effectively rise up to this challenge. The following section outlines a strategy for successfully reading advanced books. Students in my classes learn how to use it, often with outstanding results. They have—in their minds—rather lengthy reading lists. But by the end of the semester, they often say they enjoyed the reading and indicate they found the material exciting and thought-provoking. Let me explain what they learned to do.

DECIDING ON A READING STRATEGY

Selecting an effective reading strategy, students in my classes learn, is perhaps the most critical decision they make in beginning a book. Different reading materials require different strategies. (One does not read newspaper advertisements, for example, the same way one reads Shakespeare.) Students often discover that an effective strategy depends not only on the book's subject matter but also on how they, as students, are to be tested on the reading material. That is to say, the students learn that to read effectively in a college course, they often need to know the course's testing procedures. Multiple choice exams require a different reading strategy than essay exams.

I have often seen students reading books with a yellow marker in hand. Every so often they underline a passage. I am at times surprised by the sureness with which some students do the underlining. I have wondered: How do these students know, the first time through, what are the chapter's main points? How do they distinguish between what is critical and what is tangential to the chapter's overall argument before they know what the argument is? The fact, I have come to realize, is that many students do not necessarily have to know the central ideas of a chapter to do well on multiple choice exams. They only have to know salient details of the chapter.

And these, often as not, are noted in bold print or some other obvious way.

Reading for essay exams requires a different strategy. It involves, students discover, focusing on broad themes. Details are important in relation to the chapter's overall thesis, but they are less important in and of themselves. Students learn that to do well on an essay exam, they need to know a chapter's argument and how it is constructed. They need to focus on, as one student phrased it, the forest (the chapter's argument) more than the individual trees (or separate pieces of data).

Students I talk to at both Hawaii Pacific University and elsewhere offer two reasons for using this latter strategy in reading texts. First, it usually makes reading a book more enjoyable. *Assessing Cultural Anthropology*, for example, is full of broad, provocative issues. Understanding them, reflecting on them, arguing about them, is an exciting process. Second, these students recognize that they will almost certainly be tested on a book such as *Assessing Cultural Anthropology* through an essay exam. They will not have to know out-of-context details. They will not be asked to specify the American Anthropological Association's membership in 1940, for example. But quite likely they will be asked to compare and/or contrast various positions. They will be asked to assess a particular perspective.

Let me describe the skills many students in my classes use to be active, thinking readers for essay-type exams. The students and I call the method "constructing meaning."

CONSTRUCTING MEANING

To do well on an essay exam, students need to do more than passively read words on a page. They need to think about what they are reading and, like a detective, actively put together various pieces of information to construct the author's perspective. Boiled down to its basics, "constructing meaning" involves the following.

Using the Introductory Material to Advantage. When students read a challenging book, they need to first familiarize themselves with the introductory material preceding a set of chapters. The students sometimes discover they do not recognize certain studies cited in an introduction. This is understandable since a book such as *Assessing Cultural Anthropology* tends to be written for more than one audience, for more than just undergraduates. Students learn to focus on the general points made in the Introduction, particularly as they relate to, particularly as they frame, the chapters that follow. The Introduction leaves certain questions in students' minds for them to explore in the chapters and which to judge the chapters by.

Using Chapter Headings and Subheadings to Gain an Overview. Prior to reading a chapter, I encourage students to skim through a chapter focusing on its headings and subheadings. This way they get an overview of what the chapter is about. Students, tell me they often find it helpful to turn the headings into questions so as to have an idea of what to look for in reading a section. The titles of the sections in *Assessing Cultural Anthropology* were written with this objective in mind. Thus, for example, using the heading "Centrifugal Tendencies" (from page 4 in the Introduction) students might ask: What are the centrifugal tendencies in anthropology? How did they develop? How many are there?

Reading by Paragraphs. One of the most effective ways to read chapters in a book such as *Assessing Cultural Anthropology* is to read "by paragraphs." This allows a person to concentrate on a chapter's main ideas rather than get lost in a host of supporting details. Reading by paragraphs involves focusing on the key sentence (or sentences) in a paragraph. A key sentence is one that adds to the flow of the discussion, that adds to the author's overall argument in the chapter. Students learn they can often recognize a key sentence by what it is *not*: It does not involve a parenthetical aside, a brief elaboration of an already developed point, or some secondary issue not directly related to the author's central theme. Reading a particular author, students gradually develop over time a feeling for where in a paragraph the key sentence or sentences generally are. They tend to be either the first, second, and/or last sentence in a paragraph. On first reading, students in my classes discover it is best to set details in a paragraph to one side—not to ignore them, but in order to grasp the central issues raised by the chapter as a whole. Later on, after they understand the chapter's overall argument, they have the option of carefully going back through each section noting subtle details in it. A student once suggested to me that reading for salient details first is often like putting the cart before the horse. It can be done. But it creates a lot of unnecessary problems.

Students learn that it helps if they move quickly from paragraph to paragraph, focusing primarily on the key sentence (or sentences) within each paragraph. When they reach the end of a section (signaled by a new heading), I encourage students to pause to see if they have grasped the main idea(s) of the section. Students in my classes discover through experience that, when they understand a section, it often helps to mark a few salient passages for later review. (This way they do not need to read the whole book again, page by page, prior to the exam.) If students feel they have not understood a section, they often briefly skim back through the section to see what was missed. (This again is usually a paragraph by paragraph process, not a word by word one.)

The focus on reading by paragraphs, the students discover, is not really to get through a chapter quickly. Rather, it is to facilitate *the separation of details from main themes*. Undergraduates in advanced anthropology classes at most colleges are tested on their comprehension and assessment of a book's themes. You can understand why, then, students in my classes focus first on comprehending an author's argument.

Students in my classes are often surprised to discover that reading slowly does not necessarily help comprehension in a book such as this. It may, in fact, decrease comprehension. The slower one reads, the more details one becomes mired in, the less likely one will see the chapter as a whole.

While focusing on a paragraph's key sentence (or sentences), students also come to realize that it is sometimes beneficial to read through a whole paragraph carefully. The first and last paragraphs of a section are often good candidates for such careful reading because they tend to introduce or summarize ideas in a section. Other paragraphs may also state central themes. How do students learn to recognize these types of paragraphs? Usually they find a particularly cogent statement near the beginning of the paragraph. As they skim through the rest of the paragraph, they come across another (or perhaps several) similarly significant statements. They discover that the rest of the paragraph involves a lot more than illustrative details. In such cases, they learn it is important to go back to the paragraph's beginning and read the whole paragraph through slowly and carefully.

Many students discover that reading for general ideas means they need not understand every word in a paragraph to grasp the paragraph's central theme. Many terms can be figured out in a general way from the context. Those that cannot, may be looked up in a dictionary. And some terms, because they relate to minor points, may be set aside during a first reading. (Only when students go back over a paragraph and explore its meaning word for word, is a precise definition for such terms necessary.) Generally students discover they do not need to precisely know, for example, such terms as "comprador" (on page 382 of Sahlins's contribution) during an initial reading. It is sufficient to recognize that it refers to some type of trading agent. Likewise, they do not get upset when they do not precisely understand what "evolués" (on page 378 of Sahlins's chapter) refers to. They can grasp the basic point of Sahlins's illustration without it.

Reconstructing the Author's Argument. Having finished a chapter, students in my classes find it helpful to review the chapter's headings and subheadings. Having read the chapter, they are ready to perceive the construction of the author's whole argument: (1) why the chapter moves in a certain direction; (2) what points are central (and tangential) to the chapter's main themes; and (3) why one point precedes another. Students find this is often a good time to go back over the chapter's details—seeing how they fit together, seeing how they relate to the main points. Knowing what the chapter's main themes are, they can now read the details without getting lost. They gain a sense of how the chapter fits together as a whole.

Assessing the Author's Argument. After students in my classes have *identified* the author's argument, they then *assess* the author's argument. Understanding what the author intends to say, they now decide to what degree the argument makes sense, to what degree it is supported by appropriate examples. Is the author's position convincingly developed? That is, does it leave students with unanswered questions? Can students suggest counterexamples, from other chapters, to the points made? Do the students think the author's argument helps clarify important issues (such as ones discussed in the sectional introduction)? Again, based on past experience, students in my classes often decide to write down a few notes or mark a number of critical passages in the text as they reflect on these questions. This facilitates review later on.

Instead of conceiving of reading as a passive process, students come to realize that reading is an active process, in which they construct and assess an author's argument.

A Three-Stage Process

Abigail Lipson (of the Harvard University Bureau of Study Council) and I, in a set of conversations, formulated a three stage process for improving students' competence with a "constructing meaning" reading strategy. We offer it as a suggestion to students reading this book. It has worked well as a learning process in my classes.

Stage One. The first stage involves filling out a work sheet, such as the following, while reading a chapter. Though there may be more (or less) than three themes, students in my classes find it often makes sense to start with this number until they get use to the work sheet's format. In this stage, the format acts as a *guide to reading*.

Theme One:
  supporting data 1:
  supporting data 2:

Theme Two:
  supporting data 1:
  supporting data 2:

Theme Three:
  supporting data 1:
  supporting data 2:

A Brief Summary of the Chapter's Overall Argument:

In the introductory chapter for instance, students might note the following themes: (1) defining the volume's subject matter (pages 1-4), (2) centrifugal tendencies (pages 4-12), and (3) centripetal tendencies (pages 12-19). And under the first theme—defining the volume's subject matter—they might include, as supporting data, material relating to problems in defining the discipline (pages 1-3) as well as material from the section entitled "Culture" (page 3), and/or the section entitled "Cultural Anthropology" (pages 3-4). The headings and subheadings act as guides to constructing the author's argument.

Stage Two. Stage two involves filling out a work sheet, such as the above, immediately *after* an initial reading of the chapter—when the student goes back over the headings and identifies the author's key ideas. Here the work sheet acts as a *review tool.* At this stage, students in my classes tend to be more flexible about the number of themes. Though there may be three, there may also be four, or perhaps only one major theme. (Looking at major headings in a chapter tends to provide a clue as to the number of themes.)

Stage Three. Stage three involves incorporating the above format into a student's own reading and note-taking strategies. At this stage, the approach becomes a *way of thinking* about a chapter. Students personalize the above form to meet their individual needs, elaborating on it as they see fit.

Generally, students in my classes read two or three chapters at stage one and then, when they feel comfortable, move on to stage two. Likewise, after gaining some experience with stage two, they then move on to stage three. They progress to a new stage, in other words, when they feel ready. Tentatively though, I encourage most students to try to be at stage three by the middle of a book. Precisely at what point, by what chapter, is up to the individual student as she or he learns to become a more active, critical reader. But the following generally seems to be true: *The more a student focuses on "constructing meaning" as a reading strategy, the better, more active reader the student becomes, the better the student does on essay-type exams, and the more fun the student has in reading challenging books.*

RESOURCE MATERIALS

In the process of reading books such as this, students in my classes often refer to other texts—either because they need explication of a concept, or because they want to pursue a particular question further. I would suggest three additional references for *Assessing Cultural Anthropology.* Though published in 1968 (a biographical supplement was added in 1979), the *International Encyclopedia of the Social Sciences* remains a treasure trove of information. Some of the leading anthropologists of the past three decades wrote insightful, summarizing analyses of key anthropological issues in it. For briefer descriptions, Adam and Jessica Kuper's (1985) *The Social Science Encyclopedia* is excellent, including discussions of *hermeneutics, Hegel,* and *Habermas.* And finally, a student's introductory anthropology textbook often proves helpful. If you do not have one, excellent textbooks have been written by contributors to this volume: M. Harris, R. Keesing, and C. Kottak.

There is often today what Joseph Dionne (1992:5-6) terms a "rent-a-book" mentality: students come "to regard the textbook less as a lifelong reference and more as a temporary guide to the course that . . . [should] be abandoned as soon as finals are over." Students discover they usually need to keep their introductory texts if they are to pursue advanced courses in anthropology. The texts often prove invaluable reference guides. Keeping books also builds a library—it builds a resource collection students can refer to throughout college and, more importantly, throughout life.

A NOTE
TO INTERESTED TEACHERS

My experience at Hawaii Pacific University suggests that students are often quite willing to utilize a "constructing meaning" reading strategy. But what they ask of me in return is to be tested on the reading material through broad, conceptual-type essay exams. What will make them more effective readers, they suggest to me, is *not* a lot of instruction in how to read effectively. They can learn this mostly on their own. What will make them more effective readers is *a sense of trust* that they can improve their chances of success in courses by using this "constructing meaning" strategy, that trying it will not work to their detriment (as it surely will if they are tested with a multiple-choice exam after using it).

Students want to know how they will be tested. I have found that students appreciate a class period—at the beginning of the semester—dedicated to discussing the types of questions they will be asked on exams and how best to prepare for them while doing the reading. Reading a book then becomes less a matter of guessing what a teacher wants, less a matter of reaching beyond a student's personal background to pick up subtle clues from the teacher—that can be missed because of cultural, class, and/or age differences with the instructor. The session allows students to know exactly what to look for when they begin reading a book.

A FINAL NOTE TO STUDENTS AND TEACHERS TOGETHER

In *Assessing Cultural Anthropology*, we can see a discipline working its way into the future, a field in process. It is a challenging, exciting book. In the present educational climate, however, some wonder whether books such as this are above the reading level of undergraduates. It makes little sense, I have suggested, to simplify texts to a point where they are no longer challenging to you as college students. It does not train you intellectually; it does not prepare you for successfully coping with the complexities of modern life. To grow intellectually in college, you need challenges that *challenge* you.

The question we need ponder—students and teachers together—is: How can we raise the standards of undergraduate education while, at the same time, ensuring that students have the tools to succeed? All our futures—as students, as teachers, as citizens in a democracy—will be shaped by the answer we find to this question.

ROBERT BOROFSKY

ASSESSING CULTURAL ANTHROPOLOGY

Introduction

Anthropology, as an intellectual discipline, is not easily described. What comes across clearest in the literature is anthropology's diversity. It includes a breadth of subjects; its practitioners espouse a host of views. The anthropologist Clifford Geertz (1985:623) recently observed, "One of the advantages of anthropology as a scholarly enterprise is that no one, including its practitioners, quite knows exactly what it is."

People who watch baboons copulate, people who rewrite myths in algebraic formulas, people who dig up Pleistocene skeletons, people who work out decimal point correlations between toilet training practices and theories of disease, people who decode Maya hieroglyphics, and people who classify kinship systems into typologies in which our own comes out as "Eskimo," all call themselves anthropologists.

An important result of this breadth, he continues, "is a permanent identity crisis." Wolf (1980:20) phrases it more positively: "The result of anthropology's eclecticism is that the field continues to astound by its diverse and colorful activity."

Examining introductory American textbooks on the subject—as a way of trying to simplify the subtle and complex (and thereby get a handle on the problem)—only partially helps. Different authors offer somewhat different definitions of the field. Harris (1991:1) states: "Anthropology is the study of humankind—ancient and modern people and their ways of living." He divides the discipline into four major branches: cultural anthropology, archaeology, physical (or biological) anthropology, and linguistics. Ember and Ember (1985:484) define anthropology as "the study of differences and similarities, both biological and cultural, in human populations." They divide anthropology (as does Haviland 1990: 11) into two branches, physical and cultural (which in turn is divided into archaeology, linguistics, and ethnology). Kottak (1991:7) follows Harris, his one-time teacher, in dividing the field into four branches, but then raises the possibility that anthropology also includes a fifth branch, applied anthropology. These divisions contrast with those in Europe. In Sweden, for example, a distinction is made between anthropology which tends to study foreign, overseas cultures (such as in Africa) and ethnology which is focused on European cultures (and traditionally has been oriented toward peasant communities). And while, as Bloch (page 276) notes, the distinction today between British social anthropology and American cultural anthropology "is not absolute," the two branches of the field have traditionally had somewhat different emphases, the former focusing on "social structure," the latter on "cultural patterns" (cf. Herskovits 1965). In India and Japan, the situation appears different again (see Tax, Eiseley, Rouse, and Voegelin 1953:219-223). Little wonder then that many textbooks on anthropology shy away from a clear, straightforward definition of the field. The authors prefer to devote a whole chapter to clarifying what anthropology is.

Given the current concern for anthropology's unity (see e.g. Givens and Skomal 1992), it is important to note that several distinguished anthropologists perceive anthropology's unity more in terms of its historical development than in terms of a precise intellectual mission. Boas, one of the key founders of American anthropology, observed in 1908: "It will be recognized that . . . the field of work of the anthropologist is more or less accidental, and originated because other sciences occupied part of the ground before the development of modern anthropology" (1908:9). "How did anthropology come into being?" Lévi-Strauss (in Tax, Eiseley, Rouse, and Voegelin 1953:349) asks. "It made itself out of all kinds of refuse and left-overs from other fields."

Still the discipline possesses a sense of coherence—if one looks under the profusion of forms that crowd the surface. Anthropology deals with human variation through time and space in relation to what humans share as a species. Or, phrased another way, anthropology studies the cultural and physical variations that exist in human communities—both through time and throughout the modern world—and the reasons for them.

Tax (1956:317) maintains, rightly I believe, that a key tie binding anthropologists together is their desire to communicate with one another. As we see below, anthropology involves a community of scholars sharing overlapping concerns (cf. Wrong 1993).

Anthropologists, for example, share a long-time interest in process. Boas (1938:4) defined three great problems for the discipline in his 1938 textbook *General Anthropology*: "(1) the reconstruction of human history; (2) the determination of types of historical phenomena and their sequences; [and] (3) the dynamics of change." One might dispute whether all anthropologists today are interested in all three topics. But most anthropologists are concerned with at least one of them. The discipline, in a way, grew out of a concern with process, out of an interest in human and cultural evolution. Early anthropologists—such as Morgan, Tylor, and Frazer—sought to link known human cultures in a temporal scheme of progression reaching from the simplest and earliest to the most recent and complex. (In their ethnocentrism, however, they confidently placed themselves at the top while those different from them were lower on the scale.) Today, many anthropologists see historical and evolutionary processes as key to understanding present-day cultural and biological patterns.

If we explore further, we see another aspect of disciplinary unity. Anthropology's present fragmenting tendencies are part of an ongoing tradition within the discipline. Tax (1956:316) asserts anthropology has had these fragmenting tendencies since its development as a formal discipline in the nineteenth century. Barth concurs: Anthropology, he (1992:63) states, has been "always indignantly and confusingly divided." In the late 1940s American anthropology almost broke apart, in fact, because of these fragmenting tendencies (in what was phrased as a "reorganization"). But it did not, Stocking (1976:41-42) suggests, for a simple reason—power. Given that anthropology was (and still is) the smallest of the social sciences and has relatively high research costs, it made little sense for anthropologists to fragment themselves into even smaller groups. The field's limited effectiveness in gaining public recognition and financial support might well be reduced still further. (Salzman touches on this point in his chapter.)

Anthropology's wholeness as an intellectual discipline—in combining the four subfields of cultural, physical, archaeological, and linguistic anthropology—comes out clearest today when it deals with problems overlapping with those that also concerned earlier anthropologists, such as problems of biology and culture (that Levy discusses in his chapter) or problems of inferred history. When one explores how long the Philippine Tasaday have been a cultural isolate or the degree to which modern South African San Bushman culture has been shaped by European influences, the subfields of anthropology overlap nicely with one another, all providing meaningful clues to an answer. The problem is that anthropologists today not only ask such traditional questions, they also now ask a host of new ones too—hence the problem of disciplinary fragmentation.

Culture

Before turning to cultural anthropology, I should briefly discuss the term *culture*. It too needs explication. And it too seems difficult to define. Using introductory textbooks—in hope of finding a simple, direct statement regarding culture—only helps if one limits one's explorations to a single textbook. Kottak (1991:17) defines culture as "distinctly human; transmitted through learning; traditions and customs that govern behavior and beliefs." Bohannan (1992:22) defines it as "the capacity to use tools and symbols." Keesing (1981:509) states culture is "the system of knowledge more or less shared by members of a society." (His father, also a famous anthropologist, defined culture as "the totality of learned, socially transmitted behavior, or custom," F. Keesing 1958:16.)

If one explores deeper—seeing how professional anthropologists define the term for their peers—one discovers, if anything, more diversity. The standard work on the topic is a book by Kroeber and Kluckhohn (1963) entitled *Culture: A Critical Review of Concepts and Definitions*. In their examination of over 150 definitions of culture, Kroeber and Kluckhohn discuss a host of differing ways for conceptualizing the term. The definition they themselves finally adopt is:

Culture consists of patterns, explicit and implicit, of and for behavior acquired and transmitted by symbols, constituting the distinctive achievement of human groups, including their embodiments in artifacts; the essential core of culture consists of traditional . . . ideas and especially their attached values; culture systems may, on the one hand, be
considered as products of action, on the other as conditioning elements of further action. (1963:357)

The distinguishing trait of this definition, for modern anthropologists, is that few cite it today. It has gone out of fashion. It seems too broad (and hence, perhaps too unwieldy) to develop effective research questions around. Definitions of the type Kottak and Keesing present above currently pervade the field.

Cultural Anthropology

Cultural anthropology is a major subfield of anthropology. As readers might suspect, it too has been defined in various ways. But there is nonetheless significant overlap among the various definitions—if we set aside the subfields of archaeology and linguistics for the moment and focus on the general overall sense of the field today. A. Kuper in Kuper and Kuper (1985:177) provides a good definition when he states, "Cultural anthropology is used mainly in the United States to define the branch of anthropology which is concerned with man [i.e. humans] as . . . social being[s], and with learned rather than genetically-transmitted forms of behavior." Mandelbaum (1968:313) asserts "the central task of cultural anthropology . . . is to study the similarities and differences in behavior among human groups, to depict the character of various cultures and the processes of stability, change, and development that are characteristic to them." If one includes that cultural anthropology involves not only description and analysis but has traditionally framed many of its analyses in comparative terms, the definitions provided by Harris (1991:2), Kottak (1991:7), Keesing (1981:2), Haviland (1990:8), Ember and Ember (1985:485), and Bates and Plog (1990: 466) in their textbooks all fit reasonably within these parameters.

Cultural anthropology displays many of the same tendencies as the larger discipline of anthropology itself. Cultural anthropology possesses both centrifugal (or divisive, fragmenting) tendencies and centripetal (or consolidating, unifying) ones. Since cultural anthropology is the focus of this book, I will elaborate on these two tendencies in detail as a way of introducing readers to the field. Please note that I follow a common practice in the field, using anthropology to refer to cultural anthropology as well as general anthropology. While the usage is somewhat inappropriate—it conveys a sense of intellectual imperialism by equating a subfield with the general field itself—the usage does make for less complicated phrasing in a book which is primarily dedicated to cultural anthropology.

CENTRIFUGAL TENDENCIES

It is not hard to find statements regarding cultural anthropology's fragmenting tendencies. In a recent review of the field, Ortner (1984:126) observes: "The field appears to be a thing of shreds and patches, of individuals and small coteries pursuing disjunctive investigations and talking mainly to themselves." The process has been going on for some time. In the early 1950s, the British anthropologist Nadel (in Tax, Eiseley, Rouse, and Voegelin 1953:90) suggested: "Social-structure studies by Evans-Pritchard or Fortes, Firth's *Malay Fishermen*, and Mead's *Balinese Character* simply do not belong to the same universe of discourse." What are the reasons for this fragmentation?

Two Perspectives

"There are in the field at the present time," Leaf (1979:3) observes, "quite different ways of thinking about theory, about culture, and about cultural comparison." One sees this in various chapters of this book. Rappaport (page 154), for example, refers to the fact that:

Two traditions have proceeded in anthropology since its inception. One, objective in its aspirations and inspired by the biological sciences, seeks explanation and is concerned to discover causes, or even, in the view of the ambitious, laws. The other, influenced by philosophy, linguistics, and the humanities, and open to more subjectively derived knowledge, attempts interpretation and seeks to elucidate meanings.

Kuper (page 113) refers to two well-established research projects in American anthropology:

The first, effectively launched by Boas, takes as its subject culture, particularly cultural variation. It favors an insider's account of cultural experience. It asks questions about the experience of cultural differences, about the ways in which language and custom infuse actions with meaning and purpose, about the weight of tradition. It is relativistic, concerned with description and interpretation rather than with explanation, and with the particular rather than with the general. . . .

The second program has always provided the main antagonist to the Boasian program. Its central concern is human evolution, its hero is Darwin. It emphasizes material factors in the evolutionary process. . . . It seeks general principles and models itself on the natural sciences rather than on the humanities, which is where the Boasians normally find their allies.

Murphy discusses these two perspectives as well. And there are references to one or both of them in articles by Barth, Bernard, DaMatta, Das, Geertz, Harris, Keesing, Kuper, Marcus, Nader, Salzman, Scheper-Hughes, Tambiah, Tishkov, and Vayda.

Considerable controversy—or, to phrase it more positively, ambiguity—exists as to the role one versus the other of these perspectives should play in the discipline. Wolf (1964:88), in what has become a famous quotation, describes anthropology as "the most scientific of the humanities, the most humanist of the sciences" (cf. Goodenough 1989). And Lévi-Strauss (1966a:118), with a touch of poetry, suggests that anthropology nourishes "a secret dream: it belongs to the human sciences, as its name [*anthropo-* (human) and *-logy-* (study of)] adequately proclaims; but while it resigns itself to making its purgatory beside the social sciences, it surely does not despair of awakening among the natural sciences at the hour of the last judgement."

Readers should realize that a wide chasm exists between the "science" of Harris and the "interpretation" of Geertz. There are deep differences that do not lead to ready resolution. Service (1985:286) comments:

The controversies seem to come down to mutual incomprehension because of divergent aims and interests. Often . . . controversy is . . . a matter of different questions being asked, which itself results in a lack of any confrontation whatsoever between important [anthropologists]. Not only do they sometimes talk right past one another, often they are not talking toward one another at all.

The Slipping Away of a Reported Intellectual Consensus

Listening to anthropology's elders, one at times hears of an earlier disciplinary consensus. Colson (1985:178-179) observes:

We once had consensus about issues and methodology and about how we should write for our publics. . . . As of about 1930 . . . American ethnology was defined by a common set of problems, and a common methodology. It also had a growing audience of ethnologists trained in the same fashion who were able to identify with and quarrel about the same issues.

Wolf (1980:20) asserts: "An earlier anthropology had achieved unity under the aegis of the culture concept. . . . It unified the discipline around a concern with basic questions about the nature of the human species, its biological and socially learned variability, and the proper ways to assess the similarities and differences." But, he notes, "the past quarter-century has undermined this intellectual sense

of security. The relatively inchoate concept of 'culture' . . . [has been] attacked from several theoretical directions." Fitting with the discipline's diversity, different people place the break up of this conceptual consensus at different times. Colson suggests the breakup occurred in the 1930s, Leaf (1979:1) in the 1950s, Yengoyan (1986:368) in the early 1960s, and Murphy (1976:19) in the late 1960s and early 1970s. But there is no mistaking that today the cultural concept, and perhaps even the discipline's traditional methods for doing ethnography, are less able to act as broad, intellectual umbrellas under which anthropologists can unite.

One sees this in several chapters. Moore (page 369), for example, raises questions about "the usefulness of the classical idea of 'a culture.'" Vayda (pages 324-325) criticizes the "essentialist" notions implied by the concept. Nader (page 93) suggests breaking with "frameworks that are no longer yielding fruitful modes of thinking." Marcus criticizes the "realist discourse" of earlier ethnographic writers. And Bernard refers to the increasing separation between quantitative and qualitative methodologies. Something seems to be slipping away, though a close reading of earlier texts—e.g. Barnett (1940:21)—cautions against overdramatizing the intellectual coherence of earlier eras (see also Barth 1992:63 in this regard). Still, in contrast to times past, there is, to quote Marcus and Fischer (1986: 16), an "absence of paradigmatic authority" in the field today. Or to borrow a phrase from Strathern (page 213), there are pluralized visions of how the field fits together.

What will replace this bygone consensus is one of the central questions now facing anthropology. In many ways, that is what this book is about. Can some of anthropology's most distinguished scholars, in their overlapping assessments of and visions for the discipline, build a new order? It is a question readers should bear in mind throughout the book. Most of the volume's contributors—directly or indirectly—touch on this issue. At stake is the future of the discipline: How will it be shaped, who will shape it?

We will return to this topic in the book's final chapter after readers have had a chance to examine the various contributions. For now, in this introduction, I would like to turn to how this seeming paradigmatic lapse came about. What caused it? I consider three factors: (1) the expansion of anthropology beyond its early "heroic mentors," (2) changes in the world context within which anthropology developed, and (3) dynamics within the discipline itself. Other factors played a role as well, as a reading of Wolf (1969:252) indicates. But these three were central.

Beyond the Heroic Mentors

For our general purposes, we might divide anthropology's development into three periods: (1) formative, (2) heroic mentors, and (3) expansion. (Readers interested in more specific details of what happened when should refer to historical accounts of the discipline's development such as Harris 1968, Hatch 1973, Lowie 1937, Kuper 1983, Bohannan and Glazer 1988, Stocking 1968, and Voget 1975.)

The formative period begins with the founding of the discipline in the nineteenth century and might be said to end during the first decades of the twentieth century. Anthropological societies were formed, initial studies published, a small number of university appointments made. Men such as Morgan, Tylor, and Frazer postulated broad schemes of progression in which the primitive "rest" evolved into the modern West.

Anthropology's heroic mentors—Boas, Malinowski, Radcliffe-Brown, and Durkheim—were the modern founders of the discipline. Other anthropologists, before them, worked in university settings. But each of these scholars set up, during the early part of the twentieth century, their own "schools" with the financial resources and students to have a significant influence on the discipline at large. Thus their power was felt not only

through their ideas, but through their students. Stocking (1976:7), citing Kroeber, terms Boas "a true patriarch" and suggests the "Boasians"—Boas and his students—assumed the dynamics of a "large late-Victorian family." The dynamics (and ambiguities) of Boas's perspective were expressed in his students' work. Stocking (1976:8) notes:

In Boas, all four genes [i.e. scientific generalization, historical understanding, rigorous induction, and the "loving penetration of whole phenomena"] were present, although the first and the last were clearly recessive. In his students, these traits were variously manifest. The most characteristically Boasian tended to be heterozygous, either at the theoretical level (Goldenweiser), or the methodological (Spier), or both (Herskovits). Some, however, (Kroeber) went through phases in which now one, now another genetic tendency was clearly manifest.

When one looks back on this period—at the first two decades in the United States and France (for Boas and Durkheim) and the 1920s and 1930s in Britain (for Malinowski and Radcliffe-Brown)—it is critical to remember how few people were actually involved in anthropology. Firth (1975:2) states "in comparison with today, the relevant literature was very limited and the scholars involved very few." The American Anthropological Association had 306 members in 1910, 666 in 1930. "Some elders of our tribe," Stocking (1976:1) notes, "can recall an age when most anthropologists knew each other personally, and [conferences] could be held . . . in one meeting hall of modest size."

As students of a mentor passed on their knowledge to their students—Steward, for example, was a student of Kroeber who had been a student of Boas—there was an understandable diversifying of interests. Part of anthropology's present breadth, I would suggest, stems from the normal expansion of the discipline beyond its heroic mentors. This gradual process has been amplified by a major expansion of the discipline since the 1940s. Membership in the American Anthropological

Association expanded, for example, from 1,101 in 1940 to 2,260 in 1950 to 6,420 in 1970. Today it numbers approximately 10,500. The number of graduate programs and graduate students has similarly increased. Along with this expansion has come increased specialization as anthropologists seek to refine the broad formulations of earlier scholars and differentiate themselves professionally from one another. The division of anthropology into various anthropologies—medical anthropology, economic anthropology, legal anthropology, political anthropology, psychological anthropology, etc.—is part of this trend.

Some of the slipping away of a seeming intellectual consensus, then, is the result of anthropology's success as a discipline. It has expanded beyond its original heroic mentors into a much broader-based, numerically larger concern. The nostalgia that surrounds talk of earlier, more consensual times leaves out an important fact. It was easier for anthropologists to share a conceptual framework when there were only a handful of people actively involved in the discipline—people who, in all likelihood, knew each other personally and might well have been in graduate school together or at least shared some of the same teachers. Today that is much less likely to occur, given the discipline's size and number of graduate programs.

Changes in the World Context

This brings us to a second reason for anthropology's current diversity. It is not only anthropology that has changed, so has the world anthropology grew up in. The changes have called into question old conceptions without making clear what will replace them.

"It is an historical fact," Lévi-Strauss (page 425) observes, "that anthropology was born and developed in the shadow of colonialism." Decolonization has raised new, and difficult, questions for the discipline. As Godelier notes, anthropologists are being excluded from locales because of anthropology's imperialistic associations. Its concern with the less-developed, marginal groups has been taken, by some, as a morbid interest in backwardness, in the "primitive"—an image newly independent countries are often eager to shed. Prins (in Kuper and Kuper 1985:870) tells us "the image made in Accra to commemorate the achievement of political independence by Ghana shows the fleeing agents of colonialism. Along with the [administrative] District Officer is the anthropologist, clutching under his arm a copy of Fortes and Evans-Pritchard's *African Political Systems* (1940)."

It has become clear, through the works of writers such as Asad (1973) and Said (1978), that the colonial context shaped anthropological accounts in subtle ways. We now realize, Godelier (page 99) points out, that earlier "ethnographic investigation . . . [proceeded] against a backdrop of relations between observer and observed of domination, of social inequalities, and of power." Anthropological images of stability, of cultural isolation—based on functionalist perspectives and certain images of the "primitive"—downplayed the destructive nature of Western control and seemingly justified it. Wolf, Marcus, and Nader also mention this point.

The matter is complicated, however. "To the extent that [anthropologists] were trying to show coherence and order," Moore (page 374) observes in a footnote, they "had a conscious political agenda which was the opposite of that which later critics alleged was their unconscious objective. They thought they were showing how logical native peoples were" by demonstrating the systematic, functionally integrated nature of their cultures.

If good intentions are not enough to fend off subsequent criticism, what will future anthropologists suggest about our present ambiguous social activism? Barth (page 350) notes that anthropology "has had pitifully little to say . . . [about the] untranscendable poverty as it affects increasing hundreds of millions of people in all major cities of the world." And Keesing (page 307) observes, "what remains unsaid in much of current anthropological writing speaks deafeningly, if we only step back to listen."

An interesting irony exists today which should give anthropologists pause for reflection. Anthropology's unsavory association with colonialism, Lévi-Strauss points out, has not stopped people from turning to anthropological texts to reconstruct their cultural pasts—pasts filled with notions of homogeneity and stability that anthropologists now reject as too simplified. Just when anthropology's traditional conception of culture is being questioned within the discipline, Third World leaders seem to be appropriating it for their own political ends. "Our own conceptual diseases," Keesing (page 307) states, are being "deployed against us." "Culture," Sahlins (page 378) observes, "is on everyone's lips."

Who is using what cultural knowledge for which ends is now not only an intriguing intellectual question, it is also a politically explosive one. Anthropologists have yet to come to terms with this politics of knowledge and their role in a decolonized world.

The other important set of events anthropology has had to cope with, besides decolonization, is the tremendous economic and technological changes that have occurred throughout the world in recent decades. Before the Second World War, if anthropologists tried hard to ignore a host of variables, they might still believe small groups—far from the centers of European power—were bounded cultural isolates, free (or relatively free) from outside influence. One simply cannot believe that any more. "Any methodology that tries to extract the purely local from the wider system will miss much of what is going on and much that concerns the people being studied" Kottak and Colson stress (page 401). "Local concerns," they (page 400) note, "depend on engagement with wider systems." The realities of the modern world have caught up with anthropology.

This realization has affected anthropology in a number of ways. It has called into question basic assumptions about the nature of culture. As Wolf (1982:387) points out in *Europe and the People without History*, "once we locate the reality of society in historically changing, imperfectly bounded, multiple and branching social alignments . . . the concept of a fixed, unitary, and bounded culture must give way to a sense of fluidity and permeability of cultural sets." It has raised the question of linkages (in Kottak and Colson's phrasing)—how "local" sites are tied to broader forces and structures. Moore discusses three perspectives in this regard: the cultural, the political, and the economic. These three versions of how linkages take place, she (pages 373-374) asserts, "all have shortcomings. One major task for anthropology is to achieve a plausible combination of these perspectives." There is also the problem of what Sahlins (page 390) calls "the indigenization of modernity," of how larger forces are conceptualized and handled in a "local" setting. "The historic effects of capitalism," he (page 382) warns, are "not directly proportional to its material force, a simple matter of physics." They are reshaped by local conceptualizations, local cultural dynamics. The distinction between "us" and "them" has become rather ambiguous in today's world of intertwined economies and high-speed communications. The two categories almost seem to merge at times and yet remain teasingly different. The fact that so many contributors—DaMatta, Das, Geertz, Godelier, Keesing, Lévi-Strauss, Marcus, Moore, Nader, Sahlins, Strathern, Tambiah, and Wolf to name some of the more obvious cases—touch on this topic indicates how important and problematic it is.

Dynamics within the Discipline Itself

Other factors, relating to current dynamics within anthropology, also encourage the field's fragmentation.

Improvements in the Ethnographic Data Base. It might seem strange that anthropology's ever-increasing data base—which continues to improve in both quality and breadth of ethnographic coverage—could lead to doubts within the discipline. But it has. Anthropologists now have enough solid ethnographic data that they can see problems with earlier conceptualizations, with earlier approaches. Many of the volume's chapters touch on this point—those by: Barth, Bernard, Bloch, Borofsky, DaMatta, Das, Godelier, Goodenough, Goody, Harris, Keesing, Kottak and Colson, Kuper, Lévi-Strauss, Levy, Marcus, Moore, Nader, Sahlins, Salzman, Strathern, Strauss and Quinn, Vayda, Wolf, and Yanagisako and Collier.

It is now clearer than ever, for example, that cultures are not homogeneous, stable units—tending to be in equilibrium, tending to endure in the same form through time, and/or tending to involve people with mostly shared understandings. Colson (1984:7), cited by Vayda (page 322), makes this point well: "Values once thought to be fundamental for guiding the way particular people dealt with each other and their environment have turned out to be situational and time linked, rather than eternal verities that can be used to predict behavior over time, under all circumstances." Goody (page 253) asks: in what sense is "the culture of contemporary New England . . . the same as that of the beginning of the nineteenth century, [or] of the early period dominated by the Puritans, [or] of Stuart England which [the Puritans] had left?" The extensive data we have for these periods make clear how weak some of the assumptions about cultural stability are. In an attempt to rethink cultural patterns and processes, we are led into asking such questions as: (1) How do people of diverse understandings communicate effectively with one another (see e.g. Goodenough)? (2) What cultural elements tend to cohere through time (see e.g. Vayda and Borofsky) and in what ways (see e.g. Strathern)? (3) How is stability maintained in the face of change and change in the face of stability (see e.g. Sahlins and Yanagisako and Collier)?

The increasing wealth of ethnographic data also helps explain the field's increasing specialization. Given that the broad cultural outlines of many groups are now known, anthropologists today often emphasize narrower, more focused concerns. Kuper comments on this in his chapter—how anthropologists have gone from studying tribal wholes such as the Tswana to specific topics such as borehole drilling syndicates. We might note the relation of one detailed study to another is not always obvious. This understandably adds to the sense of fragmentation within the discipline.

Nor is ethnographic authority what it once was. "The credibility of our field reports" can no longer rest "on their uniqueness, that is, on the absence of any other reports," Salzman (page 35) notes (see also Geertz 1983:36). They are far more subject to challenge—as more researchers work in overlapping locales and as more indigenous peoples read and question what is written about themselves. Das raises this latter point effectively in her discussion of Dumont's work on Indian caste. DaMatta, page 124, considers it in his reference to "DeVoto's law," which states "the more anthropologists write about the United States, the less I believe what they say about Samoa."

The differing perspectives of Redfield and Lewis on the Mexican town of Tepoztlan or Mead and Freeman on Samoa make us question the objectivity and accuracy of various anthropological reports. This questioning often leads into the postmodernist concern with how anthropologists establish ethnographic authority and authenticity through certain literary devices. Reflexivity, "working into ethnographic texts a self-conscious account . . . [of] the conditions of knowledge production" (Marcus, page 45), has become increasingly important in ethnographic writing—replacing, in Marcus's (page 45) words "the observational objective 'eye' of the ethnographer with his or her personal . . . 'I.'"

As a result of these trends, anthropologists speak with much less confidence, much less certainty, than in the past. Their common set of understandings—regarding not only our conceptions of culture but also the methods used in studying it—seems more open to question.

The Discipline's Interdisciplinary Orientation. "Clyde Kluckhohn, as fondly remembered by Clifford Geertz," Salzman (page 29, see Geertz 1983:21) notes, "liked to say that a degree in anthropology is a license for poaching." Anthropologists today draw on a range of disciplines. Of Kuper's three anthropological programs, he (page 114) tells us, one is at home in the humanities, a second in the natural sciences, and a third in the social sciences. An examination of scholars cited by authors in this volume conveys a sense of the discipline's breadth. There are references to: the social historian Foucault (Borofsky, DaMatta, Geertz, Harris, Keesing, Moore, Murphy, Scheper-Hughes, Tishkov, and Wolf), the sociologist Weber (Barth, Borofsky, Godelier, Kuper, and Strauss and Quinn), the philosopher Wittgenstein (Geertz, Scheper-Hughes, Strauss and Quinn, and Vayda), the literary critic Derrida (Harris, and Keesing), the sociologist Bourdieu (Borofsky, Keesing, Kuper, Moore, Scheper-Hughes, Strauss and Quinn, Tambiah, and Yanagisako and Collier), the political economist Marx (Barth, Borofsky, DaMatta, Geertz, Godelier, Harris, Keesing, Kuper, Marcus, Murphy, Rappaport, Sahlins, Scheper-Hughes, Tishkov, Vayda, and Wolf), the literary critic Bakhtin (DaMatta, Sahlins, Scheper-Hughes, and Strauss and Quinn), the political economist Wallerstein (Kottak and Colson, Nader, and Tambiah), and the Italian activist/intellectual Gramsci (Keesing, Nader, and Scheper-Hughes).

This interdisciplinary orientation has been with anthropology for some time now. Boas (1904:523), almost a century ago, admitted that certain "knowledge is required [in the discipline] which cannot be supplied by general anthropology" itself. As Fortes (1953:1) observed, the founders of anthropology at Cambridge University "insistently taught [that] anthropological studies cannot flourish in isolation . . . advances in anthropological knowledge are inseparable from advances in related human sciences." And Tax (1956:315), in his summary of traits anthropologists share, commented that "one of the valued characteristics has always been the freedom and obligation to draw upon knowledge from any source that might be relevant to problems of anthropology."

Wolf (1964:6) adds another side to this tendency: "American anthropology owes the greater part of its theoretical armament to importations from across the Atlantic. . . . One may note wryly that, for a long period of time, Lewis H. Morgan, the major American theorist, was a prophet everywhere but in his own country." Of the six contributors citing Morgan in the volume—DaMatta, Godelier, Kuper, Marcus, Wolf, and Yanagisako and Collier—only the French anthropologist Godelier goes into any depth about Morgan's work and only he conveys a sincere appreciation for it. Bloch refers to this same pattern—of looking to outsiders for inspiration—but in reverse. He (page 350) suggests European anthropologists need to pay closer attention to the work of American cognitive scientists and cognitive anthropologists.

The tendency for American anthropologists to import ideas from across the Atlantic has, if anything, become stronger over the past decade as they turned to European (and especially French) intellectual life for new inspiration. Geertz (1991:611) notes, in a recent interview, that in earlier days "anthropologists [generally tended to] read people who were anthropologists"—"like Boas and Kroeber and Lowie." "The notion that you should read philosophers, that Wittgenstein had anything to say that anthropologists might be interested in, would be way off base." Today, in contrast, he suggests, it is "now . . . wide open . . . it's almost the opposite . . . that's what happened in the 1980s." This openness has led to innovative intellectual developments. But, he observes, it also "has led to a certain instability" in the discipline.

The point is that with anthropologists continually drawing from authorities outside their discipline, it is little wonder the field is somewhat fragmented. It is being pulled in different directions by different practitioners.

Anthropology's Nonconforming Style. Some professional anthropologists may find Salzman's (page 29ff.) discussion of anthropology as the "land of the free" overstated. But readers should realize that he is not alone in such an assertion—other scholars, both outside and inside the discipline, have said similar things. Braroe and Hicks (1967:179, 177) write in *The Sociological Quarterly* that many anthropologists "betray a restless antipathy toward authority within their own . . . culture." And they refer to "the romantic notion of the anthropologist as a dauntless adventurer, eccentric and disarmingly nonconformist." Rappaport (page 153) notes "our [anthropological] colleagues will do whatever they take to be interesting or important." Kroeber (in Thomas 1956:309), a pillar of the establishment and a student of Boas, phrased it a little more obliquely: "Old line anthropologists," he said, "are notoriously inner-directed." Elsewhere he (in Tax, Eiseley, Rouse, and Voegelin 1953:151-152) warms up to the subject:

Anthropology is certainly one of the most centrifugal of the sciences taking in an enormous territory. Sometimes we are amicably laughed at by people in fields with five or ten times as many members working at a much narrower range of problems. As Redfield says, our disposition to become concerned with questions marginal to any sector of the immense and variegated study of man . . . makes anthropology the freest and more explorative of the sciences. I think that is a claim we can justly make. Lately I have differentiated between cultural anthropology and sociology in terms of the clientele recruited by each: people with well-established centrifugal ten-

dencies for the remote and marginal become anthropologists, whereas those who have strong centripetal tendencies, who want the familiar and the repetitive, who do not want intellectual adventure, who want a certain tightness of what they operate with, become sociologists.

There are, as Salzman points out, serious implications to this disciplinary orientation. I quote Tax (1956:320): "The breadth of the enterprise . . . the openness of boundaries to both men and ideas; high tolerance for a variety of subject and tools. Out of these grows also a tolerance for a certain amount of ambiguity and vagueness." One can perhaps see why, then, there are so many different definitions of anthropology and culture. Twenty-eight of the volume's contributors refer to interpret, interpretive, or interpretation. A close analysis of the way they use these words will show sharp differences of meaning. The same is true for the fourteen contributors who refer to postmodern and the ten who refer to materialist perspectives. Contributors may use the same words, but they mean different things by them. This leads Murphy (page 55) to suggest in his paper: "Modern cultural theory suffers from a diffuseness so great that it seems to subvert discourse within our scholarly community . . . the protagonists of each perspective . . . speak past each other in a confusion of tongues; there is much talking but little dialogue."

This orientation encourages a particular intellectual style in anthropology. Persuasion and verification seem to overlap in rather elusive ways. Some notable anthropologists make some rather quotable observations about anthropology's intellectual style. Two of them are in this volume. Barth (page 350), for example, states:

Theoretical creativity requires, of course, a freedom to criticize and reject, an independence of conventions, and a willingness to explore other and radical positions. But . . . one does not enhance one's creativity by frantically shopping for the latest fashion, and scuttling all previous established (and alternative) views. There is much pressure toward a stereotyped originality in American academia.

And Wolf (page 220) comments: "In anthropology we are continuously slaying paradigms, only to see them return to life, as if discovered for the first time. . . . As each successive approach carries the axe to its predecessors, anthropology comes to resemble a project of intellectual deforestation." Anthropologists of earlier generations commented on the same tendency. Kroeber (1948:391), for example, states that sciences such as anthropology "are subject to waves of fashion." And Wallace (1966:1254) refers to the "slash and burn" nature of anthropology (cf. Lévi-Strauss and Eribon 1991:91–92).

The discipline's theories and models seem, superficially at least, to have a relatively short "intellectual half-life." Anthropologists often appear to be moving on to the "new" and downplaying the old—"slaying" it, casting it aside, or simply ignoring it. Evans-Pritchard's "stimulating essay on the importance of history to . . . anthropology [written in 1961] was provocative to some of his colleagues," Firth (1975:8) suggests, "not, as [Evans-Pritchard] argued, because of [his colleagues'] antihistorical prejudice, but because while claiming that anthropologists had turned their backs on history he totally ignored contributions already made in that field, notably by Schapera." Insights can seem newer when one's predecessors are ignored. This is especially true today—as new anthropologists, in search of positions in a tight job market and status in an expanding discipline, find it financially and intellectually advantageous to carve out their own niches by denigrating or ignoring their predecessors. Colson's (1992:51) recent comments deserve to be quoted at length in this regard:

Rapid population growth and geographical dispersal [within the discipline] have been associated with the emergence of a multitude of intellectual schools, each of which stresses both its own uniqueness and superiority and the need for the whole of the social/cultural community to accept its leadership. This never happens and even the most successful formula rarely predominates for more than a decade: at the moment when it appears to triumph, it becomes redefined as an outmoded orthodoxy by younger anthropologists who are attempting to stamp their own mark upon the profession. This has the therapeutic effect of outmoding most of the existing literature, by now too vast to be absorbed by any newcomer, while at the same time old ideas continue to be advanced under new rubrics. The history of anthropology is a splendid example of what John Barnes once called structural amnesia, the creation of convenient myths that eliminate most details and celebrate a minimal number of ancestral figures. Selective forgetting, however, obscures the continuity of ideas that in fact continue to guide much of what is done.

With such centrifugal tendencies, one might suspect cultural anthropology would self-destruct, fragment into a host of pieces. And yet it has not. There are also strong centripetal tendencies that provide the discipline with a solid, intellectual core.

CENTRIPETAL TENDENCIES

Several forces hold cultural anthropology together. Prominent among them are: (1) its shared traditions, (2) a set of similar fieldwork experiences among its practitioners, (3) the increasing quality of its ethnographic data base, and (4) its developing, self-corrective character.

Shared Traditions

The shared traditions, often inculcated during graduate school training and reinforced in the field's literature, derive from the discipline's past. Old perspectives, such as the cultural evolution of Morgan, Tylor, and Frazer and the functionalism of Malinowski and

Radcliffe-Brown, seem to live on in different phrasings or forms long after they have been seemingly rejected by the general discipline (much in the manner of Tylor's survivals). One can see this with functionalism and its relation to holism, with diffusionism in relation to "world systems theory," and with cultural evolution in relation to modern conceptions of change. Let me describe several of anthropology's shared traditions.

Holism. Holism stresses two overlapping themes. First, cultures need to be studied as wholes, not as fragmented pieces. Mauss (1967:77), a key figure in the development of French anthropology, states anthropologists "are concerned with 'wholes,' with systems in their entirety"—with, as he (1967:1) states, "total social phenomena." And second, cultural elements are often seen as interrelated and interdependent—"the intricate interdependence of all segments of a people's life" is how Kluckhohn (1949:275) phrased it. Malinowski and Boas, key figures in the development of British and American anthropology, stressed this holistic perspective. To quote Boas (1938:5): "We cannot do justice to all the important problems of human history if we treat social life as though it were the sum of all . . . separate elements. It is necessary to understand life and culture as a whole." This commitment to holism comes through in their ethnographies. Malinowski (1961), in describing overseas Kula exchanges among the Trobriand Islanders (of Papua New Guinea), for example, also refers to styles of canoe construction, magic, and social stratification. Boas (1966), in describing marriages among the Kwakiutl of the American Northwest, also takes note of property and potlatching.

A concern with holism appears in many chapters. Harris, for example, refers to the primacy of infrastructure in which changes within the sociocultural system at the interface of biology and culture—what he (1991:404) refers to as "the material costs and benefits of

satisfying basic needs in a particular habitat"—shape changes elsewhere in the system. Levy discusses the fit of personality styles with particular patterns of cultural integration in Tahiti and Nepal. Nader suggests the interrelatedness of cultural elements in her hypotheses regarding female subordination. And Yanagisako and Collier (page 192) state that "analyses of gender must begin with social wholes, rather than with individuals or . . . domains such as kinship."

Context. For anthropologists, intelligibility and understanding are achieved by placing elements within their cultural contexts. What may seem strange and exotic to those unfamiliar with a culture's practices often makes more sense when placed within indigenous contexts of meaning. The goal of the ethnographer, Malinowski (1961:25) states in what has become a famous quote, is "to grasp the native's point of view, his relation to life, to realize *his* vision of *his* world." Kroeber (1943: 6) notes that Boas too insisted "that phenomena can properly be dealt with only in their adhering context." That is why anthropologists spend considerable space in their ethnographies discussing indigenous terms and conveying the subtleties and complexities of indigenous perceptions. It draws out their meaningfulness. It clarifies, to quote Geertz (1973:16), a sense of "what goes on in such places . . . what manner of [people] these are."

In addition, placing seemingly exotic cultural elements in their indigenous contexts acts as an antidote to bigotry. It makes the strange and "savage" more comprehensible, more reasonable. Understanding between "us" and "others" is furthered through an appreciation of the contexts within which these "other" people lead their lives.

A Shared Uneasiness. We should not overstate anthropologists' commitment to holism and cultural context, however. Most anthropologists tend to accept these concepts in general form. But most, especially today, also feel uneasy in completely embracing them since they raise problematic issues.

Holism, for example, is best seen as an analytical tool, as an approach rather than a theory. It is, to quote Moore (page 364), more of "a question rather than an answer." It is a tool for uncovering "threads of influence" (in Vayda's, page 323, terms). Lowie's (1920: 441) famous statement that civilization (or culture) is a "thing of shreds and patches" has been rejected. (The great "debunker" has himself been debunked.) But as Vayda, Barth, Moore, Strathern, and I point out, it is not a settled matter how integrated culture actually is. As Strathern emphasizes, there are subtle, complex issues involved here. We need not only be aware of how indigenous groups construct wholes from parts for example, but, as she (page 204) suggests, we also need to "strive for a holistic apprehension of the manner in which our subjects dismantle their own constructs." We need to be clearer regarding how parts and wholes do (and do not) fit together.

Transformation and Change. Though anthropologists, until recently, often phrased their accounts in an "ethnographic present" (that merged past recollections and present fieldwork observations into one timeless mix) and though functionalists focused, as Beattie (1955: 7) notes, on "the present state of society" and avoided "conjecture about the remote origin of things," anthropologists have nonetheless also traditionally concerned themselves with matters of process, with questions of change. The interest did not simply arise with Evans-Pritchard's "re-discovery" of history. The early evolutionists—Morgan, Frazer, and Tylor—were concerned with cultural transformations. And the early diffusionists—such as Schmidt and Graebner—were interested in the spread of ideas and material culture. Anthropologists have been engrossed in questions of cultural change for several decades now. The topic, admittedly, has gone by a variety of names—not just evolution, history, and process but acculturation (Redfield,

Linton, and Herskovits), configurations of cultural growth (Kroeber), and innovation (Barnett).

The key questions regarding change have tended to remain the same through time. They center on causal relations—which factors, in what proportion, produce which cultural forms. "At the end of the day," Godelier (page 107, my emphasis) notes, "the essential question for the social sciences is: Of all the manifold human activities, which are those that provoke not only changes *within* society . . . but changes *of* society?" Yanagisako and Collier (page 199) add: "How [do] social systems change and, at the same time, . . . [appear] to remain relatively stable over time."

Subjects of Study. Traditionally, anthropologists have studied those under the political control of Western elites—either in faraway places such as Africa or Papua New Guinea or in settings closer to home such as American Indian reservations or rural European peasant communities. DaMatta suggests that Americans once preferred not studying their own culture (though Powdermaker 1939 and Warner and Lunt 1941 and 1942 were obvious exceptions). This has clearly changed. There are now a number of studies on a range of topics regarding American culture—such as, to name just a few, the abortion controversy in Fargo, North Dakota (Ginsburg 1989), college women in North Carolina (Holland and Eisenhart 1990), and longshoremen in Portland (Pilcher 1972).

Even with this change, however, there has been a clear, underlying continuity to what anthropologists generally study. Anthropologists tend to study "down" as Nader (1969) phrases it; they tend to focus on the "underdog" (Tax 1956:321). The emphasis is on the less empowered, on those marginal to the centers of Western political and economic power. And anthropologists usually try to describe these people—as Scheper-Hughes's article illustrates—in terms that convey dignity and appreciation for their condition.

When anthropologists step up the ladder of power and consider the colonizers (e.g. Stoler 1989a, 1989b, John Comaroff 1989, Comaroff and Comaroff 1992) not just the colonized, they usually study them in the past and in locales far from the "West"—in Indonesia or South Africa, for example. I should note, in fairness, exceptions exist to this general tendency, most notably perhaps Crapanzano's *Waiting*, Dominguez's *People as Subject, People as Object*, Taylor's *Eva Peron*, McDonogh's *Good Families of Barcelona*, and Marcus and Hall's *Lives in Trust*—though even in these cases a certain social distance tends to separate the anthropologists and their informants. The trend in anthropological research remains generally one of studying those who are seemingly less empowered than anthropologists as well as those who—in being geographically separate and/or socially distant from anthropologists— draw anthropologists away from their familiar understandings and values. It is in describing such people that the discipline has made its greatest ethnographic contributions to date.

Comparison. Forty years ago, Oscar Lewis (1956:260) emphasized that "most anthropological writing contains comparisons. Even the monographs which are primarily descriptive generally make comparisons with earlier literature, and many have a final comparative chapter." The British anthropologist Nadel (1951: 193), writing in the same decade, stressed anthropology is "wedded" to comparison. "We study variations . . . and correlate them so that from them general regularities may emerge" (1951:222). Nader (page 93) suggests: "Anthropologists have regularly identified anthropology as a comparative discipline over the past 100 years."

Godelier (page 102) describes two types of comparisons. In one, cultures are taken apart and specific aspects of them—such as their kinship system, pattern of economic exchange, or religious practices—are compared with one another. In the other, comparisons are made between more "total entities." Societies termed "states" or "chiefdoms" are compared with each other. The problem both types of comparison face is that they can, at times, run counter to certain other anthropological orientations. The first type of comparison can run counter to the concern with holism (i.e. a culture is broken down into components, cultural parts are separated from one another for purposes of analysis); the second to the concern with context (i.e. a culture is separated from its regional and historical conditions that make particular beliefs and practices comprehensible).

While comparison is basic to the discipline, we need to realize it also remains somewhat problematic. What anthropologists share, in regard to comparison, is not only a belief in its methods and possibilities but also a sense of problems still needing to be overcome. It is a tool we are still learning to use.

Participant Observation. "Anthropologists are divided on epistemological issues," Bernard (page 171) notes, "but almost all of us use the strategic method of participant observation to collect our primary data." Participant observation, as its name implies, involves two processes. Anthropologists not only observe the people being studied (with some effort of objectivity) but they also participate, with the people, in various activities (both to make themselves less aloof and to gain an experiential understanding of the activities described). Anthropologists adhere, quoting Geertz (1985:624), to "the proposition that in understanding 'others' . . . it is useful to go among them as they go among themselves."

Following Malinowski's dictum (in what has become a famous phrase), anthropologists have "come off the veranda." Few anthropologists write an ethnography by simply collecting secondhand comments on a culture or interviewing informants separately from the contexts of their everyday lives (e.g. on the porch of a European house). Anthropologists collect data by living among the people they study—not just for months but for years.

Colson, in her intellectual genealogy, notes she has been studying the Plateau Tonga and Gwembe Tonga of Zambia for more than four decades. "Because of its long-term character, involving continuous and intimate contact with those whom we study," Bloch (page 282) suggests, "participant observation makes us learn the procedures which these people have themselves learned and enables us to check up on whether we are learning [them] properly."

Participant observation is, as Bernard (page 171) states, "what makes it possible for interpretivists and positivists alike to collect life-history documents, attend sacred festivals, talk to people about sensitive topics, map the land holdings of informants, trek with a hunter to count the kill, and interview women traders formally and informally about how they cover their losses in the daily market." Despite their differences, anthropologists share a common method of data collection.

Anthropology's Vision. Finally, anthropology holds out a special vision for improving social relations and, more generally, the quality of human life. It stresses three themes.

First, it emphasizes human commonalities. It stresses what we share with those seemingly different from us in behavior, belief, and locale. To paraphrase Hymes (1969b:53), anthropology enlarges our sense of moral community, it emphasizes our connectedness with others.

Second, anthropology values cultural difference. Anthropologists "bear witness" (paraphrasing DaMatta, page 123) to other ways of life. We record them, preserve them, so they will not be lost to future generations. Today many Westerners not only know about life in distant areas of Africa or on distant Pacific islands but, equally important, see value in these people's life-styles. All sorts of knowledge from all sorts of locales has positively entered Western cultural consciousness as a result of anthropology.

And third, anthropology uses cultural difference as a form of cultural critique and,

through it, as a form of cultural enrichment. It emphasizes that other possibilities—beyond the ones we are most familiar with—exist for solving problems, for achieving meaningful lives. This is what Marcus and Fischer (1986: ix-x) refer to when they assert, "Anthropology is not the mindless collection of the exotic, but the use of cultural richness for self-reflection and self-growth." And this is what Rappaport (page 166) suggests when he states that "anthropology's future lies in helping humanity to realize . . . a vision of its place in the world." Anthropology offers a vision for reconstructing social and ecological relations, for renewing our common humanity and interdependence. *What makes anthropology special is that it affirms that those on the margin— the dominated, the disempowered—have an important contribution to make to the enrichment of others, including those at the center of power.*

To hold up a vision of what we are and what we might become is one thing. To actually realize it is another. Here anthropology has been less successful. I cited above both Barth and Keesing . Other contributors touch on this issue as well. Godelier (page 97) asks if the social sciences are only capable "of tagging along behind events." Das raises questions about the use and misuse of ethnographic data. Salzman (page 31) notes that "our work remains marginal" to most of the people we study. And DaMatta explores some of the reasons American anthropologists have been hesitant to engage in broader, social action. What we share, as anthropologists, I am suggesting, is not only a bold, intellectual vision, but limited success in achieving it.

Shared Experiences Relating to Fieldwork

Manners and Kaplan (1968:1) indicate that fieldwork is "not only the 'device' used by anthropologists to provide the discipline with its empirical material, but it has become much more . . . a kind of touchstone of adequacy, a *rite de passage* prerequisite to membership in the profession." Leach (1961:1) has termed it "the essential core" of anthropology; Cohn (1980:200) "a sacred rite."

Most anthropologists experience at least once (and some many times) the excitement and frustration of living in an unfamiliar locale with unfamiliar understandings. The ambiguities of data collection, the concern for abstracting patterns and processes from the variations of everyday life, the need to make sense of the foreign are shared anthropological experiences. They are part of becoming and being an anthropologist. Fieldwork, as Salzman (page 31) notes, is "a risky and wearing business." And anthropologists find a sense of community in their joint experience of it.

Given the varying theoretical concerns of the past several decades, this ethnographic experience often seems to provide anthropologists with a common grounding. As Wolf (1964:89) states, "There is a sense in which, in the private ranking systems of . . . anthropologists, the first-class recorder of ethnographic detail ranks more highly than the most gifted theorist." Fernandez (1975:191) adds: "We anthropologists may often decry that we make a fetish of fieldwork, yet in almost every case it is the rich data of a fulfilled field experience which is the matrix of significant accomplishment in our discipline." "Practically all our significant figures," he adds, can be tied to an ethnographic corpus—"Boas to Kwakiutl, Malinowski to Trobriands, Lowie to Crow, Kluckhohn to Navajo, Evans-Pritchard to Nuer, Griaule . . . to Dogon, [and] Firth to Tikopia."

Growing out of this perspective is a feeling, among many anthropologists, that ethnographies are more enduring than theories (see e.g. Moore, note 3). Actually, it is only partially true. Writings on groups such as the Eskimos have clearly stood the test of time. But recent writings on other groups, such as the Australian Aborigines (see Fardon 1990:39), have revised earlier perspectives. And, as we shall note in a moment, many of the same theoretical questions seem to have persisted for some time in anthropology, only their phrasings have changed. The feeling that ethnographies are relatively enduring is best seen as a reaction to the already discussed discipline's intellectual concern with continuously changing fads. Ethnography provides an intellectual and emotional grounding for the discipline.

Anthropology's Data Base

Despite the intellectual differences dividing anthropologists, most anthropologists concur that the discipline's ethnographic data base is improving. This is not only because of its ever-increasing breadth and depth as a result of constantly being added to. It is also because the ethnographies themselves are improving. Modern ethnographies tend to involve finer-grained descriptions, be more sophisticated in analyzing cultural dynamics, and demonstrate greater sensitivity to the subtleties of time and place than in the past (cf. Colson 1992:51).

Such data are making anthropologists rethink how they conduct anthropology. It is becoming increasingly clear, for example, that specialization has its limits. Dividing a culture into economic, political, or religious "systems" may prove helpful for initially understanding a group. But beyond a certain point, something is lost. Goody (page 251) notes this when he states that "it is hard to see any advantage that has accrued from treating the ideational level . . . as a distinct domain." So do Yanagisako and Collier (page 192): ". . . it is impossible to understand interaction within 'domestic spheres' without simultaneously understanding the organization of political and economic arenas." And Moore (page 370) observes: "The 'legal' like the 'economic' is a dimension of almost everything in social life." Increased specialization in data collection has pointed out the need for increased integration.

Anthropologists also share an appreciation of outstanding ethnographies. They repeatedly cite them in their writings. These ethnographies provide the basis for a common discourse, for a common frame of reference. For example, DaMatta, Goody, and Salzman all refer to Evans-Pritchard's work on the Nuer; Moore and Salzman cite Malinowski's work on the Trobriands. These ethnographies constitute standards, yardsticks, by which we measure our own and others' research. And they act as resources—allowing us to analyze old materials in new ways years after the initial research was done. The ethnographic record, Kuper (page 117) notes, is our "central, shared heritage."

Progress in Community

It might seem unreasonable to suggest that a group with such centrifugal tendencies constitutes a community. But, as we have seen, anthropologists possess shared traditions, shared experiences, and a shared literature. One other thing they share is a sense of skepticism. Many anthropologists enjoy bringing the accepted into question. Anthropologists frequently challenge their fellow practitioners' descriptions and orientations. Lowie's statement, from an earlier era, that anthropologists have "learned to view [other's] catchwords with suspicion" (in Murphy 1972:78) parallels Wolf's present one that "we need to be professionally suspicious of our categories and models" (page 220). In this volume, Harris (page 64) refers to anthropological theories as "tentative approximations"; DaMatta (page 119) acknowledges that "'ethnographic authority' must constantly be challenged"; and Godelier (page 108) asserts that the analytical language of the discipline "must constantly be watched, . . . criticized, and revised." Skepticism about the accepted is one of anthropology's strengths.

But skepticism is not enough, as the present cacophony of perspectives demonstrates. There must also be a sense of dialogue, reasoned debate, shared conversation about our differences. Differences, if properly handled,

can lead to insight. Das (page 133) emphasizes this point when she states: "What is unique about anthropology . . . is its use of the 'Other' . . . to overcome the limits of [its own] origin and location."

It is through a dialogue about differences that cumulative knowledge develops in anthropology. This is the point I (Borofsky 1987:155) suggest in *Making History:*

Anthropological ways of knowing, despite their limitations, constitute a movement toward greater cultural understanding. This understanding develops not from a single ethnography but over time. Through a dialogue with others possessing different constructions and perspectives, we move beyond the complacency of our own constructions toward increased knowledge.

In discussing conflicting ethnographic accounts of Samoans in the Freeman-Mead controversy, Kuper (1989:455) notes a similar point:

Ethnography . . . is a contribution to a debate. . . . [It] will be taken up by a community of experts (including natives) who can call upon their own experience of life in particular societies and who will refer to a body of published observations and interpretations written from different perspectives. . . . There is, then, an authority in ethnography, one which is not necessarily embodied in any one account, but which is emergent in the processes of expert research, comparison, evaluation, and debate.

Goodenough (page 271) emphasizes this same point when he states that ethnography "is a long-range, cumulative, and necessarily cooperative undertaking." Harris (1968:687) makes it too in the conclusion to his book *The Rise of Anthropological Theory.* "The vindication of the strategy of cultural materialism," he notes, lies in its capacity "to generate major explanatory hypotheses which can be subjected to the test of ethnographic and archaeological research, modified if necessary, and made part of a corpus of theory . . . capable of explaining the most generalized features of universal history and the most exotic specialties of particular cultures." Only through time, through testing and retesting, through one ethnography being piled on top of another, do we come to know the validity of various accounts.

The quest for cumulative knowledge has proven difficult in anthropology. Progress has been slow. Service (1985:318) makes this point in his conclusion to *A Century of Controversy: Ethnological Issues from 1860 to 1960*. From a review of several major questions, he suggests that cultural anthropology (he says ethnology): "has not progressed very far. . . . There is today still no clear-cut or generally accepted opinion about the 'meaning' of kinship terms, or the basic forms of social structure and totemism, or the origins of the state, law, . . . property and forms of economic exchange, or even of the very key concept of culture itself."

Still, anthropology has made intellectual progress, though admittedly it is more obvious in small rather than in big ways. As we touched on here, and as amply supported in the anthropological literature, anthropologists are accumulating a richer, "thicker," body of ethnographic data. They are developing more sophisticated methods for collecting and analyzing ethnographic materials. And they are formulating more sophisticated phrasings of old questions that still, as Service notes, remain with us. One cannot look at Rappaport's synthesis of diverging anthropological perspectives, Vayda's critique of essentialism, Keesing's and Barth's analyses of culture, Moore's and Sahlins's perspectives on history, or Kottak and Colson's discussion of linkages without gaining a sense of increasing sophistication in our approach to problems.

And if one wants to feel a greater sense of progress, one need only look back at Lowie's *History of Ethnological Theory*. Lowie (1937: 252) points out: "Within the space of half a century a number of questions have been settled. . . . No one defends the three-stage

theory of economic progress; and Hahn's distinction of plough-farming [i.e. agriculture] from hoe-and-dibble-farming [i.e. horticulture] stands unchallenged. That promiscuity now exists nowhere and is an unproven hypothesis for the past is the view" of many distinguished anthropologists. Lowie (1937: 252) also adds the discarding of prelogical primitiveness to his list. That many readers will not have heard of these issues makes my point. There has been progress if we care to look carefully at the past.

Anthropologists have been asking very broad questions with, until recently, a somewhat limited, imperfect data base. That the data base is improving offers much hope for the future. We may still yet tackle the "big questions" as our ethnographic materials increase in depth and breadth, as more anthropologists work in the same locales with overlapping perspectives, as a dialogue about differences continues to develop within the anthropological community.

I would end on a positive note. Within anthropology, there is certainly much concern about the discipline and where it is going. But, outside the discipline, as Peacock (personal communication 1991) stresses, anthropology's prestige is quite high. Geertz (1985: 624) comments that anthropologists "are cited everywhere by everybody, to all sorts of purposes. The 'anthropological perspective' is, so far as the general intellectual community is concerned, very much 'in.'"

THE BOOK'S ORGANIZATION

An Open-Ended Quality

Over the past several years a number of assessments have been made of cultural anthropology (see e.g. Harris 1968, Hymes 1969a, Hatch 1973, Honigmann 1973, Tax 1977, Ortner 1984, Marcus and Fischer 1986, Fox 1991). The assessment closest to this book in character, however, is the two-volume set

produced from a 1952 Wenner-Gren Conference (see Kroeber et al. 1953 and Tax,
Eiseley, Rouse, and Voegelin 1953). Like that
one, and unlike many more recent assessments, this volume combines three distinct
characteristics. It is an edited work involving
many of the discipline's leading scholars. Contributors do not emphasize narrowly defined,
specialized topics (e.g. economic anthropology, political anthropology, legal anthropology) . But rather, and this is the second characteristic, they tend to focus on cultural
anthropology as a whole. Third, the volume
possesses an open-ended quality. Diverse
views are represented. Readers can synthesize
these in a number of ways. I will offer one
integrative framework in the volume's final
chapter. But readers are free to look at the
same material and draw different conclusions,
to develop different assessments, of where the
field is and where it might (or should) go.

The title of this book is purposeful. *Assess,*
according to Webster's dictionary (1984:426),
"implies a critical appraisal for the purpose of
understanding or interpreting, or as a guide in
taking action." And it is in the gerund form
because the assess*ing* is still going on. The
volume constitutes part of a continuing conversation—among students and professors
alike—regarding cultural anthropology's present condition and future possibilities.

What is surprising about the volume is not
its diversity of views. One would expect that
in anthropology. Rather, what is surprising is
the degree of overlap in various authors' perspectives. One sees the threads of several
anthropological traditions discussed above—
regarding holism, contextualization, change,
domination, comparison, methods, and the
field's vision. Barth, Bloch, Goody, Goodenough, Harris, Keesing, Levy, Strathern,
Strauss and Quinn, Vayda, Yanagisako and
Collier, and I, for example, all consider the
interrelatedness of cultural elements. From this
common foundation we then go off in different directions discussing to what degree, in
what ways, and for what reasons such related-

ness exists. Bernard, Bloch, Goodenough,
Harris, Levy, Marcus, Murphy, Rappaport,
Salzman, and I are all concerned with anthropological aspects of knowing. Issues of domination and power are dealt with by Harris,
Sahlins, Scheper-Hughes, Tambiah, Tishkov,
and Wolf. DaMatta, Das, Godelier, Kottak
and Colson, Kuper, and Nader consider comparison. Barth, Bloch, Godelier, Harris, Keesing, Kottak and Colson, Levy, Moore, Rappaport, Sahlins, Strathern, Strauss and Quinn,
Tambiah, Tishkov, Wolf, and I explore issues
of process. And Barth, Geertz, Harris, Keesing, and Lévi-Strauss raise questions relating to
anthropology's proclaimed vision. It is all
rather encouraging for those who view
anthropology as an intellectual community,
especially when a careful reading of the chapters indicates that one could add additional
names to each category. It provides a sense of
hope and raises an important question: Can
anthropologists develop a general consensus
regarding where we are and where we might
go?

There is also implicit in this volume another
question—one about status and power. Most
of the contributors are senior scholars who
have had a major hand in shaping the discipline's current state. In moving ahead, understandably many lean toward retaining continuity with a present they helped create. A
younger generation of contributors might be
more interested in carving out new niches,
moving in a host of new directions to establish
their own identities, without tying themselves
to the present. We are led to ask a question:
Can the old help shape the new? Does change
have to come about, as Fox (1991:16) suggests, through "the mass retirement of the
'elders'"? Or can the "elders," with their
accumulated insight, skill, and experience help
guide the discipline toward the future?

The Organization of Sections

The thirty-one contributions did not fall into
a prearranged organization. The order of sec-

tions (and chapters) only evolved gradually as I reflected on the degree to which various contributions overlapped with one another.

Section One sets out some of the cacophonies, some of the divergence and diversity, that typify the discipline today. Underlying the positions enunciated by Salzman and Marcus is the positivist/interpretivist debate that has gone on in anthropology for decades. The argument centers on how to develop a dynamic, productive discipline. Murphy and Harris touch on another controversy, involving idealist and materialist perspectives for analyzing cultural process. This latter controversy considers the general dynamics behind cultural change.

Section Two uses one of anthropology's strengths, comparison, to reflect on the discipline's present state. Drawing on European and Third World assessments lets us see anthropology in a different way from the North American assessments of Section One. Nader sets out the need for a "comparative consciousness" in her contribution. The two European assessments—by Godelier (a French anthropologist) and Kuper (a British one)—may prove a bit disconcerting to Americans. They perceive more consensus in the field than many Americans do. And they slide over certain oppositions. (We begin to see what intrigues and upsets indigenous readers about ethnographies written on them by outsiders.) The two Third World perspectives continue this theme by looking at some uses and misuses of anthropology. DaMatta, a Brazilian anthropologist, and Das, an Indian one, raise important issues regarding present perspectives and biases in the discipline.

In Section Three, contributors play anthropologists' time-honored role as critics of the accepted. Rappaport and Bernard offer insightful comments relating to the positive/interpretivist debate. Levy, Yanagisako and Collier, and Strathern rethink old disciplinary categorizations in thoughtful, new ways. And Wolf and Scheper-Hughes consider questions relating to the dynamics of power and dis-

empowerment: Wolf suggests ways for building on traditional anthropological approaches to the subject while Scheper-Hughes considers how power relations are inscribed in the suffering bodies of sick workers.

Section Four explores the anthropological concept of culture. Goody and Goodenough help us rethink what we mean by culture— what distinctions we should make, which models we should use to help in conceptualizing the phenomenon. Bloch, Strauss and Quinn, and Keesing question old perspectives. They raise questions relating to the use of linguistic models, the degree to which culture is public versus private as well as the role of power in the cultural order.

Section Five looks at culture from a dynamic perspective—seeing it in motion, changing through time and space. Vayda, Barth, and I explore the dimension of individual diversity and how we might better conceptualize the open, fluid nature of what people know. Moore, Sahlins, and Kottak and Colson examine processual dynamics relating to change as well as linkages between local and global networks. We see culture as a fluid set of processes. And we see the problems anthropologists face in describing these processes.

Section Six considers the role of anthropology beyond the academy. In a world where cultural heterogeneity can stimulate both insight and violence, the contributions by Lévi-Strauss, Tambiah, Tishkov, and Geertz explore issues relating to ethnic conflict and cultural prejudice. Tambiah and Tishkov consider specific questions. Lévi-Strauss and Geertz reflect on the broader concerns framing these issues.

A final chapter offers my thoughts on the contributors' overlapping themes. It considers where we are in anthropology. And it queries where we might go. It stresses that the book belongs to an ongoing conversation about the discipline. It is part of a continuing anthropological dialogue in which readers, as well as contributors, are participants. On this note, let us turn to the six sections of contributions.

Diversity and Divergence
within the
Anthropological Community

I n this section, we see the tension between anthropology's centrifugal and centripetal tendencies close up. On the one hand, clear differences of opinion exist among the four contributors. Salzman and Marcus disagree, for example, on how to build a cumulative body of anthropological knowledge. Salzman (page 35) is concerned with tempering the "dazzling speed" with which "theoretical fads and fashions . . . come and go in anthropology" through (page 37) a better "process of grounded assessment" in research. Marcus emphasizes the need to experiment with new possibilities for conceptualizing and describing ethnographic fieldwork. What Salzman would view as yet another anthropological fad—postmodernism—Marcus sees as a positive, intellectual development. Murphy and Harris are critical of each other's attempts to assess the relative importance of cultural variables vis-à-vis one another in facilitating change and stability. Murphy (page 57) states that "materialists . . . fail to recognize that cultural forms have lives of their own and are not mere epiphenomena of underlying 'infrastructures.'" To which Harris (page 70) replies, "The attempt by Murphy and others to portray cultural materialism as a paradigm

in which 'the ideas by which men . . . live have no importance for their action' . . . is totally at variance with the prominence of the phrase 'sociocultural system' in the specification of cultural materialist principles."

On the other hand, there are clear overlappings of perspectives. Salzman and Marcus (as well as Murphy and Harris) are concerned with finding ways to overcome biases in the ethnographic record. They share a common concern for developing a cumulative body of anthropological knowledge. And behind the heat of the Murphy and Harris opposition is a shared concern for exploring the subtle, dynamic ways in which cultural elements interrelate. They are both interested in how cultural change arises and, especially, which variables seem to be the primary determinants of it.

What is particularly noteworthy about the debates is that they have a significance beyond this section. They run through the volume as a whole, and, more broadly, constitute tensions within the discipline itself. Service (1985), for example, touches on them in his analysis of major controversies within anthropology between 1860 and 1960. Underlying debates involving kinship terminology, social

23

structure, the origins of government, and the economic life of non-Western groups, Service suggests, are questions concerning scientific vs. humanist perspectives, determinism vs. free will, generalization vs. particularism, comparison vs. holism—questions that tie into issues raised here. Let me explain what the debates are, especially what is meant by positivism, interpretivism, materialism, and idealism.

POSITIVISM/INTERPRETIVISM

Positivism

Bernard (page 169) observes there are really two positivisms. Both emphasize "tested and systematized experience rather than . . . undisciplined speculation" (Kaplan 1968:89). But the two develop this theme in different ways.

The first type of positivism is based on writings from the early nineteenth century, especially the work of Saint-Simon, a French socialist. He coined the term "positivism" for referring to the application of scientific methods to philosophical issues. Comte subsequently applied the term to a three-stage view of human progress—the religious, the metaphysical, and the scientific. Positivism involved the tested, rational principles of the scientific age. Comte, however, seemed to get carried away (as Bernard notes) in enunciating these scientific principles, and his vision fell into disrepute.

The second type of positivism is often labeled logical positivism (though it is also known as logical empiricism, scientific empiricism, or logical neopositivism). Its perspective derives from a group of philosophically oriented scientists (and scientifically oriented philosophers) who frequently met together in Vienna in the 1920s and 1930s. The group, referred to as the "Vienna circle," viewed science as focusing on the description of experience. It opposed metaphysical speculation, not because it was not interesting, but because it often proved impossible to verify. The

group stressed that "propositions should not be accepted as meaningful unless they are [empirically] verifiable" (Passmore 1967:55).

In its present, empirically oriented, form, modern positivism (or neopositivism) is best viewed as a set of working principles, as a set of tools, for developing a cumulative body of knowledge. It emphasizes that (1) theory formation should be based on inductions from observation, (2) in case of theoretical disputes, empirical tests—rather than political affiliations—should be the judge of correctness, and (3) since theoretical disputes are resolvable over time, scientific knowledge can be cumulative and progressive in character (see Alexander 1985:632). The positivist perspective is well expressed in Harris's chapter. Scientific knowledge, he (page 64) states, "is obtained by public, replicable operations." And "the aim of scientific research is to formulate explanatory theories which are . . . testable (or falsifiable) . . . [and] cumulative within a coherent and expanding corpus of theories." Harris ends his chapter—in the tradition of Saint-Simon and Comte—with a plea that moral evaluation (and social policy) be based on scientific knowledge rather than relativistic values.

Interpretivism

Interpretivism (or more properly, interpretive anthropology) takes a different tack from positivism in establishing knowledge. The focus is less on verification than on contextualization. Understanding an action, Rabinow and Sullivan (1987:14) assert, "requires reference to its larger context. . . . The aim is not to uncover universals or laws but rather to explicate context." The interpretive stance involves different strands, and as a result has been perceived (and misperceived) in various ways. (One need only compare different contributors' use of *interpretive* in this volume to see this.) To introduce readers to the issues involved here, I provide a rough overview of the perspective. But readers are cautioned. These statements are only a foundation which readers should then use to build their own understandings on as they read through the volume.

Geertz is a key figure in the development of modern, interpretive anthropology. "Believing, with [the German sociologist] Max Weber, that man is an animal suspended in webs of significance he himself has spun," Geertz (1973:5) takes "culture to be those webs, and the analysis of it to be therefore not an experimental science in search of law but an interpretive one in search of meaning." He is concerned with "the fabric of meaning in terms of which human beings interpret their experience and guide their action" (1957:33). "Interpretive explanation," Geertz (1983:22) asserts, "trains its attention on what institutions . . . mean to those whose institutions . . . they are." "It is not against a body of uninterpreted data, radically thinned [or superficial] descriptions, that we must measure the cogency of our explications," he (1973:16) states, "but against the power of the scientific imagination to bring us into touch with the lives of strangers."

Fitting with this focus is Geertz's (1973:448) suggestion that one examine "culture as an assemblage of texts"—that "cultural forms can be treated . . . as imaginative works built out of social materials" (1973:449). Cultural works can be interpreted (and reinterpreted) as to their meanings. Festivals, rituals, cockfights are not simply events from this perspective; they also represent collections of meanings. They convey insight, emotion, and significance, much as texts do, to those who are drawn into them.

Geertz is not antiscience. "I do not believe that anthropology is not or cannot be a science," he (in Carrithers 1990:274) states, "that the value of anthropological works inheres solely in their persuasiveness." But he is against method-obsessed quantification and rigid law-seeking. And he works within a tradition—termed hermeneutic and involving such scholars as Weber, Dilthey, Gadamer, and Ricoeur—which suggests that the study of social and historical concerns requires methods different from those employed in the natural sciences. Geertz's concern is with the open-ended, layering quality of meaning, with "opposing the idea that 'there is . . . [but one] correct representation of the world'" (1990: 274). There are important social implications to his perspective regarding cultural tolerance (as he, page 465, makes clear in his own chapter):

Comprehending that which is, in some manner of form, alien to us and likely to remain so, without either smoothing it over with vacant murmurs of common humanity, disarming it with to-each-his-own indifferentism, or dismissing it as charming . . . is a skill we have arduously to learn, and having learnt it, always very imperfectly, to work continuously to keep alive.

The interpretive concern with contextualization and the construction of meaning in recent years has led to contextualizing not just the observed but the observer. "What we call our data," Geertz (1973:9) states, "are really our own constructions of other people's constructions of what they and their compatriots are up to." This contextualization—of both the known and the knower, of the described and the describer—is today termed interpretive anthropology by some and postmodernism by others.

It is deemed interpretive anthropology because it represents an extension of the interpretive framework—bringing to bear on the observer the same principles of contextualization that one applies to the observed. (The view that a description reflects both the described and the describer has, of course, a long history both inside and outside anthropology.) "Interpretive anthropology," Marcus and Fischer (1986:16) state "reflects on the doing and writing of ethnography itself," on how anthropologists present their data to others. Clifford (1988:38) suggests, "Interpretive anthropology demystifies much of what had previously passed unexamined in the construction of ethnographic narratives."

Postmodernism—if I may overgeneralize for a moment to convey its relevant sense for this context—challenges modern forms of representation. It "deconstructs" them, it critically analyzes (and contextualizes) their construction, to demonstrate how certain rhetorical forms convey credibility. "What appears as 'real' in history, the social sciences, the arts, even in common sense," Clifford (1986:10) asserts, can be analyzed "as a restrictive and expressive set of social codes and conventions." In the case of ethnography, for example, it considers how anthropologists generate a sense of authenticity—a sense of having "been there" at a field site, at having conducted effective fieldwork. The movement derives from a "crisis in representation" according to its adherents (see Marcus and Fischer 1986:8)—from an inability of modern forms of representation (especially writing and film) to convey the subtle, complex dynamics of today's world—particularly in relation to (1) the describer in the described and (2) the multiplex linkages tying fieldwork locales to larger systems.

What would postmodernists, such as Marcus, replace established ethnographic writing traditions with? "Once the conventions and rhetorical nature of realist discourse are exposed," Marcus (page 41) asserts, "the opportunity exists to formulate new questions, to materialize new objects of study, and to explore new discursive spaces through experiments with form." "What is particularly important in the discussion that hovers around self-consciously experimental texts," Marcus and Fischer (1986:41–42) suggest, "is not experimentation for its own sake, but the theoretical insight that the play with writing technique brings to consciousness, and the sense that continued innovation in the nature of ethnography can be a tool in the development of theory."

This, then, is the context for Marcus's chapter—the development of interpretive anthropology into postmodernism, the critique of ethnographic writings, and the concern with experimentation. But there is also another context. A reading of various contributions in this volume, as well as the disciplinary literature at large, indicates that many anthropologists oppose this perspective.

Criticisms center on two points. First, interpretive/postmodern anthropology is viewed as undermining established standards to the degree, some assert, that "anything goes." DaMatta (page 119) believes the overconcern with the describer in the described "tends to reduce anthropological problems exclusively to field narratives." Murphy (page 56) refers to "thick writing" (a play of words on Geertz's "thick description") "in which obscure literary allusions and baroque rhetorical forms are weapons, a kind of egghead rap-talk." Instead of ethnographic descriptions we have "navel-gazing" (as Jarvie terms it; see Sangren 1988: 428), self-absorption. Anthropological studies become a foil for talking about ourselves. Second, it downplays the context of its own productions, passing over the power plays that it itself does as if only other's power plays and intellectual constructions should be the subject of analysis. Sangren summarizes this view when he (1988:414) suggests that with interpretive/postmodern analyses:

[O]ne is free to experiment and to criticize, delegitimate, demystify, deconstruct, . . . any sort of "other," real or fabricated that suits one's purposes, without bearing responsibility for defending one's positions; . . . [it involves] an openly acknowledged freedom to engage in mystification and creative self-empowering fabrication unaccountable to any challenge of logic or fact.

What is at issue in the positivist/interpretivist debate is differing approaches for moving the discipline forward. Positivists focus on standards for differentiating, if not right from wrong, then at least better from worse research. The emphasis is on accumulating sound data, on developing an increasingly more comprehensive ethnographic data base.

Interpretivists/postmodernists caution against disembodying subtle, complex understandings in ways which may seem "scientific" but lose their original meanings and significance. They stress that much ethnographic "authenticity" is a matter of rhetorical style, with the observer hiding his or her role in shaping the observed. And they emphasize the need for being open to new possibilities, the need for experimentation in developing the discipline.

This debate has played an important role in anthropology's development. Each side has tempered the enthusiasms of the other. Interpretivists have surrounded positivists' strivings for relative objectivity with notes of caution. And positivists have emphasized the pragmatic limits of personalized, interpretive accounts in the discipline's development. What we need to explore, in the 1990s, is how to include both perspectives within a thriving discipline: How to allow them to effectively rub off one another, how to have them effectively act as catalysts to each other, in stimulating disciplinary development and cumulative understanding.

MATERIALISM/IDEALISM

One should not see the materialist/idealist debate as mainly a variant of the positivist/interpretivist debate. The relation between the two is more complicated. Harris can be equated with both positivism and materialism. But Marcus, an interpretivist, seems to find value in a materialist perspective as well. In referring to "anthropology as a situated intellectual formation in the history of Western colonialism," he (page 43) ties anthropology's development to the politics and economics of colonialism. And Murphy, despite his opposition to Harris, flirts with materialism as suggested by his (page 57) comment, "the realities of power, sex, and economic need are largely prior to and generative of . . . symbolic forms."

Materialism

The materialism/idealism debate enters anthropology through the writings of Karl Marx. "It is not the consciousness of men that determines their being, but, on the contrary their social being [that] determines their consciousness," Marx (1956:51) asserts in a famous statement. "The totality of the . . . relations of production constitutes the economic structure of society," he suggests, "the real foundation, on which legal and political superstructures arise." Or to phrase it another way, "the mode of production of material life determines the general character of the social, political and spiritual processes of life."

Harris has developed a materialist-oriented perspective based on Marx's writings (as well as those of White and Steward). As befits this ancestry, he (1991:404) terms his approach "cultural materialism." It holds that "the primary task of anthropology is to give causal explanations for the differences and similarities in thought and behavior found among human groups." He continues:

This task can best be carried out by studying the material constraints to which human existence is subjected. These constraints arise from the need to produce food, shelter, tools, and machines, and to reproduce human populations within limits set by biology and the environment. These are called material constraints . . . in order to distinguish them from constraints . . . imposed by ideas and other mental or spiritual aspects of human life. . . . For cultural materialists, the most likely causes of major variation in the mental or spiritual aspects of human life are the differences in the material costs and benefits of satisfying basic needs in a particular habitat.

Idealism

In idealist-oriented perspectives, mental processes tend to define the framework within which materialist dynamics operate. Sahlins

(1976:207) states it well: "There is no material logic apart from the practical interest, and the practical interest of men in production is symbolically constituted. The finalities as well as the modalities of production come from the cultural side." It is this belief—that materialist forces and relations of production are culturally constituted—that forms the basis for Sahlins's (page 387) view that every society "is a global society" (i.e., every society defines the world from its own indigenous perspective).

Structuralism, an idealist-oriented perspective, focuses on the underlying, relational structures of the human mind. It postulates, as Godelier (page 103) notes, that "the mind orders natural and cultural reality according to two basic rules"—*metaphor*, or association by analogy (in which, for example, the beauty of a flower is compared to a woman's beauty) and *metonymy*, or association by physical connection (in which a crown is associated with a queen because the queen wears the crown). For Lévi-Strauss—the founder of structuralism—metaphor and metonymy are conceptual, mental ways of ordering the world. Or as he (1966a:10) states, "Thought . . . is founded on . . . [the] demand for order." He perceives this ordering as taking shape through binary oppositions such as hot/cold, raw/cooked, earth/sky, male/female. He possesses a brilliant ability to see relations and oppositions in diverse myths and rituals. And he is able to use them to uncover basic contradictions in a society (as illustrated in the introduction to Section Three). A caution is in order, however. Lévi-Strauss refuses to be pigeon-holed as an idealist and draws upon other perspectives as well, including certainly a materialist one (see, e.g., Lévi-Strauss 1966a: 93, 95 and Lévi-Strauss and Eribon 1991: 108).

There is no denying the emotion generated by various forms of the materialist/idealist debate in recent decades. "One would have had to be particularly out of touch with anthropological theory," in the late 1960s and early 1970s, Ortner (1984:133-134) notes,

"not to be aware of the acrimonious debate between" them. Materialist-oriented anthropologists viewed idealist-oriented ones as "fuzzy-headed mentalists, involved in . . . unverifiable flights of subjective interpretation" while the latter viewed the former as "willfully ignoring the truth that . . . culture mediates all human behavior."

What we see in the debate, in a sense, are the strengths and weaknesses of the holistic perspective. Explicitly or implicitly, both Murphy and Harris concern themselves with the subtle, complex ways cultural elements are interrelated. But holism does not specify precisely to what degree and in what ways cultural elements interact with one another. It simply states they are related. Thus, the two contributors explore different possibilities. No consensus exists regarding the importance of different elements in facilitating change and/or stability.

DEVELOPING THE DISCIPLINE

Reading through this section, one might be reminded of Robert Frost's poem "Mending Wall." One would like to know not only what is being walled in by a particular perspective—what it specifically espouses, what it illuminates. But one would also like to know what is being walled out—what is being excluded, downplayed, passed over. The following contributions do not resolve the above intellectual debates. But readers might ponder certain questions regarding them: What issues do the contributions specifically highlight? What issues do they ignore? What questions do they raise for further research?

Ultimately, what we need consider as we read through this section is how to use the differing orientations included here to disciplinary advantage. How can we harness the tensions among contributors' opposing, yet overlapping, perspectives to move ahead as an intellectual discipline?

1

The Lone Stranger in the Heart of Darkness

PHILIP CARL SALZMAN

Whatever may be the claims of the United States in the family of nations, "the land of the free and the home of the brave" in the academic world is undoubtedly cultural anthropology. Our approach to training, research, and knowledge all bear testimony to the primacy of freedom and bravery. And it is from these most revered of characteristics that flow both the virtues and the vices, the accomplishments and the failures, of cultural anthropology.

THE FREEDOM OF THE BRAVE

Clyde Kluckhohn, as fondly remembered by Clifford Geertz, liked to say that a degree in anthropology is a license for poaching. But the freedom to do just about anything under the label of cultural anthropology (hereafter I shall use the broader term "anthropology" to represent the part which is cultural anthropology, and shall specify when I refer to other parts, such as archaeology) is evident long before one holds a degree. While other students specialize in psychology or economics, women's studies or development, politics or religion, art or history, anthropology students are free within anthropology to dip into each of them, to taste what is appealing, to switch from one to another with ease, and to select and combine as the spirit moves them. The course offerings in most anthropology departments present, not a narrow specialization, but the broad spectrum of the social sciences and humanities, and even beyond.

The extraordinary breadth of anthropology, unique in academia, has so far spawned in the American Anthropological Association no less than twelve formal groups defined primarily by topic of study (leaving aside five general, two areal, and one regional organization): feminist anthropology, political and legal anthropology, education, nutrition, agriculture, consciousness, work, cultural anthropology, humanistic anthropology, linguistic anthropology, medical anthropology, psychological anthropology, and urban anthropology. The rules for the establishment of such organizations are primarily administrative, requiring mainly that a certain number of A.A.A. members support the new group; there are no academic criteria that might, based on some restricted definition of anthropology, limit the range of acceptable topics. Similarly, members of the A.A.A., whatever their training or academic background, may join one or a few or many or all of these associations, selecting, once again, according to current interests, and limited only by considerations of pocketbook. Thus the virtually boundless range of anthropology has received validation at the most formal level of the profession.

The organization of the anthropological curriculum and of the profession in the United States reflects the examples set by the culture heroes of anthropology. Among apical ancestors, Malinowski wrote influential ethnographic books on politics, kinship, and psychology in the Trobriands, as well as important theoretical statements on ritual, myth, and religion; among second generation

29

exemplars, Evans-Pritchard contributed major ethnographic works on witchcraft among the Azande, on ecology and politics, kinship, and religion among the Nuer, and on history in Cyrenaica and among the Azande. Among contemporary champions, Geertz has enlightened through ethnographic accounts of politics and religion, and ecology and economics in Java, politics in Bali, religion in Java and Morocco, and economics in Morocco, as well as theoretical discourses on religion, ideology, common sense, art, and evolution. The great anthropological masters have felt free to range over the full spectrum of human life and its multifarious activities, strivings, relatings, construings, its outer constellations and inner forces. And indeed, the received traditional model of the ethnographic report included a chapter on each of kinship, settlement, economy, politics, religion, and so on. Nothing human is alien to anthropology.

The freedom of anthropology goes beyond the infinitude of topics open to inquiry, for it encompasses also the venue of research, the locale to be studied. Once again, in contrast to most other academics, anthropologists can choose from the wide world; any continent, any region, any locale is acceptable—from the largest and culturally most complex cities, the East End of London, the cowboy bars of Paris, the poor quarter of Cairo, the bazaar of Teheran, or the porno stores of Tokyo, to villages on tiny Pacific atolls, temporary herding camps in the deserts of Arabia, shifting settlements in the rain forests of central Africa, or the new towns in the frozen north of Canada—all are relevant to the universal scope of anthropology.

An undergraduate anthropology student in even a small-sized department can travel the world through ethnography courses. After the whirlwind one semester introduction to cultures of the world come the more restricted courses on native peoples of North America, cultures of Oceania, of the Middle East, Far East, Mediterranean, the North, and so on. If the dashing, camel-borne sheiks in turbans

fascinate, then take the course on the Middle East; if the sea and sun of Pacific islands seem exciting, take the course on Oceania; if the ecological cultures of native North Americans seem to offer another way, take the native peoples course. What rich possibilities await in the universal range of human cultures; anthropology offers it all; pick whatever appeals.

While the possibilities for undergraduate students are for the most part limited to books, lectures, and films, those that take up anthropology for a career are able to choose from the myriad possibilities a much more extended and intensive experience carrying out ethnographic research in foreign locales. Anthropologists commonly spend a year in the field, sometimes more, often followed by additional trips later. Beyond this, over the years and decades of her or his career, an anthropologist will most likely choose to carry out research in a number of different locales, not infrequently switching from one region or continent to another. I myself have conducted research in Iranian Baluchistan, in Rajasthan, India, and in Sardinia, Italy; and I am a stay-at-home compared to many of my colleagues. In fact, in my own case, circumstances acted as a push—an Islamic revolution inconsiderately carried out in Iran, coupled with a disruptive invasion of Afghanistan and chaotic rebellions and repressions in Pakistani Baluchistan; but there are always such pressures. In fact, many colleagues choose to move from one research site to a different one simply to sample more fully the rich human cavalcade. Many distinguished anthropologists have ranged across vast stretches of the globe: Geertz, as mentioned, has worked in Java, Bali, and Morocco; Edmund Leach carried out research on mountain tribes in Kurdistan, on political systems in Burma, and on land and kinship in Ceylon; and Fredrik Barth has done research in mountain villages of Kurdistan, nomadic camps of Iran, irrigated valleys and men's houses in Pakistan, fishing fleets of Norway, urban neighborhoods in Oman, tribal hill villages in New Guinea, towns in Bali, and mountain communities of Nepal. Anthropology offers us all the world; our freedom to span the world is limited only by our energies.

THE BRAVERY OF THE FREE

Be careful what you wish for, you may get it. This could be sewn across the flag of anthropology that we carry to the field, for fieldwork turns out to be a risky and wearing business. The impediments to comfort, peace of mind, and research are multitudinous. Let us count the ways.

To begin with, the people we must engage, wherever we are doing research, are busy trying to lead their lives against difficult odds, and our project rarely if ever speaks to their needs. Almost always, we are doing our research to satisfy ourselves, emotionally and intellectually, and to build our careers, to make our own lives better. If people put up with us and cooperate in our research, it is because their curiosity and generosity work to our benefit. But our work remains marginal to their lives, and we must consistently impose our research on the activity flow of local life.

Furthermore, however much we try to be open to the culture we are studying, however much we attempt to see it from the natives' point of view, the local people themselves are not obliged to do the same with us. We are the ones who purport to be cultural relativists; they do not. Our own ways will deviate from local standards in countless ways, some incomprehensible, some funny, some stupid, some dangerous, some offensive, as perceived by the people with whom we work. And they will respond to us, with a greater or lesser degree of obviousness, with puzzlement, laughter, ridicule, avoidance, and anger, all managed of course in the local fashion. Almost inevitably, we are marginal outsiders—incompetent, awkward, rude—and largely irrelevant. Being a marginal outsider is no picnic for a year of one's life; it takes considerable toughness.

Far tougher is to be a marginal outsider on one's own, all alone. Mostly we do our research on our own. Sometimes we take our boyfriends or husbands or wives with us to the field, and that does make it easier. But we are usually the lone anthropologist, doing the research on our own, facing the local people, our informants, our subjects and objects, with only our own personal resources. We have to face the puzzlement, laughter, ridicule, avoidance, and anger, accept it and deal with it as persons, and move past it as anthropologists to mold the situation so that we can extract the information that we want for our research. The fieldworker's life is strongly teleological, end motivated, goal oriented, with a constant current of immediate social and psychological discomfort.

Discomfort does not end with social marginality and cultural deviance. The physical challenge of living in new and perhaps less coddling conditions—whether constant forest rain and humidity, with mold growing over books, clothes, and skin, or scalding and searing desert heat, or the penetrating cold of mountain winters—can divert one's activities (into trying to stay dry/cool/warm) and undermine one's morale. Added to this is a whole new range of voracious microbes, often conveniently offered up by mutually accommodating sewage, drainage, and water systems, which leave the ethnographer seriously ill or functioning well below par. One colleague doing research in the Zagros mountains of Iran suffered, during one long and agonizing field research, hepatitis, cholera, amoebic dysentery, and, when there was nothing else to catch, sustained critical injuries from an auto accident on a mountain road; he knew as much about the ethnography of Iranian hospitals as he did about the tribe he was studying.

Even during periods when we manage to maintain reasonable health, the actual carrying out of research proves to be rather less straightforward and transparent than it seemed when, at graduate school, we all collectively intoned our confidence in "participant observation." Our freedom of choice in graduate school allowed us to avoid courses in methodology, just as the freedom enjoyed by graduate departments allows them to neglect offering courses in methodology. Even if a perfunctory introduction to methodology was offered, and we deigned to take it, no actual training, practice, or honing of skills could be undertaken in the brief time allotted. Such is the general profile of graduate training in methodology in North America. As regards quantitative methods and statistical tools, these are taught only in a few places and required by almost none. Training in using computers for research is virtually unheard of. So we go to the field, our hopes pinned on the vaguely formulated "participant observation," which in practice seems to mean hanging around with the folks, with some notion of watching what happens and doing some interviews. Of course, this way we are open and spontaneous, even if not very sure how to proceed. But proceed we do; girding our loins and setting our jaws, we courageously push ahead with the expectation that we shall find a way.

However, let us consider the contrary and very rare case, in which a well-developed methodology is planned and applied. A colleague of mine developed and took to the field a long structured interview to collect detailed information on family economic mobility, information relevant to theories of class. To collect the 120 interviews necessary for statistical significance, he spent most of his time for an entire year of fieldwork just doing these interviews. No calorie counting for trophic exchange analysis, no interpersonal maps for social network analysis, no descriptions of rituals, no diagrams for kinship analysis, no extended case studies of disputes for political analysis, no recording of food exchanges for caste analysis, nor any of the other dozens of types of data collection for the dozens of other types of analysis. Even if he had been trained in all of these methodological techniques and modes of analysis, really

trained, and knew how to do them, he did not even begin to have enough time to do even a few of them, not even enough time to do one other of them in a consistent, systematic, and serious way. (Oh yes, one can always catch as catch can, a bit here and a bit there on this and that subject. But how trustworthy are such scraps in the wind, and in what way do we weave them into our accounts of the things we really know?) The limits of our time and energy inevitably constrain us greatly during fieldwork; there is just so much that an individual researcher can do, and that is such a very small part of what there is to do. An important part of this, of course, is the limits on our ability to organize and control the people whom we study, for whom our research is rather marginal; their own activities directed toward the central concerns of their lives frequently take our informants out of our reach and beyond our research plans, thus slowing and inhibiting our progress. So, in the end, no matter how much we know how to do, the constraints of time and energy shackle us. Nonetheless, in spite of these constraints, we are convinced that we must not tear cultural elements out of their broad contexts, that we must strive for a holistic study, and that we are obliged to provide a full account of the society and culture that we study. We know we strive for the impossible, so impossible as to be absurd, but we nonetheless are ready to face down the absurdity, to press courageously for the necessary completeness.

Perhaps in nothing is courage more demonstrated than in our undertaking the rigors of ethnographic research without very much ability to communicate with the people we are studying. So often we go to the field with only a rudimentary knowledge of the field languages. After all, we concentrate our time and effort on the study of anthropology, and only late in our anthropological training do we decide exactly where to do our research and what languages would be necessary. Usually little time remains for language study, and often we have no access to training in the languages we need. Our own universities do not offer them and there are no funds available to support language study elsewhere. And this problem is compounded because so frequently we need to know both a national or regional language and a local one. I myself have encountered this each time I have ventured into the field: Persian and Baluchi were needed for research in Iranian Baluchistan, Hindi and Marwari for research in Jodhpur, and Italian and Sardu for research in Sardinia. The upshot of these problems in language preparation is that we must learn the language in the field, while we do our research. So, having gone off to a foreign locale to conduct research, we must learn how to live there and must initiate research without being very able to understand or make ourselves understood. It takes some courage to do this, as well as to plan, under these circumstances, to complete research within the typical year of fieldwork. (I would note that there is strong resistance among our colleagues in anthropology to the idea that fieldwork might require more than one year. In response to a recent research grant application, eventually rewarded, *all* of the assessors challenged the two-year period projected for the research, even though the length of time had no effect on the size of the grant requested. In replying to the assessors, giving the reasons for needing two years, it began to seem to me more and more doubtful that even two years would be adequate, given the obstacles to overcome and the goals to be accomplished.)

Of course all of the above presumes that one will be allowed by the political authorities to enter the country of choice and proceed to the selected field locale. Often, in fact, the question of research or residence permits is quite dicey. Recently several Ph.D. students in my department spent a year nervously waiting to hear whether they would be permitted to enter the countries for which they had been preparing the previous several years. I myself have spent long months in pre-revolution Teheran trying to get permission to go to Baluchistan, permission finally given partially and grudgingly, and eventually had the honor of being thrown out of Baluchistan by the gendarmerie for ranging too freely in the tribal territory. My later visits to sheep herding castes in Jodhpur, Barmer, and Jaisalmir, the desert districts of Rajasthan not a great distance from the border with Pakistan, roused the Indian secret police into frenzied interviewing of my Indian academic colleagues and other Indian friends, a process that did not, it seemed to me, bode well for future research and residence permits in that area. These "close calls" are the success stories, for we did get to the field(s) and were able to conduct research, even at the cost of considerable time, energy, and anxiety dealing with political obstacles. There are many other anthropologists, sometimes having waited months in a capital city, who have finally been blocked from entering the field for which they had been preparing, or chased away even after they have entered the field. There are also cases of political exclusion being of local rather than national origin; one young colleague attempting to do fieldwork among a group of American native people decided, after he discovered that the heavy buzzing was caused not by large insects but by close bullets, to shift quickly his research site to another continent. While we may go off to do fieldwork with the best of intentions—or so they seem, not always self-critically, to us—our reception may be grudging, obstructive, or totally rejecting. Because so much is at stake for us, we do our best to suppress discouragement and to press on tenaciously.

Who without great courage (or great ignorance) would undertake fieldwork under such conditions? The prospect of the many trials of fieldwork has discouraged many students from pursuing advanced study in anthropology. But how do they live there? [read: how could I live there?] is often asked by timid students nervously contemplating fieldwork. Of course, the challenge of fieldwork is an attraction to other students, students who are perhaps more daring and thus more attracted to the prospect of adventure. They will not be disappointed.

HOW SWEET ARE THE FRUITS OF ANTHROPOLOGICAL RESEARCH?

While there could be no disappointment with the freedom enjoyed by anthropologists or the courage that they display in pursuing field research, the question that we must address is whether there are grounds to be disappointed with the results of anthropological research, and whether the inadequacies are a consequence of our institutionalized freedom and courage. It has been eighty years since A. R. [Radcliffe-]Brown published *The Andaman Islanders*, and almost that long since Malinowski published *Argonauts of the Western Pacific* and the other Trobriand monographs. Anthropology should not still be a toddler, struggling to put two steps one after the other in the same direction. We do not have to rely any more on a small handful of anthropologists, one or two at Columbia, at Michigan, California, Oxford, and London. There are some 10,000 in the United States alone, and many more worldwide. If there are serious problems with anthropology, it could not be because the discipline is too young or there are too few of us. It would have to be because of the way we do things, perhaps the very freedom and courage that seem so characteristic of anthropology.

But what disappointment could there be with the results of anthropology and anthropological research? A well-known and occasionally discussed problem is the fact that the vast multitude of anthropological conferences, congresses, articles, monographs, and collections, while adding up to mountains of paper (and subtracting whole forests), do not seem to add up to a substantial, integrated, coherent body of knowledge that could provide a base for the further advancement of the discipline. L. A. Fallers used to comment that we seem to

be constantly tooling up with new ideas and new concepts and never seem to get around to applying and assessing them in a substantive and systematic fashion. John Davis, over two decades ago in *The Peoples of the Mediterranean*, seemed on the verge of tears of frustration during his attempts to find any comparable information in the available ethnographic reports that might be used to put individual cases into perspective and be compiled into a broader picture. Nor is there confidence in the individual ethnographic reports available: We cannot credit the accounts of I. Schapera, because he was a functionalist, or that of S. F. Nadel, because he was an agent of colonialism, or J. Pitt-Rivers, because he collected all his data from the upper-class *señoritas*, or F. Barth, because he is capitalistic, or M. Godelier, because he is an idealist in marxist clothing, or T. Asad, because he is a marxist in empiricist clothing, or M. Harris, because he is a crude materialist, etc., etc. So we end up without any substantive body of knowledge to build on, forcing us to be constantly trying to make anthropology anew.

Of course, making anthropology anew moment by moment is a manifestation of the freedom so woven into the structure of anthropology, and it does provide the opportunity for creativity. But are the organizational and intellectual resources necessary for fruitful creativity available? Let us consider the point of view of more narrowly restricted area specialists—whether Orientalists, Indianists, East Asianists, historians working on Europe, sociologists focusing on North America, economists concentrating on Latin America—who often receive deep training and achieve high competence in the languages, literature, geography, history, and contemporary events of their regions, knowledge which provides a sound foundation for their research. These area specialists—surely you must have encountered some yourself—marvel at the *chutzpa* of anthropologists who, usually virgin (or quasi-) in the regional languages and literatures and naked of all but enthusiasm and the certainty of the down-to-earth and with-the-people rightness of anthropology, stride off into the forest/desert/mountains/city to live for a year and to record for posterity their "newly discovered" people and culture. The dingy, stingy skepticism of these area specialists we usually brush off as cases of interdisciplinary competitiveness, and in any case they are all (are they not?) more or less caught up in Western intellectual imperialism, Orientalist prisoners of exotic fantasies of the other, whereas we anthropologists are committed to presenting "the actor's point of view," the everyday on-the-ground reality, and the cultural frame/or material circumstances/or world system context through which that reality is made. But it is hard to deny some of the above mentioned difficulties—which we prefer to think of as *practical* difficulties—in regard to our areal preparations. With our decisions about research venues being taken only a year or two before we are scheduled to leave for field research, and with the relevant languages, literatures, and other areal subjects seldom being available at our universities, and with there being commonly at least two field languages to master, the national and the local, and with the foreign scholarly literatures on the place of research often being in one or more additional languages, all too frequently ones we have not previously studied, we are not usually in a position to lay a solid foundation for our research. So we typically catch a summer language course or fit in a regional culture or history course, while we put our hopes on picking up the language in the field, learning about the culture directly from the informants, and mastering the broader context through archival research in the field. We rely on our rapid progress in the field and our ability to cover all the bases. Okay, it takes a lot of scrambling, but this is what fieldwork is all about! Fine, but, if we do our best with only moderate understanding of the language(s) and with modest areal background, and if we rely on anecdotes and impressions

because we have not been trained in the methods of collecting information, and if in any case there is not time for systematic collection of information, shall we then be surprised if all too often our ethnographic reports seem superficial, patchy, unreliable?

ARE WE THE CARPENTERS OF OUR OWN STUMBLING BLOCKS?

The credibility of our field reports rests mainly on their uniqueness, that is, on the absence of any other reports that might present contrary "findings," that is, test their reliability. Most of the cases of repeat or closely comparable studies, from Redfield and Lewis in Mexico to the Truk controversy and up to the challenge to Mead's work in Samoa, have resulted in gross contradiction, angry confusion, and a final uncertainty. The established anthropological strategy of the solitary researcher seeking a site to make her or his own—"my" village or tribe or quarter, "my" people— preferably a site previously unknown and unstudied, reinforces the sense of ethnographic fieldwork as an adventurous quest and downplays research as an informed contribution to a collective enterprise aimed at furthering knowledge.

The dubious nature of ethnographic reportage is however by no means the only source of difficulty in the building of a sound base of anthropological knowledge. At least equally debilitating are the theoretical fads and fashions that come and go in anthropology with a dazzling speed. For the last five years or so the heuristic frame of interpretationalism, stressing the symbolically constructed nature of human life and the subjective nature of research activity, has been dominant in anthropology. It is amazing to think that for the five years or so before that, anthropology was dominated by marxist analysis, focused upon oppression, conflict, struggle, revolution, and praxis. And that for the five years or so before that, French structuralism, with its formalistic deep structures and transformations, was a major influence. Before that was a similar period of transactionalism, emphasizing choice, exchange, networks, and aggregate patterns. Amongst these waves, whole literatures, often intricately entangled with other disciplines, have choked bibliographies and bookshelves, only to disappear abruptly and totally at the sound of the trumpets. And the fads continue coming, for at this very moment, medical anthropologists are telling us that "the body" should be adopted as the universal model and metaphor for human life and anthropological study. Needless to say, the heroes and followers of each new wave disparage and reject the work of the previous waves as ill-conceived and better forgotten. Only tomorrow's new theoretical look—the body? symbolic genetics? space ecology?—has any worth; as for previous errors, consign them to the flames, for they contain only falsehood and illusion. Is it any wonder, with paradigm shifts more rapid than our replacement of cars, that anthropologists have difficulty consolidating a knowledge base upon which to build?

Of course, there is a close relation between the tides of theoretical fashion and the research strategy of the lone stranger on the adventurous quest. We are so seldom in a position to ascertain the substantive value of an ethnographic account—typically even thesis supervisors know little about the people being studied by their students—to know how much of the account is the approach, imagination, and confusion of the researcher and how much reflects something real about the people being studied, that we have given up trying to judge the soundness, validity, dependability, reliability, and fairness of ethnographic reports. Indeed, the current interpretationalist and latterly postmodern view is that ethnographic reports are inherently subjective—interpretations of interpretations according to C. Geertz, stories that I brought back from the field according to J. Briggs—and so it is futile and indeed

misconceived to expect validity, reliability, and so on. Now I grant that people are subjective, an understanding shared by the way with natural science, the methodology of which is organized on that very presumption. However, the argument that ethnographic reports are personal statements by the researchers, with uncertain relation to any "reality" (if we dare posit such) in the setting studied, is in my view not so much a profound acknowledgment of epistemological wisdom, as it is often portrayed, but rather a rationalization of the slipshod training and organization and the shoddy methodology of ethnographic research and a justification of the anthropological *esprit de corps* founded on freedom and adventure. The result within anthropology is a de-emphasis on ethnography and a focus on new heuristic theoretical approaches, new conceptualizations, new keys to understanding everything, new ideologies, new slogans, *ad nauseam*. The shrewd career strategy is not to do sound and sensitive ethnography, but to come up with a sexy new approach or slogan that will make you a hero of a new anthropological "ism." And so there is a positive feedback cycle between the unassessable and dubious ethnographic literature and the raucous touting of this week's new "theoretical" slogan.

Now if my position on the current state of anthropology seems overly severe and unduly grumpy, it might be well to bear in mind the position of anthropology among its sister disciplines and among other current and potential consumers of anthropology and employers of anthropologists, and the significance of this for the future of anthropology. It is true that anthropology could probably struggle along in the academic world attracting undergraduates in search of a soft option where requirements and statistics and so on can be avoided, and attracting more young solitary adventurers to our graduate programs. But practicing anthropologists, working in government agencies or hospitals or commercial companies, who must present their findings and make their arguments among economists and agronomists, doctors and patients' lobbyists, lawyers and politicians, must present strong cases with some claim on grasping reality, or else they will be laughed out of their projects and their jobs. Even in academia, the area specialists, and colleagues in sister disciplines, have strong doubts about whether anthropologists are up to very much, other than having lots of nice vacations in exotic places. Certainly university administrators, the ones who provide funds for anthropology departments, often seem highly unimpressed by the academic merits of anthropology. Why should a university fund teaching anthropology and anthropological research when there are serious academic disciplines to fund? Similarly, why does the Social and Cultural Anthropology Program of the National Science Foundation receive only $1,400,000 annually to support research for the 10,000 U.S. anthropologists, a handsome average of $140 each? If anthropology is not considered serious by government funders, university administrators, and outside employers, we should ask ourselves why. Perhaps it is not only the ignorance and philistinism of the others, but a genuine shortcoming in what anthropology is able to offer.

While the freedom in anthropology is conducive to openness and creativity, and the courage of anthropologists conducive to tenaciousness in the face of impediments, the resulting individualism limits and inhibits the fruition of research potential and the building of knowledge. Individualism dictates that graduate students must be allowed to do what they want, whether or not what they want prepares them adequately for their research. It dictates that established anthropologists and graduate students alike may pursue any research project in any location, irrespective of its pertinence to anything else and in spite of the unavailability of established expertise. It guarantees that ethnographic reports will either be general and superficial or restricted and partial. And it results in the absence of a community of informed opinion capable of assessing ethnographic reports, which leads to the downplaying of ethnography and to anthropology's desperate vulnerability to new theories, labels, and slogans.

UNITED WE STAND

Is it possible that the individualism institutionalized in our graduate programs and in our research strategies might, with determination and care, be gently diluted by broader structures which accommodate the need of anthropology for a more adequate program of training, a more effective research strategy, an increased common discourse, a process of grounded assessment, and a basis for informed criticism? Many other disciplines, from those as close as prehistoric archaeology to the more distant biological and physical sciences, enrich the creativity of individuals through structures of cooperation and exchange, common enterprise, and division of responsibilities. A number of researchers often focus on related problems in the same milieux, or the same problem in related milieux, or investigate different aspects of the same phenomenon, thus being able to specialize without losing the larger perspective. In this way, they are able to build a small research community, cooperate in the division of tasks so that each has a feasible load, provide informed criticism, and build a fund of common knowledge from which to move forward. These research partnerships, networks, groups, or teams provide both an effective research structure and a functioning intellectual marketplace for the filtering and refinement of findings and ideas. As Ralf Dahrendorf has said, truth is not a function of morning exercises in objectivity, but rather of an effective marketplace of ideas. In such an open forum, "the truth" of research findings and theories can be tested through free criticism among scholars. Or, if "truth" is too risque a notion for our postmodern times, we can say we are seeking sounder, better-grounded, more sensitive work through new structures that assist us in producing it.

I find it ironic that anthropologists so seldom reflect on the structure of their own discipline and do not seem to consider the costs of the structures in place. It is well within our powers to institute modifications so as to provide an increased level of coordinated and cooperative research, commonality of knowledge, and critical collaboration. Ethnographic researchers, of junior and senior levels, working together at one or more field sites over a substantial period, can build together a more realistic set of complementary research responsibilities, an informed common dis-

course, provide grounded assessment and constructive criticism, and together offer to the wider intellectual community a more refined, better established, and more profound body of findings, upon which further research can more easily draw.

Of course, we could continue on as we have been, maintaining the randomness of the individualistic adventure lacking disciplinary rhyme or reason, and suffering the confusion of the repeated overlapping births and deaths of multiple fads, as long as we are satisfied with the darkness of randomness and confusion, a darkness which seems very far from the light hoped for and expected from anthropology as a research discipline.

INTELLECTUAL ROOTS

Philip Carl Salzman is Professor of Anthropology at McGill University in Montreal. He has for many years been a student of nomadic and pastoral peoples, carrying out field research among nomadic tribes in Iranian Baluchistan (1968-69, 1972-73, 1976), herding castes in Rajasthan and Gujarat (1985), and shepherd communities in Sardinia (1987, 1988, 1990-92). Publications resulting from this research include the articles "Political Organization among Nomadic Peoples" (1967), "Movement and Resource Extraction among Pastoral Nomads" (1971), "Adaptation and Political Organization in Iranian Baluchistan" (1971), "Ideology and Change in Middle Eastern Tribal Society" (1978), "Does Complementary Opposition Exist?" (1978), "Why Tribes Have Chiefs" (1983), "Shrinking Pasture for Rajasthani Pastoralists" (1986), "Labor Formations in a Nomadic Tribe" (1988), and the edited and co-edited volumes *When Nomads Settle* (1980), *The Future of Pastoral Peoples* (1981), *Change and Development in Nomadic and Pastoral Societies* (1981), *Contemporary Nomadic and Pastoral Peoples* (1982), *Nomadic Peoples in a Changing World* (1990). Salzman founded in 1978 and continues to

chair the Commission on Nomadic Peoples of the International Union of Anthropological and Ethnological Sciences—for which the Union presented him with its Gold Award in 1988—and founded, edited and published (1980–90) the international journal of the commission, *Nomadic Peoples* (currently published in Sweden). He has also published critical comment, such as "Is Traditional Fieldwork Outmoded?" (1986), "Fads and Fashions in Anthropology" (1988), "The Failure of Solitary Fieldwork" (1989), and "The Lone Stranger and the Solitary Quest" (1989). In 1988, he founded a collaborative research group, the Mediterranean Anthropological Research Equipe (M.A.R.E.), which initiated field research in Sardinia in 1990.

Having begun studying sociology with E. K. Wilson and R. Gordon at Antioch College, I was enticed by social anthropology during a year of study (1959-60) with K. Little, M. Banton, J. Littlejohn, and M. Ruel at the University of Edinburgh. When I returned to Antioch, I took up studies with Victor Ayoub, who had worked with Clyde Kluckhohn in Social Relations at Harvard, but who was intrigued by British social anthropology, as I myself became with A. R. Radcliffe-

Brown's vision of social anthropology as a division of comparative sociology and with S. F. Nadel's impressive methodological demonstration of the power of comparative analysis applied to ethnographic neighbors.

Partly because Radcliffe-Brown had taught at the University of Chicago and had influenced some of the ongoing staff, such as F. Eggan, who was a strong advocate of comparative studies, I chose to pursue graduate studies there. What I found at Chicago (1963-66), taking courses with L. A. Fallers, C. Geertz, and D. Schneider, was, however, a Weberian perspective influenced by Talcott Parsons emphasizing the interplay of quasi-independent social, cultural, and personality systems. While I was later to move toward the Parsonian view, at a time when most everyone else was rejecting it in favor of marxist materialism or symbolic culturalism, I was most inspired at Chicago by an ecological perspective, probably due to the prehistory courses that I took with L. Binfield and R. McC. Adams, which appeared to me to hold great promise for anthropological explanation and the formulation of theoretical generalizations.

The search for explanations of social and cultural variety has been one of my greatest interests, which is why I find comparative analysis, especially of the smaller scale "controlled comparison" type advocated by Nadel and Eggan, very attractive. Descriptive accounts alone, interesting though they may be, have always seemed to me incomplete. I want to know not only what a particular people and their culture are like, but why they are that way, what influences have led them to where we find them. But I did not find a basis for explanation in the powerful theories of Marx or Freud, being dissatisfied with the self-validating nature of their systems, a response informed by studies of the philosophers D. Hume and K. Popper, and also E. Gellner, whom I came to know personally later through our shared interest in nomadic peoples.

If my first contacts with the Middle East (non-Eurocentrically: Southwest Asia) came through V. Ayoub's research in Lebanon, my first exposure to the anthropology of pastoral nomads was in reading I. M. Lewis's *A Pastoral Democracy* on the nomads of Somaliland (now Somalia). I was impressed with the intrepid, independent personalities of the nomads and their democratic politics. And the factors influencing their lives seemed to me more transparent to the observer than those of some other types of society. As I pursued the study of nomads, e.g., reading E. E. Evans-Pritchard's *The Nuer* and *The Sanusi of Cyrenaica*, N. Dyson-Hudson's *Karimojong Politics*, and F. Barth's *Nomads of South Persia*, it became obvious how very different from one another different groups of nomads were. The attempt to explain these differences, using comparative analysis, underlies quite a lot of my writing.

My research among the Yarahmadzai Baluch (under the regime of the Shah called the Shah Nawazi) brought home the organizational multiplicity in Yarahmadzai society and culture, a built-in set of alternatives, sometimes overlapping and conflicting, but always providing a flexibility with which to pursue individual or group projects and to respond to changing circumstances. I had seen hints of this earlier in Nadel's *A Theory of Social Structure*, but did not realize its significance until puzzling over my field data. With this multiplicity in mind, I have addressed some ethnographic puzzles and seeming anomalies, such as the Bedouin segmentary-lineage-system-that-people-say-but-do-not-do, as reported by E. Peters, a student and latter-day critic of Evans-Pritchard.

Recently, reviewing my own experiences doing field research and the difficulties faced by my graduate students in the field and afterward, I became convinced of the serious limitations of solitary, individualistic fieldwork. In an attempt to mitigate these problems in practice, in 1988 I organized the Mediterranean Anthropological Research Equipe by bringing together graduate students and professors from several countries to carry out collaborative field research in the traditionally pastoral Ogliastra region of Sardinia. This ongoing research, begun in 1990, is providing a lively challenge to my ideas and theories.

2

After the Critique of Ethnography: Faith, Hope, and Charity, But the Greatest of These Is Charity

GEORGE E. MARCUS

AFTER THE CRITIQUE OF RHETORIC

The 1980s critiques of the rhetoric used by social science disciplines have now had an undeniable effect upon the thinking, if not practices, of most scholars. Yet the implication of such critiques for transforming disciplinary styles of research and theory over the long-term still remains an open question. Over the past decade, insiders in a number of disciplines—including history, political science, economics, anthropology, sociology, psychology, law, and architecture—have been influenced by philosophy and literary theory in their critical attention to the specialized languages used to describe, conceptualize, and explain social reality. Discourses of the "real" have been demonstrated to be of a piece with the rhetoric of fiction and to possess the fully literary character of language as narrative, subject to tropes, figuration, and self-consciousness. Blurring the categories of the literary and the scientific in language use has also raised questions that fuel the deeply skeptical element in Western philosophy, namely about the limits of representation and the referential capacity of language.

In the different versions of rhetorical critique now in play, the basic task of social science—of creating positive knowledge of the world—is much complicated. However intrinsically interesting may be the attempt to question the objectifying, realist discourse of positivism, there is a widespread anxiety about the subversion, or at least the sidetracking, of the empirical mission of the social sciences to speak with probabilistic certainty about the social world (in a manner that the natural sciences have been able to do of the natural world).

Until the implications of the strong critique of social science discourse have been articulated as fully worked out alternative projects of theory and research, the critique will be merely acknowledged, marginalized as a low-ranking specialty (like historiography, for example), or ignored with a "so what?" *Outsiders* to the traditions of social science—the philosophers, literary theorists, cultural critics, and intellectual historians who have made social science discourses their object of study—are relatively free to assert the most radical implication of the critique: that social science traditions are impossible projects that can only be perpetuated by insensitivity to their characteristics as discourse. Here, I refer to the establishment of interdisciplinary scholarship that has emerged in the humanities/cultural studies centers existing in the disciplinary interstices of many contemporary American universities. These are powered by the legacies of poststructuralist thought and the fascination with defining the present as "postmodernity." *Insiders*, who have actually delivered rhetorical critiques of their own social science disciplines (in alliance with such external critics), have much more at stake in terms of professional interest and identity. They cannot so easily banish the traditions in which they are vested.

FOUR DEVELOPMENTS FOLLOWING FROM RECENT CRITIQUES

The critique of social science discourse has generated from discipline to discipline a predictable field of reaction, debate, and polemic. Among possible positions, I want to point to two extreme and two less extreme ones. First, one finds attempts to annihilate the field and its identity with a basic challenge to the notion of representation itself. The ideology of Derridean deconstruction—of endlessly deferred meaning and the confrontation with the illusion of the real as presence—is the strong form of radical discourse critique. This position is most easily occupied by outsiders who have no stake in a particular tradition of social scientific inquiry. But versions of it are also argued by insiders who offer permanent metacritiques, like permanent revolutions, within their disciplines.

This second, or derivative position, is no less radical than deconstruction, but it does recognize a space and function for such radical critique within the historic projects of social scientific disciplines. Rather than being nihilistic, however, permanent metacritique of discourse and rhetoric confronts the mainstream's unmediated realism, taste for objectification, and belief in transparent language, in order to constantly shock and argue with these styles. Playing the minor key of skepticism against the major key of so-called logocentrism in Western cultural cognition takes on a local discipline-specific purpose of generating self-critical consciousness. This position rationalizes a place for permanent, radical critique within disciplines, but with uncertain implications for modes of theory and practice. It in fact recognizes that the mainstream is glacial and may perhaps be untransformable.

The third position is the moderate/liberal one of weak or unspecified reformism, and is fairly widespread. The awareness of one's claims and assertions as rhetorically constituted might have a therapeutic value for practitioners. The critique is something for practicing social scientists to think about. It is seen as an enriching tool that can be accommodated to current styles of theorizing and research. We only need to muddle through—qualifying to a certain degree the process of objectification and truth claims of mainstream work in the social sciences.

Experimentalism

The fourth position, experimentalism, is much more substantive and defensible. It is the one I want to dwell upon here, particularly with regard to ethnography (the practice at the core of contemporary sociocultural anthropology). The word "experiment" evokes either the central mode of the natural sciences or that of the *avant-garde* of historic aesthetic modernism in the West from the 1890s to the 1960s. These latter, through experiments with form, overturned developed, but naive, notions of realism in the arts. It is this latter sense of experiment I mean to evoke here.

The impulse governing experimentalism is that once the conventions and rhetorical nature of realist discourse are exposed, the opportunity exists to formulate new questions, to materialize new objects of study, and to explore new discursive spaces through experiments with form. The historic lesson of intellectual revitalization movements based on experiments with form may be eventual devolution into technique or the exhausting of once powerful effects in their becoming mere gesture. But I would argue that at the present moment—in which social theory and philosophy have powerfully critiqued the very process of representation—the remaking of great traditions of theory is indeed a problem of the redesign of form. Simply put, this is what the critique of social scientific rhetoric, beyond the function of critique itself, gestures toward.

Some fear that experimentalism is self-aggrandizing, chic, elitist, and nostalgic for an earlier kind of role for the creative intellectual. At worst, the fear is that there may be nothing there but free play, the overvaluation of imagination relative to shared empirical, systematic discourse and knowledge production. Finally, it might be thought that the venerable work and burden of theorizing—asking clarifications of the big questions about humanity, history, and society—cannot be born at the level of practice, at that of mere engaged experimental thinking and writing from myriad research projects which have lost faith in the ability of governing disciplinary paradigms to provide the conceptual means to represent and classify the world.

I would answer these reservations by arguing that, in the age of skepticism in which we live, the design problem in rendering accounts of the world, of rethinking how phenomena of interest in our basic descriptions have been named and conceived, is indeed the key to a broad and deep transformation of social science disciplines as they have developed in the United States since World War II. By not exempting any discourse from scrutiny, including their own, critiques of rhetoric change the generally understood relationship between theory and research practice in the social sciences. The critiques equalize them as the source of ideas and create dialogue between them—diminishing the hierarchy of authority and subordination that is conventionally understood to hold between theory and research practice. As such, the experimental mood deconstructs the categories of theory and method that organize much intellectual work in the social sciences. It offers a range of different possibilities for understanding what the purpose and process of inquiry are. Experimentation with the forms of a discipline's standard accounts

seems to me, then, to be the obvious, most promising, and most pragmatically radical implication of the recent critiques of disciplinary rhetorics that do not do away with, or recklessly challenge, whole traditions of thought themselves.

THE ROLE OF ETHNOGRAPHY IN ANTHROPOLOGY

The critique of ethnography in anthropology, to which I now direct the remainder of this paper, has attracted particular attention. This is because, of all the American social science disciplines that were formed through more or less committed adherence to an idealized model of knowledge production in the natural sciences, anthropology seems to be one where the recent critique and its implications have occupied the most prominent place in disciplinary debates. In contrast, similar initiatives in political science, history, economics, and history so far, I believe, have only been acknowledged on the margins, or assimilated as a passing fashion or subspecialty. Traditionally placed in the social sciences and humanities as the source of exotic otherness—of exceptional cases at the margins of dominant themes—ethnography within anthropology now has the possibility of redefining its position within Western intellectual discourses. It can free itself from its historic identification with the exotic and the primitive—categories of highly dubious empirical and ethical value in the late twentieth century anyway—and exemplify a discipline that not only heeds the continuing critique of its practices and discourses, but embraces such critique as the very source of its projects of knowledge.

Ethnography has been at the heart of cultural anthropology for over seventy years. It has played a critical role in overthrowing the evolutionary paradigm on which much anthropological inquiry had been founded in the nineteenth century. Indeed, one might view ethnography itself as the historic mode of experimentation made doctrine by Boas in the United States and Malinowski in England in order to move beyond the grand universalizing, evolutionary schemes of writers like Sir James Frazer and Lewis Henry Morgan. Yet a scientific, ethnography-based anthropology nonetheless retains much of the discipline's earlier central focus on the conditions of "universal Man"—interpreted as primitive humans living outside modernity, the presumed locus in which the essential questions about humanity could be addressed. Cultural anthropology might then seem to have no other contemporary overarching purpose than to create a detailed ethnographic archive of the exotic for the modern West so that certain notions of what is (or is not) universal in humans might eventually be determined.

Certainly late-twentieth-century developments in other fields, such as the cognitive sciences, and the general discrediting of progress-oriented evolutionary schemes have left the grand program for cultural anthropology and its ethnographic archive in an awkward position. What remains is a distinctive interpretive approach to knowledge production, unique in the social sciences or humanities.

Ethnography has been forged largely outside the Western notion of history through the use of such rhetorical devices as the "ethnographic present." It has been predicated on the romantic/scientific quest of fieldwork—studying life in other communities of distinctive (if not exotic) difference. This sensitive task of cultural translation and interpretation has absorbed the intellectual energies and defined the ethos of the contemporary discipline. Some indeed have resisted the ahistoricism embedded in visions of the ethnographic paradigm. Particularly after World War II, for example, the focus on the primitive expanded to include peasants, urban migrants, and the formation of ethnic groups in the era of new nation building, decolonization, and the ideology of economic development. Nonetheless even in change-oriented ethnography,

which found an intellectual home in Marxist political economy, the basic conventions and rhetoric of the ethnographic production of knowledge held fast.

The Recent Critique of Ethnography

It was only in the late 1960s and through the 1970s that effective critiques of various elements in the ethnographic paradigm emerged. First, a sophisticated and historically informed discussion of anthropology as a situated intellectual formation in the history of Western colonialism developed. Second, a critical discussion of fieldwork, as an explicitly hermeneutic method in which the observer could not be completely separated from the observed, evolved from a long-standing silence among anthropologists about this key emblem of their disciplinary distinction. There was an outpouring, from the late 1960s onward, of romantic, confessional, but nonetheless epistemologically revealing, accounts about the trials and tribulations of fieldwork. And third, anthropologists, in conjunction with intellectual historians and cultural critics, produced a critique of the historically distinctive subject of their own discipline—the primitive, exotic "other" and, behind this representation, that of "universal Man" or humanity.

These important strands came together in a focused way during the 1980s in the critique of ethnographic rhetoric and discourse perhaps most fully expressed in the 1986 volume Jim Clifford and I edited, *Writing Culture: The Poetics and Politics of Ethnography*. At the heart of the critique was the manner in which ethnographic authority is constructed rhetorically in the textual production of anthropological knowledge. For example, the legitimacy and validity of ethnographies have rested on conveying a sense of "having been there." Direct experience of another world, including knowledge of the other's language and everyday idioms, makes the ethnographer a competent translator of a distinctive form of life that should be presented vividly and holistically to the ethnographer's readerships at home. Various blindnesses, evasions, and indeed fictions, necessary to reap the important insights that ethnography has produced and their exposure in the current environment of intellectual skepticism, suggest the need for new vocabularies, new concepts, and new rhetorics. There is, in brief, a need for new modes, beyond the available legacy of nineteenth-century social theory, for describing the social and the cultural.

Innovation in anthropological thought generally has not been powered by broad meta-theoretical discourse since the nineteenth century, but rather by theory that has remained close to the manner in which ethnographic facts have been determined (e.g., Boas's historical particularism). It is perhaps not surprising, then, that the critique of ethnographic rhetoric has generated experiments with the semiliterary form that frames ethnographic knowledge claims. For example, one interesting analytic problem in cultural anthropology today concerns ways of opening up, to contemporary processes of apparent global homogenization, the local knowledge classically represented and described by ethnographers. The problem is no longer merely to place ethnography in the frame of historic meta-narratives, since they are subject to critical scrutiny, but to find new rhetorics of description for constituting the objects of inquiry that are not naive about the power of yet poorly understood transcultural processes that diversify and deterritorialize cultures just as they homogenize them. (For new work in this direction, I point the reader to the journal *Public Culture*, recently established by Arjun Appadurai and Carol Beckenridge.) This is the kind of modernist, or in its current version, postmodernist double-talk that ethnography needs to demonstrate can be made into a project of research of rich possibility. Ethnography shares this problematic with other disciplines. But its advantage, as noted, is that it functions well and creatively without a sense

that it needs a positive theoretical paradigm—that is, conventional social theory—to guide it. Instead it breeds off the critique of its own rhetoric.

By the late 1980s, the traditional interest of ethnography in culture (as lived local experience) and the acknowledged need to understand it in global perspective had come specifically to be about how collective and individual identities are negotiated in the various places that anthropologists conduct fieldwork. Such ethnography bears the burden of explaining how, in the conventional local contexts and sites familiar to ethnographic research, diversity paradoxically emerges in a transcultural world. In the face of global creolization processes, there is renewed interest among anthropologists in such topics as ethnicity, race, nationality, and colonialism. While such primordial phenomena as traditions, communities, and kinship systems continue to be documented, they can no longer, in and of themselves, serve as the grounding tropes (or figures of speech) which organize ethnographic description and explanation.

The most venturesome works in this trend concerned with the shaping and transformation of identities—of one's subjects, as well as, at the very same time, of the ethnographer and the ethnographic project itself—question most radically the frameworks which privilege exclusive identities, emergent from an authoritative cultural structure that can always be described and modeled (for example, see the recent work by Klaus Neumann 1992 whose very title signals the radical approach to the problem of identity—*Not the Way It Really Was: Constructing the Tolai Past*).

Instead, experimental ethnographies find pleasure in connecting phenomena worlds apart, in showing how cultural phenomena work systematically in decentered and fragmented ways, in overcoming the dualisms that have structured social theory and social inquiry (such as traditional-modern, rural-urban, individual-society, and the like), and finally, in discovering systematic relationships in the juxtaposition of what might conventionally have been thought to be incommensurate. In short, the practical analytic task of much contemporary ethnography (and its greatest contribution to theory at the very same time) is to redesign the spatial-temporal means for representing cultural processes in response to a perception that anthropology must deal with the fragmentation, discontinuity, and simultaneity that seem so characteristic of contemporary global and local realities.[1]

TWO KEY STRATEGIES CURRENT IN ETHNOGRAPHIC WRITING

While the critique of ethnographic discourse is still the subject of lively debate, certain changes in ethnographic rhetoric and discourse, if not widely accepted, are at least widely countenanced. The two new strategies prominently injected into ethnographies are reflexivity and what I will call the "resistance and accommodation" formula (which opens the local integrity of cultures to global or world historical forces). The danger is that these moves might be viewed as mere gestures or techniques of ethnographic discourse in response to the postmodern critique of anthropology's rhetorical styles. Indeed, unless these moves are thought through as important elements in fuller strategies for the redesign of ethnographic discourse, they will lose any analytic power they have.

Reflexivity

Reflexivity involves working into ethnographic texts a self-conscious account regarding the conditions of knowledge production as it is being produced. Crudely, this move replaces the observational objective "eye" of the ethnographer with his or her personal (sometimes pejoratively viewed narcissistic) "I." There is a move away from the naive assumption of objectivity and unmediated realism and a greater tolerance for the explicit

treatment of reflexivity in ethnographic analysis. But there is still lacking, among many, any clear understanding of the intellectual functions such explicitness about reflexivity serves.

Some might argue that it merely serves the ethical purpose of atoning for the bad faith of previously unmediated realism (in which the knower's role in the known was studiously downplayed). But there is more to reflexivity. It constitutes the basis for hermeneutic practice. It might, for example, suggest changes in the very notion of the kind of knowledge that ethnography can or should produce—knowledge that arises not from monologic authority or voice (however self-critical), but from dialogic relationships in the field that lead to experiments in intellectual collaboration which are de facto at the core of all ethnographic fieldwork. Reflexivity, then, means introducing a discussion of dialogic and collaborative relationships into the ethnographic text, that is, of how informants and ethnographer collectively construct a text. My own position is that reflexivity—deployed in different sorts of analytic and narrative tasks—is an essential dimension of any ethnography whose aim is to produce critical knowledge of its subjects' ways of life.

Resistance and Accommodation

Distinguishing the elements of resistance and accommodation in the formation of collective and personal identities has become the almost sloganlike analytic formula for retaining a sense of the coherence and locality of place in ethnographic description while also recognizing the penetrations of world systems and consumer economies. The resistance and accommodation formula might be understood, in a way, as the remaking of the salvage rationale that has served ethnography for so long. The ethnographer arrives on the scene of a world on the wane and salvages it in texts before it is lost to modernization. The alternative in the resistance and accommodation narrative that is now being experimented with locates cultural survival and authenticity in much more subtle and complex ways while still reaffirming them (for a brilliant example, see Jean Comaroff's *Body and Power, Spirit of Resistance* 1985, but now much ethnography is written in this frame).

These two contemporary features of ethnographic writing, then, are remaking the mode (unmediated realism) and rationale (salvage) of classic ethnography. In the absence of an explicit theoretical paradigm for experimentation, they are generally taken to be what experimentation is about by many anthropologists. Each of these strategies is in need of a project, a more systematic statement of their significance as experiments with ethnographic narrative and description. What follows is my admittedly programmatic and idiosyncratic attempt to provide one comprehensive scheme for the redesign of ethnography that incorporates these strategies. Far from a rejection of realism, I see the following as a move toward a revitalized and defensible practice of realism—one that arises from conversation with the most radical critics of realist narrative (those rhetoricians, skeptical philosophers, and charismatic cultural critics who question its validity, if not its possibility). What is off-stage here is that conversation and the origins of my scheme within it.

SIX EXPERIMENTAL STRATEGIES FOR REDESIGNING ETHNOGRAPHY

The following six stratagems arise from a systematic disqualification of the various structuring devices ethnographic realism has traditionally depended upon (and which the critique of its rhetoric has highlighted). Three concern changing the parameters shaping the way ethnographic subjects have been analytically and rhetorically constructed as subjects: redesigning the observed. The other three involve altering the nature of the theoretical intervention that the ethnographer deploys in

the texts he or she creates: redesigning the observer. Together they constitute a critical project for ethnography that takes it well beyond its traditional archival function of classifying and describing exotic otherness toward the postmodernist problematic of experimenting with ways of narrating (and thus understanding) the contemporary variety of simultaneously global and local forms of life.

Redesigning the Observed

Problematizing the Spatial (or breaking with the trope of community)   The concept of community—in the classic sense of shared values, shared identity, and thus shared culture—has been mapped literally onto the concept of locality to define a basic frame of reference orienting ethnography. The connotations of solidity and homogeneity (attaching to the notion of community) have been replaced in the framework of modernity by the idea that the situated production of identity—of a person, of a group, or even of a whole society—does not depend alone, or even always primarily, on the observable, concentrated activities within a particular locale. The identity of anyone or any group is produced simultaneously in many different locales of activity, by many different agents, for many different purposes. One's identity in terms of where one lives—among one's neighbors, friends, relatives, or co-strangers—is only one social context, and perhaps not the most important one, in which identity is shaped. It is the various elements of this process of dispersed identity construction—mobile, related representations in many different places of differing character—that must be grasped as social facts. Of course this presents new and some very difficult problems of research method and textual representation in ethnography. But to capture the formation of identity (multiple identities, really) at a particular moment in the biography of a person, or the history of a group of people, through a configuration of very differing sites or locales of activity recognizes both the powerful integrating (rationalizing) drives of the state and the economy in modernity, and the resulting dispersals of the subject (person or group) in multiple overlapping fragments of identity that also characterize modernity (see Marcus 1989 for a discussion of the complexities of ethnographic accounts of upper classes in this regard).

The questions for study in this parallel processing, so to speak, of identity at many sites are: (1) Which identities coalesce and under what circumstances? (2) Which become defining or dominant and for how long? (3) How does the play of unintended consequences affect the outcome in the coalescence of a salient identity in this space of the multiple construction and dispersed control of a person's or group's identities? And (4) what is the nature of the politics by which identity at and across any site is controlled?

Cultural difference or diversity arises here not from some local struggle for identity, but is a function of a complex process among all the sites in which the identity of someone or a group is defined. It is the burden of contemporary experimental ethnography to capture distinctive identity formations in all their migrations and dispersions. This multilocale, dispersed identity, vision reconfigures and complexifies the spatial plane on which ethnography has conceptually operated in the past.

Bruno Latour's *Pasteurization of France* (1989) is an example. It deals with the historic dissemination of Louis Pasteur's science in French society. Latour attempts to construct a heterogeneous (and discontinuous) space in which to render an account of a process that is refracted in the simultaneous operations of multiple sites and actors without obvious cause-effect, linear relationships to one another. There is a stretching to imagine the kind of complex space on which the cultural process of scientific innovation can be described.

Problematizing the Temporal (or breaking with the trope of history in realist ethnography).   The break is not with historical consciousness (or a pervasive sense of the past) in any site or set of sites probed by ethnography. Rather it is with historical determination as the primary explanatory context for an ethnographic present. Realist ethnography to some degree has been revived by incorporation within existing Western historical accounts of the colonial past. There is a lively effort, in contradistinction to the classic period in the development of Anglo-American ethnography, to tie the site of ethnographic observation to a stream of history within which it can be explained by reference to an historical narrative (see, for example, the entire genre inspired by Wolf 1982 and Sahlins 1985).

The contemporary experimental mood is not so sanguine about the alliance between conventional social history and ethnography. The past that is present in any site is built up from memory, the fundamental medium of ethnohistory. Collective and individual memory in its multiple traces and expressions is indeed the crucible for the self-recognition of an identity. While the significance of memory as the linking medium and process relating history and identity formation is well recognized by contemporary ethnographers, analytic and methodological thinking about it is as yet undeveloped.

The difficulty of descriptively grasping memory as a social or collective process is not unrelated to the inadequacy of the community trope (or figure of speech) to conceptualize the spatial plane of ethnography. The erosion of the public/private distinction in everyday life (on which community is constructed in Western narratives) as well as the displacement of the long-term memory function of orality and storytelling in the electronic information age make the understanding and description of any straightforward "art of memory" problematic. Collective memory is more likely to be passed through individual memory and autobiography embedded in the diffuse communication between generations than in any spectacles or performances of public arenas.

Collective representations are thus most effectively filtered through personal representations. With this insight, redesigned ethnography transforms the conventional realist concern with history—as it infuses, expresses, and even determines social identities in a locale—into a study that is synonymous with addressing the construction of personal and collective identity itself. It is probably in the production of autobiography, as this genre has emerged particularly with a focus on ethnicity (see Fischer 1986), that the sort of historical experiences carried in memory and shaping contemporary social movements can best be appreciated.

The return of an ethnographic present—but a very different ethnographic present than the one that largely ignored history in the classic functionalist anthropology of traditional, tribal society—is thus a challenge to the anthropological construction of the temporal setting. The present is defined not by historical narrative but by memory. Memory possesses its own distinctive narratives and traces synonymous with the fragmented process of identity formation in any locale, and whose distinctly social forms are difficult to grasp ethnographically.

Michael Taussig's *Shamanism, Colonialism, and the Wild Man* (1987) exemplifies this perspective. It is a vivid social history of the terror and genocide of the nineteenth-century Putumayo rubber boom juxtaposed to the present disorder in back-country Colombia. It strives to subordinate conventional historical narrative to the local media of memory found in the healing performances of shamans. This work, one of the most self-consciously experimental available, enacts with variable power most of the redesign moves that I am outlining.

Problematizing Perspective or Voice (a break with the figure of structure in realist ethnography). Ethnography has opened itself to the perspective of "voice," just as the controlling metaphor of structure has come into question. Structure as either social structure on the surface (derived from patterns of observed behaviors) or structure as underlying systematic meanings and codes (that organize language and social discourses) may continue to be indispensable in rendering descriptions of the subject matter even in experimental ethnography. But the analytic weight or focus of an account shifts, with the new emphasis, to a concern with perspective as voice, as embedded discourse in the framing and conduct of ethnographic inquiry.

In part, this comes about as a result of questioning the adequacy of structural analysis to model the complexity of intracultural diversity. The empirical recordings of actual montage flows of discourse have challenged the adequacy of structural and semiotic perspectives to account for discourse in terms of cultural models or codes and the more or less orderly transformation of components.

In part, the experimental alternative in voice, accepting the montage of polyphony as simultaneously the problem of representation and analysis, probably has had as much to do with the changing ethics of the ethnographic enterprise as with a dissatisfaction concerning the structural analysis of cultural phenomena. These changes are rooted in a marked sensitivity to the dialogic, oral roots of all anthropological knowledge, transformed and obscured by the complex processes of writing which dominate ethnographic projects from field to text, and of the differential power relationships that shape the ultimate media and modes of representing knowledge. Here, I merely want to comment on this shift in terms of the analytic difference in the way experimental ethnography creates its space-time field of discourse regardless of one's assessment of the possibilities for success in representing—ethically as well as authoritatively—voice and its diversity.

In the mode of cultural analysis that Raymond Williams developed (1977), a structure of feeling would be the goal of ethnography. It focuses on what is emergent in a setting from the interaction of well-defined dominant and residual formations with what is not quite articulable by subjects or the analyst. Making it more sayable/visible is one of the critical functions of ethnography. In this vein, recognizing such properties of discourses as dominance, residualness, and emergence (or possibility), experimental ethnography would map the relationships of these properties in any site of inquiry not by immediate structural appropriations of discourse formations but by exposing, to the extent possible, the quality of voices by means of metalinguistic categories (such as narrative, trope, etc.). Voices are not seen as products of local structures, based on community and tradition, alone or as privileged sources of perspective. Rather they are seen as products of the complex sets of associations and experiences which compose them.

Carolyn Kay Steedman's *Landscape for a Good Woman* (1987) is a good example of this move. A partly autobiographical account of an English working-class mother and her daughter, it tries to find expression for the story in given theoretical frameworks and provocatively fails. What is distinctive is that it successfully sustains the quality of voice without immediate structural determinations of the social space in which its discourses are evoked as voice. (In fact, it directly challenges the available theoretical imageries of one notion of structure or another to subsume the voices Steedman orchestrates.)

Redesigning the Observer

The Appropriation through Dialogue of a Text's Conceptual Apparatus.   The realist ethnography has often been built around the intensive exegesis of a key indigenous symbol or concept (pulled from its contexts of discourse to be reinserted in them according to the dictates of the ethnographer's analytic scheme). Much in recent cultural analysis has depended on this central organizing and analytic technique

common in ethnographic accounts. The professional assessment of a particular ethnographic work often depends on the quality and thoroughness of such exegesis.

In one sense, exegesis is a gesture toward recognizing and privileging indigenous concepts over anthropology's own. Such targeted concepts come to act as representatives of cultural identity. They stand for a system of meanings as well as the identity of a people in the anthropological literature (and sometimes beyond it). Keying an account to particular concepts, myths, or symbols thus tends to impose an identity upon a people as the contribution (or curse) of anthropology.

One alteration of the ethnography would be to remake this exercise into a fully dialogic one in which exegesis is foregrounded in the ethnography and the frame of analysis arises from the voices party to the dialogue. In this process of cultural translation, the purpose is not so much to change indigenous concepts (that is the responsibility of the anthropologist's interlocutors) as to alter the anthropologist's own. Indeed, it is the remaking of our concepts that is so much at stake in the contemporary cultural studies movement in Western academia. During a recent interview (1987:37) Fredric Jameson, in a comment about the difficulty of saying things in postmodernist discourse, calls for "a new vocabulary. The languages that have been useful in talking about culture and politics in the past don't really seem adequate to this historical moment."

From where might this vocabulary come? It might come, perhaps, from a reshaping of the translation of concepts at the core of realist ethnographies. Moments of exegesis would be replaced by moments of dialogue which involve the ethnographer's revision of familiar concepts that define the analytic limits of his or her work. A different notion of exegesis, distinctively tied to a recognition of its dialogic character, becomes a reflexive operation. While exploring the changing identity processes within an ethnographic setting, the identity of one's own concepts changes. The process of constructing an analysis thus can take on and parallel aspects of the process it describes. The key challenge here is whether an identity can ever be explained by a reference discourse when several discourses are in play, not the least of which is the ethnographer's in dialogue with specific other subjects.

There are several ways this might be represented textually. But the point is the ethnographer's framework should not remain intact if the subject's is being analytically pulled apart.

Dennis Tedlock's recent work of poetry, *Days from a Dream Almanac* (1989), appropriates more seriously and thoroughly than any other anthropological work I know a framework dialogically derived from fieldwork and makes it his own. He renders a year in his own life (a Western man traveling) in terms of the complex Maya Quiche organization of time. In so doing, he provides a new vocabulary that convincingly revises the way one might understand time in contemporary Western experience.

Bifocality (looking at least two ways). An embedded comparative dimension has always been a more or less implicit aspect of every ethnographic project. In the evolving global modernity of the twentieth century in which anthropology has been pursued almost from its professional inception, the coevalness of the ethnographer with the "Other" (as subject), however, has for the most part been denied (Fabian 1983). There is a history in ethnography of juxtapositions between one's own world and that of the "Other." But the focus is on separate, distant worlds. Only in the critique of anthropology's relationship to Western colonialism has the thoroughly blurred historic relationship of the anthropologist's own society to the subject's (under colonial domination) been argued.

Now that Western modernity is being reconceptualized as a global and thoroughly transcultural phenomenon the explicit treatment of bifocality in ethnographic accounts is becoming more explicit and openly transgressive of the previously constructed "us-them" distinction. Today, the identity of the anthropologist and his world is likely to be profoundly related to that of the particular "world" he is studying. However, only the redesigning of the observed (outlined in the earlier section), makes possible this revision of the bifocal character of ethnography. The chain of preexisting historic or contemporary connection between the ethnographer and her subjects may be long or short, thus making bifocality an issue of judgment. But its discovery and recognition remain a defining feature of the current experimental sensibility in ethnography. It stands as a critical statement against conventional efforts to sustain distanced worlds (and their separate determinations) in a world of considerable integration.

Michael Herzfeld's *Anthropology through the Looking Glass* (1987) demonstrates the communalities in the development of the culture concept in anthropology and the struggle to define the contemporary culture of Greece by Greeks themselves (in which anthropology, folklore, and the classics played a crucial role). Herzfeld develops the bifocal dimension of ethnography by revealing in his project the complex historical relationship between the ethnographic gaze and what it focuses upon. Reflexivity is brought from a mere gesture of the personal to a critical practice for ethnography that demonstrates the relationship between observer and observed in a specific moment of inquiry.

Critical Juxtapositions and Contemplation of Alternative Possibilities. The function of the experimental ethnography is primarily one of cultural critique. This involves critique not only of one's discipline (through an intellectual alliance with the subject) and of one's society that in the increasing condition of global integration is always bifocally related in transcultural process and historical perspective to the site of ethnographic attention), but of conditions within the site of ethnographic focus itself—the local world which it treats. Given the general commitment of experimental ethnographies to explore the full range of possibilities for identities and their complex expressions through voice in any one setting, the enactment of this exploration is a key form of cultural critique also. It involves the distinct and committed voice of the ethnographer in his or her text. And it operates from the critical attitude that things as they presently are need not be that way.

There are more possibilities, other identities, than those that have been enacted in any locale of research. Exploring all actual and possible outcomes is itself a method of cultural critique which moves against the grain of the given situation. The postmodernist treatment allows for tracing roads not taken or possibilities not explored. This kind of critical thought experiment—incorporated within ethnography in which juxtaposed actualities and possibilities are put analytically in dialogue with one another—might be thought to border on the utopian or the nostalgic if it were not dependent on documentation that these traces have a life of their own and are integral to the processes that form identities, including the ones that appear defining or dominant. Such clarification of possibilities against the objective, defining conditions "that matter" in any setting is the critical intervention and contribution the ethnographer can make that is uniquely his or her own.

Michael M. J. Fischer and Mehdi Abedi's (1990) account of contemporary Iranian Shi'ism, *Debating Muslims*, illustrates this approach. Developed in different genres of writing and from multiple perspectives (as well as exemplifying the collaborative ideal of ethnographic production), it critically lays out the dominant, residual, and emergent formations of a particular intellectual and cultural space—one that in recent times has been most often characterized as fanatical and monolithic. Fischer and Abedi are especially good at capturing possibility and emergence in events after the revolution and in the creation of a new and distinctive Iranian diaspora.

We have surveyed a discipline that is currently powered by innovations in its empirical practice, responding to a critique of its past aims to represent the reality of distinctive cultural forms of humanity. Such an experimental trend is identifiable in other social sciences, particularly in newly emerging interdisciplinary projects and centers. But for reasons that I hope I have made clear, nowhere does it have the disciplinary salience it does in anthropology.

I leave readers of this paper with the challenge to see in their own ethnography, or that of others, the frameworks discussed above. If they cannot (or choose not to), then they can revise and critique my own redesign in terms of other commitments and visions for what ethnography might become.

NOTE

1. I want to emphasize that experimentation is not prophesy on my part, based on the brilliant foreshadowings of a few examples, but is a documentable trend, not only in the current loosening up of the initiatory training model of ethnography in terms of what might be offered in dissertations, but in the predicament of second projects undertaken by already established scholars, who were credentialed in the late 1960s and early to mid 1970s. After all, ethnography is not only the central intellectual practice in anthropology. It is also the rite of passage that shapes careers. The initial training project of ethnographic research—one or two years of fieldwork, dissertation write-up, followed by publication of a monograph—constitutes the capital on which academic appointments are attained and then secured through tenure. While expectably the training model is conservative and tends toward orthodoxy, what is orthodox, for better or worse, both as to subject matter and conventions of writing, has changed markedly in the past decade, I believe as much through student demand as professorial will.

But for me personally and my own cohort, the most interesting source of experimentation in the conduct of research occurs very commonly at the break point with that initial career-making and conservative-tending research project in which the scholar, these days anyhow, attempts to do something very different than he or she was trained to do. Since the initial project, often lasting more than a decade, by no means achieves deep ethnographic mastery of another form of life even of research situated in a very focused space such as a village, town, or urban neighborhood, as most conventional fieldwork is, there has always been virtue attached to returning again and again to the original site of work and moving both geographically and conceptually beyond it in a painstaking manner. Yet few anthropologists now develop research careers in this manner. More commonly, these days, I find breaks with first projects to be real departures and de facto experiments both in the conception of research and in its production. Yet, since careers do not depend on such projects, they tend to be more quietly developed, more intensely personal, and more ambitious, and pursued less confidently. It is in the relatively silent production of second projects that the experimental trend that I posited exists on a widespread basis in contemporary anthropology.

The basic problem of these projects is precisely that of redesigning the conventions of ethnography for unconventional purposes, sites, and subjects—particularly moving beyond the settled community as site of fieldwork toward dispersed phenomena that defy the way that classic ethnography is framed and persuades. For example, moving from a study of Italian villagers to the multinational European parliament, from the Amazon jungles to pain centers in Boston, from a study of a Japanese factory to the international fashion industry, from the study of ancestor worship in village Taiwan to medical versus American female discourses about the body, from Transylvanian villagers to Romanian intellectuals, from the study of Sherpas in Nepal to one's own high school class, and many more shifts of careers like these each involves testing the limits of the ethnographic paradigm, and especially altering the form of the ethnography. For example, how does one reconstitute modes of ethnographic evidence and authority with nonlocalized subjects, emergent phenomena, not tied to well-articulated local history or tradition, in worlds that are not at first take that unfamiliar to the ethnographer? While there is much explicit debate about the critique and transformation of anthropology's central practice of ethnography, it is actually occurring broadly in the quiet career predicament of evolving second projects, which is very much the predicament of how to work and conceptually write one's way out of a tradition that one both wants to preserve and change.

INTELLECTUAL ROOTS

George E. Marcus is Professor of Anthropology at Rice University, where he has taught since 1975. He has been chair of the department since 1980 and oversaw its reconstitution in line with its present reputation for the critique of anthropology and the encouragement of the contemporary practice of critical ethnographic research. He received a B.A. at Yale (1968) in politics and economics, studied social anthropology at Cambridge on a Henry Fellowship, and in 1971 entered Harvard's Department of Social Relations (in social anthropology) just as its interdisciplinary graduate program was dissolving. From the early 1970s to the early 1980s, his research was on the Kingdom of Tonga. From the 1980s, he has been concerned with the study of upper classes and elite institutions in the United States and other Western societies. From 1986 to 1991, he was inaugural editor of the journal *Cultural Anthropology*. Most recently, he and his colleagues have been especially concerned with developing the relationship between anthropology and the emergent interdisciplinary arena of cultural studies. His major publications include *The Nobility and the Chiefly Tradition in the Modern Kingdom of Tonga* (1980), *Elites: Ethnographic Issues* (1983), (with Michael Fischer) *Anthropology As Cultural Critique* (1986), (with James Clifford) *Writing Culture: The Poetics and Politics of Ethnography* (1986), and (with Peter Dobkin Hall) *Lives in Trust: The Fortunes of Dynastic Families in Late Twentieth Century America* (1992).

I was first drawn to anthropology while still a high school student in the early 1960s through reading letters from the field by a sister and brother-in-law (a Yale graduate student) living among the Semai in (then) Malaya. My subsequent professionalization into anthropology cannot be told in strict genealogical terms of lineage (e.g. "Boas begat X who begat Y, etc., who begat me"). Rather, I seemed to be repeatedly passing through particular institutions of training that were rather at the intellectual end of particular trends or initiatives, so that while committed to and fascinated by the experiences anthropology offered, I always seemed to have an oblique or critically detached relationship to the specific brands of professional anthropology to which I was being exposed. First, I was at Yale during the mid-1960s after the vitality of the influence of Murdock, on the one hand, and ethnoscience, on the other, had long since peaked. Consequently, while taking anthropology courses, my real sense of excitement came from Paul Mus and Harry Benda's courses on Southeast Asian history (with strong doses of Geertz as Indonesianist), and I wound up majoring in a special program in politics and economics (composed largely of political theorists, development economists, and visiting European scholars).

Then, I spent three terms at Cambridge during 1968 and 1969, reading social anthropology for the BA Tripos. These were the twilight days of British functionalism, when the triumvirate of Goody, Leach, and Fortes (Tambiah also happened to be on the faculty) stood uncharacteristically together in the face of student radicalism among their own students and several American visitors. I remember clearly a succession of lectures by the "greats"— Evans-Pritchard, Needham, Gluckman, etc.—and I remember how tired they (and the Cambridge group) all seemed compared to the promise of their writings which I was systematically reading that year.

Next, after a two-year stint in the Army in South Carolina (when I taught anthropology in the night school of the University of South Carolina, and did some ethnographic puttering among Sea Island Gullah-speakers), I entered Harvard's Department of Social Relations (in social anthropology). Talcott Parsons and George Homans were still very much presences, but the program had nothing of its past life (for anthropologists, anyhow), when Clyde Kluckhohn led the anthropology section and David Schneider and Clifford Geertz were students. While learning much from Cora DuBois and David Maybury-Lewis, again I cleaved from anthropology and toward courses offered in other fields that seemed to have great (undeveloped) intellectual promise for anthropology—courses offered by Stanley Cavell, Barrington Moore, and Daniel Bell, for example.

I found my own experience to be similar to that of most of my fellow students in social anthropology at Harvard of the early 1970s. One was free to partake of a vast, rich range of intellectual offerings, but sooner or later, most students affiliated with one or another of the major projects which defined research opportunities in graduate work. I joined the Fiji project of the late Klaus Friedrich Koch (a legal anthropologist and a student of Laura Nader at Berkeley), since I would have the chance to work in the Kingdom of Tonga, a monarchical society that had made interesting adaptations to a long history of colonialism and modernity. My most satisfying and valuable experience in anthropology at Harvard was my participation as a teaching fellow in the social theory course taught by David Maybury-Lewis and Nur Yalman. Lunch-time meetings of the latter and the teaching fellows in this course remain memorable to this day as marking a congenial, stimulating sharing of the old, the new, and the emergent in theoretical trends that still define the horizons of social and cultural anthropology.

As formal schooling, then, my training in anthropology occurred repeatedly against the backdrop of trends and fashions winding down in institutions that were of societies (the United States, Britain), in retrospect experiencing the incipient dissolution of postwar culture and arrangements. I suppose I really first learned anthropology in' a total, committed way on the job, at Rice, and with increasing creativity after 1980, when the department literally rebuilt itself. During this period, I learned an immense amount about anthropology from my colleagues, Michael Fischer (trained at Chicago and who had been on the faculty at Harvard) and Stephen Tyler (trained at Stanford University and a major spokesperson for and critic of cognitive anthropology). A personal friendship and alliance with Jim Clifford (who had been a graduate student in history while I was at Harvard and who frequently attended department lectures and parties while I was there), beginning with his visit to Rice in 1980, opened for me new and exciting frames in which anthropology as an enterprise could be understood. A year (1982-1983) at the Institute for Advanced Study in Princeton, during which both Clifford Geertz and I were in our different ways thinking about anthropology from the angle of writing and representation, was formative for everything that I have done since. The Santa Fe (School of American Research) Seminar in 1984, which led to the publication of *Writing Culture*, crystallized my own thinking since the early 1980s and brought me into long-term association with some of the

3

The Dialectics of Deeds and Words*

Modern cultural theory suffers from a diffuseness so great that it seems to subvert discourse within our scholarly community.[1] Our theories range from sociobiology, at one extreme, through various kinds of materialism and old-fashioned functionalism to theories, at the other extreme, that locate the study of culture in language and meaning. One might hope that the protagonists of each perspective would illuminate our profession with constructive debate, but they speak past each other in a confusion of tongues; there is much talking but little dialogue. Off-hand, one might say that our future seems very bad, yet we can draw some comfort from our one tried and tested anthropological truth, which is that: *Things are never the way they seem.* Indeed, we make our living by showing that what seems to be one thing is actually something else, an alchemy that allows us to find in ritual either sublimated sex or a source of fertilizer. In this critical spirit, I will attempt to locate within the chaos of contemporary theory a different direction which, paradoxically, will call anthropology back to its center.

TWO POLAR POSITIONS

One axis of distinction between anthropological schools is the degree to which they take account of the human *mind*, and I will confine my remarks to two persuasions at polar extremes of difference on this subject: materialism and certain directions in postmodernism and interpretation.

Materialism

Some materialists say that there is no such thing as "mind." There is, rather, only the human brain, into which external stimuli flow and from which behavioral responses emanate. As for this brain, one doesn't have to know what's inside it or how it works—just what goes in and what comes out. What comes out is whatever gives the biggest bang for the least effort, which is more elegantly known as "operant conditioning." And since culture is defined by the same materialists as "learned and shared *behavior*," it follows that when enough people get the same bangs and respond in the same way, culture is born. But John Stuart Mill said it better—in his views regarding the greatest good for the greatest number—150 years ago. And 42 years ago, I took experimental psychology with my old friend and Columbia College classmate, Marvin Harris. He became a believer in the Gospel according to Thorndike, and I, reacting against behaviorism, became a devotee of Sigmund Freud.

Isaiah Berlin (1966) sorted career thinkers into two types: Foxes and Hedgehogs. The Foxes are people who have many ideas, folks like Clifford Geertz (or myself). The trouble is that after a while readers do not know where such people stand, which only becomes a problem when readers also no longer care.

*This article has been reproduced, in edited form, from *Cultural Anthropology* 1990 5(3):331-337, by permission of the American Anthropological Association.

55

The Hedgehog, to the contrary, harbors only one idea, but it is a very BIG IDEA. This, of course, again describes Harris, who underwent a materialist Pentecostal revelation early in his career, which, in conjunction with his college behaviorism, became Cultural Materialism. He has stayed doggedly with this theory for thirty-five years, adding to it here and there, but never deviating one iota from its essential outlines. The theory, however, owes less to Karl Marx than to such writers as Jeremy Bentham, Adam Smith, and B. F. Skinner. This may be why radical students in the 1970s and 1980s turned instead to various types of Marxism—a movement already waning in the faddism that now besets our profession.

Roy Rappaport has maintained that ecological studies must become more cultural and draw less on natural science models (1989), which represents a long step away from the blind mechanistic determinism of cultural materialism. In this regard, I have always thought that Julian Steward's cultural-ecological approach [described in the introduction to section four] remains our most rewarding direction because it shifted emphasis from the natural environment to culture, specifically to the penetration and embedment of labor—i .e. the social relations of production—in the total fabric of society (cf. Murphy 1970). I would add the corollary that this very embedment of labor is the pathway through which aspects of culture within the realms of value and meaning flow back to articulate and influence the organization of work, for it is to some extent a two-way street. This, I hold, is the central import of Steward's theory, albeit with my own emendations, and without the overburden of such rigid concepts as "culture core" or "infrastructure."

Postmodernism

Having discussed some moderns, I now turn my attention to postmoderns and others of kindred spirit. Postmodernism, along with the new interpretive and reflexive anthropologies,

deconstruction, dialogics, and a few others I can't remember, are growth industries in this country. Despite their success, they remain the domain of a small, albeit well-placed, minority. As for the rest of our trade, I do not think that I am overstating their mood in saying that a goodly number of them feel that there is less there than meets the eye. Much of this sentiment, I believe, derives from the writing styles of its adherents, whose sentences range from one word to involuted puzzle boxes of embedded clauses. In all fairness, however, I should note that most of the chief practitioners of what I choose to call "thick writing" are men, who seem to be engaged in a curiously competitive game in which obscure literary allusions and baroque rhetorical forms are weapons, a kind of egghead rap-talk.

With this preamble, most readers would probably expect me to launch a critique of the entirety of poststructural, postmodern scholarship but, repellant though their syntax may be, I find certain aspects of their writings to be agreeable, even familiar. It is these aspects which I will now address, saving for later in this paper the points on which they have gone awry. Among the broad directions of postmodernism and interpretation, there has been a sharp departure from the paradigm of functional positivism that has reigned in the social sciences for most of the twentieth century, and which still provides the intellectual framework of much of our profession. The functionalist model of society—as a network of causally and functionally related empirical entities forming natural systems—was implicitly based on a positivist belief in the autonomy and objectivity of the scientific observers who collect these nuggets of fact. This so-called objectivity, in turn, derived from the assumption that we, as subjects, can squat in remote villages with our notebooks and study the natives as objects. It was an innocent creed, but it bespoke an underlying imperialism of attitude.

The new anthropology has shifted its attention from structure to pattern and process, to the phenomenology of discourse, and to the processes by which culture—and reality itself—are constructed. Gone is the concern for system boundaries, and with it the linear and clockwork world of structural functionalism (espoused by Radcliffe-Brown and others). Absent as well is the objective observer standing apart from his informants and in his place is the situated, culturally constructed observer, who can no longer be separated from his ethnography. I welcome these new directions, and thus hope that you will not think it churlish of me to ask: So what else is new?

THE DIALECTICS OF SOCIAL LIFE

Some 20 years ago I wrote a book entitled *The Dialectics of Social Life* (Murphy 1971), which started with a critique of structural functionalism and went on to a more general attack on sociological positivism itself. In its place I proposed a processual view of social life that would take full account of the contradictions inherent in the flow of real human activity and our faulty comprehension of it. It called for dialectical analysis of the microhistory of social interaction and of the negative side of social life: (1) the disjunctions and distances created by every positive social bond; (2) the fabrications of consciousness that are the price and precondition of social life; (3) the misunderstandings and oppositions that make the world go around; (4) the essential alienation from self and others that delimits, and thus limits, human lives; and much more. I also collapsed the autonomy of subject and object, rebutting the notion of the objective observer. In the book I stated that human grasps on reality are in part culturally constructed, and our ethnographies themselves are a compound of the constructs of the people being studied and those that we bring to our fieldwork and impose upon our data. And I did not claim all this as newly revealed truth—rather, I drew instead on Hegel,

Simmel, Freud, Lévi-Strauss, and the phenomenological sociologist, Alfred Schutz. Much of the new anthropology isn't new at all.

Dialectics' message was far different from much of what is now being written under the banner of postmodernism, etc. *The Dialectics* called for a self-critical ethnography, not one that finds the ethnographer more interesting than the natives. On the basis of some 40 years of observing both anthropologists and natives, I can assure you that we are not. But of greater importance, in calling for a critical anthropology, the book was an extended argument for the indissolubility of praxis and thought, of deeds and words, of social activity and its cultural construction, of acts and norms—*each pregnant with the other* in a union that is primordially dialectical in nature.

It is on this point that both cultural materialism and those approaches that restrict their scope to mind, meaning, and discourse have failed. In *The Dialectics*, I held that the realities of power, sex, and economic need are largely prior to and generative of the symbolic forms in which they are expressed (or concealed). My generation didn't get these ideas from books or professors. We learned about the tyranny of privation during the 1930s, and we found that power and legitimacy came out of gun barrels in the 1940s. This gave our anthropology a quality of earthy realism that must not be lost in pursuit of a cultural iconography. Under various banners, many recent scholars have moved far away from the domain of such sensate activity into a total concern with the semiotics of meaning. This leads them into interpretive inquiries that treat both social life and ethnographies about it as texts, coming perilously close to literary criticism, the most sterile field in modern scholarship.

As for the materialists, they fail to recognize that cultural forms have lives of their own and are not mere epiphenomena of underlying "infrastructures." There is no primeval, formless praxis slime wherein culture is created.

Social behavior must take place within frameworks of meaning, and these are constructed meanings. Our actions are forged within our memories of the past, our anticipations of the future, and the reality of the present, and are perilous because, through becoming public, they are irrevocable. But our deeds, as public performances, take place in our own minds and in the minds of our beholders. Their coherence lies in the conflicting interpretations attached to them by actors and audiences alike, often making social life either low comedy or high tragedy, which are really the same thing. Behavior thus occurs within *histories* in which the actor is both producer and product, creator and victim, warden and prisoner. It was in the toils of this entrapment that Stephen Daedalus cried out: "History is a nightmare from which I am trying to awake." We anthropologists interpret these nightmares, but we also dream them and so are deeply in their thrall.

I am well aware of the fact that cultural materialists perform genuflections in the direction of symbol and norm as do postmoderns, semiologists, and interpretivists toward sensate activity. But I would submit that neither side takes proper account of the other's domain. Cultural materialism remains rooted in a mechanical, naturalistic mode that fails to reckon with the fact that the mind is far more than a *tabula rasa*, but has its own inner order and processes. And postmoderns et al. suffer disembodiment by failing to fully recognize that meanings must also be tested and molded in the arena of mundane social action. It is in this arena that we hunger and lust, labor and sweat, and in which our understandings of the world must be accommodated to our needs as humans. Cultural materialism deals mainly with the Deed and many postmoderns only with the Word. It is as if there were two sciences of Man, one concerning Man below the neck, the other above—one mindless, the other incorporeal.

AN ETERNAL CONTRADICTION

In this regard, I welcome Nancy Scheper-Hughes's (Scheper-Hughes and Lock 1987) interest in the cultural metaphors of the body, for it illustrates nicely the differences between an interpretive approach and a dialectical treatment. The body is a subject that I first wrote on in 1977 in a paper on gender roles and the anatomy of sex, which pursued the implications of the well-known fact that women can outperform men sexually (Murphy 1977). In the paper, I argued that culture inhibits this natural abundance of female sexuality, making it a scarce *commodity* relative to a male sexuality that is naturally limited but is transformed by culture into false abundance. This double inversion yields the construct of Man the Hunter (of Women) and the existential setting for the battle of the sexes. Incidentally, I did not find the inspiration for this dialectical exercise in continental philosophy, but in Mark Twain's *Letters from the Earth* (1962). I dealt with the body at much greater length in my book, *The Body Silent* (1987), which discussed paralysis as the metaphor of entropy, but which was more deeply concerned with paralysis as just plain *immobility*. I would, therefore, urge those engaged in seeing the body as a kind of text to climb down from the lofty level of metaphor to nitty-gritty social activity and regard the body as an *instrument* through which we interact with our physical and social milieus; this is in the tradition of Simone de Beauvoir and Merleau-Ponty, rather than Foucault. (The nice thing about embracing the French is that one may do so in a variety of ways.) It thus should be remembered that in *The Second Sex*, de Beauvoir commented: "If the body is not a thing, it is a situation. . . . It is the instrument of our grasp upon the world, a limiting factor for our projects." Anatomy is not destiny but, rather, a set of possibilities that anthropology has not fully explored.

I believe that I am speaking for the majority of our profession in saying that not only are both the head and the torso essential to our inquiry, but that the antithetical relationship between them, and between Act and Concept, should be the very substance of our discipline. And we will not get to the heart of this enterprise by creating either more causal daisy chains or additional subjectively contrived skeins of meaning. Indeed, in *Dialectics* I sought to stress the frailty of meaning and pattern, and to dissolve stable structures and forms in favor of a new anthropology of movement and process. And so it is that out of the antithetical positions of two schools we have forged a synthesis.

Finally, in saying that reality is in part a cultural construct, one must remain aware that this construct is not to be confused with reality itself which often gives us painful reminders of its truth. Beyond the prisms of false consciousness through which we myopically peer, there is indeed a real world, and anthropology still deals with our place in it. But we humans are not born as wet clay, plastic and malleable; humans are *constituted*, and we bend the world in our image. As a sapient species born into society with a disposition toward language and certain modes of thought, our feet are mired in dung, but our heads—our minds—reach upward to the stars. This eternal contradiction is the joy and centerpiece of our humanity, and the anthropological mission is to study and describe, in all its richness, the work of life.

NOTE

1. This is a slightly revised version of a paper delivered at the annual meeting of the American Anthropological Association on November 16, 1989, in Washington, D.C., during a symposium entitled "Assessing Developments in Anthropology" organized by Robert Borofsky. Drafts of the paper were read by Drs. Thomas de Zengotita, Barbara Price, and Joel Wallman. I am grateful for their helpful comments and suggestions.

I N T E L L E C T U A L   R O O T S *

Robert F. Murphy (1924–1990) was Professor of Anthropology at Columbia University, where he taught from 1963 until his retirement in 1990. A cultural anthropologist, he did fieldwork among the Mundurucu Indians (Brazil), the Shoshone-Bannock Indians (North America), the Tuareg (Africa), and most recently, in the field of the anthropology of disability. Murphy received the Mark Van Doren Award for distinguished teaching in 1977, and, in 1988, the Lionel Trilling Award for his book *The Body Silent* (1987). Among his numerous publications, perhaps the best known are *The Dialectics of Social Life* (1971), *Cultural and Social Anthropology* (1979), and *Women of the Forest*, co-authored with his wife Yolanda (1974).

Murphy began his career as a student of macro-structures and multilinear evolution. In mid-life he became a student of symbolically mediated social interaction, focusing on what happens between individuals in groups. Finally, his increasingly overriding concern was the nature of self, the nature of the human condition into which, in every society, we all are born. His intellectual evolution represents far less the adoption and subsequent abandonment of one "school" or another than it does the addition and integration, throughout his life, of new bodies of knowledge and theory. Indeed, much of his career was spent rejecting the constraints and confrontations of "schools" altogether. Rather, what perpetually fascinated him were the anomalies, the "exceptions" to conventional wisdoms. The investigation of these exceptions was designed not only to delineate and explain these individual cases, but to refine and reshape the original generalizations themselves.

*Prepared by Yolanda Murphy and Dr. Barbara Price.

Murphy's early life formed his character, his values, and the ironic wit with which he approached his later life and work. A child of the Depression who grew up in Rockaway Beach, New York, in a recently impoverished middle-class Irish Catholic family, he attended Far Rockaway High School along with other highly motivated and highly verbal students, most of whom had planned to attend college. Financial pressures, however, compelled Murphy to work after graduation. In 1943, he joined the U.S. Navy, saw action in the Pacific, and was discharged in 1946 with the rank of technician first class. His experiences of both the Church and the Navy left him with a lifelong skepticism of authority, whether ecclesiastical, political, or intellectual. Under provisions of the G.I. Bill, he applied to and was accepted at Columbia University shortly after his demobilization.

Accordingly, Murphy became a part of a unique upheaval in the American class system. The veterans who entered Columbia (and the other major U.S. universities) were a new generation, often brash and intellectually curious, formed in the crucible of the Second World War. Although they came from all social classes, many of them were working class in origin, who, in the days before the war, would have been discouraged from attending college. Many were the first in their families to do so, seeing in higher education a way out of poverty, out of dull, repetitive jobs. As Murphy phrased it, Columbia "formed me, brought out my potential, and encouraged me to become whatever I wanted to be, to do whatever my abilities permitted. It opened up a universe for me that was rich beyond anything I had ever imagined" (*The Body Silent*, 1987:168).

It was as an undergraduate at Columbia that Murphy discovered both anthropology and the writings of Sigmund Freud. Although he had left the Church at the age of 16, its doctrines of guilt and atonement, its symbolism, and its emphasis on sexual repression resonated in his strong response to Freud, in whom he saw the same themes, and whose work he would later draw into his investigations of the self. Still as an undergraduate, Murphy stumbled into an anthropology course given by Charles Wagley. It opened his eyes to a whole new world, gave him a new perspective on his own war experiences, and set his feet on the path of his career. Entering Columbia as a graduate student in 1949, he received his Ph.D. in 1954.

Among the graduate students at Columbia during the late 1940s and early 1950s were Eric Wolf, Morton Fried, Robert Manners, Elliott Skinner, Stanley Diamond, Rene Millon, and Marvin Harris.

While a graduate student, Murphy continued to study with Wagley, who stimulated his interest in lowland South American Indians and prepared him for his doctoral field research among the Mundurucu of Brazil in 1952-1953. The other major intellectual figure at Columbia at the time was Julian Steward, whose work in the conjoined theoretical fields of multilinear evolution and cultural ecology became a lifelong influence on Murphy, particularly so in his interests in kinship and the organization of labor. Upon his return from the field he accepted a position with Steward as Research Associate at the University of Illinois along with Eric Wolf, whom he considered a powerful intellect and whose ideas he respected. The association with Steward is especially apparent in Murphy's earlier works [*Headhunter's Heritage*, 1960; "Tappers and Trappers," 1956; and (with his wife Yolanda) *Shoshone-Bannock Subsistence and Society*, 1960].

In 1955, Murphy joined the University of California, Berkeley, as Assistant Professor of Anthropology. At this time there was great rapport between the anthropologists and the sociologists, including an intense joint seminar which involved such participants as David Schneider (whom he considered his postgraduate mentor), Rene Millon, Lloyd Fallers, Reinhard Bendix, Philip Selznick, Erving Goffman, and Talcott Parsons. The interchange of ideas in this forum led Murphy to explore the works of Simmel, Durkheim, and Lévi-Strauss, whose influences are perhaps most evident in his subsequent Tuareg research (1959-1960). Although his initial theoretical plan was to have integrated Steward's cultural ecology with a structuralfunctional model, he turned instead to Simmel and Lévi-Strauss for an analysis of the data ("Social Distance and the Veil," 1964). With this new synthesis also, he returned to his Mundurucu data and applied Simmel's work on conflict to an analysis of Mundurucu warfare ("Intergroup Hostility and Social Cohesion," 1957). In his later years at Berkeley, Murphy became increasingly interested in structuralism and gave what may have been the first seminar on this topic there in 1961 or 1962. His acceptance of this position, however, was always less than complete. Considering structuralism devoid of all systems of action and of human sentiment, he later modified and transformed a number of its elements in *The Dialectics of Social Life*.

With great gladness, Murphy returned to Columbia University as Professor of Anthropology, joining colleagues such as Wagley, Morton Fried, Conrad Arensberg, Alexander Alland, Elliott Skinner, and Marvin Harris. He felt that the diversity, not only of faculty but of students, reflected a rich and influential tradition that had generated a department committed to research and theory. *Dialectics* was written there, partly in the context of the antiwar protest movements at both Berkeley and Columbia. A formulation of dialectics of interaction, it was also a critique of anthropological positivism and perhaps one of the first attempts to bring phenomenology into anthropology. He also wrote *Cultural and Social Anthropology* and, with his wife Yolanda, *Women of the Forest*.

By the middle 1970s, Murphy was becoming increasingly ill, but continued to teach and publish. His office became a salon in which students and faculty could meet, argue, and exchange ideas. His own illness challenged him to look at paralysis as an intellectual problem, a metaphor of something deep in the human condition. Accordingly, he began a new research project to study the lives of the disabled. In *The Body Silent*, his last book, which is simultaneously autobiographical and generalizing, he attempted to integrate and synthesize all of his previous thinking, most notably to develop from *Dialectics* what he considered had been left unfinished or unaddressed in the earlier work. Quoting from *The Body Silent*:

In my hospital reveries on illness and decline, I had a haunting sense of having rehearsed for the present in all my past years, of reliving my history in hyperbole, of undergoing a savage parody of life itself. I was caught in a process from which there was not escape, one that was so inevitable that I could not resist it, only watch spellbound. In a perverse way, the progress of my physical degeneration seemed meet and proper, for in each moment of my existence were all my yesterdays and all of my tomorrows. And my recapitulation of the past—and future—was not idiosyncratic, my own private nightmare. Rather it has been in some ways an enactment in exaggerated form of the course of all of social life. (221-222)

4

Cultural Materialism Is Alive and Well and Won't Go Away Until Something Better Comes Along

MARVIN HARRIS

At the outset, I wish to disassociate myself from the impression, sometimes carelessly and sometimes deliberately conveyed, that anthropology can be equated with cultural anthropology, or much less, with ethnography.[1] Cultural anthropologists who have carried out ethnographic studies often rely heavily on historic, ethnohistoric, and archaeological materials for the fulfillment of their mature professional and intellectual interests (e.g. Sahlins, Murra, Wolf, Mintz). Moreover, many influential figures in archaeology (e.g. J. Marcus, Flannery, Hodder, Binford, Sanders) have carried out ethnographic studies on their own in order to enhance their understanding of archaic societies. In addition, field studies of nonhuman primates (e.g. by Devore, Van Lawick-Goodall, Imanishi, Teleki) provide an indispensable data base for understanding the emergence of distinctively human cultures. Studies of nonhuman primate sex roles in particular are responsible for major advances in our understanding of the evolution of human gender hierarchies. Productive scholarly interaction involving archaeology, paleontology, and ethnography takes place among many anthropologists who identify their principal interest as medical anthropology or biocultural anthropology. Nor should we forget that applied anthropologists who do surveys, write impact statements, and evaluate development programs outnumber university-based ethnographers. Surely postmodernists must have

heard it rumored that the membership of the American Anthropological Association does not consist exclusively of ethnographers.

Cultural materialism is a paradigm whose principles are relevant to the conduct of research and the development of theory in virtually all of the fields and subfields of anthropology. Indeed, it has been guesstimated (Thomas 1989:115) that half of the archaeologists in the United States consider themselves to be cultural materialist to some degree. For cultural materialists, whether they be cultural anthropologists, archaeologists, biological anthropologists, or linguists, the central intellectual experience of anthropology is not ethnography but the exchange of data and theories among different fields and subfields concerned with the global, comparative, diachronic, and synchronic study of humankind: the origin of the hominids, the emergence of language and culture, the evolution of cultural differences and similarities, and the ways in which biocultural, mental, behavioral, demographic, environmental and other nomothetic processes have shaped and continue to shape the human world.

CULTURE

It is no accident that all of the contributors to this volume who implicitly or explicitly ignore the biological and archaeological facets of anthropology operate with a definition of culture that is narrowly confined to mental and emic phenomena (see section on epistemological principles below). Culture for them constitutes a realm of pure idea which is accessible only through interactive discourse between live ethnographers and live "natives" (see Harris 1980 for the history of the definition of culture as pure idea). This unfortunate bias inevitably isolates the study of humans in the present from humans who have lived in the past and who have left no written records. For how can one carry out interactive discourse with the dead? Crucial to any effort to maintain the linkages among cultural anthropology, archaeology, and biological anthropology, therefore, is a concept of culture that embraces not only the mental and emic (see below) components of human social life but the etic and behavioral components as well.

The culture in cultural materialism refers to the socially conditioned repertoires of activities and thoughts that are associated with particular social groups or populations. This definition of culture stands opposed to the fixed, "essentialist" notions that inspire those who define culture as a realm of pure and uniform ideas hovering over the hub-bub of the daily life of specific individuals. For cultural materialists, culture elements are constructed (more specifically, abstracted) from the bedrock of the immensely variable thoughts and behavior of specific individuals (Harris 1964a). In complete accord with Borofsky's emphasis upon individual variability in this volume, cultural materialists have long argued that culture is at bottom an unfolding material process (viz. the concept of "behavior stream") rather than an emanation of a platonic archetype (see the discussion of variability and ambiguity in Brazilian color-race categories—Harris 1964b, 1970; Kottak 1967). Yet, it would be completely self-defeating to limit the definition of culture and the scope of the social sciences (as Vayda's chapter seems to propose) to the bedrock of individual thought and activity. Although we cannot see or touch entities such

as a mode of production or a transnational corporation or a sociocultural system, to the extent that these are logical and empirical abstractions built up out of the observation of individual-level events, they possess a reality that is not inferior to any other reality. Indeed, it is imperative for human survival and well-being that we learn to rise above individual thoughts and actions to the level at which we can begin to examine the aggregate effects of social life and the behavior of such higher-order entities as institutions and whole sociocultural systems. Political economies are as real as the individuals who fall under their sway, and a lot more powerful.

PARADIGMS

Paradigms stipulate the principles which govern the conduct of research. Principles fall into two classes: rules for acquiring, testing, and validating knowledge (i.e., epistemological principles) and rules for generating and evaluating theories (i.e., theoretical principles). A widely misunderstood aspect of scientific paradigms is that neither the epistemological or theoretical principles nor the paradigm as a whole has the status of a scientific theory. Principles such as creationism, natural selection, or the priority of infrastructure are not falsifiable. This does not mean however that paradigms are "ships that pass in the night." Paradigms can be compared with each other and evaluated from two standpoints: (1) their logical structure and internal coherence and (2) their respective abilities to produce scientific theories in conformity with the criteria discussed below. From this vantage point, the alternatives to cultural materialism presented in this volume offer slight hope of safe passage. I see a lot of sunken ships in the muddy waters of post-postmodernism—ships built out of flawed accounts of the history of anthropological theory, parochial agendas, inchoate conceptions of the nature of human society and human cultures, and a lack of well-formed epistemological and theoretical principles or useful substantive achievements that might justify a future—any future—for anthropology.

EPISTEMOLOGICAL PRINCIPLES: SCIENCE

Cultural materialism is based on certain epistemological principles which are held in common by all disciplines which claim to have scientific knowledge. Scientific knowledge is obtained by public, replicable operations (observations and logical transformations). The aim of scientific research is to formulate explanatory theories which are (1) predictive (or retrodictive), (2) testable (or falsifiable), (3) parsimonious, (4) of broad scope, and (5) integratable or cumulative within a coherent and expanding corpus of theories.

The same criteria distinguish scientific theories which are more acceptable from those which are less acceptable. Scientific theories find acceptance in accordance with their relative powers of predictability, testability, parsimony, scope, and integratability as compared with rival theories about the same phenomena. Since one can only approach, but never completely reach, perfection in this regard, scientific theories are held as tentative approximations, never as "facts."

This view of science derives from the logical positivist and empiricist philosophical traditions. It might be labeled neopositivism since it embodies and surmounts the critiques made by Popper (1965), Lakatos (1970), and Kuhn (1970, 1977). Note that it makes no claim to being "value free." Rather it proposes to overcome the inevitable biases of all forms of knowledge by methodological rules that insist upon opening to public scrutiny the operations by which particular facts and theories come to be constructed. The oft-repeated charge by postmodernist science-bashers that there is no community of observers who can or do scrutinize anthropological, especially

ethnographic, operations (see discussion of Tyler 1986 below) is belied by the intense criticisms to which crucial facts and theories are regularly subjected in the pages of anthropology's principal journals. Challenges by other observers to the ethnographic accuracy of the work of Boas, Mead, Benedict, Redfield, Evans-Pritchard, Malinowski, Lee, Vayda, and Chagnon just for starters, whether based on fresh fieldwork or written sources, clearly do fulfill the scientific model for independent testing by other observers. This is one of the few points of disagreement that I have with Salzman's paper, which answers "no" to whether ethnographic research involves a community of researchers at this time (page 38). It may take awhile, but ethnographers working in the same region if not the same village do help to keep each other in touch with basic ethnographic facts. However, I certainly agree with Salzman that the future of ethnography lies in greatly expanding the use of field teams and the number of restudies rather than, as Marcus proposes in his contribution to this volume, increasing the number of experimental, personalistic, and idiosyncratic field studies carried out by untrained would-be novelists and ego-tripping narcissists afflicted with congenital logo-diarrhea.

The claim is often made that even the natural sciences have had to abandon "objectivity" and determinism (because of Heisenberg's quantum indeterminacy or because of chaos theory). The idea that objectivity is no longer an issue in the physical, chemical, and biological sciences runs afoul of what it is that several million researchers worldwide actually do to earn their living. Let our anthropological science-bashers get up and tell an audience of the sick that there is no objectively valid treatment for AIDS or leukemia and that there never will be one; or tell a group of physicists that it is impossible objectively to decide whether cold fusion occurs or not; or tell the NIH panels on scientific fraud not to worry because all scientific data are equally cooked, subjective, and culturally "constructed." The reason that cultural materialists favor knowledge produced in conformity with the epistemological principles of science is not because science guarantees absolute truth free of subjective bias, error, untruths, lies, and frauds. It is because science is the best system yet devised for reducing subjective bias, error, untruths, lies, and frauds. As for determinism—the assertion that phenomena are causally determined by certain events or principles—its death is greatly exaggerated. In the social sciences nineteenth-century formulations of absolute laws were long ago qualified by the realization that science does not yield certainties and laws, only probabilities and generalizations. Incidentally, chaos theory does not lead to a renunciation of deterministic systems but to the extension of probabilistic determinism to realms of phenomena (such as hydrodynamic turbulence) which hitherto seemed to be entirely unpredictable.

Following the lead of Clifford Geertz and under the direct influence of postmodern philosophers and literary critics such as Paul De Man, Jacques Derrida, and Michel Foucault, interpretationist anthropologists have adopted an increasingly arrogant and intolerant rhetoric aimed at ridding anthropology of all vestiges of scientific "totalizing" paradigms. According to Stephen Tyler, for example, sociocultural anthropologists should abandon

the inappropriate mode of scientific rhetoric that entails "objects," "facts," "descriptions," "inductions," "generalizations," "verification," "experiment," "truth," and like concepts that, except as empty invocations, have no parallels either in the experience of ethnographic fieldwork or in the writing of ethnographies. The urge to conform to the canons of scientific rhetoric has made the easy realism of natural history the dominant mode of ethnographic prose, but it has been an illusory realism, promoting, on the one hand, the absurdity of "describing" nonentities such as "culture" or "society" as if they were fully observable, though somewhat ungainly, bugs, and, on the other, the

equally ridiculous behaviorist pretense of "describing" repetitive patterns in isolation from the discourse that actors use in constituting and situating their action, and all in simpleminded surety that the observers' grounding discourse is itself an objective form sufficient to the task of describing acts. (1986:130)

Tyler's totalizing renunciation of the search for objects, facts, descriptions, inductions, generalizations, verification, experiment, truth, and "like concepts" (!) in human affairs mocks itself so effectively that any attempt at rebuttal would be anticlimactic. I do think it may be useful, however, to point out that the "simpleminded surety" with which positivists and behaviorists are alleged to view human social life flagrantly distorts the entire history of science in general, during which all sureties, simpleminded or not, have been subject to relentless skepticism, and the history of logical positivism in particular, during which the struggle to create objective data languages has constituted the central focus of a vast and continuing philosophical effort.

Anthropology's dedicated science-bashers are not mollified by the assurance that cultural materialists seek probabilities rather than certainties, generalizations rather than laws. Shanks and Tilley (1987:38), for example, question the validity of making any kind of generalization. They ask how general a statement must be before it counts as a generalization: "two cases? three? fifty?" They also ask:

If the generalizations made are not laws, they cannot be expected to be applicable in any particular case so why are these generalizations of use to us? Why must the business of doing science necessarily be equated with the ability, or the will to generalize? This appears to be a procedural rule founded on the basis that generalizing, rather than considering all the particularity of the individual case, is a superior kind of activity. There seems to be no compelling reason why we should accept this. (1987:38)

Questions and Answers

The fallacies that embolden these queries are so transparent that one must wonder if the interlocutors really intend to be taken seriously. (This *is* a serious concern on my part since Derrida and his followers are not above celebrating the playful consequences of deconstructionism.) Yet given the current popularity of antiscientism, their questions, serious or not, cannot be left unanswered.

Question: Just how often does something have to recur in order for it to serve as the basis for a generalization?

Answer: The more times the better.

Question: If generalizations cannot be expected to be applicable to any specific case, what good are they?

Answer: The better the generalization, the more *probable* its applicability to the particular case, the more useful it is. (It is definitely useful to know that a particular person who smokes four packs of cigarettes a day is ten times more likely to get lung cancer than one who doesn't smoke, even though not all heavy smokers get lung cancer.)

Question: Why must science be equated with generalizing?

Answer: Because science is by definition a generalizing form of knowledge.

Question: Is the mandate to generalize nothing but a "procedural rule"?

Answer: Of course. And anyone is free to ignore the rule but to do so is to cease doing science. (It is also likely to get you killed the next time you step off the curb against the light, or the next time you strike a match to look inside your gas tank.)

Last question: Instead of generalizing, why not consider "all the particularity of the individual case"?

Answer: Because there are no limits to particularity. Any project that proposes to deliver *all* the particularities of any macrophysical event, human or not human, therefore makes a preposterous claim on our time and resources. For this reason, in science endless particularity is the exact equivalent of endless ignorance.

EPISTEMOLOGICAL PRINCIPLES: EMICS AND ETICS

In addition to the general epistemological principles shared with other scientific disciplines, cultural materialism is also based on epistemological principles which are specific to the study of human sociocultural systems. These involve: (1) the separation of mental events (thoughts) from behavior (actions of body parts and their environmental effects) and (2) the separation of emic from etic views of thoughts and behavior. (See below for definitions of "emic" and "etic.") The reason for the epistemological distinction between mental and behavioral events is that the operations (observational procedures) used to obtain knowledge of mental events are categorically distinct from those needed to obtain knowledge of behavioral events. In the former, observers depend directly or indirectly on participants to communicate what is going on inside their heads; in the latter observers are not dependent on actors to identify the actor's body motions and the environmental effects of those motions. The reason for the further distinction between emic and etic events is that the separation of mental from behavioral events does not exhaustively specify the epistemological status of the categories (data language) employed in the identification of mental or behavioral events. Observers have the option of describing both kinds of events in terms of categories that are defined, identified, and validated by the community of participants (emics) or by the community of observers (etics). Four types of knowledge stem from these distinctions: (1) emics of thought; (2) emics of behavior; (3) etics of behavior; (4) etics of thought.

To illustrate, consider the practice of indirect infanticide in northeast Brazil: (1) A sample of economically and socially deprived mothers condemns and abhors infanticide. (2) These mothers insist that their own behavior has been devoted to sustaining the life of their infants. (3) Observers note, however, that some of these mothers actually withhold food and drink from certain infants, especially from infants that are first and last born. (4) On the basis of the observed occurrence of maternal neglect and high infant mortality, it can be inferred that these disadvantaged women have thoughts that are contrary to or that modify their elicited emics of thought and behavior. (The foregoing has been adapted from Scheper-Hughes 1984, 1992.) Returning to participants for additional emic data may result in the elicitation of emic thought and emic behavior that correspond to the etic inferences. Emic and etic versions of social life are often but not necessarily contradictory. (See Headland, Pike, and Harris 1990 for a full discussion of the history and significance of the emic/etic distinction.) But failure to distinguish between emic and etic and between mental and behavioral data renders much of the sociocultural literature of cultural anthropology useless by literally preventing researchers from understanding the referential significance of their descriptive discourse (Harris 1968; Marano 1982; Headland, Pike, and Harris 1990).

Despite a persistent barrage of uninformed or malicious assertions to the contrary, cultural materialists insist that the proper study of humankind is both emics and etics and both thought and behavior. This brings me to Robert Murphy's paper and his claim that materialists, myself in particular, define culture as "learned and shared *behavior*" (italics in the original). I do not know how to account for Murphy's failure to have assimilated the fact that I have persistently and plainly stated, over

and over again, that culture is both thought and action, both emics and etics, and that anthropology involves the study of both mind and body. Perhaps Murphy could not bring himself to admit that his main point—namely that the "antithetical relationship between [the head and the torso], and between Act and Concept, should be the very substance of our discipline" (page 59)—does in fact constitute the very substance of my own work (e.g., race relations in Brazil; colonialism in Mozambique; cattle in India; warfare in Amazonia; and reproductive controls in preindustrial societies).

While no cultural materialist has ever advocated making the subject matter of cultural anthropology exclusively etic or behavioral, the postmodernists and their idealist predecessors have relentlessly advocated essentialist exclusions with regard to what cultural anthropologists ought to study. How convenient it would be for these critics if cultural materialists were to reject the study of mind and emics just as the interpretationists reject the study of activity and etics. ("Ah! You see, these vulgarians reject that which is most human about humans.") But words to that effect demonstrate at best an indomitable ignorance of the anthropological literature.

THEORETICAL PRINCIPLES

These rest on the assumption that certain categories of behavioral and mental responses are more directly important to the survival and well-being of human individuals than others and that it is possible to measure the efficiency with which such responses contribute to the achievement of an individual's survival and well-being. This assumption lies at the basis of the "costing" of alternative patterns of behavior which in turn is essential for identifying optimizing behavior and thought (see below) and the development of materialist theories of the causes of sociocultural differences and similarities.

The categories of responses whose costs and benefits underwrite cultural selection and cultural evolution are empirically derived from the biological and psychological sciences that deal with the genetically given needs, drives, aversions, and behavioral tendencies of *Homo sapiens*: sex, hunger, thirst, sleep, language acquisition, need for affective nurturance, nutritional and metabolic processes, vulnerability to mental and physical disease and to stress by darkness, cold, heat, altitude, moisture, lack of air, and other environmental hazards. This list is obviously not intended to encapsulate the whole of human nature. It remains open-ended and responsive to new discoveries about the human biogram and population-specific genetic differences.

This brings me to another endlessly repeated although endlessly refuted characterization of cultural materialism. In Murphy's words: "Cultural materialism remains rooted in a mechanical, naturalistic mode that fails to reckon with the fact that the mind is far more than a *tabula rasa*" (page 58). Without conceding that the minimum condition for advocating a "mechanical" or "naturalistic" mode is adherence to the doctrine of a mental blank slate, can one find such a slate incorporated into the theoretical principles of cultural materialism? Impossible, because anyone who insists that humans have definite genetically determined biopsychological drives is obviously saying that our minds are not blank at birth. Now the postmoderns and other critics of cultural materialism may not like what cultural materialism puts into the brain-mind at birth, but that is a different issue. I do not believe for example, as Murphy does, that we are wired to think dialectically, although I am prepared to change my opinion if someone can provide me with some empirical evidence from the cognitive sciences or neurophysiology.

To continue: Various currencies can be used to measure the costs and benefits of behavior that have optimizing consequences such as morbidity and mortality rates, differential sex-

ual access, monetary costs and benefits, energetic inputs and outputs, and nutritional inputs and outputs. (The omission of currencies directly linked to differential reproductive success should be noted, for it encapsulates the basic difference between cultural materialist and sociobiological paradigms. See Harris 1991 for a sustained critique of human sociobiology.)

Infrastructure, Structure, and Superstructure

The components of social life which most directly mediate and facilitate the satisfaction of biogram needs, drives, aversions, and behavioral tendencies constitute the causal center of sociocultural systems. The burden of this mediation is borne by the conjunction of demographic, technological, economic, and ecological processes—the modes of production and reproduction—found in every sociocultural system. More precisely, it is the etic behavioral aspect of the demo-techno-econo-environmental conjunction that is salient, and hence it would be more precise (but too cumbersome) to define the causal center as the *etic behavioral infrastructure* (or the etic behavioral modes of production and reproduction). Infrastructure constitutes the interface between nature in the form of unalterable physical, chemical, biological, and psychological constraints on the one hand, and culture which is *Homo sapiens*'s primary means of optimizing health and well-being, on the other. It is the unalterability of the laws of physics, chemistry, biology, and psychology therefore that gives infrastructure its initial strategic priority in the formulation of cultural materialist theories. Cultural optimizations and adaptations must in the first and last instance conform to the restraints and opportunities of the environment and of human nature.

In addition to infrastructure, every human sociocultural system consists of two other major subsystems: structure and superstructure, each with its mental/behavioral and emic/etic aspects. Structure denotes the domestic and political subsystems, while superstructure denotes the realm of values, aesthetics, rules, beliefs, symbols, rituals, religions, philosophies, and other forms of knowledge including science itself.

The basic theoretical principles of cultural materialism can now be stated: (1) optimizations of the cost/benefits of satisfying biogram needs probabilistically (i.e. with more than chance significance) determine (or select for) changes in the etic behavioral infrastructure; (2) changes in the etic behavioral infrastructure probabilistically select for changes in the rest of the sociocultural system. The combination of 1 and 2 is the principle of the primacy of infrastructure.[2]

As a guide to theory-making, the primacy of infrastructure enjoins anthropological researchers concerned with the explanation of sociocultural differences and similarities to concentrate on and to give priority to the formulation of hypotheses and theories in which components of the etic behavioral infrastructure are treated as independent variables while components of structure and superstructure are treated as dependent variables. The practical consequence of such a commitment of research effort is that the search for causal infrastructural variables will be conducted with decisively greater persistence and in greater detail than is likely under the auspices of alternative paradigms. The history of anthropological theory demonstrates that those who lack a paradigmatic commitment inevitably "quit early" when confronted with difficult, puzzling phenomena.

The primacy of infrastructure has frequently been criticized as a teleological principle that denies the importance of chance, random processes in evolution. This is clearly an incorrect portrayal, given the formulation of causality in terms of selection processes. B. F. Skinner (1984) has appropriately designated the genre of evolutionary process in question as *selection by consequences*. In biological evolution, in operant behavior conditioning, and

in cultural evolution, selection operates on variations whose origins may be indeterminate. Cultural materialism is thus no more teleological than Darwinian evolutionism. In this limited sense, cultural evolution is analogous to biological evolution (and to the development of individual learning repertories). As in biological evolution, there are innovation and selection for or against. Innovations occur at massive rates in socially conditioned human response repertories (culture). Some are selected for (retained and propagated across generations), others are selected against (extinguished). Selection for or against is probabilistically determined by the infrastructural consequences (costs and benefits) of the innovative behavior.

Despite this analogy, there are specific differences in the mechanisms of selection by consequences which characterize biological and cultural evolution. Selected biological innovations are stored in the form of information in the organism's genes; selected cultural innovations are stored in the form of response repertories in the organism's neural pathways. It is this difference that dooms the attempts to reduce the great mass of human sociocultural phenomena to the level of biology.

Another point of recurrent concern expressed by colleagues is whether cultural materialism insists that every sociocultural difference and similarity can be explained by infrastructural determinism (Magnarella 1982). This concern is misplaced. Clearly it is very likely that many sociocultural traits are the consequence of arbitrary, idiographic events. But the main task of cultural materialism is to concentrate on building a corpus of testable theories that is broader, more coherent, and more interpenetrating than the theories of alternative research strategies while attending to seemingly refractory cases as they are brought to light.[3]

Another aspect of the principle of the primacy of infrastructure that is surrounded by misinformation is the feedback between infrastructure and structure or superstructure. It would be convenient for materialist-bashers if the principle of the primacy of infrastructure meant that cultural materialists regard the mental, emic, and symbolic-ideational aspects of sociocultural systems as mere mechanical reflexes or epiphenomena of infrastructure. ("Harris thinks ideas, symbols, values, art, and religion are unimportant aspects of human life. Ugh!") Again I quote from Murphy's paper: "As for the materialists, they fail to recognize that cultural forms have lives of their own and are not mere epiphenomena of underlying 'infrastructures'" (page 57). The attempt by Murphy and others to portray cultural materialism as a paradigm in which "the ideas by which men [sic] live have no importance for their action" (Bloch 1985b:134) is totally at variance with the prominence of the phrase "sociocultural system" in the specification of cultural materialist principles. Why does one bother to talk about the systemic role of structure and superstructure if infrastructure alone has importance for action? Do cultural materialists propose that people go about producing and reproducing at random and without an idea in their heads? Could sociocultural life as we know it exist if there was nothing but infrastructure? Certainly not. No more than one can imagine people living without an infrastructure, i.e., living on ideas alone. Franz Boas was absolutely right when he noted that "no people has ever been observed that has no social structure." But who has ever been so certifiably insane as to suggest the contrary? To say that humans must think to live, however, is to say nothing about the roles of behavior and thought in the processes responsible for sociocultural evolution. The issue is not whether thought is important for action, but whether thoughts and actions are equally important in the explanation of the evolution of sociocultural systems. Cultural materialism—indeed any genuinely materialist paradigm in the social sciences—says no. The system is asymmetrical. Infrastructural variables are more determinative of the evolution of the system. But this does not mean that the infrastructure can do without its superstructure.

Moreover, to say that structure and superstructure are causally dependent on infrastructure is not to say that in the processes of continuity and change, selection pressure is exerted only from infrastructure to superstructure. Without structural and superstructural instrumentalities the infrastructural subsystem would have evolved in a radically different direction from those which we now observe. Structure and superstructure are not mere passive, epiphenomenal products; rather they actively contribute both to the continuity and change of infrastructures. But they do so within the limitations and possibilities inherent in a given set of demo-techno-econo-environmental conditions. They almost always initiate and select for change in conformity with but almost never in opposition to those conditions.

To illustrate, consider the changes in U.S. family life since World War II with reference to the disappearance of the male breadwinner role, the demise of the multiparous stay-at-home housewife, and the rise of feminist ideologies emphasizing the value of sexual, economic, and intellectual independence for women. As I have proposed elsewhere (Harris 1981a), these structural and superstructural transformations are the determined outcome of a shift from goods-producing industrialism to service-and-information-producing industrialism, mediated by the call-up of a reserve army of housewives into low-paying service-and-information nonunion jobs. The infrastructural transformations themselves were related to the use of electronic technologies and to declining productivity in the unionized smokestack industries which had created and sustained the male-breadwinner-stay-at-home-housewife families. The rise of a feminist ideology which glamorized the wage labor market and the intellectual, sexual, and emotional independence of women was the determined outcome of the same infrastructural force. However, it is clear that both the structural and superstructural changes have exerted and continue to exert an amplifying, positive-feedback effect on the infrastructural transformations. As the consequences of the call-up of the female labor force manifest themselves in higher divorce rates, lower first marriage rates, and historically low fertility rates, service-and-information industrialism is in turn amplified into an ever-more dominant mode of production and reproduction. Similarly, as feminist ideologies continue to raise consciousness against the vestiges of male breadwinner sexism, men and women find themselves locked into the labor force as competitors, wages for both are driven down, unions are driven out, and the profitability of the service-and-information industries rises, encouraging more diversion of capital from goods-producing enterprises into service-and-information production.

Although deviation-amplification can occur as a consequence of changes initiated in any sector of the sociocultural system, the infrastructural components remain causally dominant. Relations among the components remain causally asymmetrical because changes initiated at the structural or superstructural level are most likely to be selected for if they facilitate or help to optimize crucial aspects of the infrastructure. In the example under consideration, it is clear that neither feminism nor the demise of the breadwinner family selected the technological innovations which initiated the transformation of the smokestack infrastructure.

FEMINISM AND ANTISCIENCE

This is an appropriate point for me to make some observations about the relation between cultural materialism and feminism. Feminist anthropology is a distinct intellectual tradition that seeks to establish a balance between androcentic (male-oriented) and gynocentric (female-oriented) perspectives, theories, and data bases. In view of the virtual hegemony of androcentrism in anthropology during the first sixty or seventy years of this century, it is not surprising that feminism in practice often seems to give way to an attempt to substitute gynocentrism for androcentrism. It would require much more than the available space to begin to review the strengths and weaknesses of the specific modifications of anthropological data bases and theories that have been introduced under feminist auspices or in response to feminist critiques. But there is a general point that must be made if one is to understand the surge in postmodernist antiscientism and relativism.

The corpus of positivist-scientist theories about gender issues was impoverished, when not grossly counterfactual, prior to the rise of feminism. Feminists therefore tended to identify science with androcentrism. They saw scientific theories as male concoctions designed to confuse and disempower women. There was a parallel reaction to Marxism, with its claim that it was a science of society while focusing on class exploitation to the neglect of gender exploitation. In this context, postmodernist attacks on the distinction between the observer and the observed, and the advocacy of the idea that truth is relative and a political construction, seemed to constitute an appropriate paradigm for carrying out the feminist project in anthropology. (Some feminists argue that these perspectives had an independent and antecedent development within feminism itself; see, for example, Mascia-Leeds, Sharpe, and Cohen 1989.)

From a cultural materialist perspective, however, the feminist response to past inadequacies of positivist formulations of gender is both intellectually and politically counterproductive. In the long run anthropological feminism has little to gain by throwing its weight on the antiscience side. Scientific anthropology is largely if not yet completely open to feminist researchers and to their contribution to the improvement of anthropological theories in any domain of their choice. The most productive intellectual response to the exposure of biases, hidden agendas, and lack of certainties in anthropology is not to adopt paradigms that from the outset promise even greater biases, more cryptic agendas, and total uncertainty. Rather it is to work within scientific paradigms to reduce biases, expose hidden agendas, and decrease uncertainties.

For feminists whose political interests are foremost, adoption of the postmodern program portends unintended social consequences in which women are hurt more than they are helped. Some examples: the relation between no-fault divorce laws and the feminization of poverty; the relation between the feminization of the labor force and the increased marginalization of African American males with its contribution to the multiplication of impoverished black female-headed households; the low priority given by middle-class feminists to unionization and the falling take-home pay of both male and female wage earners. Like the failure of Soviet Marxist theoreticians to calculate the objective extent of the inefficiency of their command economy, these are not problems that can be identified, much less solved, by musing about the relativity of truth, or the nonexistence of such things as facts.

POWER AND CULTURAL MATERIALIST THEORIES

For proposing that changes in sociocultural systems are selected for in conformity with optimizing principles, cultural materialism has been caricatured as a form of functionalism in which all is for the best in the best of all possible worlds (Diener, Nonini, and Robkin 1978). This accusation cannot be reconciled with cultural materialism's long-standing focus on problems of class, caste, racial, and sexual inequality and exploitation (Harris 1964c, 1992; Ross 1978a; Murray 1980; Mencher 1980; DeHavenon 1990). Indeed, the critique of Panglossian functionalism—even the coining of the phrase—is a basic pre-

occupation of cultural materialism (Harris 1967:252).

The fact that modes of production and reproduction are selected for in conformity with optimizing principles does not mean that every member of a society benefits equally from this selection process. Where marked differences of power have evolved as between sexes and stratified groups, the benefits may be distributed in a completely lopsided and exploitative fashion. Under such circumstances, the costs and benefits must be reckoned not only with respect to individuals in their infrastructural context but with respect to the political-economic decisions of power holders. This does not mean that all changes which benefit ruling-class interests necessarily have adverse effects on everyone else, as Marxists have wanted us to believe. For example, as indicated above, the rise of the service and information sectors in hyperindustrial mixed economies reflects the higher rates of profit to be obtained from unorganized labor. Thus, an increasing portion of the industrial labor force consists of women who have to some extent risen above their previous condition as unpaid housewife-mothers dominated by blue-collar male chauvinist husbands. There is no contradiction involved in holding that the greater advantages accruing to U.S. capitalist interests are facilitated by a lesser but still favorable balance of benefits over costs accruing to women. The behavior of both strata exhibits the predicted optimizations even though one might hold that the gain for most women, especially for minority women, is slight by comparison.

Cultural materialism is thus no less emphatic about the importance of political-economic inequality as a modifier of optimization process than are various Marxist theoreticians who claim to have a monopoly on the defense of the oppressed (Harris 1991). Moreover, full recognition is given to conflicts engendered by unequal allocations of costs and benefits between stratified groups and the system-changing potential of such conflicts. One can never escape the question of benefits for whom or of costs for whom. Far from neglecting or "covering up" the effects of political factors on optimizations, cultural materialists recognize regular systemic feedbacks from the structural to the infrastructural level which give rise to political economy, political demography, political technology, and political ecology. One cannot for example explain the adoption and spread of technological devices such as shotguns, of new varieties of wheat and rice, tractors, or solar cell generators apart from the interests of trading companies, agribusiness, and petrochemical transnational corporations, local landowners, banks, etc.

It seems to me that in his contribution to this volume, Eric Wolf embraces a very similar perspective when he declares apropos of Sahlins's subordination of Hawaiian history to Hawaiian "culture": "To explain what happened in Hawaii or elsewhere, we must take the further step of understanding the consequences of the exercise of power" (page 227). I should also note in connection with Wolf's contribution that his call—for "an anthropology that is not content merely to translate, interpret, or play with a kaleidoscope of cultural fragments, but that seeks explanations for cultural phenomena" (page 227)—is completely isomorphic with the aims of cultural materialism. But aside from presenting specific examples of the effects of power, Wolf does not offer a coherent set of principles for achieving the desired alternative to postmodern relativism and nihilism. Perhaps he is a closet cultural materialist.

WHERE IS CULTURAL ANTHROPOLOGY GOING?

A popular myth among interpretationist science-bashers is that positivist anthropology deservedly collapsed because of its failure to produce a coherent body of scientific theories about society and culture. Marcus and Fischer for example assert that there is a crisis in anthropology and related fields because of the "disarray" in the "attempt to build general and comprehensive theories that would subsume all piecemeal research" (1986:118). This implies that the postmodernists have made a systematic study of the positivist corpus of theories that deal with the parallel and convergent evolution of sociocultural systems. But they have not done this. It was only after World War II that nonbiological, positivist cultural and archaeological paradigms gained acceptance among anthropologists. In the ensuing years unprecedented strides have been made in solving the puzzles of sociocultural evolution through a genuinely cumulative and broadening corpus of sophisticated and powerful theories based on vastly improved and expanded research methods. The cumulative expansion of knowledge has been especially marked within archaeology and at the interface between archaeology and cultural anthropology (see e.g. Johnson and Earle 1987). It is ironic, then, that at the very moment when anthropology is achieving its greatest scientific successes, anthropologists who have never tested the positivist theoretical corpus which they condemn hail the death of positivist anthropology and the birth of a "new" humanistic paradigm. Only those who know little about the history of anthropological theories could hail such a paradigm as "new," much less as "a refiguration of social thought" (Darnell 1984:271).

This raises the question of why antipositivistic humanism has become so attractive to a new generation of anthropologists (and other practitioners of social "science"). One reason may be that the generation of students reared during the 1960s and early 1970s believes that positivist social science is responsible for such twentieth-century scourges as fascism, Stalinism, U.S. imperialism, corpocracies, and the educational-industrial-military complex. No doubt hyperindustrialism, high tech, and the "technological fix" lead to feelings of dehumanization and alienation. But the association between all of this and positivist social science is spurious. The problem is not that we have had too much of positivist social science but that we have had too little (Harris 1974: 264ff). The atrocities of the twentieth century have been carried out precisely by people who were ignorant of or vehemently opposed to positivist social science (e.g., Lenin, Stalin, Hitler, Mussolini). Too many anthropologists seem to have forgotten that there is a flip side to relativism, phenomenology, and antipositivism—the side on which relativists who denounce reason and scientific knowledge construct the world in their own image. Benito Mussolini put it this way:

Fascism is a super-relativistic movement because it has never attempted to clothe its complicated and powerful mental attitude with a definite program but has succeeded by following its ever changing individual intuition. Everything I have said and done in these last years is relativism by intuition. . . . If relativism signifies contempt for fixed categories and men who claim to be bearers of an external objective truth . . . then there is nothing more relativistic than Fascist attitudes and activity. . . . From the fact that all ideologies are of equal value, that all ideologies are mere fictions, the modern relativist deduces that everybody is free to create for himself his own ideology and to attempt to carry it out with all possible energy. (Quoted in Ross 1980a: xxvii)

The proposal that there is an association between antiscience relativism and fascism cannot be dismissed as a mere intellectual scare tactic. Mussolini's fascist philosophy borrowed heavily from Friedrich Nietzsche, especially the latter's concept of the "will to power" as the source of truth. Paul De Man, who was as important as Derrida in the development of deconstructionism, warmed up for his role as literary critic by studying Nietzsche and by broadcasting propaganda for the Nazis during World War II, a fact which he effectively concealed from his colleagues at Yale until after his death (Lehman 1988). And Michel Foucault, the postmodernist whose cachet among anthropologists is ascendant, is also

much indebted to Nietzsche, as his aphorism "another power, another knowledge" reveals (Foucault quoted in Hoy 1986:133).

NOTES

1. My assigned task in the 1989 session "Assessing Developments in Anthropology" was that of discussant. Since my critical reaction to the papers in this volume is guided by the advocacy of a cultural materialist paradigm, and since the principles of cultural materialism are misstated in several of the papers, my discussion will consist to a considerable extent of an exposition of what cultural materialism is and is not.

2. The substitution of "primacy of infrastructure" for "infrastructural determinism" is a purely strategic or cosmetic change intended to placate a generation that feels its dignity is compromised by any deterministic paradigm and that chooses to ignore the probabilistic nature of the determinism in question. In the same vein, I have suggested elsewhere that we substitute "symbolic-ideational" for "superstructure," i.e. to avoid the implication of a superfluous or unimportant component.

3. This corpus includes theories about: General evolution: Leavitt (1986); Sanderson (1990). The origin and evolution of sex and gender roles: Divale and Harris (1976); Harris (1977, 1981a); Hayden et al. (1986); Maclachlan (1983); Margolis (1984); Miller (1981); Leavitt (1989). Warfare: B. Ferguson (1984, 1989); Morren (1984); Balee (1984); Harris (1984); J. Ross (1984). Class caste and ethnic relations: Harris (1964b, 1964c); Despres (1975); Mencher (1980); Abruzzi (1982, 1988); E. Ross (1978a). Origin of religions: Harner (1977); Harris (1977, 1989). Origins of food preferences and avoidances and of major world cuisines: E. Ross (1980b, 1983, 1987); Harris (1985); Vaidyanathan, Nair, and Harris (1982). Settlement patterns, demographic trends, and modes of population regulation: Good (1987); Gross (1975); Harris and Ross (1987); Hayden (1986); Keeley (1988). The origins of agriculture: Hayden (1990). The origin of chiefdoms and the state: Kottak (1972); Sanders and Price (1968); Price (1984); Webster (1985); Sanders, Santley, and Parsons (1979); Haas (1982); Paulsen (1981). Anthropologists who carry out research in conformity with cultural materialist principles to avoid controversy often prefer not to label themselves as contributors to the cultural materialist corpus. The unmarked influence of cultural materialism has been especially significant in American archaeology, where as one archaeologist has written: "The principle of infrastructural determinism of course underlies modern archaeology at least in North America" (Schiffer (1983: 191). An interest in cultural materialism among behavioral psychologists should also be noted: Biglan (1988); Glenn (1988); Malagodi (1986); Vargas (1985); R. Warner (1985).

INTELLECTUAL ROOTS

Marvin Harris was a member of the faculty of Columbia University in the Department of Anthropology from 1953 to 1980, and chairman there from 1963 to 1966. Since 1980 he has been Graduate Research Professor of Anthropology at the University of Florida. He has carried out field research in Brazil (most recently—1992—in Rio de Contas, Bahia, which he first visited in 1950); Mozambique; India; and East Harlem, New York City. He has also conducted field training programs in Brazil and Ecuador. Of his seventeen books, the most influential are *Patterns of Race in the Americas* (1964); *The Rise of Anthropological Theory* (1968—designated a "Social Science Citation Classic" in 1991); *Culture, People, Nature: An Introduction to General Anthropology* (six editions since 1971); *Cultural Anthropology* (three editions since 1983); *Cows, Pigs, Wars, and Witches: Riddles of Culture* (1974); *Cannibals and Kings: The Origins of Cultures* (1977); *Cultural Materialism: The Struggle for a Science of Culture* (1979); *America Now: The Anthropology of a Changing Culture* (1981); *Good to Eat* (1985); and *Our Kind* (1989). These books have been translated into a total of sixteen languages. Harris is past chair of the General Anthropology Division of the American Anthropological Association and Distinguished Lecturer for 1991.

I committed myself to anthropology after taking Charles Wagley's four-field introductory course at Columbia College. Wagley was my fieldwork supervisor, chair of my doctoral committee, and lifelong friend. Under his tutelage, I became a good eclectic Boasian particularist-relativist and shared his rejection of Steward's cultural ecology approach. Although I took a course with Steward, it had little effect on me until several years later (perhaps because he was ill and absent most of the time). Being a Boasian in those days, however, meant being a positivist—the image of Boas as the consummate scientist was an article of faith among his intellectual heirs at Columbia such as Bunzel, Lesser, and Mead. Courses in Skinnerian psychology and independent readings in logical positivism also helped to inspire my interest in convincing others that anthropology was or should be a science. After 1953 when I began to teach and shared an office with Morton Fried, I was attracted by Leslie White's critique of the Boasians and by White's emphasis on energetics. What bothered me about White, however, was that he had not actually measured energy inputs and outputs, a fault I intended to remedy when I next went to the field, but never did.

Alfred Kroeber was and continues to be a very important role model for me. He twice taught at Columbia, first when I was an undergraduate, and again when I was in graduate school. As an undergraduate I wrote a paper for him that showed why neither he nor Leslie White understood the logico-empirical operations that validate the abstractions we call "culture" and related "superorganic" entities. (The paper foreshadowed *The Nature of Cultural Things*, 1964. Most anthropologists still remain incapable of supplying an epistemologically sound operational model of "culture.") I admired Kroeber for his erudition, especially his four-field approach as embodied in his masterpiece, *Anthropology* (1948), which was the inspiration for my own (1971) foray into four-field textbook writing.

The big change in my intellectual outlook came about as a result of the field trip to Mozambique. While I had hoped to carry out research on energetics in Bathonga households, as well as to trace the history of changes since the beginning of the century using Henri Junod's ethnography as a baseline, my most important objective was to compare race relations in Brazil with race relations in another part of the past and present Portuguese empire. All my intentions were overwhelmed by the reality of Portugal's system of colonial apartheid and labor exploitation. The discrepancy between what people were doing and what they were saying made the problem of subjectivity and objectivity, of mental and behavioral events, and of emic and etic perspectives (words which I did not yet possess) altogether inescapable. Furthermore, the more I learned about the difference between race relations in Mozambique and Brazil, the clearer it became that different systems of production and of exploitation of labor accounted for much of the divergent evolution of Africa and the Americas. Portuguese or Anglo-Saxon values and traditions had little to do with it but were themselves largely dependent on what I later called the demo-techno-econo-environmental infrastructure. Finally, the Mozambique experience made it clear to me that, as an anthropologist, I could not escape the moral consequences of a feigned relativist neutrality.

Returning to Columbia, I wrote a pamphlet for the American Committee on Africa, *Portugal's African Wards* (1958), describing the operation of the Portuguese *Indigenato* (plus other articles). At the same time, I read Marx, Plekhanov, and Kautsky with new insight. I realized that Marx was the common ground under Steward and White, although both had shied away from public acknowledgments in deference to the anti-Marxist terror that reigned in academia during the late 1930s and early 1950s. Another crucial figure for me in the early 1960s was Karl Wittfogel, who despite his rabid and treacherous anticommunism, was responsible for Steward's treatment of ecological factors in the rise of early agro-managerial states.

Before Mozambique, my scientism had existed apart from the special epistemological and theoretical principles necessary for establishing a positivist materialist (nondialectical) paradigm in the social sciences; after Mozambique, all the components came together. The basic materialism came from Marx and B. F. Skinner; the importance of economic factors also from Marx; the overall evolutionism from White; and the environmental and demographic foci from Steward and Wittfogel (but ultimately of course from Darwin and Malthus).

In 1963 I presented my first paper on the material conditions that select for Hindu India's beliefs about cattle. And in 1964 *Patterns of Race in the Americas* appeared along with *The Nature of Cultural Things*. While teaching the History of Anthropology course at Columbia, I began to assemble the materials for *The Rise of Anthropological Theory* in which I coined the phrase "cultural materialism" and presented it as a specifically anthropological alternative to all forms of idealism and to dialectical, Stalinist, and antipositivist as well as biological reductionist forms of materialism. I have sought ever since to refine and improve the formulation of cultural materialist principles by testing them against a widening corpus of puzzles ranging from food preferences and avoidances to changes in U.S. family structure, and most recently, to the collapse of Soviet and East European state socialism.

My plans for the near future include a renewed effort to confront the elitist, obscurantist, and nihilist posturing of postprocessual and postmodernist anthropology, not as an end in itself, but as part of an attempt to gain for anthropology a more central intellectual and applied role vis-à-vis the great issues of our times such as the ecological consequences of the spread of consumerism and capitalism; the rise of country-less global corporations; the resurgence of ethnic and racial chauvinism; the deepening poverty of the poor; and the prevention of war.

Enhancing
the Comparative Perspective

I n the disciplinary literature at large as well as in chapters of *Assessing Cultural Anthropology*, one senses uncertainty regarding the field's direction. It is not just a question of the discipline's intellectual diversity. That, I noted in the Introduction (citing Tax and Barth), has been going on for a long time. What seems to distinguish the present mood has to do with the discipline's efforts to move in two directions at once—attempting to preserve a sense of continuity with past perspectives while developing new ones significantly different from them. The concern for continuity is apparent in various contributions. In the last section, for instance, Salzman (page 34) criticizes the effort to make "anthropology anew moment by moment." And Murphy (page 55) talks of returning "anthropology back to its center." The concern for innovation is equally obvious. Marcus (page 46ff) suggests ways for redesigning ethnography, and Nader (page 86) (in this section) calls for revitalizing comparison by "violating . . . generally accepted canons."

In this section we focus on the comparative perspective as a way of reflecting on the discipline at large. Many view comparison as central to anthropology. Contributors as diverse as Harris (page 62), Marcus (page 50), Yanagisako and Collier (page 198), and Wolf (page 219), to mention a brief sampling of the volume's anthropologists, emphasize its importance. Over two-thirds of the contributors make reference to it in their chapters. Nader (page 93) observes "anthropologists have regularly identified anthropology as a comparative discipline over the past 100 years." And Godelier (page 97) adds, anthropology's "ambition is to learn enough about each of these societies to be able to compare them." Yet comparative studies seem to be declining in importance within the discipline. While a range of comparisons are still being done, relatively speaking, comparison seems to play a less significant role—numerically and intellectually—than in times past. "The sheer number of comparative articles and books published" in the early 1950s, Nader (page 85) notes, reminds us "that energetic debates about the intellectual place of comparison are missing from today's anthropological agendas." Kuper (page 116) adds "comparison is no longer the central interest of many field anthropologists." And Holy (1987:8, 13), in a book entitled *Comparative Anthropology*, observes "these days, a great proportion of empirical research is distinctly non-comparative" and "comparisons aimed specifically at generating cross-culturally valid generalizations seem to be conspicuous by their absence."

Such statements contrast with those of earlier times when Lewis (1956:260) could write "Within the past five years there have appeared an unusually large number of theoretical writings dealing with comparative method in anthropology" and Eggan (1965:357) could observe "in the last decade there has been an unusually large number of theoretical writings in anthropology concerned with comparative method." A question we might ponder with the following contributions is how, in reinvigorating the comparative perspective, we might enhance the discipline of anthropology as well.

REMEMBERING THE PAST: RECALLING SOME OF ANTHROPOLOGY'S NOTABLE COMPARISONS

Remembering past comparisons is not only a form of nostalgia. It is a way of understanding where we have been in relation to where we are now, as well as, perhaps, where we might go in the future. We need consider: What do past comparisons say about the discipline of anthropology—its understandings, its approaches, its hopes?

In reviewing certain notable comparisons in anthropology, we might make a distinction between implicit and explicit comparison. Implicit comparison is inherent in most description. When we describe someone as hopeful, we mean hopeful in relation, in comparison, to our understanding of the term, not in regard to some absolute sense that can be instrumentally measured. Explicit comparison is different. It involves overtly comparing two (or more) groups to illuminate a set of cultural dynamics. It is this explicit sense that Nadel (1951:222) refers to when he suggests that the comparative perspective is the "equivalent of the experiment in the study of society." By bringing more than one case to bear on a problem, it offers suggestive possibilities for explaining how cultural trait A influences B or how trait C causes D. In what are termed "controlled comparisons," for example, anthropologists explore a select number of related contexts involving a limited number of cultural differences to assess how certain social variables affect one another (see Eggan 1954, 1955:499 plus Eggan's and Nadel's studies below).

Nineteenth-century anthropologists—such as Morgan, Tylor, and Frazer—developed an evolutionary form of comparison. They compared cultural differences in space to establish cultural differences in time. Existent societies throughout the world were arranged on a temporal scale from the simple to the complex or, really, from societies unlike European ones to societies more like them. "In working out this unilinear sequence of institutions, the comparative method was utilized to document the various stages," Eggan (1965:363) notes. "Existing societies were [deemed] surviving examples of earlier stages through which more advanced societies had passed. . . . Once the evolutionary structure was established in outline, the comparative method became essentially a procedure by which new information was pigeonholed." The focus was less on what we might term "cultures" than on "culture"—on "the progressive accumulation of . . . art, science, knowledge, refinement—those things that freed man from control by nature" (Stocking 1968:201). Given this orientation, it is not fair to assert, as some have, that these evolutionists ignored the cultural contexts of certain practices. They had a different frame of reference. They were more concerned with the evolution of culture in general, with its stages of development, than with its operation in specific contexts at specific times. It was in this tradition that Tylor (1889) used a cross-cultural statistical analysis of between three and four hundred cases relating to post-marital residence, in-law avoidance, and the levirate (involving widow remarriage) to uncover "a tendency of society to pass from the maternal to the paternal system" (1889: 256).

Murdock, in his book *Social Structure*, similarly used statistical data to suggest a set of evolutionary changes but on a less grand scale. He postulated—based on certain statistical correlations involving descent, marriage, residence, and kinship terminologies—a particular direction to change in social organization. "When any social system . . . begins to undergo change," Murdock (1949:221) suggested, "such change regularly begins with a modification of the rule of residence." A change in the form of localized aggregations of kin followed; this was followed in turn by changes in the rule of descent and kinship terminology respectively. Using patrilocality and patrilineally oriented kinship terminology, one might represent the changes as: patrilocality → patrilocalized extended families → patrilineages → patrilineally oriented terminology. (So as not to overstate the case, readers should note that Murdock offered qualifications to the directional relationship—see e.g. Murdock 1949: 222.)

Another set of comparative studies grew out of Boas's critique of the evolutionary perspective. "Even the most cursory review," Boas (1940:273-276) observed, "shows that the same phenomena may develop in a multitude of ways." "Before extended comparisons are made, the comparability [i.e. the similarity of development] of the material must be proved." Boas contrasted what he labeled "the comparative method" of the evolutionists with his own "historical method" which—while still comparative—involved:

a detailed study of customs in their relation to the total culture of the tribe practicing them, in connection with an investigation of their geographical distribution among neighboring tribes. . . . [This] affords us almost always a means of determining with considerable accuracy the historical causes that led to the formation of the customs in question and to the psychological processes that were at work in their development.

"If anthropology desires to establish the laws governing the growth of culture," Boas (1940: 280) continued, "it must not confine itself to comparing the results of the growth alone, but whenever such is feasible it must compare the processes of growth." Sapir (1916) nicely summarized many of the principles involved in this form of comparative method in *Time Perspective in Aboriginal American Culture*.

Spier's (1921) *The Sun Dance of the Plains Indians*—which traced the Sun Dance's spread across the Great Plains from a postulated origin among the Arapaho and Cheyenne—is a commonly cited illustration of this approach. But a more recent and perhaps better example of the perspective is Eggan's (1955, 1968:396-397) comparison of kinship terminologies and subsistence patterns among North American Plains Indians. Eggan divided North American Plains Indian kinship into two major types: one stressing lineage unity, the other generational unity. Indians in the eastern portion of the Great Plains were primarily horticulturists and lived in permanent villages organized as unilineal descent groups (e.g., the Omaha, Iowa, Illinois, Hidatsa, and Pawnee). The Indians of the High Plains were seminomadic hunters in bilateral bands centering around a camp circle (e.g., the Cheyenne, Kiowa, and Dakota). Their classificatory kinship system emphasized generation and sex, drawing in a wide range of other relationships with (unlike the lineage system of the horticulturists) only a vague sense of outer limits. Eggan suggested that the principle of lineage unity—as manifested in unilineal descent organization—provided the settled horticulturists of the Eastern Plains with a sense of stability and continuity through time. The concern with generational unity among the Indians of the High Plains, in contrast, stimulated ties of wide-ranging extension, but shallow depth—a pattern fitting with the flexible forms of solidarity needed among seminomadic hunters adapting to a variable set of ecological conditions. What made Eggan's analysis particularly interesting was his suggestion that Indian groups, such as the Crow, altered their kinship systems as they moved from one region of the Plains to another. Eggan, in other words, related differences in kinship patterns to differences in subsistence within a geographical region to gain a better sense of how certain adaptational pressures affected kinship organization.

Durkheim and Mauss used a comparison of Australian, Zuni, Sioux, and Chinese classificatory schemas to uncover what they perceived to be the underlying basis for classificatory thought—the social organization of human beings. As they phrased it in 1903:

Society was not simply a model which classificatory thought followed; . . . its . . . divisions . . . served as divisions for the system of classification. The first logical categories were social categories; the first classes of things were classes of men. . . . It was because men were grouped, and thought of themselves in the form of groups, that in their ideas they grouped other things. (1963:82)

Nadel's (1952) study of four African societies is a seminal controlled comparison regarding the underlying dynamics of witchcraft. (Because of length considerations, I limit my summary to the two West African societies discussed.) The Nupe and Gwari, he noted, shared a number of cultural similarities regarding social, economic, and political organization. But they differed on one significant point. Among the Nupe only women were witches, among the Gwari both men and women were. Why the difference? Nadel pointed out that Nupe women were traders. And this trading often provided Nupe women with economic power and wealth. Moreover, it allowed Nupe women the freedom to become involved in a number of extramarital sexual liaisons. Gwari women did not have this power or freedom. They were unable to challenge the cultural norm of male dominance existing in both cultures. Only Nupe women could. Nadel suggests that the gap between the ideal power (of men) and the real power (of women) focused witchcraft accusations on female traders among the Nupe. Social stresses among the Gwari were more diffuse and, as a result, so were their witchcraft accusations.

Wolf (1957) used historical material drawn from various archives to develop a comparison between Meso-America and Central Java in colonial times. He suggests that a type of peasant village—termed "closed corporate communities"—arose in both locales due to similar pressures during the colonial era. Wolf identifies "closed corporate communities" as communities with communal jurisdiction over land, restricted membership, redistributive mechanisms for surplus, and barriers against outside goods and ideas. Part of the reason they developed, he suggests, was because of administrative efforts to restrict the power of colonial settlers. "By granting relative autonomy to the native communities, the home government could at one and the same time ensure the maintenance of cultural barriers against colonist encroachment, while avoiding the huge cost of direct administration" (1957: 10). Another formative factor concerned the enforced economic dualization of the colonial society—involving a dominating entrepreneurial sector and a dominated peasant sector. Indigenous peasants were relegated "to the status of part-time laborers, providing for their own subsistence on scarce land, together with the imposition of charges levied and enforced by . . . local authorities" (1957:12). What Wolf uncovered, in his historical comparative study, were some of the similar dynamics that helped shape peasant communities during the colonial era in widely separate parts of the globe.

Drawing on information from the Human Relations Area Files—an encyclopedic collection of ethnographic materials involving hundreds of societies that Murdock also used in his research—Beatrice Whiting (1950) statistically analyzed the relation between sorcery and dispute settlement in fifty non-Western societies. The essential characteristic of societies with what she (1950:82) termed "coordinate" political controls was "the absence of an individual or group . . . with delegated authority to settle disputes and punish offenses." The major mechanism of social control, in such instances, was retaliation by peers. In societies with "superordinate" political controls, individuals with recognized authority (e.g. judges) solved disputes and punished offenders. "Hence, societies in which murder was settled by retaliation were classified as coordinate, and those in which murder cases were referred to a delegated authority [were classified] as superordinate" (1950:84-85). Whiting found that out of 25 societies with coordinate controls, sorcery was important in 24 of them. Out of 25 societies with superordinate controls, sorcery was only important in 11. From this Whiting concluded fear of sorcery often constituted an important means of social control, especially in societies which lacked superordinate control mechanisms. (See Swanson 1960:137-152 for a related analysis of the same problem.)

In these examples we perceive some of anthropology's hopes for itself. We see the types of questions particular anthropologists deem important. And we see how these anthropologists seek to answer them. We perceive something of anthropology's goals and methods.

TWO PROBLEMS

We face at least two key problems in relation to comparison today. One derives from our discussion of the positivism/interpretivism debate: We need a reliable body of materials to develop valid comparisons. Ethnographies tend to cover different topics in different depths and from different perspectives. This makes comparison difficult. Salzman (page 34) cites the case of John Davis who "seemed on the verge of tears of frustration during his attempts to find any comparable information in the available ethnographic reports." And in the Introduction, I noted a study by Steward [1950, quoted by Lewis (1956:262)] which found "difficulties in comparability due to the

uneven coverage which seems to depend largely upon individual interests." As a result of this problem, samples are often based less on systematic selection techniques than on opportunistic collection. Researchers primarily select groups for which they readily have information. Schapera (1953:353) comments: "the principles . . . that govern the selection of societies for comparison seem to be anything but scientific; nor . . . is there even any consistency about what is meant by a 'society,' i.e. about the nature of the units between which comparison is being made." By way of illustration, Schapera criticizes the technique Murdock used in *Social Structure*. "We cannot but conclude that Murdock's sampling technique was influenced more by literary convenience than by adherence to scientific discipline," he states (1953:357). Murdock rarely relied, he notes, on ethnographies written in foreign languages (1949:353-377). "When he asks us, in effect, to condone incomplete research because he could not spare the time to do his job thoroughly," Shapera continues, "we may perhaps be forgiven for being skeptical about the validity of his correlations and conclusions." The first problem then is how to systematically collect representative data.

The second involves the question of linkages. In times past, anthropologists might think they were comparing seemingly independent groups who, though perhaps related to one another, had their own distinct cultural boundaries and identities. Such independence hardly, if ever, exists today. And following Keesing and Kottak and Colson (in later sections), we might wonder if it has existed for centuries. This question of linkages draws us into the "Galton problem" in which the statistical validity of certain comparisons is undermined because the items compared might be historically related to one another. When one observes similar sorcery beliefs in two distinct societies, for example, one must not immediately jump to the conclusion that the same underlying cultural dynamic produced both of them. Group A's beliefs might have simply spread instead, through diffusion, to group B. Because of various historical linkages, in other words, difficulties exist in sorting out the causes of relationships observed in comparisons—whether they stem from historical connections or are related to similar social dynamics. Whiting notes, for instance: "The question might be raised as to whether the connections between sorcery and coordinate control are not in many cases historical rather than functional. . . . The problem of factoring out historical connections is a difficult one" (1950:88). In today's world of overlapping linkages and complex interactions among cultural groups this is even more the case. We are then led to ask how effective comparisons can be made today.

FRAMING THIS SECTION'S CONTRIBUTIONS

I have used Nader's chapter—particularly her concern for "comparative consciousness"—to frame the contributions in this section. Nader raises questions about how to reinvigorate comparison and, in the process, suggests a means for enhancing the discipline of anthropology as well. In an increasingly interlinked world, she stresses that our overlapping perspectives of one another form a fertile field for comparative analysis. She explores how others see us in relation to how we see them and/or ourselves. In her suggestion lies hope for a fertile new form of comparison—different from, but building on, earlier ones.

Drawing on her ideas, I would ask readers in this section to compare different assessments of anthropology—in this section and in the volume more generally—in order to explore how we might reinvigorate the discipline. All of the authors in this volume assess the field of cultural anthropology in one way or another. But I have selected four—two European contributors (Godelier and Kuper) and two contributors from beyond the traditional centers

of anthropology (DaMatta and Das)—to explore how different people assess the issues anthropology needs to address in the 1990s. In their overlapping but divergent assessments of where the field is and where it should go we perceive much about anthropology's present state and something, perhaps, about its possible future.

I urge readers to not only compare the perspectives enunciated in this section with one another but to compare this section's perspectives—individually and collectively—with those in other sections. The perspectives in this section, for example, differ in rather interesting ways from the first section regarding the issues raised, the concerns stressed. While Section One involves American and Canadian assessments, the last four contributions in this section involve European and Third World assessments. Both Harris and Godelier share a "materialist" orientation. But their approaches are distinct. And while Marcus and Das hold a common interest in interpretive perspectives, they develop this interest in separate ways. Different contributors, moreover, cite different authors. Interestingly, the French anthropologist Godelier is far more complimentary regarding the early American anthropologist Morgan than American anthropologists are in this volume.

We should not see one individual's (or section's) perspectives as correct and the perspective of others as wrong. Rather, we need be attuned to the subtle overlappings and divergences of their assessments and to see what insights we can draw from a comparison of them. What are the reasons behind Harris's and Godelier's or Marcus's and Das's differing assessments of the discipline, for instance? Asking this question draws us into a different sense of comparison, as Nader suggests. We are encouraged to consider: What do their differences and similarities illuminate about both the assessors and the assessed?

In the four contributions following Nader's initial chapter, we see the complication of polarizing the world into "us" and "others."

Four of the section's contributors are non-American anthropologists. Are they "us," meaning anthropologists? Or are they "other," meaning non-American? However one splits the categorization, First World versus Third World, American versus non-American, ambiguities abound. Yet the dialogue of perspectives proves intriguing and the basis for much insight.

Godelier and Kuper provide two European assessments of the discipline. (Bloch, Goody, Lévi-Strauss, Strathern, and Tishkov provide others in later sections.) Intriguingly, Godelier and Kuper perceive more coherence in the field than many American anthropologists might. Their descriptions are probably a bit unsettling to some American anthropologists. (Readers may begin to sense the uneasiness that develops as one becomes the described rather than the describer.) We see traditional French and British anthropological concerns expressed in the way Godelier reflects on a broad set of theoretical issues relating to power, politics, and economics (in his discussion of Lévi-Strauss and Marx), while Kuper reflects, more empirically, on the importance of fieldwork and the reanalysis of ethnographic materials.

The chapters by two Third World anthropologists, DaMatta (a Brazilian) and Das (an Indian), likewise raise a number of issues. DaMatta, for example, takes aim at interpretive anthropology. But his comments regarding why anthropological questions get drawn into general political and intellectual life in some countries and not others are relevant to much of the discipline. To what degree, we are led to ask, is Third World anthropology different from Western anthropology? Das begins with a critique of Dumont's work on the hierarchical nature of Indian social organization. Dumont sought to overcome the ethnocentric, egalitarian biases of Western accounts of India by presenting his analysis of India in Indian terms. But we have the intriguing problem of an Indian anthropologist taking exception to it. Her reflections lead into the broader question of what role anthropologists can (and should) play in the analysis of their own versus other cultures. Who speaks for whom? In what ways and for what purposes?

As readers examine these chapters, then, they might keep certain questions in mind: How do various assessments of the field overlap? Where and why do they differ? Viewed collectively, what do they indicate about anthropology's past development as a discipline? And similarly, what do they suggest regarding anthropology's future direction?

5

*Comparative Consciousness**

LAURA NADER

INTRODUCTION

Much has been written about the reasons for doing anthropology that implies that the very existence of a disciplinary anthropology was due to colonialism or more generally to imperialism. Anthropology has also been described by many as the study of the non-Western "Other." From such assumptions—that anthropology has its roots in imperialism and that it is the Western study of non-Western peoples—there has flowed a sometimes enlightened, sometimes flawed critique of fieldwork and writings about other cultures. Much of this wide-ranging critique, in which people outside of the discipline participate, has implied that field research has been part of an effort to "maintain a certain type of relation between the West and its Other" (Fabian 1983:149).

Sigfried Nadel wrote about this relation between the West and its Other, and the role introduced religions played in changing African societal structures in *The Nuba* (1947). He observed that "Religious education uproots first, and rebuilds afterwards. Christianity, even more than Islam, plans to build a new society" (1947:512). However, Nadel's observation lay dormant for decades as a research question of interest and importance precisely because of what I call the *positional predicament* of a Western anthropology which excludes observation *on the West* by other cultures and which may be part of an effort to manage a certain relation with the Western "Other."

A Missing Component in Current Debates

Disagreements have been plentiful among academic anthropologists, and if they result in debate they are part of our strength (Nader 1989c). For example, disagreements taught us that convenience enters into theory development: thus the notion of culture and behavior as consensual was convenient both for colonizers, and for a newly developing anthropology, and even for those colonized who actively constructed their self-presentation. When, through accumulated ethnographic experience, attention was called to variation as a response to the criticism of consensual models, reaction was still within the range of a positivist ethnography. Eventually, however, the cumulative critiques of a flawed positivism inspired approaches that emphasized the rich, multiple nature of symbolic meanings and the need to calibrate the observer as an instrument of record.[1]

The idea accompanying each successive criticism, however, was that one approach was supreme and exclusive. This notion was inconvenient (1) for those concerned with the enormous complexity of the subject matter, (2) for those contending with the problems stemming from a West-centered or "Occidental" anthropology, or (3) for those interested in comparison as first and foremost a discovery

---

*I would like to acknowledge the help and stimulation of Saddeka Arebi, JoAnn Martin, Lori Powell, and Tarek Milleron as well as many student members of my seminar, "Orientalism, Occidentalism and Control."

process. Dissatisfaction was followed by assessments indicating the need for a composite theory, some call it unified (Collier and Yanagisako 1987), and the need for multidimensional approaches that embraced different ways of knowing (Ong 1987). But the obvious question is: How did *anthropology*, a discipline that prides itself on its holistic perspective, come to develop unidimensional models and, the corollary, that methods must be exclusive of one another?

Anthropologists tend to conform to the canons of their societies—in this case the canons of a positivist science based on an ideal laboratory model in which specialization of methods and increasing control over variables were key.[2] Critiques of the past twenty years have turned our attention to the rhetoric of science and to the limitations of positivist science in anthropology, a useful antidote to the arrogance of scientists in a nuclear age. They also revealed the limitations of nonscientist humanists in a postmodern period, who also arrogantly conceive of understanding as possible from unidimensional frames. The obsession with method in both camps has been continuous, and the obsession with models, charts, and numbers, and the resulting illusory concreteness, was repeated by those obsessed with writing, those who see anthropology as a narrative art form. Some of my functionalist colleagues call this obsession with writing "fluff," a concern with aesthetics, not a serious concern with problems of presentation, and not responsible anthropology. Putting accusation and argument to one side, the critiques are indicative of a vigorous anthropology.

Comparison is not a major issue in contemporary discussions; however, the absence of interest is illustrated by recalling Oscar Lewis's 1956 survey of anthropology in which he reported examining a total of 248 writings dealing with comparison (from 1950 to 1954). The sheer number of comparative articles and books published in that period is a reminder that energetic debates about the intellectual place of comparison are missing from today's anthropological agendas.

THE NEED FOR COMPARATIVE CONSCIOUSNESS: I

In thinking about positivist and interpretive models, I am reminded of another tradition in anthropology, one with different assumptions, one concerned as much with commonalities as with differences. For many of us anthropology is not solely about non-Western colonial or isolated island societies. The subject for anthropology is human existence in all its diversity, including all cultural forms found on the globe: in the suites, in the streets, in the villages, on the steppes, in the cities, in the institutions, and in the mind. In this inclusive tradition there are many kinds of intellectuals, not just European and American ones. Anthropologists not only range over the whole earth but span the entire period of human existence. From such a vantage point one would say that our anthropology/ethnography has been incomplete—in terms of our experience of place and problem, which led me to advocate for a vertical slice in "Up the Anthropologist" (Nader 1969); in terms of unidimensional approaches espoused by each successive generation of anthropologists, which led me to write about postinterpretive anthropology (see Nader 1989c); and in terms of an anthropology which is not as self-conscious as it might be about the implications of its Western (Occidentalist) origins (see Nader 1989b).

In the examples that follow, the particularist approach in which the native is mute (or heard through anthropological interpretation) is distinguished from the universalist one which allows for the Other's Other. The difference between universalizing and particularizing theories underscores a comparative consciousness that is linked to a consciousness about the uses of comparison. There can be a division of labor in anthropology, one that incorporates directly (without interpretation) insight from non-Western observers about us in the West as well as one that utilizes and scrutinizes categories used in comparisons made by nonanthropological commentators. A "big" anthropology would resonate to the problems of a Western monopoly of "knowledge" production.

In his book *Mirror for Man*, Kluckhohn observed, "Studying primitives enables us to see ourselves better. Ordinarily we are unaware of the special lenses through which we look at life. . . . The scientist of human affairs needs to know as much about the eye that sees as the object seen" (1949:16).[3] That was 1949; today we use the term cultural critique, but it is somehow not critical in the sense of looking back with serious *comparative consciousness* because we still do not know enough about the eye that sees. Navel gazing is not enough.

When the ethnographer goes to another culture and tries to understand that which is different, difference becomes the primary attraction. Both critical and comparative consciousness fall out and there are costs thus incurred. If in looking at Egyptian women's lives we get caught up in clitoridectomy (Morsy 1991), we miss the opportunity to examine simultaneously breast implants in the United States. If we debunk comparison as part of debunking positivist science and the comparative methods associated with positivism (cross-cultural and controlled comparison), we throw out possibilities for examining those dimensions of the human experience that are shared (see Kapferer 1988). Without comparison we literally lose consciousness and become victims of the bounds of thinkable thought (Chomsky 1985; Borofsky 1987).

The need for an increased consciousness about comparative methodologies in anthropology is compelling precisely because of current controversies. It is useful to notice that the recent postmodern critiques in anthropology have marked a broadening of the situatedness of ethnographic research. Explanations of cultural dynamics are no longer focusing primarily on factors internal to a cultural unit but are being enriched by the inclusion of external explanatory factors of a global, demographic, political, economic, or ideational nature as well. However, the focus on the wider contextualization of ethnography has also encompassed a rejection of generalist goals as, for example embodied in positivist science, and, with this, a rejection of explicit comparison.

In turn, comparativists have been slow to respond beyond entrenchment in and elaboration of earlier models. The challenge is an intellectual one, and not merely technical or ideological as some have assumed: Can contemporary comparative methodologies cope with questions of process and hegemony?

It is a disservice when histories of anthropology portray a continuous conflict between those who cherish the unique and those who wish to generalize, between comparativists and noncomparativists. It leaves on the margin those who are doing both. The historical, functional, and interpretive schools of ethnographic research are idealized examples of particularist modes, while developmental, crosscultural, and controlled comparative methodologies are examples of generalist modes. This essay is about the area in-between, a place which holds the possibility of a comparative consciousness that illuminates connections—between local and global, between past and present, between anthropologists and those they study, between uses of comparison and implications of its uses. In other words, this essay is about comparative methodologies that engender a capacity for thinking about fluid situations, those that embrace both humanism and science, both "expert" and nonexpert observers.

REVITALIZING COMPARISON

Comparative approaches which might elucidate the kinds of connections mentioned above depend on violating two generally accepted canons of comparative research:

(1) that the items compared must share certain fundamental traits (the notion of controlled comparison) and (2) that the items compared must be discontinuous, that is, they must not directly influence one another. These two methodological assumptions restrict research questions to those that can be phrased with neatness and with elegance, and, as a result, they have served to give rise to particularistic findings.

Comparative methodologies that are useful in examining the current world situation must include the interactive aspects of the global movement of people, goods, and ideas.[4] Monographs written in search of the native and comparativists in search of scientific "truth" have at times treated colonialism, missionizing, and schooling as contaminating the subject under study. For example, in 1941 Llewelyn and Hoebel described the disputing processes of the Cheyenne without mentioning that they were a decimated culture and people. By contrast I (1990) recently described dispute processes among the Zapotec as enmeshed in local considerations of global forces, thereby transcending the boundaries of the microcosm to incorporate common experience in dispersed locales.

Attention to comparative consciousness and the development of a plurality of comparisons are ways to understand our subject matter more adequately. By means of comparative consciousness anthropologists evolved a way of thinking about human life as a response to repeated observations that in other disciplines might be considered discoveries: (1) culture is not homogeneous, nor always consensual; (2) culture may be constructed and spread instrumentally; (3) social organization does not operate on principles that predict everything important; (4) organization may stand still while meaning changes; (5) change is ubiquitous; (6) some changes indicate the force of global impact for millennia; and (7) anthropologists did not invent the study of society and culture, only the disciplinary study of "man," allowing

space for observations our subjects may have about us.

Anthropologists have made creative responses to such discoveries: (1) time reorders both the anthropologist and her informants (Colson 1984); (2) history is part of the interpretivist's tools (R. Rosaldo 1980); (3) both the people and the anthropologist make history (Borofsky 1987); and (4) the weight of century-old ideologies may be found in the daily routine of both Western and Westernized peoples (Nader 1990). Comparative frames may arise from ethnographies within large or small geographical regions, but they are set within the overall framework of interaction among world systems which give rise to change locally (Nash 1979, Taussig 1980). By means of comparative consciousness we tease out the historical interactions between large areas of the world from more limited regional interactions, an approach which allows us to capture the dynamic while maintaining a holistic or ecological perspective (Nader 1989a). Comparison may also elucidate by means of juxtaposing the unique components of an area, an approach which led to discovery of the cultures of nationalism (Kapferer 1988) and to recognizing the impact of national history on local history and an intolerance for conflict (Greenhouse 1986), which then reverberates back on national culture (Nader 1989).

A contemporary predisposition against comparison (especially against controlled experiments) may be attributed to an inability of any one kind of comparison to illuminate the conditions in a world that is increasingly characterized by interdependence, in the context of dynamic global power relationships, while also maintaining the integrity of the communities described. The solution to the predisposition against cross-cultural or controlled experiments, or a predilection for one particular kind of comparison, is to use all comparisons in their historical, functional, and contrastive forms so as not to inhibit raising *and* addressing interesting questions related to the dynamics of interaction. Composite approaches are never neat, and as compared to more orthodox positions do not attract a constituency. Yet to expand comparative consciousness that serves the universal challenge to anthropology is not to narrow or constrict the concept of comparison, but to enlarge its methodological scope and its intellectual style.

FILTERING THE WEST[5]

So-called primitive and third world cultures have been described as laboratories by anthropologists, places of exploration that could be used, it was thought, to discover "truth." Another view of the study of human activity is that it can change our ideas of what it means to know something. In this regard it is interesting to understand the functionally equivalent ways in which other cultures have perceived their "Other." In the following pages my examples come from reading "Orientalist" and "Occidentalist" literature as dialogues. My focus is on "Occidentalisms"—material written about the West by non-Westerners. There is only scattered reference to how the Occident has been perceived, and comparatively little has been written or translated about the West by some parts of the East. What writing there is should be carefully examined because it is especially relevant to the notion of positional predicaments.

From 1826 to 1831, the Egyptian director of Mohammad Ali's first scientific expedition to Europe, Rifa'ah al-Tahtawi, traveled in France. In 1836 Edward W. Lane, an English representative of the British foreign office, published his book on Cairo. A comparison of these works was published in an article by Sandra Naddaf (1986). Naddaf compares the differences between the two writers. Both authors describe an institution which the East *shares* with the West. The manipulation of mirrors is used by both authors as a descriptive and narrative device. The English traveler establishes himself as a detached observer, hides

his existence in the scenes he describes, and holds the mirror to reflect Egyptian society without being a part of the reflected image. In his description of the cafes of Cairo, Lane establishes the cafe as an institution specific to the culture by the intensive use of Arabic terminology which can only be parenthetically translated. The Egyptian traveler holds the mirror in a position so as to reflect both subject and object. Although al-Tahtawi speaks of Paris, he brings the Oriental tradition into the background. His representation of another culture, as Naddaf points out, is not a means of distancing himself from the Other but a means of integration. In fact, since al-Tahtawi assumes the role of translator between the two cultures, he tends to find common points of reference and elements of self-recognition. Both of these traditions—the particularist approach and a more universal approach—are present in anthropology, though (as I mentioned earlier) recently the particularizing approach has overwhelmed the creative possibilities of comparative consciousness.

Lebanese-born Faris al-Shidyaq's nineteenth-century account of his encounter with European music is consciously comparative, pointing to distinctions between Arab and Western music. For al-Shidyaq, like his Egyptian contemporary al-Tahtawi, first contact inspired comparison. In his description of what he calls "Frankish music" al-Shidyaq cites several differences between the music of these two worlds. The first relates to the innovation of musical notation. Al-Shidyaq marvels that "even without previous knowledge of a piece of music, if twenty of them were to assemble with such graphic signs before them you would find them all following as one" (Cachia 1973:43). However, al-Shidyaq is aware of the constraints which notation places on the musician, for skillful improvisation was highly valued in Arab music. A second difference relates to harmony. Arab music is characterized by heterophony, a style of music in which all instruments and voices play a single melodic line, each with their own style of ornamentation. Western harmony employs voices and instruments playing different melodic lines simultaneously. Al-Shidyaq goes on to notice differential effects of the two musics, referring to "Frankish" music employing military instruments as thematically concerned with fighting, revenge, or defense of truth. In contrast, Arab music is concerned with tenderness and love aimed at a state of enchantment. And finally he notes that Western music tends to use only two modes whereas Arab music regularly uses many more modes than major and minor. He sums up his comparison by reiterating that "their songs of zeal and enthusiasm are unknown among us" (Cachia 1973:46).

These observations are significant because the changes that were to be made in Arab music lead toward greater dramatic and expressive range and away from improvisatory forms. The Arab view of Western music was constructed and became a model for musical change in twentieth-century Arab music, as music became an arena for asserting international cultural competence, often causing local controversy (Stokes 1992).

The term comparative consciousness implies that people are sometimes not conscious about comparison, although the act of thinking comparatively is probably universal. In travel observations comparison is sometimes implicit, sometimes explicit dependent on the context. But comparison is always part of the observational substratum.

Further scrutiny of Eastern writings about the West indicates several relevant contexts— political, economic, psychological, or more generalized conditions. For example M. Gandhi's small monograph *Indian Home Rule* (1922) is a response to a political situation. Gandhi has reform in mind, rather than an account of history. The book is positioned, a comparison of a Western civilization which is immature, impure, and diseased to an Indian civilization that is mature, pure, high, and moral. Indian civilization for Gandhi is alive, it is present, not off in the past somewhere.

The book pits soul force or passive resistance against brute force. Resistance to invasion from the West is to be accomplished by inner transformation. To quote Gandhi, "Peasants have never been subdued by the sword and never will be" (1922:92). Comparison is a critical part of Gandhi's call for change.

There is a similar positioning in the records of Arab historians and chroniclers contemporary with the Crusades, 1096-1291 (Maalouf 1984). These Arab writers quoted in *The Crusades through Arab Eyes* saw the confrontation as one between the culturally superior East and the technologically superior "wild beasts" of the West, who knew mainly blood, torture, and cannibalism. Arabs of the period compare the rationality of the Arab who values books with the Westerner who destroys books. The observations are comparative and made in relation to technology, medicine, judicial behavior, the lack of tolerance for diversity, and religious fanaticism attributed to Crusaders. The *Franj,* a word used in colloquial Arabic even today, designates Westerners. The French, in particular, were for Arab observers technologically sophisticated barbarians in need of Eastern civilization.

Two observations are pertinent. First, the Eastern view of Westerners (which is an old one) as barbarian is a mirrored image of the East in the West. Secondly, these excerpts remind us that while Westerners may think of Islamic, Indian, or Chinese civilizations in the past tense, members of these societies see their civilizations as part of the present, even if a spiritual present. In their rhetoric they thus continue to compare themselves as positionally superior to the barbaric West, even if the West is technologically superior.

An interesting reversal of the usual comparisons appeared recently. Usually the West is portrayed by Eastern cultures as technologically superior, but spiritually inferior. An early release of a manuscript written by top Japanese corporate executives illustrates a view of American Westerners as spiritually inferior *and* technologically inferior. The manuscript was titled *The Japan That Can Say No: The New U.S.-Japan Relations Card* and widely reviewed by the American press before official publication (Ishihara 1991).

Comparisons utilizing notions of positional superiority are not always clear-cut, as illustrated in the case of Chinese observers of the West. The writing of travel notes about people and places visited has been a major literary genre from early times in China. Observing the Other is a Chinese custom at least as old as an early Chinese manuscript by Hiuen Tsiang, a Chinese Buddhist pilgrim who lived in the seventh century A.D. and wrote about India (Coon 1948), which for him was West. In his excerpts from this work (1948:452-463), Coon points out there is a contemporary ring to Hiuen Tsiang's observations made over 1200 years ago. An examination of the full manuscript generates a respect for Hiuen Tsiang's abilities in describing the social structures he encountered (Beals 1957-58).

A similar comment can be made about a collection of work about America by Chinese authors writing from the mid-nineteenth century to the present. In *Land without Ghosts* (Arkusch and Lee 1989), the writers render explicit observations about United States culture against changing Chinese attitudes about the United States: as exotic, menacing, a model to emulate, a flawed model. And as we move through these different attitudes, which are influenced by real political happenings both in China (as with the Boxer crisis of the 1800s), and in America (specifically in regard to American treatment of Chinese workers), the tone changes—from tidbits of barbarian exotica, to respect for democratic process and fear of introducing individualism and liberal democracy in China. There are somber notes in discussing racism in the United States, alternating with delight over the warships and guns. The uses of comparison change, although a continuous critique of the American family extends throughout more than one hundred years of observation. The Chinese are particularly out-spoken about the way Ameri-

cans treat their kinsmen, both old and young. One has the keen sense that these observations are coming from members of an old and continuous civilization looking at the members of a very young civilization.

COMPARATIVE CONSCIOUSNESS AND THE POSITION OF WOMEN

Feminist scholarship in the United States and Western Europe produced a dramatic increase in research on the position of women in other parts of the world. By and large this research on women of other cultures examined the position of women using internally generated conceptions of gender relations. For example, Ortner (1974), Rosaldo and Lamphere (1974), and Strathern (1981b) approached the arrangement of gender relationship through an analysis of the binary oppositions underlying symbolic classification: "self interested"/"socially interested," public sphere/private sphere, nature/culture. Additionally, Biersack (1984) argues that binary opposition is inherent in the social construction of gender. Harris agrees that contrast plays an important role in the construction of gender identity, although she argues that binary oppositions fail to account for important features of gender identity (O. Harris 1978).

While internal contrastive comparison reveals societal gender arrangements, less attention has been given to the ways in which complexes of male/female relations can be organized around contrastive comparison *between* societies, the ways in which gender arrangements are related to macro-level distinctions between "us and them," as between East and West and the ways in which cultural categories of a Western anthropology contribute to changing conceptions of gender. Important in this regard is Nelson and Olesen's (1977) observation that Western feminist research is based on a premise of equality as compared to the Middle Eastern premise of complementarity.

If we are to understand the place of women as dynamic and contextual but not unilineal (that is progressing from worse to better), account must be taken of the purpose of gender ideologies in the larger framework of the attempts of nations and societies to maintain separate identities within the context of increasing interaction. In short, women's place may be profitably viewed in the context of male attempts to maintain authority in societies increasingly threatened by the dynamic of international power relationships. In this manner, gender structures emerge as more than a product of internal debate between males and females of particular societies. Bringing different dogmas of gender construction into the arena of comparison reveals the common as well as the unique dimensions of women's subordination which may be obscured by the absence of comparison.

Both historical and functional comparative methods are useful. When a woman's status in one sociopolitical arena is juxtaposed to the "Other" and to global economic movements, it becomes clear that women, by virtue of their custodial positions, are key to larger indigenous control mechanisms (Knauss 1987). First and Third World systems are part of a common interactive process in which ideas are transmitted from one world to another, shaping and reshaping the construction of gender. The dynamics of diffusion can catch women in a spiral. Without a comparative consciousness, observations of the dynamics, and the appearance of multiple systems of gender in single locales may go unnoticed. Interactive processes generated by economic and political dependence between cultural areas bring about diffusion. In the disjuncture resultant from focusing on the particular, or on the cross-cultural, gender is a missing link, as I indicate in the following example of comparison as control.

The use of comparison as control may be illustrated by brief reference to East/West image material (see Nader 1989b). Value judgments are beside the point here; the popular images of women in the other culture are the subject. Unfortunately, scholarly writings on Arab Muslim women have been kept separate from scholarly writings on Western women, and such separate treatment has exacerbated the making of images through the media.

In 1987 a Middle East specialist, Barbara Stowasser, analyzed a popular contemporary guide for the Muslim woman by Egyptian Shaykh I-Sha'rawi. Sha'rawi published his guide as the ideal paradigm by which a woman's life may be measured as truly Islamic in Cairo of 1982. In the selections that Stowasser presents there are recurrent comparative statements about East and West. Sha'rawi extols the civil rights of the Islamic woman, noting the rights that women in the West do not have: "When a woman marries in Europe, she calls herself by her husband's name. She does not have the right to retain her name or her father's or mother's name. Under French law she does not have the right to stipulate individual property for herself. The West does not give the woman any rights, neither concerning her name, nor concerning her wealth." I-Sha'rawi continues to note that "as mothers, women find themselves in high regard in Islam as compared to the West" (Stowasser 1987:267-268).

The work is an example of a genre now common to activity that uses comparison to defend the Islamic order, to correct errors of external interpretation, to respond to provocative criticisms from the West, and, most importantly, to prevent Islamic women from Westernizing. Examples from the genre illustrate that the West plays an important part in the Islamic construction of Islamic womanhood and as I show is key to holding Western women in place. Paradigms are legitimized by their very contrast with the West, especially a barbaric, materialistic West.

I-Sha'rawi is not a theologian or a revolutionary or a scholar, but rather a highly visible media personality, an educated figure who is one of the contemporary traditionalists who see themselves as rearming Islamic women to counter the impact of the imperialistic West. The women who listen to him are part of a class of women who believe that Western women in general and U.S. women in particular are not respected as a class. At every occasion and without prodding, such women recount that American women are sex objects and cite the multibillion-dollar pornography industry as evidence. Women in the West are said to be under daily threat of rape, while they are not in Cairo. U.S. incest and family violence rates are cited, and always we are reminded that the portrayal of women in American magazines is disrespectful.

The Western media reciprocate, and their images show that the East plays an important part in the construction of Western womanhood. Images of the Muslim woman show her as pitiable and downtrodden. Usually these media images focus on selected areas of comparison (contrast). Muslim women wear the veil, a symbol of subordination for the Western observer. Islamic society fixates on the cult of virginity, and female children are abused by various techniques such as *Jabr* or forced marriage, or by clitoridectomy. Also polygamy and easy divorce subjugate women psychologically and materially.

The implications of both implicit and explicit comparisons are fundamental to the control of Western women and, through development, Eastern women as well. Female subordination is increasingly rationalized in terms of the Other. Downtrodden Arab females make Muslim culture in general seem less human, and by comparison the treatment of Western women seem more human, and more enlightened. The reverse is also true; images of the West are of a barbaric and immoral people. The result of using comparison as control I argue is *perpetuation of female subordination in both East and West.*

Comparative consciousness requires comparisons that are not only of a dichotomous nature, comparisons that draw on the differences between us and them, but comparisons that indicate points of convergence and commonality. Both East and West have male-dominated governments. In both East and West women increasingly work double shifts, and as a class along with their children constitute the majority of the poor and impoverished. Although in both areas there are ideologies that glorify the status of women, in both places the lower status of women is still popularly explained as due to the inherent inferiority of women. In other words, in both the East and the West, women's subordination is institutionally structured and culturally rationalized, and leads to deference, dependency, powerlessness, and poverty. Yet in both cultures the manner of gender construction, whereby the inside culture is idealized in comparison to the outside culture, allows members of both East and West to feel superior each to the other, a part of the apparatus controlling women's place. Dichotomies tend to stress the unique features of each—the West appears to possess the highest standards of technological apparatus, and the East portrays itself as spiritually superior.[6] Comparison serves to control in both the East and the West, and it is one process not two.

For those who use the language of hypotheses, the process of discovery through the use of such comparisons might generate some working hypotheses. Evans-Pritchard's hypothesis about the worsening condition of women with increased cultural ascendancy or with the development of an increasingly complex civilization is a starting point (1983). Subparts of this general hypothesis might include the following less general hypotheses:

1. Female subordination may increase in the context of male attempts to maintain authority in societies increasingly threatened by the dynamic of international power relationships. Under conditions of colonialism, migration, and modernization, female subordination would tend to increase, although the indicators may vary from increased rape in one society to increased seclusion in another.

2. Female subordination increases with the rise of "civilizations" because multiple systems of female subordination result from conquest, change, and the general increase of interaction common to civilization. Such would be the case, for example, if a Mexican woman was married to an Egyptian man living in Dallas, Texas, under subordination patterns from all three cultures.

3. Female subordination categories follow lines of complementary distribution when First World positional superiority is being asserted or when positional superiority is raised as a defense against the possibilities of Third World women becoming Westernized. For example, a Moslem construction of female subordination in the West includes the high rape rate, pornography, women as sexual objects, the loss of family name at marriage, and absence of respect as indicated by unequal pay structures. A Western construction of Moslem female subordination includes forced marriage, veiling, clitoridectomy, easy divorce, and general exclusion of women from public life.

The idea is to use comparison in its historical, contrastive, and controlled forms to break with the frameworks that are no longer yielding fruitful modes of thinking.

THE NEED FOR COMPARATIVE CONSCIOUSNESS: II

Anthropologists have regularly identified anthropology as a comparative discipline over the past 100 years. But being conscious about comparison has been less consistent. Each era in anthropology has produced a theoretical framework within which the comparative dimension is defined (Kobben 1956). The evolutionists used comparison to understand the development of social and cultural institutions. Diffusionist theory was aimed instead at comparative procedures that would establish historical relationships between cultures, how an idea spread from one cultural grouping to another. The advent of functionalism introduced interest in identifying functionally significant relationships and comparing them across cultures where similar conditions obtain.

When functionalism came under attack in the sixties and seventies there was another shift in the use of comparison. With the influence of linguistics and componential analysis, and later of interpretive anthropology, interest in comparison waned. A positive value was placed on the unique and the particular, and there was a de-emphasis on generalizing. In addition, there were assertions as well as evidence that societies were not neatly bounded (and that maybe they had not been for centuries), indicating that the units under study were more dynamic and fluid than we had thought (see, e.g., Wallerstein 1974, Wolf 1982, and Gramsci 1971).

Still, anthropology remains comparative in spite of fluctuating trends. There has always been an implicit comparison in ethnographies between us and the so-called Other. It is not only with regard to cafes and subordination of women that comparative consciousness and consciousness about the use of comparison become critical to understanding. In my work on harmony ideology the exercise of comparative consciousness stimulated a search for the past and present uses of this ideology by Christian missionaries and colonial governments (Nader 1990). And it was a comparative consciousness that helped me understand that the same Christian harmony that was used as pacification in the initial European colonization of the peoples of the world was, and is, being employed to quell the proclivity for contentiousness among Americans in the post-1960s period (Nader 1989a).

The basic premise in this essay is that a well-honed comparative consciousness leads to important discovery. It is written from a vantage that argues for increased intellectual discussion among comparativists of the advantages of loosening the technical grip on explicit comparison, and for ethnographers to tighten up the implicit comparisons in ethnographic work. If knowledge is power, comparison is critical in the dynamic of knowledge production.

NOTES

1. Critical discourse also called into question the fixity of meaning. This, during the visibly politicized sixties and seventies, was also convenient, and some say escapist.

2. The external critiques had utility. Anthropologists became more conscious that they are the instrument of their work; they benefited from increased sophistication about the manner in which knowledge is created. Debate sharpened our critical assessments about knowledge produced by previous generations and for some has made anthropologists realize that this moment in time will also become "the work of previous generations," and a subject that will generate its own debate and criticism.

3. In the late 1950s Clyde Kluckhohn taught a course on American society at Harvard University using only

novels for reading assignments. Only novels, he argued, could fill in the blanks that result when anthropologists are unidimensional and when some locales (such as studying elites) are taboo.

4. As we articulate varieties of comparison, anthropologists will take to comparison with renewed vigor because ethnographies that are extremely localized and comparisons that squeeze the unique into the narrow definition of scientific variables gloss over both hegemonic and counterhegemonic influences, thereby neglecting historical processes.

5. Paul Bohannan's declaration (personal communication) that today "culture is loose on the streets" and Richard Rorty's observation that "We have become so open-minded that our brains have fallen out" (1989:526) have stimulated me to think carefully about what it costs to lose the power of comparison in anthropology. The answer to my question causes me to address some general predicaments of contemporary social-cultural anthropology.

6. Goody's (1983) analysis of Western and Eastern structures utilizes a method of comparison in which the compared features are looked at not only from the standpoint of the East or the West but also from a third angle. Seen from such a vantage differences may seem relatively slight.

INTELLECTUAL ROOTS

Laura Nader is Professor of Anthropology at the University of California, Berkeley, where she has been a member of the Anthropology Department since 1960. She worked among the Zapotec and Trique of Mexico, the Shia Moslems of south Lebanon, urbanites in Morocco, and among people of the United States. Her most intensive fieldwork is among the Zapotec of Oaxaca, Mexico (1957-1968), and in the United States (1970—). Her research resulted in numerous articles. Her most outstanding books are *Talea and Juquila—A Comparison in Zapotec Social Organization* (1964), *The Ethnography of Law* (1965), *Law in Culture and Society* (1969), *The Disputing Process* (1978), *No Access to Law* (1980), and *Harmony Ideology—Justice and Control in a Zapotec Mountain Village* (1990). With colleagues she published on *Energy Choices in a Democratic Society* (1980) and on the future of American children (*All Our Children* 1980). She is a member of the American Academy of Arts and Sciences.

I began my studies in the Department of Anthropology at Harvard University under Clyde Kluckhohn as a consequence of reading his popular book *Mirror for Man* at a critical intellectual juncture. Although Kluckhohn had studied at Oxford under Robert Marett and worked in Vienna with Father Schmidt and others of the Kulturkreise School, when I knew him he was most influenced by his linguistic study with Edward Sapir and was involved in work with A. L. Kroeber on the concept of culture. It was because of Kluckhohn that I attended the Summer Institute of Linguistics at the University of Michigan, Ann Arbor (summer 1956). Later when I expressed interest in spending a year of study in England due to my admiration for the work of E. R. Leach and Raymond Firth, Kluckhohn said I could read what the British had to say whereas the imaginative thinking was in France with people like Lévi-Strauss. I stayed at Harvard. For Kluckhohn an education in anthropology was a breadth not a specialist education. He encouraged students to carefully read Kroeber's 1948 *Anthropology*, to visit the experimental psychologists in Mem Hall, to be critical in our readings of the sociologists, not to forget the importance of reading novels (which was his way of teaching about American society), to recognize the importance of evolutionary biology and the importance of time. Anthropology was about all of us, everywhere.

Douglas Oliver taught the Harvard first-year course; he also studied in Vienna. He introduced students to anthropology through a year-long course in which we read classic monographs. It was in the reading that I encountered Gregory Bateson's *Naven*. Bateson was self-conscious about the construction of ethnography when hardly anybody else seemed to be, and along with Kluckhohn raised the difference between the scientific and artistic modes of presenting a culture. At the same time, Oliver lectured the class on his work in the Pacific discussing methodological innovations applied from Eliot Chapple's work. Fine-grained fieldwork was the standard for Oliver, but it was contact with Beatrice and John Whiting of the School of Education's Laboratory of Human Development where I learned about comparison. The why of it was to understand human universals and variations. The Whitings had completed their degree work at Yale, and the influence of Sapir and Malinowski, who was visiting there, was a strong part of what they imparted to me. The influences at Harvard were of a heterogeneous nature.

As a student among the Mountain Zapotec I found myself struggling to record a fine-grained ethnography while feeling that I was missing what came later through film and cultural analysis. I compared two very similar villages; the comparison was on a continuum rather than posed as variables present or absent. The Mexican anthropologists who informed me were Julio de la Fuente and Roberto Weitlaner. De la Fuente's monograph on the Yalalag Zapotec and his work with Malinowski on indigenous market systems were important markers for Oaxacan ethnography. The model from the market research illustrated a network of relationships between seemingly autonomous vil-

lages. De la Fuente warned me of E. C. Parsons's failure to document variation in her Mitla work because of too great a dependence on a single informant. Roberto Weitlaner took me into Otomi villages where he taught me how to take a genealogy, how to ask questions that made sense to the Otomi. He was a model of a rapport builder. Weitlaner was trained as an engineer, then educated in American linguistics, and the many hours over coffee in Sanborns were the best field seminars anyone could have had in historical reconstruction.

In 1960 I joined the Department of Anthropology at U.C. Berkeley. Clyde Kluckhohn and A. L. Kroeber both died that year, and Geertz, Fallers, and Schneider had departed for Chicago, leaving an age break between younger and older Berkeley anthropologists. I was to teach about the anthropology of law. Law was not a subject taught to me at Harvard, but I was thoroughly familiar with the literature. Malinowski's work on law appealed to me because his vision was wide-angled, and although I admired Gluckman's work, I found his focus on courts too lawyerly. When I initiated the Berkeley Village Law Project I decided to continue to center the work on the dispute case (as Gluckman did) because I thought of it as a minimal unit, comparable to units such as phonemes and morphemes that were part of the discourse in linguistics. Disputing is a universal phenomenon in human culture, but not to be confused with the dispute resolution paradigm, the use of which is sometimes found to be insular. As a unit of action the dispute case may be manipulated by the parties or by power structures. It was Eric Wolf's work that helped me understand such manipulations as powerful mechanisms of global colonization and pacification.

Berkeley in the 1960s had its intellectual impact. Sherwood Washburn was writing about race as a social and cultural concept. Elizabeth Colson was writing about tradition and change; George Foster was studying how people behaved under conditions of scarcity; and Robert Heizer was studying long continuities in Nevada cave sites in the context of a nuclear age. Dell Hymes encouraged many of us to write a critical anthropology. *Reinventing Anthropology* (1969) included my piece on studying up, an effort to broaden the ethnographic domain. The notion of public interest ethnography was pioneered (Spradley 1970), but the movement was overwhelmed by trends that had little tolerance for anthropological precursors or even an anthropology that could use both scientific and artistic methods of understanding. Yet for me the heterodoxy of the earlier period persisted and new worlds opened.

My teaching and research reflect these heterogeneous influences. I teach the Introduction to Sociocultural Anthropology, the Anthropology of Law, and a course called Comparative Society, and maintain area interests in Middle America and the Middle East. Most recently I teach an undergraduate course on Controlling Processes—the dynamic components of power. My related seminar—"Orientalism, Occidentalism and Control"—I write about in this volume as a new venture in historical ethnography. The inspiration for this current work stems from the discovery that concurrent use of comparative methodologies yields new understandings more profound than the use of single approaches. I am currently writing a series of essays on contemporary practices which use the concepts of social and cultural control together with the now common idea that *ethnographers and their cultures* are an instrument of writing ethnography and, therefore, part of the analysis of hegemonic forms of culture.

6

"Mirror, Mirror on the Wall . . ." The Once and Future Role of Anthropology: A Tentative Assessment

MAURICE GODELIER

I have been asked to assess the present state, nature, and future of anthropology in a few pages. It is an impossible task, of course. But it is a challenge and a fine pretext for asking the questions that, sooner or later, everyone must ask. And now is as good a time as any, perhaps better, for during the past few years, a whole epoch has come to a close. Ten years ago who could have predicted that such a widespread economic and social structure as the socialist system would crumble and that entire walls of the edifice would disappear within the space of a few months? No politician, no social scientist foresaw it. Are the social sciences capable only of tagging along behind events, of analyzing societies without noticing that they are already in the process of vanishing? Are they never able to predict new developments? Or perhaps, these events and others yet to come will usher in an epoch that will have an even greater need for the social sciences.

Should this be the case, what can anthropology contribute? Before going any further, though, I would like to return for a moment to the original challenge: assessing the state of anthropology today. The best tactic is to convert the challenge into a number of simple questions: Who are we? Where are we coming from? What have we done? What should we do?

WHO ARE WE?

Anthropologists trade in "knowledge." Our explicit goal is to find out how human societies function, why the various societies living side by side on this planet—which comprise the present multifaceted essence of humanity—live and think as they do and what this means. Our ambition is to learn enough about each of these societies to be able to compare them. Whether it admits it or not, anthropology aims to be a universal science. This can be understood in one of two ways: (1) universal because it is a science, that is, a field of thought which claims that its propositions, methods, and conclusions can be subjected, as in physics and biology, to testing and objective evaluation, whether the anthropologist is American, Japanese, or Mexican; and (2) universal since by definition no society is excluded from its sphere of analysis because it aims to discover the mechanisms present in all societies.

Once this is said, however, the paradoxes immediately leap from the page. If anthropology is to be the comparative study of all human societies, must it then invade the customary domain of history and add to the present-day societies all those of the past? And, another paradox, even if it sticks to present-day societies, how is anthropology to fit in with sociology, which also takes them as its object of study?

In fact, we all know that these paradoxes are still unresolved and that we are working within a compromise tacitly agreed to among the three disciplines. In practice, anthropologists work more on present-day societies than on those of the past and more on other societies than on our own; more on non-Western societies than on those in the West. This compromise was present from the beginning. Where, then, did we begin?

WHERE ARE WE COMING FROM?

The Historical Context

The following two personal anecdotes will help bring our origins into focus. Six months after I arrived in 1967 among the Baruya—an isolated tribe in the mountains of New Guinea which had in 1960 just come under the control of the Australian government—I was asked separately by the Australian patrol officer heading the military post and by the German missionary responsible for the Lutheran mission to provide them with information that might be of use to them. The officer wanted me to give him the names of the tribe's traditional "fight leaders," knowing full well that the men he had appointed in Her Majesty's name as village heads possessed no real authority over the others. As for the missionary, he was anxious for me to teach him about these people's religion, their secret rites, and especially their witchcraft. Like his military colleague, he wanted to know the names of the men and women reputed to be "witches" (note that the Baruya designate these people by a term of respect that means "one who deals with the spirits"). Of course, professional ethics forbade me to say anything, and I was viewed with suspicion by these other whites.

On another occasion, on the contrary, I agreed to collaborate with the Australian authorities. Here is why. A man returned after several years of plantation work only to discover that his wife had left their home to go and live with her married lover. The husband went to demand his wife back, but the lover beat him and humiliated him in front of the whole village. The next day the husband followed his wife into the field and hacked her to death with an ax. Then he gave himself up to the officer who arrested him. He was convicted of murder. The judge called me to explain Baruya customs to the court. I said that, in killing his wife, the man had been acting in accordance with Baruya law. By right she belonged to him since her own lineage now owed a woman to the murderer. The judge took these facts into consideration when he sentenced the man.

There was surely more than one reason for my conduct. Obviously, by accepting or refusing—depending upon the case—to collaborate with a colonial administration or an occidental church, I was following principles not all of which are an intrinsic part of our trade. Whenever I was able, I tried to cushion the impact that the pressures and power exerted by the West had on the Baruya. My attitude was conditioned by scientific and ethical reasons, but also by political ones. And we all know anthropologists who would have acted differently. They would not necessarily have shared my scruples about helping to propagate the "true" faith. But I am sure that, over and above these divergences, all anthropologists would like to have been there before it changed for the very simple and logical reason that it is not possible to measure change unless the previous state is known. Every anthropologist dreams of being the first on the spot. That is the "scientific" fantasy we all share.

But, in a colonial situation, which was the anthropologist's main working context until after the Second World War, the anthropologist was not the only arrival on the scene. He was preceded or followed by other figures, whose functions were indispensable in this type of setting: soldiers, missionaries, merchants, and sometimes European mine or plantation owners. Thus these personal anecdotes show us (1) that anthropology can be of use to others and be recognized as such and (2) that, like any other science, anthropology does not itself contain the criteria for deciding how it should be used. These criteria exist, but they lie beyond anthropology.

In what ways do these anecdotes refer us back to our origins, at least for those of us in the West? For anthropology did not simply appear full-blown one day in the Western world and stake its claim as a universal science. It emerged gradually out of the need to better understand two areas that were, at the outset, totally unconnected. On the one hand, there were the peoples of Africa, pre-Columbian America, and Asia, who were slowly being discovered and subjected to the lure of Western commerce or its powerful weaponry. Wherever colonizers wanted to trade, govern, or evangelize, they had to learn the local languages (for the most part unwritten), observe the customs, and make note of them. In Europe, too, from the sixteenth century at least, numerous civil servants of various states or clergymen of different churches were writing down the customs of the Basques, the Slovenes, the Vlachs, the Lithuanians, etc. This was done for a wide variety of reasons—in order to settle differences with a commune, for example, when communal lands had been expropriated and the people protested in the name of their "former rights." In short, there were many reasons in Europe to seek a better knowledge of the diverse ethnic groups or the peasant communities, which had (to a greater extent than in the cities) retained their customs and brandished them in their fight to resist change. And so the professional anthropologist was preceded by a number of figures who did more or less the same thing as he did, but for different reasons. These travelers, administrators, merchants, and missionaries remained his fellow travelers, even once anthropology had established itself in all its

difference. And here we come to the essential point—just what is this difference?

What Makes Anthropology Distinct

Lewis Morgan's work will help us define just how anthropology is distinct from these seemingly similar activities. But first we must take a last look at the conditions in which our discipline took shape. Anthropology is a strategy of knowledge acquisition that must be used when a living society has no written archives or other historical documents to tell us how it functions. It is a technique that makes it possible to extract knowledge from observation, from information gathered inside the society under study. Essentially our discipline was constructed around a method, participant observation, which postulates the more or less long-term immersion of an observer (usually an outsider) in the group observed. The two contexts within which Western anthropology developed—(1) occidental colonial expansion and, in Europe, (2) the subordination of the ethnic groups and peasant communities to the process of national state-formation and the development of the market economy—mean that ethnographic investigation tends to proceed against a backdrop of relations between observer and observed of domination, of social inequalities, and of power. And this backdrop intrudes incessantly throughout the entire investigation.

But the West is not unique in this. Other civilizations have subjected many peoples about whom they subsequently seek more precise knowledge. There is no need to turn to the Middle Ages or to the accounts of Chinese administrators and travelers. In present-day "communist" China, anthropology is almost exclusively reserved for the study of national "minorities," that is ethnic groups such as the Yao and Lesu which are supposed not to have attained the same degree of civilization as the Chinese Han. These groups are the object of special political measures that emphasize their inferiority. The slogan "one child per family" does not apply to them since it would be too great an affront to their customs. Families are allowed up to three children, whence the paradox that today we see Chinese applying to the state to be recognized as non-Han in order to benefit from the advantages of this status. In India, one of the world's great civilizations, early anthropology seemed destined to be relegated to the study of those tribes still not included in the caste system. In sum, in these countries as in the West, anthropology is seen as the study of culturally backward, economically and socially less-developed peoples and groups. Our profession still bears the marks of this attitude. The foregoing explains why today many newly independent countries refuse entry visas to anthropologists. "We are not bush Kanaka for Europeans to observe," they say. "We are people like everyone else. We are interested in sociology, not anthropology."

This rejection is one of the reasons why anthropology, sometimes given a frosty reception in parts of Oceania and Africa, is turning its attention to Europe and America. But there are more positive reasons for the reorientation. Sophisticated observation techniques have been developed and a critical self-awareness has emerged which enables anthropologists now to go beyond the limitations imposed by the original context. Today anthropologists are undertaking to analyze cities, systems of education, and male/female relations in all classes and societies. In short, we are involved in a twofold, somewhat contradictory movement. Improvements in our method have broadened the field of application to include many areas not previously targeted. At the same time, our history, our past associations, our complicity with the relations of power our societies entertained over other cultures tend to exclude us today from the areas we occupied in the past.

None of this is mysterious, and the work of Lewis Morgan, one of our founding fathers, will explain why. This lawyer from Rochester, New York, friend and defender of

the Indians, became drawn to the study of Iroquois customs. In the course of his research, he discovered that Iroquois kinship relations are not at all absurd but follow a logic different from our own. They are based on a matrilineal descent rule that serves as a principle for recruiting members to a social unit as well as to define those one is prohibited from marrying. To designate this type of lineal exogamous group, he used the Latin term *gens*. This was not a matter of chance. Morgan discovered that kinship terms and descent and residence rules constitute a "system." He set out personally to compare a dozen other Indian societies already living on reservations. Later, as he discovered regular patterns, he had the idea of launching a worldwide study. More than a thousand questionnaires were sent out to missionaries, administrators, etc. On the basis of the data collected, which brought together the broadest range of facts ever gathered on kinship, Morgan developed the first synthesis in the *Systems of Consanguinity and Affinity of the Human Family* (1870).

Therein lies the difference between professional ethnography and the notes made by missionaries and travelers. It resides in the idea that social relations form a "system," in the hypothesis that their enormous diversity can be "reduced" to a few basic types, and that their evolution as well as their transformations follow patterns or even obey laws. Anthropology did not become a true scientific discipline until it adopted the explicit aim of discovering these logics, of reducing the diversity to a few types, and of discovering what (among the many accidents of history) produced these transformations. In order to accomplish this, it had to perfect its concepts, making them systematic and verifiable.

But Morgan was also a man of his times. As he was founding our discipline as a science, he was simultaneously weakening it by forcing his discoveries into an imposing, but artificial, mold that presented human evolution as a parade of progress. He believed he could trace the stages of evolution from long periods of primitive savagery and barbary to the civilized state which, for the West, culminated in Europe and nineteenth-century Anglo-Saxon America. It was at this point that the relation of domination that had always been in the background now shifted to the very heart of anthropological theory. All non-Western societies, as well as European ethnic groups and peasant communities, were portrayed as not only remnants, but as vestiges of the stages through which mankind had passed on its way to civilization. The world became the mirror in which all mankind could at last contemplate its origins and evolution. The Occident became not only the mirror, but the measure of history as a whole. That is why Morgan chose a Latin term to designate the Iroquois' matrilineal lineage. He saw the Iroquois as a vestige of the *gens* organization that had characterized Europe in Greek and Roman times but which it had now outgrown.

It is precisely this type of evolutionism, this particular ideological vision of mankind, that proved to be the weak point of his theory and the obstacle to be overcome if further advances were to be made. The schools of anthropology that have grown up since Morgan's time have all had to start by repudiating this unilineal version of evolutionism. What have we done since?

TOWARD AN UNDERSTANDING OF KEY SOCIAL RELATIONS

Anthropology started out with a postulate shared by all the social sciences at the beginning of the century. It can be stated as follows: every society is an organic unit that (1) exists only because certain functions are performed by various institutions and which (2) subsists only insofar as the internal or external transformations undergone by the society are compatible with the reproduction of these institutions and functions.

For a long time this postulate was the basis for our analyses. But behind the formal abstract presupposition, we find something of the image of Western societies within which (for some centuries now) economic, political, and religious institutions as well as kinship relations have been leading separate lives. In Europe, economic relations split off centuries ago from the political and religious institutions (e.g. of a feudal type). The development can, it seems to me, be explained by the interplay of market forces and laws. In Western societies, separate functions are carried out by separate institutions. This has not always been the case, however, and it is not the case in all cultures today. In many societies of Africa and Oceania, for instance, kinship relations subsume such economic functions as overseeing the land, mobilizing the labor force, and redistributing the products of labor. In other societies like lamaist Tibet, religious institutions (such as temples and monasteries) supervise many of these economic functions.

Anthropologists used the above-noted postulate regarding the organic nature of social units as a framework for analyzing other societies. At the same time, they saw that their framework never corresponded exactly with the picture the members of these societies had of their own social organization. From the outset anthropology found itself faced with the problem of taking seriously and explaining the discrepancy between its own frame of analysis and the concepts and principles of the populations whose way of life it was seeking to understand. Our theory expresses this difference by the idea that anthropology must combine an "emic" analysis (analysis of native actors' representations) with an "etic" analysis (analysis of the "scientific" observers' representations). Certain anthropologists such as D. Schneider (1984) carry this distinction to its logical limits and are not far from thinking that the "emic" approach excludes or demolishes the "etic," that kinship as it is conceived and experienced by the "natives" has nothing to do with the version conceived and reconstructed by the anthropologists.

Whatever their differences, anthropologists found themselves faced with three tasks.

1. Description. To make an exhaustive description of individual societies, reconstructing as faithfully as possible their ways of thinking and the principles of action explicitly followed by members of these societies. This effort has manifested itself in the mountain of monographs written by anthropologists based on their fieldwork.

2. Comparison. Since there is no science without comparison, anthropologists assiduously compared observations in an attempt to find patterns or, better yet, laws. Now this comparing can be done in two ways.

First, the societies can be taken to pieces and the pieces compared (but not the societies). Comparisons are made of institutions—kinship relations, religious beliefs and practices, etc.—by choosing examples from a large number of societies and ignoring the links these may have with other aspects of social practice in each society. That is what Morgan did when he compared systems of "consanguinity" (descent) and "affinity" (marital ties). That is what Lévi-Strauss did in his *Elementary Structures of Kinship* (1969 [1949]). That is how the subdisciplines of anthropology came about: political anthropology was separated out from religious anthropology which was separated out from the anthropology of law. But then came the hard problem of how these specialized fields tied in with the other social sciences that deal with the same areas. How does economic anthropology, for example, relate to political economy and economic history? Can anthropology simply turn its back on them? Should it absorb them or will it be absorbed by them? Will anthropology illuminate, criticize, or complement?

Societies can also be compared as total entities; in this case they are placed into broad categories: acephalous (or chiefless) societies,

chiefdoms, states. These categories can be subdivided: for instance, acephalous societies can be broken down into bands and tribes, etc. This was the method used by E. Service and M. Sahlins (in his early writings) following the lead of L. White, who in turn took his own cue from Morgan.

The difficulties (and doubts) encountered are obviously greater when comparing total societies than when comparing their parts. But this type of overall comparison provides anthropologists with better insight as to the reasons for the variety and distribution of total social structures in space and over time. The reasons may be ecological, technological, or ideological. In other words, we are looking for a logic to history. I am not being ironical about this attempt. Ecological anthropology, for instance, has taught us a lot. It has taken on the difficult task of identifying and measuring the material constraints imposed on a society by its techniques and ecosystem (from which it draws its means of existence). It has also opened up a whole new field of ethnoscience since researchers needed to discover how human groups represented plants, wild and domestic animals, the seasons, the forest, the plain, the sea. Today, thanks to the theoretical interest in the material conditions of existence of human groups and their representations of their natural environment, ethnobotany, ethnozoology, ethnoecology are thriving subdisciplines. But in another area the dream of certain researchers has not come true, for, as Marshall Sahlins once reminded Harris, all that this can tell us is what is materially possible to do in a society, not why one of these possibilities became socially necessary.

3. Metatheory. It is here that we come to the metatheoretical level. Anthropologists who venture this far cannot avoid referring to broad theoretical paradigms such as those of Max Weber, Karl Marx, or Emile Durkheim. But even if prudence or critical distance dictates that they stop short of such theoretical paradigms, some very difficult problems remain. Why and how do kinship relations in one society take on a whole series of functions that they do not perform in another and, in so doing, dominate the overall logic of this society? Why, in another society, is it religion that plays the dominant role (in our eyes), as L. Dumont (1971) suggests in his *Homo Hierarchicus* in India? Anthropology has not been able to come up with a universally satisfactory answer to these questions. The most frequent reply, which begs the question, is that every society "chooses its culture." Indeed. Societies and cultural systems are not individuals; they are not invented by any one person. No single person invented Chinese or Finnish.

Mining Lévi-Strauss's and Marx's Metatheories

Is there something that resides within the individual (but is not identical to his irreducible singularity) which is the source of these cultural and social worlds?

Lévi-Strauss. Durkheim, Lévi-Strauss, and others look beyond the single individual to the unconscious structures and working rules of the human mind in general. They postulate that the mind orders natural and cultural reality according to two basic rules of analogy: metaphor and metonymy (see note 1 for their definition). Thinking means discovering or positing relations of equivalence (or nonequivalence) between beings and things and between aspects of these beings and things. On a more abstract level, it means thinking about relations between relations. Metaphor and metonymy are ways of establishing relations. This was Lévi-Strauss's starting point for his analysis of myths and systems of thought. And it gave him good mileage. He detailed the role played in the formation of myths, and in the rituals that often accompany them, by pairs of principles and binary oppositions (such as hot/cold, raw/cooked, earth/sky, male/female) which may in turn enter into even more complex combinations.

Having gotten this far, however, we find ourselves confronted with two unresolved problems. If the principles operating in myths and religions are found in the mind and if the unconscious part of the human mind is the same in everyone, then why are there such different classifications in the world? Could it be that other mental principles or different contents of social practice come into the genesis of myth and religion and thus account for the diversity? This raises a second question. Even if we do not deny the creative role played by thought in the production of social relations, are we not in danger of seeing social relations as merely "applied" thoughts? It is with this argument in mind that empiricists accuse Lévi-Strauss of "intellectualism," while he in turn charges them with simplistic functionalism, and the Marxists blast away at the former without sparing the latter. It would seem that we are standing at a crossroads of opposing views, and yet, however fond the protagonists may be of their differences, their theses have never been entirely contradictory.

Lévi-Strauss criticizes the empiricists for confusing the description of the visible forms of social organization—institutions and their visible interconnections—with the analysis of their true logic which is that of the structural properties of these social relations. These properties can never be seen with the naked eye, however, and must therefore be mentally reconstructed with the aid of models. Lévi-Strauss rejects the accusation of idealism claiming that, if his models provide a better explanation of how observed reality fits together, it is because they correspond to something "inside reality." He insists that he is a "realist," if not an out and out materialist. In *The Savage Mind,* he goes as far as to write that in dealing with kinship systems and myths, he is only dealing with the "superstructures" of social life and he maintains that he accepts Marx's proposition of the "primacy of infrastructures" (the primacy of the structures organizing material production) over super-structures (the structures of ideas and ideals). He thus postulates the existence of an "order of orders," a concept that he never fully explores, but which he credits Marx with having invented. When Lévi-Strauss claims that in studying primitive myths and religions he is merely studying the shadows on the wall of the cave, the platonic metaphor suggests that reality (which is not a shadow play) exists somewhere outside the cave. In order to understand reality it is necessary to come out of the cave of representations and ideologies. Here Lévi-Strauss is not far from Marx who, in his *Capital* (1906 [1867-1894]), speaks of the "fetish-like" character of commodities which stems from the fact that the appearance of a commodity does not reveal the secret of its essence. Its appearance dissimulates the fact that a commodity's value lies in the human labor needed for its production.

Marx. And so we now turn to Marx, then, and those who, like myself, have attempted to apply Marxism to anthropology. (In actual fact, many followed Althusser rather than Marx, at least among French anthropologists—for example Terray and Meillassoux. I was not one of them.)

Let us look at the main ideas that have been borrowed from or attributed to Marx which have influenced the social sciences. The cornerstone is that people do not just live in society like other social animals, they produce society (and its social relations) in order to live. If they produce new forms of society, it is because (unlike animals) they are capable of modifying their natural environment through the very relations they entertain with nature and with other people. Humans domesticated plants and animals, they developed farming and animal husbandry, and in so doing entered a new stage of social development. This line of reasoning is not peculiar to Marx. Many believe that the development of farming and animal husbandry was more instrumental than hunting and gathering in creating the condi-

tions for the regular production of a surplus that made possible the emergence of classes or castes specialized in political or religious functions (and which did not have to produce their own material means of existing). This, in their view, was the origin of kingdoms and states.

"Marxism" postulates then that the development of the material and intellectual forces of production entails a series of consequences for the organization of society. This hypothesis is not devoid of truth, with one formidable reservation: productive forces never develop in isolation, the economy is not driven by economic reasons and forces alone; Marx knew this. His theory oscillates between two hypotheses.

One is that the emergence of new productive forces gives rise to new relations of production, which in turn affect the corresponding superstructures (kinship systems, political and religious structures, art forms, etc.). This is Marx revised by Althusser. The infrastructure determines the superstructures and the ideologies, which are the superstructures' superstructure. Here ideas are indeed shadows on the wall of the cave.

But there is a second version of Marx that begins with his rejection of the idea that productive forces develop on their own. It postulates, on the contrary, that they develop only within and driven by fixed relations of production. This time it is the social relations surrounding production and not the productive forces themselves that are the point of departure for social transformations.

There is a problem with both hypotheses, however. It is only in capitalist societies that relations of production (within firms or in the marketplace) are totally separate from political and religious relations. In noncapitalist societies, the relations organizing production are embedded in and constitute functions and aspects of what we call kinship relations (as among the Australian aborigines) or political and religious relations (as in the kingdoms of Africa or in ancient pre-Columbian empires).

Marx's whole theory is in danger of toppling in this case, for it would mean that it is kinship or religion that structures the social forms of production and imposes on the productive forces a certain type and rate of development. Furthermore, the more noneconomic factors that go into shaping the way a society divides labor between the sexes, orders, and castes, the less likely it is that this division corresponds *directly* to a set level of productive forces and the less chance Marx's hypothesis—that there exist "laws of correspondence" between productive forces and relations of production—has of being true.

What this shifting proves is that the metaphor infrastructure/superstructures/ideologies does not work and must be eliminated. A society does not have a top and a bottom. When we talk about first or last causes, we mean only that one human activity weighs more or less than the others in the process of the production and reproduction of societies, not that it is the prime or final cause of its existence.

We still have to take a close look at some of Marx's other ideas which have caused far fewer doubts and discussion. For instance, Marx thought that the material relations people entertain among themselves are also relations of power. Whoever controls the access to people's means of existence and means of producing wealth has power over them and subordinates them to himself. This is almost a truism. The problem involves the conditions governing the appearance of this inequality of access to the sources of subsistence and wealth. Is this inequality of access regarded as legitimate (or not) by those who benefit from it as well as by those who are subjected to it?

The crucial question here is what roles do violence and consent, respectively, play in the genesis and the perpetuation of social inequalities? To this question, Marx suggests an answer in his famous phrase "In a class society, the dominant ideas are those of the dominant class." And he adds that these ideologies are accepted by the underdog both because they pass off relations of exploitation as conditions for attaining an illusory "common good" and because they remain silent about a whole area of reality. For Marx, the functions of ideology, as opposed to those of scientific knowledge, are to *disguise* reality and to *create a silence* in the consciousness. (Freud was to hit upon the same ideas in another domain, when he brought to light the mechanisms of sublimation of desire, displacement of meaning, and censorship of the body or conscious thoughts.) Order depends not only on repression, but on silence and disguise as well.

None of this, however, resolves the problem of how and why representations are shared among classes, castes, and sexes having opposing interests. It is precisely this sharing which, together with and beyond the direct violence inflicted upon dominated groups, is the source of their voluntary consent (even when passive) to the social order that dominates them. In order for this consent to exist, the unequal relations (containing forms of domination or oppression) must, in one way or other—by means of some mysterious process that we must analyze—present themselves as a *reciprocal exchange* of services. The exercise of power must ultimately be seen as a service provided by the dominant group for those it dominates. And it must make the latter feel *indebted* for these services and bound to reimburse the debt by giving of their wealth, their labor, their services, and their lives. From this perspective it is possible to show how, in India for example, religion functions as a relation of domination and production. Because the Brahman caste, by virtue of its purity, appears as the only caste capable of performing the religious rites and offering the appropriate sacrifices, it is seen to perform an irreplaceable service for the other castes. This, in turn, entitles Brahmans to gifts of these other castes' labor and services. Here it is the monopoly of access to what we see as imaginary realities and to imaginary conditions of reproduction of the universe and society which founds the inequality of access to the material conditions of existence—to land, work, and wealth.

And so where do we stand, now that we have come to the end of our attempt to untangle the various theoretical approaches, all of which comprise elements of truth, all of which raise major questions for which, because of some of their basic assumptions, they are not sure of having an answer?

A Perspective on Kinship

On the theoretical level, it now seems safe to say that there is no direct correspondence between a given mode of production and a particular descent rule or kinship system. This was already clear before Murdock or Meyer Fortes. At the same time, no one has yet explained why so many different systems of kinship—patrilineal, matrilineal, cognatic, etc.—are found scattered over the face of the earth. The conflict between those who have focused on ties of descent (Fortes, Goody, etc.) and those who have focused on marriage or affinal ties (Lévi-Strauss, Dumont, Needham, and, a more cautious exponent, Leach) as primary in establishing ties of kinship has been quite helpful in furthering our understanding of the subject.

Kinship As Descent/Kinship As Marital Alliance. The distinction between filiation—biologically based bilateral ties—and descent—the more exclusionary cultural constructs dealing with genealogical transmission (e.g., patri- and matrilineality)—suggests that all kinship systems include a layer of bilateral or cognatic relationships. Going along with Fortes, it is possible to accept the idea that some descent rules (which favor certain lines of filiation to the disadvantage or exclusion of others) work together with other social relations such as political relations. In this case, the way lineages are organized could be related to the structure of power. But having advanced the idea and instigated serious research into the political systems of Africa, Fortes was unable to explain the reasons for the diversity of

African systems (ranging from acephalous, chiefless tribes to chiefdoms to kingdoms).

Nor was Lévi-Strauss wrong in claiming that marriage rules are an intrinsic part of the logic of kinship—that they are more than a secondary imported element useful only for the reproduction of descent groups. This is where incest comes to the fore. The existence of this prohibition is what makes alliances between kinship groups a necessary and permanent condition for their reproduction. But is it necessary to accept his claim that the incest taboo is at the origin of "authentic" human society and the source of culture? Does this not fallaciously credit man with having "invented" society? We did not have to invent society. We are social animals by nature, and it was natural evolution that made us this way. But man is the only animal that has the ability to modify his original conditions of existence, to produce new forms of social existence. This is a capacity he probably owes to the size of his brain (which enables him to understand relations between relations) and to his upright posture (which frees his hands and endowed him with an exceptional ability to act upon his surrounding environment).

But Lévi-Strauss advanced another idea which today seems unacceptable. To say that marriage is an exchange is true. The idea is a fundamental one. But to say that this exchange must always take the form of the exchange of women by men is to posit male domination as a fact of nature, a transcultural and transhistorical presupposition of kinship relations. This is not to say that male domination does not exist. But all that can be deduced from the analysis of kinship systems is that, when male domination exists (and it can exist for many reasons that have nothing to do with kinship), it works its way into kinship relations and uses them for its own reproduction. In our present-day Western societies, marriage does not present itself as an exchange of women between men but as an exchange of men and women between families. Marriage *as such* does not presuppose male domination even though it permeates our societies.

What Kinship Relations Do and Do Not Explain. Kinship relations change and evolve. They do this for a number of reasons. But the result of their evolution is the appearance of another system of kinship. A matrilineal system may become bilineal; a cognatic system may become patrilineal. The evolution of kinship produces kinship. No conceivable transformation of a kinship system will be able to explain the emergence of classes, or castes, or other similar groups in society.

Another fact of great theoretical import is that a kinship system can survive large social changes and (at the price of some internal rearranging) get along quite well for long periods of time with highly diverse economic and political structures. If Jack Goody is to be believed, most European kinship systems were cognatic for centuries and first adapted to the appearance, then the disappearance, of feudalism and then to the development of capitalism (with its attendant massive industrialization and urbanization). In the end, and this is a critical continuation of Meyer Fortes's (1969) thesis, kinship relations appear as support systems—they are channels for transmitting from one generation to the next political titles and/or rights to land, and/or religious offices. Social, political, economic, and religious relations are constantly undergoing metamorphoses, working their way into the functioning of kinship systems where they become attributes, aspects of certain kinship relations.

The imposition of a descent rule subjects the relations of filiation to manipulations that have the effect of underrating certain relations because they overrate others. This is what underlies "native" theories concerning the body and the representations of what each child receives from his or her father and mother (blood, bone, flesh, sperm, etc.). It is the mechanism for the appropriation of children by adults (claiming to be in a given kinship relation with them) that is legitimated.

Recent research on kinship and on representations of the individual in various cultures has shown that sex acts like a ventriloquist's dummy, that from the outset gender is forced by culture and society to serve as a language—to legitimize aspects of reality that have nothing to do directly with the sexes and with sexual reproduction. In all the societies studied, bodies are used not only to bear witness to but also to testify for or against the existing order.

But neither kinship nor sexuality accounts for this order. The fact that a kinship system is cognatic or patrilineal does not explain or even shed much light on why the titles that are channeled through kinship from one generation to the next are feudal titles. Nor does kinship explain why property inherited by a person's descendants takes the form of private ownership or seigneurial ownership of the land. There is, then, no direct connection in the form of a necessary correspondence, in any one society, between the nature of the kinship relations, on the one hand, and the nature of the forms of ownership and power, on the other. And yet they co-penetrate each other. A similar analysis could be made of religion, which would show that Christianity, whose original dogmas crystallized over two thousand years ago in the Middle East, subsequently became associated with the development of feudalism and capitalism, neither of which has any connection with the origins or dogmas of the Christian religion.

Two Key Social Relations

At the end of the day, the essential question for the social sciences is: Of all the manifold human activities, which are those that provoke not only changes within society, an ordinary everyday occurrence, but changes of society? Now I believe that it has just about been demonstrated that these forces and reasons lie neither in kinship, nor in religion, nor in art. It seems to me that they reside in the actions of two series of relations and activities, themselves closely interrelated. Together these comprise the source of the forces and constraints which lead to changes of society.

These two series of relations are those that, on the one hand, *organize man's action on nature and redistribute the material effects to society;* and, on the other hand, *organize the relations of power among men and enable society to reproduce itself as a community,* as a whole that is greater than the sum of its parts. This theoretical vision of the components of social life is like a nucleus of forces that outweighs the other forces of social production. These forces are associated with economic and political functions: power, subsistence, wealth. But this heavier nucleus of forces is also necessarily associated with kinship, art, and religion, *without* this association ever taking the form of a *necessary correspondence.*

Marx occupies an important place in this vision. But his hypothesis that the economic sphere constitutes the *general* foundation of social life—that it is the infrastructure upon which all other social relations are built and from which they flow—is invalidated by what now can be accepted as proof that no necessary correspondence exists between this nucleus, the economic and political spheres, and the other aspects of social practice.

AND NOW WHAT SHOULD WE DO? THE BROKEN MIRROR

By now the reader will have gathered that anthropology is alive and well. It has its crises and conflicts like the rest of the social sciences. But for some time to come, it will have an indispensable role to play in social thought because anthropology is irreplaceable. Of all the social sciences, it alone presents such a vast array of information about the various ways of living and thinking that coexist on the earth today. It has the advantage of presenting us with two versions, as it were, of this data: on the one hand, the analytical, theoretical perspectives of the discipline, which must constantly be watched, and criticized, and revised, if not actually destroyed; on the other hand, the multitude of ethnographic studies of societies anthropologists have described and analyzed over the last one hundred and fifty years. Neither sociology nor history offers such a broad field for comparisons.

Of course the context of anthropology has changed since its birth, or rather its births. The era of great discoveries and "travels in America" is over. The great colonial empires have disappeared, although certain countries still bear clear traces (for example the French influence in West Africa or English culture in Asia). Our epoch will certainly be one of a new expansion of the system born in the West, the capitalist-type market economy associated or not with a political regime of parliamentary democracy. The combination does not occur everywhere and is perhaps not even necessary, as Max Weber hinted. South Africa is a capitalist country whose entire population, black and white, is Christianized. But it is characterized by apartheid and the absence of democracy.

The originality of our epoch lies also in the paradoxical fact that the Westernization of the world is now partly in the hands of the East. Japan, which was never a colony, which has always maintained its political sovereignty, and which rejected Christian attempts at evangelization, now leads all other capitalist countries in the development of state-of-the-art technologies and capitalist economic mechanisms.

Another original feature of our times and one that is just beginning to emerge is that Europe, which has been cut in half for the last several decades (and in fact has not been united for centuries), may be reunited under the banner of the market and democracy. But there is a danger of going from a totalitarian form of socialism to a new brand of unbridled capitalism. It will have to confront all the centuries-old, still unresolved (and denied or brutally repressed by the socialist regimes) problems of the manifold dominant or dominated ethnic identities that make up Central and Eastern Europe. The analysis of ethnic groups and "ethnic identity" is one of anthropology's strong points.

Anthropologists should also concern themselves with the resurgence of the great religions such as Islam and the appearance in the West itself of new forms of spiritual life. Also, the relations between men and women, especially the forms of denial and oppression involved in these relations, is a field of political debate and theoretical reflection not only in the West but in many societies. Anthropology today is in the vanguard of the disciplines exploring this area. And behind the relations between the sexes lurks the problem of intergenerational relations, relations between adults and young people, and all the problems that accompany changing generational attitudes, changes that call into question systems of education.

On a more abstract plane, anthropology is a front-runner among the disciplines capable of analyzing the mechanisms and foundations of "belief." Sharing the same representations, believing in the same ideas while being separated by opposing interests remains both an essential problem of human practice and a particularly difficult point of theory. What were the circumstances surrounding the death of the Greek gods; did they cease to be the objects of active belief and worship? We have

not yet gotten very far with our investigation of the black box containing the mechanisms of belief and we do not yet know why and how a given belief or practice becomes associated with a given symbol. Symbols are not simply embellishments derived from certain practices and representations. They are one of their inner components, an intimate part, by means of which beliefs and practices take on life.

By now it must be evident that, if it is to address all these problems, anthropology cannot be governed by a single doctrine. Now is the time for a rational theory of pragmatism rooted in permanent critical vigilance that never stops learning—learning from our past, from our origins as well as our evolution. All studies, all theories, all anthropological stances are not equal. Those that prove useful—such as the work of Lévi-Strauss, Leach, Firth, Rivers, for example—must be given due credit. We must build on what we have taken from them in order to continue on our common and contentious way.

NOTE

1. **Editor's note:** Metaphor, or association by analogy, occurs, for example, when the beauty of a flower is compared with a woman's beauty. Metonymy, or association by physical connection, occurs when a crown is associated with a queen because the queen usually wears the crown.

INTELLECTUAL ROOTS

Maurice Godelier is a Professor of Anthropology at the Ecole des Hautes Etudes en Sciences Sociales in Paris. In 1990 he was awarded the Von Humboldt International Prize for the Social Sciences. Former Vice President of the Société des Océanistes, Scientific Director from 1982 to 1986 of the French National Center for Scientific Research (CNRS) and head of its Department of Humanities and Social Sciences, he has done intensive fieldwork in Papua New Guinea among the Baruya and other members of the Anga cultural group. Among his numerous publications: *Rationality and Irrationality in Economics,* New Left Books, 1972 (French edition, 1966); *Perspectives in Marxist Anthropology,* Cambridge University Press, 1977 (French edition, 1972); *The Making of Great Men,* Cambridge University Press, 1986 (French edition, 1982); *The Mental and the Material,* Verso, 1986 (French edition, 1984); co-editor with Marilyn Strathern of *Big Men and Great*

Men: Personifications of Power in Melanesia,
Cambridge University Press, 1991; and editor
of *Transitions et Subordinations au Capitalisme,*
Maison des Sciences de l'Homme, 1991.

When I began my studies at Lille in 1951, I had no
idea that I would one day become an anthropologist. Philosophy was my passion, but I was also interested in psychology. In 1952, Michel Foucault,
fresh from the Ecole Normale Supérieure and
having just passed his *agrégation de philosophie,* came
to Lille as a professor of philosophy and psychology. We became friends, and it was he who ad-
vised me to go to Paris to continue my studies
there.

I entered the Ecole Normale Supérieure in 1955
and began working on logic in Husserl, Kant, and
Hegel, and then set out to read Marx's *Capital*
from cover to cover. In 1958, I passed my
agrégation de philosophie. At this time a debate was
raging over the death of philosophy, which many
felt could not possibly withstand the development
of the sciences and the revolutionary changes
taking place in society. I took the stand that what
had to die was the presumption that philosophy
could by itself discover the foundations of the
sciences and social practice. I came to the conclusion that I would need more than philosophy to
philosophize about anything and decided to
continue my studies. I was torn between medicine
and economics, but because of my interest in Marx
and my political activities, I chose economics.

In 1960, the historian Fernand Braudel engaged
me at the Ecole Pratique des Hautes Etudes, of
which he was president. This was a great opportunity for me. Braudel gave me two years of complete freedom to do as I pleased, and I read
copiously.

Ultimately three questions intrigued me: Under
what conditions can economic systems be "compared"? What explains their appearance and disappearance at certain moments in history? To what
extent can the Western conception of "economic
rationality" be used in comparing socioeconomic
systems? The last question seemed to be at the
center of violent discussions that would break out
between economists any time someone wanted to
demonstrate the superiority of capitalism and market economy over socialism and planned economy,
or vice versa. And it was in search of answers to
these questions that I turned to anthropology. It

seemed to me that it would be more productive to
study economic systems in contemporary living
societies organized according to social and cultural
logics totally different from our Western models.

It was at that point that a second important
opportunity arose. Having just published three
articles on the notion of "structure" in Marx's
Capital, I sent them to Lévi-Strauss, whom I did
not know personally. He responded with a note
saying that these texts interested him, and all the
more because, in his younger days, before his own
agrégation de philosophie, he had written an essay on
"The Logical Structure of Marx's *Capital.*" He also
invited me to call on him, and, when I told him I
wanted to go into anthropology, he suggested I
join him at the Collège de France.

In 1962, *La Pensée Sauvage* had just been published, and in it Lévi-Strauss adopted Marx's
position that infrastructures prevail over superstructures, and he presented himself as the superstructure specialist. One day he jokingly suggested
that I take infrastructures and research all the
anthropological material on the economy of primitive societies. In 1963, I was appointed Senior Lecturer in his department, and I organized the first
course in France on economic anthropology. The
only French scholar working in the area at the time
was C. Meillassoux, a student of G. Balandier. A
lively debate was running between substantivists
(Polanyi and his disciplines) and formalists (Firth,
Schneider, etc.). It seemed to me that the discussion was headed in the wrong direction. I felt
that there was a need to look further and to try to
understand why the economy of a society was
embedded in kinship or political relations or, on
the contrary, nonembedded, as in capitalist economies. It was at that time that I began to see the
distinction between infrastructure and superstructure no longer as a distinction between institutions, but as one between functions which could
be located in very different areas of social practice.
I would develop this view some ten years later
in *Horizon, Trajets Marxistes en Anthropologie* (1977),
for which I was immediately attacked by
Meillassoux, Terray, Kahn, and others, who
claimed to be Marxists, but who in reality followed
Althusser's interpretation of Marx.

I met George Dalton, Marshall Sahlins, and
many others on trips to the United States and then
returned to France to complete *Rationality and
Irrationality in Economics,* which came out after I had
left for New Guinea (1966). In it, I concluded that

there was no such thing as economic rationality, but that there existed various social rationalities and that the reasons for the succession of socio-economic systems down through the ages were to be sought in the largely unintentional structural changes and conscious reorganizations that had occurred in social relations, which taken alone were not enough to bring about a changeover from one system to another.

One of Marx's ideas that seemed important to me was that the relations that organize the production and circulation of means of subsistence and wealth imply the development of conflicting interests and social contradictions. Another was that ideologies either pass over these contradictions in silence or disguise them as reciprocal exchanges, thereby masking the domination and exploitation they imply. The Marxist outlook, which stresses material constraints and the evolution of systems, brought me closer to the new school of ecological anthropology which was emerging in the United States with R. Rappaport and P. Vayda and in France with J. Barrau, who had worked with H. Conklin at Yale. Nevertheless, I felt that the ecological approach did not always pay enough heed to the existence of social contradictions and forms of exploitation in the dynamics of systems.

At the end of 1966, I left for New Guinea, after having taken E. Leach's advice and gone to Cambridge to meet A. and M. Strathern, who had just returned from their first fieldwork with the Melpa. On my way to Australia, I stopped in New York to consult M. Meggitt and R. Rappaport and then in Canberra to see W. Stanner. My first stay lasted three years (1967-1969), as I wanted to combine a quantitative and qualitative approach, and the size of the Baruya group (approximately 1700 persons) seemed to allow this. In 1969, M. and A. Jablonko came to film the production of salt and other aspects of Baruya life; and Ian Dunlop came to film the big male initiation ceremonies which were held in October-November of that year. Analyzing these images with my Baruya friends, translating the dialogues, and then presenting the Baruya with copies of the films were very important experiences in my life.

The time I spent with the Baruya profoundly altered my theoretical views, not to speak of my own self. I was struck by the fact that the myths and rituals worked systematically to raise men and lower women in people's minds by a series of imaginary explanations that justified each gender's place in society. I was also struck by the fact that male domination always combined two forces: the use of physical, political, and symbolic violence, of course, but also the women's own consent to this domination. Therefore, instead of writing the usual monograph dealing with the economy, kinship, etc., I decided to describe Baruya society from the standpoint of male-female relations, which seemed to be the centerpiece—whence *The Making of Great Men* (1982). It was the Baruya, then, who got me interested in analyzing gender relations, or at least made me see and hear more clearly what was going on around me in my own society. Paradoxically, this also led me, beginning in 1974, to spend much more time reading about hunter-gatherer societies, as these were being tapped by feminist and antifeminist movements in anthropology to prove either that male domination had always been the universal rule or, on the contrary, that it had only come about with the emergence of more complex types of society and social stratification. In 1978, I organized a meeting on "Hunters and Gatherers," the results of which appeared as *Politics and History in Band Societies* (edited by Eleanor Leacock and Richard Lee, Cambridge University Press, 1982). My acquaintance with E. Leacock influenced me all the more perhaps because I did not share a number of her views.

My work among the Baruya also had theoretical consequences for me as a specialist on Melanesia. Twenty years ago, many anthropologists looked to M. Sahlins's model of Melanesian Big Man vs. Polynesian Chief when analyzing the forms of power they encountered in New Guinea. Unfortunately, try as I might, I could not fit the Baruya into this mold. Nowhere did I find a Big Man amassing wives and wealth and trying to outdo others with gifts and counter-gifts in ceremonial exchanges. The prominent men in Baruya society were the masters of the male initiations, great warriors, shamans, in a word, persons whom I chose to call "Great Men," to distinguish them from the others. This led me to scour my colleagues' work on some fifteen New Guinea societies to see if this distinction between Big-Men and Great-Men societies occurred elsewhere. I had a hunch that these were two poles of a set of social and cultural logics whose variations were not simply the product of chance. In 1987, M. Strathern and I organized a meeting on "Big Men and Great Men: Personifications of Power in Melanesia."

But there was one problem that kept cropping up: while the power to dominate always combines violence and consent, for this consent to exist, in some way dominators and dominated, exploiters and exploited must share the same representations. This plus the conviction that there were no direct links between a given mode of production and any one kinship system or religion—Christianity, for instance, and capitalism, which appeared fifteen centuries later—led me to attempt a synthesis in *The Mental and the Material*. It no longer seemed possible to make the economic sphere the general foundation of society and thus the primary key for analyzing forms of society, as Marx had tried to do. It now seemed to me that two force fields, economic relations and relations of power, entertained structural affinities which were more than simply the effect of reciprocal adaptations and which outweighed all other areas of human practice (art, kinship, etc.) in the processes which not only induce societies to change but to change into another type of society.

Bearing all this in mind, I have, for the last ten years, been exploring two directions. On the one hand, I have been looking at the process of subordination and disintegration/reproduction in peripheral societies subjected to the expansion of Western capitalism. And, on the other hand, I have returned to the classic study of kinship. Why kinship? Once again the story begins with my work on the Baruya. The feeling that there must be some connection between the existence of a kinship system based on the direct exchange of women and the existence of a collective political and symbolic organization—male initiations—uniting the men against the women incited me to compare the kinship systems found within New Guinea, first of all, and then further afield. For the last three years I have been going through numerous works on kinship with the intention of one day writing something on "Incest, Kinship, and Power(s)," and I must admit that I find many of the widely discussed theories unconvincing.

7

Anthropological Futures

ADAM KUPER

What can we expect of anthropology in the 1990s? I think it will be recognizably like anthropology today, for its main constituents have been stable throughout the twentieth century. At the same time, tendencies which will bring about some shifts in direction and emphasis must already be apparent.

THE THREE DOMINANT PROJECTS

There are three well-established research projects in anthropology. Two are most fully institutionalized in the United States, while the third is characteristic of Western Europe.

The first, effectively launched by Boas, takes as its subject culture, particularly cultural variation. It favors an insider's account of cultural experience. It asks questions about the experience of cultural differences, about the ways in which language and custom infuse actions with meaning and purpose, about the weight of tradition. It is relativistic, concerned with description and interpretation rather than with explanation, and with the particular rather than with the general.

This research program has undergone a number of transformations over the generations, but it is still recognizable in the second half of the century in a range of projects, especially within interpretive and psychological anthropology. Recently it took a radical form—but one which would have been immediately intelligible to Boas—in postmodernism. Its long-established psychological interests are expressed mainly in the anthropology of the "self." Current tendencies favor a cognitive definition of culture and imply—they are seldom explicit—a form of cultural determinism. There are close affinities with the social constructivist movement in philosophy and the sociology of science. And often language is given prominence—or "privileged" as they say in their Franglaise dialect.

The second program has always provided the main antagonist to the Boasian program. Its central concern is human evolution, its hero is Darwin. It emphasizes material factors in the evolutionary process: first, the biological parameters of human development and behavior and, second, the ecological and technological forces at work in different periods of human history. It seeks general principles, and models itself on the natural sciences rather than on the humanities, which is where the Boasians normally find their allies. This program is the automatic choice of most archaeologists and physical anthropologists, though it has also always been favored by a significant number of cultural anthropologists, beginning with the followers of Morgan at the Bureau for American Ethnology and including (in the second half of this century) the intellectual progeny of Stewart and of White, the ecologists of the sixties and seventies, and, most recently, the sociobiologists.

Obviously some individuals have straddled both of these programs, and others have identified themselves with one modality of a particular tradition but reacted against others.

113

(The evolutionist tradition has always had a right wing and a left wing, as it were, the one more concerned with biological constraints, the other with technology and the environment.) Nevertheless, it is fair to say that most anthropologists in most American departments of anthropology have worked within one of these two broadly defined programs, and, usually, repudiated the other.

There are not only spiritual differences between these two programs. Each has been funded by different sources, and anthropology departments have often been divided politically between the advocates of one or other research trajectory.

The third program—characteristic of social anthropology in Western Europe—tends to be Durkheimian (though it has been hospitable to some readings of Weber and Marx). It is concerned with the relationship between social structure and what is variously labeled culture, religion, or ideology. If the Boasian program is typically at home in the humanities, and the evolutionist program aspires to acceptance by the natural sciences, then social anthropology is a social science, closely related to sociology. Between the two World Wars, its center was England, but its more recent transformations have usually evolved in Paris. These include Lévi-Straussian structuralism in the sixties and structuralist Marxism in the seventies, but the tradition has been remarkably unimpressed by other Parisian movements in philosophy or literary theory that have so influenced contemporary American cultural anthropology. Today social anthropology draws ideas from the sociologies of Bourdieu, Habermas, and Giddens and from the structural history which the Annales school developed from Durkheim.

This program has a virtual monopoly position in European social anthropology, and social anthropology in Europe is beginning a phase of demographic and institutional growth, particularly in the German-speaking countries and in Spain and Portugal. A new European Association of Social Anthropolo-

gists has been formed, and its first conferences, held in Portugal in 1990 and in Prague in 1992, gave evidence of a fresh vitality. The Western Europeans are now more open to influences from American cultural anthropology than they have been in the past, and recent work in American cultural anthropology has stimulated some European emulation (as the December 1989 number of *L'Homme* and recent conferences of the British Association of Social Anthropology bear witness). In the United States, however, social anthropology remains a minority interest, though it has some well-established outposts. In Europe, social anthropology has little or no relationship to physical anthropology and only a remote and occasional link with archaeology. These disciplines tend to take their cue from developments in the United States.

These three research programs are well-established, viable, dynamic, and institutionally entrenched. It is a fair bet that they will all be in place in the coming generation. This is not to say that academic disciplines are immortal, though they certainly are robust. Within anthropology, the intertwined European traditions of ethnology and folklore studies are today so feeble that they probably cannot survive. They have been pushed onto the nonacademic periphery in most Western European countries, and in Eastern Europe, where they have persisted, they will probably be among the many unremarked casualties of the present political reorientation. In contrast, the vitality of the three traditions I described is very striking. One diagnostic feature is their capacity to spawn fresh, often unexpected, sometimes dazzling transformations of their basic programs.

SOURCES OF CHANGE: REGIONAL DIVERSIFICATION

If these are the massive elements of continuity, there are also two significant sources of change. It is no longer adequate to define cultural or social anthropology in terms of metropolitan traditions, even if the definition of the metropolis is broadened, as it surely must be, to include Japan. There are fascinating developments outside the metropolitan centers, and they will become increasingly significant in the near future.

The most stimulating conferences I have attended in the past few years were a small gathering of Indian social anthropologists, economists, and development personnel in New Delhi and a huge meeting in Campinas of the Association of Brazilian Anthropologists, over two thousand strong. These may stand for dozens of similar meetings in India, Indonesia, Brazil, Mexico, and South Africa. In these countries, social anthropology has taken on more or less the role of sociology in many Western countries. It trains the personnel and provides the intellectual resources and the methods for the study of national social processes. Anthropologists in these countries are typically engaged in programs of social development, and in policy-making (either directly or as critics). They are extremely sensitive to the political implications of their work. There are also many who are passionately interested in more traditional ethnographic research because of a commitment to the free cultural development of particular communities in their countries. I feel a fresh pride in my profession when I consider the way in which colleagues have used the resources of our discipline to understand and sustain the interests of the urban poor in Mexico or India, of the migrant laborers of South Africa or Brazil, and of the threatened tribal minorities of the Amazon or the Himalayas, and probed ethnic conflicts all over the world.

The anthropology in these countries is typically eclectic in its intellectual inspiration. It draws, on the whole, upon metropolitan theoretical models (though Latin American dependency theory, for example, influenced many metropolitan scholars in the seventies). Debates in local scholarly communities nevertheless help to shape the study of particular regions in the metropolitan centers. This influence will grow. Ethnographers from the West who go out to work in these countries are now (necessarily and rightly) joining up with these local communities of scholars, engaging in common debates, and finding themselves liable to stinging criticism for failures in empathy, political sensitivity, and local knowledge. There are some excellent regional journals, and the best ethnographic monographs are now quite frequently published in India or Brazil rather than in England or the United States.

SOURCES OF CHANGE: THE ETHNOGRAPHIC RECORD

This regional diversification of our discipline—its institutional diffusion in some of the liveliest intellectual communities of the Third World—reinforces the other major process which I see as making for change. This is in one sense methodological, in another demographic. The generation of Malinowski and of Boas saw themselves as explorers, opening up a new world, and their students still had the mentality of pioneers. They may have been deceiving themselves, but in our times such illusions are in any case impossible. My old friend Isaac Schapera recently remarked to me that when he began working in what was then the Bechuanaland Protectorate (now Botswana), over sixty years ago, he understood his task to be the description of every aspect of the social life of every Tswana tribe. Recently a young fieldworker came to see him en route there to make a field study of borehole drilling syndicates. This is a perfectly reasonable and feasible project because so much is known today about rural life in Botswana. In all probability several other social scientists are even now engaged in overlapping research projects in the country. They will be in touch with officials in the Ministry of Local Government in Gaborone and perhaps with World Bank officers who may be funding projects that have to do with water resources, or cattle marketing, or the ecological consequences of pastoralism.

I do not want to exaggerate the contrast: Malinowski told his students to study problems, not peoples (echoing Collingwood's admonition to historians, that they should study problems, not periods). But if instead of contrasting two caricatured extremes, I suggest that there has been a clear trend of development, there can be little argument. The trend has been toward more specialized ethnographic fieldwork, and towards more complex and detailed ethnographic coverage. Ethnography, in short, has become increasingly intensive.

There are several important consequences. I shall mention two. First, each contemporary ethnographer must master a library of secondary sources and keep up with a stream of relevant local studies—by anthropologists, but also by linguists and historians and students of religion, by demographers and economists and geographers. Second, it is no longer necessary for every ethnography to address a metropolitan academic audience and to make a general theoretical argument. The ethnographer's readership is more and more weighted toward people with local expertise. They may be perfectly satisfied with an ethnographic critique of the excessively literary and Brahman-oriented interpretation of some Hindu folk cults. Or they may value a description of the ways in which a pastoral people have reacted to the diversion of a river to supply a dam. And to the extent that the ethnographer is addressing a local readership, he or she must take into account its political and cultural sensibilities.

These tendencies are all familiar enough perhaps, but it is well to consider some implications for the development of cultural and social anthropology. Comparison is no longer the central interest of many field anthropologists, and in any case the comparative enterprise—which is, I believe, the core of theoretical anthropology—is changing its nature.

The most suggestive and subtle comparisons are, today, regional in scope and historical in conception. There are good theoretical reasons for this, but it also follows from the intensive ethnographic research that is characteristic of our time.

Given these tendencies, some of the leading university departments in the Third World will become the centers for this theoretically informed regional comparison, as Leiden once was for Indonesian studies, or Oxford for Sudanic studies. The old Rhodes-Livingstone Institute under Max Gluckman or the East African Institute of Social Research under Audrey Richards perhaps foreshadow some of the anthropological centers of the next generation.

INTERDISCIPLINARY RESEARCH

Implicit in these developments is another large issue, which is the relationship between new directions in our discipline and in others. Social and cultural anthropologists outside the metropolitan centers take it for granted that they work in an interdisciplinary milieu. After all, they are interested above all in a region. They consume all the information they can find about it, and they engage in continual debates with others who share their concerns. Nevertheless, theoretical innovations will continue to come mainly from the metropolitan centers, precisely because of their less regional and more generalizing orientation, but also because it is here that new developments tend to occur in other disciplines and first become available to anthropologists.

The one sure prediction is that most theoretical innovations in the next generation will be interdisciplinary, but the source of outside stimuli in the coming years is hard to predict. In the past quarter century, we have drawn models and ideas from sociology, historiography, linguistics, philosophy, literary theory, ecology, and sociobiology. One strange omission has been cognitive psychology, whose lively promise is only just beginning to be tapped by anthropologists.

SHARED THEORETICAL CONCERNS AND METHODS

I began by sketching the three main traditions in cultural and social anthropology. I predicted that they will continue to define the major research programs in the metropolitan centers. They differ in all sorts of ways, and above all they set distinctive questions about human history. They are frequently in institutional competition with one another, and at times regard themselves as virtually distinct disciplines. Yet they are not always, or necessarily, at odds with each other. One source of intellectual vitality in anthropology may lie in the rediscovery of our shared theoretical interests, in creative confrontation, and in the pooling of our resources.

Outsiders are inclined to suppose that there is a program common to all the various anthropologies. I think that their intuition is not as naive as it may appear at first blush.

Anthropology is about the unity and diversity of human beings. We wish (1) to establish the extent to which people vary in their social institutions, their values and beliefs, and even in their physical makeup, (2) to chart the range of these variations and uniformities, and (3) to account for these findings and to consider their implications.

The broad enterprise is usually defined with reference to three shared abstractions: "evolution," "culture" and "social structure." Admittedly, each of the three main anthropological projects has made one of these abstractions its particular focus. But these notions take their meaning from their relationship with each other. They form a set. And every anthropological theory is in effect a hypothesis concerning their interconnections.

There is also a remarkable convergence of methods. Here the key terms are "fieldwork"

and "comparison," but there is also a third common procedure, which we sometimes neglect to define—the reanalysis of ethnographic materials, particularly of the classic case studies of the discipline.

Anthropologists from the major disciplinary traditions tend to deploy similar methods of data collection, based upon participant observation. They are also alert to the possibilities of comparison, characteristically combining a fascination with the intricacies of ethnographic cases, a sense of the relative significance of particular instances, and a sophisticated recognition of the pitfalls of the established comparative procedures. Yet although we may lack confidence in some conventional forms of comparison, we may still implicitly accept their basic premise—that ethnographic materials can be recast in new contexts and reanalyzed. The postmodernist critique has made us creatively uneasy about our procedures, but some of the most suggestive recent essays in reevaluation proceed by the persuasive critique and reanalysis of ethnographic data, not just of ethnographies.

These theoretical concerns and methods also have a shared point of reference. This is not some abstract notion of human history, but a very concrete, familiar body of materials that constitutes the central, shared heritage of anthropology: the ethnographic record. The theories of anthropology are attempts to make sense of this record; the methods of anthropology are procedures for adding to it, criticizing it, exploiting it. Anthropologists are trained to respect and appreciate this record. We honor those who know it well and revere the handful in every generation who contribute significantly to it. Anthropologists are sophisticated in the uses of this record. In contrast, outsiders who make raids on it typically seem to us naive, uncritical, falling into traps which even undergraduate anthropologists should be canny enough to avoid. (If outsiders see anthropologists as a community, we also recognize how different they are from ourselves.)

A CONTINUING INTELLECTUAL ENDEAVOR

There are, then, both centripetal and centrifugal forces—often creative forces, fostering innovation—that are working upon the anthropological world. While the central core is there, it does not have the same magnetic attraction for all anthropologists. A social anthropologist probably knows as much—perhaps more—about contemporary sociology as about current theories of human evolution or of semantics, and an archaeologist working on the Neanderthals may know next to nothing about "social structure."

The main fault lines in the discipline run perhaps not between the great intellectual research programs but between disciplinary specialties—social and cultural anthropology, archaeology, physical anthropology. Linguistics has virtually severed its links with the rest, however much cultural anthropologists may regret the fact. In the seventies, several leading anthropologists predicted the collapse of the discipline as an academic institution. The organizational fragmentation of the American Anthropological Association may presage yet further disintegration.

I am very aware that this review has been conducted from within social and cultural anthropology. A review of anthropology conducted from within archaeology or physical anthropology would probably identify rather different disciplinary trajectories. And yet much of the excitement in contemporary archaeology comes from the exploitation of social anthropological theories and of the ethnographic record; and human biology is engaged with the dynamic interaction of biological, cultural, and social processes. The central concerns—the deep structure of the discipline—will surely survive into the next millennium (which is not so far away). And it will continue to find expression in organizations, university departments, and journals, and, above all, in intellectual endeavour.

INTELLECTUAL ROOTS

Adam Kuper was born in South Africa and studied social anthropology at the University of the Witwatersrand and at Cambridge University, where he took his doctorate in 1966. He has taught at universities in Uganda, Britain, Sweden, the United States, and the Netherlands and has been a fellow at the Center for Advanced Studies in the Behavioral Sciences at Stanford. His books include ethnographic monographs dealing with villagers in the Kalahari desert and with modern Jamaica, comparative ethnographies of Southern Africa, and historical critiques of social anthropology. His most recent book is *The Invention of Primitive Society* (Routledge, 1988). He has edited *Current Anthropology* since 1986, and was the first chairman of the European Association of Social Anthropology.

Every social anthropologist is trained to work both as an ethnographer and as a comparativist or social theorist. I find that I try to justify myself on both fronts, but through perhaps slightly unconventional projects. My own work has two main foci, one the comparative ethnography of Southern Africa, the other the history and theory of social anthropology. My present research concerns the preconquest political systems of Southern Africa. I tend to switch from one set of projects to the other every few years, but this is not a planned rhythm, and I am aware of it only when I look back at what has happened.

Though my most intensive period of training occurred at Cambridge, under Meyer Fortes, the greatest intellectual influence on my work has been the writings of Claude Lévi-Strauss. Editing *Current Anthropology* greatly enlarged my intellectual horizons and brought me into contact with anthropologists all over the world. More recently, however, I have been caught up in the revival of European social anthropology.

8

Some Biased Remarks on Interpretivism: A View from Brazil*

ROBERTO DAMATTA

I would like to discuss some aspects of the "interpretivist" perspective which has developed recently in American cultural anthropology. I do not intend to write an exhaustive, detailed study, nor do I want to write a thesis against a movement many of whose points I am in full agreement with or tend to accept. Brazilian anthropologists have always worked in highly authoritarian political environments and wrote their first studies about "contact situations" in which the tribal societies they wanted to do ethnographies of were on the verge not only of cultural, but sometimes of tragic physical, extinction. For these anthropologists I think it would come as no surprise to say that: (1) the world is shrinking, (2) a rhetorical style exists whenever one speaks of "the other," speaks about those whom anthropologists study, and (3) "ethnographic authority" must constantly be challenged and put to the test.[1]

What I am trying to accomplish here is to present my opinion about a perspective which in my view has some fatal flaws. I am referring to the fact that American "interpretive anthropology," besides lapsing into abstract philosophical arguments, tends toward rhetorical and programmatic exaggeration, at times slipping into what can be called an irritating righteousness. Furthermore, it tends to reduce anthropological problems exclusively to field narratives, systematically avoiding a historical and theoretical contextualization which has been the basis for both anthropology's scientific and humanistic claims.[2]

The basic argument of this article is that it is impossible to discuss questions of this kind without addressing two fundamental problems. The *first* is that the basis of ethnographic authority goes beyond a mere question of stylistics. It is linked to the success with which ethnographic studies present, resolve, or bungle a given theoretical question in the period in which the work was written. The *second* problem is that the interpretive position must be learned and judged in a particular context—that is, within the bounds of a social universe in which the academic life (and I am thinking obviously of American academic life) has certain characteristics. One of these characteristics is its extreme compartmentalization; another is its size and massive political and institutional security; a third is its firm belief that the world is undergoing a fragmentation into individualism (with a "cosmopolitanization" of everything and everyone in which individual choice plays a fundamental role). No one has summed this up better than James Clifford (1986, 1988), the intellectual leader of this position. For Clifford—who is a professor at the cosmopolitan and thriving University of California at Santa Cruz—the world is a place in which "the pure products go crazy."

---

*Translated from the Portuguese by Patrick Kennelly.

I think that much of "interpretivism" has a direct correlation with the American cultural and academic scene—a universe constituted by cosmopolitan, egalitarian individualism, where one is entitled to eat Chinese, Mexican, or French "food," and where one lives in a social context singularized by the fact that the local culture is defined negatively and by means of a paradoxical absence.[3]

One can develop, I believe, an interesting discussion of the "interpretivist" position based on observation of the movement's ideological and/or cultural properties, especially when we bear in mind the contrasting kinds of anthropologies produced in Brazil. Without this effort of mutual and reciprocal assessment, our criticism will always be made in terms of universalistic presuppositions. What is supposed to be a "dialogical" and polysemic dialogue becomes once again an authoritarian monologue.

THE CONTEXT OF AMERICAN INTERPRETIVE DISCOURSE

In my opinion the irritating feature of "postmodern anthropologies"—inspired by the "discovery" that subjectivity and history permeate everything we do—is their relative inability to be theoretically inspired by the society, culture, and value system of the scholars who produced them. This represents a remarkable turnaround. While the founders of European hermeneutics and critical studies in general—from Dilthey to Ricoeur and Foucault—were concerned with problems, categories and circumstances intimately linked with their own culture, and society, the modern representatives of this trend in American anthropology have continued to shrink from the study of their own culture as the Devil from the cross.

We have here a curious situation. A new "interpretive anthropology" is vigorously advanced (in good American style) as a denunciation of traditional ethnographic authority paradigms. Instead of "monologic" style ethnographies, it is insisted, we need a carnivalesque, "polyphonic dialogical" style in which the researcher and the object of research finally (and justly) trade places.[4] At the same time, however, the majority of works of this movement continue to focus on exotic phenomena—phenomena which require the presence of an interpreter for discussion even to begin. The greatest challenge for "cultural anthropologies," and for the "fieldwork" which gives rise to them, should be not only to reconcile subjectivism with "scientific objectivity"—to combine personal, humanistic perspectives with scientific ones—but to present the basic text of a given situation or human circumstance. The ethnographic account, the documentation of fieldwork, portrays a particular humanity in the landscape of societies and cultures.

This privileged, positive side of fieldwork—in spite of its risks, errors, and exaggerations—has, in my opinion, been undervalued by American "interpretivists." Perhaps this is because some of them have never carried out field research; or because they have had disillusioning research experiences; or because they have worked in national societies where there is a sensitive political problematic—a situation for which American students' preparation is notoriously deficient.

Let it suffice to point out, by way of ethnography, that in the 1960s the required reading for Ph.D. candidates in social anthropology at Harvard University included works by Maine, Morgan, Tylor, and Frazer, but not Engels or Marx. I recall lively discussions among vociferous students and nice professors, but they stayed off political questions which were not considered part of a social anthropologist's training. The texts were thus discussed with reference to whether or not they were helpful to the project of fieldwork in some exotic land, an activity truly fetishized by its professional practitioners at that time.

A Brazilian Contrast

All this contrasted with my Brazilian anthropological initiation, in which, quite to the contrary, political questions and the great moral dilemmas were by far the primary topics of discussion. In Brazil, we began by reading Marx and Engels and postponed the works of Frazer, Maine, Morgan, and the others. What was lacking in American academics was, in a sense, abundant in Brazil's intellectual life.

I am afraid that there exists a negative perception of fieldwork among the heralds of American interpretive anthropology. In their eyes, ethnographic practice is a sort of magician's hat, a space in which ethnographers can pull off rhetorical nasty tricks and transform their burdensome and biased subjectivities into supposedly objective theoretical rabbits. In fact, in one of the most important chapters—if not the central one—of *The Predicament of Culture,* James Clifford speaks of "ethnographic authority" as essentially derived from the rhetorical power of the formula: "You are there . . . because I was there" (1988:22). (Leave aside the fact that such a formulation is practically non-sensical in Portuguese.) "You are there . . . because I was there" makes complete sense only in a highly mobile collectivity of travelers, a culture of postcards, *of individuals* who journey to the ends of the "civilized world" to return bearing novelties. This idea contrasts sharply with the Brazilian experience, in which it is precisely rootedness to a particular place that defines social superiority and economic and political privilege. For Brazilians, it is the *absence of movement* (and of journeys, particularly solitary or migratory journeys) that denotes social well-being. But in a system which makes mobility its credo, these "eyewitness accounts" which masterfully combine a first-person discourse with perfect narrative control, are as far from our ethnographic style as the sky is from the earth. In this context it is appropriate to recall Louis Dumont's cautionary observation in speaking about the way social anthropology has developed as a discipline: "It would seem that a feverish impatience is driving us headlong to forget or swiftly compromise our most valuable acquisitions. *This is a trait that may come from the United States, where transitory fashions rapidly succeed each other in an ideological and institutional climate of competition which favors overbidding*" (Dumont 1986:203; my emphasis).

THE CONTEXT OF BRAZILIAN ETHNOGRAPHIC DISCOURSE

What would the Brazilian "ethnographic text" look like? An overview may prove revealing. In three ethnological studies written by three well-known Brazilian anthropologists of diverse theoretical tendencies and generation—Cardoso de Oliveira (1960), Schaden (1965), and Ribeiro (1974)—the overall style is strikingly marked by the first person plural. The three authors write with an impersonal and formalizing "we" that displays an authoritarian, majestic, sovereign, and professional bias.[5] To some interpretivists, who believe the ethnologist should be a dialogic author, writing about living people and transcribing ambiguities and dialogues from an individualistic point of view, all (or nearly all) of Brazilian ethnology must certainly appear mystified and authoritarian. Nevertheless, in Brazil we do have an anthropological tradition that is genuinely concerned with the paradoxes of cultural contact and the fate (and voices) of tribal groups, and is engaged in a systematic criticism of the national state.

Can one really judge authority by an ethnographic style as some of the interpretivists would have us believe? I fear that to do so would be to draw an overly simplistic caricature of ethnographic discourse, losing sight of the fact that such narratives begin and end with a set of questions that have been defined before the fieldwork is undertaken. In the examples used above, Cardoso de Oliveira, Schaden, and Ribeiro all shaped their reflections around the problem of "cultural contact"—a critical topic in the field of Brazilian anthropology. It bridges the gap between the local diversity of native cultures and the representation of the nation as a dominating totality. It also touches the classic question of national identity, a critical problem in the case of a self-defined "mestizo country" of mixed racial ancestry like Brazil.[6] Any attempt to produce a less formal, pompous, and impersonal text would run the risk of being impugned as a fanciful or false narrative.

Before categorically (and universalistically) discrediting "ethnographic realism" we need to understand the cultural and historical contexts in which it is produced. In the Brazilian case, what emerges as monological formalism can be understood as part of a well-established cultural style in which to write with an individualizing "I" was (and still is) often seen as a mark of immodesty, egocentrism, and poor taste. Besides, the use of a solemn and formal "we," by blending the author and his discipline, also serves—through its ambivalent combination of authority and modesty—as a powerful way to command the attention of government elites in a public context marked by hierarchy, corporatist centralism, and the absence of egalitarian democratic representation.

In summary, then, a comparison with other cultural traditions, such as so-called "peripheral anthropologies" in which individualism is not a dominant value, shows that neither the use of the first person nor an individualist-inspired "dialogism" can be taken as a sure sign of a novel or prejudice-free anthropology. Thus, to report on a case I know well, when I wrote my book on the Apinayé, I wrote in the first person. I did so because I wanted to show that this more individualist and monograph style of doing anthropology, where each society is read as a "case," should be tried out more regularly in Brazil. What moved me to experiment with this individualist style was my motivation to disturb the routinized ethnographic authority inspired by crass Marxist evolutionism which led to the production

of dormant and lineal ethnographic narratives.[7] My goal was to show the possibility of constructing a text in which the researcher located himself as a concrete, flesh-and-blood, *fragile observer* within the field situation—as a true and accountable author of his narrative.[8]

The attentive reader will note once again that discourses and styles can have different values in different cultural and historical situations. What appears orthodox and even "authoritarian" to American interpretivists might have a positive and liberating value in Brazilian and other kinds of nonindividualistic centered anthropologies.

TESTIFYING TO OTHER HUMANITIES

In order to grasp deep motivations in ethnographic styles, one has to deal with how natives are represented as "others"—as different, as distinct—in divergent national contexts. In Brazil, the "other" is incarnated by a small native population, scattered in the empty Amazon and Central Brazil, a population generically called by the name, "Índio" (Indian). But the "Indian" is not alone, for with the category "Negro" they form the basis of a singular and intriguing view of the immediate human diversity for Brazilians. The "Negro" (who is fundamentally the ex-slave) is an intrinsic element of Brazilian social structure, haunting with his massive presence the "whiteness" of a bourgeois life-style. The "Indian" is an outsider, giving rise to the romantic fantasies of the noble savage who has to be either isolated and protected from the evils of civilization or be eliminated from the national landscape for incapacity to take part in modern progress.

In this context, to be with "Indians" is, for a Brazilian anthropologist, more than having the opportunity of living with another humanity. It is also to have the privilege of getting in touch with a mythical other. And by doing so, have the honor of being the one to overcome all manner of discomforts in order to describe a new way of life in the midst of Brazilian civilization. Thus, for Brazilian anthropologists, "to be there" is also an opportunity of being a *witness* to the way of life of a different society. This is particularly true when that way of life runs the risk of succumbing to a contact situation that is brutally unequal in political terms.

In my view, this consciousness of *testifying about* other humanities recuperates anthropology's humanistic project, while at the same time it reminds us of the severe limitations of that project. Claude Lévi-Strauss said many beautiful and wise things in *Tristes Trópicos* (1957), a book whose title seems to be trying to rescue that nostalgia—that immense Luso-Brazilian *saudade*—with which every anthropologist speaks of his or her field experiences. Without that multivocal blend of nostalgia, love, sympathy, youthful craziness, and, last but not least, anxiety about objectivity, no monograph would ever be written about any "other." It is precisely this mixture of authority and fragility which typifies the anthropological discourse. The authority derives from being the one who testifies and produces the account. The fragility comes from the painful realization that the "ethnographic present" is an illusion which in a few years will be corrected by another ethnographer who, in another research project, will ask different questions.

The "tropics" really are sad. Not because Lévi-Strauss scorns them entirely, but because they beckon with those dubious feelings of intense conviviality (which brings fragile comprehension) and with that formidable distance (which leads to objective authority)—sentiments which, in its most optimistic moments, the anthropological bridge (or, better put, anthropology as a bridge) hopes it can get beyond. From this comes the intimate relationship between good anthropology and confession (perceived by Lévi-Strauss), and between good ethnography and a novel. In my opinion, it is to be regretted that the practitioners of this interpretive anthropology have lost

sight of the *testimonial* aspect of all fieldwork, attempting to substitute for it—in good American fashion—another formula: a dialogistic one, individually interpreted.

Bearing Witness

One cannot forget that *bearing witness* is a critical part of our practice as scholars. Above all in Brazil, where a true tropical sadness comes from the realization that some of the societies we study with such affection, sacrifice, and sympathy are about to perish! It was for this reason that, copying Lévi-Strauss, I spoke of an "anthropological blues" associated with field research (DaMatta 1987b). What moved me to this position was a double objective: to try to record the melancholy that comes from working with societies which my country does not recognize as nations, and to reflect on the personal uprooting I was undergoing. Could it be that this is all a thing of the past, that today these societies can no longer be distinguished one from another and from the Brazilian community as distinct cultures?

For all this, it can be understood that when we refer to Tikopia, Tallensi, Crow, or Nuer, we must necessarily cite Firth, Fortes, Lowie, and Evans-Pritchard. Not only did they write excellent English and are "experts" on these realities. Their works also make up the exclusive or most complete way of speaking sociologically about these humanities. If it were not so, no one would need to cite the work of Curt Nimuendajú (cf. Nimuendajú 1939, 1946), a collection of ethnographic pieces which precisely describe some collectivities who had never before been known.

Nimuendajú had little formal anthropological training prior to his fieldwork. And Nimuendajú's ethnographic writing involves an ethnographic style all its own—a mode of writing in which a "dialogic" interest for the fate of the studied societies runs parallel to a detached and realistic description in the best Malinowskian style. Could this be the result of the association between Nimuendajú (a scholar without a stable institutional affiliation) and Robert H. Lowie (an established and internationally known professor at the University of California—Berkeley's already famous anthropology department)? What the association between Lowie and Nimuendajú reveals is the prospect of discussing "ethnography" as a narrative which claims to be fundamentally cumulative. Without the association with Lowie, who asked Nimuendajú the questions capable of ordering the reality the latter had visited, Nimuendajú would not have been able to produce ethnographic texts full of authority. Whoever has studied Nimuendajú's work knows that his early studies presented a narrative with severe descriptive problems due to an obvious absence of a viewpoint or, if you will, "theory." This stands in stark contrast to the work he produced years later, under the aegis of Lowie. In this later work we have a narrative—a text in the fullest sense of Ricoeur (1971)—with the conciseness and the unity which typify modern ethnographic writing.

ETHNOGRAPHIES OF THE FAMILIAR

I must insist that all this is much different from accounting for popular religiosity, studying race relations, trying to understand the popularity of Brazilian soccer, or discussing the chronic clientelism that permeates the Brazilian political system. What would Clifford Geertz's interpretive anthropology look like if he set out to interpret a football game at Notre Dame, Indiana, instead of talking about cockfights in Bali? Could Bernard DeVoto's "law"—that states "the more anthropologists write about the United States, the less I believe what they say about Samoa"—be also applied to him?[9]

As Max Gluckman (1957) and Mary Douglas (1975) have called to our attention, describing and interpreting the familiar can trigger a much more powerful "counter-interpretive" reaction, more so, than merely cataloging exotic kinship terminologies or interpreting tribal dualism. After all, how many people are interested in such phenomena in our society? But if we write about the structure of carnivalesque ritual, everything changes. Now we are no longer dealing with a text produced to delight a handful of initiates, but with a social phenomenon lived and thought by millions of people.

Description and Narration

When we are dealing with our own culture, it becomes remarkably difficult to achieve realistic and descriptive "ethnographic distance." In fact, the very exercise of such a literary mode—a cool, monological description in which the narrator stands miles removed from the thing being described—is sufficient to provoke such a sense of estrangement that the phenomenon being described, even though it is familiar, becomes unrecognizable. This is what happens to Americans when Horace Miner (1956)—in his "Body Ritual among the Nacirema" (i.e., American spelled backwards)—describes such American practices as brushing one's teeth or visiting a dentist from the perspective of an outsider who sees these experiences as magical rites (related to improving one's appeal to others).[10] Since such distantiating descriptions are seldom done, we tend—in describing our society—to slip into the realm of "interpretations" transformed in the wink of an eye into "opinions," which undermine, in turn, the supposed authority of our "objective" descriptions. This occurs in Brazil, where authority is by definition suspected and where nobody has a straightforward and candid attitude toward "the law" and its representatives. Pompous "objectivistic" descriptions of well-known facts and institutions may, contrary to the usual accepted American expectation, lead to ridicule and rampant criticism.[11]

It might be said, recalling a famous old distinction made by Georg Lukács (1965), that when we speak about strange societies we *"describe,"* but when we speak of our own system we *"narrate."* Such studies inevitably lead to a critical attitude with respect to the researcher's own culture, causing the idyllic distance between observer and observed to be swept away. In this way, the wisest method of preserving an aspiring "scientific" social discipline from these debates—in which the subject of research and the opinion of the researcher can become dangerously intermingled—would be to keep miles of distance between the two by inventing the myth of fieldwork in distant locales. Could it not be for precisely this reason that many of the great academic centers of the West have tended to avoid and resist studies of their own culture?[12] It is as if the study of the "distant other" sometimes were an excuse for impeding the "defamiliarization" of ourselves—viewing ourselves as outsiders might, in unfamiliar ways. It avoids a certain kind of radical political questioning that often permeates the anthropologies of so-called "Third World" countries.

The point is that, in the classic case of studying distant cultures, the result tends to be a description, whereas in speaking of one's own culture the tendency is to replace description with interpretive narration which (as proved by Bernard DeVoto's quip) quickly becomes "opinion." As I pointed out some years ago (DaMatta 1976b), there is a tendency, in traditional anthropology, to establish a totemic association between the researcher and the object studied. In the same way that "natural scientists" christen newly discovered species of animals, plants and microbes with their own names, each anthropologist had *"his"* and/or *"her"* own tribe.

The Problem that Arises from Not Doing Endo-Ethnography

In the ethnographies of the anthropological center—the leading Western schools of the discipline—we have a disjunction: a radical discontinuity which at various levels separates the researcher's society from that of "the natives." This sort of attitude has been questioned by many critics, who often invoke the fragmentation of the contemporary world as being responsible for a "postcolonial" crisis which is said to have gradually and systematically eroded cultural frontiers. I do not wish to enter here into a discussion of the sociological merit of this thesis, which seems to me highly questionable. But I do want to emphasize that inasmuch as such critics do not address their own societies, they are unable to comprehend the deepest differences between the descriptive posture required by an "exo-ethnography" (in which the other is a stranger, is of another, often radically different, culture) and the complex narrative displacement provoked by an "endo-ethnography" (which involves the study of what is familiar, or at least known, in our culture).

It seems to me that one of the greatest shortcomings of "interpretivist anthropologies" has been their failure to take full account of this paradox. As a result, they skirt the basic problem that each and every anthropology has to face: how studying the "other" can lead to a better understanding of oneself. As Maurice Merleau-Ponty has observed, it is not a question of an anthropology which seeks to "vanquish the primitive or give him reason to oppose us, but instead to situate ourselves on a terrain on which we can be mutually intelligible to each other, with neither reduction nor brash transposition. . . . The task . . . consists of enlarging our reason in order to be able to comprehend that which, in us and in others, precedes and exceeds reason" (1962: 183).

ANTHROPOLOGIES OF THE PERIPHERY AND THEIR PRODUCTION OF TEXTS

If the anthropologies practiced in the great academic centers of the West show a remarkable unwillingness to take their own societies as the object of study and of theoretical inspiration, just the opposite is true among anthropologies of the periphery. Here the recurring theme is no longer the "other" as a polar opposite within the boundaries of the known world, but rather that "other" who disguises himself behind carefully straightened hair, and an elegant European suit.

What seems to me to be most distinctive, and certainly most authentic, about these "national anthropologies" is that they—despite themselves—are not mere applications of theoretical models invented in the great Western academic centers but involve impassioned search over several generations for an answer to the question, "Who are we?" For as all who have trod that path have discovered, even the most "well brought-up" anthropological theories do not recognize the full implications of interpreting familiar things. This is because: (1) everyone seems to know what is being described (which in a sense renders most description unnecessary); (2) everyone feels and takes sides in what is being spoken about (which means that the speaker's rhetorical devices will be immediately recognized and denounced by the interlocutors, whether they are experts or lay persons); and (3) when one speaks about that which is in our midst, one inevitably commits an act of self-recognition that is political and simultaneous to sociological study. In Brazil and many other "Third World" countries, one often speaks of "social anthropology" and of "Brazilian anthropology," "Mexican anthropology," and so forth, which are supposed to be in some way different from the "original." In assessing anthropology, it is about time to take all anthropologies as variants of the very same myth, by realizing that all—even when they constitute the vanguard—have their blindness.[13]

There are differences between studying an exotic system (which is basically learned through intellectual means) and seeking to understand one's own system. If one goes through this sort of experience, it is easy to perceive the enormous contrast between discussing the value system of an exotic society, and trying to comprehend familiar social practices like Carnival (for Brazilians) and football (for Americans).

How could I have been distant in studying the phenomenon of Carnival (as a Brazilian) when it stirred up emotions, fantasies, feelings, and postures—especially political postures? Like Dostoyevsky's characters, it "dialogically" insisted in escaping my control, to gain a sort of space of its own in my studies. I had to deal *with* varieties of people in order to do justice to its complexity. When studying a distant tribe located on the other side of the world, one has "authority." One speaks *alone*. And one has total control over the phenomena to be presented for discussion. Here, the separation between me as investigator and my object of study was a given. I did not need a Geertz to tell me that the Apinayé ran the risk of becoming a "text."[14] My entire experience among them, and above all my efforts to *express this experience anthropologically,* confirmed that.

In my studies of Brazilian society, I found myself always facing versions and variations of phenomena that could from the outset have multiple texts. In this context, it is worth pondering if all social phenomena have a "text." What really takes one by surprise in studying one's own society is the discovery that there are social practices, institutions, and values virtually without a fixed form (or a text). There are in every society certain things that are to be talked about and others that are hidden. The latter are classified as taboo, mystery, secret, dogma—that which cannot be spoken, or even thought. Could a native of certain parts of New Guinea "textualize" his secret initiation? Could a priest reveal the secrets of a confession, transforming it into a titillating story? Could an Apinayé openly describe a case of witchcraft? Could a Brazilian betray a friend, telling the whole world the friend's sins and fears?

Two Fundamental Problems

These questions lead us to two fundamental problems. The first is the social (and political) conditions that govern the production of a text, which leads us back to the old problem of how one collects data in the field. Fieldwork, despite its rhetorical tricks, still is hard—and one could add—dirty work. (God knows that some anthropologists in the field would give anything for a good story.) The production of documents in ethnographic field research is as opportunistic and dependent on random events and good luck as the work of historians. One does not always have an opportunity to have a "dialogic" interaction.

The second fundamental problem is whether this relationship between society and narrative might become less visible when we are dealing with the study of our own system. As everyone who has studied controversial themes of Brazilian society knows, it is important to not talk about that which is classified as "taboo." It is just as problematic to talk about rope in a hanged man's house as it is to challenge the principle of authority in Brazil or to textualize—as Louis Dumont did—the hierarchy and inequality of India. It came as no surprise that Dumont's "textualization" of inequality in India (whose consequences are politically liberating) provoked negative, and frankly self-centered and solipsistic reactions among some Indian social scientists. A few even went so far as to question whether social anthropology was capable of transcending the distance that separates Indian culture—for these social scentists founded on incommensurable religious values—from the modern Western world dominated by its civic and political dimensions. It is clear that the problem is not only the Dumontian style of anthropology—easily seen as yet another form of ethnographic authority—but instead his revelation of a system based on inequality and hierarchy. The reaction to Dumont's work shows how anthropological discourses can be transparent in terms of their political implications, a feature that the design of Western academic institutions and "exo-ethnography" frequently disguises. A case similar to Dumont's with respect to Brazil is that of Gilberto Freyre (1933), who in writing *Casa Grande e Senzala* textualized a series of practices of the Brazilian elite—above all certain sexual activities—which were never supposed to be discussed openly. Gilberto Freyre told me that in 1933 there was a movement to burn *Casa Grande e Senzala* publicly under the allegation that it was a pornographic text. It was common to prohibit the book because it was seen as "very strong" for people of my generation. The book was shocking because it was a veritable textualization of the elite's intimate practices, and worse still, a textualization written by an insider.

THE ACADEMIC CONTEXTS OF ANTHROPOLOGY

An academic attitude which refuses to engage in "endo-ethnography" inhibits the most radical and profound critique of its own academic scene. The more established a university system is—the more individualistic the intellectual career, the more compartmentalized and autonomous and market-oriented the system of promotions and raises—the more debate tends to be viewed as "theoretical," "technical," and frankly "academic."

For the purposes of this discussion it is vital to try to understand the much-talked about distinction between "academic life" and "intellectual life," in relation to the American academic establishment.[15] I am inclined to think that the more compartmentalized a university system becomes—as is the case in North America and England—the more it has an "academic" rather than an "intellectual" life. But in countries like France, Italy, and throughout Latin America, where "intellectual activity" tends to encompass university life, the situation is reversed. In these countries, the goal is to be an "intellectual," read and known outside the academy. The academy is frequently viewed as limited, formal, and reactionary, or as a place where one has a mere "job" or does a little prestigious moonlighting. But it is not seen as socially significant. In Brazil, in order to become an intellectual, an academic has to reach beyond the "university walls" and try to affect the entire society.

In these systems, debates about ideas tend to turn into "endo-ethnographies"—into a lively discussion in which one argues not so much the theoretical problems which gave rise to the debate as questions that affect the society as a whole. In a system bounded by such parameters, it becomes very difficult to promote a moralistic and programmatic critique that tends to end up in "how-to" prescriptions, as is typical in the United States, where the academic system is made up of well-established islands (or fiefdoms) and the discussion of ideas often takes place in a compartmentalized manner.[16]

In criticizing a type of anthropology practiced by a colleague, a North American (or English) professional can afford the luxury of exaggerating to make a point. But rarely would an attack on an opponent's anthropological approach be linked to a particular political line—least of all to a specific party affiliation. The result is that debate tends to confine itself to one realm of the system, rarely overflowing the ivy-covered walls of the universities. But in countries in which the university system is not as compartmentalized, things happen in a different way. In these countries, specialized debates overflow the academic realm, get mixed up with politics, and end up by becoming truly "dialogic"— mobilizing a public which, even without understanding the technical aspects, declares itself in favor of one or the other side of the debate. What is at stake here is not the subject itself (which becomes a mere worthless "fact") but the "hidden agendas" that lie behind

the debate and reveal its true political character.[17]

It seems to me that these social situations give rise to different kinds of anthropologies. In societies where university life is fragile, where the education and research system tends to be pervaded by party politics, and where the public power structure is highly centralized, debates tend to be a "(pre)text" for radical and frequently demagogic proposals for reshaping the whole social system. One passes quickly from anthropological discussion to a debate about the whole society, and particularly about its system of power—a debate in which the most radical critique spares nothing and leaves nothing standing in its wake.

I believe that the most empiricist traditions tend to emerge and proliferate in countries where the academic systems are most compartmentalized. Another characteristic of academic movements is their purely programmatic and methodological approach. The direction is clearly stylistic, as if the discipline did not have more fundamental questions to confront and "resolve." Cultural problems should not be reduced to a poetic or to a politics of narrative style, nor should one dimension be radically separated from the other.

When all is said and done, it would be useful—if not indeed imperative—to discuss these academic movements in terms of the contexts from which they arise. Such a position would have three main aspects. First, it would reveal the maturity of a more critical, and less formalist and mimetic, "Brazilian anthropology." Secondly, it would demonstrate that the liberation from colonial limitations leads to taking the "center" as an object, with its prestigious creativity, challenging provocations, and severe limitations. Finally, it shows that the job of assessing anthropology is basically linked with the understanding that all anthropological ventures are made of flesh and bones, having a cultural, national, and historical context also filled with desires, values, and fantasies.

NOTES

1. I write from a "relativist" posture, and with a structuralistic bias, moved by what I suppose to be a healthy skepticism, justified by my professional experience. My arguments are aimed at several aspects of "interpretivism," some of which, it seems to me, have not been sufficiently contemplated. I am also motivated by the fact that I have experimented with a wide variety of "anthropologies." In my thirty years of anthropological practice I have studied two tribal societies (the Gê-speaking Gavies and the Apinayé of Central Brazil), as well as my own value system. I have also experimented with the sociological study of literary texts which I have treated as ethnographic documents.

2. We are dealing with an anthropology which, as Wilson Trajano Filho (1988) has noted, has been more concerned with questions of technique than with the traditional problems of the discipline.

3. The United States is perhaps the only known society which in many contexts defines itself as not having a culture—as being a "melting pot" or as possessing a multiplicity of "customs" which are "natural" and "universal" as self-evident truths. This contrasts with well-known North American legal and/or civic procedures which, besides being local, are rigidly applied and defined by the expression "it's the law!" Such civic procedures are omnipresent in the collective life of the United States. One might say that the United States denies itself as a "society" only to affirm itself as a "nation." As Louis Dumont says: We ourselves are made to look back to *our own modern culture and society as on a particular form of humanity* that is exceptional in that it denies itself as such by its profession of universalism (see Dumont 1986:207, italics in the original).

4. From my point of view, the idea of the "dialogic," which is intimately linked with the concept of "carnivalization," does not dismiss a holistic (and dynamically ambivalent) view of society. Moreover, the dialogic idea does not by itself guarantee nonauthoritarian, less distant and cold ethnographies, as Clifford himself is aware. In fact, it is quite possible to be extremely authoritarian and dialogic, as it is to be dialogic and still produce *impersonal ethnographies*—reports where relationships with the "other" are suppressed or repressed. On the question of individualism as an implicit value in American social sciences, see Hervé Varenne (1989). For important, if forgotten, thoughts on the absence of emotions (and I would add *personal involvement*) in anthropological fieldwork, see Francis Hsu (1983:172-173).

5. The use in Portuguese of a normative "plural of modesty" indicates the simultaneous (and ambiguous) use of a rhetoric of humility and authority. As specialists have pointed out, this modality of plural also implies "majesty" (Cunha, 1975:206) and/or "sovereign authority" (Lima, 1975:290). I owe these observations, as well as the relevant bibliography, to Professor Enylton de Sa Rego. For provocative considerations on the rise of the "I-form" in English, and some of its social, psychological, and political implications, see Franz Borkenau (1981).

6. In my opinion, it is "indigenism" *as an ideology* that will relate the unwieldy diversity of tribal cultures—with small populations and little voice in the national arenas—to a typically Ibero-Brazilian centralized (and essentialistic and antimodern) conception of "national society." Thus, "acculturation" and "assimilation" studies, so popular in Brazilian anthropology, can be read as ways of "overseeing" the trajectories of tribal societies which must take a single path—that which leads them into the "national society."

7. I must note that up to 1960, Brazilian anthropological studies were dominated by the classic "indigenist schema" proposed by Darcy Ribeiro. This is a paradigm based on a reinterpretation of Leslie White's evolutionism. For Darcy Ribeiro, in the same manner that societies evolve from primitive to civilized states, tribal groups within the national territory would also evolve in the direction of the national system. The two processes parallel each other. In this model, it is postulated that tribal societies enter the national order by means of an evolutionary, gradual process. First they enter into "intermittent contact" with pioneers; then in a phase of "permanent contact" they establish routinized links with segments of the national society; finally, they are "integrated" into the nation. This schema forgets that indigenous societies are not in fact uniform blocks, capable of being "properly" integrated into the national order. As I have noted elsewhere (DaMatta 1976b), territorial, political, and economic integration can occur without automatic assimilation of other spheres of tribal life. A tribal group may be economically assimilated while remaining relatively "isolated" (and autonomous) in terms of kinship system, ceremonial, and religious beliefs.

8. In order to do so, I had the example of David Maybury-Lewis, who had been my advisor at Harvard and who, in his works, treats this fragility most frankly (see Maybury-Lewis 1967, 1965). When I came into contact with Maybury-Lewis's work I was astonished by two facts: first, to find an anthropologist who had traveled with his family—something quite rare among Brazilian fieldworkers; and, second, to encounter an anthropologist who *related everything*. For us Brazilians, the project of traveling to the field certainly included a degree of distance, but our relationships with Indians and rural folk would soon acquire a familiar tone through

links of patronage and government agencies, potential political prestige, and the omnipresent Brazilian hierarchy. Moreover, the tradition of fieldwork in Brazil was much more *personalized*, and the journey became a sort of "macho" adventure in the style of the mythical "bandeirante," the historical explorer and exploiter of the Brazilian wild backlands.

The experience of traveling with a wife and child, however, as it is related by Maybury-Lewis, indicates a remarkable degree of isolation and fragility. The sum of these experiences certainly explains Maybury-Lewis's distanced, *but* sharp, perception of the social and institutional milieus of the society he visited. Thus, what I think should be pointed out is that fieldwork heightens this fragility, which is handled differently by diverse anthropological traditions. The English ethnographic style tends to incorporate it into a "scientific" impersonal report. In Brazil such experiences are not even mentioned.

To a good ethnography, one can apply Oscar Wilde's observations on Dostoyevsky's art: that he "never completely explains his characters" (Bakhtin 1981b:50). It seems to me that Evans-Pritchard's work and Malinowski's work are good instances of this authentic "dialogism"—a situation where native practices, beliefs, and cosmologies are more important than the ethnographer's own background and convictions. The characters of good anthropological monographs take over the author, speaking and living for themselves.

9. Bernard DeVoto's quip is aimed at Margaret Mead's works on American society and is cited by Geertz (1983:9).

10. Brushing one's teeth, having bathrooms, going to the dentist, and caring obsessively for the mouth as part of physical hygiene are relativized and transported from the realm of "science" applied and embedded in our common sense into the realm of pure "culture" and ideology by an "alien" observer. The result is a diatribe against the distinction between magic and science—"savage" and "civilized"—and, at the level of ethnographies and hermeneutics, an elegant demonstration of the power of distance and estrangement. Miner's article shows that what really matters is not only rhetoric, but a *vantage point* or a "theoretical perspective"—a fact which the "interpretivists" do not like to talk about. Thus, even when one tries to deconstruct standardized modes of "objective" description, one must not forget that the arguments also represent a "theoretical position" and that the new mode proposed also presents another way of doing—another formula.

11. After all, only a "quiet" anthropologist would really think (and believe) that the ethnographies he reads were always written in a cold and honest way, and are to be taken as expressions of "reality" in a true objective fashion. Malinowski's *Diary* could have only shocked the Anglo-American academic establishment, accustomed to think that nobody should lie or show deep ambiguities and contradictions. When read by Brazilian students, this work is taken as a proof that, thank God!, at least one of *them* is human!

12. It is known that at Oxford and Cambridge it tended to be taboo to carry out anthropological studies of one's own culture. Such studies were carried out at Manchester, where Max Gluckman acted unorthodoxly, provoking negative reactions to his work. Even today, graduate students in anthropology in many leading departments in North American academia are not encouraged to study their own society.

13. Writing about Gilberto Freyre's "originality," I emphasized (in DaMatta 1987a) that when Freyre wrote about the "Brazilian reality," he treated it as an encompassing moral universe—a world in which he had patent interests. Freyre seldom adopted a "disinterested," "distant," or "scientific" attitude with respect to his subject. On the contrary, he was always its proponent and wholehearted partisan (DaMatta,1987a:4). Freyre himself was well aware of this attitude when he wrote, in *Casa Grande e Senzala*, that the practice of sociology does not involve discovering scientific formulas, but rather "wanting to complete ourselves" (Freyre 1933, in DaMatta 1987a:5). Gilberto Freyre is one in a Ibero-American lineage of truly "dialogic anthropologies" in which the hermeneutic position is richly presented and where characters tend to overcome the author, speaking for themselves. One has to know and take this tradition more seriously in order to be so assertive about the nature of description and writing in the social sciences.

14. **Editor's Note:** As indicated in the introduction to Section One, "Diversity and Divergence," Geertz (1973:448-449) suggests that one examine "culture as an assemblage of texts"—that "cultural forms can be treated . . . as imaginative works built out of social materials."

15. For a classical discussion of the sociological position of the "American intellectuals," see Lipset (1959). It is worth recalling that in this essay, Lipset, significantly for what I am arguing here, provides a narrow definition of the "intellectual." This was noted and criticized by a commentator of European origin, Professor Karl Deutsch (see Deutsch 1959).

16. It may be suggested that behind the "interpretivist" movement, there is the hope of changing American academic life, bringing it out of the ghettos where it tends to be carried on. In this sense, their views reveal perhaps a deep dissatisfaction not only with anthropology but with the organization of American intellectual life.

17. The reader will allow me to indulge in a personal experience. In 1979 I wrote a response to some of the opinions espoused by Darcy Ribeiro ("A Antropologia Brasileira em Questo," in *Encontros com a Civilizaáo Brasileira,* September 1979) which were critical of the kind of anthropology practiced in the Museu Nacional's graduate program, where I had been the Director and held a senior post. My intention in responding to Darcy Ribeiro was threefold. First, I wanted to demonstrate that it was possible to exercise individual liberty in a tangible way, breaking out of the long-standing authoritarian and hierarchical pattern then governing Brazilian intellectual life, which held that no one should challenge a well-established person like Darcy Ribeiro. Secondly, I wanted to show that the social world could really be egalitarian and could permit various anthropologies to coexist simultaneously (that is, the ch ce of one anthropological style would not delegitimi or eliminate all others). Finally, I wanted to show that it was possible to practice an anthropology centered around theoretical problems, an anthropology that could prevent a Victorian, "evolutionist" indigenism from being used to stigmatize certain theoretical schools and from serving as a straitjacket to hinder certain experiences. If "indigenism" was a valuable legacy, it should not be transformed into demagogy which talked a lot about defending "Indians" while doing little to understand or respect them. In sum, I was coming out against the authority of a famous "boss" of the discipline. But as soon as my response had been published, I immediately realized that I was alone and that my academic point of departure had become a political issue.

INTELLECTUAL ROOTS

Roberto DaMatta is the Edmund P. Joyce, c.s.c., Professor of Anthropology and Senior Fellow of the Helen Kellogg Institute for International Studies at the University of Notre Dame. He studied two Indian societies of Central Brazil, the Gavioes in 1961, and the Apinayé, from 1962 to 1971. His best known books are *A Divided World: Apinayé Social Structure* (1982); *Carnivals, Rogues, and Heroes* (5th Brazilian edition, 1991; first American edition, 1991); and *A Casa & a Rua* (5th Brazilian edition, 1990). He was the Director of the Graduate Program in Social Anthropology of the National Museum (Federal University of Rio de Janeiro), Brazil, and the Chairperson of its Department of Anthropology. His edited books include *Universo do Futebol* (1982) and *E. R. Leach* (1983).

I came to Social Anthropology after receiving a B.A. in History from the Fluminense School of Philosophy, in Niteroi, State of Rio de Janeiro, in 1959. I first came into contact with the discipline through Professor Luis de Castro Faria. Castro also held a post at the National Museum in Rio and had field experience in ethnography (he was Claude Lévi-Strauss's companion in his researches in Brazil) and archaeology. Through him I became an intern at the museum, and started an association that lasted twenty-eight years. At the museum I met Professor Roberto Cardoso de Oliveira, who had a fundamental influence upon me. Cardoso de Oliveira had been a student of Florestan Fernandes at the University of Sao Paulo, and had also been a collaborator of Darcy Ribeiro at the Museu do Índio, in Rio. In 1961, he started an experimental graduate course at the museum that was basic in my life. Cardoso de Oliveira exposed me to Brazilian anthropology, American cultural anthropology, British social anthropology, and the French school of sociology. This approach was later to be reinforced by the association between Cardoso de Oliveira and David Maybury-Lewis—at the time, an assistant professor at Harvard—who was interested in doing comparative work with the Gê tribes of Central Brazil. Since I had done fieldwork with the Gavioes and the Apinayé, I went to Harvard as a special student in 1963-1964. This was decisive for my intellectual life. For a parochial Brazilian student from Niteroi, without international experience, but full of life and desire to learn, Harvard was pure paradise, and David Maybury-Lewis was of basic importance as a host, as a friend, and as an intellectual mentor. Harvard was also the center of a paradigmatic experience with a democratic nation and with the American way of life. In 1963-64, Thomas Beidelman was also teaching at Harvard, and he and James Fox (who was there in 1967-70 and had a great deal of interest and enthusiasm for structural studies) also influenced me. Since Maybury-Lewis, Beidelman, and Fox had all been Rodney Needham's students at Oxford, I soon became an avid reader of kinship theory and social organization. The work of Lévi-Strauss had the greatest impact in my intellectual life. This phase gained more importance with the beginning of the Harvard-Central Brazil Research Project, which brought to fieldwork in Brazil a group of young, bright, and well-prepared Harvard graduate students: Terry Turner, Joan Bamberger, Jean Carter Lave, Dolores Newton, Jon Christopher Crocker, and Cecil Cook Jr. They gave a cosmopolitan touch and a confident style to our mode of thinking. Our joint discussions at Harvard, where we were also in close contact with Pierre and Elli Maranda, and in Rio, where we had Julio Cezar Melatti (who studied the Kraho and was a member of the Project) and Roque Laraia, were certainly the most intense moments of these basic formative years. My relationship with Harvard lasted up to 1970, when I wrote my dissertation on the Apinayé and returned to Brazil to be the director of the Graduate Program in Social Anthropology of the National Museum.

In the 1970s Brazil was under a brutal authoritarian regime. Facing many critical challenges, I reoriented my intellectual focus and started to study Brazil. This interest increased my interest in the work of Victor Turner and Louis Dumont, who influenced a great deal of my work with Brazilian national rituals, daily life, mythical heroes, and literature. That change of focus also made me think of using my Brazilian and American experiences in a comparative way. This brought to my attention the work of Conrad Kottak. It also led me to read social history and political science. Right now, I am working with the implications of liberal and egalitarian social practices and values in relational societies like Brazil.

9

The Anthropological Discourse on India: Reason and Its Other

VEENA DAS

The Eurocentric nature of anthropology, as of several other social sciences, has long been recognized. What is unique about anthropology as a discipline, however, is its use of the "Other"—of societies and cultures radically different—to overcome the limits of anthropology's origin and location. In this paper I shall examine the "otherness" of Indian society and the role it has played in anthropological theory. It is ironic that controversies of anthropological theory are not only mirrored in the ideological conflicts in modern Indian society but may be also seen as having provided new spaces for these conflicts to be articulated.[1]

THE PROBLEMATIC ROLE OF THE INDIAN ANTHROPOLOGIST IN A "SOCIOLOGY OF INDIA"

I begin by asking a question—to whom is the anthropological text addressed and does the addressee influence the choice of the object? One of the most influential writers on Indian society, Louis Dumont, characterized the "predominant ideological note" of the social system in India as being one of traditional hierarchy. Hierarchy was chosen as the appropriate object of study because it constituted an absolutely contrasting pole to what he called "modern ideology," which was egalitarian in orientation. The purpose of studying this contrasting pole, according to Dumont (1971:2), was to isolate our ideology's essential qualities

in order to transcend them "because otherwise we get caught in it as the very medium of our thought."

This framing sentence makes it quite clear that taken as a charter for the legitimacy of anthropological research, the subjects of this research—the "we" as well as the audience to whom it is addressed—belong by definition to societies with "modern ideologies." Located spatially in the West, its very "modernity" puts an obligation on the audience to cultivate the ability to comprehend other values intellectually. As Dumont (1971:2) states:

The reader may, of course, refuse to leave the shelter of his own values; he may lay it down that for him man begins with the Declaration of the Rights of Man, and condemn outright anything which departs from it. In doing so, he certainly limits himself, and we can question not only whether he is in fact "modern," as he claims, but also whether he has the right to be so-called. In actual fact, there is nothing here like an attack, whether direct or oblique, on modern values, which seem in any case secure enough to have nothing to fear from our investigation. It is only a question of attempting to grasp other values intellectually (emphasis supplied).

Within such a description of the anthropological project, what intellectual space can anthropology create for itself in India? Is it better to characterize sociology/anthropology as *in* India, in the sense that India provides a location for the observation of cultural difference and its articulation? Or is it preferable to

133

think of a "sociology *of* India," as contended by Dumont, which could provide the means through which the Western yearning to escape the limits of its ideology intellectually could be fulfilled?

The danger for the Indian anthropologist is that she is vulnerable to the charge of being either "defensive" or "chauvinistic." The educated Hindu cannot speak with an authentic voice on matters pertaining to caste or religion since she is condemned to seeing the institutions of her society from a Western point of view.

Nowadays Hindus often assert to Westerners that caste is a social and not a religious matter. It is clear that motivation here is quite different; it is mainly a question of finding some justification for the institutions from a Western point of view, the point of view usually accepted by the educated Hindu. (Dumont 1971:26)

If, however, she speaks from a point of view that may be characterized as "Indian," or "Hindu" or "Islamic" she will be accused of being "backward looking." The only legitimate orientation to the traditions of one's own society that is permitted, it seems, is to place them squarely in the past. Let us revisit an old controversy between Dumont and two Indian anthropologists in order to appreciate the double bind in which the Indian anthropologist finds herself.

Dumont's Vision Regarding a "Sociology of India"

In his inaugural lecture on assuming the Chair of The Sociology of India in France in 1955, Dumont initiated the project of establishing a (new?) sociology of India which lay at the "confluence of sociology and Indology." In this project Dumont identified the caste system as the fundamental institution of Indian society which could be studied both at the textual and observational levels. The identification of caste as the fundamental institution

of Indian society, he maintained, allowed India to be conceptualized as *one*, despite observed regional and historical variations. Dumont was not unaware that to assert that the unity of India lay in its caste system could be construed as both a sociological proposition and a political statement. Thus, he wrote in 1960 (Dumont 1960:8-9) that he feared a misunderstanding of his project by some of his Indian readers. In his own words:

Have not some of our Indian readers found in the affirmation of the basic unity of Indian caste society more than a sociological proposition, something of the kind of a political affirmation, not to say a weapon? . . . To clear up all misapprehension it should suffice to recall that the unity to which we have referred not only is not a political unity but is a religious unity. In terms of the "ends of action," artha *is made subservient to* dharma *. . . this means here political disunity for the sake of religious supremacy. And the course of Indian history as a whole confirms this.*

While for the Western reader, the identification of the fundamental unity of India in the caste system is a question of apprehending other values *intellectually,* at least some Indian readers are likely to use this sociological proposition as a *political* weapon. We shall argue later that the concept of the nation (as essentially opposed to the traditions of the society within which it was being instituted) and of a time consciousness (that views the past as a threat to the future of the political stability of India) forms an important ideological debate in the public culture of Indian society. It is through these dual notions of "nation" *versus* community (read here caste), and a "past" that has to be consciously discarded that the political debate takes shape.

Dumont deals with the political implications of this by a methodological device. The spatial distance between India and the West allows Western scholars to study "caste" and its values at the level of the intellect. But these "obsolete" values provide neither political opportunities nor political challenges to the Western reader. To the Indian anthropologist who lives in societies imbued with these values, according to Dumont, the challenge is to overcome these traditional institutions and values in order to build a modern nation-state. The only attitude that the modern Indian can take to her own traditions is to place them in the past. In no case can these traditions offer an intellectual resource to contemporary societies. The functions of spatial distance (for Westerners) are performed by temporal distance (for Indians) so that her own past appears as the "other" for the Indian anthropologist.

The Ambiguous Role for Indian Social Scientists in Dumont's Vision

In 1962 the Indian sociologist A. K. Saran, who has shown a consistent concern with the implications of sociology as a Western discipline for the development of knowledge systems of India, wrote a review of some of Dumont's work (Saran 1962). In this review, Saran argued Dumont's claim that an external view of Indian society was more objective than an internal view was a positivist trap. An external view, he contended, is nothing else but one culture interpreted through the categories of another, alien, culture. Such a questioning of the concept of an external view—that it is somehow more objective—is neither startling to philosophy nor to anthropology. Indeed, the idea of reality independent of its description would be very difficult to sustain in modern philosophical discourse. Geertz (1973) commented upon the epistemological proximity of ethnography and fiction. He suggested that conventions whereby truth is asserted and accepted in ethnography and fiction are part of a nonfictional narrative tradition which achieves an illusion of fact through innocent fictions.[2] Indeed it may be almost considered conventional now to discuss the "crisis of representation" in the context of the

dismantling of the claims to ethnographic authority with reference to an "objective" or "external" reality.

Yet Dumont's reaction to Saran was not framed in terms of a dialogue about the nature of the world that the ethnographer creates or represents, but rather to castigate Saran as a fascist. The following two quotations speak for themselves:

While the Western social anthropologist longs for seeing his own culture—i.e. the culture which at present dominates materially the world—"in perspective," Dr. Saran wants to be left alone in blissful possession of his neo-Hindu creed. This is understandable, for Hindu religion and philosophy is at least as all embracing in its own way as any socio-logical theory may be. (Dumont 1966:26).

The ambiguity contained in this statement is overthrown in the next page:

What I find most disquieting is that Dr. Saran seems to be unaware of the dangers of the large scale implications of his stand. We Europeans have had one master who would have taught us the impenetrability of cultures (he said races); his name was Adolf Hitler. Solipsism is far from incompatible with violence. . . . I hope that this much justice may be rendered us: that we have brought some contribution to smoothing the path of understanding, without underestimating the difficulties and obstacles. I should have thought that a scholar of Dr. Saran's standing would not lend a hand to neo-Hindu "provincial" and backward feelings. (Dumont 1966:27)

In these remarkable passages, Dumont seems to construct in a single moment, both, India as an anthropological object and the conditions under which (modern?) Indians may lay claim to a legitimate place in the world of anthropological scholarship. For the Western anthropologist, it is part of her modern enlightenment values to comprehend values of other cultures intellectually. This aids her attempt to convert ideology into an instrument of scientific reasoning. This intellectual attempt, however, poses no threat to her present values since the "otherness" of alien cultures can remain hermetically sealed—being separated as it is by distance—from the regular life of the anthropologist and the audience for which she usually writes.[3] For the Indian anthropologist, however, there is no possibility of participation in the demystification of "universalist," "objectified" categories of Western sociology by showing the traces of an alien culture in the making of these categories. The possibility of transcending their own ideology through an intellectual appropriation of other values is open to the Western anthropologists. But Indian anthropologists have no legitimate way of applying the same method to the ideology of their own culture. The knowledge categories of non-Western cultures are simply unanchored beliefs, whereas the Western categories acquire the status of scientific and objective truths.

The future of a sociology that may be rooted in the values of a culture different from that of the West is foreclosed, for it is known beforehand that such a sociology would be a fascist sociology—"neo-Hindu," "provincial," and "backward." Thus the fate of Indian systems of knowledge is sealed. They can have a place in the history of ideas; they can be intellectually apprehended to provide means by which "we" of the West can transcend the limits of "our" ideology. But they are not present as resources for the construction of knowledge systems inhabited by the modern Indian. Other cultures acquire legitimacy only as objects of thought, never as instruments for thought. I do not say that the value of Dumont's work is exhausted by this description[4]—only that where the Indian anthropologist is the direct addressee of his discourse, her role is limited to that of an informant. The condition for participation in the making of the sociological discourse for the non-Western anthropologist is an active renunciation of contemporary possibilities in her own culture.

INDIAN CONSTRUCTIONS SHAPING WESTERN CONSTRUCTIONS OF INDIA

I turn now to another important strand in Dumont's sociology—his commitment to the notion of totality, to a stable reality and with it, to a stable system of representation. I argue that this stability of representation is achieved by privileging one worldview—that of the (or to be more accurate, one of the) Brahmanical concepts of tradition and assuming that it can represent Indian society as an "objective totality" of the world. I hasten to add that this objective totality is not an empirical or quantitative notion for Dumont. Rather Dumont uses the notion of hierarchy to exclude contingent particulars in order to grasp the underlying laws of Indian society and history.

It is the linkage between the principle of totality and the principle of hierarchy that allowed Dumont to accommodate criticisms about his neglect of other values in Indian society by treating them as empirically present but theoretically residual. Thus practices of lower castes were contemptuously dismissed with the following remark, "Because barbers shave one another, someone [who Dumont does not even care to name] would like to conclude that 'equality and reciprocity' have the same importance as does hierarchy in the system." The whole point of drawing attention to practices among lower castes that stood in opposition to Brahmanical practices was to interrogate the notion of a "system" or of a "totality" which privileged the worldview of the Brahmin, giving it the status of an "objective" truth. In positioning the Brahman as the only "voice," Dumont was in fact participating in the creation of a master narrative of Indian society which saw Brahmanical worldviews as somehow representative of the whole of Indian society.

Burghart: The Brahmanic Shaping of Dumont's Analysis

Why has the Brahmanical worldview been so privileged in the anthropological discourse on India? Burghart (1990) gives an interesting reason for the centrality of the Brahmin as the "other" of anthropological discourse. When anthropologists began to look at the Indian subcontinent as an arena of anthropological interpretation, Burghart (1990:261) argues, they discovered that "it was already occupied and defined by local counterparts—Brahmins and ascetics who spoke about the social universe in the name of Brahma."

The encounter between these two modes of constructing knowledge—that of the Brahmin and of the anthropologist—was of interest, according to Burghart, because "both types of persons totalize social relations as a system in which they act as knowers and in which their knowledge transcends that of all other actors" (1990:261). He then goes on to describe the different anthropological modes in which knowledge about India was constructed, primarily as a function of the different kinds of dialogues between anthropologist and the Brahmanical tradition. These dialogues, he argues, range from an active avoidance of the Brahmanical tradition (as in the work of the Indian anthropologist M. N. Srinivas) to complete imitation of it as in Louis Dumont. In Burghart's reckoning, then, far from the Orient being a European projection as argued by Said (1978) and more recently for India as argued by Inden (1986, 1990), the subjectified peoples, the objects of anthropological research enter the text of the anthropologist not only as suppliers of raw data but also as people who have actively framed the research project and its outcome.

Applying this insight to an analysis of Dumont's work, Burghart argues that the Brahmanical counterparts of Dumont were not passive objects of scholarly perception but, rather, they enabled and framed his representation of caste. In fact "representation" is not even the right word to use in this context. Burghart states that "My reading of Dumont starts from [the] observation [that Dumont is a European Brahmin] and culminates in the view that the singularity of *Homo Hierarchicus* lies not in Dumont's representing the Brahman's view of Hindu society but in his imitating the Brahmin's representation of Hindu society" (1990:268). It is precisely because the Brahmanical tradition sees history as a series of resemblances, for example, that Dumont can talk of caste as it appeared in the texts of Manu in the second century A.D. and caste as it functions in village society in contemporary India as if they pertained to the same ethnographic reality.

The distinction between local circumstances (for which customary rules were valid) and authoritative knowledge (which was only contained in texts) was crucial to the Brahmanical construction of tradition. Srinivas came to terms with this disjunction by positing a sharp difference between "book view" and "worldview" in Indian society and reserving the latter as the legitimate domain of enquiry for the anthropologist.[5] Dumont, according to Burghart, simply imitated this distinction between empirical truths and ideology, allowing him, like the Brahmins, to treat diversity as a residual, or leftover remainder, in relation to textual truths. Far from India being a projection of the European imagination, then, the Brahmanical imagination manages to shape the European representation of India within an order of mimesis.

If Burghart's characterization of Dumont's work as an imitation of the Brahmanical view of tradition is correct, then it is all the more interesting that this counterpart of Dumont, the Brahmin, must be located in India's past. For many, any attempt at developing a language of sociology that has its roots in Indian tradition is not worthy of an intellectual confrontation. It is simply considered dangerous for the building of an Indian nation based on modern values.

Burghart does not carry his reflections further. But questions remain. Are native social anthropologists to be regarded as native spokespersons? Do they earn membership in the anthropological community on condition that they renounce (not simply transcend) all forms of knowledge acquired through membership in the society of which they now write?[6] With these issues we come back to the question we posed in the introduction—what intellectual space can anthropology create for itself in India?

LOCATING THE ROLE OF ANTHROPOLOGICAL (AND SOCIAL SCIENCE) DISCOURSE IN INDIAN SOCIETY TODAY

Critiquing Past Politics: The Underlying Agenda of Colonial Representations

It was stated in the introduction to this paper that anthropology as a discipline not only mirrors the ideological conflicts of modern Indian society but has also helped to create new spaces for their articulation and enactment. I shall take one contemporary conflict which has been the subject of considerable discussion, both in the public realm and in the social science literature, in India. I do not enter into this discussion in order to provide a "solution" to a vexed debate but rather to show how much of social science literature in India shares the assumptions of the modern nation state and indeed, construes itself in response to contemporary political needs.

The controversy that I refer to is known as the Ramjanmabhumi-Babri Masjid dispute and it relates to rival claims made by Hindus and Muslims over a sacred site in the city of Ayodhya. Certain Hindu groups have claimed that on the basis of historical evidence, they can prove that this was the site of a temple built to commemorate the birthplace of Lord Rama, a much revered kingly

deity of the Hindus. They claim that this temple was destroyed by the orders of Babur, a Muslim king in the sixteenth century, and a mosque was built to commemorate his victory over the Hindu kingdoms. Several Muslim organizations, on the other hand, claim that there is no firm historical evidence that a mosque was built on the site of a temple. This issue has led to unprecedented mobilization on both sides. Every major political party has been involved in the controversy, and the mobilization of people on either side has been accompanied by much violence in the form of communal riots and police violence in which the Muslims have suffered more because of their vulnerability as minorities.

Although this dispute has now taken a volatile form, historians have been quick to point out that narratives of this dispute figure in the administrative records of the British. As most social scientists have now become aware, the administrative record cannot be treated as documentary evidence of an "undiluted" truth. If the record gives such an impression, it is because it evolved certain conventions for the assertion of truth borrowed from, and framed by, dominant anthropological theories of the time. The manner in which this "official" truth may be read reflects British understandings of the nature of Indian society. Pandey (1990:21) states the problem succinctly:

The modern history of India, in this sense, was first written in colonial times and by colonialists. It was colonialist writers who established the pattern of the Indian past pretty much as we know it today. And in that pattern sectarian strife was an important motif.

By the end of the nineteenth century, the dominant strand in colonialist historiography was representing religious bigotry and conflict between people of different religious persuasions as one of the more distinctive features of Indian society, past and present—a mark of the Indian section of the "Orient."

Pandey and others have shown how this particular representation of India led to such crystallized narratives as "the colonial riot narrative" in which there was "an emptying out of all history—in terms of the specific variations of time, place, class, issue—from the political experience of the people, and the identification of religion, or the religious community, as the moving force of all Indian politics" (Pandey 1990:24). Regardless of the time when a riot occurred, or the space in which it occurred, or the issue (e.g., desecration of sacred space, abduction of a woman, or protest over government legislation), the British official discourse saw the same event structure in every riot.

Given this framework within which Indian history was viewed, it is not surprising that in the case of the dispute in Ayodhya, the British would have seen themselves as the fair and neutral arbiters of an age-long dispute between Hindus and Muslims. It is from this point of view that the problem of ascertaining the historical merits of rival claims became a major issue for the British officials. In the official narrative of the dispute as it was framed, the following are muted: (1) the events which pointed to cooperation between Hindus and Muslims, (2) the rivalry between different Muslim groups to establish their own influence and patronage and, most importantly, (3) the role of the British administration in making decisive interventions to alter the local power structures in order to establish loyal Muslims in positions of power. From the official narrative it is difficult to guess that the patronage offered by several Muslim Nawabs to Hindu worship as well as rivalries between different Hindu sects played an important role in the evolution of Ayodhya as a pilgrim center.

The result is a master narrative evolved by the colonial state in which the dispute over the temple and the mosque appears as one more instance of the eternal conflict between Hindus and Muslims in which the British appear as neutral mediators. It is not my case

that the Indians were passive pawns in these events. Rather I am suggesting there was a complex agency at work in which British concepts of Indian society, altered configurations of local and regional forces, and new ways of defining legitimacy played a role in the evolution of this, and several other similar, disputes. The narrative of the colonial state was constructed so as to give an impression of the sealing of local codes of conduct from the encompassing bureaucratic and legal institutions that a colonial power had illegitimately introduced.

Supporting Present Politics: The Imaging Power of the Nation-State

In contemporary India, social science discourse provides a charter, on scientific grounds, to legitimize the right of the state not only to govern but also to shape modern Indian identity. I cannot emphasize enough that I am not posing a contrast in intellectual stances between "foreign" anthropologists (such as L. Dumont) and "native" social scientists (such as S. Gopal), but showing the routes by which convergence has occurred. Let me illustrate this point with the help of a discussion on the Ramjanmabhumi-Babri Masjid dispute by the distinguished social historian Sarvepalli Gopal (1991).

Defining Religion in Terms of the State's Needs. Gopal sees this dispute as reflective of a general sickness in Indian society. "The Ramjanmabhumi issue . . . brings into sharper focus than at any time since 1947 a sickness which free India has not been able to shake off and demands reappraisal of many basic features of our society" (1991:11). This sickness which comes in the way of "civilized principles of national cohesion" (1991:13) is directly related to the deep entrenchment of religion in the Indian soil. "The logical attitude of getting rid of religion altogether," says Gopal, "was too utopian for Indian society, where many religions were deeply entrenched" (1991:13).

Thus the practical solution was not opposition to religion but the relegation of religion to the private life of the individual, expelling it from all forms of public life. This is not the place to examine such a version of secularism in any great detail except to point out that the distinction between private and public is by no means as simple or uncomplicated as Gopal assumes it to be.

What interests me here is the attempt to define religion in a manner that would be consistent with the needs of the nation-state. On the true nature of Hinduism, Gopal (1991: 14) has this to say:

While there is no Hindu religion in the sense in which that term is generally used, there is an atmosphere, a structure of feeling, which governs the different sects and lifts them to higher levels. This common element in the faith which binds together those who call themselves Hindus in the various parts of India is the acceptance of religion as spiritual experience, as the direct apprehension of the reality of the one supreme Universal Spirit. Devotion to truth and respect for all human beings, a deepening of inner awareness and a commitment to compassion form the essence of the Hindu religion.

Although the construction of this passage is in the indicative tense—as if a timeless truth about the essence of Hinduism is being asserted—it is obvious that what is being constructed is a view of religion that is consistent with the political needs of the state. A Hinduism that is emptied of all political content and all other functions except the other-worldly ones of meditation on the supreme universal spirit leaves the political arena free for the play of other forces. (This view of Hinduism corresponds only to the highly Brahmanical great tradition in which involvement with worldly affairs was considered suspect.)

Portraying Religious Communities in Terms of the State's Own Constructed Image. Romila Thapar uses the phrase "imagined religious communities" to characterize the nature of community as it was "imagined" in the administrative discourse of the British rulers. The sense of imagined here is that of something that is fabricated and thus false. It is important to recall here that Benedict Anderson (1983), who used this phrase to characterize the nature of modern nations, was interested in capturing the constructed nature of nations rather than declaring them to be inauthentic or false. In proposing the definition of a nation as an imagined political community, he also proposed that we treat all communities, with the exception of primordial village face-to-face communities, as imagined communities in the sense that their members do not know each other in their concrete existence and yet in each member lives an image of their communion. For Anderson, the "political" power of nationalism is only matched by its philosophical poverty and even incoherence. It is, then, interesting to note that despite this philosophical poverty the discourse of nationalism provides the image for the shaping of other communities, including religious communities in modern India.

As counterparts of the nation-state, religious "communities" also create images of communion between people who do not have any concrete relationships with each other. In the controversy on the temple and the mosque, for instance, certain Hindu groups came into being whose main agenda was the creation of such images of communion. The literature produced by militant Hindu groups emphasized issues such as the high fertility rate of the Muslims and the fear that Hindus would become "minorities" in their own land. Clearly this vision of the community as purely a numerical entity can exist only within the framework of a governmentality that takes for granted the collection of regular statistical information about the different communities that form the "nation" because it has no other definition of community except a numerical one.

From the point of view of the nation-state, religion occupies an illegitimate space when it lays claims to the construction of the past that is in conflict with the institutionalized memories sacralized by the nation-state. What the Hindu groups in this case seem to be doing is challenging this distribution of functions by imaging themselves in the same mold as the nation-state. Anderson had argued that the nation as an imagined community has strong religious roots but that it is by limiting the religious imagination that the nation as a sovereign and essentially limited community can be imagined.

We now see that by defining themselves essentially within the same arena of historicity as the nation-state, the religious community limits its own possibilities of addressing fundamental human questions of suffering and redemption and becomes narrow and parochial. This, however, does not represent a perversion of religion but rather a simple testimony to the simultaneous power and philosophical poverty of nation-state ideologies.

Is there a vision in the traditional construction of community that could escape the imaging power of the nation-state which acts as the touchstone of all modern values? In the next section we consider the attempt of Saran to offer such a possibility and we critique the nostalgic rendering of the traditional community which marks the other pole of social science research in contemporary India.

Critiquing Modern Life: The "Traditional" Community

The concept of community was closely tied, in the classical sociological literature, to the idea of a spatially bound, face-to-face sphere of human relationships based upon an innate moral order. According to Benedict Anderson (1983), the community institutes itself in the modern world not as a face-to-face sphere of human relations but as an imagined community that demands allegiance from people who have no concrete relations with each other by creating images of communion and oneness among them. It is interesting to observe that

the crisis of modernity, represented as the death of God, evoked a nostalgic construction of loss of community (in classical sociological reflections) and loss of virtue (in contemporary philosophical commentaries). The contrast made by Tonnies (1957) between *Gesellschaft* and *Gemeinschaft* posited community as arising out of a response to the needs of real, organic life. Society was characterized as a form of social relationship based upon artificial and mechanical relationships of reflective will. His formulation suggests that one goes into Gesellschaft (society) as one goes into a strange country.

In more recent studies, community has been treated as a resource for remoralizing areas of life denuded of moral meaning by the growth of a bureaucratic, impersonal rationality (see especially Unger 1975). We see two major problems in this nostalgic rendering of community. The first is that by ignoring the extent to which violence plays a role in defining community, the nostalgic view gives a rather sanitized view of tradition and community. Secondly it overlooks the fact that community, in the contemporary context, is defined as much by structures of modernity, including bureaucratic law, as by a customary innate order.

The view that a sociology that has its roots in India finds its justification in the radical critique of the modernist vision of life inspires the work of many social scientists in contemporary India. Saran represents a powerful voice in the articulation of this vision. For him the articulation of tradition is not so much a return to a glorious past as the development of a different notion of "normality" that may challenge (what he considers to be) the pathologies of modern society. The most developed political credo that is capable of mounting this challenge, according to Saran, is found in Gandhian thought. However, Gandhian thought cannot be studied, according to Saran (1989:681), in isolation from the tradition to which it belongs.

One has to go beyond Gandhi's [writings] and plumb deeper and deeper into his life-and-thinking in an endeavour to reach the center of Gandhian thinking, that is the center from which Gandhi starts and to which he returns. . . . Gandhi strove to discover a center wholly beyond the modern Western civilization. This center is what has usually been called the "primordial Tradition."

Saran considers the political sphere to be *the* domain for the exercise of such a "radically spiritual" critique. Fundamental to this critique is an examination of human life in terms of three kinds of relationships—that of man to nature; of man to man; and man's relation to the divine. Saran contends that the fragmentation in human life which has come about in the modernist vision of life is premised upon a division between these three types of relationships. In the traditional vision the man-god relation provides the paradigm for all other kinds of relations. It follows that such modern concepts as the principle of competition, the desire to overcome suffering, and the idea of progress are based upon "untruth." Thus Saran has no difficulty in supporting Gandhi's ideas about the evils of modern Western medicine as well as modern Western education. Saran (1989:721), incidentally, bases his support of Gandhi not only on the excesses of modern medicine but on a different theory of suffering altogether.

Sickness can affect both man's body and mind, but the distinction between bodily and mental and spiritual sickness is not sharply drawn in traditional civilizations which always cater to the needs of both together. All sickness and suffering has a spiritual and cosmological significance just as ignorance is ultimately ignorance of who one is. Accordingly, all knowledge is knowledge of one's true Self . . . and all healing is healing of the wound of ignorance of one's real Self.

This passage also signifies the limits of such a vision for the building of an anthropological space in India in the context of contemporary

theories of knowledge. What Saran has been seduced by is the vision of traditional Indian civilization as the "Other." While Dumont was quite misleading in suggesting that Saran was only capable of cultural solipsism, the totalizing tendency of his thought makes the concept of tradition rise above that of contested sites. Yet the experience of tradition in Indian society, as in many similar societies, is that it has a double entrenchment—one in institutions that may be considered traditional, such as caste or religion, and second in institutions that may be considered modern, such as bureaucracy and law.

It is this double articulation which makes such institutions as caste or religious community into a new and original entity—it is not a matter of aggregation in which new features are added on to old ones. When, for instance, Gandhi uses *satyagraha* as a form of nonviolent resistance to the British rule, he transforms a traditional concept into a *new* concept. It is only within the Brahmanical theory of time, alluded to earlier in this paper, that Saran can treat this as an instance of "traditional" thinking.

CONCLUSION: A PLURALITY OF VIEWS

Ranajit Guha puts across the argument extremely well when he talks of an ensemble of overdetermining effects constituted by a double meaning in which "the ideological moments of social contradictions in pre-colonial India and modern England were fused with those of the living contradictions of colonial rule to structure the relation" of dominance and subordination. If this double articulation is the feature of both tradition and modernity in contemporary India, then we cannot have a simple recourse to the notion of progress, as an uncontested notion, to critique tradition. Conversely, a nostalgic construction of ideas of traditional community, as a resource for building an alternate vision to that of modernity, is also not available.

We cannot uphold the claims of the nation-state to be the provider of all value; but we cannot also go along with Saran and construct a total "traditional man." It seems that given the constructed nature of culture, and the contests over the ethical spaces within which the social sciences may place themselves, the only honorable place left for anthropology is one in which the seductions of consensus in the name of both modernity and tradition have to be avoided.

Unlike the social scientists who came into the world of knowledge as part of the anti-colonial, nationalist enterprise, the modern generation of social scientists in India has to live with a destruction of certainty as the condition under which they engage in the production of knowledge about Indian society. They cannot "represent" India as if India were absent and silent. They can only insert their voices within a plurality of voices in which all kinds of statements—prescriptive, normative, descriptive, indicative—are waging a virtual battle about the nature of Indian society and the legitimate space for social sciences in this society.

NOTES

1. This paper does not intend to provide a comprehensive survey of the problem. It only makes certain incisions into the literature of social sciences to illuminate certain problems in the anthropological discourse of Indian society.

2. For an analysis of this view, see Steven Webster (1982).

3. Dumont was quite mistaken to imagine that "other cultures" would remain hermetically sealed from modern Western life. In France, the decision of Muslim girls to wear the veil to school has created much controversy. The Salman Rushdie affair brought to light the fact that in England, laws against blasphemy applied to Christianity but not to other religions. It seems that in the context of modern global societies it will become very difficult to keep cultures apart in hermetically sealed compartments. The otherness experienced in faraway places is already part of one's own life-world in European societies.

4. The centrality of Dumont's writings on India is attested by several symposia on his work in which Indians (including myself) have participated and expressed their admiration for his remarkable abilities to bring together a wide range of materials within a single theoretical frame. What one senses, however, in Dumont as in several other scholars is an impatience with modern Indian scholarship which is seen as imbued with the experience of colonialism—as if to be touched by one's own history is to have become inauthenticated.

5. For a critique of this distinction, see Das (1977).

6. The compulsions of having to signal the entry into the field, as if the field were an alien land, is evident in Srinivas' (1977) account of Rampura. Its most poignant expression may be found, however, in Madan (1978) who speaks of living intimately with "strangers." The strangers were Kashmiri Pandits, members of his own community in a village not far from where Madan grew up. We find several interesting reflections in Srinivas of the consequences of his being a Brahmin. But whereas the problems of representing the other who is outside have received much attention in the last decade, a similar concern with the otherness within has hardly received any attention.

INTELLECTUAL ROOTS

Veena Das is Professor of Sociology at the Delhi School of Economics, University of Delhi. She is the author of *Structure and Cognition: Aspects of Hindu Caste and Ritual,* Oxford University Press, Delhi, 1977; and editor of *The Word and the World: Fantasy, Symbol and Record,* Sage Publications, Delhi, 1986; and *Mirrors of Violence: Communities, Riots and Survivors in South Asia,* Oxford University Press, Delhi, 1990. She has taught in the University of Delhi since 1968. She has held visiting appointments at the University of Chicago, University of Harvard, Amherst College, and University of Heidelberg. She is currently one of the editors of the journal *Contributions to Indian Sociology.* She has been awarded the Ghurye Award in 1977 and the VKRV Rao award in 1986.

I cannot find any systematic pattern in my development as an anthropologist. I was privileged to be a student of M. N. Srinivas at the University of Delhi. Srinivas had been a student of G. S. Ghurye at Bombay University and Radcliffe Brown at the University of Oxford. Although at Delhi University, Srinivas emphasized the "field view" of Indian society and opposed it to the "book view," he encouraged me to use my training in Sanskrit for the construction of sociological problems. That is how I began to work on the lesser known Sanskrit texts of thirteenth-century Gujarat for my doctoral dissertation. Since I had a consuming interest in relocating Sanskrit texts in modern knowledge systems, I found the work of Louis Dumont absolutely fascinating. The structuralist method for the study of myth opened many doorways for me in my early twenties. I used to imagine that Claude Lévi-Strauss was perhaps a modern-day avatar of an ancient or medieval Sanskrit scholar who had to risk his salvation when he chose one theory of language as against another! All this is to say that the ideas of structuralism and later of narrative analysis were made available to me not only in the texts in which they were contained but also by creating a different genealogy for them in the Sanskritic tradition. In 1982 I explicitly tried this method by posing the *mimamsa* school of ancient Indian philosophy as interlocutor to contemporary anthropological theories of sacrifice in the Henry Myers Lecture that I was privileged to deliver. I am happy that categories of knowledge emanating in non-Western cultures are engaging the social anthropologists but regret the totalizing frames within which these are formulated.

Now when I reflect back I can recognize in my intellectual preoccupations the desperate need to escape to a collective past that would overcome the violence all around me. But the immediacy began to press on me and I began to resent the role of anthropology as a purveyor of dreams. Slowly I learnt to engage the problems of my immediate environment. Since 1984 I have been engrossed with the understanding of violence and the way in which moral communities are created through suffering. These concerns stem from some aspects of my personal biography, some contingent events which threw me right in the middle of catastrophic violence, and the advice Srinivas once gave me, that a social anthropologist must feel her way into the environment as an animal feels it—not only as an intellectual preoccupation but as a way of being. How I have been able to translate this vision will be tested in my forthcoming book, *Critical Events*, where I have tried to show how social anthropology helps us to redescribe such critical events as communal riots during the partition of India, the emergence of *sati* in modern India, the chemical disaster in Bhopal, by recreating pain as an anthropological object. In this process I have learnt to read classical scholars like Durkheim and Nietzsche as intensely preoccupied with the problem of pain. Although I cannot claim descent from the long line of venerable scholars who created social anthropology as a discipline, I think the kind of work being done in so-called marginal spaces like India and Brazil will claim this tradition and shape its future.

The community of scholars in Delhi, especially Andre Beteille, Ashis Nandy, J. P. S. Uberoi, Ritu Menon, and Upendra Baxi, and, elsewhere, Richard Burghart, Audrey Cantalie, and Arthur Kleinman, have acted as critical anchors in my development. I cannot emulate them in being able to define a central focus to my research for I seem to live intellectually as a completely contingent being. This too, as Kierkegaard said, is a reflective choice.

Rethinking Past Perspectives

I n describing (and offering appreciation for) cultural orientations different from those we are familiar with, anthropology tends to call into question—either implicitly or explicitly—taken-for-granted understandings. It emphasizes that our norms are not the only norms; our values not the only values. Anthropology stretches us intellectually. It encourages an appreciation of the culturally unfamiliar, helping us to see ourselves in broader perspective. As Boas (1928) observed in his 1928 forward to Margaret Mead's *Coming of Age in Samoa*: The "attitudes of foreign cultures . . . set off in strong light our own."

Anthropology not only applies its role as an agent of "cultural critique" (in Marcus and Fischer's 1986 phrasing) to Western culture. It also applies the same role to itself. Part of the impetus behind what Wolf (page 220) views (in this section) as the continuous "slaying" of paradigms is the constant anthropological concern with rethinking the intellectually accepted of the discipline. It is, in some ways, how anthropology has theoretically progressed to date.

In this section we consider a number of such "rethinkings." Rappaport and Bernard offer two perspectives on the positivist/interpretivist debate. Levy, Yanagisako and Collier, and Strathern reconceptualize respectively: the relation of person to context, gender to kinship, and social parts to social wholes. And Wolf and Scheper-Hughes suggest new ways of looking at the dynamics of power and disempowerment.

Continually rethinking the accepted has its problems as various authors in this volume emphasize. If one is not careful, it can leave the discipline without a common core, without a firm foundation on which to build. But the rethinking process can also be positive. It can lead to new insights, new syntheses, that move the discipline forward—as the contributions in this section illustrate.

STANDARDS OF EVALUATION

How does one evaluate "rethinkings" of past perspectives in anthropology? How does one separate the wheat from the chaff, the positive from the negative? It is not easy. Ideally, one would prefer to test new perspectives against specific data—to determine their effectiveness in explaining that which remains unclear. Harris (page 64), Goodenough (page 263), and others set out criteria for such evaluations. But as the first two sections of this volume make clear, anthropology has generally not reached the stage where it can carry out precise, effective, scientific tests—at least not yet. (That is why Bernard lays such stress on methods in this section.) Presently, a host of difficulties—including the quality, completeness, and comparability of data available for evaluation—

145

make a straightforward confirmation or rejection of a new perspective problematic.

Still, there are criteria many, perhaps most, anthropologists use in judging intellectual innovations. The key criteria center around the perspective's intellectual power: Does it suggest new, productive ways for resolving old problems, old oppositions? Is it more effective than existing perspectives in handling particular concerns? Does it lead to suggestive, new insights? Numerous intellectual innovations have fit these criteria in the discipline's history.

The Malinowskian-Boasian concern for fieldwork is a prominent one. Prior to the early part of this century, a different "economy of ethnographic knowledge" (in Clifford's 1988:27 terms) prevailed. There were "armchair" anthropologists who did little ethnographic research. And there were the "men on the spot" (as Frazer phrased it)—missionaries, travelers, administrators, traders—who knew a culture from extensive, firsthand experience. The problem that arose was the abstract theories spun back in the metropole by "armchair" anthropologists often went astray in the interpretations of ethnographic data. Cultural meanings got lost in the letters written back and forth between the two groups. Informants' suggestive, figurative associations in the field, for instance, became assertions of actual belief back in the metropole (see Lewis 1986). Malinowski and Boas stressed anthropologists needed to engage, as part of their training, in lengthy community-oriented fieldwork with extensive participant observation to understand a culture. One had to live, Malinowski asserted, "right among the natives" (1961:6). The innovation gained widespread acceptance. Where previously some anthropologists had conducted fieldwork, by the 1930s almost all anthropologists did. It became established practice. Today, fieldwork experience generally constitutes a rite of passage for obtaining a Ph.D. in anthropology. Only now, with linkages beyond local communities so clear, the variations among locales so obvious, are we reaching the limits of this community-based fieldwork approach. We can no longer explain broad cultural phenomena by restricting ourselves to intensive fieldwork in one locale at one moment in time.

Another example of a successful innovation is Lévi-Strauss's analysis of myth. Prior to his development of structural analysis, myths were usually interpreted anthropologically from one of two perspectives. They were analyzed in psychological terms. Kluckhohn (1942) suggested, for instance, that myths reduced anxieties through establishing a sense of a cultural order and continuity. Or they were, following Malinowski (1948), seen as mythological charters for the present, as ways for grounding and justifying existing institutions. Lévi-Strauss (1963) formulated three key innovations. First, he suggested that the analysis of myths should focus less on specific details of content, regarding who did what when, and more on "bundles" of relations, on the relationships among events, objects, animals, and/or humans in a myth. Second, he stressed the importance of different versions. One account was not simply an imperfect copy of another, "correct" version. Rather, all collected versions were important and needed to be analyzed. They expressed, to use a musical analogy, variations on a common theme. And third, Lévi-Strauss (1963:234) stressed that mythic thought "progresses from the awareness of oppositions toward their resolution." Myths dealt with the resolution (or at least diminishing) of important cultural oppositions. The story of Asdiwal, for example, explored the American Northwest Coast Tshimshian tension between egalitarian and hierarchical orientations in marriage. "All the paradoxes conceived by the native mind . . . geographic, economic, sociological, and even cosmological, are, when all is said and done," Lévi-Strauss (1967b:27-28) stated, "assimilated to the less obvious yet so real paradox which [a particular form of] marriage . . . fails to resolve."

I have been a bit misleading. Implicit in what has been said is that these innovations were so obviously powerful, so clearly significant, that they were readily accepted. That is not true. Initially, it is often unclear which innovations will (and will not) be accepted by the discipline.

Two overlapping principles tend to be involved in this process. The first is: Who cites the perspective? Or to rephrase this slightly: How many anthropologists of what stature refer to the innovation in their writings? Harris implicitly emphasizes this principle when he notes, in a footnote (page 74), the host of scholars drawing on cultural materialism for insight. "To survive or to be turned into fact," Latour (1987:38) states, "a statement needs the *next generation* of papers." That is, there is a waiting period for assessing innovations. One has to see who refers to the innovation in what ways and in what contexts. (This helps explain why some scholars repeatedly cite one another, or themselves, in support of a point and why others feel hurt at the lack of citations.)

Lévi-Strauss's approach to myth has proved quite successful in this regard. It has been analyzed and reanalyzed, critiqued and praised, and, most significantly perhaps, imitated by a host of scholars. One can find literally hundreds of citations to his work. Evans-Pritchard's (1937) now classic *Witchcraft, Oracles and Magic among the Azande* took a long time to achieve this status. His student, Mary Douglas (1970:xiii-xiv), writes: "For a good decade . . . [after] its publication . . . [the book] had little influence. . . . But in the next twenty years it came to dominate the writings of anthropologists in a remarkable way."

A lack of citations may not only be a sign of neglect. It may also be a sign of failure. Leach (1961) proposed a rethinking of anthropology thirty years ago. He suggested that the "organizational ideas" present in a society constitute "a mathematical pattern" (1961:2). Few, if any, have taken up this idea in the precise form expressed. Today his *Rethinking*

Anthropology is cited more for its criticism of Radcliffe-Brown's structural typologies as "butterfly collecting" than for its own intellectual innovations. Ethnoscience and componential analysis have, to a certain degree, met a similar (though less drastic) fate. In 1972, Keesing (1972:299) pondered: "The articles on folk classification that filled the journals several years ago have dwindled away. What ever happened to ethnoscience?" Today, twenty years later, we see the lack of citations all the more clearly. Its classical works are only sparingly cited now.

A second evaluative principle, intricately bound together with the first, is: Does the perspective stimulate new ethnographic research? This principle might seem fairly straightforward. But there is a subtle complication. Senior scholars often direct graduate student projects. Stimulating new research may come down to having a set of compliant students. This was a factor in the acceptance of the Malinowskian-Boasian perspective on fieldwork. These two heroic mentors exerted tremendous influence on the following generation of scholars by training many of its prominent members (e.g. Firth, Evans-Pritchard, Fortes, Leach, Kroeber, Lowie, Benedict, and Mead). We can understand then how their joint vision became accepted so quickly, independent of its obvious merits.

It is interesting to speculate as to why a French fieldwork tradition—growing out of the work of Griaule and others—has, until recently, been ignored in North America in comparison to the Malinowskian-Boasian one. As Clifford (1983:126) notes, "The Griaule tradition offers one of the few fully elaborated alternatives to the Anglo-American model of intensive participant-observation . . . portraying research as inherently . . . fraught with power" relations. Clifford (1983:140) also adds: "Griaule never thought of being an unobtrusive participant. . . . Research was manifestly an intrusion." "His accounts assumed a recurring conflict of interests . . . resulting in mutual respect, complicity in a productive balance of power." Intriguingly, while theoretical innovations by various French scholars—such as Durkheim, Mauss, and Lévi-Strauss—are cited repeatedly in the literature, several French classics related to this ethnographic tradition tend to be ignored by British and American anthropologists. One cannot help but suspect the downplaying of such French works relates to the seeming competition between the two ethnographic traditions and an Anglo-Saxon difficulty (discussed in DaMatta's and Wolf's chapters) of coming to terms with questions of power.

THE INTELLECTUAL CONTEXT OF THE CONTRIBUTIONS

It may prove helpful, in reading the contributions that follow, to note some of the contexts they derive from for those unfamiliar with them. But first let me add a brief note. Most, if not all, of the volume's papers might be seen as part of a "rethinking" process. There is an artificiality in allocating certain papers, and not others, to a section entitled "rethinking past perspectives." The following papers should be seen as illustrations, as representatives, of a general anthropological trend that the other papers participate in as well. This section, then, illustrates some of the thinking, and rethinking, going on in the field.

As already noted, Rappaport's and Bernard's contributions focus on the discipline's positivist/interpretivist debate. We have discussed this debate in Section One and need not further elaborate upon it here. Readers should take note, however, that each contributor develops his synthesis from a different perspective. Readers might also consider an issue, raised by Rappaport (and previously Das), that is discussed later on in the volume: What significant role can anthropology play in modern life? And, following on this, they might query: To what degree are the methods discussed by Bernard critical for the effective assessment of today's problems?

Levy's contribution relates to a different context. It concerns the relationship between culture and personality. From the 1920s into the 1950s, various anthropologists (especially American anthropologists such as Sapir, Mead, Benedict, Linton, Kluckhohn, and Hallowell), addressed this topic. They did not form a school, LeVine (1991:3) notes. Rather they belonged to what he terms a "field of inquiry"—"in which scholars seeking to bring together psychological with . . . cultural perspectives experimented in devising a variety of new theoretical models, empirical methods, and research programs." Different scholars postulated different relationships between "culture" and "personality." (Scholars, moreover, defined both terms in a variety of ways.) Some emphasized culture shaping personality; others personality shaping culture. Some saw culture and personality as essentially the same thing. And still others suggested personality acted as an integrator of cultural variables—shaping some variables and being shaped by others. For LeVine (1991:4), "The culture and personality field in its first two decades . . . was one of the most exciting intellectual explorations launched by American social science in the 20th century." However, by the late 1950s the field had lost much of its momentum and was in decline. Its theoretical postulates were deemed imprecise; its methodologies limited (see LeVine 1973, Shweder 1991, Lindesmith and Strauss 1950). It never came to terms, for example, with the problem of variability. It exaggerated the consistency of cultural elements and personalities across different contexts and through time.

What took its place in the 1960s was a "new" culture and personality—now called psychological anthropology—which was much more concerned with cognitive matters. It often concentrated on the cultural categorization of knowledge, especially the indigenous classification of social and physical worlds. Questions regarding how informants organized their knowledge (in terms of what was deemed "psychological reality") became salient. But again, with time, this focus seems to be losing momentum.

What is replacing it is an increased concern with questions of selfhood, motives, learning styles, and the relation of cognitive processes to cultural contexts (see e.g. White and Kirkpatrick 1985, D'Andrade and Strauss 1992, Chaiklin and Lave 1993, and Holland and Quinn 1987). Levy's contribution draws our attention back to some of the earlier questions of the field. Here is an example of a paradigm slain (in Wolf's page 220 phrasing) returned to life in a more sophisticated form.

One might argue that gender issues have concerned anthropologists for some time (see e.g. Richards 1939, 1940, 1956; Kaberry 1939, 1952; E. Parsons 1991 [1915-1924]; and Underhill 1936). But starting in the 1960s, a number of factors, both within and outside anthropology, led to a decidedly greater recognition of their critical role. Initially, the focus was on counteracting male (or androcentric) biases in ethnographies. Reiter (1975:12) conveys a sense of what these were: "Kinship studies . . . usually centered on males, marriage systems . . . analyzed . . . the exchanges men [made and] . . . evolutionary models explain[ed] the . . . development of human society by giving enormous weight to the male role of hunting without much consideration of female gathering." Restudies of well-known cultures from more female-oriented perspectives (such as Weiner's famous 1976 study of the Trobriands) made clear to what degree androcentric biases missed key social dynamics of interaction.

Another important concern was the questioning of male dominance and the biological essentialism implicit in it. One aspect of this questioning was the formulation of cross-cultural polarities in gender relations—between, for example, nature/culture (Ortner 1974) and domestic/public (M. Rosaldo 1974)—that reconceptualized the issue of male dominance. Another was the suggestion that early band societies possessed a sexual equality later lost with cultural evolution toward states (see e.g.

Leacock 1981). Male "dominance"—in quote marks because it was defined in a variety of ways as were "culture" and "nature"—was not deemed universal. Rather, as Sanday (1981:11) indicated: "Male dominance and female power are consequences of the way in which peoples come to terms with their historical and natural environments."

The most recent trend in gender studies has been away from what is *missed* by the exclusion of gender issues toward what is *included* by a thoughtful analysis of them. Because gender concerns overlap and are entwined with numerous other aspects of culture, they constitute a powerful vehicle for examining a host of issues. Collier (1988), for example, discusses the cultural implications—in terms of world view and ritual—of different types of marriage transactions in classless societies. And Stoler (1989a:634) explores "how the very categories of 'colonizer' and 'colonized' were increasingly secured through forms of sexual control which defined the common political interests of European colonials and the cultural investments by which they identified themselves."

Kinship, once the focus of much anthropological analysis, has declined in theoretical importance in recent decades. (It is another of Wolf's slain paradigms.) One might find a variety of explanations for this—increased analytical sophistication, a changing world, different anthropological concerns. But it is important to note that the political, economic, and religious issues once addressed by kinship have not gone away. They have simply been conceptualized in other ways. Yanagisako and Collier suggest a way for drawing kinship back into the anthropological mainstream through an analysis of gender. We see what a focus on gender clearly adds to an ethnographic analysis.

Strathern addresses a different but related issue. As she (1992:150) states (concerning her recent book *The Gender of the Gift*): "I regard as a misplaced intellectualism the way in which Western anthropologists have read the concept of 'society' into Melanesians' understandings. . . . I [have] set myself the task of imagining what the intellectual counterpart to such a concept could plausibly be." As she (page 215) notes in her paper, "'Our' project should not be mistaken for 'theirs.'" In exploring "how to conceptualize a society that . . . [is] not composed of groups" (page 206) she reflects on alternative orderings of parts and wholes or as she (page 206) phrases it: "If groups were the vehicles through which societies presented themselves to their members, then without group membership what was a person a part of?"

Her exploration touches on a number of historically important concerns within the discipline. British anthropologists of the 1940s and 1950s used the concept of descent group to relate individuals to bounded groups and bounded groups to larger collectivities one might term societies. In the 1950s and 1960s their efforts were challenged on two fronts. First, there arose the question of cognatic groups—how could people effectively belong to groups that were seemingly unbounded by descent? This led to research on additional criteria, besides descent, that might bind people into collectivities. Second, marital alliances (and the exchanges implicit in them), rather than descent, were asserted as the key shapers of group boundaries. Instead of emphasizing the internal organization of groups, the focus shifted to a group's exchanges with other groups. Descent theorists such as Fortes used the concept of "complementary filiation"—of matrilateral ties in patrilineal systems and patrilateral ties in matrilineal ones—to theoretically deal with ties beyond the descent group. Entangled in these discussions—or really arguments—is a question relating to the value (and validity) of differentiating between politico-jural and domestic domains within groups—an issue addressed in both Yanagisako and Collier's and Strathern's papers. The point is the issue Strathern raises—the bounding of individuals into groups and groups into larger collectivities—

has been an important and continuing topic of concern in anthropology.

Strathern's emphasis is not on groups or individuals but on social relationships. Quoting Brown (1992:124): "Strathern's thesis [is] that the relationship, rather than society as an entity or the individual as autonomous, is anthropology's subject. . . . It is a defect of Western thinking to make the person an agent at the center of social relations. For Melanesia . . . the relationship is the crux of social action." This leads into her conception of gender which is different, in a sense, than Yanagisako and Collier's:

By "gender" I mean those categorizations of persons, artifacts, events, sequences, and so on which draw upon sexual imagery—upon the ways in which the distinctiveness of male and female characteristics make concrete people's ideas about the nature of social relationships. (Strathern 1988:ix)

This explains why Strathern (page 207) discusses "the division of persons into male and female elements." The focus becomes less one of bounding collectivities and more one of differentiating relationships. To quote her (page 215) again:

[What was separated from one another] were persons and relations themselves: person from person, relation from relation, not persons cut off from relations. Far from being fixed in time at the moment of birth, relations were the active life on which the person was forever working. What differentiated relations in Melanesia was the exchange of people's perspectives on one another.

Many anthropologists would admit Strathern is not an easy writer to follow. There are subtleties, complexities, and partial connections in her writings that bear reading and rereading. But she leaves us with a powerful set of questions to contemplate: (1) What do (or should) anthropologists mean by their often-used concept of "society"? (2) What sorts of relations in what ways and in what contexts bind people together in one versus another part of the globe? And (3) how are the seeming parts of social life—individuals (with their divisible elements) as well as the relations individuals have with one another—tied, if at all, into larger wholes?

Given the anthropological tendency to study "down" (as Nader phrased it)—to study the less powerful, those marginal to dominant centers of power in the world today—one might think that power would be a prevailing concern in anthropology. In past decades, it has not been as much as one might wish. "The nature of power has been obscured within our own society," Adams (1977:409) notes, "because of our long emphasis on the fundamental equality of" humans and, I might add, because of our affirmation that government derives from the governed. Wolf (1964: 63) suggests: It is not "too much to say that Americans have had some difficulty in thinking about . . . power . . . as long as . . . power differential[s] had to be denied in favor of an ideology holding that . . . power is potentially accessible to all." We see here DaMatta's point regarding academic life. In France, where academic debates overflow the university and get caught up in general intellectual and political life, power is very much an object of analysis. One sees this in Godelier's contribution and in Griaule's view of fieldwork (cited above). In the United States and Great Britain, where academic concerns are more "compartmentalized," kept separate from public life, manifestations and manipulations of power are less passionate foci of analysis. Wolf suggests we need to pay more attention to the dynamics of power in American anthropology—a theme that resonates with recent feminist writings (such as those by Rapp, Sacks, Morgan, and DiLeonardo).

Scheper-Hughes's chapter overlaps with Wolf's in that medical anthropology, while retaining its traditional concern with the cultural determinants of illness and healing, has increasingly moved toward also considering the power relations implicit in biomedical discourse and practice. Estroff (1981), for example, analyzes the uses and abuses of power relations in psychiatry, E. Martin (1987) and Lock (1988b) in gynecology, and Taussig (1992) in general medical practice. In another paper, Scheper-Hughes (1990:190-195) suggests that medical anthropologists often act today in ways reminiscent of earlier anthropological relations to colonial agents—putting their knowledge at the service of authorities interested in developing Western programs without necessarily helping indigenous populations resist the negative effects of such programs.

Building on Kleinman's (1980:72) distinction between *illness* (disorders perceived by the patient) and *disease* (disorders as diagnosed by the physician), a number of clinically oriented studies today explore the dynamic tensions and interactions between indigenous and biomedical perspectives in particular settings. In contrast, more critically oriented approaches to medical anthropology, quoting Singer (1989:1196), focus on "the necessity of situating the examination of ill health within the 'wider field of force' [of power relations] . . . that determine what is produced, how it is produced and who benefits (or suffers)" as a result. The theoretical background for this work often derives from Foucault (see, for example, 1975, 1979, 1980a, and 1980b) whose "analyses of the body," in the words of Dreyfus and Rabinow (1982:111), indicate how "the most minute and local social practices are linked up with the large scale organization of power." This critical perspective is exemplified in Scheper-Hughes's paper, which analyzes social class and gender relations at the level of the body. She reconceptualizes the conventional Freudian analysis of conversion hysterias and the psychological somatization model to suggest the production of "unruly" bodily signs and symptoms in people should not be viewed as pathology but rather as a legitimate form of "body praxis"—in which the body speaks "truth to power" in the form of symptoms that reveal the "unspeakable"

10

Humanity's Evolution
and Anthropology's Future

ROY A. RAPPAPORT

As one who, with others, was engaged a couple of decades ago in the development of a certain ecological approach, I might be expected to assess the past twenty years in ecological anthropology and, on the basis of that assessment, make suggestions for future directions. I will confess at the outset, however, to reservations about prescriptions and predictions generally. Our colleagues will do whatever they take to be interesting or important, and whatever that might turn out to be can hardly be foreseen and certainly can't be legislated. My remarks, therefore, indicate nothing more than what I, who have been a student of both ecology and ritual and, more recently, have worked on some problems of contemporary society, find interesting and important. I like to think, however, that I am trying to glimpse something toward which the field as a whole may be groping. It's not altogether clear to me what it is yet, but let's say it's to become a discipline, a field, a science, a way of knowing, the characteristics of which conform to those of the species that constitutes its subject matter. We are, I think, alone among social sciences in attempting such a thing, and although it may be disciplinary chauvinism to say so, for the very reasons that anthropology has been rather backward as a modern science it may well become preeminent as a postmodern science.

TWO ANTHROPOLOGICAL TRADITIONS

By "postmodern science" I mean something quite different from the cluster of ideas and attitudes coming to anthropology from architecture by way of literary criticism. I am, rather, following Stephen Toulmin (1982), who uses the term to contrast with "modern science," that is, the program codified by Descartes and his followers. Toulmin's postmodern science, as it would develop in anthropology, might share some features with the more familiar literary postmodernism but the two are diametrically opposed in fundamental respects. This may be obvious because in the literary-critical sense "postmodern science" could well be an oxymoron. I will return to Toulmin's conception after first paying a visit home to anthropology.

Someone once said—it may have been Gregory Bateson—that there are two styles of thinkers in this world, the simpleminded and the muddleheaded. It may be a little simpleminded to say so, but it seems to me that anthropology selects for muddleheads or may even be in its very constitution muddleheaded, whereas the other social sciences, at least so our stereotypes go, may incline toward simplemindedness. Be this as it may, we have never been very trustful of simplicity, and we have always taken the world to be messier and more complicated than any method or combination of methods could account for. This stance has not only been an appropriate product of humility, but also an entailment of our peculiar and ambivalent epistemology.

Two traditions have proceeded in anthropology since its inception. One, objective in its aspirations and inspired by the biological sciences, seeks explanation and is concerned to discover causes, or even, in the view of the ambitious, laws. The other, influenced by philosophy, linguistics, and the humanities, and open to more subjectively derived knowledge, attempts interpretation and seeks to elucidate meanings. Our ancestry, thus, lies in both the enlightenment and in what Isaiah Berlin (1980) calls the "Counter Enlightenment." We are descendants of Vico as well as Descartes.

Our two traditions have not always lived very easily together even when, or perhaps especially when, they have cohabited in the same minds. But any radical separation of the two is misguided, not only because meanings are often causal and causes are often meaningful but because, more fundamentally, the relationship between them, in all its difficulty, tension, and ambiguity, expresses the condition of a species that lives, and can only live, in terms of meanings it itself must construct in a world devoid of intrinsic meaning but subject to natural law. Any adequate anthropology must attempt to comprehend the fullness of its subject matter's condition.

But one of the most remarked upon developments over the past two decades has been the increasing estrangement of the two traditions. This estrangement should not be exaggerated, however, nor should it be measured by the radical declarations of those on the extremes. It is as yet far from a divorce, and the separation may have been helpful in allowing each tradition not only to explore the limits of its own possibilities but in doing so to rediscover its dependence on the other. I think, however, that the time has come for their reunion, as problematic as it may continue to be.

More may ride on it than the future of a minor discipline. Let me turn from our discipline to its subject matter. Ours is, after all, not only an endangered species but one whose endangerment endangers all others. I don't for a minute believe that anthropology has the answers to all, or even, perhaps, any of the world's pressing problems. But it may, at least, have helpful ways to conceptualize some of them, ways that differ in important respects from the conceptions, dreamt up by economists, that dominate public discourse, often through appeals to that conceptual triumph of simplemindedness, "the bottom line." On the other hand, tangling with such problems will stretch us theoretically as well as substantively.

I would suggest that important among the reasons for our endangerment is disconformity between natural law and constructed meaning. By the term "natural law" I mean to designate nature's regularities and their causes whether or not recognized or understood. On the one hand it is extremely unlikely that the laws of nature will ever be fully known, but even if they are, the operations of nature are of such complexity and so subject to chance that their outcomes will ever remain in high degree unpredictable. On the other hand, there is nothing in the nature of human thought to prevent it from constructing self-destructive follies, follies which, empowered by ever more powerful technologies, have now developed world-destroying capacities. That this observation is trite only confirms its truth.

I will only note in passing that one of the problems of cultural relativism in its more extreme forms is that it does not seem to have any room for errors of the sort that may possess entire cultures. I mean by "errors" to refer to conceptions, no matter how produced, that so disconform to the world's structure that the actions they guide are destructive. The reigning economic conception of ecological systems as, essentially, concentrations of resources, a conception which contributes to the destruction of the ozone layer and global warming, is an example which, in addition to familiarity and gravity, has the virtue of demonstrating that "errors" are not simply, or even mainly, matters of empirical misunderstanding, and that they are likely to be, in some degree, functions of power. But the main point I wish to make here is that anthropology cannot approach the general problem of disconformity between natural systems and cultural constructions if the two traditions are radically separated.

Before we can further consider anthropology's future in the context of the disconformity that may well constitute the essence of what is sometimes called rather portentously and perhaps pretentiously, "the human condition," it will be helpful to consider that disconformity itself, and its emergence in the course of humanity's evolution.

LANGUAGE AND HUMANITY

Please note. I did not say that I will deal with "hominid" or "human evolution" but with "the evolution of humanity." The difference is one of connotation. The phrases "hominid evolution," or "human evolution," would have emphasized what our species has in common with other species, namely that we are animals living among and dependant upon other organisms, and, further, that our species emerged through processes of natural selection no different in principle from those producing limpets or lions. I assume these commonalities, but the phrase the "evolution of *humanity*" emphasizes the characteristic that sets our species apart from all others. Our hominid forebears became what might loosely be called "fully human" with the emergence of language. All animals communicate and even plants transmit information, but only humans, so far as we know, are possessed of languages composed, first, of lexicons made up of symbols in Peirce's (1960, vol. 2:143ff.) sense, that is, signs related only "by law" or

convention to that which they signify, and second, of grammars, sets of rules for combining symbols into semantically unbounded discourse.

The possession of language makes possible ways of life inconceivable to nonverbal creatures, and the ability to use it must have been selected for strongly. With language, communication not only can escape from the here and now to report upon the past and the distant but can also order, to a degree, the future by making more precise planning and coordination possible. Other entailments of language were as consequential although not as unambiguously advantageous. With language, discourse can escape from the here and now not only to enter the actual past and distant or to approach the foreseeable future but it can also search for such parallel worlds as those of the "might have been," the "should be," the "may always be." It can, this is to say, explore the realms of the desirable, the moral, the possible, the imaginary, the general.

To explore such realms is not simply to *discover* what is there but to create it. Language expands by magnitudes what can be thought. This expansion in conceptual power as much as an increased ability to communicate underlies the general human mode of adaptation. As such language has been absolutely central to human evolutionary success.

I just introduced the term "adaptation." By "adaptation" I mean the processes through which living systems maintain themselves in the face of continuous disturbance and occasional threat. Bateson (1972) put the matter in informational terms, stating that adaptive systems operate to preserve the truth value of certain propositions about themselves in the face of threats to falsify them. In infra-human organisms these propositions are descriptions of crucial aspects of their structure or physiology. Among humans these propositions may be propositions properly so-called, and about other matters to which we shall return. Adaptive responses include both short-term reversible changes of state and long-term irreversible changes in structure. The two, often contrasted, are closely related, for structural transformations in subsystems make it possible to maintain more basic aspects of encompassing systems unchanged, and thus the fundamental question to ask of any evolutionary transformation is "What does it maintain unchanged?"

Flexibility is central to adaptation so conceived, and the adaptive flexibility of humans following from the possession of language seems to be unparalleled. Language is, thus, fundamental to the human mode of adaptation. But even such an assertion does not do language's momentousness justice, for its significance transcends the species in which it appeared. Leslie White (1949) claimed many years ago that the appearance of language was the most radical innovation in the evolution of evolution itself since life first appeared. White's claim was not extravagant, for language was not simply a new way to communicate old types of information. With language, an entirely new form of information appears in the world. This new form brought new content, and the world as a whole has not been the same since.

The epochal significance of language for the world beyond humanity did not become apparent for many millennia after it had emerged. But effects upon the lifeways of the hominids must have been enormous in earlier times. Language not only permits thought and communication to escape from the solid actualities of here and now to discover other realms, but both *requires* such thought and *makes it inevitable*. As I said at the outset, humanity is a species that lives and can only live in terms of meanings it itself must construct. These meanings and understandings not only reflect or approximate an independently existing world but participate in its construction. The worlds in which humans live are not fully constituted by geological and organic processes, but are also symbolically conceived and established by performative

actions (see Austin 1962), and thus come to be filled with the likes of honor, evil, democracy, and gods. All of these conceptions are reified, made into *res,* real things, by social actions contingent upon language. It is in terms of their existence, no less than in terms of the existence of physical things, that people operate in and transform ecosystems which in all but the cases of hunters and gatherers, they have dominated since the emergence of agriculture 10,000 or so years ago. Language has ever more powerfully reached out from the species in which it emerged to reorder and subordinate the natural systems in which populations of that species participate.

SOME IMPLICATIONS

It conforms to this account to say that language is central to human adaptation, but it is clear that such a statement is inadequate or even misleading as a characterization of the relationship of language to language user. *If people act, and can only act, in terms of meanings they or their ancestors have conceived, they are as much in the service of those conceptions as those conceptions are parts of their adaptations. There is, this is to say, an inversion or partial inversion, in the course of human evolution, of the relationship of the adaptive apparatus to the adapting species.* The capacity that is central to human adaptation gives birth to concepts, like God, Heaven, and Hell, that come to possess those who have conceived them. To argue that all such concepts or the actions they inform enhance the survival and reproduction of the organisms who maintain them is not credible.

That the implications of these suggestions may be obvious does not make them any the less profound. First, if the metaphor of inversion (surely a simplification) is at all apt, the extent to which concepts like inclusive fitness and kin selection account for cultural phenomena is rather limited. Second, and related, whatever the case may be among other species, group selection (selection for perpetuation of traits tending to contribute positively to the survival of the groups in which they occur but negatively to the survival of the particular individuals in possession of them) is not only possible among humans but of great importance in humanity's evolution. All that is needed to make group selection possible is a device that leads individuals to separate their conceptions of well-being or advantage from biological survival. Notions like God, Heaven, Hell, heroism, honor, shame, fatherland, and democracy, encoded in procedures of enculturation representing them as factual, natural, public, sacred (and, therefore, compelling), have dominated every culture of which we possess ethnographic or historical knowledge. In more general terms, this is to say that if adaptive systems can be characterized as systems that operate (consciously or unconsciously) to preserve the truth value of certain propositions about themselves in the face of disturbances tending to falsify them, then it is appropriate to propose that the favored propositions in human systems are about such conceptions as God, Honor, Freedom, and the Good. That their preservation has often required great or even ultimate sacrifice on the parts of individuals hardly needs saying. Postulates concerning the unitary or trinary nature of God are among those for whom countless individuals have sacrificed their lives, as are such mundane slogans as "Death before dishonor" or "Better dead than red."

A final implication: we approach here a generally unrecognized evolutionary law or rule, possibly the evolutionary equivalent of the old adage about the nonexistence of free lunches: every evolutionary advance sets new problems as it responds to and ameliorates earlier ones, and language was no exception.

We have been led from a celebration of language to the contemplation of its vices. In addition to the unprecedented possibility of contradiction between the preservation of symbolic constructions and the survival of the organisms that imagined them into existence,

two other problems are intrinsic to language's very gifts. First, when a sign is only conventionally related to what it signifies as in Peirce's sense of symbol, the sign can occur in the absence of the signified and events can occur without being signaled. The same conventional relationship which permits discourse to escape from the here and now also facilitates lying. If humans are not the world's first or only liars they are the world's foremost liars. Second, language makes the conception of alternatives to prevailing conditions and customs unavoidable. The very capacity that enhances flexibility presents a continuing challenge to prevailing social and conceptual orders. The dark side of enhanced flexibility is increased possibility for disorder. It is of interest that Buber (1953) took lie and alternative to be the grounds of all evil. Be this as it may, if there are to be any words at all it may be necessary to establish what may be called *The Word*; the "True Word," to stand against the dissolving power of lying words and of many words, of falsehood and babel.

The question we face is close to the one asked by Hans Kung (1980:1) in the very first paragraph of his massive *Does God Exist?*

And since the emergence of modem, rational man there has been an almost desperate struggle with the problem of human certainty. Where, we wonder, is there a rocklike, unshakable certainty on which all human certainty could be built?

I would modify Kung's question only by dropping the terms "modern" and "rational." Modern rational man may be faced with the breakdown of ancient means for establishing certainty but that is another matter. First we must turn to those ancient means, to Logos and its establishment.

LOGOS

I use the term "Logos" to designate a category of conceptions ordering many societies, perhaps most premodern societies. Each conception is unique in particulars, but they all bear each other a "family resemblance." In some societies they are only implicit, but in many they are named: *Ma'at* in ancient Egypt, the Zoroastrian *Asha, Hozho* of the Navajo, *Nomane* of the Maring. And, of course, there is the ancient Greek *Logos,* the "type species," so to speak, from which I have derived the genus name.

In the New Testament, Logos is usually glossed into English as "Word" but I am taking the term in its earlier pre-Socratic sense. By Heraclitus's time it denoted an enduring and even divine principle ordering the world (Debrunner 1967; Kahn, 1979). The Logos possessed certain general characteristics, some of which are quite widespread among the world's *Logoi,* but we shall be concerned first with the Greek species in particular.

First, the notion of unity may be implicit in any concept of order, but it is an explicit feature of the *Logos.* One of the crucial fragments is translated by G. S. Kirk (1954: 65) as follows: "Listening not to me but to the *Logos* it is wise to agree all things are one."

Second, the *Logos* is accessible to human comprehension because the same *Logos* that orders the universe orders human minds as parts of the universe. Only one activity is genuinely wise, understanding how everything in the world is part of a unified whole. This understanding is radically different from other forms of cleverness, and only through it can humans assimilate themselves to the ordered whole of which they are parts. Several comments follow.

To begin with, it is clear that comprehension of the *Logos* is not merely intellectual. One grasps it by becoming part of it. As one modern commentator puts it, "It claims a man" (Kleinknecht 1967:85). "The particular *Logos* of Man . . . is part of the general *Logos* . . . which achieves awareness in man, so that through it God and Man . . . the true man who . . . has *Orthos Logos,* and thus who

lives as a follower of it, are combined into a great cosmos."

This modern interpretation recognizes its social aspects. For one thing it is normative—there is a *Logos* which is *orthos.* People *should* follow it, but it is possible for humans to do otherwise. It is, indeed, likely that they will do otherwise because the *Logos* is hidden.

This broaches another of its general features. The unity that wisdom's is to grasp encompasses obviously disparate and conflicting things, but one of *Logos's* explicit qualities is harmony. In view of the strife with which the world is obviously filled this can only be a harmony arising out of, or underlying, conflict itself. Heraclitus's hidden harmony is a harmony of tension. The violence of a Nature maintained by creatures eating each other is apparent to those participating in it, the order or harmony at the level of the ecosystem of which the participants are parts is not. In transcending them it is concealed from them.

We are brought here to another of *Logos's* qualities, *Alethia,* which etymologically, according to Heidegger (1959), denotes non-concealment, but is usually glossed "truth." It is, however, a special sort of truth, not the truth that some statements may possess by virtue of their correspondence to states of affairs but "the real state of affairs to be maintained against different statements" (Bultmann 1964: 238). The contraries of *Alethia,* and prominent among the enemies of *Logos,* are *pseudos,* "deception," and *doxa,* "opinion." *Alethia* is that which is the case regardless of opinion. In English it is not mere veracity but verity. Although *Logos* orders the universe, the existence of *doxa* and *pseudos* indicates that it is likely to be ignored or violated. Another of its enemies is *idia phronesis,* "individual calculation," perhaps what classical economists mean by "rationality." More fundamentally, *Logos* is often ignored simply because, being hidden, it is unrecognized. Its unconcealment must be achieved by work of some sort, the work of words in poetry, of stone in statues, and perhaps most importantly, the work of people in ritual. It is of interest that the English word "liturgy," which is a synonym for ritual, derives from *Laos ergon*, "work of the people."

I should make it clear that there is no evidence for any connection between Heraclitus's conception of *Logos* and the liturgical practices of his day. His conception is virtually unique in this respect. In all of the other cases cited, *Logos* is established and sanctified in ritual. I have been concerned, so far, with the establishment of orders that are cultural fabrications. For such orders to be established they must be accepted as true and certain. Having spoken of *Logoi* (the plural of *Logos*), I will now take up how they are made true and certain. This leads to a discussion of, first, the concept of the sacred and then of ritual.

SANCTITY AND RITUAL

Central to the bodies of discourse constituting *Logoi* represented in Liturgy are certain sentences which I call "Ultimate Sacred Postulates." Familiar examples include "The Lord our God, the Lord is One." Such sentences typically contain no material terms, and sometimes seem internally self-contradictory. They thus seem invulnerable to empirical falsification, and beyond the reach of logical falsification. Nor can they be verified. Nevertheless, they are taken to be unquestionable. I take this unquestionableness to be of the essence and elsewhere have defined sanctity as "*the quality of unquestionableness imputed by congregations to postulates in their nature absolutely unfalsifiable and objectively unverifiable*" (1971:29, 1979c:209). As such they may seem indistinct from axioms but there are differences. For one thing they cannot be derived as theorems from logics of a higher type. Reciprocally, sentences contingent upon them are not derived from them logically, but are, rather, sanctified, which is to say certified, by them.

This definition, be it noted, takes sanctity to be a characteristic of discourse rather than of objects of discourse. It is not, for instance,

Christ that is sacred. It is the expression of his divinity (in discourse) that is sacred. Sanctity flows from ultimate sacred postulates throughout the bodies of discourse constituting the *Logoi* at the tops of which they stand, and in this flow escapes from ritual to enter into social processes generally. If, for instance, kingship is part of the *Logos*, and if kings are crowned in the name of God in coronations, then even their mundane directives are sanctified. Expressions commonly sanctified include cosmological axioms, commandments, testimony, and oaths as well as those ordaining rituals and legitimizing authorities. Sanctity, this is to say, escapes from ritual not only to sanctify *Logoi*, but to underwrite discourse generally. And in its flow the generalized unquestionableness which is sanctity's essence takes on related but more specific characteristics, namely propriety, morality, legitimacy, efficacy, and truth.

We must now ask, how do certain postulates attain their ultimately sacred, which is to say unquestionable, status? I believe that their representation in ritual confers such status upon them. Ritual is a means, possibly the only means, for manufacturing sanctity. I have not yet defined ritual. I take the term to denote *the performance of more or less invariant sequences of formal acts and utterances not encoded by the performers* (see Rappaport 1979c:175).

I have argued at length elsewhere (1979c) that ritual grounds the unquestionableness of the sacred in three ways, two of which are dependant upon the relative invariant characteristic of the ritual form. I do not have time to discuss them in detail here. I can only note, first, that to perform an invariant order encoded by another than the performer is perforce to conform to that order. This is, at minimum, to recognize the order's authority. But it is more than that. To perform a liturgy is to participate in it. To participate in it is to become part of it. To deny an order of which one is a part while a part of it I take to be self-contradictory and thus impossible. Therefore, to perform a liturgical order is to accept whatever is encoded in its canon. To accept it is to agree not to question it. This is one ground of unquestionableness. (It is important to note that acceptance does not entail either belief or compliance. Acceptance establishes obligation to comply but does not itself guarantee compliance.) The second ground of unquestionableness lies in the significance of invariance for the text itself.

If ritual is a mode of communication it is, in information theoretical terms, a peculiar one. To the extent that a ritual order is invariant its unfolding in performance reduces no uncertainty. Inasmuch as information (in a technical sense) is that which reduces uncertainty this is to say that ritual is devoid of information. But to say that it is informationless is not to say that it is meaningless, for *the meaning of informationlessness*, A. F. C. Wallace noted (1966: 234), is *certainty*. The certainty of that which is invariantly encoded is the second ground of unquestionableness.

A further consequence of invariance is that to perform a liturgy is *ipso facto* to "follow the *Logos*." Although there is room for private understandings of a publicly realized *Logos*, that is, for performers to interpret it in idiosyncratic ways, the *Logos* itself, constituted by acts and utterances performers do not invent but find encoded in the invariant liturgy, is held in common and stands beyond *doxa*.

The unquestionable status of ultimately sacred postulates must, however, stand on more than formal acceptance and a trick in information theory. I have defined the sacred in a way which associates it with the *discursive*, or linguistic, aspect of religious phenomena. It is not the whole of the Holy. The other aspect of the Holy, the nondiscursive, affective, experiential aspect which is also generated in ritual, may, following Rudolph Otto (1923), be called "the Numinous." The Numinous is experienced as a direct and immediate awareness of an extraordinary presence or even as participation in such a presence. Informants agree that it is deeply, even ultimately, meaningful.

Unlike sacred postulates, which are unfalsifiable, *numinous experiences, because immediately and directly felt, seem undeniable*. Such experiences are engendered by common features of ritual, not only invariance but such related features as unison, rhythmicity, stylization, and antiquity as well as others—strangeness, sensory overload, pain. Numinous experience, when it occurs, reinforces formal acceptance with belief, with a conviction which claims those convinced more profoundly than the merely moral claims of obligation or the persuasions of mere certainty. This is the third of ritual's ground for unquestionableness. And so we come to an answer to Hans Kung's question, "Where . . . is there a rocklike . . . certainty on which all human certainty can be built?" but what we have found is hardly rocklike. We are faced with a remarkable spectacle. The unfalsifiable supported by the undeniable yields the unquestionable which transforms the arbitrary, dubious, and conventional into the apparently correct, necessary, and natural. This is, I have argued so far, the ancient foundation upon which the human way of life was built, and it was laid in ritual. It is doubtful, however, that it still stands there. It is well to remember that every evolutionary advance sets new problems as it ameliorates older ones, and that sanctity is no exception, for it has problems of its own.

PROBLEMS GENERATED BY SANCTITY

There are many such problems and space is limited. Among the most obvious is the capacity for differing sacred truths to engender conflict and persecution between or among groups whose discourse and trust is founded upon them.

There is next the problem of oppression. In simple tribal societies such discrete authorities as exist depend for their prerogatives upon their sanctification, but their sanctification derives from rituals in which those presumably subject to them participate. *This is to say that in such societies a cybernetic process is operant. Subjects can deprive authorities of sanctity should they perform incompetently or oppressively*, either passively by withdrawing from the rituals sanctifying the authority, or actively, by participating in rituals sanctifying alternative authorities or by participating in rites of degradation.

In more developed societies, in which authorities have at their command armed men, the situation changes. Authorities can now stand on power rather than sanctity. They do not abandon their claims to sanctity, but their relationship to it is inverted. *Whereas in the simpler society the authority is contingent upon its sanctification, in the more developed society sanctity may be degraded to the status of the authority's instrument.*

Ritual participation may continue, of course, but if it is coerced, as it sometimes is, it does not constitute acceptance, and even when participation is eager it is likely to be profoundly different in orientation and consequences. The established religions of state organized societies tend to focus upon salvation in the hereafter and to become detached from the correction of the ills of here and now. As Marx said, religion becomes the opiate of the masses.

Sanctity has further problems of a subtler sort. First, characteristic of social evolution is increasing differentiation of society into specialized subsystems which inevitably come to differ in power. It follows that the narrowly drawn interests of the most powerful can come to dominate the values of society as a whole. As a consequence, these subsystems are able to usurp greater degrees of sanctity than is appropriate to their specialized and instrumental nature. If, for example, America is as stated in some documents and in its pledge of allegiance, "One nation under God," and if "the business of America is business," as was asserted by one of our presidents (a man, that is, sworn into our highest office), then business becomes highly sanctified, and the logic of "What's good for General Motors is good for the country," a statement made by one of

our high officials, becomes compelling. In the terms of our earlier discussion of adaptation, highly specific propositions are raised to the status of ultimate truths. This elevation of the specialized, instrumental, and profane to the status of general, fundamental, and sanctified is an instance of what the theologian Paul Tillich (1957) called "idolatry," in which the relative and contingent is mistaken for the absolute, and the absolute is, consequently, relativized. He took it to be evil. Whatever the moral case may be I would argue that to invest specialized and instrumental institutions, like business, with high degrees of sanctity makes them increasingly resistant to change, thus reducing adaptive flexibility and impeding orderly evolutionary transformation (see Rappaport 1979d).

"Oversanctification," of which idolatry is a form, can also develop within religious traditions themselves. Minor rules can be mistaken for the fundamental, and inappropriately high degrees of sanctity accorded to them. A case in point is the Catholic church's stand on birth control. A degree of sanctity appropriate only for matters of faith, like the doctrine of the immaculate conception, is being accorded to a low-order rule concerning nonimmaculate nonconception. As a result there have not only been widespread defections from the Catholic church, but challenges by such theologians as Hans Kung to papal authority generally.

A related but less obvious ill of sanctity is a consequence of another epochal advance, namely writing. With writing come scriptures. Being written, they easily become absolutely invariant and also long and full of specifics. Fundamentalists are inclined to take whole scriptures to be ultimately sacred, which is not only to say unquestionable but immutable. If flexibility is central to adaptiveness, loss of adaptive capacity is a general consequence. Political and social conservatism is a likely outcome, and so may be resistance to secular scholarship. Such developments, however, endanger sanctity more than they impede intellectual exploration. To put sanctity into the service of the geocentric theory in the seventeenth century or creationism in the twentieth has, among its effects, discrediting sanctity itself as a principle of certification.

THE EPISTEMOLOGY OF MODERN SCIENCE

Moderns have been inclined to celebrate the liberation of knowledge from sanctified domination, but this liberation has had its costs. With the emergence of modern science the order of knowledge was inverted. Ultimate knowledge in *Logoi* is sacred knowledge, which, because numinously known or ritually accepted, is unquestionable. Ultimate sacred postulates, taken to be eternally true, sanctify, which is to say certify, hierarchies of expressions and institutions in terms of which thought and action are organized. Knowledge of mundane facts is, as it were, at the bottom of such hierarchies. Facts are taken to be obvious, transient, low in or devoid of sanctity, and contingent.

When science is liberated from religion, ultimate knowledge becomes knowledge of fact. Facts are subsumed under generalizations called "theories" but theories continue to fall victim to anomalous facts. If facts are both ultimate and transient, certainty disappears. Theories, moreover, are also of limited scope; thus attempts to apply concepts developed in one domain to another tend to be dismissed as "mere analogies." The result is a fragmentation of knowledge, and if oneness is intrinsic to the conception of *Logos*, *Logos* is threatened with dissolution. There is a loss of any sense of the world's wholeness.

What, when facts become sovereign, is the fate of that which had been ultimate knowledge? It is now no more than "mere belief," belief being reduced to the status of opinion, or *doxa*. Values sanctified by the ultimately sacred are degraded to the status of tastes or preferences. Unlike *Logoi,* which make moral

and emotional claims upon those who follow them, the new order of knowledge makes explicit that its claim upon those operating in accordance with it is no more than intellectual. Explorers are *supposed* to become disengaged from the worlds they objectively explore. Participation in scientific acts of observing and analyzing the world in accordance with natural law are very different from participation in ritual acts constructing and maintaining the world in accordance with *Logos.* Rituals, once ultimately meaningful acts of participation in orders the performances themselves realize, become "mere rituals," empty or even hypothetical formalisms. Ritual as an instrument for establishing the foundations of human worlds has been seriously damaged and it is not clear that other means for establishing such foundations are as effective as rituals once were.

In sum, we face a terrible contradiction. The reordering of knowledge that has liberated humans to discover the laws of the physical world is antagonistic not only to superstition, dogmatism, and irrationality, but hostile to the very processes by which the peculiarly human components of the world are constructed and ordered. The epistemology of modern science threatens to destroy the ontological ground of meaning. To put it a little differently, in discovering the physical aspects of the world we undermine its conventional foundations.

LAW AND MEANING

That modern science may threaten meaning is no reason for anthropology to turn its back on it, however. To recognize that science, by *itself,* does not provide a comprehensive understanding of humanity is not to say that it is wrong.

Adequate comprehension of humanity must encompass both law and meaning, for humanity is a species that lives, and can only live, in terms of meanings it itself must construct only loosely constrained by its nature from fashioning self-destructive or world-destroying follies, in a world devoid of intrinsic meaning but subject to physical laws that can neither be changed nor, perhaps, ever fully understood. Physical law and conventional meaning: the lawful and meaningful are not coextensive, and they are differently known. If physical laws and the states of affairs they constitute are to be known they must be *discovered*. In contrast, humankind's meanings must be *constructed* and accepted. Laws and facts and the scientific procedures for discovering them may provide some of the materials out of which meanings are made but they do not, by themselves, constitute meaning, nor can they do meaning's work of organizing human action. Conversely, although constructed meanings are often represented as discovered law, they do not constitute nature. The laws of physics, chemistry, and biology, and the states of affairs contingent upon them, are the case whether or not they are known. The lawful emergence, in the course of evolution, of the ability to construct meaning has provided humans with no exemption from physical law but has increased by magnitudes their capacity not only to conceive the world but to misconstrue it as well. Subsequent evolution has armed our powers of misunderstanding with an ever-increasing capacity, technological, economic and political, to destroy the world for increasingly narrow, trivial, or abstract reasons.

Human worlds, then, are worlds whose operations must be constructed as well as discovered by those participating in them. But a *caveat* should be introduced here. Although we may *distinguish, as classes,* the physically constituted from the culturally constructed, they *cannot be separated* in nature, and the world is increasingly an outcome of their interaction. The reconciliation and continuing accommodation of discovery and construction, difficult at best, becomes ever more difficult as our capacities to destroy the world increase and the certainty of our symbolic constructions crumbles.

POSTMODERN SCIENCE

We may, against this background, now return to anthropology. The primary aim of a postmodern science may be to conceive of ways to effect such reconciliation. I don't claim to know how to do this but harbor the belief that anthropology is in a favorable position to move toward reconciliation because both unreconciled elements are built into its very constitution.

Stephen Toulmin provides some leads in his 1982 *The Return to Cosmology*. In his view, "postmodern science" will differ from "modern science" in several ways that suggest that anthropology has already begun to qualify as a postmodern science. First, it will return scientists to the systems from which the Cartesian program banished them, relegating them to the status of detached observers. In Toulmin's view, such a status is no longer tenable on any grounds because such developments as Heisenberg's recognition of indeterminacy, the recognition of transference and countertransference in psychoanalytic theory, the effects of the study of ecological systems on the systems studied, and of opinion polls on the opinions of those polled, and the growing awareness that living systems under study have subjective as well as objective characteristics all demonstrate that "scientific detachment" simply cannot be achieved. And, of course, even if scientists could be detached, others use their results not only for acting in but for transforming the world in which scientists, among others, live.

This leads to a second difference. Whereas modern science has attempted to develop "theory," that is, detached intellectual understandings derived from "objective" or "outside" knowledge of particular constituents of the world, leaving "praxis" to farmers, carpenters, engineers, priests, or politicians, a postmodern science, recognizing that participation in the world it observes is inescapable, will incorporate into itself considerations of practice. In incorporating into itself considerations of practice it must develop a theory of practice. Such a theory cannot be simply, or even mainly, methodological in nature. It must also be, or even be primarily, a moral theory. A third difference, then, is that whereas modern science claims to be value-free, postmodern science will be candid about its value dimension.

A fourth difference is implicit. If postmodern science is to be a science of thinking and acting subjects and not merely of inanimate objects, or of subjects treated as inanimate or passive objects, then it will take as valid "inside," subjective knowledge as well as objective, "outside" knowledge, Vico's *verum* as well as Descartes' *certum*. It is of interest to note that Toulmin, a philosopher, approaches postmodern science (discussion of which comprises part three of *The Return to Cosmology*), through consideration of the work of an anthropologist, Gregory Bateson, who, he says, "gives us a tantalizing glimpse of what, in the new era of 'postmodern science,' an overall vision of humanity's place in nature will have to become."

It does not denigrate Bateson's originality and genius to suggest that what Toulmin reacted to in his work consisted in part of characteristics that, despite recent particularistic tendencies, continue to underlie much of anthropology. These qualities, which are the very factors that sometimes lead others to regard anthropology as the most "backward" or "primitive" or "undeveloped" of the modern social sciences, are the very factors which suit it for leadership in the emergence of the postmodern science toward which Toulmin, following Bateson, points: (1) its qualitative concerns, (2) its commitment to context and to holism, (3) its respect for subjective as well as objective knowledge, (4) its consequent emphasis upon *participant* observation, rather than observation, pure and simple, and its willingness, therefore, to take *verum* as well as *certum* seriously, (5) its worries about ethnographic representation, (6) its willingness to quantify tempered by awareness of the epistemological limitations of quantification, (7) its humanistic concern with what it is to be human.

There is a fifth difference between modern and postmodern science. The detailed and specialized observations specified by the methods of modern science have required, as a practical matter, an ever finer division of scientific labor. Disciplines have multiplied and, as they have, knowledge has become increasingly fragmented. As a consequence the organization of the world as a whole has become no serious scholar's business. Indeed, attempts to generalize that have involved the application of principles developed in one field to others are often regarded with suspicion, and are likely to be dismissed as amateurish, reductionistic, or metaphysical. Postmodern science, in Toulmin's view, will, on the contrary, revive concern with Cosmos, banished from the considerations of serious scientists since the seventeenth century when the New Astronomy and the subsequent Cartesian revolution made forever untenable the simplistic cosmological model, based upon astronomy, that had dominated thought since antiquity. That astronomy ultimately proved an inadequate ground for a cosmological model does not mean, however, that no good cosmological models are possible, Toulmin observes, and in his view postmodern science will be ultimately concerned (I use Paul Tillich's expression deliberately) with the world's unity, *both* with understanding the principles of that unity *and* with maintaining its integrity. In sum, what Toulmin calls "postmodern science" is an order of knowledge *and* action in which both those who seek to discover natural law and those who seek to understand the nature of the world's constructed meanings are reunited with a world which they do not merely observe but in which they participate for better or for worse.

Whereas premodern cosmology was based upon astronomy, postmodern cosmology, grounded in a revitalized *Logos*, could be founded, Toulmin suggests (as have, in other words, many others), upon ecology. There are important differences between cosmologies built upon astronomy on the one hand and ecology on the other. It may once have been plausible to believe that the stars' courses could affect us, but it has never been easy to believe that we could have any effect on them. Indeed, their imperviousness to our manipulation was part of their cosmological appeal. In contrast, the reciprocity of our relations with our environments is not only undeniable but manifestly obvious. Whereas the relationship of human lives to the movements of heavenly bodies was one of correspondences between radically separate systems, the relationship of humans to the plants and animals and soils surrounding them is one of ceaseless interaction. Whereas humans could relate to heavenly bodies only through observation, they relate to ecosystems of which they are elements through participation, and in these times humans are clearly the most consequential participants in the systems they seek to understand.

Toulmin speaks of "a return to Cosmos" as crucial to our future. I earlier spoke of "Logos," for I take the conception of Logos to be crucial to Cosmos. The conception of Logos entails a realization that the world's unity is not only constituted by galactic, geological, meteorological, chemical and organic processes, but since the emergence of humanity, it is also in part constructed culturally, and since the emergence of plant cultivation, the cultural component has become ever more determining. With cultivation humans come to construct and dominate anthropocentric systems that, with increasingly powerful technology, have demanded ever more comprehensive management at the same time that they have become increasingly vulnerable to disruption by humans. It is now at least possible that humans could so seriously insult the planet's chemical cycles and physical variables that natural self-regulatory processes could no longer correct them. There is a second reason for my preference for the term "Logos." In

characterizing it I noted that commentators agree that its comprehension is not merely intellectual. As one of them put it, it "claims" those who grasp it. Intrinsic to conceptions of Logos is commitment to realize, participate in, maintain, correct, transform—and not merely observe—orders grounded in and conforming to the world's order. How comprehension is to be turned into commitment is not clear. Earlier we discussed liturgy's capacities in this regard but later observed that it has been damaged in recent centuries and its weakened powers may not be sufficient to lay claims on those who matter. Nevertheless it, or related forms of action, should not be ruled out. I have found in my own recent work on the social and economic impacts of outer continental shelf oil leasing that participation in concerted actions conforming to ecological value and theory and directed toward the amelioration of ecological or other social disorders is likely to be found by participants to be "deeply" or "highly" meaningful and as such committing. With some judicious increase in the formalization of some aspects of such action it might become as committing as ritual. It could, in fact, itself become ritualized.

It seems obvious to me, at the end, that given humanity's powers to construct and destroy, and its position of dominance in ecosystems it itself destabilizes, its responsibility can no longer be to itself alone but must be to the world as a whole. If evolution, human and otherwise, is to continue humanity must think not merely of the world but on behalf of the world of which it is a very special part, and to which, therefore, it has enormous responsibilities. If this is true in some general sense for humanity as a whole it is particularly compelling for those whose profession it is to think about such matters, prominent among whom are anthropologists. We may recall here one of Heraclitus's modern commentators (Kleinknecht 1967:85): "The particular Logos of Man . . . is part of the general Logos . . . which achieves awareness in man."

The *Logos,* this is to say, can reach consciousness in the human mind and, so far as we know, only in the human mind. This proposes a view of human nature very different from *Homo economicus,* that golem of the economists into which life has been breathed not by the persuasiveness of their theory, but by its coerciveness. It is also very different from that alienated and fragmented creature, dazzled by surfaces and mystified by language's opacities, of whom literary post-modernists speak. Humanity, in this view, is not only a species among species. It is the only way the world has to think about itself. In my view anthropology's future lies in helping humanity to realize, that is, to understand and make real, such a vision of its place in the world.

INTELLECTUAL ROOTS

Roy A. Rappaport is the Walgreen Professor for the Study of Human Understanding at the University of Michigan where he has been a member of the Anthropology Department since 1965. A past president of the American Anthropological Association (1987-1989), he has done ethnographic fieldwork in Papua New Guinea (1962-64, 1981-82) after brief archaeological fieldwork in the Society Islands (1960). More recently, he has worked on environmental issues in the United States, most particularly on nuclear waste disposal and oil drilling on the outer continental shelf. His best known publications are *Pigs for the Ancestors* (2nd enlarged edition, 1984) and *Ecology, Meaning, and Religion* (1979).

I came to anthropology from an earlier career in inn-keeping because I felt decreasingly comfortable in the world of the late nineteen fifties and wanted to come to a deeper and more rigorous understanding of my own growing sense of alienation. I first thought of sociology, but one of the other contributors to this volume, Robert Levy (my first matrilateral parallel cousin), counseled me toward anthropology. A friend, Kai Erikson, and his father, Erik, also urged me to enter anthropology, the latter setting up an appointment for me with Clyde Kluckhohn at Harvard. In deference to Erik Erikson, Kluckhohn saw me, taking the occasion to deliver a monologue on why Harvard would not admit a 33-year-old with a ten-year-old bachelor's degree in Hotel Administration who had a B-grade-point average. I can't say I blame him, but at any rate I went to Columbia, an institution which, through its School of General Studies, had a mechanism for provisionally accepting anyone who walked in off the street.

The dominant paradigm at Columbia in those days was White's general evolution, which was most articulately represented by Morton Fried, an important early influence on me. Although I quickly rejected the Whitian perspective, the vision of a lawful and unified order underlying the multiplicity of structures and events more apparently constituting the human world was, and remains, exciting to me. Harold Conklin had not yet departed for Yale, and I found his classes in both ethnoscience and ecology very useful. In retrospect, Conrad Arensberg's courses in political anthropology, which focused upon the formal characteristics of hierarchies and their operation, had an abiding effect upon my thinking about the structure of adaptive systems. Two fieldwork seminars with Margaret Mead were invaluable, but, as an adjunct professor, she was seldom present and had, unfortunately, little influence upon most of the students. I took only one course with Marvin Harris, but the materialism he was developing at the time was something that we all needed to contend with.

Four months of archaeological fieldwork in the Society Islands in 1960 with Kenneth Emory and then with Roger Green were also important, for firsthand knowledge of Polynesian land and sea-scapes suggested to me the explanatory potential of general ecology. Upon returning to the United States I encountered Marshall Sahlins's recently published *Social Stratification in Polynesia* and also read widely in biological ecology which, at the time, was more or less committed to ecosystemic approaches. Pete Vayda, also centrally interested in ecology, joined the Columbia faculty at the time, and I began to work with him. He eventually became my dissertation chairman. Fred Barth visited from Norway that year and offered a course in ecological anthropology. By the end of the winter semester I was pretty much committed to ecological studies. Vayda and I coauthored two papers for the Pacific Science Congress in Hawaii in 1961 and then wrote a grant proposal for ecological work in Papua New Guinea which he, Ann Rappaport, Cherry Lowman-Vayda, and I commenced in 1962.

In reaction against the special form of ecology that Julian Steward thought necessary to accommodate the concept of culture, I had intended to study a local group of tribal horticulturalists in the same terms that animal ecologists study populations in ecosystems, and made observations and measurements to that end (e.g. areas under cultivation, yield per unit area, per capita intake, energy input per unit area). I was therefore surprised, to say the least, to discover that environmental relations among the people studied seemed to be regulated by a protracted ritual cycle. After completing *Pigs for the Ancestors,* I realized that I could provide an account of the place of ritual in a particular ecological system, but did not know why those functions were vested in ritual, nor anything about ritual itself. I subsequently became as interested in ritual and related matters (e.g. the concept of the sacred and religion in general) as in ecology and have remained so ever since.

I joined the Michigan department in 1965. My senior colleagues included Leslie White, with whom I shared an office one year, Elman Service, Eric Wolf, Marshall Sahlins, and Mervyn Meggitt. Rob Burling, Aram Yengoyan, and Norma Diamond were a bit in advance of me; Conrad Kottak, Kent Flannery, and Henry Wright came a year or so later. All influenced me to some degree. Perhaps most important initially were Sahlins, Wolf, and Meggitt: Wolf for the capacity of his mind, Meggitt for his rigor and erudition, Sahlins,

himself in transformation from evolutionism and ecology to structuralism, for simply challenging the materialist truisms of ecology and evolutionary anthropology.

I met Gregory Bateson in Hawaii in 1968 and he immediately became—and has remained—the most profound of influences upon me. Formally a student of Alfred Haddon, but, more deeply of his own father, the biologist William Bateson, his view of evolution and adaptation as informational processes, particularly as developed in a number of essays in *Steps to an Ecology of Mind,* seems to me to be synthetically promising. As Stephen Toulmin has observed, Bateson points not only to directions in which *anthropology* should move but to directions in which *science* in general should move.

My interests in ritual in particular and religion in general owe something to both Durkheim and Weber but are more obviously and directly indebted to other figures, both ancient and modern, outside as well as inside anthropology. They include importantly: Heraclitus of Ephesus, St. Augustine, Giambattista Vico, Charles Sanders Peirce, Gershom Sholem, J. L. Austin, Herbert Simon, Claude Shannon, Arnold van Gennep, Victor Turner, and Anthony F. C. Wallace. At present I am trying to find the time to complete the final draft of a large work on ritual that has occupied me intermittently for many years.

I have, in recent years, become increasingly interested in the ecological, social, and political problems troubling the late twentieth century. I have been serving on a very active National Academy of Science panel on the social and economic impacts of outer continental shelf oil drilling and a State of Nevada panel on the effects of locating the national high-level nuclear waste repository at Yucca Mountain. While president of the American Anthropological Association, I established a number of task forces and panels on contemporary problems. I plan to devote myself further to such matters in the future.

11

Methods Belong to All of Us

H. RUSSELL BERNARD

*Respect the nature of the empirical world
and organize a methodological stance to reflect that respect.*
Herbert Blumer (1969:60)

INTRODUCTION

The word "method" in anthropology, indeed
in all of social science, has at least three meanings.

First, method refers to *epistemology,* to sets of
assumptions about how we acquire knowledge. The phrase "scientific method," for example, encapsulates a set of such assumptions
(as well as some rules of practice). The assumptions are: (1) there is a reality "out there"
(or "in there" in the case of ideas and emotions); (2) it can be apprehended, more or less,
by human beings through direct experience
(or through some proxy for direct experience);
(3) all natural phenomena can be explained
without recourse to mysterious forces beyond
investigation; and (4) though the truth about
phenomena is never known, we do better and
better as old explanations are knocked down
and are replaced by better ones. Competing
epistemologies reject one or more of these
assumptions.

Second, method refers to *strategic approaches*
to the accumulation of actual data. Experimentalism and naturalism are two strategic approaches within the scientific method. Experimentalism involves the direct manipulation of
variables under the most controlled conditions
possible. Naturalism involves observing phe-

nomena in their natural environment. Sea-
going oceanographers, astronomers, wildlife
biologists, and anthropologists are all naturalists. Participant observation is a strategic approach to data gathering used by some
naturalists in the social sciences.

And third, method refers to *techniques* or sets
of techniques for collecting and analyzing
data. The survey questionnaire method is a set
of techniques (involving sampling, construction of instruments, interviewing, and other
things) *for collecting data.* Spot observation is
another set of techniques for gathering data
(for example, about how much time people
spend in various activities). Content analysis,
componential analysis, multidimensional scaling, and ethnographic decision tree modeling
are techniques for *analyzing* (extracting meaning from) data.

Anthropologists receive little formal training
in any of these three kinds of research methods. Many graduate programs in anthropology
offer *no* required course in ethnographic
methods (Trotter 1988; Plattner 1989). I believe that training in all three kinds of methods—epistemology, strategy, and technique—
should be a major part of both the undergraduate and graduate curriculum in anthropology.

How much training in methods is enough?
I'll address this question at the end of the

chapter. First, I discuss method as epistemology and method as strategy.

METHOD AS EPISTEMOLOGY

Positivism

One might draw a broad distinction between two epistemologies in cultural anthropology—positivist and interpretivist. I will focus on the former here and leave others (in this volume) to describe the latter for, in my view, the positivist perspective has not always been understood. Positivists and interpretivists may disagree on matters of epistemology. But when we talk about methods at the level of strategy and technique, methods belong to all of us.

At its birth, positivism was simple enough. Here is John Stuart Mill in 1866 explaining "le positivisme" to an English-speaking audience.

Whoever regards all events as parts of a constant order, each one being the invariable consequent of some antecedent condition, or combination of conditions, accepts fully the Positive mode of thought. . . . (15)

All theories in which the ultimate standard of institutions and rules of actions [is] the happiness of mankind, and observation and experience the guides . . . are entitled to the name Positive. (69)

Positivism[1] in the mid-nineteenth century was science applied to the study of humanity, and done in the exuberant and optimistic spirit of service to human happiness.

The French social philosopher Auguste Comte didn't just believe in science as an effective means for seeking instrumental knowledge, though. He envisioned a class of philosophers who, with support from the state, would direct all education. They would advise the government, which would be composed of capitalists "whose dignity and authority," explained Mill, "are to be in the

ratio of the degree of generality of their conceptions and operations—bankers at the summit, merchants next, then manufacturers, and agriculturalists at the bottom" (1866:122). Comte attracted admirers who wanted to implement the master's plans. Mercifully, they are gone, but the word "positivist" still carries the taint of Comte's ego.

Logical Positivism

The modern version of positivism was developed by members of the Vienna Circle, a group of philosophers, mathematicians, physicists, and social scientists who met from 1923 to 1936 in a series of seminars. The members of the circle were committed to empiricism and against metaphysics. Hunches could come from anywhere, but scientific knowledge, they said, is based only on experience, and scientific explanation is based only on logical, mathematical principles. Hence the label "logical empiricists," by which they were known for a while.

For these positivists, logic was paramount. They understood that the assumptions of science are assertions. They also understood that the assumptions of science are not *mere assumptions*. The members of the Vienna Circle were committed to a scientific, that is logical, mode of thinking and to the benefits that this would bring to humanity. This was the component of positivism that they shared with Comte. It's what motivates many social scientists today, including me, to count ourselves as positivists.

It is clear, of course, just how dangerous this commitment can be. My ideas about what is good may not be the same as yours. This is what makes the study of ethics a critical part of method as epistemology.

Numbers and Science

In the early decades of this century, many luminaries of cultural anthropology supported the collection of both quantitative and qualitative data. They collected texts and counted things as necessary in their research.

For example, one of Tylor's enduring contributions to anthropology was his paper "On a Method of Investigating the Development of Institutions" (1889). In that paper, Tylor described a numerical method for doing systematic cross-cultural comparisons. One of Boas's great contributions was a monograph in which he demonstrated the relationship of nutrition to body size among immigrants, rendering useless much racist rhetoric of the day against allowing Eastern Europeans into the United States. Kroeber's study of 300 years of women's fashions is a landmark in the quantitative study of cultural trace materials (Richardson and Kroeber 1940).

When I was a graduate student at the University of Illinois thirty years ago, the tradition of using both qualitative and quantitative data was still strong. Oscar Lewis, for example, advocated the use of survey methods to complement ethnographic field studies.[2] Joseph Casagrande taught cross-cultural hypothesis testing using the Human Relations Area Files. Both, of course, were ethnographers who had collected reams of qualitative data.

There was, to be sure, another tradition in anthropology, one opposed to the use of quantitative data. The cause against quantification in anthropology was eloquently taken up by one of Boas's students, Paul Radin, in 1933. In *The Method and Theory of Ethnology,* Radin praised his teacher for criticizing Tylor's and Frazer's evolutionary doctrines. But he accused Boas of being "naturwissenschaftlich eingestellt" or science-minded (Radin 1933:10), of believing that cultural facts could be transformed into physical ones and counted. He railed at Boas for training a generation of students like Kroeber, Sapir, Lowie, Wissler, and Mead who, Radin said, sought to tag cultures and habitats, like animal and plant species, and compare them statistically (Radin 1933:10).

Radin was right about that crowd, but he had a different idea of what anthropology should be about. An ethnographer had to live a long time with the people whom he or she studied, and had to learn the native language fluently. Above all, said Radin, the ethnographer must provide readers with the original texts, the materials from which he or she makes observations.

Those texts, and the exegesis of the ethnologist, should show current cultural realities "as seen through the mirror of an actual man's heart and brain and not through the artificial heart and brain of the marionettes with which Boas and Sapir and Kroeber operate" (Radin 1933:10). Radin didn't mince any words. To demonstrate his method, Radin presented a meticulous analysis of a series of texts from three Winnebagos about the Peyote Cult. In one of those texts, John Rave discussed his conversion to the Peyote Cult. Radin drew on his knowledge of local history. He showed that Rave's account reflected acceptance by Rave of particular components of Christian faith and particular components of earlier Winnebago beliefs. Rave failed to achieve a vision during his Winnebago puberty rite, and was denied membership in the Medicine Dance. This, said Radin, accounted for Rave's proselytizing zeal.

You can object to all this as just so much pop-psych, but Radin was the consummate fieldworker: he knew the language, he spent years working with the Winnebagos and with these particular informants, and he had the texts to back up everything he said. If Kroeber and Boas and Sapir didn't like his arguments, Radin said, "there still remains the document for them to interpret better and more profoundly" (1933:238).[3]

Radin would not have wanted to be remembered as a scientist, but in my terms he was—and a gifted one, at that. He was empirical in the extreme; he built arguments only from observations; he was committed to the open-endedness of truth. With all his texts on the Peyote Cult, he had the data on which to postulate a theory of revitalization. That he left this nomothetic exercise to others who would come later diminishes not one whit the contribution of Radin's effort.

Many anthropologists today who share Radin's views about primary data also want to contribute to the development of knowledge about regularities in human behavior. They may have some well-founded doubts about whether *all* the phenomena in which they are interested can be quantified accurately. But I believe that what keeps many cultural anthropologists (I haven't counted them, but I'm guessing hundreds, not dozens) from conducting quantitative research is that they are just unequipped to do it when they leave graduate school.

METHOD AS STRATEGY: PARTICIPANT OBSERVATION

Anthropologists are divided on epistemological issues, but almost all of us use the strategic method of participant observation to collect our primary data. Even anthropologists who use questionnaires in their research engage first in participant observation in order to build the questionnaire instrument.

Participant observation is what makes it possible for interpretivists and positivists alike to collect life-history documents, attend sacred festivals, talk to people about sensitive topics, map the landholdings of informants, trek with a hunter to count the kill, and interview women traders formally and informally about how they cover their losses in the daily market. Among other things, participant observation helps us build rapport. Rapport is what makes it possible for us to observe and talk to people and record information about their lives.[4]

Improving Participant Observation

Anthropologists developed the method of participant observation, and we have seen with satisfaction its acceptance by researchers in many other disciplines. But we haven't fol-

lowed up. After decades of experience with the method of participant observation, we are not much further along than when we started. We haven't studied participant observation systematically; we haven't improved it.

At least five things affect the kind and quality of data we can collect as participant observers: (1) personal characteristics, such as age and gender; (2) language fluency; (3) objectivity; (4) informant accuracy; and (5) informant representativeness.

Personal Characteristics. By the 1930s, Margaret Mead had already made clear the importance of gender as a variable in data collection. Gender has at least two consequences: it influences how you perceive others; it limits your access to certain information.

In all cultures, you can't ask people certain questions because you're a [woman][man]. You can't go into certain areas and situations because you're a [woman][man]. You can't watch this or report on that because you're a [woman][man]. Even the culture of anthropologists is affected: your credibility is diminished or enhanced with your colleagues when you talk about a certain subject because you're a [woman][man]. (See Golde 1970; Whitehead and Conaway 1986; Scheper-Hughes 1983b; Altorki and El-Solh 1988.)

When she worked at the Thule relocation camp for Japanese-Americans during World War II, Rosalie Wax did not join any of the women's groups or organizations. Looking back after more than forty years, Wax concluded that this was just poor judgment.

I was a university student and a researcher. I was not yet ready to accept myself as a total person, and this limited my perspective and my understanding. Those of us who instruct future field workers should encourage them to understand and value their full range of being, because only then can they cope intelligently with the range of experience they will encounter in the field. (1986:148)

Besides gender, we have also learned that being old lets you into certain things and shuts you out of others. Being a parent helps you talk to people about certain areas of life and get more information than if you were not a parent. Being wealthy lets you talk to certain people about certain subjects and makes others avoid you. Gregarious anthropologists may be unable to talk to shy people.

Being divorced has its costs. Nancie González found that being a divorced mother of two young sons in the Dominican Republic was just too much. "Had I to do it again," she says, "I would invent widowhood with appropriate rings and photographs" (1986:92). Even height may make a difference: Alan Jacobs once told me he thought he did better fieldwork with the Maasai because he's almost 6 1/2 feet tall than he would have if he'd been, say, an average-sized 5 feet 10 inches.

Language Fluency. Thirty years ago, Raoul Naroll (1962:89-90) found suggestive statistical evidence that anthropologists who speak the local language are more likely to report witchcraft than those who don't. His interpretation was that local language fluency improves your rapport, and this, in turn increases the probability that people will tell you about witchcraft.

Does the credibility of our data depend on control of the local language? In his 1933 diatribe against his science-minded peers, Radin complained that Mead's work on Samoa was superficial because she wasn't fluent in Samoan (1933:179). Fifty years later, Derek Freeman (1983) raised questions about whether Mead had been duped by her informants, perhaps because she didn't know the local language well enough.[5]

According to Brislin, Lonner, and Thorndike (1973:70) Samoa is one of those cultures where "it is considered acceptable to deceive and to 'put on' outsiders. Interviewers are likely to hear ridiculous answers, not given in a spirit of hostility but rather sport." Brislin et al. call this the "sucker bias," and warn fieldworkers to watch out for it. Presumably, knowing the local language fluently is one

way to become alert to and avoid this problem.

If participant observers run the risk of being suckered, then research is called for to determine (1) the conditions under which that's most/least likely to happen and (2) how to recognize and avoid it. Research is called for on the kinds of data available to "indigenous anthropologists" that are not available to outsiders, and vice versa (see Messerschmidt 1981 for papers on doing fieldwork in your own culture). Research is called for on making participant observation the best strategic method it can be.

Objectivity. No one I've ever known in the social sciences has seriously thought that humans could become robotic, completely objective field researchers. But just because perfect objectivity is impossible, this does not let us off the hook. The economist Robert Sarlow is reported to have observed that, while a perfectly aseptic environment is impossible, this doesn't mean we might as well conduct surgery in a sewer (cited by Geertz 1973:30). Objectivity clearly varies from person to person. Some people achieve more of it, others less. More is better.

Objectivity means becoming aware of one's biases, and transcending them, not the lack of any biases. Some people do better at transcending, some do worse. Striving for objectivity is important even if perfect objectivity is unobtainable.

Laurie Krieger, an American woman doing fieldwork in Cairo, studied physical punishment against women. She learned that wife beatings were less violent than she had imagined, and that the act still sickened her. Her reaction brought out a lot of information from women who were recent recipients of their husbands' wrath. "I found out," she says, "that the biased outlook of an American woman and a trained anthropologist was not always disadvantageous, as long as I was aware of and able to control the expression of my biases" (1986:120).

The need for objectivity is recognized by even the most qualitative fieldworkers. Colin Turnbull says that the key to good fieldwork is "to know ourselves more deeply by conscious subjectivity" because in this way "the ultimate goal of objectivity is much more likely to be reached and our understanding of other cultures that much more profound" (1986:27).

Objectivity does not mean (and has never meant) value neutrality. No one asks Cultural Survival, Inc., to be neutral in documenting the violent obscenities against indigenous peoples of the world. No one asks Amnesty International to be neutral in its effort to document state-sanctioned torture. We recognize that the power of the documentation is in its objectivity, in its irrefutability, not in its neutrality.

Informant Accuracy. In 1940, C. Wright Mills wrote that "the central methodological problem of the social sciences" is the fact that what people say and what they do is so different (1940:329). He was right, and the problem remains central today.

Informants lie, of course. But lying appears to be a small part of the problem. Informants, like all of us, make honest errors of commission (they say they did things that they didn't do) and of omission (they neglect to report things that they did do) in reporting their own behavior.

The problem was articulated clearly by Richard La Pierre in 1934. Accompanied by a young Chinese couple, he crisscrossed the United States by car. They stayed at and ate at 66 hotels and 184 restaurants. Six months after the trip was over, La Pierre wrote a letter to all those hotels and restaurants, telling the managers that he was planning a trip and would they mind serving Chinese people? More than 90 percent said they would not serve Chinese people. Irwin Deutscher picked up the theme in 1972, in his book *What We Say, What We Do*. He made it clear that the problem had not been solved, despite the fact

that scholars from many disciplines had read La Pierre's study and had recognized its importance.

My colleagues and I conducted a series of studies during the 1970s to find out if people could accurately report their social interactions (see Bernard and Killworth 1977, for example). A lot of social science, after all, is based on data collected by asking people "*who did you* [talk to] [exchange memos with] [interact with] [call on the telephone] *in the last* [24 hours] [week] [month]?" In 1984, my colleagues and I reviewed the literature on informant accuracy. A long list of studies, including our own, showed that a fourth to a half of what informants say about their behavior is inaccurate.

This finding shows up in studies of what people say they eat, how often they claim to have gone to the doctor in a given period of time, and in how much money they say they have in their savings accounts. It shows up in the most unlikely (we would have thought) places: in the 1961 census of Addis Ababa, 23 percent of the women underreported the number of their children. Apparently, people don't "count" babies that die before reaching the age of two (Pausewang 1973:65).

Progress is being made in explaining informant inaccuracy. Thirty years ago, Cancian (1963) showed how informant errors conformed to expected patterns in prestige rankings in a Mexican village. D'Andrade showed in 1974 that there is a general pressure to think in terms of "what goes with what" even if this creates errors in reporting factual events. (Also see Shweder and D'Andrade 1980.) More recently, Freeman, Romney, and Freeman (1987) found that, for some behaviors at least, informants report *typical* behavior to social scientists rather than specific behavior when asked to dredge up what they actually did and who they actually interacted with (see also Freeman and Romney 1987; McNabb 1990).

People round off, in other words, and report behavior according to rules of central tendency. This may go for informants' reports of their own behavior as well as for their reports of the behavior of others. (Cognitive psychologists, of course, have done careful investigations of how people store and retrieve information.)

Still, the question remains: When people report their behavior to us, do we get inaccurate answers, or answers that are accurate proxies for some other question about norms?

Informant Representativeness. Even if informants tell us accurately what they know, there remains the question of whether what they know is representative of the population we are studying.

Since the 1930s, cultural anthropology and sociology have gone their separate ways largely over this issue. Sociologists have focused on developing systematic instruments (like questionnaires) and applying those questionnaires to representative samples of respondents in a population. This places emphasis on reliability (whatever the instrument measures today it will measure tomorrow, more or less) and on external validity (whatever we find out from the sample can be extended to the rest of the population, within some known limits of error).

Anthropologists have focused on internal validity. What good is it to know that data are reliable or generalizable if they are inaccurate? Every social scientist knows horror stories of questionnaires that force people to produce nonsensical answers (because the questions are culturally inappropriate, for example).

On the other hand, why would we want to know what a handful of informants think or do, if the information cannot be generalized beyond those informants? This is one area where considerable progress has been made in anthropology. Jeffrey Johnson's recent book (1990) on selecting ethnographic informants summarizes much useful information in this area. Romney, Weller, and Batchelder (1986) offer a technique called consensus modeling

for selecting informants who are experts in particular cultural domains (like ethnozoology, local medical practice, or whatever). Romney et al. demonstrate that, when assumptions of their model are met, just six informants may be enough to achieve representative, valid information about a cultural domain. It is an intriguing line of research.

METHODS TRAINING IN ANTHROPOLOGY

I believe that training in methods should be a key part of both the undergraduate and the graduate curriculum in anthropology. How much is enough? Well, given the three meanings of the word "method" (epistemology, strategy, and technique), it takes a lot to be enough.

Epistemology

All anthropologists need a thorough grounding in the various approaches to knowledge that have characterized our discipline. This means exposure of all students, whatever their initial predilections, to the philosophical foundations of structuralism, symbolism, interpretivism, hermeneutics, phenomenology, positivism, and empiricism.

Training in ethics should be part of the training in epistemology. Plattner (1989:33) makes the case:

Training in the ethics of research is as important as training in the techniques of research design, data collection and data analysis. Research consists of a series of decisions (where to study, what to study, who to interview, what questions to ask, when to leave the field), and every decision . . . has an ethical component.

Every anthropologist has stories to tell about how his or her ethics were tested by circumstances in the field. We have accumulated a large collection of these cases, in the *Newsletter* of the *American Anthropological Association*, for example, and in Cassell and Jacobs (1987). We ought systematically to use the wisdom they provide and not rely on the telling of stories informally to disseminate that wisdom. The case-study method is used in teaching law and business administration. A case-study course on ethics should be part of every graduate curriculum in anthropology.

Strategy

All anthropologists need *formal* training in participant observation. This means familiarity with the accumulating literature on the subject. It means studying what we already know about how good and bad participant observation is done—about culture shock, about gender roles in the field, about violence, disease, and other hazards of field research, about maintaining objectivity without the pretense of value neutrality.

This kind of training will give anthropologists the skills they need to do better fieldwork. It will also give them the means to contribute concretely to improving participant observation.

Technique

This is where it gets tough. College graduates in the social sciences these days simply must know how to use a computer—not just for word processing but for data entry, data management, data retrieval, and data analysis. Students of anthropology who manage to escape getting these skills before going to graduate school will need compensatory education before they can study formal data collection and analysis.

Once the basics are out of the way, anthropologists need training in research design, in data collection (structured and unstructured interviewing, for example), and in data analysis. Students who hope to do any serious work with survey data, for example, need at least two courses in applied statistics (through

multivariate analysis). Students who want to work with a large corpus of field notes, or with life history material, need training in computer-based text management.

All anthropologists need formal training in *the collection and analysis of both qualitative and quantitative* data. Photography, videography, audio taping, stenography, and sketching are methods for collecting qualitative data. Coding, counting, and measuring produce quantitative data. People's responses to open-ended questionnaire items are qualitative. Coding and attaching numbers to the responses create quantitative data. Observing people and recording their behavior in words produce qualitative data. Counting the behaviors creates quantitative data. Transcribed texts are qualitative data. Counting the number of times people use a particular word or theme in a text creates quantitative data.

Pawing through field notes is qualitative data processing. Putting the notes on a computer and using a text management program to paw through them is still data processing. Doing a chi-square test with a hand-held calculator is quantitative data processing. So is putting thousands of numbers into a computer and having the machine calculate the chi-square value.

Much of what is called statistical analysis is, in my vocabulary, data processing, not data analysis. Thinking about the themes in a text, like field notes, is data *analysis*. Thinking about what a chi-square (or any statistical) value *means* is also data analysis. All analysis is ultimately qualitative. But we can't even get to that stage unless we've collected solid (valid, credible) data.

Besides learning to use research methods, we should be improving them. Every field trip provides information on how personal characteristics and language fluency affect data collection. Every field trip is an opportunity to test the relationship between what people say and what they do. We need to monitor and publish the results of all these naturally occurring experiments.[6]

CONCLUSION

In the past, cultural anthropologists were more concerned with description than with explanation and prediction. A good description is *still* its own analysis; being right about what causes a problem is still the best contribution anyone can make to solving it; and good writing—telling a good story—is still the best method any anthropologist can acquire.

Many anthropologists today, however, are interested in research questions that demand explanation and prediction, questions like: Why are women in nearly all industrial societies, socialist and capitalist alike, paid less than men for the same work? Why is medical care so hard to get in some societies that produce plenty of it? Does cultural pluralism support or undermine the stability of states (as in Canada, Belgium, India, Azerbaijan, Yugoslavia, or Kenya, for example)?

Answering such questions demands greater sophistication in research methods than is now customary in anthropology. It requires skills in comparative statistical research and in gathering data from published sources including data that are only available on computer tapes. Anthropologists who are involved in multidisciplinary team research on complex human problems—in agricultural development, fertility control, health care delivery, and education—need more methods training than has been the norm to date.

Knowing about methods for collecting qualitative and quantitative data is more difficult in some ways today than it was forty years ago. There are simply more methods now than there were then.[7] In some ways, though, learning research techniques is easier now. Microcomputers and efficient software make text management, statistics, and cultural domain analysis less intimidating.[8] No one can control all research methods. But those who control a certain fraction will be unintimidated about learning new methods that become available and that seem appropriate to particular research projects.

As I said at the beginning of this essay, anthropologists may disagree, even vehemently, about method as epistemology. But they share a common interest in and concern for method at the level of strategy and technique. Controlling many different methods for collecting and analyzing qualitative and quantitative data liberates us to investigate whatever theoretical questions attract us. And conversely: limited training in methods limits our ability to think about and solve many important theoretical questions. Knowing more is better than knowing less.

NOTES

1. Mill felt that the French word *positivisme* was not suited to English, but decided in the end to use Comte's word, properly anglicized to refer to Comte's concept. I've long wished Mill had decided otherwise.

2. See Lewis's contribution to the 1953 volume *Anthropology Today*, edited by Alfred Kroeber. See also Lewis's article on family studies in the 1950 volume of the *American Journal of Sociology*. In those days, family studies was still the province of sociologists. When Lewis wrote for anthropologists, he stressed the need for survey research as a complement to ethnography. When he wrote for sociologists, he stressed the need for ethnographic research as a complement to survey data.

3. I was inspired as a graduate by Radin's work on the production and presentation of native texts. Radin followed Boas's lead in native ethnography of indigenous North American peoples. Boas trained George Hunt, a Kwakiutl, to write ethnographic descriptions of Kwakiutl culture. Hunt produced over 5,000 pages of notes that served as the basis for much of Boas's published work on Kwakiutl life. Radin trained Crashing Thunder to write in Winnebago, and Crashing Thunder wrote his classic autobiography of the same name.

Native ethnography has long held great promise as a means to develop an authentic emic data base about Indian and other indigenous cultures. I can only surmise that the physical difficulties involved must have kept native ethnography from becoming a major method in cultural anthropology.

In recent years, I have found that microcomputers make native ethnography much easier to do. I simply program a word processor to handle whatever special characters are needed in a particular language, teach native speakers of previously nonwritten languages to use the equipment, and hand the equipment over to them.

For many years, my partner in this effort has been Jesús Salinas Pedraza, a Ñähñu (Otomí) Indian from the Mezquital Valley of Mexico. Salinas has written an extensive ethnography of the Ñähñu, which I translated and annotated (Bernard and Salinas 1989).

Since 1987, Salinas and Josefa González Ventura, a Ñuu Saavi (Mixtec) Indian from Oaxaca, Mexico, have run the Native Literacy Center at the Centro de Investigaciones y Estudios Superiores en Antropología Social in Oaxaca City. They have now trained 75 other Indians from Mexico, Peru, Bolivia, Argentina, Ecuador, and Chile to use microcomputers to write books in their respective native languages.

There are many social and ethical issues raised by this effort. I deal with these, and the history of the project, in Bernard 1992.

4. In this sense, participant observation, like everyday life, is also an exercise in impression management (see Berreman 1962:11).

5. Was Mead duped? Whether she was or not has nothing to do with her overwhelming contributions to anthropology. All ethnographers run the same risk.

6. How much, for example, can we rely on informants to tell us about their income? The size of their landholdings? Where their grown children are? Data on the nature and causes of informant inaccuracy would help illuminate the relation between cognition and behavior, between the internal and the external worlds of human beings around the world.

7. Methods do come and go, however. No one uses so-called "culture free" tests anymore to investigate cognition cross-culturally. Those tests were discredited and abandoned by most researchers thirty years ago (Brislin, Lonner, and Thorndike 1973:109).

8. For handling relatively small amounts of text material (up to say, a thousand pages of field notes, transcribed interviews, etc.) GoFer is an excellent product. Write to Microlytics, Inc., Two Tobey Village Office Park, Pittsford, NY 14534. For handling large amounts of text material, ZyINDEX is highly recommended. Write to ZyLAB, Information Dimensions, Inc., 100 Lexington Drive, Buffalo Grove, IL 60089. For coding and analyzing text, consider the following: (1) The Text Handler, by Gery Ryan. This package works with WordPerfect. Write to Gery Ryan, Dept. of Anthropology, University of Florida, Gainesville, FL 32611. (2) TALLY 3.0, by Jeffrey W. Bowyer. This program works with ASCII files. Write to Wm. C Brown Publishers, 2460 Kerper Boulevard, Dubuque, IA 52001. (3) DtSEARCH, by David Thede. DtSEARCH works with all of the top word processors, as well as with ASCII files. Write to DT Software, Inc., 2101 Crystal Plaza Arcade, Suite 231 Arlington, VA 22202. (4) THE ETHNOGRPH, by John Seidel. This program works with text from major word processors. Write to Qualis Research Associates, P.O. Box 2240, Corvalis, OR 97339. ANTHROPAC, by Stephen Borgatti, helps researchers collect and analyze numerical data. It is particularly useful for multidimensional scaling, hierarchical clustering, consensus modeling and other methods that operate on similarity matrices. Write to Analytic Technologies, 306 South Walker Street, Columbia, SC 29205.

Most of the programs mentioned here have been reviewed in *Cultural Anthropology Methods* from 1989 to 1993.

INTELLECTUAL ROOTS

H. Russell Bernard is Professor of Anthropology at the University of Florida. He has done field research in Greece, Mexico, and the United States and on ships at sea. Bernard was editor of *Human Organization* (1976-1981) and of the *American Anthropologist* (1981-1989). Recently Bernard has been working with Jesús Salinas and other Indian colleagues in Oaxaca, Mexico, to establish a center where native peoples can publish books in their own languages. Bernard's best-known contributions are *Research Methods in Cultural Anthropology* (1988); *Native Ethnography* (with Jesús Salinas Pedraza, 1989); *Technology and Social Change* (edited with Pertti Pelto, 2nd edition, 1987); and a series of articles on social network analysis (with Peter Killworth and others).

In the summer of 1959, as a junior at Queens College, I went to Mexico to study Spanish and came back knowing that I wanted to be an anthropologist. As an undergraduate, I studied with Ernestine Friedl, Hortense Powdermaker, and Mariam Slater. Late in my senior year, Powdermaker told me about a new Ph.D. program just opening at the

University of Illinois. Perhaps I could get in there, she said.

Illinois in 1961 was an intense intellectual environment. I studied with Kenneth Hale and Duane Metzger for my M.A. in anthropological linguistics, and then with Edward Bruner, Oscar Lewis, Julian Steward, Dimitri Shimkin, Kris Lehman, and Joseph Casagrande for the Ph.D.

Metzger was part of the (then) new ethnoscience camp. The goal was to write the grammar of a culture—to learn what a native speaker of a language knows about, say, ordering a drink and to lay that knowledge out clearly.

Making cultural grammars turned out to be harder than anyone imagined. Metzger offered a hands-on seminar. With a few other students, I spent a semester working with one Japanese housewife, learning and mapping the implicit rules she used for deciding how to cut and arrange vegetables on a plate.

It was an enormous effort just to keep track of the data. One of the other students got the computer to sort and print the whole corpus every time we learned a new rule. The people over at the computer center thought this was pretty quaint, but this systematic approach to data gathering and the idea of using computers to make light work of complex data-management tasks have stayed with me ever since.

Ken Hale was Carl Voegelin's student. Like Carl (and like Boas and his early students before him), Ken worked closely and collaboratively with Indian colleagues. The model was to help Indian colleagues produce their own texts, in their own languages, and then to use the texts for linguistic analysis and for cultural exegesis. Ken's example, and the tradition it represented, led to my lifelong collaboration with Jesús Salinas, a Ñähñu Indian from the Mezquital Valley in Mexico.

Jesús was my informant in 1962 when I did the research for my M.A. thesis on the tone patterns of Ñähñu (called Otomí in those days). In 1971, I became Jesús's informant, teaching him to write in Ñähñu and, in the 1980s, to use a Ñähñu word processor. I'm still working with Jesús, who now heads CELIAC, the Native Literacy Center in Oaxaca, where Indians from around Latin America train in using computers to write and print books in their own languages.

Much of my career, then, was shaped by my work at the M.A. level. I learned from that experience how important it is for students to become involved in research projects early and often.

During my Ph.D. studies, Julian Steward, Dimitri Shimkin, Joe Casagrande, and Kris Lehman encouraged me to pursue my interests in quantitative data analysis. In Casagrande's seminar on cross-cultural research, I first learned to use the Human Relations Area Files and to test hypotheses using cultures as units of analysis.

I don't recall anyone labeling all this "positivism" in those days, or worrying about whether my interest in scientific, quantitative research was unhealthy. I read works by Tylor, Boas, Kroeber, Driver, Wissler, Murdock, and Roberts and noticed that all of them did quantitative work and published reams of ethnographic work as well. I found this mix of qualitative and quantitative methods to be very sensible.

My major doctoral professor was Ed Bruner. Ed became identified with symbolic anthropology and I went in a different direction. But Ed taught me to write, and to understand that seeking knowledge was only half the battle. You have to be able to tell others what you have learned, to engage their attention, and to keep them from closing the book before you have finished your argument. This may be one of the few things that positivists and interpretivists fully agree on; but for my money, it's the most important thing of all.

In 1972, I spent a year at the Scripps Institution of Oceanography, where I met Peter Killworth, an ocean physicist. We decided to study problems together that (1) neither of us could tackle alone, (2) both of us agreed were sheer fun, and (3) were not in the mainstream of research in either of our disciplines. We also agreed that we would not let our joint projects get in the way of our separate research careers. (He is in ocean modeling.)

We did, in fact, have a great time doing a series of papers on informant accuracy, and we are having just as much fun now testing a network model for estimating the size of populations that you cannot count (like the number of rape victims in a city). Peter has taught me a lot about data analysis.

I have also benefited greatly from my association with Pertti Pelto. We began the National Science Foundation Summer Institute on Research Methods in Cultural Anthropology in 1987. Stephen Borgatti joined the teaching team of the summer institute in 1988, and I have learned a lot from him about new analytic methods.

My intellectual biography is still being written. I can look back and see the influences of my professors clearly. But just as clearly, I see the influence of contemporaries, of junior colleagues, and of students. This is what makes anthropology so exciting for me. The learning never has to slow down.

12

Person-Centered Anthropology

ROBERT I. LEVY

PEOPLE AND THEIR CONTEXTS

One of anthropology's central achievements has been the isolation of "culture" as a coherent way of understanding aspects of human behavior and experience. That achievement has been an important moral and intellectual accomplishment. But like all such generative simplicities, it split the world up in ways that have generated new conceptual problems while managing to perpetuate some old ones in a new language. The problems we are concerned with here are those suggested by such conventionally contrasted terms as culture and the culture carrier, role and self, culture and mind, and culture and personality.[1] We will call investigations which are centered on the problems of examining and thinking about the relations of people and their contexts person-centered anthropology.[2]

A shifting, divided view of conditions of life on the one hand and of the people who live lives on the other is probably universal. In seventeenth- and eighteenth-century European encounters with brand-new worlds, explorers, who were expected to contribute to European knowledge as well as power, were interested—as the British Admiralty's statement of mission to Captain Cook put it—in "the genius and temper" of the natives as well as such strategically interesting material matters as their spatial "disposition and number."[3] Europeans wanted to know not only how the natives lived but what they were like, that is, what kinds of humans they were. The "noble and ignoble savages" that the times were obsessed with were fantasies about the "inner" qualities of the people out there as well as about the lives they lived.

These two commonsensical ways of looking at people require a skillful shifting of viewpoints. Trouble comes when, having accepted the reality (or usefulness) of "context" and "individual" as separate spheres, one tries to conceive of context (culture, society, location in history and the world) and "inner natures" (self, personality, temperament, mind) at the same time and in some logical or causal interrelation.

There are deep conceptual and, in fact, ideological problems troubling attempts to deal with people and contexts in some coordinated vision. Anthropology, in keeping with its discovery (or invention) of culture, dealt with the problem of the people in the communities it studied in various more or less offhanded ways. Sometimes it assumed that there was no distinction between culture and people, culture being written into people as it was into baskets. In this mood we talked of patterns and styles of culture, national character, ethos, eidos, and values. Most commonly, we assumed that there was a distinction. But in our obsession with culture, we either played down the "actor" in a consideration of actorless scripts, or assumed an unproblematic "anthropological man," some universal role player who learned to find his way through the local cultural maze and whose pan-human peculiarities had to be taken into account in one way or another by all communities. Individuals were, generally, not seen as proper topics for central anthropological investigation. But anthropology's obsessions with the contexts of experience abstracted from the particular people who do the experiencing left a peculiarly shaped void, motivating attempts to fill the gaps by such things as life histories, humanistic essays, and the various approaches of the subdiscipline called "culture and personality" or, in latter years, "psychological anthropology."

This void-filling was institutionalized and made into elegant and, for a while, bewitching imagery in Harvard's mid-century Department of Social Relations, where the analysis of human social action was to be exhaustively compartmentalized into three different "systems"—"personality," "society," and "culture"—conveniently corresponding to the three established academic disciplines, psychology, sociology, and anthropology.

Once split and bounded, a search for "transactions" between the separate spheres became necessary. Culture and personality theory, for example, is full of miscellaneous ingenious attempts to relate cultural institutions to psychological structures and vice versa. By and large, the various theories of the individual (for the most part, originally, psychoanalytic ones) used in these enterprises were fitted into the residual spaces left by theories of culture and society.

The Boasian Legacy

In early anthropology, conceptions *condensing* alien actor and his or her alien action—usually to the detriment of the actor and the elevation of ourselves—enabled romantic assumptions about the personal bravery and ferociousness of Native American warriors. They helped generate patronizing convictions about the fundamental licentiousness and (at the same time) innocence of South Sea Islanders, the persisting infantile thought processes of cannibals who seemed to believe that eating the heart of their enemies would make them brave. Or, closer to the Euro-American homeland, they helped generate images of the incorrigible avariciousness and clannish nature of Jews, the wired-in dishonesty of Gypsies, the laziness of Southern Europeans (produced by eons of too much sunshine), and the like.

Liberal and optimistic thinkers sometimes blamed such "inferior natures" on imperfect education and the bad examples of others. But in the late nineteenth century and early twentieth century, European and American views of the world generally held by the prejudiced, the privileged and the powerful thought of such "inferior natures" as biologically and racially based. The actions of primitive people and the actions of, say, Southern Europeans or Irish or Blacks were thought to be (1) direct indexes of the nature of those peoples' "minds," and (2) evidence of the limits and generally unpleasant qualities of their *fixed* abilities.

It was against this background of assumptions, with their powerful implications for social attitudes and policies, that the seminal articulation of anthropology's "culture theory" by Franz Boas developed.[4] The behavior of the exotic other was now interpreted in a different way. Action and actor were now split apart by means of a new use of the concept of "culture."

It is useful to follow Boas's arguments in the first edition of *The Mind of Primitive Man*, published in 1911, to glimpse this new anthropological common sense in the making. "We recognize that there are two possible explanations of the different manifestations of the mind of man," he wrote (Boas 1911b:102):[5]

It may be that the minds of different races show differences of organization; that is to say, the laws of mental activity may not be the same for all minds. But it may also be that the organization of mind is practically identical among all races of man; that mental activity follows the same laws everywhere, but that its manifestations depend upon the charac-

ter of individual experience *that is subjected to the action of these laws (emphasis added)*.

The first move, then, away from racist assumptions was to deny comparative differences in the "organization" of the mind. It is important to note that Boas in 1911 accepted his opponents' assumption that such "mental characteristics" as "inhibition of impulses," "power of attention," and "power of original thought," if they were taken to be indexes of different kinds of "laws of mental activity"— that is of different sorts of "organization of the mind"—would necessarily be "hereditary."

The second move was to separate an actor's *behavior* from his *essence*. Boas's solution to the problem of exotic behaviors—particularly those looked down on by Europeans—was that they were responses of equivalent universal actors to different "situations." "The proper way to compare the fickleness of the savage and that of the white is to compare their behavior in undertakings which are equally important to each" (Boas 1911b:107). The comparative "importance" of a "situation" or "undertaking" was in itself, as Boas was aware, a "mental" phenomena, so he added an essential, concluding point:

The explanation of the activity of the mind of man . . . requires the discussion of two distinct problems. The first bears upon the question of unity or diversity of organization of the mind, while the second bears upon the diversity produced by the variety of contents of the mind as found in the various social and geographical environments. (1911b:104)

In this powerful use of the conception of "culture," it was natural for Boas to reject a radical assumption—that "the organization of mental activity" might well be in part determined by local experience. He sensed, perhaps, that even experientially determined differences in the "organization of the mind" could be used for the same sorts of discriminatory actions which genetic theories had supported. He solved the problem of exotic behavior by separating situations (and their re-

flections in "contents of the mind") from the rest of the person. The remainder, the common humanity, was now in a sense quantitatively enlarged. The "savage" was made very closely akin to the "civilized man" and the suspect Southern and Eastern European to his Northwestern European judges.

The now critical *internal* variable, the informational "content" of minds, was derived from the structure of local situations and experiences and was more or less similar to—an "internalization" of—what was taken to be people's "cultures" conceived of as local systems of definition and information that were somehow external to individuals. The individual actor, now part of the human species as defined by Western assumptions, became uninteresting to anthropology, and became simply a subject for one or another supposedly pan-human psychology. If anthropology was now to consider the universally similar actors at all, it was "contents of the mind," "meanings," which were—and are in contemporary cognitive and symbolic anthropology—the acceptable local differences to be found in the dancers of strange dances. Beyond that lay forbidden territory and the danger of backsliding.

As this sketch of Boas's mission suggests, different ways of thinking about people who act differently from us have profound ideological consequences. How we think about them determines what we think about ourselves. And if we have the power to affect their lives, then the way we think about them profoundly affects what they will think about themselves, and what we will do to them.

THE DANCER AND THE DANCE

Privileging culture and subordinating universal people to it was a powerful achievement, but it made the relations of context and person into a methodological and ideological axiom instead of treating them as an empirical problem. The best succinct expression of the problem of dissecting others and ourselves into outer and inner realms is probably a verse by Yeats:

O chestnut-tree, great-rooted blossomer,
Are you the leaf, the blossom or the bole?
O body swayed to music, O brightening glance,
How can we know the dancer from the dance?[6]

Our personal experience suggests to us, whether delusively or not, that sometimes we *are* the dance—are constituted by the dance—and sometimes we are distinct from it and are *doing* it for some purpose or other—willfully putting the dance to use. It is important to us in our judgment of others in everyday life to know if they are "being" or "acting."[7] A breach of expectations in either direction—being when acting is appropriate, acting when being is appropriate—can lead to judgments of insincerity, of weirdness, of inappropriateness, of untrustworthiness, or even of mental illness.

An intriguing documentary film, *Holy Ghost People*—of a meeting in West Virginia in the 1940s of the poor-white members of a poisonous snake handling, Pentecostal group—shows people who are possessed by the Holy Spirit, speaking in tongues, and undergoing classical "hysterical" epileptoid convulsions. Among them is one man, at least, who (to my certain conviction) unable to become possessed is dancing around *pretending* to be possessed. The others, in contrast, are—whatever this may mean—not pretending. Life as we experience it, prior to some sort of powerful and simplifying "totalizing" analysis, informs us that the relations of people to aspects of contexts are complex and various. Their delineation is an empirical problem, and, for anthropologists, the proper subject of a person-centered anthropology.

ETHNOGRAPHIC EXPLORATIONS

To understand the person in context we must refuse to be either culturologists or sociologists, on the one hand, or psychologists, on the other. We must be investigators and theory builders who take the shifting phenomena of dancer/dance as our focus of concern, as the basis for a "discipline."

We must, while taking full and critical account of psychological and sociocultural matters, examine the *person* as an active center of history and context and of psychological and biological potentials and constraints, in terms adequate to our field of problems. Such a stance should lead to surprises and to the possibility of productive comparison, explanation, and contributions to general anthropological theory.

What We Should Look At

What are some of the things we might look at in an investigation of the danced dance, that is when the relations of person and context are at the center of our concern? What will we find at the interface of the public and private worlds, sometimes separating them, sometimes condensing them? Looking at some of the traditional concerns of psychological anthropology and adding some recent emphases a list would include, to begin with, some of the following matters.

(1) The formation and nature of the subcomponents of an individual's inner world and public experience referred to by such terms (with different implications) as "self," "person," and "identity." (2) The structure of coercive controls which play over the socially formed "self" (or "identity" or "person"), that is, the personal and public aspects of a community's system of "moral controls." (3) The private and public sorting of what is *known* in one way or another, and of what is *hidden* from private and/or public knowledge. How are things known? How are they hidden? In what distorted forms may they be expressed? In what components of private or community life are they expressed? This is related to the traditional question of the "nature of the unconscious," with the qualification that there are importantly different degrees and ways in which things exist, and are then known and not known. (4) The connection between what people experience, and what they think they "know." This is the

question of the kind of embedded "epistemology" which operates in a community. (5) The different kinds of "realities" that are thought by community members to exist in their private and public realms. How are they labeled and related? What differing kinds of thinking, logic, discourse are related to them? How does an individual relate himself or herself to those different realities? For example, through a conviction of common sense? Through play? Through faith? (6) The personal and public forms that affect the meanings and uses of the various aspects of space and time and their relations, and that thus affect, for example, the meanings and consequences of events, and of "history." (7) The private and public dimensions of the structuring, recognition, management, and uses of the emotions. (8) The private and public aspects of what psychoanalytic theory calls "defense mechanisms," devices which allow the individuals to deal with conflicts within and among self, the moral system, and what the community defines as "reality" with, ideally, minimal disruption to the dance. (9) The ways in which the dance and/or the dancer go wrong, or break down. What are the pathologies characteristic of a particular community, or of any community?

Some Examples

The people I studied in "Piri," a very small horticultural Tahitian village in the South Pacific, and in Bhaktapur, a highly integrated, "premodern," agriculturally based, densely populated, Nepalese Hindu city in the Himalayas[8] differed in all these matters. Where it was possible to tease apart context and person, it seemed to me that the two communities' inhabitants were not only unique individuals on the one hand and very generally human on the other. They were also in many aspects precisely the kinds of people who are likely to be produced by such places, places which were—at the same time—in many interesting aspects exactly what they had to be insofar as

they were inhabited by such people. Furthermore, insofar as such interdependencies were characteristic of other communities that resemble Piri or Bhaktapur in one or another respect, I supposed that I was glimpsing something beyond the local particularistic relations of people and context in the two places—namely the possibility of a more general understanding of the relations of *kinds* of places to the *kinds* of people who live in them.

Starting from properly targeted studies of people acting in different sorts of communities, we should be able to delineate progressively how and within what limits aspects of the dancing person relate not only to the immediately constituting, enabling and restraining aspects of the particular environing dance, but to such larger and more general aspects of social context as, for example, community scale and complexity, population density, larger areal integrations, technology and economy, colonial history, local cultural structures and traditions, and whatever else we may turn up.

Let me sketch briefly for illustration some possible implications of one difference between Piri and Bhaktapur, the difference in scale and complexity. Much of tiny Piri's order is produced, as nineteenth-century theorists of *Gemeinschaft* utopias argued it should be, through the cognitive and moral resources of very small face-to-face communities. People assent to a body of truths generated by relatively common experience. They are true because, as Gregory Bateson once put it, everyone believes them. An imperious commonsense reality is constructed at many levels of experience, joining the small group of villagers in a compelling structure of seemingly perceptually based reality. Adherence to this system is backed up, when necessary, by the consistent moral pressures of, in Erving Goffman's phrase, a "total community" (Goffman 1956).

Bhaktapur's comparatively enormous urban scale and complexity transform the possibilities and effects of this kind of order. Although people in Bhaktapur are rooted, like people everywhere, in the intimate face-to-face moral and reality-constructing units of household, extended family, and neighborhood, they must also move competently and extensively in a nested structure of quite different, larger, highly organized urban orders in a way that—in comparison with Piri—transforms their sense of self, their ways of thinking, their moral organization. Piri's modalities are not sufficient for social order in Bhaktapur. In Bhaktapur's wider realms beyond its elemental face-to-face communities, sacralized symbolism—a special "premodern" mode of integration that is used only sparingly in Piri—is enormously elaborated to integrate people into larger community spheres and to orient them in the city's complex space, time, and social order. For these larger integrative tasks, the city makes use of the highly elaborated and minutely detailed resources of a dramatic, compelling, and relentlessly instructive religion, Hinduism, whose claims to "reality" are of a different sort from those of the common-sense secular forms of everyday life.

Such different conditions of life are associated with quite different sorts of danced dances and, less obviously, of local dancers. A Tahitian response to the question "Who are you?" for example, is puzzlement at the question, although the nature of the Tahitian self can be deduced from other kinds of discourse and action (Levy 1973:213-239). But "self" is not a problem for rural Tahitian discursive thought or public discourse.

The same question asked of a Bhaktapurian tends to elicit a self-conscious and complicated analysis. "Who are you?" I ask an upper-caste man in Bhaktapur. (He is able to grasp the peculiarity of this question, as I know him well and have been interviewing him for many hours at this point.) He remarks that this is an interesting question, and that he has, in fact, discussed it with his friends. "To a great extent," he answers after a preliminary discussion of relevant passages about self from the *Bhagavad Gita*, "it seems that I am everything other—because whenever I cook, I am a cook; whenever I love some girl, I am a lover; whenever I have a son or a daughter, I am a parent, I am a father; whenever I am with my father, I am a son; whenever I am alone with a friend, I am a friend; whenever I am with foes, I am an enemy." This response is, although particularly elegant, typical of much Bhaktapurian talk, and certainly would surprise (and probably bore) a citizen of Piri. The nature, quantity, discontinuity, and paradoxical conflicts of different "roles" in the complex and large society of Bhaktapur have profound implications for "self" and its allied "psychological structures."

Let us note another contrast between people in Piri and Bhaktapur which also seems to be an implication of the kinds of communities they live in. Rural Tahitian informants tended to take the forms of their culture more or less literally, as places where analytic thought and discourse must or should stop. "Why do you do that?" "It is our custom."

Bhaktapurians, on the other hand, under certain circumstances, put traditional cultural explanations into tension with other sorts of explanations, with a knowledge generated through experiences which, so to speak, resist the dominant ordering forms of culture. Thus a farmer in Bhaktapur, pushed repeatedly and annoyingly by me on contradictions in his culturally provided justification for the repression of untouchables (a repression that serves to assure that they will continue to serve their traditional stigmatized social roles and that is justified by salient theories of purity and of *karma*), finally says in pleading exasperation, "If we eat with them, we will lose our whole caste system. We will lose the whole system of hierarchy in our society. And people will be able to do whatever they want, there will be chaos."

This kind of analytic thinking[9] generates understandings which are often potentially subversive to public doctrine—and which often have the interesting quality of seeming to express some relatively culture-free general truth. In Bhaktapur many "cultural" doctrines are problematic or counterintuitive for individuals; they are nevertheless firmly supported through a movement in the face of doubt into the *secondary* certainty of faith, a movement which is powerfully motivated through the deeply moving personal messages delivered by many rites of passage and public rituals. This balance of certainty, doubt, analysis, and faith comes to characterize for many, perhaps most, Bhaktapurians some very general ways of thinking about and responding to their world.

Bhaktapurians have as a result of the kind of place they live in, as a result of the dances they must dance, developed certain features of the "organization" of their thought—a sort of orderly layering of different kinds of contradictory knowledge, which we might designate as "sophisticated" in relation to the "naive" thinking of many village Tahitians.[10] Such observations on the significant clustering of belief, doubt, faith, aspects of cognitive organization, community scale and complexity are an example of the sorts of phenomena that person-centered anthropology should be able to clarify and to make use of in the building of theory.

TRAINING FOR A PERSON-CENTERED ANTHROPOLOGY

As sociocultural anthropology has become progressively differentiated into specialized subfields, university departments have faced the problem of how to train students in both general anthropology and in one or another of the subfields that require special theoretical and technical preparation.

Person-centered anthropology has, like other subfields, its own problems in training and technique. We have suggested, for example, its need for an understanding of the data and theory of both sociocultural and individual "realms," as well as an ability to select among these data and to criticize and modify such theory in order to recenter its concerns.

Perhaps the most critical and difficult task of prefield training is to teach—and learn—how to recognize and gather relevant data. A probably indispensable tool for this purpose is supervised interviewing. In the version we have used for many years, students, in the context of relevant reading, interview selected "respondents" at length—say, for two one-hour interviews a week during the course of a term. The interview subject should be someone with an interesting social role (mortician, poet, priest). The role, because it is "interesting," provides for the student the sort of alienation which makes the sociocultural situation of other communities visible and problematic. "Respondents" are individuals who are treated as problems, as "objects" to be studied in themselves, in contrast to "informants," expert witnesses who provide us with "objectively valid" descriptions or explanations. Anthropology's "culture and personality" studies inherited a tradition from psychology in which the analysis of "respondents" was firmly believed to be more or less mechanically derivable from measurements, tests, and observations of factlike signs and symptoms. We are aware now that understanding of the "other," which is to say the understanding of "respondents," requires much humility, reflexive self-consciousness, and hermeneutic subtlety. These contemporary anthropological virtues must inform the methodology of such a course in technique as well as the fieldwork which is to follow it.

Interviews must be tape-recorded to capture the multiple layers of significant form that they carry. By using techniques originally rooted in the tradition of "psychodynamic interviewing" and modified for our nonclinical purposes, respondents' interviews turn out to be full of richly illuminating clues bearing on Yeats's dancer/dance problem. When properly conducted, they amply illustrate the organization of themes, the hesitations, the decision branches, the paralinguistic and kinesic clues, the "defensive operations," which in conjunction with the verbal "content" of the interview illuminate the shifting relations of the speaker to his or her "surface" discourse (the danced dance), to the interviewer, to the various phases of the interview, to the various kinds of material discussed, and beyond that, to the respondent's life course, roles, membership in various communities, and so on. Selections played from the interviews, supported by typescripts of the selections, can be used to illuminate problems in interviewing, in discerning potentially significant phenomena in the various patterns captured by the recordings, and in learning to build modest theoretical models as firmly based as possible on specific and demonstrable interview materials. In the field this kind of interviewing requires a particularly good knowledge of the local language. In contrast to many other anthropological investigations one cannot work through the areal lingua franca,[11] and, more evidently, not through an interpreter.

Field studies in person-centered anthropology cannot be done in a hurry. We must in a first long stage learn enough about the context, culture, social organization, and language of a community so as not to be foolish, and not to add to some centuries of foolishness, when we turn to studies of and assertions about the community members' intimate environing and constituting worlds.

The pursuit of person-centered anthropology, like all anthropology, is full of difficulties. But who is in a better position than the anthropologist to observe such interesting dances and who is in a better position to meditate on Yeats's challenge?

NOTES

1. The splitting of "culture" from "society" has created another set of problems.

2. "Person" is used here in a general and unspecified sense for "a human being" or "an individual" and not in the particular moral sense (of great interest for anthropology) of a human or corporate entity conceived by a community (or body of law) as having enforceable rights and duties.

3. Several sections of this chapter are adapted, some sentences more or less verbatim, from an article for a different audience (Levy 1989). Some issues which are touched on briefly here are developed at length in that earlier article. I am grateful to Roy Rappaport for useful, critical comments on a draft of this paper.

4. On Boas and culture theory in American anthropology see Stocking (1968).

5. This discussion of Boas is adapted from Levy (1973:245).

6. W. B. Yeats, "Among School Children."

7. This distinction has a different shape in different kinds of societies. It is, perhaps, a particular problem in modern societies where "formal" behavior is not guaranteed and made dependable by some more or less inviolable code of honor or some binding social convention. In modern societies (as David Riesman 1952 once suggested for the particularly American obsession with "sincerity") a sense of an individual's "inner state" is of special importance.

8. See Levy (1973, 1990).

9. "Analytic thought" can be distinguished from the passive reproduction of "cultural doctrine" by the ways that individuals arrive at and defend assertions.

10. A statement of this kind, or for that matter almost any comparative statement about culturally produced differences in individuals' "mental organization," insofar as it seems to threaten the achievement of Boas is immediately irritating to most anthropologists, who would set to work to find apparently disconfirmatory data. There are, in fact, discrete data which can seem to disconfirm almost any anthropological claim, but such claims are usually about general *tendencies* in behavior. We judge people to be kind in spite of occasional unkind acts, or intelligent in spite of occasional stupidities. Assertions about organizational tendencies must be countered not with particular acts, but at the same *level* of analysis in which claims are made.

11. I noticed while working in French Polynesia that the responses of the same bilingual Polynesians interviewed in French or Tahitian were quite different. The two languages seemed to tap different aspects of the self and somewhat different defenses, and to activate different schemas of the world. Systematic studies of responses in both the languages of bilingual respondents would be of potentially great anthropological interest.

INTELLECTUAL ROOTS

Robert I. Levy is Professor Emeritus of Anthropology at the University of California, San Diego, and Research Professor of Anthropology at the University of North Carolina at Chapel Hill. His first career was in medicine, psychiatry, and psychoanalysis. Between 1961 and 1964 he conducted his first anthropological studies in two small Tahitian communities in French Polynesia. From 1964 to 1968 he worked at the University of Hawaii. During this period he helped coordinate studies and programs on comparative psychiatry in East and South East Asia. In 1969 he became one of the founding members of a new Department of Anthropology at the University of California—San Diego, organized by Melford Spiro as a center for the study of psychological anthropology. In 1973 Levy began the study of Bhaktapur, a premodern, traditional Hindu city in Nepal's Kathmandu Valley. He has published ethnographic and theoretical papers on Tahiti and works on many issues in psychological anthropology, including several influential papers on emotion in anthropological perspective. His book *Tahitians: Mind and Experience in the Society Islands* (1973) describes the person-centered worlds of understanding and action of some Tahitian villagers. *Mesocosm: Hinduism and the Organization of a Traditional Hindu City in Nepal* (1990) describes the symbolic and religious organization of Bhaktapur. He is currently working on a volume on the private worlds of some citizens of that city and the interrelations of those private spheres and the larger public sphere of the city.

My intellectual biography has some of its beginnings in medicine, with its special insights and limiting prejudices, its vision of tightly interrelated systems more or less bounded within human skins, and its emphasis on pathology and breakdown as a privileged way of understanding healthy functioning. Encounters in psychiatric courses with "psychotic" patients initiated a lifelong interest in the behaviors and inner worlds of exotic others and their slippery connections to "our" realities and normality. In mid-century the frontiers of psychiatry seemed to be in psychoanalytic theory, and during the psychiatric residencies which followed medical school the thing to do was to enter psychoanalytic training at one of the psychoanalytic "Institutes" which were beginning to proliferate in New York and other major American cities. I picked the William Alanson White Institute, a "neo-Freudian" group (whose members had included the social philosopher Erik Fromm and Harry Stack Sullivan, a then influential theorist of "interpersonal" relations). The faculty of the institute, like other "neo-Freudian" schools, emphasized what they took to be "cultural" factors in human development and psychopathology, in the face of what they considered to be an overly "biological" Freudianism. But, in spite of that "cultural" emphasis, the Institute kept much of the medical-psychiatric model of some sort of focal pathology centered in the "patient." After some years of practice in New York, and—after an informative spell in the army where I saw some radically non-middle-class patients and pathogenic situations—in San Francisco, I began to feel progressively dissatisfied with the limitations of both the theory and the practice of psychoanalysis. It seemed to me then that the useful next step would be an attempt to understand the relations of person-centered phenomena to wider sociocultural processes.

I was influenced by contemporary research in what was variously called social or transcultural or comparative psychiatry, among which were the important studies of the anthropologist Alexander Leighton on the relations of community disorder and personal stress, and by the then-flourishing field of "culture and personality studies," whose most stimulating writers, for me, included Ernest Beaglehole, Abram Kardiner, Melford Spiro, Margaret Mead, George Devereux, and Geza Roheim. But the most important, transformative, and longest-lasting influence on me was Gregory Bateson, whom I first met when he was working near San Francisco on schizophrenia, work which lead to elaborations of his theory of learning (of great anthropological usefulness) and the double-bind theory of schizophrenia. Bateson's work, particularly the theoretical papers eventually collected in *Steps to an Ecology of Mind*, introduced me to the revolutionary shift in models of behavior initiated by cybernetics and communication theory, which allowed behavior/mind/thought to be understood (in part) as located and learned in a structured field of dynamic and mutually constructive relations in which individuals were nodes. He provided an entree into the developments of late twentieth-century thought (including the French thought of recent decades, which traverses much of the same new ground from a different entrance place) and a partial corrective to the (still flourishing) mechanistic, intrapsychic, and "culture-personality" models which were residues of nineteenth-century ways of understanding. It should be noted that with all the enormous corrective power of these late twentieth-century models, they, in their turn, underspecified and undervalued the complex intrapsychic processes and activities of the "nodes"—that is, of "individuals"—and overemphasized cognition or "mind" as precipitates of dominant cultural schemas at the expense of such determinants of human understanding and action as conscience, emotion, defense mechanisms, intuition, and the like—all of which have their own sorts of relations to and resistance to "culture."

By the mid-sixties, to take up the genealogical thread again, I was anxious to leave a problematic psychiatric practice and to try to learn something from new experiences and observations. I was able, through the invitation of the anthropologist and specialist on Oceania, Douglas Oliver, to work in a Tahitian-speaking village and a small urban enclave from 1961 to 1964. In later years I worked in a greatly contrasting community, a traditional Hindu city in Nepal (from 1973 to 1976). In both places my central interest was in the relation between the structures and forms of community life and the forms of "mind and experience" of dwellers in different kinds of communities. These relations have continued to preoccupy me.

13

Gender and Kinship Reconsidered: Toward a Unified Analysis*

SYLVIA YANAGISAKO AND JANE COLLIER

INTRODUCTION

Our goal is at once to revitalize the study of kinship and to situate the study of gender at the theoretical core of anthropology by calling into question the boundary between these two fields. In challenging the view that kinship and gender are distinct, albeit closely linked, domains of analysis, we hope to renew the intellectual promise of these two fields while reconstituting them as a whole.

Kinship Studies

As an attempt to demonstrate the creative power of ignoring the distinction between two well-established analytical domains, we steer a course that diverges from a recent theoretical trend in anthropology. During the past two decades, kinship has declined from its position as the central focus of ethnographies and as the privileged site for theoretical debate about the character of social structure. Recent reviews and commentaries on theory in anthropology (for example, Ortner 1984, Yengoyan 1986, Hannerz 1986, Appadurai 1986b) render it obvious that kinship studies no longer generate either the controversy or the conceptual innovation they did during the first half of the century. Certainly neither the ethnographies nor the comparative studies that currently excite the anthropological imagination concentrate on what were once considered the basic building blocks of kinship—descent rules, marriage prescriptions or preferences, and terminology systems.

In retrospect, it seems apparent that the waning theoretical importance of kinship studies in anthropology was heralded in the 1960s and 1970s by various attempts to rethink its core concepts and methods (Leach 1961, Schneider 1964, 1972, Needham 1971). These efforts were themselves symptomatic of a general erosion of faith in the structural-functional model of society, whose rise to hegemony in anthropology had coincided with kinship's increase in importance.

The postwar critique of the structural-functional paradigm eventually undermined confidence in the notion that kinship everywhere constituted a domain of relationships readily accessible to any ethnographer armed with a genealogical chart. Direct challenges to kinship as a discrete domain of analysis (Schneider 1976, 1984) capped off a period of increasing skepticism about the institutional model of society that structural-functionalism had provided. Just as we realized we could no longer assume the existence in every society of

---

*Reprinted, in edited form, from Jane Fishburne Collier and Sylvia Junk Yanagisako (eds.), *Gender and Kinship: Essays toward a Unified Analysis,* Stanford, Calif.: Stanford University Press, 1987, by permission of the publishers. ©1987 Board of Trustees of the Leland Stanford Junior College.

a sphere of politics that provides authority and the orderly exercise of power and coercion, or a sphere of religion that provides cognitive resolution of universal dilemmas concerning the meaning of human existence, so we realized we could not assume a sphere of kinship that provides a system of rights and duties for the orderly reproduction of human life. By taking for granted the existence of these domains, structural-functionalism sacrificed the analytical power of asking how such domains come to be constituted in particular ways in specific societies and with what social consequences.

Recent analyses of kinship that have retained a conceptual vitality and have made innovative contributions to theoretical discussion in anthropology have not focused on kinship per se, but on kinship as an aspect of political economy (Meillassoux 1981, Terray 1972, Friedman 1974) or on kinship as an aspect of broader systems of inequality in which gender is a key dimension (Collier and Rosaldo 1981, Ortner and Whitehead 1981). In short, the call for the dissolution of conventional analytical boundaries has offered these kinship studies the greatest theoretical promise.

Rather than accepting without question conventional analytical boundaries, we ask what new understanding can be gained by ignoring the line between gender and kinship. This question itself has developed out of the questioning of kinship studies by feminist scholars.

The Feminist Challenge to Kinship Theory

With the revival of the women's movement in the 1960s, feminist anthropologists turned to kinship studies for tools to understand women's place and possibilities. Not only was ethnographic information on women and their lives found primarily in chapters on kinship, marriage, and the family, but Fortes's distinction between the domestic and politico-jural domains (1958, 1969) suggested a reason

why women's association with the "domestic" might make them and their activities seem universally less valued than the activities and attributes of "public" men (Rosaldo 1974).

The relationship between kinship and gender studies, however, was soon reversed in the 1970s by the development of feminist anthropology. As feminist scholars shifted their concern from understanding the position of women (for example, Rosaldo 1974, Ortner 1974, Friedl 1975, Schlegel 1977), to charting variations in women's roles and experiences, and then to understanding the construction of gender in specific social systems (for example, MacCormack and Strathern 1980, Ortner and Whitehead 1981), they began to call into question the central assumptions of kinship theory.

At the heart of kinship theory lies an analytic dichotomy between "domestic" and "political-jural" domains. This dichotomy, used implicitly by kinship theorists since Morgan and elaborated by Fortes (1949, 1958, 1969, 1978), remains influential in anthropology and related disciplines. Fortes developed the concept in order to challenge Western assumptions about the biological basis of kinship, claiming that kinship has a jural, political dimension. But, ironically, in carving out a politico-jural domain of kinship based on legal rules, Fortes left intact the assumption of an invariant domestic domain built upon the affective ties and moral sanctions of the mother-child bond. The domestic/politico-jural dichotomy assumes a "domestic" sphere dedicated to sexuality and child-rearing, associated primarily with women, and a "public" sphere of legal rules and legitimate authority, associated primarily with men (Yanagisako 1979).

Feminist anthropologists who first turned to kinship theory for analytical tools soon began to question the assumption of a domestic sphere organized by the affective and moral constraints of the mother-child bond, to which other functions—economic, political, and ideological—might be added without changing its primary "natural" role of human reproduction. Because of their concern with variations in gender conceptions, women's strategies, and women's powers, feminists began to relate observed differences in women's experiences to different forms of economic, political, and cultural organization—thus questioning (1) the apparent naturalness of mother-child dyads and (2) the relationship between supposed male "authority" and the actual dynamics of power and privilege in particular social systems.

In focusing on women's strategies, feminist scholars did not simply record that women, like men, have goals and work toward them. Rather, they demonstrated that it is impossible to understand interaction within "domestic spheres" without simultaneously understanding the organization of political and economic arenas that provide goals and resources for both sexes. Similarly, feminists focusing on gender conceptions demonstrated that symbolic conceptions of femininity can never be understood apart from a cultural order, because biological facts achieve significance only within wider systems of meaning (Ardener 1975, 1978).

Feminists have not been alone in questioning the central assumptions of kinship theory. Goody's theory of the evolution of the domestic domain (1973, 1976) challenged the view of kinship as an autonomous system by showing how productive processes and the transmission of property shape domestic groups. Bourdieu (1977a), in rejecting Lévi-Strauss's formalistic "rules of marriage," analyzed the "marriage strategies" through which people in particular societies reproduce relations of production and social inequality.

At the same time, Schneider's cultural analysis of kinship (1968, 1972) provided a tool for understanding the interrelationship between kinship and other domains. He and others have argued that kinship is not a discrete, isolable domain of meaning, but rather that the meanings attributed to the relations and actions of kin are drawn from a range of cultural domains, including religion, nationality, gender, ethnicity, social class, and the concept of "person" (Alexander 1978, Chock 1974, Schneider and Smith 1973, Strathern 1981a, Yanagisako 1978, 1985).

RETHINKING KINSHIP AND GENDER

In light of the feminist challenge to kinship theory, it now seems the time for kinship theorists to turn to gender studies for tools to reconsider their analyses. As feminists have shown, it is no longer adequate to view women as bringing to kinship primarily a capacity for bearing children, while men bring primarily a capacity for participation in public life. Consequently an analysis of gender in, for example, traditional Chinese and Nuer societies may well reveal that labeling both as involving "patrilineal descent" obscures more than it illuminates. Along similar lines, an analysis of gender may provide a rather different understanding of the kinds of "alliances" men form through exchanging women. It might, furthermore, demonstrate the impracticality of separating marriage transactions from other property transactions. We disavow merely using gender studies to understand the traditional concerns of kinship theorists. Instead, we argue that gender and kinship are mutually constructed. Neither can be treated as analytically prior to the other, because they are realized together in particular cultural economic, and political systems. In short, analyses of gender must begin with social wholes, rather than with individuals or with functional domains such as kinship or gender.

Kinship and the Biological "Facts" of Sexual Reproduction

Among kinship theorists, Schneider (1964, 1968, 1972, 1984) has been the most consistent in refusing to take for granted what others have, namely, that the fundamental units of kinship are everywhere genealogical relationships. In his cultural analysis of American kinship (1968), Schneider first demonstrated that our particular folk conceptions of kinship lie behind our assumption of the universality of the genealogical grid. By explicating the symbolic system through which Americans construct genealogical relationships, Schneider denaturalized kinship and displayed its cultural foundations.

Most recently, in his 1984 critical review of the history of kinship studies, Schneider argues that, for anthropologists, kinship has always been rooted in biology because (by our own definition) it is about relationships based in sexual reproduction. When we undertake studies of kinship in other societies, we feel compelled to start from some common place. And that place has always been sexual reproduction. We do not ask what relationships are involved in the reproduction of humans in particular societies. Instead, we assume that the primary reproductive relationship in all societies is the relationship between a man and a woman characterized by sexual intercourse and its physiological consequences of pregnancy and parturition. The only time we bother to ask questions about reproduction is when we discover that the natives do not draw the same connections we do between these events (as in the case of the Trobriand Islanders), or when we discover that the natives permit marriages between people with the same genital equipment (as among the Nuer or Lovedu). In other words, we assume that creating human offspring—through heterosexual intercourse, pregnancy, and parturition—constitutes the biological process upon which we presume culture builds such social relationships as marriage, filiation, and co-parenthood.

Although it is apparent that heterosexual intercourse, pregnancy, and parturition are involved in human reproduction, it is also apparent that producing humans entails more than this. M. Bridget O'Laughlin (1977) put it very succinctly when she wrote, "Human reproduction is never simply a matter of con-

ception and birth." There is a wide range of activities in which people participate besides heterosexual intercourse and parturition that contribute to the birth of viable babies and to their development into adults. These activities, in turn, involve and are organized by a number of relationships other than those of parenthood and marriage.

Given the wide range of human activities and relationships that can be viewed as contributing to the production of human beings, why do we focus on only a few of them as the universal basis of kinship? Why do we construe these few activities and relationships as natural facts, rather than investigating the ways in which they are, like all social facts, culturally constructed? The answer Schneider has proposed is that our theory of kinship is simultaneously a folk theory of biological reproduction.

Gender and the Biological "Facts" of Sexual Reproduction

Schneider's insight that kinship is by definition about sexual procreation leads us to realize that assumptions about gender lie at the core of kinship studies. Moreover, not only are ideas about gender central to analyses of kinship, but ideas about kinship are central to analyses of gender. Because both gender and kinship have been defined as topics of study by our conception of the same thing, namely, sexual procreation, we cannot think about one without thinking about the other. In short, these two fields of studies are mutually constituted.

Gender assumptions pervade notions about the facts of sexual reproduction in the kinship literature. Much of what is written about atoms of kinship (Lévi-Strauss 1969 [1949]), the axiom of prescriptive altruism (Fortes 1958, 1969), the universality of the family (Robin Fox 1967), and the centrality of the mother-child bond (Goodenough 1970) is rooted in assumptions about the natural characteristics of women and men and their natural roles in sexual procreation. The standard units of our genealogies, after all, are circles and triangles about which we assume a number of things. Above all, we take for granted that they represent two naturally different categories of people and that the natural difference between them is the basis of human reproduction and, therefore, kinship.

The literature on gender is sensitive to the many ways in which pregnancy and childbirth are conceptualized and valued in different societies and to the different ways in which the activities surrounding them can be socially organized. But the conviction that the biological difference in the roles of women and men in sexual reproduction lies at the core of the cultural organization of gender persists in comparative analyses.

Like kinship theorists, analysts of gender have assumed that specific social consequences necessarily follow from this difference between men and women. For example, the assumption that women bear the greater burden and responsibility for human reproduction pervades gender studies, in particular those works employing a reproduction/production distinction. Yet this notion often appears to be more a metaphorical extension of our emphasis on the fact that women bear children than a conclusion based on systematic comparison of the contribution of men and women to human reproduction. In other words, the fact that women bear children and men do not is interpreted as creating a universal relation of human reproduction.

The centrality of sexual reproduction in the definition of gender is reflected in the distinction between sex and gender that has become a convention in much of the feminist literature. Judith Shapiro summarizes the distinction between the terms as follows:

[T]hey serve a useful analytic purpose in contrasting a set of biological facts with a set of cultural facts. Were I to be scrupulous in my use of terms, I would use the term "sex" only when I was speaking of biological differences between males and females, and use "gender" whenever I was referring to the social, cultural, psychological constructs that are imposed upon these biological differences. . . . [G]ender . . . designates a set of categories to which we can give the same label cross-linguistically, or cross-culturally, because they have some connection to sex differences. These categories are, however, conventional or arbitrary insofar as they are not reducible to, or directly derivative of, natural, biological facts; they vary from one language to another, one culture to another, in the way in which they order experience and action. (1981:449, italics ours)

The attempt to separate the study of gender categories from the biological facts to which they are seen to be universally connected mirrors the attempt of kinship theorists, reviewed by Schneider (1984), to separate the study of kinship from the same biological facts. Like the latter attempt, this one seems doomed to fail, because it too starts from a definition of its subject matter that is rooted in those biological facts. It is impossible, of course, to know what gender or kinship would mean if they are to be entirely disconnected from sex and biological reproduction. We have no choice but to begin our investigations of others with our own concepts. But we can unpack the cultural assumptions embodied in them, which limit our capacity to understand social systems informed by other cultural assumptions.

Bringing Gender and Kinship Together

Although gender and kinship studies start from what are construed as the same biological facts of sexual reproduction, they might appear to be headed in different analytical directions: kinship to the social character of genealogical relations and gender to the social character of male-female relations (and even to male-male relations and female-female relations). However, because both build their explanations of the social rights and duties and the relations of equality and inequality among people on these presumably natural characteristics, both retain the legacy of their beginnings in notions about the same natural differences between people. Consequently, what have been conceptualized as two discrete, if interconnected, fields of study constitute a single field.

Our realization of the unitary constitution of gender and kinship as topics of study should make us wary of treating them as distinct analytical problems. Like "economics," "politics," and "religion," kinship has been posited as one of the fundamental building blocks of society by anthropologists (Schneider 1984:181). At the same time, neither should we assume that in all societies kinship creates gender or that gender creates kinship. Although the two may be mutually constituted as topics of study by our society, this does not mean they are linked in the same way in all societies.

We should seek rather than assume knowledge of the socially significant domains of relations in any particular society and what constitutes them. Having rejected the notion that there are presocial, universal domains of social relations, such as a domestic domain and a public domain, a kinship domain and a political domain, we must ask what symbolic and social processes make these domains appear self-evident, and perhaps even "natural," fields of activity in any society.

TRANSCENDING DICHOTOMIES: A FOCUS ON SOCIAL WHOLES

Understanding the folk model of human reproduction underlying the explicit and implicit analytical categories and dichotomies that have dominated both gender and kinship studies is the first step toward transcending them. The next step is to move beyond the dichotomies by focusing on social wholes. Instead of asking how the categories of "male" and "female" are endowed with culturally specific characters—thus taking the difference between them for granted—we need to ask how particular societies define difference. Instead of asking how rights and obligations are mapped

onto kinship bonds—thus assuming the genealogical grid—we need to ask how specific societies recognize claims and allocate responsibilities.

Analyzing Social Wholes

Given our tendency to reinvent the analytic dichotomies that limit our ability to understand gender in our own and other societies, we need an explicit strategy for transcending them. The one we propose rests on the premise that there are no "facts," biological or material, that have social consequences and cultural meanings in and of themselves. Sexual intercourse, pregnancy, and parturition are cultural facts, whose form, consequences, and meanings are socially constructed in any society, as are mothering, fathering, judging, ruling, and talking with the gods. Similarly, there are no material "facts" that can be treated as precultural givens. The consequences and meanings of force are socially constructed, as are those of the means of production or the resources upon which people depend for their living.

Just as we reject analytic dichotomies, so we reject analytic domains. We do not assume the existence of a gender system based on natural differences in sexual reproduction, a kinship system based on the genealogical grid, a polity based on force, or an economy based on the production and distribution of needed resources. Rather than take for granted that societies are constituted of functionally based institutional domains, we propose to investigate the social and symbolic processes by which human actions within particular social worlds come to have consequences and meanings, including their apparent organization into seemingly "natural" social domains.

Systems of Inequality

We begin with the premise that social systems are, by definition, systems of inequality. This premise has three immediate advantages. First, it conforms to common usage. By most definitions, a society is a system of social relationships and values. Values entail evaluation. Consequently, a society is a system of social relationships in which all things and actions are not equal. Every society has a "prestige structure," as Ortner and Whitehead (1981) presume. A system of values, however, is not "male," and in analyzing any particular society, we must ask why people appear to hold the values they do.

Second, the premise that all societies are systems of inequality forces us to separate the frequently confused concepts of equality (the state of being equal) and justice (moral rightness). By presuming that all societies are systems of inequality, we are forced to separate the study of our own and other people's cultural systems of evaluation from considerations of whether or not such systems meet our standards of honor and fairness.

Finally, the premise that all societies are systems of inequality frees us from having to imagine a world without socially created inequities. If we assume that all societies are systems of inequality, then we, as social scientists, are forced to explain not the existence of inequality itself but rather why it takes the qualitatively different forms it does.

The premise that all societies are systems of inequality forces us to specify what we mean by inequality in each particular case. Instead of asking how "natural" differences acquire cultural meanings and social consequences (a strategy that dooms us to reinventing our analytic dichotomies), a presumption of inequality forces us to ask why some attributes and characteristics of people are culturally recognized and differentially evaluated when others are not. This requires us to begin any analysis by asking, What are a society's cultural values? And what social processes organize the distribution of prestige, power, and privilege? We may find that in some societies neither cultural values nor social processes discriminate between the sexes (that is, a nongendered system of inequality). But this conclusion must follow from an analysis of how inequality is organized.

Given our premise that social systems are systems of inequality, we propose an analytical program with three facets. These facets are arranged not in order of theoretical importance but in the sequence we feel they should be employed in any particular analysis. Some researchers, depending on the particular question or type of society that is the topic of study, may find another sequence preferable or may choose to focus on one facet more than the others. But, we suggest, no attempt to analyze social wholes can proceed very far without employing all three.

(1) The Cultural Analysis of Meaning. The first facet of our program entails an analysis of cultural systems of meanings. Specifically, we must begin by explicating the cultural meanings people realize through their practice of social relationships. Rather than assume that the fundamental units of gender and kinship in every society are defined by the difference between males and females in sexual reproduction, we ask what are the socially meaningful categories people employ and encounter in specific social contexts and what symbols and meanings underlie them. Just as Schneider (1968) questioned, rather than took for granted, the meanings of blood, love, and sexual intercourse in American kinship and their influence on the construction of categories of relatives, so we have to question the meanings of genes, love, sexual intercourse, power, independence, and whatever else plays into the symbolic construction of categories of people in any particular society. This analytical stance toward gender is well summarized in the following statement by Ortner and Whitehead (1981:1-2):

Gender, sexuality, and reproduction are treated as symbols, invested with meaning by the society in question, as all symbols are. The approach to the problem of sex and gender is thus a matter of symbolic analysis and interpretation, a matter of relating such symbols and meanings to other cultural symbols and meanings on the one hand, and to the forms of social life and experience on the other.

By attending to the public discourses through which people describe, interpret, evaluate, make claims about, and attempt to influence relationships and events, we can extract the relatively stable symbols and meanings people employ in everyday life.

These symbols and meanings, as will be stressed in the next section on systemic models of social inequality, are always evaluative. As such, they encode particular distributions of prestige, power, and privilege. However, because they are realized through social practice, they are not static. As will become apparent when we discuss the importance of historical analysis, we do not assume cultural systems of meaning to be timeless, self-perpetuating structures of "tradition." Yet, even when the meanings of core symbols are changing, we can tease apart their different meanings in particular contexts and, thereby, better understand the symbolic processes involved in social change (Yanagisako 1985, 1987).

Once we have investigated the various ways in which difference is conceptualized in other societies—including whether and how sex and reproduction play into the construction of differences that make a difference—we can return to examine the biological model that defines gender in our own society. In other words, just as our questioning of the domestic/public dichotomy as the structural basis for relations between men and women in other societies has encouraged us to question its analytical usefulness for our own society (Yanagisako 1987), so we can ask what a conception of gender as rooted in biological difference does and doesn't explain about relations between men and women in our society. Having recognized our model of biological difference as a particular cultural mode of thinking about relations between people, we should be able to question the "biological facts" of sex themselves. We expect that our questioning of the presumably biological core of gender will eventually lead to the rejection of any dichotomy between sex and gender as biological and cultural facts and will open up the way for an analysis of the symbolic and social processes by which both are constructed in relation to each other.

The cultural analysis of meaning cannot be isolated from the analysis of patterns of action. We do not view systems of meaning as ideational determinants of social organization or as solutions to universal problems of meaning and order. Rather, we conceptualize the interrelated, but not necessarily consistent, meanings of social events and relationships as both shaping and being shaped by practice. Our refusal to dichotomize material relationships and meanings or to grant one or the other analytic priority derives from our conceptualization of practice and ideas as aspects of a single process.

(2) Systemic Models of Inequality. The second facet of our analytical strategy requires the construction of systemic models of inequality. These models are of a particular type. Following Bourdieu (1977a), we analyze a social system not by positing an unseen, timeless structure but rather by asking how ordinary people, pursuing their own subjective ends, realize the structures of inequality that constrain their possibilities. This is why the first facet of our strategy requires an analysis of the commonsense meanings available to people for monitoring and interpreting their own and others' actions. But this analysis of meaning must be followed by an analysis of the structures that people realize through their actions. Because we understand the commonsense meanings available to people not by positing an unseen, timeless culture but rather by exploring how people's understandings of the world are shaped by their structured experiences, we must move back and forth between an analysis of how structures shape people's experience and an analysis of how people, through their actions, realize structures.

Although a systemic model of inequality may be constructed for any society, developing a typology of models aids in the analysis of particular cases. In the end (as we will discuss in the next section) each society must be analyzed in its own, historically specific terms. But a set of ideal typic models helps us to see connections we might otherwise miss. All attempts to understand other cultures are, by their nature, comparative. It is impossible to describe a particular, unique way of life without explicitly or implicitly comparing it to another—usually the analyst's own society or the society of the language the analyst is using. Since comparison is inevitable, it seems more productive to have a set of models available for thinking about similarities and contrasts than to have but ourselves as a single implicit or explicit standard of comparison.

In seeking to develop such models, we do not view either technology or socially organized access to productive resources as determining traits (see Collier and Rosaldo 1981: 318, Collier 1987, 1988). Given our assumption that no biological or material "fact" has social consequences in and of itself, we cannot begin by assuming the determining character of either the forces or relations of production. We therefore do not classify societies according to technologies—such as foraging, horticulture, agriculture, pastoralism, and industry (for example, Martin and Voorhies 1975)—or according to social relations governing access to resources—such as egalitarian, ranked, and stratified (Etienne and Leacock 1980) or communal, corporate kin, and class (Sacks 1976).

An example of the kind of model of inequality we are proposing is Jane Collier and Michelle Rosaldo's ideal typic model of "brideservice" societies (1981). The classification scheme employed in this essay and others (Collier 1984, 1987, 1988) uses marriage transaction terms—brideservice, equal or standard bridewealth, and unequal or variable bridewealth—as labels for systemic models, treating marriage transactions not as determinants of social organization or ideas but rather

as moments when practice and meaning are negotiated together. Marriage negotiations are moments of "systemic reproduction" in those societies in which "kinship" appears to organize people's rights and obligations relative to others. Societies with different bases of organization will have different moments of "systemic reproduction."

Just as we do not posit determining traits, so the kind of understanding we seek is not linear. Rather, the type of model we propose traces complex relationships between aspects of what—using conventional analytical categories—we might call gender, kinship, economy, polity, and religion. The principal virtue of such models is that they provide insights into the cultural meanings and social consequences of actions, events, and people's attributes by tracing the processes by which these elements are realized. Such systemic models privilege no domains over others. Unlike Ortner and Whitehead, who advocate a focus on "male prestige-oriented action" as the key to understanding gender relations in any society (1981:20), we suggest that "prestige systems" also need explanation. When men, for example, talk as if male prestige is generated through activities that do not involve relations with women, such as hunting and warfare, we ask why men make such statements and what social processes make them appear reasonable. A "brideservice" model suggests that—at least in societies of foragers and hunter-horticulturalists—people celebrate "Man the Hunter" not because male prestige is actually based on hunting, but rather because hunting is a principal idiom in which men talk about their claims to the wives whose daily services allow them to enjoy the freedom of never having to ask anyone for anything (Collier and Rosaldo 1981).

Because systemic models specify the contexts in which people articulate particular concerns, such models can help us to understand the apparently inconsistent meanings we discover through cultural analysis. In their analysis of "brideservice societies," for example, Collier and Rosaldo (1981) suggest why male violence is feared even as it is celebrated, why women who contribute as much or more than men to the diet do not emphasize their economic contribution but rather stress their sexuality, why bachelors are lazy hunters when sex is portrayed as the hunter's reward, and why notions of direct-exchange marriage coexist with the belief that men earn their wives through feats of prowess. Systemic models, by allowing us to understand such apparent inconsistencies, provide the analytic tools necessary for overcoming our own cultural bias toward consistency.

(3) Historical Analysis. The third facet of our analytical strategy is motivated by our belief that change is possible in all social systems, regardless of their particular configuration of inequality. We thus need an explicit strategy to counterbalance the emphasis on social reproduction in our systemic models, so that we can see how social systems change and, at the same time, better understand the processes that enable them to remain relatively stable over time. A historical analysis that interprets current ideas and practices within the context of the unfolding sequence of action and meaning that has led to them provides this balance.

Such an analysis broadens the temporal range of our analysis of social wholes by asking how their connection with the past constrains and shapes their dynamics in the present, whether that connection is one of relative continuity or of radical disjunction. In other words, whereas historical analysis is of critical importance for understanding societies and communities that are undergoing dramatic transformations (for example, Sahlins 1981, Yanagisako 1985, Collier 1986), it is of no less importance for understanding societies characterized by seeming social and cultural continuity (R. Rosaldo 1980). For, given that change is inherent in social action, the reproduction of social systems requires no less explanation than does their transformation.

Grounding our analysis of social wholes and fashioning our systemic models of inequality within particular historical sequences will enable us to see how the dynamics of past actions and ideas have created structures in the present. By taking such a historical perspective on the constitution of social wholes, we avoid assuming that present systems of inequality are the timeless products of identical pasts; instead, we question whether and how these systems developed out of dissimilar pasts. We can see how aspects of ideas and practices, which in our systemic models seem to reinforce and reproduce each other, also undermine and destabilize each other.

CONCLUSION

In conclusion, we suggest that feminism's next contribution to the study of gender and kinship should be to question the difference between women and men. We do not doubt that men and women are different, just as individuals differ, generations differ, races differ, and so forth. Rather, we question whether the particular biological difference in reproductive function that our culture defines as the basis of difference between males and females, and so treats as the basis of their relationship, is used by other societies to constitute the cultural categories of male and female.

We suggest calling into question the universality of our cultural assumptions about the difference between males and females. Both gender and kinship studies, we suggest, have foundered on the unquestioned assumption that the biologically given difference in the roles of men and women in sexual reproduction lies at the core of the cultural organization of gender, even as it constitutes the genealogical grid at the core of kinship studies. Only by calling this assumption into question can we begin to ask how other cultures might understand the difference between women and men, and simultaneously make possible studies of how our own culture comes to focus on coitus and parturition as the moments constituting masculinity and femininity.

In this essay, we have argued for the need to analyze social wholes and have proposed a three-faceted approach to this project: the explication of cultural meanings, the construction of models specifying the dialectical relationship between practice and ideas in the constitution of social inequalities, and the historical analysis of continuities and changes.

We have no illusions that the strategy we propose will resolve all the issues we have raised. We know that we can never be free from the folk models of our own culture, and that in questioning some folk concepts we privilege others. We expect that the studies we hope to generate by questioning the difference between women and men will, in time, reveal their own problematic assumptions. These will generate new questions that will, in turn, give rise to new strategies and new solutions.

INTELLECTUAL ROOTS

Sylvia Yanagisako is Professor of Anthropology at Stanford University, where she has been teaching since 1975. She has conducted research among American Indians and Japanese Americans in the state of Washington and among Italian capitalist families in Como, Italy. Her book *Transforming the Past: Kinship and Tradition among Japanese Americans* offers a theoretical framework for understanding the historically specific processes through which people interpret and transform their kinship relationships. She coedited the collection *Gender and Kinship: Essays toward a Unified Analysis* with her colleague Jane Collier, with whom she co-authored the theoretical overview appearing in this volume.

The initial intellectual influences on me can be traced to the pre-World War II plantation political economy of Hawaii and its post-World War II transformation. I grew up in Hawaii at a time when a plantation society dominated by a white, landholding oligarchy was being rapidly transplanted by a more diversified military-tourist economy controlled by a more ethnically diverse coalition of interests. My family's history of plantation labor and petty entrepreneurship endowed me with a vigilant suspicion towards all myths of a unified Social Good. At the same time, the ethnically heterogeneous and racially mixed population of students who were my classmates in

Honolulu taught me the fluidity and negotiated character of ethnic identity and cultural practices, albeit within a structure of political-economic inequality.

The first teacher to have a major intellectual influence on me was Ms. Setsu Okubo, my teacher at Roosevelt High School in Honolulu, who turned a required civics course for seniors into a compelling critique of North American military-industrial interests. In the context of the issues facing the United States in the early sixties—including the Cold War and the Cuban missile crisis, the Black civil rights movement, and the war on poverty—I came to question the ideology of those who claimed they governed in the interests of all people.

During my undergraduate and early graduate career at the University of Washington in the sixties, my intellectual perspective was shaped less by my professors than by the national and international dialogue generated by the anti-Vietnam war movement, the youth cultural revolt, and the Black civil rights and Black power movements from which the former two drew a good deal of their inspiration, political analysis, and tactics. The explosion of underground publications and other fora for political and cultural critique provided me with alternative theories and concepts to the structural-functionalist, Durkheimian models of society then dominant in American anthropology.

After completing an M.A. thesis on the educational problems faced by Indian children in white-controlled public school systems which left me unsatisfied with anthropology, I dropped out of graduate school with friends to organize a commune in Hawaii. This experiment in communal living taught me a great deal about the pervasiveness of gender inequality, including my own internalization of ideologies of gender and power. Although I was somewhat isolated from the developments unfolding outside my community, I soon realized that my personal experience paralleled the emergence of the second wave of feminism in the rest of the country.

When I returned to the University of Washington after a three-year break in my graduate studies, I found much had changed. My plan to continue research among American Indians was precluded by the growing Native American movement and its critique of the role of anthropologists in their cultural domination. My advisor Laura Newell, a physical anthropologist interested in population issues among Japanese Americans, suggested I do a kinship study of them, because she wanted to understand the cultural forces shaping population processes. At the same time, another faculty advisor, Michael Lieber, introduced me to David Schneider's book *American Kinship: A Cultural Account*. This book, along with Schneider's articles, challenged the course kinship studies and anthropological theory had taken for the past century. Although Schneider drew upon a tradition of cultural theory that can be traced through Max Weber, Franz Boas, Ruth Benedict, and Talcott Parsons, his treatment of American folk and anthropological ideas about biological kinship as a symbolic system denaturalized kinship in a way that had never been done before, opening up new lines of analysis which are still being explored today.

My first years as a faculty member in the Stanford anthropology department (1975-1980) introduced me to a broad range of critical cultural theory which had been lacking in my graduate career. I learned much from Jane Collier, Bridget O'Laughlin, Michelle Rosaldo, Renato Rosaldo, and later Donald Donham about how cultural analysis could be made a more powerful tool when it attended to issues of power and inequality. In the second half of the 1980s, the interdisciplinary faculty seminar on Cultural Studies at Stanford provided an intellectual home for me and for my exploration of cultural theory in other disciplines.

In the eighties, my perspective was also strongly influenced by my graduate students. Lisa Rofel, Anna Tsing and Kath Weston taught me, among other things, to question the heterosexist assumptions of kinship studies and cultural theory, including much of feminist theory. Roger Rouse taught me to locate anthropological theories within their own national and transnational material histories of political crises and cultural movements. This lesson is quite obviously reflected in the way I have constructed this narrative of my intellectual development.

I am currently writing a monograph on the transformation of gender, family, and industry in capitalist family firms in the silk industry of northern Italy. In focusing on the ways in which changing ideas about gender have shaped the transformation of industrial firms in an advanced industrial society, my study extends feminist analysis beyond its conventional domain of the study of women and institutions that have been construed as "female" to the heart of the presumably "male" sphere of industrial structure and the economy.

INTELLECTUAL ROOTS

Jane F. Collier is Professor of Anthropology at Stanford University, Stanford, California, where she has been teaching since 1972. She has done fieldwork among the Maya Indians of Zinacantan, Chiapas, Mexico, and with Andalusian peasants who became urban wage workers in Spain. Her publications include *Law and Social Change in Zinacantan* (1973) and *Marriage and Inequality in Classless Societies* (1988), and two coedited volumes, *Gender and Kinship: Essays toward a Unified Analysis* with Sylvia J. Yanagisako (1987) and *History and Power in the Study of Law* with June Starr (1989). She is interested in studying systems of social inequality. Her work focuses on how legal and customary norms organize the unequal distribution of wealth, power, and prestige, fostering differentiation by class, gender, and ethnicity/race.

I became an anthropologist because, as an undergraduate at Radcliffe, I had the opportunity to participate in a summer fieldwork program in southern Mexico organized by Evon Z. Vogt of Harvard. The Zinacanteco families who hosted me in 1960, particularly the Vaskis family of Navenchauk, changed me from an aspiring archaeologist into an aspiring social anthropologist. Although I never mastered the weaving and tortilla-patting skills they tried to teach me, I learned that I wanted to know more about Maya culture. I returned to Zinacantan the following summer to study courtship customs, and wrote an undergraduate honors thesis under Vogt's direction.

It was a privilege to participate in the Harvard Chiapas Project. E. Z. (Vogtie) and Nan Vogt were outstanding leaders, creating an intellectual and social environment that promoted learning and cooperation. Vogtie shared his immense knowledge of Zinacanteco religion while encouraging each of his students to pursue an individual project, and Nan taught us to work together. Through sharing experiences and field notes with other project members—particularly my husband George Collier, Frank and Francesca Cancian, Robert and Miriam Laughlin, John Haviland, Leslie Devereaux, Victoria Bricker, and Stuart and Phyllis Plattner—I learned that knowledge and understanding grow by building upon each other's ideas.

I trace my present interest in law and social inequality to the coming together of my Harvard training in cultural values with my later participation in the feminist movement. Although I never took a course from Clyde Kluckhohn, all my teachers studied with him. Vogt, my undergraduate advisor and sponsor during the five years I postponed schooling for motherhood, encouraged me to continue working in Zinacantan. When I decided to focus on customary law, he introduced me to Laura Nader at Berkeley, who, through correspondence and later in person, generously instructed me in how to collect and analyze case materials. Her article and film on Zapotec judges who "make the balance" inspired me to search for a comparable norm underlying Zinacanteco legal procedures. B. N. Colby, who hired me to work part-time on a cross-cultural study of values inspired by Kluckhohn's classification scheme, taught me to extract norms from ethnographies. And Munro Edmonson, my advisor during graduate study at Tulane, helped me to appreciate the complex, and often contradictory, ideas encompassed within Mayan and Hispanic cultures.

I became interested in the role of social processes in creating and perpetuating cultural values after reading Fredrik Barth's "Models of Social Organization," which convinced me to focus on litigants' strategies rather than on judges' decisions when writing my dissertation on Zinacanteco customary law. Later, at Stanford, Katherine Verdery introduced me to Ralf Dahrendorf's article on "The Origin of Inequality among Men," which led me to ask how legal norms create and perpetuate the unequal distribution of prestige, power and privilege. And M. Bridget O'Laughlin introduced me to marxism, an intellectual tradition that had been significantly missing from my education. The excitement of discussing works by Marx and his twentieth-century French followers with Bridget, Donald Donham, Michelle (Shelly) and Renato Rosaldo, and George Collier led me to experiment with developing ideal typic models connecting the role of power in producing knowledge with the role of knowledges and ignorances in distributing power. My 1988 book on *Marriage and Inequality in Classless Societies* proposes models for analyzing groups where age and gender organize obligations, and my current study of Andalusian peasants who became wage workers traces the effects of replacing amount of inherited land with labor market success as the apparent determinant of status.

Although marxism gave me the conceptual tools to study the relationship between values and inequality, feminism provided the incentive. My growing awareness of gender asymmetry stimulated me to study the creation and perpetuation of cultural concepts of femininity and masculinity. In 1971, Shelly Rosaldo and I, as faculty wives, participated in a six-woman collective to develop and teach Stanford's first anthropology course on "Women in Cross-Cultural Perspective."

The following year, Benjamin Paul, the department chair, obtained affirmative action funds to hire us both as half-time assistant professors. Shelly and I continued to coteach the course on women, changing its name and content as our interests shifted from studying women to analyzing the social construction of gender differences. While Shelly wrote her book on Ilongot concepts of self and society, *Knowledge and Passion*, and I searched for cross-cultural correlations between legal procedures and forms of political organization, we built upon each other's ideas to develop an ideal-typic model linking cultural conceptions of gender to stratification processes in what we called "brideservice societies." Shelly's death in 1981 left a large hole in my life and in Stanford's Anthropology Department. But her influence lives on. Sylvia Yanagisako and I organized the conference on "Kinship and Gender" that the three of us had planned. And Sylvia's and my article, reproduced in this volume, develops ideas we shared.

14

Parts and Wholes:
*Refiguring Relationships**

MARILYN STRATHERN

HOLISTIC AND DISSOLVING CONSTRUCTS OF "SOCIETY"

De Coppet (1985:78, original emphasis) has put forward a powerful plea for the study of societies as totalities: "Comparison is only possible if we analyze the various ways in which societies order their ultimate values. In doing so, we attempt to understand each society as a *whole*, and not as an object dismantled by our own categories." The task is to compare not subsystems but "societies in their own right," a holistic vision apt for "holistic societies."

If I endorse de Coppet's observation, it is to remark that conceptualization is inevitably reconceptualization. The society we think up for the 'Are 'Are, Melanesians from the Solomon Islands, is a transformation of the society we think up for ourselves. For instance, de Coppet says of the 'Are 'Are that far from their society's imparting its own character of permanence to the individuals who compose it, it builds up its character (of permanence) through repeated dissolution into "the ritual and exchange process of the main elements composing each individual" (1981:176). Instead of dismantling holistic systems through inappropriate analytical categories, then, perhaps we should *strive for a holistic apprehension of the manner in which our subjects dismantle their own constructs.* At least as far as Melanesia is concerned, the constructs thereby dismantled or dissolved include life-forms:

persons, bodies, and the reproductive process itself.

Contemporary Melanesian ethnography, especially but not only from the Austronesian-speaking seaboard, is developing its own microvocabulary of dissolution. It describes the processes by which the elements that compose persons are dismantled so that the relationships persons carry can be invested anew. This may include both the relations created during life and the procreative (conjugal) relations that created them. A North Mekeo is "de-conceived" first at marriage and then finally at death (Mosko 1985); Muyuw on Woodlark Island "end" a parent's marriage when the child dies (Damon 1989); Barok mortuary feasts "obviate" previous relationships in finally killing the dead (Wagner 1986), a process that for the Sabarl is a "disassembling" (Battaglia 1990) and on Gawa a "severance" or "dissolution" of social ties (Munn 1986). These recall Bloch's (1986) arresting account from elsewhere in the Austronesian-speaking world of the literal "regrouping" of the dead in their tombs. But if relationships reproductive of persons sometimes have to be dissolved at death, other Melanesians see birth as the principal substitute act by which new re-

*Reprinted, in edited form, from Adam Kuper (ed.), *Conceptualizing Society*, New York: Routledge, Chapman, & Hall, 1992, by permission of the author.

lations displace previous ones (Gillison 1991). Indeed, all knowledge of a revelatory kind may appear as decomposition (Strathern 1988).

These counterimages to the received anthropological metaphors of structure and system have a late-twentieth-century, even postmodern, ring to them. However, as Battaglia notes (1990:218, note 49), it is important to distinguish postmodernism as "a movement with roots in the specifically historical problem of the alienating and fragmenting effects of Western socioeconomic and political influences on other cultures" from analytical perspectives (hermeneutic, deconstructivist) that have as their goal "respect for indigenous ways of conceiving the cultural reproduction of knowledge that are themselves 'perspectivist.'" Indeed, one should be as cautious as one is creative with the resonances between cultural fragmentation perceived in the world at large, specific analytical tactics such as deconstruction, and the discovery of relationships being indigenously conceptualized through images of dissolution.

What clouds the anthropologists' holistic enterprise in the late twentieth century is the Western dismantling of the very category that once carried the concept of a holistic entity, that is, "society." Society was a vehicle for a kind of Western holism, a totalizing concept through which modern people could think the holisms of others.[1]

This chapter is a late-twentieth-century attempt to refigure certain relationships as they have been conceptualized in the recent, and pluralist, past. The relationships in question belong to an apparently small domain of anthropological enquiry, those Melanesian kinship systems known as cognatic. This is because of the assumption that, despite the insignificance of kinship in Western or Euro-American society, Euro-American systems are similarly cognatic in character. I suggest that failure to attend to the particularity of our "own" kinship thinking has also been failure to attend to symbolic processes in anthropological thinking. It is these that have, over the last century or so, both endorsed the concept of society and dissolved it before our eyes.

THE VANISHING OF GARIA SOCIETY

I start with the rebirth of a modernist paradigm. The mid-century in British Social Anthropology saw, in Kuper's phrase, a phoenix arise from the ashes. In a reconceptualized form segmentary lineage systems, as he observes (1988:204), turned up everywhere. Among other things, they afforded a powerful equation between societies and groups.

Conceptualizing a Society Not Composed of Groups

When Lawrence finally published his account of the Garia, he rather daringly had Fortes write the foreword. It was all very well for Fortes to say that eventually the Garia concept of "thinking on" kinsmen inspired his formulation of kinship amity. The truth is that, in 1950, Lawrence's description of these Melanesians had been a scandal. Looking back, Fortes (1984:ix) set out the problem.

When, fresh from the field, Peter Lawrence enthusiastically described Garia social organization to me, my initial reaction was, shall we say, cautious. What later came to be designated the African segmentary descent group model was still a novelty and to many of us full of promise. Melanesia meant, above all, the Trobriands, Dobu, Manus, the Solomon Islands, and descent groups resembling those of the African Model seemed to occur in all of them. The Garia were conspicuously different. . . . [T]hey seemed to have a structure without boundaries: no genealogical boundaries marking off one group of people from another . . . no local boundaries fixing village sites . . . no political boundaries with neighboring peoples, no closed ritual associations or exclu-

sive access to economic resources—a society based, in short, not on unilineal descent groups but on ramifying cognatic kinship relations. . . . [T]his fluidity of structure posed the problem of how any sort of social continuity or cohesion could be maintained.

The only visible basis for social relations appeared to lie in the way the individual was conceived to be at the center of radiating ties that formed a security circle.

The essence of their social organization . . . is the right of the individual to align himself . . . freely with kin on the side of either of his parents. . . . This gives rise to the main problem that, as Radcliffe-Brown . . . points out, confronts all such systems of social organization: how to counteract— how to put boundaries to—the outward extension of kinship ties to farther and farther zones of cousinship. (1984:x)

Garia social organization was there, but where was Garia society?

Lawrence was battling against the then prevailing cartographic images of social structure that insisted on a boundedness to the division of social interests. The concept of cognatic kinship made it appear as though it were the overlapping demands of kin alignments that created divisions. Social order was thereby apprehended as a plurality of external interests; cohesion was to be found in the security circle, where the kindred could at least be diagrammed (1984:figs. 7, 9). Yet the significance of these relationships to a person was stated in a disconcertingly casual manner. "They are merely those individuals . . . with whom he has safe relationships" (1971: 76).

The problems that Garia posed in 1950 were twofold. First, how to conceptualize a society that was not composed of groups; and second, the relationship of parts to wholes. If groups were the vehicles through which societies presented themselves to their members, then without group membership what was a person a part of?

The Relation of Person to Group in Mid-Century British Anthropology

The problem (for British anthropology) had been posed by Radcliffe-Brown: "It is only a unilineal system that will permit the division of a society into separate organized kin-groups" (1950:82).[2] Larger kin groups such as clans "consisted of" smaller ones such as lineages (1952b:70) and lineages were composed of "persons" such that "the principle of the unity of the lineage group" provided a relation which linked "a given person and all the members of the lineage group" (1952b: 87). Persons could also be seen as linked in a network of kin relations that constituted "part of that total network of social relations that I call social structure" (1952b:53). With the demonstration of structure came the assertion that between "various features of a particular kinship system, there is a complex relation of interdependence" such that one may conceptualize "a complex unity, an organized whole" (1952b:53). Radcliffe-Brown could thus call for the comparison of whole systems elucidated by different kinship structures such as those manifest in lineage groups. The whole was known by its internal coherence, and thus its closure.

System, structure, group: these terms are not identical, and are not identical with society, but as a set of comprehensive, organizational categories, each provided a perspective from which that whole entity could be imagined. The recognition of groups "by society" was further visualized in the notion that individual persons became part of society by becoming a part of a group. Descent-group theory literally focused on the mediating role of lineages and other corporate constructs in effecting social adulthood, adulthood being equated with membership. In one flight of fancy, Fortes imagined this process in the manner of a child growing from infant to adult status. The maturation of the individual is of paramount concern to society at large, he argued. Thus the domestic group "having bred, reared and educated the child" then "hands over the finished product to the total society" (1958: 10). As a preexisting whole, society makes individuals into parts of itself by severing them from other preexisting domains. Thus "the whole society" sets itself against "the private culture of each domestic group" (1958: 12).

If individual persons were, in this mid-century view, made into members of groups or of society as a whole, they were also regarded as having naturally preexisting identities. These derived both from their biological or psychological makeup and from the domestic domain. Since domestic and politico-jural domains were conceptualized as cutting up social life into components that were not reducible to one another, each gave a different perspective on social life, and while they combined in single persons ["Every member of a society is simultaneously a person in the domestic domain and in the politico-jural domain" (Fortes 1958:12)] they represented quite distinct relational fields. Society appeared simultaneously exclusive of and inclusive of the domestic domain. What made a person a member of society by virtue of his or her politico-jural relations was not what made him or her a member of the domestic group that supplied "the new recruit."

In short, what gave the part ("the individual") distinctiveness as a whole person was not what made the person a part of the whole society. The Garia problem can be rephrased: by contrast with what made a Garia a person it seemed in the 1950s impossible to discern what made a Garia a member of society.

EXCHANGING PERSPECTIVES

The Person as a Model for Relationships

Seeking the groups by which to specify membership led to much travail. But suppose the problem at which we have arrived were also a fact: suppose Garia conceived the person as a model for relationships. Instead of trying to find the groups of which a person is a member, one would then consider what modelling of relationships the person him- or herself contains. And if Garia society were modelled in the encompassing unity of the singular human being, a person would in this sense not be a part of anything else. A multitude of persons would simply magnify the image of one.

As it turned out, Lawrence placed little weight on jural relations and social cohesion. Instead he emphasized Garia pragmatism and self-interest: "Statements about moral obligation . . . are no more than short-hand terms for considerations of interdependence or mutual self-interest and social survival" (1969: 29). Social conformity, he alarmingly stated, is mere by-product. A relationship valued for the practical and material advantage it confers appears subject to that person's efforts, so that even where expectation is greatest, as among close kin, any sense of indebtedness must be created. Consequently, moral obligation is limited to the circle of effective social ties.

If in the Garia view there are no relationships that are not submitted to the person's definition of them, then what the person contains is an apprehension of those relations that he or she activates externally. If they preexist, it is as internal differences within his or her composite body. This I believe is also an image of the Garia cognatic stock or "group."

The Division of Persons into Male and Female Elements

What do we do with the recurrent internal division of persons, including the cognatic stock, into male and female elements? I wish to suggest that what distinguishes Garia formulations from the familiar groupings of the so-called lineal systems of their neighbors lies in a temporal modality. What is at issue is the divisive figuring of gender to create a future image of unity.

The point at which persons ("groups") appear as a composite of male and female elements and the point at which a single gender is definitive are temporal moments in the reproduction of relations that take a mode imagined across all of Melanesia. Unity emerges once a dual gender identity has been discarded in favor of a single one. The process entails an oscillation between the person conceived as androgynous and the person conceived as single-sex. Single-sex persons are presented through the bodies of men or of women or through the mobile female or male items of wealth that pass between them. The decomposition of the composite person thereby reveals the relations, at once internal and external, of which he or she is composed.

Such a Melanesian person—androgynous or single-sex—is not some kind of corporation sole,[3] and the singular person is not conceptualized as a group with relations extrinsic to it. The matrilineal Trobriands, whom Fortes so eloquently claimed for descent-group theory, present a case in point.

Throughout their lifetimes, Trobrianders activate relationships in a mode that makes the form that every living person takes a composite of maternal and paternal kin. The person can be conceptualized as a vessel, like a canoe containing matrikin, adorned on the outside by its relations with others and especially relations through men. Indeed, the entire kula exchange system is a kind of adornment to matrilineality. At death, the person is divided and, as Annette Weiner (1976, 1979, 1983) has shown, the descent group achieves unitary form as a collection of ancestral spirits waiting to be reborn. This is a moment at which it appears as a single-sex entity—as it also appears in the images of land or of blood that contain the living body. When it takes after the living person, however, the descent group appears in the form of its numerous extensions and relations to others: land attracts

sons to stay and the fetus is nourished by the father.

If relationships give a person life, then at death what is extinguished are those relationships embodied by the deceased. Indeed, a significant effect of Massim mortuary ceremonies is to strip the deceased of social ties: the enduring entity is depersonalized. Relationships created during the lifetime are thus refashioned, for the living can no longer embody them. In some cases (see, for example, Mosko 1989; Battaglia 1990), it is as though people have to recompose the world as it was before the person existed. The cognatic entity built up during a lifetime is partitioned at death.

What anthropologists have classified as differing principles of Melanesian social organization can also be understood as an effect of modalities in temporal as well as spatial sequencing. The mode of dissolution is various, but the "social organization," the person, is similarly construed everywhere. To apprehend this, we need to apprehend the nature of Melanesians' "perspectivism." For they live in a world in which perspectives take a particular form, namely, that of analogies. The result is that perspectives can be exchanged for one another.

Where Perspective Becomes Important

Relations appear at different times and in different locations. This is where perspective becomes important. A male member of a matrilineage is both like and unlike a female member, a collectivity of men giving birth to an initiate is both like and unlike a solitary woman in labor, the yams that swell the belly of the Trobriand brother's garden are both like and unlike the yams with which a father feeds his children. There is constant diversification of the forms in which persons and relations appear. Indeed, one may turn into another: my sister is your wife.

These are switches of perspective between the positions that persons occupy: donor becomes recipient, daughter's paternal substance becomes mother's maternal substance. A temporal perspective is evident, for instance, in the patrilineal clan groups of the Papua New Guinea Highlands. The groups exist in anticipation of action, the spatial reminders of clan unity—men's house, territorial boundary—expectant of the moment when the clan will act as one. As one body, one gender, the clan in turn will act to dispose or rearrange the focus of others in relation to it.

The "cognatic" or androgynous person becomes depluralised, decomposed, in the creation of the "unilineal" single-sex person. Heterogeneous internal relations are thus everted, and appear to the agentive clan(sman) as the network of external affines and consanguines it can focus on itself.

Instead of providing the bases from which to conceive radically different worlds of knowledge, Melanesian forms allow perspectives to exist at once as analogues and as (potential) transformations of one another. For they contain the possibility that persons can exchange perspectives. My center is not your center, but your detached sister/brother (wealth) can be incorporated as the mother/father of my children (my means of reproduction). What is not at issue is that switch of perspective required to perceive an individual as an entity differently constituted from the relationships of which it is part.

In the way that Melanesians present social life to themselves, it would seem that there are no principles of organization that are not also found in the constitution of the person. External relations have the same effect as internal ones. To imagine the person in this manner means that no switch of perspective between person and relations is required in order to "see" social relations. Exchanging perspectives only differentiates one set of relations from another, as it does one kind of person from another.

COGNATIC KINSHIP?

English Kinship: The Person as Less Than the Whole

It may seem curious to resurrect British descent-group theory of the mid-century, but I do so to remark that at its core was an interesting symbolic device. The nature of the debate that it precipitated over non-unilineal kinship systems reveals in retrospect the character of an indigenous Euro-American kinship system—less in the classification of relations it purported to offer than in the conceptualization of kinship with respect to society. The English are my example, and I take an insider's view.

The matter can be put simply. The English person conceptualized as an individual was in one important sense incomplete (after Carrier n.d.). There always appeared to be "more than" the person in social life. When the singular person was taken as a unit, relationships involved others as like units. Social life was thus conceptualized as the person's participation in a plurality. As a result, an individual person was only ever a part of some more encompassing aggregate, and thereby less than the whole.

Where a prototypical Melanesian might have conceptualized the dissolution of the cognatic person as making incomplete an entity already complete, our prototypical English took the person—powerfully symbolized in the child that must be socialized—as requiring completion by society. To focus on the individual person inevitably dissolved this larger category, fragmenting the "level" at which holism could be seen.

Radcliffe-Brown called for the comparison of whole systems because (from the point of view of systems) only systems were whole. The English paradox was that holism was a feature of a part—not the whole—of social life! That is, it was a feature more evident from some (e.g. systemic) perspectives than from others.

That the English imagined themselves living between different orders or levels of phenomena, in an incommensurate world of parts and wholes, both created and was itself a precipitate of the manner in which they handled perspective. I have suggested that an example of this way of thinking was evident in the mid-century British debates over cognatic kinship.

How Could One Have Both Cognatic Systems and Groups?

Unilineal descent groups were taken as evincing the characteristics of orderly social life. Above all, membership could be demonstrated. Indeed, in their kinship organization, many non-Western peoples seemed to be doing what the anthropologist was also doing in elucidating social structure: classifying according to conventions of social life. The individual person was situated within an order of sociality—descent and succession—whose identity clearly endured beyond the life of any one member. "Life" as such became an attribute of abstract social systems (Fortes 1958:1). From the perspective of descent, a group could be conceptualized as a (single) juristic person (Fortes 1969:304). Yet, as we have seen, the same argument assumed that what made individual persons members of a whole group was not what made them whole persons.

A particular significance seemed to inhere in those parts of the kinship system that regulated the disposition of assets, the loyalty of members, and their own definition as sociocentric entities. Hence the significance of the distinction between "descent" and "kinship" and between those (politico-jural) relations that affected group affiliation and those focused on ego as an individual. To the extent that the first set of relations (i.e. descent) appeared social, the second (i.e. kinship) appeared based on natural connections. The domestic domain was thus seen to deal with reproduction as a biological necessity; there was an internal logic to its own developmental cycle (Mosko

1989), and the network of kin ties focusing on the individual ego appeared a natural ground to other kin conventions. "Society" and "nature," we might say, mapped different domains of social relations, the former being more obviously molded by convention than the latter.

Indeed, consanguineal relations as such indicated a virtual fact of nature, a universalism in human arrangements. There were, it seemed, no societies that, in taking account of parentage, did not take account of the presence of both maternal and paternal kin: "Filiation . . . is universally bilateral" (Fortes 1970:87 [1953]). Recognition of consanguinity was unremarkable. What varied was the extent to which kin relations were the social basis for group membership. British Social Anthropology became preoccupied not only with types of descent, but with whether peoples had descent groups at all.

It is a pity that the term "cognatic" should have been so emphatically developed as a complement to the lineal "agnatic" or "uterine." Cognatic ties, wrote Fortes (1970: 49 [1943-1944]) are "ties of actual or assumed physical consanguinity." For Tallensi, it is in the domestic family that we have "the sharpest picture of the interaction between cognatic kinship and agnatic ties. We have there the elementary ties of cognatic kinship linking parent to child and sibling to sibling, and we also have the agnatic tie which sets apart the males as the nuclear lineage" (1970:50 [1943-1944]).

Cognatic kinship thus emerged as a kind of ground against which the social relations based on agnation appear. The creation of the latter came to look like the creation of society (out of nature). One may depict it thus: (1) Descent groups exemplified the creation of social difference—bounded sociocentric entities cut out of the ramifying networks of individuals. Society was evident in conventional differentiation. (2) The field of cognatic kin thus appeared as a set of consanguines naturally undifferentiated—the raw material of kinship. In descent-group systems nonlineal cognates were acknowledged through complementary filiation or the residual claims of subsidiary ties.

The term "cognatic" was unfortunate if only in that it was in use, and had been for a century (Derek Freeman 1961), for those many other systems in which unilineal descent groups did not exist at all. The prototypes were European as well as English. Without unilineal privilege, each parent was of equal weight and equally differentiated. What became interesting was the effort anthropologists put into redeeming the social significance of kin ties in such societies.

The question was how you could both have cognatic systems and have groups. It seemed commonly the case that cognatic kin-reckoning coexisted with cutting or bounding classifications that rested on other-than-kinship criteria such as residence (cf. Scheffler 1985). Cognatic systems thus came to have a dual theoretical status, marginalised both in relation to lineal systems and in terms of their own internal kinship constructs. The latter seemed either thoroughly uninteresting or else thoroughly familiar. Interest lay rather in the (nonkinship) conventions by which such systems achieved the kind of closure necessary if they were to be, in the parlance of the time, the building blocks of society.

Kinship systems that produced groups were no trouble. The trouble with cognatic systems was that tracing cognatic kinship could neither in a strong sense produce groups nor in a weak sense yield a sense of convention or society. Here, in the absence of lineality, was the inverse case: (1) Cognatic kinship reflected natural difference in the bilateral reckoning of relations. (2) But the field of cognatic kin was thus socially undifferentiated and groups had to be cut out of this field by criteria of a different order.

Society, like the analyses anthropologists produced, was to be made visible in its internal differentiations and categorizations, the social segments it cut from nature. Yet in the cognatic case one saw only the endless re-combination of elements devolved from and focusing on individuals. Natural proliferation, ties stretching for ever: as Fortes voiced in his comments on the Garia, there seemed no structure to the mode of kin-reckoning itself. Conceptualized as a kind of inverse to lineal holism, the workings of cognatic kinship seemed incapable of yielding a model of a whole.

Part-Whole Relations: Switching Between Two Totalizing Worlds

If "society" were most visible in groups, it was because they too exemplified classification and convention. For society was held to inhere in the "level" of organizing principles, not in what was being ordered; levels were literally conceived as of a different order from persons concretely imagined as so many individuals.

Hence the central problematic of mid-century anthropology: the relationship between individual and society. Each comprised an irreducible perspective on the other, and the result was *pluralism*. To think of society rather than to think of the individual was not to exchange perspectives, for there was no reciprocity here. Rather, it was to switch between totalizing worlds. Here each perspective encompassed the other perspective as "part" of itself.

In this presentation of part-whole relations, the whole was composed of parts, yet the logic of the totality was to be found not in the logic of the individual parts but in organizing principles and relations lying beyond them. To perceive life from the perspective of the discrete parts thus yielded a different dimension from the viewpoint gained from the whole.

Depending on what was taken as a whole and what was taken as a part, one could always generate (whole) new perspectives and new sets of elements or components. Each part was potentially a whole, but only from other perspectives. Thus an individual person was a potentially holistic entity—but, for anthropologists, only from the perspective of another discipline such as psychology. From anthropology's own disciplinary perspective, the concept of society stimulated the "more" holistic vision.

THE VANISHING OF ENGLISH KINSHIP

To argue that the symbolic strategy at the heart of this kinship theorizing was based on the idea that parts cannot be defined by what defines wholes, recalls David Schneider's (1968) formulation of American kinship. What makes a person a relative, he stated, is not what makes a relative a person. It is to such a switch of perspectives that the kinship constructs of the mid-twentieth century gave facticity and certainty. What was embedded in anthropological kinship thinking was, I suspect, reflected back by the folk models of the "wider society" of which it was a part.

Now while I take "English" as my exemplar of a folk model and thus illustrative of Euro-American kinship thinking, there is also good reason to suppose that the trivialization of kinship in social life is a characteristic that may well distinguish it from some continental or southern European models (though it may give it an affinity to aspects of "American" kinship). It is of interest insofar as it has helped shape British anthropological theorizing on kinship. Both belong to a cultural era I have called "*modernist*" or "*pluralist.*"

The short question is why a kinship system of the English kind has been so hard to conceptualize theoretically. Part of the answer must lie in conceptualizing it as cognatic. For that meant it became profoundly uninteresting. Either its mode of kinship reckoning is entirely unproblematic because it self-evidently follows natural distinctions or it is entirely problematic because it solves so few of the other questions we would ask about social life. It disappears in studies of local communities or class or visiting patterns. We have a

feeling that kinship in English society ought to have a significant social dimension, despite the fact that all we can see is the number of times daughters visit their mothers or who gets what at Christmas. But what we then "see" is the incompleteness of kinship as an explanatory device. We reintroduce dimensions of class and income and neighborhood and our grasp of what might be distinctive about kinship has again vanished.

Incompleteness as an Artefact of the System

That the English cannot pin down a sense of society when they reflect on their own kinship systems is an artefact of the system itself. And that is because of the way they make kinship vanish. Collaterals do not, of course, go on forever; they fade out rather quickly (Firth, Hubert, and Forge 1969:170-171), but not for reasons to do with the nature of the kin connection. Other factors intervene; and this is the point. Kinship seems less than a complete system.

From a British view, despite our best efforts as anthropologists to see our own conventions, we somehow take the manner in which the English (say) trace kin along lines of consanguinity as socially trivial. Society lies "beyond" kinship, impinging as a different order of phenomena.

But suppose that this problem were also fact: suppose that this incompleteness were part of English kinship thinking. Instead of trying to specify what the social significance of kinship might be, we would consider what modelling of plurality kinship formulations themselves contain. Let me rephrase the modelling at issue and reinstate the tense that indicates the temporal perspective from which I write.

What I have called modernist or pluralist in this kinship thinking produced the figure of the person as an individual, made up of the physical materials that made up other individuals but recombining them in a unique way. In this sense, the person was a whole individual. But what made the person a whole individual was not what made him or her a part of any wider identity. In relation to society, the individual was incomplete—to be completed by socialization, relationships and convention. The problematic at the heart of mid-century British anthropology was also a proposition at the heart of twentieth-century English kinship.

The proposition neatly encapsulated the manner in which anthropologists produced plural and fragmented worlds for themselves as much as it did the manner in which they produced totalizing and holistic ones. For the moment one switched from looking at a person as a unique individual to his or her relations with others, one added a dimension of another order. Each perspective might be used to totalizing effect, yet each totalizing perspective was vulnerable to other perspectives that made its own purchase on reality incomplete. The individual person was both a part of society and a part of nature. Society both was cut out of nature and encapsulated nature within itself. To switch from one perspective to another was to switch whole domains of explanation. The parts were not equal since perspectives could not be matched. They overlapped; one whole was only a part of another. Thus social convention could be conceptualized as modifying and encompassing natural givens.

Such modernist perspectives had their own pluralizing effect. When perspectives cannot be exchanged, one perspective can only capture the essence of another by encapsulating it as a part of itself. Parts in turn thus always appear to be cut from other, larger wholes.

POSTPLURAL VISIONS

Clifford's Pluralized Vision

Some people in the West think they now live in a world that has lost the unifying perspective of modernism. This leaves the problem of

what to do with parts and wholes. I offer an American example.

I have been struck by the organizing images of Clifford's *The Predicament of Culture* (1988), his concern with the rootlessness that off-centers persons and scatters traditions. This mood of lost authenticity—the idea that the world is full of changed, part-cultures—is not new. What is new (he says) is the setting that the late twentieth century provides: "A truly global space of cultural connections and dissolutions has become imaginable: local authenticities meet and merge in transient . . . settings" (1988:4). The task is how to respond to an unprecedented overlay of traditions.

Intensive ethnography must be an ethnography of conjunctures, moving between cultures, a cosmopolitan practice which participates in the hybridization he sees everywhere. Yet (he argues) ethnographies have always been composed of cut-outs, bits extracted from context, brought together in analysis and narrative. What is also new is the way we think about the hybridization. Texts that once celebrated the integration of cultural artefacts have been displaced by deliberate attention to the uniqueness of fragments. Creativity can only lie in their recombination. Clifford sees this as a salvation not just for texts but for the concept of culture itself, for cultures have always been hybrids, "the roots of tradition [forever] cut and retied" (1988:15). Tradition?

The therapeutic hope of his own efforts is for the "reinvention of difference" (1988:15). Elements cut from diverse times and places can be recombined, though they cannot fit together as a whole. Clifford's problem is not that of simple multiplicity or of the multiculturalism of contact. Rather, it is a postplural vision of a composite world forever the result of borrowings and interchanges. In his view, such a habitation significantly resists the global vision of (say) Lévi-Strauss's *Tristes Tropiques* (1955), with its 1950s nostalgia for authentic human differences disappearing in an expansive commodity culture. Rather than being placed at the end of the world's many histories, the European narrative of a progressive monoculture is to be set beside the creolization of culture itself. He evokes the Caribbean: a history of degradation, mimicry, violence, but one that is also rebellious, syncretic, and creative. Without wholes, the only thing to do is recombine the parts.

Ethnography as Collage; Thinking Kinship

Listen, then, to how the images of recombination and cutting work. Listen to what happens when one imagines Clifford's vision of the postmodern world as though he were thinking kinship of the English kind.

Clifford's criticism is of those who mistook people's collections for the representation of a collective life: there never were any authentic indigenous master narratives for which the anthropologist's master narrative was an appropriate genre. The classifier of ethnographic collections "invents" a relationship between artefact and culture. Cut out of their (living) contexts, artefacts are made to stand for abstract wholes, a Bambara mask for Bambara culture. Creolization, by contrast, makes incongruity evident, as in ethnographies which leave "the cuts and sutures of the research process" visible (1988:146).

Ethnography as collage "would be an assemblage containing voices other than the ethnographer's, as well as examples of "found" evidence, data not fully integrated within the work's governing interpretation" (1988:147). Here is the potential creativity of ethnography. Rather than the creativity of convention, of human kinship "reduced to discrete differential systems" (1988:241), ethnography must remain open to registering the original act of combination—the procreation of a hybrid.

Clifford's presentation of cultures as bits and pieces cut up and recombined contains borrowings of its own. On the one hand, like rootless persons cultures are always in fragments; on the other hand in their collecting it is past anthropologists who have cut up cultures into the bits reassembled in their narratives. Cultures are always hybrids, yet cultural future lies in further creative recombining, including the recombinations of the ethnographic enterprise. As Clifford depicts the late-twentieth-century ethnography, its skilled differentiations will apply to differences already there. He quotes Said: "A part of something is for the foreseeable future going to be better than all of it. Fragments over wholes. . . . To tell your story in pieces, *as it is*" (1988:11—original emphasis).

This is the old reproductive idiom of biological kinship. Clifford does not, of course, talk kinship. Yet transmuted into his language of ethnographic creativity are, I suggest, ideas equally applicable to mid-century notions of procreation. Persons are natural hybrids: the creative recombination of already differentiated genetic material makes everyone a new entity. The past might have been collected into ancestral traditions, but the future lies in perpetual hybridization.

Clifford finds it unproblematic to convey the hybridization of a hybrid world, with its particulate nature and unique moments. Yet hybrids are not to be stabilized as wholes. For him, all the "problems" lie in those master narratives which purported to reveal holistic societies—in which case the real problem lies in being heir to them, and thus to the supposition that parts are always cut from something else: how to conceptualize a part that is not a part of a whole?

Clifford speaks for a world that has ceased to see either unity or plurality in an unambiguous way. What lies behind him are years of modernist scholarship with their vision of a *plurality* of cultures and societies whose comparison rested on the unifying effect of this or that governing perspective. Each perspective simultaneously pluralized the subject matter of anthropological study and held out the promise of a holistic understanding that would show elements fitted together and parts completed.

Rethinking Anthropology's Holistic Concept of Society: Apprehending Alternative Orderings of Parts and Wholes

At least for British anthropology, I suspect it was an intimacy between anthropological and folk models that in fact made an indigenous cognatic system impossible to analyze; it either appeared as a negative version of other kinship systems, or was universalized as displaying the facts that others tried to conventionalize. Such conventions were found in societies where kinship seemed central to the manner in which society itself was represented. "Kinship" was, of course, already conceptualized as a "system," and systems were seen to be wholes made up of (interdependent) parts. But to give "parts" their distinct identity would draw one into other perspectives, other totalizing systems of relations. In Western society one could take the perspective of kinship but this could not also be the perspective of society.

Think again of the Garia person. It was a fancy, of course, ever to have supposed that this Melanesian figure contains an image of "society," for the very idea of society in Western thinking entailed an encompassment of perspectives. Society did not in Garia modelling provide a perspective on the singular person any more than the singular person provided a perspective on society. There was in that sense no perspective; or, rather, only the one perspective, from the center, of which others were always analogies or transformations. Thus to imagine another person was to exchange perspectives: one person's periphery appeared as another person's center (Werbner, 1989).

New dismantling idioms might give anthropologists a vocabulary with which to apprehend other people's dismantling projects, but "our" project should not be mistaken for "theirs." We are not devolved from and do not reproduce the same worlds.

Parallels between "Melanesian" and "Western" conceptualizations always were elusive. The Garia security circle looked at first blush like the ramifying kin network of consanguines with which many Europeans were familiar. Yet the figure of the Garia person was never a genetic hybrid, complete by inheritance and endowment but incomplete when thought of as a part of a wider society. Rather, socially complete, it was made incomplete in its engagement and exchange with others. Nor did the holism of Melanesian imagery mean that Melanesians did not envision cutting. On the contrary, images of partition, extraction, severance were commonplace. But what was "cut" were persons and relations themselves: person from person, relation from relation, not persons cut off from relations. Far from being fixed in time at the moment of birth, relations were the active life on which the person was forever working.

What differentiated relations in Melanesia was the exchange of people's perspectives on one another: the transfer of valuables that guaranteed that a woman would bear her husband's child and not her father's or the work of spouses in procreation that must be repeated before birth and supplemented by nurture afterwards. A person was created, so to speak, out of the same materials by which it created its own life: composite but not unique; "cut" and partitioned but not from a sphere that lay external to it. The Highlands woman being prepared for marriage might be both severed from her clan and internally divided—detached from and made to void paternal substance. Everything was partible.[4] But this partitioning did not create different orders of being out of parts and wholes.

The modernist imagery of parts and wholes worked to different effect, and it is to this that we are heir. It made us see persons as parts cut from a whole imagined as relations, life, and, for the anthropologist, society. Conversely, in the discourse of systems and structures it was relations, life, society that creatively recombined the fragments and parts. The "cognatic kinship" of Western society reproduced unique individuals whose procreation was perpetually modified by an overlay of other principles of social life. Take the individual away and, the English would say, society will still endure. But a Melanesian death required the active severance of persons and relations—living persons rearranging their relationships among themselves when the deceased could no longer embody them. This included "undoing" the cognatic ties which constituted life.

What was creative about the recombinations that Melanesians enacted—the wealth and children they made—was that they anticipated and were made of acts similar to those which subsequently partitioned them. Parts were never dislocated in this sense, left on the cutting-room floor, so to speak, to be recombined by someone else. Contrary to understood wisdom, Melanesians have never needed salvage ethnography. For their vision of the world had no problem with how parts fit together. There were no bits and pieces that had to be put back again, for the sake of a culture to restore, a society to conceptualise. I doubt that nostalgia for either culture or society figures in their present cosmopolitanism.

NOTES

1. Nowadays it seems to belong more to text than to life. Thornton argues that much of the significance of "society" lay in its power as a rhetorical trope for the organization of anthropological data. Positing analytical components capable of theoretical integration presumed an entirety to the object of study as a whole made up of parts, so that society emerged as a holistic precipitate of analysis. "The imagination of wholes is a rhetorical imperative for ethnography since it is this image of wholeness that gives the ethnography a sense of fulfilling 'closure' that other genres accomplish by different rhetorical means" (1988:286). Conversely, "it may be that it is impossible to conceptualize society, except in terms of holistic images" (1988:298).

2. While Fortes (1970:81 [1953]) allowed himself to refer to "[a] society made up of corporate lineages," it was an image that he later took great pains to undo (e.g. 1969:287). On the disjunction between Fortes's own rich documentation of the Tallensi case (including their overlapping fields of clanship) and his theoretical axioms, see Kuper (1982:85); and for a similar point with regard to the relationship of "descent" and "group," see Scheffler (1985:9).

3. Editor's note: Maine (1861:181) (quoted in Fortes 1969:292) explains a corporation sole as follows: "A Corporation sole is an individual, being a member of a series of individuals, who is invested by a fiction with the qualities of a Corporation. I need hardly cite the King or the Parson of a Parish as instances of Corporations sole. The capacity or office is here considered apart from the particular person who from time to time may occupy it, and, this being perpetual, the series of individuals who fill it are clothed with the leading attribute of Corporations—Perpetuity."

4. Where persons are cut from persons (or relations from relations), as we might imagine a female agnate severed from her clan or donor distinguished from recipient, then one position or perspective is substituted for another of comparable order. Thus Molima substitute the division of maternal and paternal kin at death for their combination in the living person. When persons die, they become reconstituted as siblings—their marriages, so to speak, undone and their children de-conceived (Chowning 1989). Now insofar as one set of relations (siblingship) substitutes for another (conjugality), it is also anticipated, and in that sense "already there." How different from the novelty with which English kinship (say) perceives the natural creation of individual persons and the social creation of relations!

I N T E L L E C T U A L   R O O T S

Marilyn Strathern is Professor of Social Anthropology at Manchester University and William Wyse Professor Elect at Cambridge. Initial fieldwork in the Papua New Guinea Highlands led to *Women in Between* (1972), the coauthored *Self-Decoration in Mt. Hagen* (1971), and then to two New Guinea Research Bulletins on dispute settlement and Hagen migrants.

A critical assessment of that earlier work was among the reasons for writing *The Gender of the Gift* (1988), while *Partial Connections* (1991) addressed comparison after postmodernism. *Kinship at the Core* (1981) was a study of an Essex village, whose gender of the gift is so to speak *After Nature* (1992), a critique of the relationship between anthropological theorizing about individual and society and indigenous ("English") kinship. Most recent works are the collected essays *Reproducing the Future* (1992) and the coauthored *Technologies of Procreation* (1993). She is a Fellow of the British Academy.

Going to Cambridge in 1960 cured me once and for all of the illusion that the universe might have a center; my own students have since demonstrated that there is nothing lineal about the transmission of ideas from teacher to pupil; and when they were little my children taught me that time comes in, also rather small, lumps. I have little faith in genealogies then; rather, I imagine my work as contextualized and recontextualized by others.

In making the selective nature of this self-account apparent, I restrict myself to female figures. This is not to say that I have not been influenced by men. On the contrary, as a student I was deeply affected both by Jack Goody's sociological precision and by Edmund Leach's cultural transgressions, a duplex to some extent repeated in the difference between Andrew Strathern's heady pragmatism (I owe much of my fieldwork style to him) and Roy Wagner's relentless powers of recursion. If there is a descent line between A. Strathern and J. Goody, one of their inspirations was also initially mine: Radcliffe-Brown's *Structure and Function*, picked up in Foyle's, a once-famous secondhand bookshop, excited me before I even got to Cambridge, and the thesis (1968) that became *Women in Between* was gripped in the problematics of social order. In an odd interlude in Port Moresby, I read among other things Ann Oakley's newly published *Sex, Gender and Society* (and in 1973 wrote a book on gender that was never published). But in the summer of 1978 I was struck sideways by Wagner's *The Invention of Culture*. The book derived much of its power from the antecedent it unwrote for me (*Structure and Function*); reading Michelle Stanworth's *Reproductive Technologies* ten years later in turn rewrote for me what a feminist agenda in the 1990s might look like.

My mother, Joyce Evans, had led me to take for granted the rightness of focusing on women's affairs, a confidence broken by Annette Weiner's early criticism. Another duplex: between the complacency induced by a known audience and the shift that a critical one brings. Always polemical myself—divided between those for whom I write

and those against whom I write—I realize I deserve what I get. And, when it matters, as in this case, eventually find gratitude.

The first audience for my anthropological efforts was Doris Wheatley (Director of Studies at Girton, Cambridge), while Esther Goody and Audrey Richards marked—with a care I still recall—my second- and third-year essays. E. Goody became my Ph.D. supervisor (in the same graduate cohort as Maurice Bloch and Adam Kuper), Paula Brown happily being appointed to oversee the fieldwork part in Papua New Guinea, and instilled in me a respect for social detail. Much later, Richards generously made available the materials she had accumulated on Elmdon, Essex, and on which Marianne Leach had subsequently worked, though I think she (i.e. Richards) never really liked the book I wrote from them. A steadying ethnographic influence in Port Moresby (1972-1976) was Ann Chowning, whose staggering personal knowledge of the country defied most generalizations.

It was coming away from the 1977 ASA conference organized by Jean La Fontaine that Carol McCormack and I found we both had problems with the nature-culture dichotomy. The collection of essays that followed (*Nature, Culture, and Gender*, 1980), further stimulated by a year at Canberra with the Gender Relations study group and a brief visit to Berkeley (where Elizabeth Colson was in her last year), threw me into *The Gender of the Gift*. Its moments of clarity owe much to the insights of more recent fieldworkers in Melanesia, including Debbora Battaglia, Aletta Biersack, Gillian Gillison and Margaret Jolly.

At this point, as with my present colleagues at Manchester, history can only find expression as a current sense of debt. Indeed, if history requires a distance on moments thus made previous, then perhaps it is the uninvited guest who is always most influential: oneself. While I might otherwise have continued fieldwork in Papua New Guinea, I am grateful for the circumstances that have instead forced me into un-writing and rewriting my own work. Kinship has recently resurfaced among my concerns, and in new form—recontextualized by the biological and cultural possibilities joined in the technologies of procreation. Brought up to think that anthropology's contribution always lay rather uniquely in this domain, I find the once luxury of rethinking has in fact become an urgent and thoroughly practical necessity.

15

Facing Power:
*Old Insights, New Questions**

ERIC R. WOLF

I want in this essay to engage the problem of power and the issues that it poses for anthropology. I want to argue that we actually know a lot about power, but have been timid in building upon what we know. This has implications for both theory and method, for assessing the insights of the past and for raising new questions.

The very term makes many of us uncomfortable. It is certainly one of the most loaded and polymorphous words in our repertoire. The Romance, Germanic, and Slavic languages, at least, conflate a multitude of meanings in speaking about *pouvoir* or *potere*, *Macht*, or *mogushchestvo*. Such words allow us to speak about power, as if it meant the same thing to all of us. At the same time, we often speak of power as if all phenomena involving it were somehow reducible to a common core, some inner essence. This conjures up monstrous images of power, Hobbes's Leviathan or Bertrand de Jouvenel's Minotaur, but it leads away from specifying different kinds of power implicated in different kinds of relationships.

MODES OF POWER

I shall argue instead that it is useful to think of four different modes of power. One is power as the attribute of the person, as potency or capability, the basic Nietzschean idea of power (Kaufmann 1968). Speaking of power in this sense draws attention to the endowment of persons in the play of power, but tells us little about the form and direction of that play. The second kind of power can be understood as the ability of an *ego* to impose its will on an *alter*, in social action, in interpersonal relations. This draws attention to the sequences of interactions and transactions among people, but it does not address the nature of the arena in which the interactions go forward. That comes into view more sharply when we focus on power in the third mode, as power that controls the settings in which people may show forth their potentialities and interact with others. I first came across this phrasing of power in anthropology when Richard Adams sought to define power not in interpersonal terms, but as the control that one actor or "operating unit" (his term) exercises over energy flows that constitute part of the environment of another actor (Adams 1966, 1975). This definition calls attention to the instrumentalities of power and is useful for understanding how "operating units" circumscribe the actions of others within determinate settings. I will call this third kind of power *tactical* or *organizational power*.

*Reprinted, in edited form, from *American Anthropologist* 1990 92(3):586–596, by permission of the American Anthropological Society.

But there is still a fourth mode of power, power that not only operates within settings or domains but that also organizes and orchestrates the settings themselves, and that specifies the distribution and direction of energy flows. I think that this is the kind of power that Marx addressed in speaking about the power of capital to harness and allocate labor-power, and it forms the background of Michel Foucault's notion of power as the ability "to structure the possible field of action of others." Foucault (1984:427, 428) called this "to govern," in the sixteenth-century sense of governance, an exercise of "action upon action." Foucault himself was primarily interested in this as the power to govern consciousness, but I want to use it as power that structures the political economy. I will refer to this kind of power as *structural power*. This term rephrases the older notion of "the social relations of production," and is intended to emphasize power to deploy and allocate social labor. These governing relations do not come into view when you think of power primarily in interactional terms. Structural power shapes the social field of action so as to render some kinds of behavior possible, while making others less possible or impossible. As old Georg Friedrich Hegel argued, what occurs in reality has first to be possible.

What capitalist relations of production accomplish, for example, is to make possible the accumulation of capital based on the sale of marketable labor power in a large number of settings around the world. As anthropologists we can follow the flows of capital and labor through ups and downs, advances and retreats, and investigate the ways in which social and cultural arrangements in space and time are drawn into and implicated in the workings of this double whammy. This is not a purely economic relation, but a political one as well: it takes clout to set up, clout to maintain, and clout to defend; and wielding that clout becomes a target for competition or alliance building, resistance or accommodation.

This is the dimension that has been stressed variously in studies of imperialism, dependency, or world-systems. Their questions are why and how some sectors, regions, or nations are able to constrain the options of others, and what coalitions and conflicts occur in the course of this interplay. Some have said that these questions have little relevance to anthropology, in that they don't have enough to say about "real people doing real things," as Sherry Ortner put it (Ortner 1984:114); but it seems to me that they do touch on a lot of what goes on in the real world, that constrains, inhibits, or promotes what people do, or cannot do, within the scenarios we study. The notion of structural power is useful precisely because it allows us to delineate how the forces of the world impinge upon the people we study, without falling back into an anthropological nativism that postulates supposedly isolated societies and uncontaminated cultures, either in the present or in the past. There is no gain in a false romanticism that pretends that "real people doing real things" inhabit self-enclosed and self-sufficient universes.

THE TASK OF ANTHROPOLOGY

I shall address here primarily the relation between tactical (or organizational) power and structural power. I do this because I believe that these concepts can help us to explain the world we inhabit. I think that it is the task of anthropology—or at least the task of some anthropologists—to attempt explanation, and not merely description, descriptive integration, or interpretation. Anthropology can be different things to different people (entertainment, exotic *frisson*, a "show and tell" of differences), but it should not, I submit, be content with James Boon's "shifting collage of contraries threatening (promising) to become unglued" (Boon 1982:237). Writing culture may require literary skill and genre, but a search for explanation requires more: It cannot do without naming and comparing things, and formulating concepts for naming and comparison. I think we must move beyond Geertz's "experience-near" understandings to analytical concepts that allow us to set what we know about X against what we know about Y, in pursuit of explanation. This means that I subscribe to a basically realist position. I think that the world is real, that these realities affect what humans do and that what humans do affects the world, and that we can come to understand the whys and wherefores of this relationship.

We need to be professionally suspicious of our categories and models; we should be aware of their historical and cultural contingencies; we can understand a quest for explanation as approximations to truth rather than the truth itself. But I also believe that the search for explanation in anthropology can be cumulative; that knowledge and insights gained in the past can generate new questions, and that new departures can incorporate the accomplishments of the past.

In anthropology we are continuously slaying paradigms, only to see them return to life, as if discovered for the first time. The old-time evolutionism of Morgan and Engels reappeared in ecological guise in the forties and fifties. The Boasian insistence that we must understand the ways "that people actually think about their own culture and institutions" (Goldman 1975:15) has resurfaced in the anthropology of cognition and symbolism, now often played as a dissonant quartet in the format of deconstructionism. Diffusionism grew exhausted after biting too deeply into the seductive apple of trait-list collecting, but sprang back to life in the studies of acculturation, interaction spheres, and world-systems. Functionalism overreached itself by claiming to depict organic unities, but returned in systems theory as well as in other disguises. Culture-and-personality studies advanced notions of "basic personality structure" and "national character," without paying heed to history, cultural heterogeneity, or the role of hegemony in shaping uniformities; but

suspiciously similar characterizations of modern nations and "ethnic groups" continue to appear. The varieties of ecological anthropology and the various Marxisms are being told by both user-friendly and unfriendly folk that what they need is "the concept of culture." We are all familiar, I trust, with Robert Lowie's image of "diffusionism laying the axe to evolutionism." As each successive approach carries the axe to its predecessors, anthropology comes to resemble a project in intellectual deforestation.

I do not think that this is either necessary or desirable. I think that anthropology can be cumulative, that we can use the work of our predecessors to raise new questions.

THREE PROJECTS

Some of anthropology's older insights into power can be the basis for new inquiry. I want to briefly review three projects that sought to understand what happens to people in the modern world and in the process raised questions about power, both tactical and structural. These projects yielded substantial bodies of data and theory; they opened up perspectives that reached beyond their scope of inquiry; and all were criticized in their time and subjected to reevaluation thereafter. All three were efforts toward an explanatory anthropology.

Puerto Rico

The first of these projects is the study of Puerto Rico in 1948–1949, directed by Julian Steward; the results are in the collective work, *The People of Puerto Rico* (Steward et al. 1956). The original thrust of the project stemmed from Steward's attack on the assumptions of a unitary national culture and national character which then dominated the field of culture-and-personality. The project aimed instead at exhibiting the heterogeneity of a national society. It was also a rejection of the model in which a single community was made to stand for an entire nation. It depicted Puerto Rico as a structure of varied localities and regions, clamped together by island-wide institutions and the activities of an insular upper class, a system of heterogeneous parts and levels.

The project was especially innovative in trying to find out how this complex arrangement developed historically, by tracing out the historical causes and courses of crop production on the island, and then following out the differential implications of that development in four representative communities. It promised to pay attention to the institutions connecting localities, regions, and nation, but actually confined itself to looking at these institutions primarily in terms of their local effects. It did carry out a study of the insular upper class, which was conceived as occupying the apex of linkages to the level of the nation.

The project's major shortfall, in terms of its own undertaking, was its failure to take proper account of the rapidly intensifying migration to the nearby U.S. mainland. Too narrow a focus upon agricultural ecology prevented it from coming to grips with issues already then becoming manifest on the local level, but prompted and played out upon a much larger stage.

Central Africa

While the Puerto Rico project averted its eyes from the spectacle of migration, another research effort took labor migration to the towns and burgeoning mines of Central Africa as its primary point of reference. This research was carried out under the auspices of the Rhodes-Livingstone Institute, set up in 1937 in what was then Northern Rhodesia and is now Zambia. Its research goal was defined by the first director, Godfrey Wilson, whose own outlook has been characterized as an unconscious effort to combine Marx and Malinowski (Richard Brown 1973:195). Wilson understood the processes affecting Central Africa as

an industrial revolution connected to the workings of the world economy. The massive penetration of the mining industry was seen as causal in generating multiple conflicts on the local and regional scene. Then Max Gluckman, the director from 1942 to 1947, drew up a research plan for the Institute which outlined a number of problem-oriented studies, and enlisted a stellar cast of anthropologists to work on such problems as the intersections of native and colonial governance, the role of witchcraft, the effects of labor migration on domestic economy, and the conflicts generated by the tension-ridden interplay of matrilineal descent and patrilocal residence.

Dealing with an area of considerable linguistic and cultural diversity, the researchers were able to compare their findings to identify what was variable and what was common in local responses to general processes. But where the project was at its most innovative was in looking at rural locations, mining centers, and towns not as separate social and cultural entities but as interrelated elements caught up in one social field. It thus moved from Wilson's original concern with detribalization as anomic loss toward a more differentiated scenario of variegated responses to the new behavior settings of village, mine, and urban township. In doing so, it opened perspectives that the Puerto Rico project did not address. Its major failing lay in not taking systematic and critical account of the colonial structure in which these settings were embedded.

Guatemala

The third project I want to mention was directed by Richard Adams between 1963 and 1966, to study the national social structure of Guatemala. It is described in the book *Crucifixion by Power* (Adams 1970). The project took account of the intense growth of agricultural production for the market and placed what was then known about life in localities within that context.

Its specific innovation, however, lies in the fact that it engaged the study of national institutions in ways not broached by the two other projects I have referred to. Adams showed how local, regional, and supranational elites contested each other's power, and how regional elites stabilized their command by forging ties at the level of the nation. At that level, however, their power was subject to competition and interference by groups operating on the transnational and international plane. The study of elites was followed by accounts of the development of various institutions: the military, the renascent Guatemalan Church, the expanding interest organizations of the upper sector, and the legal system and legal profession. Adams then showed how these institutions curtailed agrarian and labor demands in the countryside, and produced individualized patron-client ties between the urban poor and their political sponsors in the capital. What the project did not do was to bring together this rich material into a synthesis that might have provided a theoretical model of the nation for further work.

Their Significance

It seems clear now that the three projects all stood on the threshold of a promising new departure in anthropological inquiry, but failed to cross it. They were adventurous, but not adventurous enough. First, in my view, they anticipated a move toward political economy, while not quite taking that next step. The Puerto Rico project, in its concentration on agriculture, failed to come to grips with the political and economic forces that established that agriculture in the first place, and that were already at work in "Operation Bootstrap" to transform the agricultural island into an industrial service station. We did not understand the ways in which island institutions, supposedly "national" but actually interlocked with mainland economics and politics, were battlegrounds for diverse contending

interests. Thus the project also missed an opportunity to deal with the complex interplay of hegemonic and subaltern cultural stances in the Puerto Rican situation. In fact, no one has done so to date; the task remains for the doing.

The Central Africa project was similarly confined by its own presuppositions. Despite its attention to conflicts and contradictions, it remained a captive of the prevailing functionalism, especially when it interpreted disjunctions as mere phases in the restoration of continuity. There was a tendency to take the colonial system as a given and thus to mute both the historical implications of conquest and the cumulative confrontations between Africans and Europeans. New questions now enable us to address these issues. Colonialism overrode the kin-based and tributary polities it encountered. Their members were turned into peasants in the hinterland and into workers in mine and town; peasantization and proletarianization were concomitant processes, often accompanied by force and violence. New ethnic and class identities replaced older, now decentered ties (Sichone 1989). Yet research has also uncovered a multiplicity of African responses in labor and political organization (A. L. Epstein 1958; Ranger 1970), in dance societies (J. C. Mitchell 1957; Ranger 1975), in a proliferation of religious movements (Van Binsbergen and Schofeleers 1985; Werbner 1989), in rebellion and resistance (e.g. Lan 1985). These studies have reemphasized the role of cultural understandings as integral ingredients of the transformation of labor and power.

Adams's project came very close to a new opening. It embodied a historical perspective, it understood the relations among groups as conflict-ridden processes, and it included the operations of multinational and transnational powers in this dynamic. It did not, however, move toward a political economic model of the entire ensemble—perhaps because Adams's own specific interests lay in developing an evolutionary theory of power. It thus also neglected the complex interplay of cultures in the Guatemalan case. Such a move toward synthesis still awaits the future.

The significance of these three projects lies not only in their own accomplishments but in the new questions they lead us to ask. First, they all call attention to history, but not history as "one damned thing after another," as Leslie White used to say. "History," says Maurice Godelier, "does not explain: it has to be explained" (1977:6). What attention to history allows you to do is to look at processes unfolding, intertwining, spreading out and dissipating over time. This means rethinking the units of our inquiries—households, localities, regions, national entities—seeing them not as fixed entities, but as problematic; shaped, reshaped, and changing over time. Attention to processes unfolding over time foregrounds organization—the structuring arrangements of social life—but requires us to see these in process and change. Second, the three projects point us to processes operating on a macroscale, as well as in microsettings. Puerto Rico was located first in the Hispanic orbit, then in the orbit of the United States. Central Africa was shaped by worldwide industrialization as well as by the policies of colonial governance. Guatemala has been crucified by external connections and internal effects at the same time. The point continues an older anthropology which spoke first of "culture areas," then of oikumenes, interaction spheres, interethnic systems, and symbiotic regions, and that can now entertain "world-systems." Macroscopic history and processes of organization thus become important elements of a new approach. Both involve considerations of power—tactical and structural.

UNDERSTANDING ORGANIZATION AS PROCESS

Organization is key, because it sets up relationships among people through allocation and control of resources and rewards. It draws on tactical power to monopolize or share out liens and claims, to channel action into certain pathways while interdicting the flow of action into others. Some things become possible and likely; others are rendered unlikely. At the same time, organization is always at risk. Since power balances always shift and change, its work is never done; it operates against entropy (Balandier 1970). Even the most successful organization never goes unchallenged. The enactment of power always creates friction—disgruntlement, foot-dragging, escapism, sabotage, protest, or outright resistance, a panoply of responses well documented with Malaysian materials by James Scott (1985) in *Weapons of the Weak*.

Granted the importance of the subject, one might ask why anthropology seems to have relinquished the study of organization, so that today you can find the topic more often discussed in the manuals of business management than in our publications. We structure and are structured, we transact, we play out metaphors, but the whole question of organization has fallen into abeyance.

Many of us entered anthropology when there were still required courses in something called "social organization." It dealt with principles of categorization like gender, generation, and rank, and with groupings, such as lineages, clans, age sets, and associations. We can now see in retrospect that this labeling was too static, because organization was then grasped primarily as an outcome, a finished product responding to a cultural script, and not visualized in the active voice, as process, frequently a difficult and conflict-ridden process at that. When the main emphasis was on organizational forms and principles, it was all too easy to understand organization in architectural terms, as providing the building blocks for structure, a reliable edifice of regular and recurrent practices and ideas that rendered social life predictable, and could thus be investigated in the field. There was little concern with tactical power in shaping organizations, maintaining them, destabilizing them, or undoing them.

If an idea is judged by its fruitfulness, then the notion of social structure proved to be a very good idea. It yielded interesting work and productive insights. It is now evident that it also led us to reify organizational results into the building blocks of hypostatized social architectures, for example, in the concept of "the unilineal descent group." That idea was useful in leading us to think synoptically about features of group membership, descent, jural-political solidarity, rights and obligations focused on a common estate, injunctions of "prescriptive altruism," and norms of encompassing morality. Yet it is one thing to use a model to think out the implications of organizational processes, and another to expect unilineal descent groups with all these features to materialize in these terms, as dependably shaped bricks in a social structural edifice.

How do we get from viewing organization as product or outcome to understanding organization as process? For a start, we could do worse than heed Conrad Arensberg's advice (1972:10-11) to look at "the flow of action," to ask what is going on, why it is going on, who engages in it, with whom, when and how often. Yet we would now add to this behavior-centered approach a new question: For what and for whom is all this going on, and—indeed—against whom? This question should not be posed merely in interactionist terms. Asking why something is going on and for whom requires a conceptual guess about the forces and effects of structural power that drives organization and to which organization on all levels must respond. What are the dominant relations through which labor is deployed? What are the organizational implications of kinship alliances, kin coalitions, chiefdoms, or forms of state? Not all organizations or articulations of organization answer to the same functional requisites, or respond to the same underlying dynamic.

Furthermore, it behooves us to think about what is entailed in conceiving organization as a process. This is an underdeveloped area in anthropological thinking. Clearly dyadic contracts, networks of various sizes and shapes, kinship systems, political hierarchies, corporations, and states possess very different organizational potentials. Understanding how all these sets of people and instrumentalities can be aggregated, hooked together, articulated under different kinds of structural power remains a task for the future.

Models as Discovery Procedures

In the pursuit of this task we can build upon the past by using our concepts and models as discovery procedures, not as fixed representations, universally applicable. For example, Michel Verdon developed a strong critique of lineage theory in his book on the Abutia Ewe (Verdon 1983). Yet the critique itself is informed by the questions raised by that theory and by the demands for evidence required for its corroboration. Verdon investigated the characteristics and distribution of domestic units, residential entities, and matrimonial practices, treating these as prerequisites for defining linkages by kinship. He then used the model of lineage theory to pose further queries about the relation of kinship to political synchronization, taking this connection as a problem, rather than an assumption a priori. The model served as a method of inquiry, rather than an archetype.

A similar redefinition of problem has taken place in the study of chiefdoms, where interest, as Timothy Earle has said, "has shifted from schemes to classify societies as chiefdoms or not, towards consideration of the causes of observed variability" (Earle 1987:279). Social constellations that can be called chiefdoms not only come in many sizes and shapes (Feinman and Neitzel 1984), but they are now understood as "fragile, negotiated institutions," both in securing compliance within and in competition with rivals outside. Emphasis in research now falls on the mixes of economic, political, and ideological strategies which chiefdoms employ to these ends, as well as on their variable success in shaping their different historical trajectories (Earle 1989:87). Similarly, where people once simply spoke of "the state," the state is now seen less as a "thing" than as "a process" (Gailey 1987). A new emphasis on "state-making processes" takes account both of the "diversity and fluidity of form, functions and malfunction" and of "the extent to which all states are internally divided and subject to penetration by conflicting and usually contradictory forces" (Bright and Harding 1984:4).

STRUCTURES OF SIGNIFICANCE

Finally, I want to address the issue of power in signification. Anthropology has treated signification mainly in terms of encompassing cultural unities, such as patterns, configurations, ethos, eidos, epistemes, paradigms, cultural structures. These unities, in turn, have been conceptualized primarily as the outcomes of processes of logico-aesthetic integration. Even when the frequently incongruous and disjointed characteristics of culture are admitted, the hope has been—and I quote Geertz—that identifying significant symbols, clusters of such symbols, and clusters of clusters would yield statements of "the underlying regularities of human experience implicit in their formation" (Geertz 1973:408). The appeal is to the efficacy of symbols, to the workings of logics and aesthetics in the movement toward integration or reintegration, as if these cognitive processes were guided by a *telos* (or ultimate end) all their own.

Questioning Traditional Approaches to the Subject

I want to call this approach into question on several grounds. First, I draw on the insight of Anthony Wallace who in the late fifties contrasted views of culture that emphasize "the replication of uniformity" with those that

acknowledge the problem of "the organization of diversity." He (Wallace 1970:110) argued that

all societies are, in a radical sense, plural societies. . . . How do societies ensure that the diverse cognitions of adults and children, males and females, warriors and shamans, slaves and masters articulate to form the equivalence structures that are the substance of social life?

This query of Wallace's continues to echo in many quarters: in a feminist anthropology that questions the assumption that men and women share the same cultural understandings; in ethnography from various areas, where "rubbish-men" in Melanesia and "no-account people" on the Northwest Coast do not seem to abide by the norms and ideals of big-men and chiefs; in studies of hierarchical systems in which different strata and segments exhibit different and contending models of logico-aesthetic integration. (India furnishes a telling case.) We have been told that such divergences are ultimately kept in check and on track by cultural logic, pure and simple. This seems to me unconvincing. It is indeed the case that our informants in the field invoke metaphoric polarities of purity and pollution, well-being and malevolence, *yin* and *yang*, life and death. Yet these metaphors are intrinsically polysemic, so abundant in possible signifiers that they can embrace any and all situations. To put them to work in particular scenarios requires that their range be constricted and narrowed down to but a small set of referents. What Lévi-Strauss called "the surplus of signifiers" must be subjected to parsimonious selection before the logic of cultural integration can be actualized. This indexing, as some have called it, is no automatic process, but passes through power and through contentions over power, with all sorts of consequences for signification.

Wallace's insights on the organization of diversity also raise questions about how meaning actually works in social life. He pointed out that participants in social action do not need to understand what meanings lie behind the behavior of their partners in interchange. All they have to know is how to respond appropriately to the cues signaled by others. Issues of meaning need not ever rise into consciousness. This is often the concern only of certain specialists, whose specific job or interest it is to explore the plenitude of possible meanings: people such as shamans, *tohunga*, or academics. Yet there are also situations in which the mutual signaling of expectations is deranged, where opposite and contradictory interests come to the fore, or where cultural schemata come under challenge. It then becomes apparent that beyond logic and aesthetics, it is power that guarantees—or fails to shore up—the structures of significance.

The Role of Power

Power is implicated in meaning through its role in upholding one version of significance as true, fruitful, or beautiful, against other possibilities that may threaten truth, fruitfulness, or beauty. All cultures, however conceived, carve out significance and try to stabilize it against possible alternatives. In human affairs, things might be different, and often are. Roy Rappaport, in writing on sanctity and ritual (Rappaport 1979b), has emphasized the basic arbitrariness of all cultural orders. He argues that they are anchored in postulates that can neither be verified nor falsified, but that must be treated as unquestionable; to make them unquestionable, they are surrounded with sacredness. I would add that there is always the possibility that they might come unstuck. Hence symbolic work is never done, achieves no final solution. The cultural assertion that the world is shaped in this way and not in some other has to be repeated and enacted, lest it be questioned and denied. The point is well made by Valerio Valeri in his study of *Kingship and Sacrifice* in Hawaii. Ritual, he (1985:xi) says, produces sense

by creating contrasts in the continuum of experience. *This implies suppressing certain elements of experience in order to give relevance to others. Thus the creation of conceptual order is also, constitutively, the suppression of aspects of reality.*

The Chinese doctrine of "the rectification of names" also speaks to this point of the suppressed alternatives. Stipulating that the world works in one way and not in another requires categories to order and direct experience. According to this doctrine, if meanings multiplied so as to transcend established boundaries, social consensus would become impossible—people would harm each other "like water and fire." Hence, a wise government had to restore things to their proper definitions, in clear recognition that the maintenance of categories upheld power, and power maintained the order of the world (see Pocock 1971:42–79).

Modes of Power in Relation to Modes of Categorization

I have spoken of different modes of structural power, which work through key relations of governance. Each such mode would appear to require characteristic ways of conceptualizing and categorizing people. In social formations that deploy labor through relations glossed as kinship, people are assigned to networks or bodies of kin that are distinguished by criteria of gender, distinct substances or essences of descent, connections with the dead, differential distributions of myths, rituals, and emblems. Tributary formations hierarchize these criteria, and set up distinct social strata, each stratum marked by a distinctive inner substance that also defines its positions and privileges in society. Capitalist formations peel the individual out of encompassing ascriptive bodies, and install people as separate actors, free to exchange, truck, or barter in the market, as well as in other provinces of life. The three modes of categorizing social actors, moreover, imply quite different relations to "nature" and cosmos. When one mode enters into conflict with another, it also challenges the fundamental categories that empower its dynamics. Power will then be invoked to assault rival categorical claims. Power is thus never external to signification—it inhabits meaning and is its champion in stabilization and defense.

Perceiving Power's Role in Transformations of Signification

We owe to social anthropology the insight that the arrangements of a society become most visible when they are challenged by crisis. The role of power also becomes most evident in instances where major organizational transformations put signification under challenge. Let me offer some examples. In their study of the Plains Vision Experience, Patricia Albers and Seymour Parker (1971) contrast the individualized visions of the egalitarian foragers of the Plains periphery with the standardized kin-group controlled visions of the horticultural village dwellers. Still a third kind of vision, oriented toward war and wealth, emerged among the buffalo-hunting nomads who developed in response to the introduction of horse and gun. As horse pastoralism proved increasingly successful, the horticulturists became riven by conflicts between the personal-private visions of young men involved in buffalo hunting, and the visions controlled by hereditary groups of kin.

The development of the Merina state in Madagascar gives us another example (see e.g. Berg 1986; Bloch 1986). As the state became increasingly powerful and centralized around an intensified agriculture and ever more elaborate social hierarchy, the royal center also emerged as the hub of the ideational system. Local rites of circumcision, water sprinkling, offerings to honor superiors, and rituals ministering to group icons and talismans were increasingly synchronized and fused with rituals of state.

The royal rituals of Hawaii furnish a third case. Their development was linked to major transformations that affected Hawaii after 1400, when agriculture and aquaculture were extended and intensified (see e.g. Earle 1978; Kirch 1985; Spriggs 1988). Local communities were reorganized; lineages were deconstructed; commoners lost the right to keep genealogies and to attend temples, and were assigned as quasi-tenants to nonlocal subaltern chiefs. Chiefs and aristocrats were raised up, godlike, into a separate endogamous stratum. Conflicts within the elite brought on endemic warfare and attempts at conquest; both fed the cult of human sacrifice. Innovations in myth and ritual portrayed the eruption of war and violence by the coming of outsiders, "sharks upon the land." Sahlins (1985) has offered the notion of a cultural structure to interpret how Hawaiians understood such changes and revalued their understandings in the course of change. But reference to a cultural structure alone, or even to a dialectic of a structure of meaning with the world, will not yet explain how given forms of significance relate to transformations of agriculture, settlement, sociopolitical organization, and relations of war and peace. To explain what happened in Hawaii or elsewhere, we must take the further step of understanding the consequences of the exercise of power.

I have in these pages put forward the case for an anthropology that is not content merely to translate, interpret, or play with a kaleidoscope of cultural fragments, but that seeks explanations for cultural phenomena. We can build upon past efforts and old insights, but we must also find our way to asking new questions. I understand anthropology as a cumulative undertaking, as well as a collective quest that moves in ever expanding circles, a quest that depends upon the contributions of each of us, and for which we are all responsible.

INTELLECTUAL ROOTS

Eric R. Wolf is Distinguished Professor of Anthropology at Herbert Lehman College and the Graduate Center of the City University of New York. He has done fieldwork in Puerto Rico, Mexico, and the Italian Alps. He has contributed to the comparative study of peasantries and to work on the articulation of complex societies. His best known books are *Sons of the Shaking Earth* (1959), *Peasants* (1964), and *Europe and the People without History* (1982). He is a member of the American Academy of Arts and Sciences.

I suspect that my intellectual drive springs from the predicaments of growing up in a thoroughly assimilated Jewish family in multiethnic, but ever more nationalist and anti-Jewish Central Europe. As a child I was fascinated by the life-ways of animals. In my early teens I discovered mountaineering and Germanic folklore. Displaced to England in my late teens, I encountered natural science, and read J. B. S. Haldane. I began college in New York (1940) with the idea of studying biochemistry, but then vagabonded through the social sciences, eventually coming to rest in Hortense Powdermaker's course on culture and personality and Joseph Bram's lectures on the anthropology of Asia. Powdermaker had studied with Malinowski at L.S.E.; Bram had been a student of Boas.

Three years in the U.S. mountain troops then provided the funds, on the G.I. Bill, to finish college and pursue graduate anthropology at Columbia University. In the war years I also expanded my understanding of socialist perspectives, especially through reading the economist Paul Sweezy, the Caribbean polymath C. L. R. James, and—in the summer preceding graduate school—Karl Wittfogel's ecological/political-economic study of China (1931). At Columbia I first took courses with Ruth Benedict, and later with Julian Steward, who invited me to join his fieldwork team in studying Puerto Rico (1948-1949). This work, in turn, led to further immersion in the problems of Latin America. Studies at Columbia also put me in contact with an unusually able group of fellow students—Stanley Diamond, Morton Fried, Robert Manners, Daniel McCall, Sidney Mintz, and

Elman Service. We formed a study group and learned much from one another. John Murra sometimes joined the group, when in New York on visits from Chicago.

Benedict and Steward, each in their own way, had intensified my own interest in how subgroups and regions came to be welded into overarching nations, and I pursued this interest further in library and field research in Mexico (1951-1952). There I encountered two gifted Spanish refugees—Pedro Armillas, who introduced me to a new kind of archaeology, and Angel Palerm, with whom I came to share convergent intellectual and political concerns. These contacts and engagements then made the fifties a period of productive inquiry into the interplay of groups and institutions during the course of Mexican history.

After teaching at a variety of institutions, I returned to fieldwork on ecology and nationhood in two peasant communities located on either side of a language frontier in the Italian Alps (1960-1961). I was then fortunate to join a group of colleagues at the University of Michigan who were working on a synthesis of ecological and evolutionary perspectives, a group that then included Marshall Sahlins, Elman Service, and Roy Rappaport. Where I had focused on Mexico in the fifties, the decade of the sixties at Michigan allowed me to pursue further the comparative study of peasantry. I was also able to take part, with William Schorger, in sending students into the field to both the European and the African shores of the Mediterranean; and John W. Cole, then a graduate student, and I carried forward our field study of the communities in the Alps that would eventually result in a book, *The Hidden Frontier* (1972). In 1971 I moved to the City University of New York to teach undergraduates at Lehman College in the Bronx, and graduate students at the Graduate Center. I expanded the scope of my inquiries to deal with the inclusion and participation of widely diverse societies and cultures in global systems of interaction. This work led to the writing of *Europe and the People without History* (1982). I remain both fascinated and puzzled by the way in which the social and cultural entities studied by anthropologists are at once interlinked with one another, and yet repeatedly insistent on their separateness and distinctive character.

16

Embodied Knowledge: Thinking with the Body in Critical Medical Anthropology[1]

NANCY SCHEPER-HUGHES

My body is made of the same flesh as the world.
Merleau-Ponty (1962)

In the fall of 1989 at a public lecture at the University of California, Berkeley, Ronald Frankenberg remarked that it came as a great revelation to him to learn, by way of medical anthropology, that "humans live in bodies whereas previously [he] thought they lived in communities." Frankenberg was referring to his own training in the tradition of classical British social anthropology which assumed an ahistorical and universal human body and which concerned itself with the particularities of social structure, function, and social roles into which individual (and largely interchangeable) bodies were inserted. (Individual bodies could be viewed as bundles of roles.) It was only after many years, Frankenberg added, that he came to realize that in order to understand social conflict, the community, rather than too "micro" or small a unit of analysis (as marxist social theorists had supposed), was really too "macro" or large.

Had Frankenberg taken, he said, the study of Durkheim on anomie theory or Marx on alienation theory, or even Freud on conversion hysterias, more seriously, he might have foreseen why the body would emerge as the primary action zone in the late twentieth century. As it was, however, his revelation was to come largely through the more humble, empirical studies of his medical anthropological colleagues laboring in the clinics, hospitals, fields, and factories among people with sickness, madness, pain, disability, and distress.

I will take this theme—anthropology's "discovery" and new consciousness of bodies—and situate it in a brief discussion of the invention of a critically interpretive medical anthropology (see Lock and Scheper-Hughes 1990) and to show its potential contributions to anthropological theory and to medical/psychiatric practice and to political praxis. In a way this discussion takes up where Sherry Ortner (1984) left off in her review of "Theory in Anthropology Since the Sixties." While the sixties were dominated by the themes of "symbol, nature, and structure," and the seventies were preoccupied with anthropology's belated discovery of Marx, political economy, and world systems theory, I might characterize the decade of the 1980s as theoretically driven by a concern with the overlapping domains of body, self, emotion, reflexivity, and resistance.[2]

LOCATING THE STUDY OF THE BODY IN MEDICAL ANTHROPOLOGY

Let me suggest at the outset that it is medical anthropology's "preferential option" for the body that represents this subdiscipline's unique vision as distinct from social and cultural anthropology (where the body is largely absent) and from physical anthropology and the biomedical sciences (where the body is present but silent). But even as I introduce *embodiment* as a central paradigm in medical anthropology, I am keenly aware of how unstably the field is situated between biological/biomedical and sociocultural/symbolic worlds and meanings.

Medical Anthropology's Argument with Biomedicine

On the one hand there is the basic irreconcilability between anthropological and biomedical ways of knowing and seeing. Anthropological knowledge is fundamentally *esoteric* (concerned with difference, basic strangeness, and "others"), *local* (in the Geertzian sense), *symbolic*, and doggedly *relativist*. Biomedical knowledge is intrinsically *mundane, universal* (and universalizing), *objectivist*, and radically *materialist/reductionist*.[3] On the other hand, however, medical anthropology stands closer to biomedicine than to social anthropology with respect to medicine's *regard*—its focused and sustained gaze on (or inside) the body. It is social anthropology's characteristic disregard of the body that sets it apart from medical anthropology in this instance. The hypothesized "body" of which I speak—*mindful, nervous, consuming, commoditized, fetishized, laboring, anguished*, or *disciplined*[4]—is for critical medical anthropologists both unquestioningly real and existentially given, even though its very giveness is always historically and culturally produced. Although bodies are, to a certain extent, "made-up," there are limits to their made-upness, and critically interpretive

medical anthropologists (see Lock and Scheper-Hughes 1990) understand the body as more than the signifying, symbolizing, aestheticized abstraction that it is for social anthropologists.

The "unquestionability" of the body was, for Ludwig Wittgenstein (1969) where all knowledge and certainty began. "If you do know that here is one hand," he began his last book, *On Certainty* (1969:2), "we'll grant you all the rest." But having said this, Wittgenstein, who was then working with hospitalized patients who were dismembered and otherwise physically and spiritually compromised by World War II, wanted to pursue just those circumstances that eroded or took away the "certainty" of the body. In my recent writings on the nervous-hungry (1988b) and the "disappeared" bodies (1992) of rural Brazilian sugarcane workers, I have explored a set of circumstances that give a great many people grounds to lose their bodily certitude to bouts of existential doubt and despair.

Ideally, the medical anthropologist in the field is as "at home" with the body as the proverbial country doctor making his (or her) rounds. I am often pulled along roughly by the people of the Brazilian shantytown of Alto do Cruzeiro to come closer, to look, touch, probe an angry, inflamed wound or a badly set bone jutting out at a ridiculous angle from beneath a torn pants leg. But medical anthropologists are not frustrated doctors and the "medical anthropological gaze" (or perspective) is not to be confused with the penetrating, dissembling, "clinical gaze" described by Michel Foucault (1975). For while the clinical, biomedical gaze has reduced the body to smaller and smaller invisible particles (Valery 1989), and while the epidemiological gaze has retreated from individual bodies and even social groups in order to study disembodied and detached "high risk behaviors" (Bolton 1992), the medical anthropological perspective remains focused on, around, and between real, living, experiential, and suffering bodies. The medical anthropological gaze grazes the body's surface and then moves outward to catch the play of metaphors, figures of speech (tropes), and symbolic meanings within the web of exchanges among the "three bodies" (Scheper-Hughes and Lock 1987)—the representational *body social*; the controlling, bio-power forces of the *body politic;* and the not unrelated but self-conscious, more or less alienated, attribution of meanings to the individual and existential *body personal*.

Medical Anthropology's Argument with Social Anthropology

So much for medical anthropology's argument with scientific and clinical biomedicine. Its argument with social anthropology is different. It is that the body has made only occasional and cryptic appearances in the discipline. Consequently, most debates about human relations and social life in social anthropology have swirled around an analytic gap at the core of the discipline—the absence of the body. Traditionally, the body, insofar as it was treated at all, figured in the writings of social anthropologists (including Durkheim 1951, Van Gennep 1960, Lévi-Strauss 1967a, Mary Douglas 1970, Clifford Geertz 1974, Robert Hertz 1960, Victor Turner 1969, and Terrence Turner 1980) as an instrument of social inscription, as a medium on which to inscribe symbols and homologies of the social world. In this way societies could make claims of coherence, consensus, and of the unconscious cultural loyalty that Pierre Bourdieu (1977a: 164) refers to as "*doxa*"—the "quasi-perfect correspondence between the objective order and the subjective principles of organization . . . [so that] the natural and social world appears as self-evident." The cultural body "naturalizes" the fictive social body, making society appear to be "unquestionably" certain, "real," and existentially "given." So it must seem when "social categories" are taken in with mother's milk.

The body in social anthropology emerges as a passive, inert, dead weight attached to a lively, responsive, nomadic mind, the true agent of culture. Terrence Turner (1980:113) describes the surface of the body as its "social skin," a template and a "symbolic stage upon which the drama of socialization is enacted." Pierre Bourdieu (1977a), following Marcel Mauss (1979), describes a Chaplinesque image of Algerian peasants whose body movements are determined by their insertion into a particular cultural, technical, and productive order. While there are grace and meaning to be found in the rhythmic movements of peasants, portrayed as embodied metaphors suspended in time and space, the bodily order is stretched out on the rack of cultural and technical imperatives. In Bourdieu's powerfully evocative writings, the body emerges as the embodiment (or somatization) of culture. The social order is primary and reproduces individual bodies that are comfortably compatible with it. This is what Bourdieu seems to mean by "habitus," the habituated, bodily expression of social identity, belonging and cultural affirmation. We might call this the "positivity" of the body.

Foucault

By contrast, Michel Foucault has explored the opposite: the "negativity" of the body, particularly the *destructive* effects of power relations on the socially and politically constituted body. In his essay "Body/Power," Foucault (1980b:55) asserts: "The phenomenon of the social body is the effect, not of social consensus, but of the materiality of power operating on the bodies of individuals." This, Foucault demonstrates most forcefully in his histories of medicine and psychiatry with their mass production of medicalized and violated bodies and psychologized and defeated sexualities (see Foucault 1979, 1980a, 1980b). The "Foucaultian body," as the nexus of power struggles originating in the "state" of things (that is, in the body politic), is readily transferred to interpretive medical anthropology where the body in question is more often afflicted, alienated, and suffering than it is ecstatic, decorated, and affirming. The Foucaultian question, "*What kind of body does society want and need?*" has stimulated a great deal of critical thinking in contemporary medical anthropology.

Nonetheless, the body of Foucault's imagining is still, to a great extent, a body devoid of subjectivity, and hence without a real experience of affirmation and alienation or of power and powerlessness. What is missing in both the body social of the symbolic anthropologists, and in the bio-power of Foucault's body politic, is the existential experience of the practical and practicing human subject. The first two bodies, each a product of social inscription and of political control, leave behind a project that is "self-defeating" in that it ignores the lived experience of the body-self. It is this third dimension, the "missing," self-conscious, often alienated individual and collective experiences of the body-self that critically interpretive medical anthropology returns to anthropology in the form of the "mindful body" (Scheper-Hughes and Lock 1987). It does so through the pressure exerted by its very subject matter: suffering bodies that refuse to be merely aestheticized or metaphorized.

Medical Anthropology's Body

The medical anthropological body, then, represents the intersection of the three bodies—the bodies personal, social, and political. These are understood not only as three separate but overlapping levels of analysis, but as the working synthesis of three theoretical approaches: existential phenomenology (the individual body-self); structural and symbolic anthropology (the social body); and critical theory, especially via Gramsci's (1971) notion of hegemony and Foucault's poststructuralism (the body politic). In critical medical anthropology, the body is the most immediate, most proximate terrain where social truths are forged and social contradictions played out, as well as the locus of personal resistance, creativity, and struggle. In returning the missing, subjective body to the center of their inquiries, critical medical anthropologists invert the Foucaultian question to ask: "*What kind of society does the body need, wish, and dream?*"

THE SUBVERSIVE BODY

> *The body is the first and most natural tool of man.*
> Marcel Mauss, 1979:98

Embodiment concerns the ways that people "inhabit" their bodies so that these become "habituated." This is a play on Mauss's notion of "habitus," a term later appropriated by Bourdieu, by which Mauss meant all the acquired habits and somatic tactics that represent the cultural arts of using and being in the body (and in the world). From the phenomenologically oriented perspective of some medical anthropologists (concerned with the "lived-in" sense of illness), pain, disability, and other forms of human suffering are habituated bodily expressions of dynamic social relations. Sickness is more than just an unfortunate brush with nature. It is more than something that "just happens" to people. Sickness is something that humans do in uniquely original and creative ways. Illness is a form of body praxis, of bodily action.

It is to this secret language of the body—illness symptoms—that the following remarks are addressed. They may be taken as an attempt to supersede the psychosomatic idiom of "somatization" that is so popular in conventional medical anthropology. Here, I will focus on the body's "wisdom," its intentionality and purposefulness in its production of unruly and "chaotic" symptoms that continually breech the boundaries between mind and body, nature and culture, individual and social bodies. The body is "naturally" subversive: it refuses to conform to epistemologies that traffic in oppositions and dualisms or in reductionist and radical materialisms.

At first, medical anthropologists were fairly content to work within the psychiatric and psycho-somatic framework of Eisenberg's (1977) and Kleinman's (1980) conceptual distinction between subjective *illness* as perceived by the patient and objective disease as diagnosed by the biomedical physician. The patient's experience of sickness was understood as an important modifier of otherwise reified and universal categories of biomedical diagnosis and classification. Later, following the writings of more critical medical anthropologists,[5] illness was gradually rescued from the individualizing domain of doctor-patient relations and understood in more collective and social terms as cultural narratives, as dramas and performance, as rituals of bodily resistance and social reform.

For, while the body may be used to express a sense of belonging and affirmation (as symbolic anthropologists have long indicated), the body can also be used to express negative and conflictual sentiments, feelings of distress, alienation, frustration, anger, resentment, sadness, and loss. These two forms of bodily expression exist in a dialectical relationship, expressing the tensions between belonging and alienation that characterize social life everywhere. In social systems characterized by a great deal of institutionalized inequality (whether in the form of gender, racial, class, or caste hierarchies) feelings of oppression, frustration, and submerged rage are common, though disallowed, personal and social sentiments.

Medical Weapons of the Weak

James Scott (1985:xv) has noted that while powerless social classes are rarely afforded the "luxury of open, organized political activity," the aggrieved often do put up a remarkable assortment of resistances, including "foot dragging, dissimulation, desertion, false compliance, pilfering, feigned ignorance, slander, arson, sabotage, and so on" (xvi). To these weapons of the weak, the critically interpre-

tive medical anthropologist would add those somatic tactics and "remedial institutions" that appear with great frequency in our chosen domain: (1) witchcraft, sorcery, evil eye and counter sorcery; (2) trance and possession illness; (3) nervous frenzy and madness; and (4) organized rituals of reversal and of fantasy play.

Witchcraft and sorcery accusations and illnesses are invoked in many parts of the world to explain misfortune and to correct ailing social relationships. Leith Mullings (1984), for example, notes that in the context of the increasing "commodification" of personal and social life in urban Ghana, witchcraft-produced ills and sorcery accusations are an expression of social tensions and hostilities related to the introduction of industrial capitalism. Witchcraft accusations focus especially on those individuals who engage in unfair competition, who are "greedy" and materialist, and who are, consequently, violating more collectivist values and making others in the community weak and sick. Favret-Saada (1977, 1989) has shown that witchcraft plays a formidable role in the social relations of a traditional peasant economy in the Bocage region of western France. In the Bocage, male heads of small farm households often fall victim to illness through bewitchment. They find themselves paralyzed, unable to work or to produce. Witchcraft illness is often an expression of the farmer's guilt concerning his legally and culturally sanctioned acts of "violence" against his closest relatives that is entailed in the acquisition, through inheritance, of a farm household. Farm inheritance means that one's own siblings have been dispossessed and that as head of household one will exploit the free labor of a great many kin—wife, children, and unmarried and disinherited siblings. Techniques of "un-bewitching" serve to redirect the tensions and sources of hostility to distant neighbors (who are identified as the key suspects), to those with whom there is virtually nothing at stake. Unbewitching then, serves as a remedial institution that allows the conflicted farmer to go about his business free of guilt and fear of reprisals against him for assuming the role that fate has bestowed on him through primogeniture.

Fantasy play offers aggrieved people another way of circumventing or managing conflict and contradictions that often beset social relations in societies characterized by class or gender inequality. One form of institutionalized play found worldwide through which women and men have expressed their frustrated longings are the rituals of forgetting, reversal, and travesty, such as the New Guinea gender-crossing Naven ceremony (Bateson 1958), the Indian feast of love, Holi (Marriot 1966), and Brazilian carnaval (DaMatta 1983, Scheper-Hughes 1988a, Parker 1990). Common to all these is an inversion of the normative social order and of the moral economy that governs behavior in everyday life. Thrown into the upside down, topsy-turvy, carnavalesque atmosphere of license and laughter that these pageants allow, a space is created for the powerless, the weak, the exploited, and the oppressed to assume symbolic domination, to take center stage. Oppressive social roles are reversed: peasants mock landowners; wives berate husbands; men dress as women; sexuality is displayed rather than hidden. A creative chaos and liminality replace structure and order. Although the potentially revolutionary or the socially conservative character of these rituals has long been heatedly debated (see Gluckman 1955, Babcock 1978, Hobsbawm 1965, Illich 1982, Davis 1975, Ladurie 1979), there has been no examination of the psychosocial-bio-physiological therapeutic nature of these rituals of redress and complaint for the poor and marginalized individuals who throw their bodies into them with such evident enjoyment. Similarly, some forms and expressions of illness, disability, and madness may also be viewed as acts of embodied refusal, as mockery, and as protest by the relatively powerless against oppressive social roles and ideologies.

Of all the tactics for expressing dissent, defiance, and discontent, illness is by far one of the most common but also one of the most problematic. A critically interpretive view of illness as body praxis (or bodily action) must overcome the prevailing psycho-somatic and psychoanalytic paradigms which, through the idiom of "somatization," largely serve to reinforce negative stereotypes and to stigmatize those who choose to speak truth to established powers through the vehicle of their own bodies.

Somatization Reexamined

Somatization is conventionally understood as the unconscious and generally maladaptive amplification and exaggeration of psychological symptoms by the individual sufferer. In this regard, conventional, clinical medical anthropologists (see Kleinman 1980, 1986) have shared the view of those doctors and psychiatrists who view somatization as a fairly "primitive" mind-body mechanism, as an inchoate expression of mental and social distress in the form of nonspecific and "neurotic" bodily complaints. Somatization was seen as characteristic of marginalized, relatively powerless, psychologically unsophisticated and un-self-reflexive, indeed mostly lower-class or non-Western, women and men. Kleinman's (1980) early work on somatization in Chinese and Chinese-American clinic patients as symptomatic of "masked depression" (as the real, underlying disease) is a case in point. Ian Lewis's (1971) classic study of possession sickness as a manipulative, unconscious, individualistic strategy of redress used by marginalized people in the third world, but especially by women, is another. In this view, spirit possession is a culturally exotic form of conversion hysteria, one that offers the poor, the weak, and women a "safe" way of communicating their anger, fear, resentment, anxiety, and envy. Communicated in these conventional interpretations is the unattractive, cowardly, petulant quality of those who would stoop to so primitive a strategy. The somatization paradigm conjures up as well the negative, sexist images of Freud's pampered female hysterics, and the likes of Elizabeth Barrett Browning and Alice James (James 1964), the "lesser" of the famous James siblings, querulously commanding their small world from the reduced confines of the sick room. In place of Kafka's "Hunger Artist" we have the "Sickness Artist."

A limitation of the somatization model is that while it *pretends* to advocate an indissoluble unity of mind and body, individual and social bodies, and of nature and culture, it has, in practice, failed to overcome the dualisms. Illnesses are understood as the subjective, transparently psychological manifestation of real, identified physical diseases, or else they are nothing at all, except perhaps the illusory traces, figments of imagination, "bits of undigested beef," like Scrooge's vision of the ghost of Marley. If mind and body are truly one, as even the most conventional medical anthropologists assert, then *all* diseases, without exception, are and must be psychosomatic—all are "somatized" as well as "mentalized." But medical anthropology has never lived up to the strength of its convictions and has never been prepared to support so radical and consequential a thesis.

BODY PRAXIS: DRAMATIZING PROTEST AND COMPLAINT THROUGH THE BODY

People *everywhere*, men as well as women, and people of *all* social classes, employ their bodies in expressing complicated, contradictory, and hostile sentiments. Negative sentiments often explode in an epidemic of unruly bodily complaints and in symptoms that may fail to materialize under the penetrating gaze of the X-ray and CAT scan. These very unruly and chaotic symptoms continually and simultaneously breech and bridge the boundaries between mind and body, nature and culture,

personal and social. If we begin with a notion of the embodied person living out and creatively responding to their assigned place in the social order, the social origins of distress and disease and the "sickening" social and moral order come into focus.

Then, it becomes possible to see the outbreak of archaic spirit possession on the modern, sanitized shop floor of multinational microchip factories in Malaysia (see Ong 1987, 1988) as part of a complex negotiation of reality in which young female factory workers are reacting both to the violation of their traditional cultural identity and to the demanding and overly disciplined work conditions by invoking ancient ancestral spirits, thereby bringing production to a temporary halt. In place of the demeaning clinical notions of malingering or psychoneurotic "somatization," we can see the beginnings of a "sickness strike," a strategy not dissimilar to the factory slowdowns, the "Italian strikes" (that are often used when open strikes are likely to fail or to lead to permanent dismissal).

We can also look to the production of "new," chronic and annoying, if not disabling or life-threatening, diseases in our own society and among all social classes, and ethnic groups [see American Psychiatric Association 1987, DSM-III(R)]. The contemporary overproduction of disease in advanced industrial societies has been the subject of much medical anthropological inquiry. Alan Young (1989), for example, has studied the social and political meanings of posttraumatic stress in Vietnam war veterans. Emily Martin (1987) has interpreted the medical invention of PMS, premenstrual syndrome, as a clinical discourse on the control of socially unacceptable female irritability and rage. Margaret Lock (1988b) has followed the medical "discovery" of the menopause in Japan as an expression of moral panic over the modernization and Westernization of the Japanese family and gender and age roles. And Lock and I (Scheper-Hughes and Lock 1986) have explained the channeling of more and more personal dissatisfaction, longing, and protest into the idiom of sickness as a consequence, in part, of the secularization of social life and public institutions and where other forms of everyday resistance, such as witchcraft accusations, trance, fantasy play, and the carnavalesque have disappeared or lost their powers of enchantment.

On the other hand, the existence of these "remedial institutions" and somatic tactics does not obliterate the uses of the body in dramatizing protest and complaint. The creative uses of sickness are also present (1) in rural peasant communities, (2) in societies undergoing an early and rapid stage of industrialization, and (3) among manual and wage workers. The conventional psychiatric observation that poor and working-class people are particularly prone to "invent" illness and to "embody" their discontent in fictive symptoms diminishes, trivializes, and misunderstands an alternative and widespread form of body praxis. The tendency in biomedicine, psychiatry, and clinical medical anthropology is to standardize our own medically constructed and socially prescribed mind-body tactics and to label those that do not conform to them as psychologically primitive, deviant, pathological, irrational, or inadequate.

Against this view I will offer an interpretation of the embodied lives and somatic culture of the Nordestino sugarcane cutters (see Scheper-Hughes 1992) as both normative and less "alienated" than the psychologization of social and political distress that is accepted in our society as a universal norm and standard. When personal and social distress is expressed "psychologically" rather than through a bodily idiom, the "natural" language of the body is suppressed, silenced, and denied. Among the cane cutters the structure of both individual and collective sentiments (down to the feel of their bodies and the uses to which the body is put) are an expression not only of their habituated systems of dispositions (i.e. Bourdieu's "habitus," 1990b:61) but also their position and role in the technical and productive order.

EMBODIED LIVES, SOMATIC CULTURE: *NERVOS* IN ALTO DO CRUZEIRO, BRAZIL

In referring to the "somatic culture" of the displaced and marginalized sugarcane workers of northeast Brazil, I mean to suggest that theirs is a social class and a culture that privileges the body and that instructs them in a close attention to the physical senses and to the language of the body as expressed in symptoms. Here I am following the lead of Luc Boltanski (1984), who has argued that somatic thinking and practice are frequently found among the working and popular classes who extract their subsistence from physical labor. Boltanski noted the tendency of the French working classes to communicate with and through the body so that, by contrast, the body praxis of the bourgeois and technical classes appears impoverished.

Among the agricultural wage laborers living in the hillside shantytown of Alto do Cruzeiro, on the margins of a large, interior market town in the plantation zone of Pernambuco, Brazil, and who sell their labor for as little as a dollar a day, socioeconomic and political contradictions often take shape in the "natural" contradictions of angry, sick, and afflicted bodies. In addition to the wholly expectable epidemics of parasitic infections and communicable fevers, there are the more unexpected outbreaks and explosions of unruly and subversive symptoms that will not readily materialize under the health station's microscope. Among these are the fluid symptoms of *nervos* (angry, frenzied nervousness): trembling, fainting, seizures, hysterical weeping, angry recriminations, blackouts, and paralysis of face and limbs.

These nervous attacks are in part coded metaphors through which the workers express their dangerous and unacceptable condition of chronic hunger and need (see Scheper-Hughes 1988b) and in part acts of defiance and dissent that graphically register the refusal to endure what is, in fact, unendurable and their protest against their availability for physical exploitation and abuse. And so, rural workers who have cut sugarcane since the age of seven or eight years will sometimes collapse, their legs giving way under an *ataque de nervos,* a nervous attack. They cannot walk, they cannot stand upright; they are left, like Oliver Sacks (1984), without a leg to stand on.

In the exchange of meanings between the body personal and the body social, the nervous-hungry, nervous-angry body of the cane cutter offers itself as metaphor and metonym[6] of the nervous sociopolitical system and for the paralyzed position of the rural worker in the current economic and political dis-order. In "lying down" on the job, in refusing to return to the work that has overly determined their entire lives, the cane cutters' body language signifies both surrender and defeat. But one also notes a drama of mockery and refusal. For if the folk ailment *nervos* attacks the legs and the face, it leaves the arms and hands intact and free for less physically ruinous work. Consequently, otherwise healthy young men suffering from nervous attacks press their claims as sick men on their various political bosses and patrons to find them alternative work, explicitly "sitting down" work, arm work (but not clerical work for these men are illiterate).

The analysis of *nervos* does not end here, for nervous attack is an expansive and polysemic form of dis-ease. Shantytown women, too, suffer from *nervos*—both the *nervos de trabalhar muito,* "overwork" nerves from which male cane cutters suffer, and also the more gender-specific *nervos de sofrir muito,* the nerves of those who have endured and suffered much. "Sufferers' nerves" attacks those who have endured a recent, especially a violent, tragedy. Widows of husbands and mothers of sons who have been abducted and violently "disappeared" are prone to the mute, enraged, white-knuckled shaking of "sufferers' nerves." Here Taussig's (1990) linking of the "nervous system," anatomical and sociopolitical, is use-

ful. One could read the current "nervousness" of shantytown residents as a response to the nervous and unstable democracy just now emerging in Brazil after more than twenty years of repressive, military rule. Many vestiges of the military state remain intact, and, on the Alto do Cruzeiro, the military presence is most often felt in the late-night knock on the door, the scuffle, and the abduction of one's husband or teenaged son.

The epidemic of *nervos, sustos* (fright sickness), and of *pasmos* (paralytic shock) signifies a state of alarm, of panic. It is also a way of communicating a state of affairs where one moves back and forth between an acceptance of the situation as normal, or expectable, and an awareness of the real state of emergency in which one has been plunged (see Taussig 1990). The people of the shantytown are thrown into a state of nervous agitation, shock, crisis for which *nervosos, doenca de nervos* sets off the alarm, warning others in the community that their bodies and their lives are in danger. The epidemics of *nervos* among the wives and mothers of the politically disappeared is a form of resistance that is both effective and safe. It publicizes the danger, the fright, the "abnormality of the normal," yet it does not expose the sufferers to further political reprisals. The political nature of illness and of the communicative subversive body remains an only partly conscious (and thereby protected) form of protest. Who would reduce this complex, creative, somatic, and political idiom to an insipid discourse on patient "somatization"?

A PEDAGOGY FOR PATIENTS: ILLNESS AS RESISTANCE

In conclusion, illness and illness metaphors are coded messages in the bottle tossed on turbulent seas by the suffering and the aggrieved in the hope that a passing navigator will retrieve the bottle and decipher the hidden meanings, the S.O.S. of its contents. The rub is, however, that whenever defiance and protest are expressed in the bodily language of symptoms, there is always the danger of an individualized, medicalized response. When anger, frustration, dissatisfaction, and social and political contradictions are expressed through the body, drawing on ethnomedical syndromes such as *nervos*, there is always the consequent danger of these being absorbed and "treated" as disease alone. Broad, flexible socially constructed afflictions—whether *nervos* in Brazil or "spirit attack" in Malaysia or worker "burnout" in the United States—create a space for medicalization and domestication. They can be tranquilized or psychoanalyzed, depending on the level of technology available. And so, in northeast Brazil, nervous-angry cane cutters do sometimes show up in public clinics and pharmacies looking for strong, powerfully acting drugs that will reinvigorate the body, "animate" the senses, and "fortify the bones." A man will slap at his wasted, emaciated legs, as if they were detachable appendages from the self, and say to the clinic doctor that they are completely "useless." In the clinic, self-loathing and self-blame take the place of class anger and the political implications of the afflictions are concealed. The possibility of using bodily distress to generate a radical critique of the social order is lost.

So, too, Ong (1988) notes that the managers of microelectronic factories in the Free Trade Zone of Malaysia, aided by Western models of hysteria, are all too ready to convert dissident female workers into psychiatric cases. Medical and religious specialists are called into the factory, and the "spirits of resistance" are summarily fumigated and dispersed to be replaced, one is tempted to say, by the spirit of capitalism. Biomedical practice invites all manner of somatic complaint to be interpreted in light of its essentializing, universalizing discourse and so signals the worldwide defeat of traditional idioms of resistance and noncompliance. In northeast Brazil, by the time that nervous hunger and nervous frenzy reach the clinic, the sufferers of *nervos* are already defeated. It is

a certain bet that their suffering will be heavily sedated, so that medicine, even more than religion, comes to actualize the Marxist platitude regarding the drugging of the oppressed masses.

Whatever else illness is, and it is many different things—an unfortunate brush with nature, a fall from grace, a social rupture, an economic contradiction—it is also, at times, an act of refusal. The refusal can express itself in various ways: a refusal to work, a refusal to struggle under self-defeating conditions, a refusal to endure, a refusal to "cope" (as with the nervous collapse of those paralyzed sugarcane cutters who had had enough and had reached the end of their rope).

As Talcott Parsons (1972) recognized in his classic analysis of the sick role, sickness can pose a real threat to the stability of the social and moral order. Assuming the sick role is an available weapon of the weak. Parsons recognized the destructive effects of industrialized relations of capitalist production on the human body and spirit, and he understood that the overproduction of bodily symptoms and complaints was a "sigh of the oppressed," an expression of worker frustration. Medicine offered an escape in the lure and haven of the sick role, in disability pay, and sick leave—in terms of what Parsons viewed as sanctioned deviancy. But these covert functions of the sick role had to be carefully monitored lest a sickness strike spread among other dissatisfied workers. It was essential, therefore, that clinical medicine play dumb, that it fail to see the secret indignation of the sick and that doctors transform the fluid symptoms of bodily protest into passive, reified, individualized, and contained forms of breakdown, into disease alone.

The sufferer of *nervos*, of PMS, of worker stress and burnout has two choices. She (or he) can be open to the secret language of the organ that contains within it the seeds for critical reflection and consciousness. "My nerves," concluded one Alto woman who had recently suffered the abduction-mutilation of her adult son, "is really just my life." Another resident reached a similar conclusion: "My sickness is both physical and moral."

On the other hand, the sufferer can silence the bodily scream of protest, cut it off by relegating more and more of her pain and her consciousness to the technical domain of medicine where anger, frustration, anxiety, fear, and panic, as well as nervous hunger, can be transformed into diseases and treated with injections, nerve pills, hormone replacement, and sleeping pills. Once safely medicated the message in the bottle, the desperate and socially significant S.O.S., is forever lost.

And so, the debate as to how ethnomedical categories of distress can best be subsumed under biomedical diagnostic categories of disease is really beside the point. The translation of a culturally rich form of communication into the restricted and individualizing language of physiology, psychology, or psychiatry is inappropriate and distorting. Rather, the critically interpretive medical anthropologist can show how such polysemic terms as *nervos, susto,* spirit possession, and stress can provide links between the social and political orders and personal distress. If this form of communication (that keeps the body metaphorically linked to mind and society) is reduced to the "truthful" language of science, then one of the most common sources of personal resistance is made unavailable to people in their struggle against oppressive social conditions.

The presence of suffering, especially when it is expressed in the language of symptoms, exposes the gap between bodies that refuse the demand to suffer quietly and the requirements of antagonistic economic and social orders. The task of bridging the three bodies—individual, social, and political—remains the missing link in a critical discourse on illness.

NOTES

1. This article has its origins in several years of productive collaborations with my colleague Margaret Lock with whom I locked pens on many occasions in the attempt to create a critical, reflexive medical anthropology. In our coauthored article, "Speaking Truth to Illness" (1986), we began to articulate a positive theory of the creative uses of sickness.

2. The past decade has seen a revision of the meanings of popular culture and everyday practice, animated, as it were, by a heady postmodernism Bakhtinian (1984) vision of the subversive meanings and intent that lie behind even the most ordinary and mundane activities, from sports and play (see Edward Bruner 1983) to dance and carnival (see Moreno 1982, DaMatta 1983, Limon 1989) to popular religion and ritual (see Comaroff 1985, Lancaster 1988, Kligman 1988) to shamanistic healing (Taussig 1987) to tropes and figures of speech (de Certeau 1984). Within this arena critical medical anthropology, with its focus on embodied knowledge and body praxis, moves comfortably and offers a unique set of propositions.

3. There is a lingering Cartesian (body/mind) orientation to this materialist/reductionist heritage. As Foucault noted, the Cartesian answer to the question "Who am I?" is that you are anyone, anywhere, at any time. Whereas biomedicine presupposes a universal, ahistorical subject, medical anthropologists are confronted with rebellious and "anarchic" bodies, bodies that refuse to conform (or submit) to presumably universal categories and concepts of disease, distress, and medical efficacy.

4. Where Mary Douglas (1970) refers to the "Two Bodies," the "natural" and the social representational, John O'Neill (1985) distinguishes among the physical body, the communicative body, the world's body, the social body, the body politic, consumer bodies, and medical (and medicalized) bodies. The "disciplined" body is, of course, the invention of Michel Foucault (1979). I am also indebted to Bryan Turner's (1984) volume, *The Body and Society: Explorations in Social Theory,* and to Michel Feher, Ramona Naddaff and Nadia Tazi, the editors of the handsome three-volume series *Fragments for a History of the Human Body,* published in 1989. In some circles, at least, the body has never been absent, missing, or detached from social theory.

5. Among critically interpretive medical anthropologists are Alan Young (1980, 1982, 1988); Ronald Frankenberg (1988a, 1988b); Jean Comaroff (1982, 1985); Michael Taussig (1987, 1990, 1992); Margaret Lock (1986, 1988a, 1988b); Merrill Singer (1989); Singer, Davidson, and Gerdes (1988); and Arthur Kleinman's (1986) *Social Origins of Distress and Disease,* which modifies his earlier and more decontextualized notion of somatization.

6. Editor's note: Metaphor, or association by analogy, occurs when the beauty of a flower is compared with a woman's beauty. Metonymy, or association by physical connection, occurs when a crown is associated with a king because the king usually wears the crown.

INTELLECTUAL ROOTS

Nancy Scheper-Hughes is Professor of Anthropology, Director of the Graduate Program in Medical Anthropology, and 1992-1993 Director of the Center for Latin American Studies at the University of California—Berkeley. Beginning in July 1993, she will hold the Chair in Social Anthropology at the University of Cape Town in South Africa. Previously, she taught at Southern Methodist University in Dallas, Texas, and at the University of North Carolina, Chapel Hill. Extensive fieldwork has taken her to a mountain village in western Ireland (1974-1975), to psychiatric institutions in Boston, Massachusetts (1979-1980), to Spanish-American villages and the Taos and Picaris Pueblos of northern New Mexico (1979, 1985, 1986), and to a twenty-five-year involvement with the people of an impoverished shantytown in northeast Brazil (1964-1992). Most recently, she has been studying AIDS and public policy in Brazil and in Cuba. Her best known publications include *Saints, Scholars and Schizophrenics: Mental Illness in Rural Ireland* (1979, 1982), *Child Survival: Anthropological Approaches to the Treatment and Maltreatment of Children* (1987), and *Death without Weeping: The Violence of Everyday Life in Brazil* (1992). She was the recipient of the Margaret Mead Award (1981), the Stirling Award (1985), a John Simon Guggenheim Fellowship (1987), and the Eileen Basker Memorial Prize in Medical Anthropology (1992).

I was born in 1944 in the Eastern European Catholic and Hasidic immigrant neighborhood of Williamsburgh, Brooklyn. It was at a time when recent refugees from war-torn Europe were about to confront a new wave of impoverished and dislocated immigrants from rural Puerto Rico. It was within that clash of cultures, missed interpretations, and racial/religious misgivings, phobias, and hatreds that my anthropological education began, quite unbeknownst to myself.

At Queens College in New York City, I began my studies in English literature and philosophy and took my first course in anthropology—"Peoples and Cultures of Africa" taught by Hortense Powdermaker—as an elective and a bit of a lark. The assigned readings for that course, which included the classic writings of A. R. Radcliffe-Brown, Monica Wilson, Ira Schapera, E. E. Evans-Pritchard and others, captured my imagination even more than the seminars in existential literature and philosophy. By the end of the semester (spring 1964), I decided to leave college to join the still nascent organization of the U.S. Peace Corps (see Scheper-Hughes 1993).

Assigned to northeast Brazil (1964-1966), I lived and worked as a paramedic and community organizer in a hillside shantytown for recently expulsed sugarcane cutters who had come to reside on the margins of a sugar plantation market town in the state of Pernambuco. It was there in the Alto do Cruzeiro that some initial traumas, doubts, and questions regarding the effects of scarcity, hunger, and infant death on what is commonly called "mother love" first arose. I treated the subject in a series of short stories when I returned to the United States and reenrolled in Queens College, this time as a student of creative writing. Once again, however, I was drawn to anthropology and to Hortense Powdermaker and I took her class on "culture and personality" which introduced me to the neo-Freudians in addition to the writings of Margaret Mead, Edward Sapir, Cora DuBois, George Spindler, Yehudi Cohen, and Melford Spiro, among others. But it was Powdermaker's own writings on the cultural psychology of race relations in the deep south (see Powdermaker 1943) that most excited me, and at the end of *that* semester (spring 1967), I again left school to work with SNCC (the Student Non-Violent Coordinating Committee) and other civil rights groups in Selma, Alabama. I was put in charge of a field project that explored hunger and malnutrition among more than 500 black farm families living in the blackbelt counties of southwest Alabama. The field reports were used in a civil rights class action suit, *Peoples vs. the Department of Agriculture* (Civil Action No. 544-68, U.S. District Court, Washington, D.C., April 1968) that helped bring the food stamp program into counties where the local white officials had initially tried to block it.

As a graduate student in anthropology at the University of California—Berkeley, I worked as a research assistant for Hortense Powdermaker, who had retired to California (see Scheper-Hughes 1991), while studying under the direction of May Diaz, Gerald Berreman, George Foster, George DeVos, and Margaret Clark, though I was also influenced by Elizabeth Colson and Eugene Hammel through their seminars on theory and method respectively. There was no single, dominant paradigm at Berkeley during these years when the campus politics of Vietnam, Cambodia, and the Third World Strike often eclipsed organized seminars. Meanwhile Dell Hymes's (1969a) radical challenge to conventional anthropology, *Reinventing Anthropology*, convinced my cohort of graduate students that if anthropology were to survive at all it must take a new and critical form. Some of my classmates chose the way of marxist and neomarxist anthropology while others chose the way of inventing a feminist anthropology.

I participated in both critical movements at Berkeley, though much to the perplexity of some of my peers, I chose to study schizophrenia among bachelor farmers in rural Ireland as a projection of cultural themes for my dissertation research. Working in the early 1970s with the first translations of the writings of Michel Foucault, I was taken by his perception that madness was a cultural construction with a specific history that needed to be explored in a variety of social contexts.

My first book, *Saints, Scholars and Schizophrenics*, was a blend of old and new approaches (of socialization and adult personality, TAT tests, and of reflexive/interpretive and critical anthropology). It was theoretically eclectic, combing and applying the insights of Erik Erikson, Gregory Bateson, R. D. Laing, and Michel Foucault to a tiny population of Irish-speaking shepherds and fishermen. Soon after receiving the Margaret Mead Award, however, my Irish book became embroiled in a large and distressing controversy. The approach I was developing—a kind of existential cultural critique—was viewed as "ethnocentric" in that it deviated from the implicit anthropological premise to write only about what is "good" and "right" about a given society and culture, especially (as in the case of western Ireland) a postcolonial society. One was not to use anthropology, as I had, in order to diagnose the ailing parts of the social body gone awry, and I was labeled a dangerously "skillful pathologist of the human condition" by one Irish critic.

My Irish book departed radically from Conrad Arensberg's (1937) description of Irish country life in *The Irish Countryman* because it was a child-centered ethnography told, not through the perspective of the old men seated comfortably at the pub and at the hub of rural life, but from the perspective of their sons, the young lads and boy-o's who would have to wait until their 40s and 50s to come into their own, and from the perspective of the young Irish village girls who could not wait to escape village life and its constraints. *Saints, Scholars and Schizophrenics* offered a counterhegemonic view of Irish country life, but one that seemed to some sensibilities "anti-Irish," "anti-Catholic," or "anticlerical." The fact that I had written only about "public secrets," those that everyone in the village knows—such as the high incidence of alcoholism, depression, and madness, sexual alienation, and frustration—but that no one wants to talk about, was not consolation to Irish villagers who preferred to be "left alone" with their culturally derived defenses.

As a postdoctoral fellow at Harvard University, I studied the problematic return of large numbers of hospitalized mental patients to the tough, working class neighborhood of South Boston. A series of papers (1981, 1983, 1987) diagnosing the "dilemmas of deinstitutionalization" in the United States was followed by the publication of *Psychiatry Inside Out* (1987), a coedited translation of the writings of Franco Basaglia, a radical Italian marxist-phenomenologist, whose Democratic Psychiatry Movement contained the elements I saw as necessary for the kind of cultural revolution needed to return severe mental patients to a real place in society. Because of its uncompromisingly anti-institutional analysis, *Psychiatry Inside Out* was met with considerable hostility from the American psychiatric profession.

Since 1982 my field research in Brazil has concentrated on the topics of mother love and child death, the medicalization of hunger, illness as protest, and on the ontological insecurity of the body for marginalized rural workers who are prey to the violence of hunger, medical maltreatment, and death squad torture and executions on a daily basis. A preliminary article, "Culture, Scarcity and Maternal Thinking" (1985), generated a heated controversy about the interpretation of emotions. The publication of *Death without Weeping: The*

Violence of Everyday Life in Brazil (1992) concludes a decade of anthropological research in the shantytowns of northeast Brazil in the form of an experimental, "womanly-hearted" ethnography that weaves elements of narrative, plot, suspense, irony, and other literary forms into a broad thesis on the effects of chronic scarcity, sickness, and death on the human spirit and on maternal thinking and practice in particular.

At present, I am writing a book, *The Rebel Body*, that brings together a series of reflexive essays on the body as a primary site of resistance and defiance in the postmodern world. "Embodied Knowledge" (the above chapter) is drawn from that work in progress.

Many of the topics I have written about—stigma, scapegoating, and distributive injustice within families; the everyday violence of medicine and psychiatry when it is practiced in bad faith; the madness of hunger and destructive hunger of motherhood in the shantytowns of Brazil—are concerned with the need to ground anthropology in ethics. If anthropologists cannot begin to think critically about social institutions in moral or ethical terms, our discipline strikes me as quite weak and useless. But the problem of *how* to articulate a standard (or divergent standards) for moral reflections that does not privilege our own "Western" cultural assumptions and presuppositions remains open and unresolved.

Rethinking the Cultural

G iven the importance of the cultural concept in anthropology, it is understandable it would become drawn into the discipline's centripetal/centrifugal tensions. Few deny the concept's importance. Historically, Yengoyan (1986:368) notes, "Culture was the most important concept that held American anthropology together." But, as Hatch (1973:1) states: "Even though the term has been discussed in countless books and articles, there is still a large degree of uncertainty in its use—anthropologists employ the notion in fundamentally different ways." And Goldschmidt (1985:171) adds that the cultural paradigm is "so global in its character and so diffuse in its formulation that scholars have increasingly focused their attention on particular aspects" of it. One can understand why, then, over 150 definitions of the term exist (see Kroeber and Kluckhohn 1963).

To help readers with the contributions that follow, let me offer a sampling of definitions—provided by three of the volume's contributors in their introductory texts—to give a sense of the concept's present usage. Harris (1988a:597) refers to culture as "the learned patterns of behavior and thought characteristic of a societal group"; Keesing (1981:509) states that culture is "the system of knowledge more or less shared by members of a society"; and Kottak (1991:17) defines it as "distinctly human; transmitted through learning; traditions and customs that govern behavior and

beliefs." For reasons to be explained below, I prefer using "the cultural" to "culture" as a label for the phenomena being described here. The jarring usage is purposeful. It reminds us we are dealing with an anthropological construction, a concept, not a living entity.

THE CULTURAL AS COHERENT

Though varied, the definitions of the cultural tend to share at least one common trait—they portray it as relatively coherent. The idea is that certain items co-occur, are somehow interrelated, and/or support one another in a particular manner. Without such coherence, Kroeber (1953:373) notes, "One has a thousand disparate items which add up to little." With it, there is a semblance of order.

Anthropologists have traditionally emphasized two general sets of factors as shaping cultural coherence—those deemed as relatively intrinsic to a group and those which, though conceptualized in cultural terms, may be assessed as more extrinsic to it (such as the environment). These two sets of factors should not be seen as totally distinct from one another. They really represent two poles of a continuum with considerable overlap between them.

Before describing them, let me add a parenthetical note. For anthropologists steeped in today's trends, a description of these factors

243

may appear a bit dated. Disciplinary attention has moved on to other issues. Yet these newer concerns, in some ways, developed out of older ones. And the present generation of students need know what models framed conceptions of the cultural in times past to place present conceptions in perspective. Several issues noted below, I might add, also live on in various forms.

Intrinsic Factors

Anthropologists have traditionally phrased their intrinsic analyses in terms of two conceptual models: the organic and the linguistic. Spencer, Durkheim, and Radcliffe-Brown stressed the organic; Boas, Sapir, Benedict, and Lévi-Strauss the linguistic.

Based on a biological analogy (in which different parts of the body work together to maintain physical health), the organic model views social institutions as supporting one another to maintain a healthy social order—which is often defined in terms of possessing stability and integration. Associated with the organic model is the concept of function (and the label functionalism). "To explain a social fact," Durkheim (1938:97) notes, "we must . . . show its function in the establishment of social order." Durkheim (1915:63) suggests that the function of religion, for example, is to unite adherents "into a single moral community." Religious rites, Durkheim (1915:432) states, "are means by which the social group affirms itself periodically." Through them, people "become conscious of their moral unity" (1915:432) (cf. R. Rosaldo 1989:20). Early in his career, in *The Andaman Islanders*, Radcliffe-Brown explicitly stresses the organic analogy. "Every custom and belief of a primitive society," he (1922:229) writes, "plays some determinant part in the social life of the community, just as every organ of a living body plays some part in the general life of the organism." In later works (1950:82), this notion is refined: "The social function of any feature of a system is its relation to the struc-

ture and its continuance and stability." Or, phrased slightly differently, functional unity is "a condition in which all parts of the social system work together with a sufficient degree of harmony or internal consistency, i.e. without producing persistent conflicts which can neither be resolved nor regulated" (1952b:181). Incest taboos illustrate his point. They prevent the disruption not only of "the social life of a single family, . . . [but] of the whole system of moral and religious sentiments on which the social order rests" (1950:72). They order life, they prevent disrupting conflicts.

The linguistic model takes a different tack. Here the cultural is analyzed in terms of conceptual frameworks and insights borrowed from linguistics (see e.g. Aberle 1957). "It seems necessary to dwell upon the analogy of ethnology and language," Boas (1911a:70-71) writes, because "language seems to be one of the most instructive fields of inquiry" for understanding indigenous ideas (cf. Kroeber 1952:107). Just as language is patterned, Sapir (1949:161) asserts, so is culture: "The network of cultural patterns of a civilization is indexed in the language." Benedict (1934:23-24) suggests: "It is in cultural life as it is in speech; selection is the prime necessity. The numbers of sounds that can be produced by our vocal cords . . . are practically unlimited." "In culture too," she continues, "we must imagine a great arc on which are ranged the possible interests. . . . A culture that capitalized [on] even a considerable proportion of these would be as unintelligible as a language that used all the clicks, all the glottal stops." For Benedict, such cultural patterns tend to have a psychological consistency. Or as she (1934:46) phrases it: "A culture, like an individual, is a more or less consistent pattern of thought and action." The Zuni are described, for instance, as "a ceremonious people, a people who value sobriety and unoffensiveness above all other virtues" (1934:59). Relying on insights from structural linguistics, Lévi-Strauss emphasizes a different side of the linguistic analogy. For Lévi-Strauss language and culture constitute related codes of communication. "Without reducing society or culture to language," he (1963:83) states, one can interpret "society as a whole in terms of a theory of communication. . . . Rules of kinship and marriage serve to insure circulation of women between groups, just as economic rules serve to insure the circulation of goods and services, and linguistic rules the circulation of messages."

Goodenough and Bloch, in their contributions, differ on the linguistic analogy's value. Goodenough, in his chapter, restates and updates a position he has made famous. In just the way one learns a language, he (page 265) notes, learning about a culture involves discovering "what one needs to know to participate acceptably as a member in . . . [its] affairs." Bloch challenges the linguistic analogy's value. Drawing on recent cognitive research, he distinguishes between different types of knowledge and suggests the linguistic analogy is appropriate only in some cases for modeling cultural knowledge. The tension between Goodenough's and Bloch's positions helps bring into focus not only the strengths and weaknesses of the linguistic analogy, but, more generally, the value and problems of conceptualizing the cultural in terms of analogies in general.

Extrinsic Factors

For Boas and Benedict, the environment was a mildly restraining influence. For Steward it constituted a major shaping force as his (1963: 37) notion of "cultural core" makes clear. This core involved "the constellation of features which are most closely related to subsistence activities and economic arrangements"—those cultural features, in other words, that are most readily shaped by the environment. This core of cultural features, he suggested, played a critical role in shaping both a group's social organization and its development through time. Among the Shoshonean Indians of the Great Basin, for example: "Owing to the cultural ecological

processes—to the exploitation of their particular [dry] environment by means of the techniques available to them—families functioned independently in most cultural activities . . . the few collective interfamilial pursuits did not serve to give permanent cohesion to [different] extended families" (1955:119). As a result, "the economic and social relations of Shoshonean families . . . [were to] be likened to a net in that each family had occasional associations with families on all sides of it . . . [but] the net lacked knots; each family was at liberty to associate with whom it pleased" (1955:116-117). Kroeber (in W. Thomas 1956:304) went further in one ecological analysis. From a study of American Indians, he suggested: "An unproductive habitat, which enforced nearly constant but scattering food quest, tended strongly to be accompanied by meager and undifferentiated institutions as well as personalities."

Anthropologists might, in some ways, also be referred to as extrinsic variables shaping cultural coherence. From an interpretive perspective, cultural coherence lies as much in the eye of the describer as in the realities of the described. Or as Said (1989:224) stated, "Anthropological representations bear as much on the representer's world as on who or what is represented." Cultural elements are fitted together in ethnographies in ways that not only reflect indigenous perspectives but also in ways that make sense to anthropologists and their readers (see e.g. Borofsky 1987).

The cultural, properly speaking, is not a concrete, living entity, it is not something one can touch. It is a way for conceptualizing a set of beliefs and practices, a set of continuities and changes. That is why, following Keesing (page 309), I use the term "cultural" rather than "culture." The adjectival form downplays culture as some innate essence, as some living, material thing. Culture is an anthropological abstraction.

Goody's contribution builds on this theme by considering problems in delineating the cultural. The specific focus of his contribution—questioning the difference between the "cultural" and the "social" as concepts—touches on an old debate in the discipline. Kroeber (1948:267) viewed culture and society as "two faces of a sheet of paper." They "are so interwoven as actual phenomena," he (1948:268) stated, "they are often quite difficult to disentangle." By contrast, his colleague and friend Lowie (1953:531) emphasized the primacy of the cultural and viewed "social structure . . . [as] one aspect of . . . culture." Goody, like Goodenough and Bloch, leads us to consider how we might best conceptualize the cultural: How should we define it? For what ends?

Ultimately, cultural coherence is best seen as a guiding hypothesis. It has proved a valuable one. But it still is only that—"a question rather than an answer" in Moore's (page 364) phrasing. As Lowie emphasizes (1937:142-143), "many of the cohering elements in the life of a people are not chance, . . . but it has never been proved that *all* . . . [cultural] traits are linked."

CONCEPTUALIZING THE CULTURAL

Today certain issues repeatedly arise in discussing the cultural concept. Let me briefly note some of them.

The Cultural Concept as a Historically Situated Idea

The cultural concept developed within a set of historical contexts. An important one was Western industrialization. Commenting on Raymond Williams's (1983) book *Culture and Society*, Herbert (1991:22) notes:

The idea of culture appears on the scene as the central element of a long, closely knit English tradition of social criticism directed against the disintegrating and debasing effects of industrialization. Starting with Burke, what writers began calling "culture" was an ideal of harmonious personal and collective perfectibility, "a body of values superior to the

ordinary progress of society," "the true standard of excellence for a people."

Another important context was the politics of nationalism. As Keesing (page 307) observes, our modern sense of "cultural identity has its origin in nineteenth-century cultural nationalism in Europe, expressed in an intense search for ethnic roots and folk origins, for primordiality and cultural tradition." Importantly, the nation-states that arose in Europe at this time were different in conception from earlier kingdoms on the continent. Quoting Anderson (1991:19):

Kingship organizes everything around a high center. Its legitimacy derives from divinity, not from populations who, after all, are subjects, not citizens. In the modern conception, state sovereignty is fully, flatly, and evenly operative over each square centimeter of a legally demarcated territory. But in the older imagining, where states were defined by centers, borders were porous and indistinct, and sovereignties faded imperceptibly into one another.

The nation-states, in order to support their new conception of statehood, developed, Anderson suggests (1991:6), "imagined communities"—"*imagined* because the members of even the smallest nation will never know most of their fellow-members, meet them, or even hear of them, yet in the minds of each lives the image of their communion." Language played a key role in these imagined communities. Anderson (1991:145) continues, "there is a special kind of contemporaneous community which language alone suggests—above all in the form of poetry and songs." With the singing of national anthems, for example, "no matter how banal the words and mediocre the tunes, there is in this singing an experience of simultaneity. At precisely such moments, people wholly unknown to each other utter the same verses to the same melody. The image: unisonance."

These two historical contexts—industrialization and nationalism—help explain some of the present implications and ambiguities of the cultural concept. One can see, implicit in many writings, the notion that non-Western cultures possess a homogeneity and community lacking in the industrialized West. And one can perceive an ambiguity regarding the degree to which the cultural represents an elitist ideal versus a group's actual shared beliefs and behaviors. In defining religion as a cultural system, Geertz (1966:7-8) makes an important distinction between a model *for* reality and a model *of* reality. The former "is a model under whose guidance physical relationships are organized" involving, for cultural models, "doctrines," "melodies," and "rites"—things which inspire one to act in certain ways. The latter describes "physical relationships . . . as to render them apprehensible," comprehendible. The difference between the two lies in viewing the cultural as an inspiring ideal versus a summarizing description. Variations of the former were common in nineteenth-century anthropology; variations of the latter in the twentieth (see Stocking 1968; cf. Wolf 1964:18).

I would caution readers against seeing one or the other model as definitively correct. Certainly, models *of* reality pervade most anthropological and popular discussions today. But important ambiguities exist in the concept. There is the problem, for example—discussed in both this and the next section—of defining cultural boundaries and of delimiting cultural sharing. Where does a "culture" specifically end? What do people within it specifically share?

Readers might reflect for a moment on the political implications of these two conceptual models. In regard to the relation between political and cultural conceptions of state, Anderson (1991:19) intriguingly notes "premodern empires and kingdoms [which used an elitist "*for*" model of the cultural] were able to sustain their role over immensely heterogenous, and often not even contiguous, populations for long periods of time." One might wonder whether many modern nation-states—with their shared, homogenous "of" models for the polity—will be able to demonstrate such political stability over the long term, especially given the intense ethnic conflicts now confronting them.

Salient Ambiguities

Exploring the cultural concept further, we might note at least two enduring ambiguities. One is the overlapping of continuity and change. Despite appearances to the contrary, it is not always easy to tell continuity from change. They tend to merge into as well as define one another. Two examples illustrate some of the complexities involved in differentiating between change and continuity.

In describing the *Political Systems of Highland Burma*, particularly that of the Kachin, Leach (1954) explores the difference between two forms of organization: *gumsa* (emphasizing chiefs and hierarchically ranked lineages) and *gumlao* (a more egalitarian structure). Leach (1954:227) asserts, "In Kachin society as a whole, *gumlao*-type communities have a general tendency to develop *gumsa*-type characteristics, while *gumsa*-type communities have a tendency to break up into sub-groups organized on *gumlao* principles." "The real Kachin society is not," he (1954:195) suggests, "a rigidly structured hierarchy of fixed classes and well-defined offices, but a system in which there is constant and at times very rapid social mobility." There is a continuous pattern of cyclical change with *gumsa* developing into *gumlao* and *gumlao* developing into *gumsa*. Clarifying this point, Leach (1954:212) adds: "The ultimate 'causes' of social change are, in my view, nearly always to be found in changes in the external political and economic environment; but the form which any change takes is largely determined by the existing internal structure of a given system."

Sahlins (1981, 1985) deals with the cultural dynamics of the early contact period in Hawaii. In applying the traditional ritual power of tabu to a new context—regulating trade with Westerners—Sahlins (1981:45) suggests that "the Hawaiian rulers went some way toward redefining it." "The commercial uses of the tabu" by the Hawaiian chiefs, Sahlins (1985:142-143) states, "meant that, for the common people, the sacred restrictions which promised divine benefits (when respected) were now directly counterposed to the general welfare"—the tabus were used to restrict commoners from trading with the British. As a result, "ordinary Hawaiians did not . . . hesitate to violate tabus of all kinds, in more or less open defiance of the powers-that-be." The consequence was an undermining of the tabus and of the chiefly ritual authority related to them that foreshadowed, and led up to, the famous abolition of tabus in 1819 by Liholiho. In applying a traditional concept to a new context, the chiefs helped alter both the concept and the contexts within which it operated. Paraphrasing Sahlins (1981:8), efforts at reproducing a structure (i.e. extending the use of ritual tabus to regulate exchanges with Europeans) developed over time into a transformation of the structure (i.e. a challenging and eventual abolition of the tabus). "The more things remained the same," Sahlins (1985:144) observes (turning the famous French expression *plus ca change, plus c'est la meme chose* on its head), "the more they changed." "One may question," he (1981:67) observes, "whether the continuity of a system ever occurs without its alteration or its alteration without continuity."

Another ambiguity regarding the cultural concerns the difficulty of demarcating boundaries. Cultural groups do not necessarily possess clear, distinct borders. One need only recall Kroeber's (1948:284) definition of peasants—as part-societies with part-cultures—to see the problem. We know from our own experiences, in a global economy, that political and cultural intertwinings between "us" and "others" can be subtle, intricate, and extremely complex. "The amount of cultural material . . . of foreign origin which gradually accumulates within any one culture," Kroeber

(1948:257) notes, "may . . . be said to be normally greater than what is originated within it." But, he continues, "as soon as a culture has accepted a new item, it tends to lose interest in the foreignness of origin." It thus becomes difficult to separate out the "indigenous" from the "foreign" in any absolute sense. They overlap too much. Linton (1975:405 [1937]), in a famous article entitled "One Hundred Per-Cent American," makes this point well regarding what we might consider the American way of life. The average American:

on awakening . . . glances at the clock, a medieval European invention, uses one potent Latin word in abbreviated form, rises in haste, and goes to the bathroom. . . . He will have heard stories of both the quality and frequency of foreign plumbing . . . but the insidious foreign influence pursues him even here. Glass was invented by the ancient Egyptians, the use of glazed tiles for floors and walls in the Near East, porcelain in China, and the art of enameling on metal by Mediterranean artisans of the Bronze Age. Even his bathtub and toilet are but slight modified copies of Roman originals.

Describing "the cultural" as a neatly demarcated entity, coterminus with a certain social grouping, may make us (and/or others) feel distinctive. But it does not fit with the facts. Important ambiguities are passed over.

As background to Strauss and Quinn's contribution, I would discuss another matter regarding the cultural. It relates to a dispute between Geertz and Goodenough. The cultural, for Geertz, is located in public institutions, performances, and symbols, not private, individual cognitive models. "Culture is public," Geertz (1973:12) asserts, "because meaning is." "No one would, I think, identify [a Beethoven quartet with] . . . the skills and knowledge needed to play it, with the understanding of it possessed by its performers or auditors" (1973:11). Goodenough (1981:53-54) opposes this perspective and suggests: "A Beethoven quartet is an abstraction in the minds of each of us who has any familiarity with it. . . . The quartet . . . exists in each individual's comprehension of it. . . . If culture is learned, its ultimate locus must be in individuals rather than in groups." The question boils down to this: For what reasons and in what ways does it make sense to view the cultural as embedded in public and/or private (that is, mental) activity. Strauss and Quinn try to bridge this gap. They (pages 295-296) suggest, "It is time to say that culture is *both* public and private, both in the world and in people's minds . . . [so] we can better account for what we have learned about culture so far and begin to develop a deeper understanding of the problems that still elude us."

Foreshadowing the theme of his contribution to this volume, Keesing (1987:161-162) elsewhere observes: "We need to ask who *creates* and who *defines* cultural meanings, and to what ends." Keesing questions the political agenda inherent in traditional conceptions of the cultural and emphasizes that we need to be attuned to the historical situatedness of cultural meanings. In the process, he touches on some of the politics surrounding the cultural concept today. Keesing refers to hegemony, a concept now popular among anthropologists. For Gramsci (1971:12), the individual most associated with the term, hegemony refers to "the general direction imposed on social life by the dominant fundamental group"—the intellectual contexts and frameworks within which discussion, opposition, consensus, and conflict take place. Hegemonic influences can be obvious as in the imposing of one's beliefs on others or they can be subtle as in framing the terms within which political dialogue proceeds. One should not, however, assume the dominated necessarily accept domination passively under such circumstances. Thompson (1966), Willis (1981), and Scheper-Hughes (in this volume) suggest that cultural resistance manifests itself in a host of subtle, complex ways.

The contributions that follow, then, present a range of views regarding the cultural—such a range, in fact, readers may well not accept all of them. And yet, we should note they share certain common elements. All, for example, focus on embedding the cultural concept in social activities. And none describes the cultural in abstract, essentialized terms.

The contributions leave us with a set of important questions: How might we move beyond the cultural concept's present ambiguities and limitations? How might we better come to terms with the concept's historical, linguistic, and political overtones? How do we build an effective cultural concept for the 1990s?

17

Culture and Its Boundaries: A European View

JACK GOODY

The concept of culture, accepted as unproblematic in most everyday discourse, and indeed in many academic discussions, has had a rocky history.[1] There have been strong pleas from philosophers of science to tighten up the definition, accompanied by suggestions as to the way that should go (Kroeber and Kluckhohn 1963; Moore 1952; Goldstein 1957; Cafagna 1960). There have been a number of comprehensive reviews, which have all too often ended on a pessimistic tone (Singer 1968; L. Schneider and Bonjean 1973; Keesing 1974).

There are broadly two ways in which social scientists use the term. First there is "culture" in the sense of learned behavior (and its products) that which in general but not in detail distinguishes mankind from the other animal species that are overwhelmingly dependent upon genetic transmission. Learned behavior (social action) is in some sense (often in a very weak one) goal-oriented, at least during the learning process. Secondly, there is "a culture" comprising the patterned behavior of a particular group, tribe, nation, class, locality. This latter usage can be deceptive in a number of ways, especially in the hands of those anthropologists who see the cultural in opposition to the social as designating a particular field or aspect of human behavior concerned with symbols and beliefs, "an array of beliefs locked together into relational patterns," to use the phrase of Mary Douglas (see also D. Schneider 1976:198: "a system of symbols and meanings"). Those who follow Talcott Parsons (1973) call for the recognition of a separate field of "cultural" studies concerned with the analysis of "symbols" and "meaning," a field that stands opposed to, or is at least distinct from, the social (social structure, social organization, etc.), despite the fact that Parsons's concept of "social action" includes both elements (Geertz 1965; D. Schneider 1976). Geertz distinguishes between social structure as "the ongoing process of interactive behavior" and culture as "the framework of beliefs, expressive symbols, and values in terms of which individuals define their feelings, and make their judgments" (Geertz 1957:33).

As I sit on a balcony and watch my neighbors in a rural French village, I find it difficult to distinguish two such fields. They act and interact in ways that may allow one to discern beliefs, symbols, and values, but these are intrinsic to their interaction; social action must include such a dimension and would be meaningless without it. The statement of beliefs, the use of symbols, the "expression" of values, these are part of "the ongoing process of interactive behavior." Any more separable notion of a "framework" emerges from the analytic perception of the observer rather than from the action perspective of the actor. That does not make it wrong, but it may make it unnecessary.[2]

DIFFICULTIES IN DIFFERENTIATING THE CULTURAL FROM THE SOCIAL

The European tradition is less inclined to accept a dichotomy between culture and society. Like the earlier nineteenth-century approach, it has tended to treat these categories as being virtually synonymous. Certainly Sir James Frazer recognized no such distinction when he accepted the chair in Social Anthropology at the University of Liverpool. Nor does the French usage of "anthropologie sociale" exclude the study of what American scholars might think of as "culture." Indeed, having earlier been the instigators of the study of "social structure" under Durkheim, they have continued to display the greatest interest in the study of myths, symbols, and "meaning," all under the heading of the social. Even if one does accept the dichotomy, I would suggest that beliefs (in Douglas's definition), or symbols and meanings (in that of Schneider and others) are only one element in what most scholars recognize as the cultural domain; from an analytic standpoint these elements need to be treated not so such as distinct, but perhaps as having a similar kind of relation to the "social" as "myth" to "ritual" (Kroeber and Kluckhohn 1963:291).

In a widespread European view, culture is seen as the content of social relations, not as some distinct entity (e.g. Firth 1951:27). That is to say, it is the "customary" part of social action, not one which constitutes their entire field of study and about which one can have a separate body of theory.[3] Indeed it is difficult to visualize what a general "theory" of culture would look like. While there has been some gain in the examination of aspects of knowledge systems, for example, in the classification of phenomena, it is hard to see any advantage that has accrued from treating the ideational level, including the level of symbols and meanings, as a distinct domain. For one thing, such an approach tends to overstress a line of division between "material" and "nonmaterial" phenomena, reflecting long-established but often misleading folk dichotomies. Goodenough was very explicit when he affirmed that "culture is not a material phenomenon," being a mechanism of behavior rather than behavior itself (Goodenough 1957:167). In other words culture is a secondary phenomenon which we derive from the study of behavior. Where do the book and painting come in if we are only dealing in the immaterial? And is thought itself devoid of a material aspect?

Such an approach has a distinctly "idealist" tonality which plays down not only *material* culture but the material aspects of culture generally. While there is every reason to stress the role of ideas, values, norms in "sociocultural" analysis, there are no grounds for neglecting the role of material elements in behavior (in which an ideational, that is linguistic, element is intrinsic, at least as respects human interaction). In an all too obvious way the coming of the automobile has changed the way goods are acquired in the village as well as the relations between work and house. In another sense of communication, the coming of writing has affected the potentialities for sending messages at a distance and of receiving them from the past, that is, from writers long dead, as well as for influencing not only the content of those messages but the mental operations of the members of literate societies. The separation of the material and the nonmaterial implied, and often explicitly asserted, in many recent approaches to the study of "culture" is severely confining from the perspective of analysis and profoundly unsatisfactory from that of general theory. It leads to the neglect of important questions without itself raising many others that can be profitably asked.

Indeed, whatever the theoretical assertions of cultural anthropologists, in their practice they deal with much more than the specialized field that some declare as their particular domain, that of symbols and meaning. Geertz understands culture as "an historically transmitted pattern of meaning embodied in symbols, a system of inherited conceptions expressed in symbolic forms by means which men communicate" (Geertz 1973:89). He distinguishes between cultural symbols as "vehicles of thought" and social structure as "forms of human association," with a "reciprocal interplay" occurring between them. Despite this potential interplay, the human situation is phrased in terms of a radical dichotomy. Many other scholars would see language as the primary example both of a vehicle of thought and of the means of human association (Rice 1980:171). In many spheres there seems little to be gained and much to be lost in so strongly separating "content" from "interaction," especially as this is hardly required in Parsons's (1973) concept of social action nor yet by the earlier social analysts of whom his work was a kind of synthesis. In any case in European usage social structure can include an analysis of the realm of symbols, as in much of Lévi-Strauss's work, or it may involve a study of "interplay" as, for example, in Evans-Pritchard's study of Nuer religion or in Fortes's enquiry into the worship of ancestors (Evans-Pritchard 1956; Fortes 1987).

Attempts to differentiate the cultural from the social, or the symbolic from other forms of human interaction, seem then open to question. The terms may serve as general signposts to areas of interest within a wider field of social action, sometimes areas in which one is lost for an (alternative) explanation.

It is the historian Berkhofer (1973) who provides the context for the change in the (American) definition of culture after the Second World War. The earlier artifactual component became excluded in favor of the "symbolic," a shift from the "real" to the "ideal" orders, the "material" to the "immaterial" which he sees as consistent with changes in historiography from oppositional to consensus approaches to American politics during the period of the Cold War. It is a shift from the more concrete, more general, more comprehensive, definition offered by E. B. Tylor to one concentrating on the ideational or symbolic level.[4]

QUESTIONS OF UNITY AND DIVERSITY IN LITERARY AND HISTORICAL NOTIONS OF CULTURE

In his *Notes towards the Definition of Culture*, T. S. Eliot (1948) attempts to reconcile three senses of "culture" ("a culture" rather than "culture"), depending on whether it is attached to an individual, to a group (or class), or to a whole society. Beginning with tribes, he turns to the totalizing anthropological definition as it was offered in E. B. Tylor's seminal work of 1871, *Primitive Culture*. But he goes on to remark that "if we are considering highly developed societies, and especially our own contemporary society, we have to consider the relationship of the three senses. At this point anthropology passes over into sociology" (Eliot 1948:20). That is to say, one can apply the notion of homogeneity to "tribes" but not to more complex units.

A similar point is made by Keith Thomas (1971) in his historical account of belief in Tudor England, *Religion and the Decline of Magic*. In the introduction he writes of the diversity of England at that period due to the huge variation in standards of living, educational level, and intellectual sensibility which makes this society so diverse, and therefore so hard to generalize about. Not only did conditions change over the two centuries, but at any one point in time there were so many different layers of belief and levels in sophistication. The invention of the printed word, moreover, had made possible the preservation and dissemination of many different systems of thought, deriving from other societies and sometimes dating from the remote classical past. The task of the historian is thus infinitely harder than that of the social anthropologist, studying a small homogeneous community in which all inhabitants share the same beliefs, and where few of those beliefs are borrowed from other societies. This was no simple unified primitive world, but a dynamic and infinitely various society, where social and intellectual change had long been at work and where currents were moving in many different directions (Thomas 1971:5).

Both literary critic and social historian take the view that holistic definitions do not apply to post-Renaissance societies but only to the "tribes" the anthropologists are examining which have cultures of an undifferentiated kind. The implied division of labor between sociology and anthropology has serious theoretical objections that involve assumptions about the nature of "other cultures." We can of course regard the "simpler societies" as less dynamic and more static because they are small-scale, more homogeneous, and more "primitive." But that would be a circular argument. I would wish to qualify this description as well as pointing to a mechanism that might account for some part, at least, of the difference, a mechanism that is suggested by both writers. We may agree that most small-scale societies of the kind exemplified by the Nuer or the Tallensi are relatively homogeneous in terms of culture. There is little political or economic stratification, and subcultural differences tend to get ironed out in face-to-face interaction. However, such a state of affairs does not necessarily mean that they are static over time since we may be faced with a moving homogeneity. Any homogeneity has a temporal dimension, being disturbed from time to time by external forces and by internal tensions or contradictions.

Even for these simpler societies it is easy to overemphasize the homogeneity of culture, which is always relative. In any system of human interaction, there are common understandings of a cultural kind between the participants, negotiated certainly, but at the same time those participants each retain their own different understandings. Even in oral societies these are not simply deviations from a fixed norm but may differentiate one individual or group from another at any one point in time, while over the longer duration they may constitute creative acts that redefine culture and social relationships themselves. It is easy to assume that such creative acts are variants of a single "culture," and in one sense that is true by definition. But the dangers of such an assumption are apparent when we look at the question of the spatial and temporal extent of "culture" or of elements of culture. For instance, lengthen the time perspective and ask in what sense the culture of contemporary New England is the same as that of the beginning of the nineteenth century, of the early period dominated by the Puritans, of Stuart England which they had left, of the earlier Chaucerian England to which their ancestors belonged.

Moreover not all nonliterate societies are equally homogeneous. If we look at the earlier kingdoms of Africa we find forms of stratification that turn on access to high offices, whose incumbents have magico-religious powers conferred upon them. Those powers are by no means always passed down by heredity in the strict sense, even when political office is so transmitted. The ruling estate, usually comprising the descendants of incoming conquerors, have exclusive access to the major political offices, and specialist groups surround the king and his court, weaving cloth, drumming, interpreting, and carrying out similar tasks. Differences of role and occupation abound.

What is the difference between this African situation and the one in Renaissance Europe that Burke (1978) describes in terms of subcultures of artisans and other groups? Patently it is partly a matter of degree. It is also a matter of the nature of the boundary. In Eurasian societies the boundaries between groups were often reinforced by marriage. In Africa, that was rarely the case, except with the ruling groups in the Interlacustrine states of East Africa, among some specialist groups in West Africa, and for adherents to world religions, all of whom tended to be endogamous. In all these cases there was not only marriage within but also a tendency to develop subcultures. In general however there was not an advanced hierarchy of culture, so that it is difficult to talk, for example, of a popular culture in opposition to some high culture.

While it is a mistake to overstress the homogeneity of nonliterate societies, there is certainly a broad distinction to be made between cultures in "simpler" and "complex" societies that relates to their means of communication; this is the mechanism to which I referred as having to be taken into account to help clear the conceptual ground. Obviously, oral societies are spared what Benjamin Franklin called "the restless interventions of the printer." They are also spared the disturbing and creative presence of the writer. And the absence of writing clearly has some relation to their homogeneity, since at the very least new forms of knowledge, new symbols, and new meanings are created in this medium that affect the culture in far-reaching ways. I doubt if we can speak of "popular culture" except in societies with writing, although writing is not always the only means of differentiation.

Social layering of the more complex kinds means differential access to and involvement in sociocultural activity in a more subtle way but it also entails granting a certain autonomy and power to the written word, even when that word is not necessarily controlled by the political or religious authorities. The nature of writing promotes the notion of the externality of culture—that culture is partly out there in books to be bought or burnt, in the theatres to be subsidized or suppressed, in ministries of culture rather than in the hearts and minds of men. Embeddedness of the latter kind is often assumed by anthropologists when they define culture as learned behavior—taking language as the model and then generalizing the particular characteristics of that means of communication (which have to be relatively precise and quasi-universal) to the content of communication (in which differentiation can often be much greater).

Actors generally define their culture in terms of the dominant political, linguistic, or religious units to which they owe affiliation, so that they readily speak of American English, of American Catholicism, of American culture, presuming a bounded unity which is often problematic (since many others share the basic components of the English language and the Catholic religion). In this sense the concept of "a culture" tends to have a highly nationalistic flavor about it, certainly highly political. Culture may be visualized as homogeneous, as a way of covering up the cracks in the fabric of society. The notion is often attached conceptually to political units, or to units that desire to play a political role. Not by chance, therefore, that Schama's analysis of Dutch culture in the golden age has an early chapter entitled "Patriotic scriptures" which begins with the question, "Just who, exactly, did the Dutch think they were?" (Schama 1987:51). Attention is thereby centered upon the commonalities among members of a political unit, most usually their language. But from the outsider's vantage point, a similar language (though a different religion) and many other behavioral features were present among the inhabitants of Flanders, with the activities of Antwerp closely resembling those of Amsterdam. The outsider sees the overlap, the insider emphasizes singularity.

These problems that are inherent in the use of the concept of culture emerge clearly in Eliot's (1948) discussion of Europe at the end of the Second World War, not only from a temporal but also from a spatial standpoint. He writes of the unity of European culture (which was the title of his postwar broadcast to Germany on the subject). In his eyes that unity was essentially Christian; and in different forms religious unity characterizes all higher cultures. Cultures, he sees, not only as stratified internally but the strata are culturally higher or lower, having more or less culture. Higher cultures are distinguished by "differentiation of function, so that you can speak of the less cultured and the more cultured strata of society" (Eliot 1948:124). It is one of the functions of education to maintain the higher culture; "education should help to preserve the class and to select the 'elite'" (Eliot 1948: 163). In other words, Eliot seeks to combine the sociological use of "a culture" with the evaluative, elitist view of "culture" that is present in much everyday usage, especially in literary circles where it often refers to a particular written or artistic tradition. This he does by insisting on the differentiation not so much between elite and popular cultures, as between the more and the less cultured.

From the political standpoint Eliot was trying to revive the notion of European "culture" in the postwar period when notions of reconstruction were everywhere in the air, not only the political reconstruction of conquered countries—the rehabilitation of Germany, the abandonment of notions of imperial rule, and the creation of new world orders—but also the reconstruction of culture when so much had been destroyed on the material level, so much neglected on the level of performance. The first book I bought after the War was called *The Bombed Cities of Europe*, a record of what had been lost. Nowadays a casual observer would scarcely recognize the scars. Then one regretted each lost masterpiece, one was hungry for each artistic performance. Culture in the sociological sense was in the air, too, as Eliot (1948) saw, because it drew attention to ongoing features on which a new world might be built, taking up the best of the old. Hence perhaps part of the attraction of Benedict's *Patterns of Culture* as well as the work of Mead, Bateson, Gorer, and others, that stripped societies down to supposedly continuing elements, to themes and patterns that persisted through all adversity, immaterial components that no bomb could destroy, neglecting the tensions and contradictions that gave rise to strife, or the varied complexity that Thomas (1971) finds in Renaissance England.

Leaving aside the objections to such an approach that were a common feature of European social science, especially in British social anthropology, there was something flawed in these notions to those who had witnessed the transformation of Germany under Hitler, of France under Petain, and later on the sudden collapse of Fascist culture in Italy

and of Nazi culture at the end of the War. Were these changes simply matters of political shifts at the top? Certainly not. The fascist regimes gained much popular support, as we saw in the prosecution of the War. What emerged from their ruins was partly new, partly imposed from above and largely accepted below. Such shifts were replaced by totalitarian rule and vice versa. Racism alternated with tolerance; great musicians, artists, writers were abandoned and then welcomed again into the fold.

Literary studies such as Eliot's (1948) remind us of the evaluative element embedded in many uses of the concept; historical ones such as Thomas's (1971) bring out the associated notion of differentiation. In addition we need to be fully conscious of the varying boundaries, not so much of a culture but of cultural practices. A recognition of these features may make us wary of simplistic notions of cultural homogeneity, of the commonality of sense and non-sense. It may indeed make us wary of the drift towards establishing a dichotomy between the cultural and the social, or even using the term "cultural" altogether.

BOUNDARIES IN CULTURE AND ITS CONSTITUENTS

Different cultural components have different boundaries. First, there are those between the internal domains of a given sociocultural system, religious, political, interpersonal (gift-giving), culminating in the highly contextual usages of individual creative writers. Then there are the local boundaries between adjacent social groups and individuals' boundaries that differ for different kinds of social action. Thirdly, there are the hierarchical boundaries of estate or class. The nature of these boundaries will vary with the type of social system; the simpler societies are relatively undifferentiated not only hierarchically but with regard to domain, the religious merging with the political.

Domain

In European gift-giving red roses usually stand for sexual love; in the context of Christianity for the Virgin, for the love of Christ as well as for his martyrdom; in that of politics, red is often the blood of socialist martyrs. Interpersonal, religious, and political contexts define the usage quite differently, indeed in contradictory fashion. The nineteenth-century "language of flowers" tried to list single referents for each flower, an impossible task—if it was supposed to conform to accepted usage—since that was multiple, determined by domain. Moreover such usages were subject to creative extension, in the arts as well as in life. For the artist the communication of symbolic meaning was not only a matter of giving expression to an existing, customary, cultural, pattern of meanings but of extending and elaborating what was already present (which might include "specialist" or "created" sets of meanings). And these notions may differ according to the individual or group as well as according to the domain, topic, or other context of their discourse. If one looks for the common set of cultural meanings, in a linguistic sense, one arrives at a particularly impoverished set of equivalences, because that would omit differences of the spatial, geographical, temporal, and hierarchical kinds. And taking those differences into account, it is not at all clear that one ends up with a coherent system, let alone a code, in the usual way this term is applied.

Spatial Boundaries

Secondly, there are spatial boundaries of varying kinds and extent. We often speak of culture as if it were an attribute of distinct social groups in a bounded fashion, but that may not be at all the case when one looks at specific elements of behavior. In the seventeenth century the question received attention from Abbé Jean-Baptiste Thiers who noted in his *Traité des Superstitions* (printed in 1697) that "popular" is opposed to Catholic belief as the particular to the universal: "every kingdom, every province, every diocese, every town, every parish has its own beliefs" (quoted by Revel 1984:299). Why? As Thiers saw it such beliefs had no foundation in canonical authority. Looking at it from the other end we can attribute the diversity to the generative nature of culture particularly where not reined in by political or religious hegemonies. What these beliefs and practices lacked, Thiers was right, was canonical authority. The words reinforce one another; the canon was not only a document which constituted an authority, but also a rule, a duty authorized and accepted. It provided a discipline for belief and practice, both in the sense of disciplining students or soldiers, even forming their character, and in the sense of a field of study, a field with its own body of writings.

In relating the "universal" or Catholic to the written, and the particular or local to oral custom, the intention is not to reduce the notion of high and popular culture to that between text and utterance. Even if such a simple dichotomy were appropriate, the one influences the other, differently over time as each is creative in its own way; the oral replaces, the written accumulates. Moreover there are levels of differentiation within both spheres. Nevertheless, one long-term effect of the addition of a written register is undoubtedly towards standardization of rituals, law, and customs over wider areas. That is not to say these are static, but a measure of a standardization is established by their incorporation in writing.

In the Middle Ages the canon was not confined to one country, to one "culture." It belonged to the whole of Catholic Christendom in which similar religious ideas, similar religious symbols were current throughout. The red rose stood for Christ and the Virgin Mary. Similarly the heraldic symbolism of flowers was not confined to one society: it spread across the aristocracies of the West among whom the horizontal solidarities of estate were at times stronger than the vertical ties of political affiliation. Even at the popular level there were similarities throughout Europe, for example, in the activities centered on May 1st (which do not appear to represent an ancient cult of the kind visualized by Robert Graves). Nevertheless, such activities were widely adopted at a popular level and fitted into the interstices of the liturgical calendar, perhaps with the encouragement of the Church, who regarded May as Mary's month, or of the polity, interested in ceremonial safety valves. Nevertheless, it was by and large the oral that diverged in very parochial fashion, whereas the written tended to extend its sway well beyond those boundaries.

At the other pole of the dialectic of culture lies not the canon but the creation, which is confined neither to the written nor to the oral. There is some reason to see Shakespeare's use of the symbolism of flowers in *Hamlet* as more a literary creation than a code, although one bearing some relation to popular usage. So too the tradition of the "language of flowers" in nineteenth-century France, which was one aspect of the "high" culture of Paris. It was rather an aspect of the culture of the growing urban bourgeoisie, one which drew on some elements of both popular and upper culture to establish a new, temporary tradition of restricted circulation and limited viability, but one that had a variety of consequences.

High and Low

Compared with the complexities of horizontal variation, vertical differences appear relatively straightforward. But that is not fully so. In the first place features that are characteristic of particular groups tend to seep down and less frequently to mount up the hierarchy. These hierarchical differences may be partly restated as urban-rural ones. Before the present tendency to universal suburbanization, the European uses of flowers in town and country were highly diverse. Even such a widely accepted meaning as the sexual connotations of red roses appears to have been primarily

urban and upper, extending gradually to other levels of society. That has often been the case with wedding practices where women and men tend to dress up in the clothes and paraphernalia of higher groups, as witness the evening dress worn until recently in rural France and England, as well as the decorating of the bride in China as the Empress or in Islamic societies as a queen. Dressing "up" means adopting the costumes and practices of upper groups, at least for the specific occasion, a process that is especially characteristic of weddings although also found in other rites.

Such adaptation does not put an end to differentiation. The ceremonies of the upper group are unmistakably their own, even if only because of the wealth displayed. But subtle criteria may distinguish a group's behavior. Criteria are sometimes arbitrary and half-concealed and are continually emerging in another guise. Such mutations may well start as individual expressions of likes and dislikes.

There is a notion, cultivated by many literary critics and anthropologists alike, that popular and oral cultures are virtually indestructible, possessing a living tradition enduring through all the adversities that Fortune can throw at them. And in this they contrast with high culture, which is more subject to changing fashion and the fickleness of circumstance. The notion needs modifying not only because for the literate classes writing provides a fixed and, in the ritual domain, often enduring text (as well as encouraging cumulative innovation in other spheres), but because of the generative aspects of oral cultures and their willingness to adopt features from other social groups. That is also the case with "popular culture," which is necessarily complementary to "high culture." In societies with writing the popular is more dependent upon, more influenced by the "high" or hegemonic than is often realized, in some instances devastatingly so. That is especially true under reformist movements of a religious kind. When Christianity became dominant, it had just such a transformative effect on Europe. One can dimly perceive elements of earlier cultures that persisted, but in domains that were significant to Christianity the new creed took over in such an overwhelming manner as to present grave problems for any hypothesis of deep-rooted continuity. What emerged untouched were often the marginalia of culture, or those elements that were relatively independent of the main structures of practice and belief.

In some cases such features are actively diffused from "upper" to "lower," or from "written" to "oral," as part of the processes of social incorporation, of deliberate control, or of aggressive missionizing, in which "education" may be included; these are the processes of hegemonic transfer. Alternatively, or even concurrently, lower groups or individuals may seek to appropriate cultural features from above in a number of classic ways that have been documented by seventeenth-century dramatists in France, in England after the Restoration, by folklorists in many lands—the Regency beds in French farmhouses, the widespread building of turrets and dovecotes after the Revolution. Such adaptations occur even in the presence of sumptuary laws which attempt to limit these democratic transfers.

There is therefore no simple division into "great" and "little" and a number of historians have argued against a binary opposition between high and popular culture. As Hall and Chartier (D. Hall 1984:5; Chartier 1984:231) show, a radical dichotomy is patently inadequate if it neglects the interaction and exchange between the various levels; for example, the interface between the "written" and the "oral" produces a layered set of interactions of considerable complexity. Indeed the very notion of "popular culture" is itself a complex one. Revel's (1984) analysis of changing ideas in early modern France points to the way in which the establishment of a national culture was linked to the process of political centralization.

The differentiated popular culture of complex societies (implying the coexistence of both a low and a high) is contrasted with the traditional (generally seen in a holistic manner). We may think of "tribal" societies in Africa as being relatively homogenous in their ways of thinking and acting, definitely so among small, acephalous (noncentralized) groups like the LoDagaa; less so among states such as Gonja, also of northern Ghana; less so yet where a conquering group of a different socioethnic background has imposed itself on the indigenes, as in the Interlacustrine kingdoms off East Africa. But there is relatively little tendency, compared with Eurasia, to form distinct subcultures on a "class," professional, or sectarian basis. There are some differences in ways of acting and thinking in the strata of many African states, in cultures that are effectively without writing. Some specialists make their appearance, keeping their forms of knowledge to themselves. I think specifically of the tendencies to "caste" formation in occupational groups in the Mande region of West Africa, groups that not only retain skills but do so by means of endogamy, by taking spouses from within the group. However, over large areas of social intercourse there is a process of internal homogenization that I have tried to describe for cooking, a process in which continual interaction restrains the emergence of gentry or other subcultures.

In Europe, by contrast, such differences were constantly emerging, especially in the context of estate and class—and in particular of the court, giving rise to a cultural hierarchy. At the same time the transfer of ways of acting occurs in the process of popularization or vulgarization. This aspect of the interaction between such groups or groupings raises once again the problem of boundaries and their permeability. Members of different "subcultures" always participate with each other in wider exchanges; indeed subgroups often merge into wider collectivities for ritual and political ceremonies. The degree to which they come together or hold themselves apart (or are held apart) varies greatly. In parts of Europe, Jewish communities participated in little but economic activities, along the lines of Furnival's model of a "plural society" in Southeast Asia, each group pursuing its own social life (Furnival 1948). Other groups confined their separate activity to guild affairs. Broadly speaking, in all the major preindustrial societies of Eurasia there is a distinct dimension of high and low, of elite and popular cultures, whether this be viewed as a division or continuum. On the other hand interaction takes place not only in the public sphere of national ceremonies or military action but in the more private domains of domestic life, when village brides adopt the wedding garb of the upper orders, just as musicians to the court adapt country airs to please their patrons. Such boundaries and borrowings, such interaction and adaptation, manifest certain general trends and characteristics but they have to be looked at empirically in each context since the variables that influence particular situations are multifold. So, irrespective of how the concept of "popular culture" emerged in European history, we still require some method of characterizing polarities or segments within the wide range of cultural activities in any political unit. The nature of this range and the characteristics of its components will vary with the sociopolitical system.

Some recent studies have attempted to make further broad distinctions in the type of cultural divisions that exist, and these should be looked at in a broad historical and comparative perspective. The development of new techniques for addressing a mass audience rather than a face-to-face community has led to the gradual penetration of many of the boundaries we have discussed. That tended to be the case much earlier when writing itself became a mass phenomenon, whereas restricted literacy had exacerbated any incipient cultural divisions between high and low, elite and popular, by adding the dimension of literate and nonliterate to other axes of stratifica-

tion. That is not to say that all elites were literate; far from it. But all were strongly affected by the presence of writing that had helped to transform the social order upon which their status depended.

A complex series of changes in communications, that is, in transport as well as in media, taking place over a long period of time, have tended to increase the movement of people as well as of goods and of messages. Cultural practices such as the trend to adopt a Western marriage dress (with orange blossoms in the hair and carnations for the man), not to mention popular music, multinational advertising, and the cinema, have been radically affected by the extension of interaction on a worldwide scale by means of cheap transport and the electronic media. Culture is no longer encapsulated in local communities. Indeed the "culture of flowers"—the significance and use of flowers among various groups through time (Goody 1992)—suggests that it was never entirely constrained in such a fashion.

When one gets beyond the signposting use of the term "culture" what is problematic about the concept lies in the questions of hierarchy (internal differentiation) and boundaries (external differentiation). In terms of hierarchy the division between high and popular, or great and little traditions, does not always allow for reciprocal influences, nor yet for the further distinctions we often need in talking about working-class culture, or gentry subculture, or the subcultures of professional groups. And what are they sub(ordinate) to? Both in ordinary speech and in analytic discourse we talk of American culture, or Navaho culture, tying the notion of cultural unity to a social group, a political or tribal unit. At other times, as in Eliot's (1948) notion of a European culture, which he saw as religiously grounded, we link it to wider geopolitical or religious groupings (e.g. Arab or Islamic culture, Jewish culture). Then increasingly we speak of consumer cultures, public cultures, even the world culture of the global village, associating cultural phenomena with economic, religious, and especially communications variables, that is, with mass consumption, with "world" religions, with electronic media. Each of these usages has their rationale but the analytic base is weak. It becomes even weaker when we look at the component (cultural) elements, traits in the earlier American terminology. These may be clustered into "areas," but these areas often differ for different "traits." Linguistic ones I may share with some, religious with others; both these formidable cultural components stretch across the usual boundaries of a culture. The same is true, on a more specific level, of how one uses red or yellow roses. Such usages may mark out a major sociocultural unit (essentially political) such as we normally conceive them (i.e. French or American culture). They may characterize the behavior of subgroups, of classes or of townsfolk as against country folk. Often they are distributed in "areas" that crosscut such groups and link, in an uneven fashion, neighboring groups, not altogether unlike the relations between adjacent groups among the Tallensi of northern Ghana described by Fortes (1987) or among the LoDagaa of the same area described by myself, though they rarely constitute explicit diacritical features.

In this essay I have tried to discuss some of the problems in setting a boundary to the concept of culture and to viewing such boundaries in terms of shared ways and products of thinking and acting. From this point of view it is not something which one can have a theory about though one can about particular clusters of ways and products of thinking and acting. I have stressed the varying boundary dimensions, spatial and hierarchical, as well as the broad temporal differences in cultural forms that are linked to differences in the modes of communications and production. The "cul-ture of flowers" has to be considered, for example, in relation to the participants and to the factors that influence its development over time, which include cultivation and the market as well as botanical knowledge, ritual practice, and artistic and literary traditions. Such "cultural" aspects are not to be dissociated from ecological, economic, and other social factors. Nor is that any less true of other topics such as food, shelter, burial, and "performance." The cultural, in other words, is the social viewed from another perspective, not a distinct analytic entity.

NOTES

1. This paper is a shortened, revised version by the editor of a paper printed in the first number of *Social Anthropology*. Themes developed in it are augmented in the author's *The Culture of Flowers* (Cambridge University Press, 1993).

2. In practice I see little difference except of emphasis between these views. In societies where literacy is of greater importance a more radical separation might seem to emerge, but that is more adequately dealt with by considering the differences between oral and written discourse.

3. Note, in contrast, the titles of D. M. Schneider's article (1976)—"Notes towards a Theory of Culture"—and Keesing's review (1974)—"Theories of Culture."

4. L. Schneider (in Schneider and Bonjean 1973) questions the inclusion of an artifactual element in Tylor's initial definition of 1871. While it is true he refers to art rather than artifact, nevertheless Tylor's account of "primitive culture" makes it clear that "material culture" is an important element, as it certainly was in the teaching of anthropology and especially of archaeology. One would not expect food to be excluded, in concrete as well as symbolic form, from an analysis of French culture nor the circulation of consumer goods from the American version, nor painting from either.

INTELLECTUAL ROOTS

Jack Goody is a Fellow of St. Johns College, Cambridge, and held the William Wyse Chair in Social Anthropology at the University from 1972 to 1985. He has carried out fieldwork extensively among the LoDagaa and Gonja of northern Ghana, and briefly in Gujarat, as well as doing survey work or particular studies in other parts of the world (e.g. flowers in South China, "may" in the Lot, and cemeteries in the United States). His best known publications are *Death, Property and the Ancestors* (1962), *Technology, Tradition and the State in Africa* (1971), *The Myth of the Bagre* (1972), *Production and Reproduction* (1976), *The Domestication of the Savage Mind* (1977), *Cooking, Cuisine and Class* (1982), *The Development of the Family and Marriage in Europe* (1983), *The Logic of Writing and the Organization of Society* (1986), *The Interface between the Written and the Oral* (1987), *The Oriental, the Ancient and the Primitive* (1990), and *The Culture of Flowers* (1993).

What is my intellectual genealogy? It differs depending on the topic. Topics can rarely be encapsulated by the word "anthropology" taken in its academic sense. My initial training at Cambridge was in English Literature, though I was also interested in history and in politics. Already before going to the university, I was attracted to the moral and cultural analyses of F. R. Leavis and his associates. At this time I read around the sociology of literature and took up references to the "Cambridge anthropology" of Frazer from studies on medieval literature.

Returning to Cambridge after the Second World War, I switched to reading anthropology, having been stimulated by the wider ranging historical studies of Gordon Childe and the social psychoanalytic work carried out by the Tavistock Institute of Human Relations. Once there, I was influenced by the lectures of Evans-Pritchard but more by my fellow students (especially G. Lienhardt and E. L. Peters, who followed him to Oxford).

Later, when I joined them there, I was supervised by Fortes and got to know the other past and present members of the department—M. Gluckman, P. Bohannan, M. N. Srinivas, L. Dumont, and J. Peristiany, many of whom looked up to the work of Radcliffe-Brown and, to a lesser extent, Malinowski. Behind Radcliffe-Brown lay the nineteenth-century tradition of jurisprudence, Maine and Maitland in England, as well as the remarkable school of the Scottish enlightenment, culminating in Robertson Smith. Above all, it was the works of Durkheim and other members of the *Année Sociologique* that constituted the core of our reading, though I also became familiar with the writings of Talcott Parsons (with whom I later took a seminar) and through him of Weber. Marx and Freud were not central to our teaching but they played a large part in life as a whole. I have elsewhere expressed my debts to French sociology, to Parsons, Shils, and Homans, as well as those influenced by the early "Cambridge anthropology" of Sir James Frazer, Jane Harrison, E. K. Chambers, and Jessie L. Weston.

I did not set out to become an anthropologist in the usual sense of the term. A major interest has always been in trying to place the cultures and societies I know in the framework of the wider history and distribution of mankind. Essentially, I have been heir to the same set of interests in history and literature that moved my contemporaries, Raymond Williams, Eric Hobsbawm, E. P. Thompson, Ian Watt, and a host of others, some of whom, like Godfrey Lienhardt, Kathleen Gough, and Peter Worsley, also made the move from "literature" to "anthropology" in an academic sense but always retained an interdisciplinary (i.e. human) concern with the world as a whole.

18

Toward a Working Theory of Culture

WARD H. GOODENOUGH

We anthropologists need a good working theory of culture. The need is evident in current anthropological writings. Without a good working theory, we remain unclear as to the goals and methods of ethnography. In this paper, I present how I have come to think about culture in the course of my own work. I do so in the hope that it may offer possibilities for a suitable working theory.

Notable in much current writing is concern for the place of people as individuals—each different from the other and all bent upon their own purposes. We see them defying custom, creating new ways of doing things, and negotiating with one another the terms by which to conduct their affairs. Seeing this, we ask how it is possible to think of culture as a socially shared body of customary ways of thinking and acting, a social consensus, that determines how a society's members act. Edward Sapir questioned this view of culture over sixty-five years ago, making the same point that cultural theory requires attention to how individuals contribute to the formation and maintenance of cultures and how they see customs and traditions as serving their interests and needs (Sapir 1924).[1]

WHY A THEORY OF CULTURE?

Seeing people as having an active role in the maintenance of their societies and the creation of their cultures has implications for what has been the predominant anthropological view of culture and society. In that view, a culture is the collective property of a society and exists, somehow, apart from and independently of the society's individual members. If that view now appears untenable, does it follow that culture, as a concept, has outlived its usefulness? Given so much variation in what different people in the same community say about their beliefs and practices, does their lack of consensus make the idea of culture an anthropological myth that is best abandoned? Shouldn't we just discard the term as having outlived its usefulness? If we do, does there remain a phenomenon or set of related phenomena we will still have to talk about?

The answer to the last question is clearly yes. Anyone who has dealings with people from other geographical areas or from different sectors of a complex society finds that they do a lot of things differently. They speak differently, they carry themselves differently, they have different expectations regarding social behavior, they play different games, and they organize their family and kin relationships differently. In Kiribati (Gilbert Islands) people talk about *te-katei-ni Kiribati*, "customs of Kiribati," as distinct from those of others. Likewise in Chuuk (formerly Truk), people speak of the differences in *wussun Chuuk*, "Chuuk ways," *wussun Sapan*, "Japanese ways," and *wussiy*, "my way (of doing things)." Whatever these differences consist of, they are a phenomenon of experience that people remark on virtually everywhere. People differ in their explanations of such differences, but they all note them.[2]

From a natural science point of view, there are observable differences in speech, behavior, social arrangements, and expressions of belief that characterize different populations. The content of speech, behavior, and belief—whatever it is—requires description; and similarities and differences in those contents, as described, need explanation. We use the terms language and culture to refer to such content. Our problem is not with the terms but with our understanding of the contents of what they refer to.

DESCRIPTION

Obviously our understanding of the contents of the phenomena we refer to as languages and cultures is limited by our ability to describe them.[3] Description is fundamental to all science. As thoughtful scientists know, and contrary to widely held assumptions, description is not a simple process. Description presents what we have been able to construe cognitively from records of phenomena. We do not have the means to record everything going on in the real world. What we can do is necessarily limited. Scientists, like human beings generally, try to make sense of the "real world" by looking for recurring patterns and relationships in what they have recorded of it. Some patterns can be intuited directly from the record, others cannot. It is necessary to map the record into some notational system, amenable to analysis, before patterns can be seen. (Thus, for example, we map tape recordings of speech into writing or sound spectrograms in order to analyze them.) Scientists construct models of content and process and project them upon their external world. But these are never more than approximations, or working theories, of reality. Advances in scientific understanding are based not only on better technology for making records but on devising notation systems that improve the possibility of discovering the patterns in them.

To describe languages or cultures is to create models and theories of the understandings humans have constructed from their experiences. We make these models and theories by analyzing the material manifestations of these understandings, their artifacts, as we have recorded them. How often one hears ethnographic description referred to as "mere" and therefore not a proper scientific enterprise. Description is not only the record one has made, but the sense one has made of it: the model or theory of content and process that one has constructed from the record in order to represent what lies behind it. Like other scientists, we anthropologists are limited by our technology for recording and by the suitability for analysis of the ways we notate the record. Our bodies are our principal recording instruments, and we largely map what we record with them into ordinary language.

The criteria scientists use to assess the acceptability of their constructions have to do with how well these constructions seem to make coherent and consistent sense of the recorded data. They base their evaluations of theories or interpretations on several things. One is the replicability (within recording limitations) of the data. Another is richness. A theory or interpretation that accounts for more of the phenomena under consideration is preferable to one that accounts for fewer of them. One that is consistent with interpretations that account for other kinds of phenomena is preferable to one that is not. Scientists are also concerned with how well a theory or interpretation continues to account for new records of the phenomena under study. They prefer constructions that clarify other bodies of phenomena that have been baffling previously. Finally, all else being equal, scientists prefer parsimony and elegance. It is these same criteria that we use in anthropology for evaluating descriptions of languages and cultures—whether we do so as scientists or as humanists.[4]

How the foregoing considerations apply to cultural description and its evaluation needs to be examined further in light of what we already believe we know about the content of specific languages and cultures.

DESCRIBING WHAT ONE NEEDS TO KNOW TO PARTICIPATE ACCEPTABLY

If languages and cultures are learned in the course of participating in the activities of social groups, and if what is learned are *criteria* for speaking, acting, and interpreting that enable one to participate to one's own and others' satisfaction in those activities, it follows that those criteria—whatever they consist of—are among the things we need to describe. Our problem in this, as indicated above, is essentially no different from the problem of description in science generally. We record what we see people do and what they say about what they do and then try to infer from this record what it is we need to know in order to participate, ourselves, in what is going on and do so in ways that those people accept as showing we are knowledgeable. Their judgments are the measure of our success. A model of what one needs to know that meets this judgmental criterion is an "emic" description.[5]

A widespread misunderstanding among cultural anthropologists who have no training in linguistics is that an emic description has to do with presenting a group's culture in the terms members of the group use to talk about it. How people talk about their culture is both interesting and useful information, a valuable part of the record from which an emic account is constructed. The more contextually bound such information is, the more useful it can be for developing such an account. But if one takes people's generalizations literally as a basis for participation with them in their affairs, one is not likely to be honestly judged as knowledgeable. (The degree to which such

generalizations differ from what, in practice, one needs to know varies, obviously, with the subject matter.) An emic account relies more on analysis of the patterns in people's judgments of what is or is not acceptable in specific situations and contexts than it does on their explanations or generalizations. An emic account, then, is a model of what one needs to know to speak a language like a native speaker or to behave acceptably by the standards for socialized persons within a society. It is not merely an account of what they say about it. A model of what one needs to know is, of course, a model of what competent people in a society under study are presumed to know. As such, it is a model of that part of their cognition that enables them to function acceptably in their society.

We understand all of this well in describing languages. A description of a particular dialect of English that was not an accurate guide to speaking it in a manner acceptable to its recognized speakers would be judged inadequate. We expect grammars and dictionaries of languages to do this for us. Rarely have ethnographers sought to do the equivalent in describing cultures. We have not thought of our task as telling the reader what he or she needs to know in order to function acceptably as a member of the society reported on.[6]

Describing a group's culture in this sense of the term requires that we be able to formulate in words many things that people know subjectively but that they have not formulated to themselves. These things may include what no one has tried to formulate in words before. Mapping subjective knowledge into words for descriptive purposes objectifies it, makes it an object of scrutiny, and transforms it into something other than what it is as a subjective feel. Mapping into words formalizes subjective knowledge, and formalization tends to state as rules the subjective criteria (the feel) for what is and isn't appropriate. Formal analysts of culture, indeed, have been accused of reducing culture to rules. The error in this, if it is one, is not peculiar. It represents what humans do generally when they seek to objectify what have been subjective and, as such, personally more varied criteria for governing their behavior and appraising that of others. We have good reason to formalize. But we must guard against the temptation to reify such formalizations and, moreover, the formalizations of the people whose cultures we study. (The rules of "proper" English grammar I was required to learn in the eighth grade in my youth are but one example of such overformalization and reification.)

The prospect of trying to describe cultures adequately is daunting. For some aspects of culture we simply do not know how. For others the necessary recording technology may be available, but we lack notational systems to make the record susceptible to analysis. Existing notations, such as the one Birdwhistell (1953) devised for kinesics, require considerable training, and there has been little incentive for anthropologists to get the necessary training. For those aspects of culture where we do know how to record and analyze the relevant data, the task is often beyond what a lone fieldworker can readily do in a year or two.

I have been struck over the years how we cultural anthropologists have stressed the importance of cultural knowledge in dealing with people in other parts of the world when, at the same time, there has been no attempt by an anthropologist to describe comprehensively a people's customs relating to etiquette. I submit that making comprehensive descriptions of what one needs to know to participate acceptably as a member in a society's affairs is one of the objectives at which ethnography should aim—a necessary one on which to build a theory of culture.

I hasten to add that it is by no means the only objective of ethnographic field study. There is much more out there than language and culture to be recorded and described. There are, for example, (1) existing artifacts of the culturally structured human activities of the past, (2) distributions of landholdings and wealth, (3) political power centers, (4) threatening enemies, and (5) disease—all the things to which people apply their culture in order to cope with life's problems. These, too, must be carefully described. Otherwise we cannot see how people use their cultures, and we lack the data for comparative study on which theories of cultural change and adaptation (or maladaptation) necessarily depend. There is good reason, as cultural materialists have insisted, in having these things on our agendas for ethnographic description. But we cannot deal with such things as cultural adaptation if we have incomplete or fuzzy accounts of the culture that is being adapted.[7]

WHAT A THEORY OF CULTURE MUST EXPLAIN

Implicit in what I have been saying is an assumption that what we refer to as languages and cultures are the same order of phenomena. A language is appropriately seen as one kind of cultural tradition, just as a cuisine, a body of religious dogma and ritual, or prescriptions for social arrangements are. Both method and theory relating to language and other kinds of cultural tradition, while differing in specifics from one tradition to another, are productively to be regarded as basically similar (Goodenough 1981). What we learn about language can be useful in helping to think about culture. Just as a theory of language rests on what we learn about specific languages, a theory of culture rests on what we learn about specific cultures.

We have traditionally thought of a language as being shared by its speakers and a culture as being shared by a group's members. We know, however, that much is not shared (Wallace 1970:22-36, Keesing 1976:138-145). Even what people do seem to share is not understood in exactly the same way in all respects by any two individuals. It is not, in Wallace's terms, a "replication of uniformity." Each individual's understanding of the language of his or her speech community differs somewhat from that of every other member of the speech community. Each person has his or her idiolect (or personal speech pattern). The same is true of people's understanding of what they consider to be the customary practices, values, and beliefs—the culture—of the groups in which they function as members. Even when there seems to be a high degree of consensus, close scrutiny reveals individual differences.

A theory of both language and culture must account for what individuals know and how they come to know it. It must also account for the processes that work toward an appearance of consensus in what people know—that give rise to what can be seen as a group's language and culture—and it must account for the processes that work against such consensus. Such theory should help account for how languages and cultures change over time (see e.g. Goodenough 1981). It must be concerned not only with learning at the individual level of emotional and cognitive development. It must also be concerned with what goes on in social interaction: imitation, play, behavioral conditioning, and, above all, communication in its verbal, nonverbal, and subliminal forms. And a theory of language and culture must be informed by what is known about psychological and social interactive processes and, importantly, how these processes affect one another. So informed, it can serve as a stimulus to the study of these processes in ways that will contribute even more to cultural, social, and behavioral theory.

SOCIAL GROUPS AND ACTIVITIES IN A THEORY OF CULTURE

A major mistake in what has been the common anthropological view of both culture and language is that they pertain to a community or society as a whole. It is important to stress that it is more productive to think of a community as having a cultural and linguistic makeup, rather than a uniform culture and language (Goodenough 1981:26, 102-111). A community carries among its members a number of different traditions, each with its own history. Some of these traditions, such as that for public decorum, are widely known within the community. Others, like those involving technical expertise, are not. Some are widely known in general but vary in specifics from subgroup to subgroup within the community. Some of these differences are conspicuous and function as badges of subgroup identity. People may pay no attention to or even be unaware of other such differences. What there is to be known is one thing. Who knows it, who is eligible to know it, and the circumstances under which knowledge can appropriately be put to use are also important considerations.

I have found it theoretically helpful to think of both culture and language as rooted in human activities (rather than in societies) and as pertaining to groups insofar as they consist of people who engage with one another in the context of those activities (Goodenough 1981:102-103). People who interact with one another regularly in a given kind of activity need to share sufficient understanding of how to do it and communicate with one another in doing it so that they can work together to their satisfaction.[8] All they need to share, in fact, is whatever will enable them to do that. If some people always perform in one kind of role and others always perform in another, it may facilitate the conduct of activity if they do not have the same understanding of it (see Wallace 1970:27-28). There is a different culture of the activity for each set of role performers. These differences form a part of the cultural makeup of the overall group of people who perform the activity, but there is no one culture of that activity for the group as a whole, one that all its members share.

From this point of view, the problem of studying culture in complex societies (as against simple ones) disappears. In small, relatively isolated communities, everyone has dealings with almost everyone else in most kinds of activity and in relation to nearly every kind of subject matter. Sharing will be extensive but, even here, by no means complete. In complex societies, individuals deal with different sets of people in the various activities in which they engage, and no one is involved in all activities. Yet they have their understandings of how to conduct the activities in which they participate and with which they judge the adequacy of the performances of their fellow participants. They have, that is, their cultures for those activities. There is much diffusion of cultural understanding across activities and from one activity to another. The result is that what is understood about the conduct of one activity may apply to the conduct of many others, but is unlikely to apply to all.

Cultural description in complex societies—and, indeed, in relatively simple ones, as well—is, in my experience, greatly facilitated by focusing on activities and on the individuals and groups, whether ad hoc or standing, that perform them. There is, I think, no question but that in practice field researchers have tended to focus on activities as the contexts for much gathering of data, but our practice in this regard has not informed our theorizing as well as it could.

The cultural makeup of a society is thus to be seen not as a monolithic entity determining the behavior of its members, but as a melange of understandings and expectations regarding a variety of activities that serve as guides to their conduct and interpretation. The content of these understandings keeps changing over time as the frequency and contexts of interaction change. Frequent performance of an activity promotes greater sharing of understandings among its participants over time. Discontinuity of personnel and infrequent performance both militate against shared understanding. People responsible for a rarely performed activity have to sit down and negotiate among themselves their understanding of how it is properly to be done.

From this perspective, a theory of culture must try to explain how (1) frequency of interaction, (2) continuity of people, and (3) motivation of people to participate help to promote (or inhibit) the development of shared understandings about an activity—about its reasons and occasions for, and its modes of conduct. It is this set of shared understandings that constitute, for these people, their culture for that activity.

As Geertz (1973:10–13) has stressed, a culture arises and is maintained in the course of human interaction. But a theory of culture gets into trouble if it sees a culture as having an existence apart from the individual people whose interactions give rise to it. It is natural for people to see their culture as having such a separate existence. They feel constrained by the expectations of others. It is not surprising, therefore, that we anthropologists have done what comes naturally to us as humans and have thought of cultures that way, too. But theory requires the contrary view, namely that a culture (and language) exists as an aggregate of the somewhat different individual understandings that each participant attributes to the group. A culture is an aggregate of individual understandings that each individual attributes to the group along with the affective associations each individual has with those understandings. A theory of culture must, therefore, address the processes that reduce (or increase) the differences among individuals in their respective understandings and affective associations.

In a way, linguistic and cultural communities are analogous to biological species (Goodenough 1981). Each species is at any point in time an aggregate of genotypically and phenotypically diverse individuals that can mate productively with one another. Each human community is, similarly, an aggregate of individuals who are diverse in idiolect and personal understanding of their group culture (analogous to genotype) as well as in manifested habits and styles of behavior (analogous to phenotype). But in neither case is the diversity so great that people cannot interact with one another productively in the activities through which they accomplish their personal and collective purposes. Just as biologically selective processes affect the kind and degree of variance within a species that will allow it to continue as such, so social and psychological selective processes limit the kind and degree of variance in idiolect and in personal understanding of social expectations that allow a human community or society to continue as such and to have a group culture. Such a view of the relation of language and culture to society provides productive possibilities for examining the processes by which human communities come into being, are maintained while changing through time and, ultimately, disintegrate.

THE SPECIAL PLACE OF LANGUAGE IN CULTURE

We carry in our bodies subjective records of experience—as in memory and recall. We have subjective understandings that we speak of as a "feel" for how things work. But what we can do with these records and understandings in their subjective form is limited. With language, people have a means of mapping the subjective record into overt behavioral forms, and thereby they make their experience an object to themselves and to others. They make it public. The mapping is not one-to-one, and people's use of language affects, in turn, how they make and maintain their subjective records. But language allows them to compare records and to establish a sharable or group record. The group or public record cannot be a subjective one, subjectivity being in individuals. The public record consists of what people have said about their experiences (not what they have individually experienced or how they individually interpret what has been said).

The advantage of such objectified records and understandings is that they can be added

to and revised. They allow people to expand their phenomenal world vicariously. We can imagine things, review possibilities for the future, and consider alternative courses of action. We can air and discuss differences in our expectations of one another and in our understandings of how things work. And we can resolve those differences so that whatever remains of them does not get in our way.

Other processes, such as imitation, play crucial roles in reducing individual differences in behavior. But verbal communication is crucial in reducing individual differences in experience by making vicarious experience possible. And it is crucial in reducing variance in individual understandings, making possible the intellectual traditions that are so important in human life.[9]

DESCRIBING A SOCIETY'S CULTURAL MAKEUP

The comprehensive description of a society's cultural makeup requires giving an account of what one needs to know to perform acceptably in every kind of activity its members engage in—ranging from the things that everyone in the society is expected to know to the things that only specialists know. The ethnographic product would be a cultural encyclopedia of the society.

Because one must learn, at least vicariously, what one is going to describe, such comprehensive description is beyond the capabilities of any one individual. Ethnography requires collaborative and cumulative research. A lone anthropologist spending a year or two in the field, even with a good working knowledge of the local language, cannot hope to do what no individual member of the society being studied does in a lifetime.

At best, field research allows one to learn the things that everyone is expected to know and, perhaps, some of the more specialized bodies of knowledge. Simply focusing on what every responsible man and woman in the community is expected to know is a formidable task, especially in simpler societies where people are not confined to participation in only a few of its activities.

It is often valuable to concentrate on a single complex of interrelated activities, such as farming. Manolescu (1987) provides an instructive example. She undertook to describe how a community of Schwenkfelder dairy farmers in a valley in Pennsylvania actually farmed, focusing on their criteria for doing what they did and for judging good from poor farm practice. She began by working for one of the farmers as his helper for over a year. In this way she learned, through her own active participation with him, all of the operations as he performed them—in every one of the pertinent activities—and, in the context of actual performance, the reasons he gave for doing them the way he did. On the basis of what she learned, she was then able to construct a schedule of critical topics for observation and interview to be used with each of the other farmers in the community. The results allowed her to discern several different approaches to dairy farming among them—their selection of one or another seeming to represent differences in their value orientations toward farming and motivations for doing it.[10]

I mention her study, because it illustrates an important point about the strategy of cultural learning. If Manolescu had constructed a questionnaire survey based on a priori assumptions about dairy farming, she would not have learned much about the culture of dairy farming and its subcultural variations in that community. It was more important for her to work with one person as her teacher. Afterward, being perceived by the other farmers in the community as personally knowledgeable about dairy farming, she was able to have highly productive interview and observation periods with almost every one of them, including access, with due regard to confidentiality, to their records of earnings and expense.

This is, of course, the way cultural learning takes place generally. People grow up learning from a small number of people—from parents and siblings about some things, a few other persons about others. The more knowledgeable about the subject one's teacher is judged by others to be, the better one's learning opportunity. Having learned to a point where they can interact with others in the context of the subject matter, people discover inadequacies in their understandings and find, also, that not everyone does things in the same way. Manolescu was using the natural process of cultural learning in a self-conscious and systematic way in her ethnographic study.

The development of good ethnographic data bases depends on cultural learning by the investigator. If there are things to be counted, one needs to know what it is meaningful to count. When I mapped the land plots and took inventory of holdings on them in Romonum, Chuuk, in 1947, it was the locally known and named plots that I mapped. It would have been a waste of effort to make an arbitrary grid of the island and then collect data on who owned what in each square of the grid. Surveys are especially vulnerable to this problem. A survey made before one knows what are the culturally relevant matters to be sampled is likely to have little ethnographic value. Surveys need to be based on a good prior understanding of the local cultural makeup of the activities and groups being studied.

In the course of learning their culture, people have a few experiences of something and then come to a conclusion about how it works. They put their conclusion to empirical test by acting on it in the course of daily life. Subsequent experiences are (or are not) consistent with it. As consistent experiences accumulate, people get increasing confirmation of their conclusion. Inconsistent experiences are critical here. They call one's conclusions into question and lead to revised understandings of how things work. Such, too, is the process by which an ethnographer learns the cultural traditions of the people he or she studies. Early conclusions that are disconfirmed are followed by increasingly cumulative confirmations of revised conclusions, though even here there is always the lurking possibility that some further revision will be necessary.[11]

In doing ethnography, one does not always wait for a host of instances to accumulate in the normal course of living. Doing ethnography requires that we work with locally knowledgeable people to accumulate, as exhaustively as possible, records of cases—both real and hypothetical—from which to derive the patterns that inform our understanding. Our records of this kind stand as enduring data bases for future analysis (and reanalysis). One thinks in this regard of the rich data bases on which many of our best ethnographic works rest (e.g., Conklin 1957, 1980; Firth 1936; Kelly 1977; Netting 1968; Pospisil 1963).

Focusing on activities is a productive route to cultural learning. One makes, cumulatively, a record of all the different kinds of activities in which people engage, individually and in groups. (Long ago Malinowski, 1944, presented a useful outline of the underlying structure of what he called an "institution," an outline that fits the structure of activities, whether they are institutionalized or not.)[12]

In this regard, data as to how different modes of personnel organization and the structuring of management and authority are distributed across activities are important for the study of social organization. They free kinship, for example, from the relatively sterile consideration of a few abstract principles, such as descent, to an account of how organizing principles work in practice. One cannot consider what are understood to be appropriate times, places, and occasions for the conduct of activities without getting into the way they are scheduled in relation to one another and in relation to such considerations as seasons, conflict, illness, and the other contingencies of human existence. Such knowledge regarding activities is also crucial for the study of change,

and it is especially so for the design of programs for planned change and the monitoring of their progress.

THE END PRODUCTS OF ETHNOGRAPHY

Given an approach to ethnography like that outlined above, what are its end products? Are we any closer to knowing what is the culture of the people we study as they understand it, or are we still trapped in our own imperfect constructions of it?

In answer to the latter question, let me repeat that a "people's culture as they understand it" consists of the aggregate of different individual understandings of the expectations of others. Each individual projects his or her understanding on the group of which he or she is a participant or observer. For that individual all the group's members are assumed, for practical purposes, to have as their collective property what is thus attributed to them. People deal with one another on the assumption that groups share the understandings they attribute to them, on the assumption that there really are collective understandings and representations.

This assumption serves our social needs. As long as the differences in individual understandings are small enough or complement one another in ways that do not interfere with productive social interaction, the assumption works.[13] From this perspective, the best an anthropologist can do is the best every other human can do: arrive at his or her own understanding of the expectations of the set of others being studied and attribute it to them as a group.

What is important for us to achieve is an understanding such that members of the group studied accept what we manifest of our attributions to them as falling within the acceptable range of variance among their own manifestations of their own understandings. If it meets this criterion, an ethnographer's understanding is a *valid* specimen of the aggregate of understandings comprising the group's culture in the same way that a grammar and dictionary of a language aims at being a valid specimen.

In this regard, let us consider again Manolescu's study of dairy farming in a Schwenkfelder community. Suppose that after learning how to do dairy farming from the farmer for whom she initially worked for over a year, she had then written an account of what she had learned and presented it as the culture of dairy farming in that community. She might thus have produced a specimen of the culture that would have been more valid for one of its subcultures than for the cultural aggregate of the whole community, but one that would still have been in the ballpark of acceptability. By going on, as she did, to interview and observe the other farmers in the community, she was able to develop her understanding of variant ways of farming. Thus she was able to present an account of different subcultures of farming within the community.

Much ethnography is, of course, of the kind that Manolescu would have produced if she had stopped her research after working intensively with the one farmer. As such, an ethnography may be less than adequate for some purposes and very adequate for others. Its utility depends on what it is to be used for. If I want to compare how kin relations are organized in Chuuk with how they are organized in the Trobriand Islands, one good ethnographic specimen of such organization from each place can give a fair picture of how the two places differ culturally and can serve to raise all kinds of questions for further research. But I must have specimens from a number of localities in Chuuk to see the range of variation there. What we now know of culture in Chuuk is very informative for cross-societal studies in Micronesia, the Pacific, and the world generally, but it is still far from an adequate picture of the cultural composition of Chuuk as a whole.

From this perspective, we can see ethnography progressing from the collection of what we hope are reasonably good single specimens of the cultural composition of the world's many culture-bearing groups to getting several specimens for each group and, through time, increasingly more sophisticated specimens. Thus we gradually obtain a picture of a society's cultural makeup, showing what people know and don't know, what they argue about and disagree on. To develop knowledge of the cultural makeup of even a representative sample of the world's societies is a long-range, cumulative, and necessarily cooperative undertaking.

There is a much repeated canard about the practice of cultural anthropology to the effect that anthropologists jealously guard their particular research turfs from other anthropologists and thus protect themselves from having their ethnographic reports challenged. There are some known cases of this. In anthropology's earlier days, there was good reason to cast a wide net and avoid duplication of cultural specimen collecting. There was so much to be done—so much of interest seemed to be disappearing under colonialism and under the effects of the newly emerged industrial societies.

From the beginning, however, and increasingly since World War II, there have been growing numbers of societies to which different anthropologists have returned again and again to follow up and expand on earlier work, to study hitherto neglected topics, and to chronicle change.[14] There is by now what can be considered a field of Zuni studies, Hopi studies, Navaho studies, Mayan studies, Hawaiian studies, Maori studies. For Pohnpei, Chuuk, Belau, and Yap in Micronesia there is, for each, a growing body of ethnographies, beginning with the work of the German ethnographers early in this century and continuing actively to the present with studies by American and Japanese ethnographers (as well as by other social scientists). Not only has this work expanded upon subject matters already covered previously, it has cumulatively revised and enlarged our understanding of the complicated cultural makeup of each of these island communities. We also now have respectable grammars and dictionaries of all the languages spoken in Micronesia; and they are in the course of being upgraded by further research. Similar developments are beginning to take place in ethnographic study in Melanesia, where they have been understandably slowed by the greater number of cultural communities to be studied.

The Association for Social Anthropology in Oceania self-consciously conducts its annual meetings in a way that successfully emphasizes ethnography as a cooperative endeavor. Its members contribute to an expanding pool of knowledge and constructively evaluate one another's work with the object of upgrading the quality of future contributions.

I conclude, then, with the assertion that ethnography is not in the crisis that some postmodernists attribute to it. As conducted in at least some parts of the world, it is alive and well and shows every sign of continuing to develop as both a scientific and humanistic endeavor. As more cooperative and more systematic research continues to be done, we shall find ourselves increasingly able to refine our theory of culture, taking fuller account of the cognitive, emotional, and interactive processes in individuals and groups from which cultures arise.

NOTES

1. Significantly, there is now a renewed interest in Sapir's thinking. My own way of looking at culture, like Sapir's, has derived from some exposure to linguistics and social psychology. When I undertook the task of writing a book about social and cultural change, especially planned change, I found it essential to focus not on society and culture but on people pursuing their interests as they understood them, abandoning them when it suited them in some instances and clinging compulsively to them in others (Goodenough 1963). I was struck by how much the record of development showed that, even with the great power and resources

they often had for trying to effect change, planners could in the end be no more than proponents of change. They could greatly disturb things as they were, but the people for whom they planned controlled much of the outcome, if only by sitting on their hands. It was evident that a theory of the processes affecting social and cultural change and stability over time must focus on people.

2. Whatever the nature of these differences, they cannot be explained in biological terms. A child from anywhere in the world that is reared in another part of the world grows up speaking and acting in ways that conform with how things are said and done where he or she was reared. Anthropologists have necessarily concluded that observed differences in language and custom are socially learned. There are biological factors that enable and constrain the possibilities for speech and other forms of behavior, but within those constraints, differences in speech and behavior from one group to another are a product of historical contingencies.

3. Our efforts to explain their apparent similarities and differences across human groups are similarly constrained. Description of what characterizes human groups linguistically and culturally is the foundation on which both the scientific and humanistic studies of language and culture rest.

4. That this is so is not obviated by our often having problems applying these criteria, given the way much research is conducted. Nor is it obviated by widespread misunderstanding of how these criteria may be—and, informally, often are—employed as a part of the process of field research.

5. The term "emic" was generalized to describing all meaningful behavior, by Pike (1954), in an analogy with what was called a "phonemic" description in linguistics—an account of the categories of sound of which one needed to be aware in order to distinguish between meaningfully different utterances in a given language (see Sapir 1925).

6. The importance of aiming at description that will do this was impressed on me during my doctoral research in Chuuk (Truk) in 1947 (Goodenough 1951). I was seeking information on traditional ways of managing land tenure. I was also aware that what I had to report might serve as a basis for helping American administrators deal with property disputes that came before them for resolution. When I asked myself what I would need to know if I were in such a position, it was immediately obvious that I would have to know how to conduct the equivalent of what we call a "search of title" in that tenure system. I had, therefore, to learn and describe what were the different kinds of transactions that could

be made and what were the consequent rights, duties, privileges, and powers of the parties to them. I was amazed to find that anthropologists had not described property systems in nonliterate societies in that way before. There were no emic accounts of the culture of property in the anthropological literature.

7. Methods for gathering and analyzing data relating to population, physical environment, disease, objects of emotional concern, and the like are matters to which disciplines other than anthropology primarily address themselves. Culture remains the peculiar concern of anthropology. Method and theory relating to it, even though challenging to develop, must have top priority for anthropologists.

8. Chapple and Coon (1942) referred to a society's standing groups whose members regularly engage together in recurring activities as "institutions" in a systems analysis approach to culture and society that is not unlike one that I have found useful. I center it more comprehensively on activities rather than on standing groups, however.

9. The processes by which people learn to meet one another's expectations of behavior and to achieve the appearance of common understandings and bodies of knowledge about how the world works are necessarily the same processes by which we, as anthropologists, can learn to meet the expectations of the people we study and then describe what we think we have learned. We cannot transcend our human nature in this. But we can use these processes self-consciously and systematically. We can devise strategies and tactics from them, develop them into a methodology for empirical ethnographic research, and thereby greatly enhance the richness and replicability of the ethnographic records we create in pursuit of our scientific and humanistic goals.

10. Interestingly, hers stands as apparently the only study of how any community of farmers actually farms that has been done in the United States.

11. People do not ordinarily go out of their way to look for disconfirmations of their understandings. They are content to go along with what they think they know until forced to modify it. By contrast, ethnographic method, like scientific method generally, requires searching for disconfirmations and welcoming them as providing opportunities for better understanding. To do this requires systematic data gathering.

All insights are perceptions of patterns. Insights that lead to cultural understandings come from perceptions of patterns in how two or more kinds of significant things are appropriately (or inappropriately) distributed with regard to one another. We may derive these insights haphazardly in the way most people acquire their cultural knowledge, or we may use distributive analysis systematically to this end. Such analysis is the method by which linguists formulate the principles governing a language's phonology and grammar. Ethnographers are less consistent in their use of it, but I have found it very productive.

In studying customs relating to property in Chuuk, for example, I was dealing with different culturally recognized objects of value, such as space, soil, trees, gardens, canoes, houses, and ceremonial bowls. There were different kinds of entitlements people could have in them. These entitlements resulted from the different kinds of transactions Chuuk's people could engage in. And there were different social entities, individuals and groups, that could be party to these transactions. Distribution analysis showed that the same kind of entitlement involved different rights and duties depending on whether the objects were classed as productive of food or not. All kinds of objects could be subjected to some transactions but only some to others. And so it went. By systematically seeing how kinds of transactions, their resulting rights and duties, kinds of entitlement, kinds of objects, and kinds of social entity could and could not be mutually associated, I developed my understanding of the workings of property in Chuuk.

12. I need not repeat here my elaboration in relation to activities of Malinowski's formulation (Goodenough 1963:322-337). Suffice it to say that every activity has public justification for being undertaken (Malinowski's "charter"), unless, as in stealing, it is publicly disapproved. (In the latter event, of course, it has a private justification.) Analysis of how public justifications distribute over different activities, and of the priorities (and their justification) given to competing activities, can provide evidence of public values. Analysis of how strategies, techniques, and resources for getting things done distribute over activities is evidence of a society's overall technological organization.

13. Human existence as we know it is based on our making this assumption and our having the motives to learn from one another in order to make the assumption work much of the time, especially in those matters where it is most crucial for it to do so.

14. On the little island of Romonum in Chuuk, for example, four anthropologists and a linguist worked as a team in 1947. Within the next few years two more anthropologists had done work there, and one of the original team had returned in 1965. At least seven others have worked in other localities in Chuuk's lagoon in the years since 1947, including two students of one member of that year's team.

INTELLECTUAL ROOTS

Ward H. Goodenough is Emeritus University Professor of Anthropology at the University of Pennsylvania, where he has served on the faculty since 1949. His books are *Property, Kin, and Community on Truk* (1951), *Cooperation in Change* (1963), *Description and Comparison in Cultural Anthropology* (1970), *Culture, Language, and Society* (1971, 1981), *Trukese-English Dictionary* (with Hiroshi Sugita, 1980, supplementary volume 1990), and the edited volume *Explorations in Cultural Anthropology* (1964). He was editor of the *American Anthropologist* (1966-1970), president of the American Ethnological Society (1962), and President of the Society for Applied Anthropology (1963), and on the board of directors of the American Association for the Advancement of Science (1972-1975). He is a member of the National Academy of Sciences, the American Philosophical Society, and the American Academy of Arts and Sciences.

Up to my senior year at Cornell University, my studies were in Old Icelandic and the Icelandic saga literature, Germanic languages, Latin and Greek, and history. I turned to the social and behavioral sciences in my senior year, taking a course in cultural anthropology from Lauriston Sharp and in personality theory from Leonard S. Cotrell.

From Cotrell's course, I learned that our sense of self—cognitively, kinesthetically, and affectively—emerges from our experience of ourselves as objects in interaction with our environment, most importantly other people. It emerges, that is, out of the transactions that take place in "self-other" relationships. From Sharp, I learned that what anthropologists call culture is learned, not transmitted biologically. It, too, emerges from and is sustained by the transactions that take place in "self-other" relationships. Culture and an individual's sense of self, I saw, were in some way products of the same processes. It was also evident to me that while theory was able to say something about the processes by which a sense of self and culture come into being, we were still without any good procedures for describing the *content* of either one. Here was a challenge.

In my first year of graduate study at Yale, I took courses with Bronislaw Malinowski, John Dollard, Irving Rouse, Clellan Ford, George P. Murdock, and Wendell Bennett, and worked under Murdock on the Cross-Cultural Survey. I got a good exposure to Malinowski's ideas and to the ways that behavioristic psychology and psychoanalytic theory might be applicable to anthropology's holistic approach to the study of human nature and human phenomena. That year, also, I had a course in phonetics and phonemics from George Trager. This course was an inspiration to me in that it seemed to offer an answer to the question that had emerged from my studies the year before at Cornell: how to get at the content of culture and of what is learned in the course of social interaction. I saw that linguists had developed fairly rigorous procedures for arriving at testable hypotheses about the content of what people had learned and knew subjectively in regard to the language they spoke. It seemed to me that if we could put the linguists' approach to content together with the social and behavioral psychologists' to process, we had the possibility of creating a productive theory of culture and also making a significant contribution to the science of human behavior. I have been at work chipping away at trying to realize this possibility ever since.

In World War II, I was for three years with the field staff of the Research Branch of the Army's Information and Education Division. There I got a grounding in the methods of attitude and opinion research and learned Guttman scaling. (My first scientific publication in 1944 was on a technique for doing such scaling.)

When I returned to Yale, I had a rewarding apprenticeship with Murdock as his research assistant when he was writing *Social Structure*. Ralph Linton, then also at Yale, had considerable influence on my thinking as well, stimulating me to try to put together his formulation of "status" and "role" with what I had learned about Guttman scale analysis. His work with Kardiner on "culture and personality" added to my growing interest in the role of culture in the interactive processes leading to the construction of a sense of self. I was fortunately able to continue to develop my thinking on these matters after joining the faculty at the University of Pennsylvania in 1949, where I learned much from A. I. Hallowell and Anthony Wallace. My wife, Ruth Gallagher Goodenough, herself trained in social psychology, has also been an important continuing influence in my work. Pervasively influential has been my father, Erwin R. Goodenough, a noted historian of religion, who contributed greatly to theory and method in the study of religious symbols in his *Jewish Symbols in the Greco-Roman Period.*

In my forty years at Penn, I have continued to work at how to describe the content of culture and at how we are to understand the human processes from which culture emerges and which affect its content in the course of time. In this, my methodological approach, following the example of linguistics, has been to develop data bases of specific cases sufficient to reveal patterns in events and to suggest the criteria with which people in specific groups appear to judge whether or not behavior is acceptable and appropriate. My theoretical approach has been that human behavior is largely aimed at accomplishing purposes, taking care of wants and needs, not only in regard to physical survival but also to social relationships and, perhaps most important of all, to emotional well-being. My primary concern has been to contribute to our understanding of how particular human groups work as expectation-governed systems, whether the expectations involve speech or other kinds of activity. It has been my premise that the better we understand how such systems work, each in their own terms, the better we shall be able to understand what is common to or underlies all such systems and thereby what it means to be human. In all of this, I have, of course, been far from alone and owe much to more people than there is space to mention here.

19

Language, Anthropology, and Cognitive Science[*][1]

MAURICE BLOCH

COGNITIVE SCIENCE AND CULTURE

Cognitive science is usually described as the attempt to bring cognitive psychology, philosophy, neurophysiology, artificial intelligence, linguistics, and anthropology together in order to understand cognition. In this alliance anthropology is, in fact, a rather shadowy partner. Only cognitive anthropology is usually taken into account by cognitive scientists and, even then, only the further reaches of cognitive anthropology which many anthropologists, especially European anthropologists, would fail to recognize as their business at all. This state of affairs is unfortunate, because some of the theories emerging in cognitive science are *central* to the concerns of anthropology, whether social or cultural, and should lead anthropologists to reexamine many of the premises of their work.

Cultural anthropologists study culture. This can be defined as that which needs to be known in order to operate reasonably effectively in a specific human environment.[2] Social anthropologists traditionally study social organization and the behavior by means of which people relate to each other. Both cultural and social anthropologists, however, are well aware that the distinction between the two branches of the discipline is not absolute. Cultural anthropologists know that they cannot get at culture directly, but only through the observation of communicative activity, verbal or otherwise, natural or artificially simulated. Social anthropologists are aware that they cannot understand action, verbal or otherwise, if they do not construct, probably in imagination, a representation of the culture of the people they study, since this is the only way to make sense of their activities (Winch 1958).

Some concept of culture is therefore essential to all social and cultural anthropologists. However, a further assumption of anthropology, sometimes stated and sometimes unstated, is that this culture is inseparably linked to language, on the grounds either that culture is thought and transmitted as a text through language, or that culture is ultimately "language-like," consisting of linked linear propositions. It is these two assumptions about culture that I want to challenge here.

If culture is the whole or a part of what people must know in a particular social environment in order to operate efficiently, it follows first, that people must have acquired this knowledge, either through the development of innate potentials, or from external sources, or from a combination of both, and secondly that this acquired knowledge is being continually stored in a manner that makes it relatively easily accessible when necessary.[3] These obvious inferences have in turn a further implication which is that anthropologists'

---

[*]Reprinted, in edited form, from *Man* 1991 (26:183–198).

concerns place them right in the middle of the cognitive sciences, whether they like it or not, since it is cognitive scientists who have something to say about learning, memory, and retrieval. Anthropologists cannot, therefore, avoid the attempt to make their theories about social life *compatible* with what other cognitive scientists have to say about the processes of learning and storage.

CONCEPT FORMATION

All classificatory concepts are at least partially learned, and recent work in this area has brought about certain fundamental changes in the way we envisage the process. The old idea that the child learns classificatory concepts as minimal and necessary definitions, an idea taken for granted in most of anthropology and which was more particularly implied in structuralism and ethnoscience, was shown to be untenable some time ago (Fillmore 1975; Rosch 1977, 1978a; E. E. Smith 1988). The more generally accepted position now is that such concepts are formed through reference back to rather vague and provisional "prototypes" which anchor loosely formed "families" of specific instances. For example, the concept of a house is not a list of essential features (roof, door, walls, and so on) which have to be checked off before deciding whether or not the thing is a house. If that were so we would have no idea that a house which has lost its roof is still a house. It is rather that we consider something as "a house" by comparing it to a loosely associated group of "houselike" features, no one of which is essential, but which are linked by a general idea of what a typical house is.

It seems that the mental form of classificatory concepts, essential building blocks of culture, involves loose and implicit practical-cum-theoretical pattern networks of knowledge, based on the experience of physical instances sometimes called "best exemplars" (Smith, Sera, and Gattuso 1988:372). A significant aspect of looking at classificatory concepts in this way is that it makes them isomorphic with what are known as "scripts" and "schemata," although these latter may be on a much larger and more elaborate scale. These "scripts" and "schemata" are, in effect, chunked networks of loose procedures and understandings which enable us to deal with standard and recurring situations, for example "getting the breakfast ready," that are clearly culturally created (Abelson 1981; Holland and Quinn 1987; D'Andrade 1990).[4]

If classificatory concepts such as "scripts" and "schemata" are not like dictionary entries, but are instead small networks of typical understandings and practices concerning the world, then the question of their relation to words becomes more problematic than it was with the old "checklist of necessary and sufficient conditions" view. That there is no inevitable connection between concepts and words is shown by the now well-established fact that concepts can and do exist independently of language. This is made clear in the many examples of conceptual thinking in prelinguistic children, first presented by Roger Brown (1973). Children have the concept "house" before they can say the word. We also have studies which show that the acquisition of lexical semantics by children is very largely a matter of trying to match words to already formed concepts. This is the so-called "concept first" theory. Contrary to earlier views in cognitive anthropology (Tyler 1969), therefore, language is not essential for conceptual thought.[5] It is possible to go beyond this initial distancing between the lexicon and mental concepts, however, thanks to work on semantic acquisition by Bowerman (1977). This demonstrates a continual back and forth movement between aspects of classification which are introduced through language and mental concepts, as the child learns to express these concepts through words. This dialectical movement is not only interesting in itself but also suggests a much more general process, to which I shall return, by which originally nonlinguistic knowledge is partly transformed as it becomes linguistic, thereby taking on a form which much more closely resembles what structuralists, among other anthropologists, had assumed to characterize the organization of all human knowledge (Keil and Batterman 1984).

This brief review of concept formation enables us to reach the following provisional conclusions: (1) that much of knowledge is fundamentally nonlinguistic; (2) that concepts involve implicit networks of meanings which are formed through the experience of and practice in, the external world; and (3) that, under certain circumstances, this nonlinguistic knowledge can be rendered into language and thus take the form of explicit discourse, but changing its character in the process.

SOME IMPLICATIONS OF HOW WE LEARN SKILLS AND DEVELOP EXPERTISE

Another area of joint concern to anthropology and cognitive psychology also reveals the importance of nonlinguistic knowledge. This is the study of the way we learn practical, everyday tasks. It is clear that we do not usually go through a point-by-point explanation of the process when we teach our children how to negotiate their way around the house or to close doors. Much culturally transmitted knowledge seems to be passed on in ways unknown to us. Perhaps in highly schooled societies this fact is misleadingly obscured by the prominence of explicit instruction, but in nonindustrialized societies most of what takes people's time and energy—including such practices as how to wash both the body and clothes, how to cook, how to cultivate, etc.— are learned very gradually through imitation and tentative participation.

The cultural specificity, complexity, and embeddedness of such tasks, and their character as not linguistically explicit, have been commented upon by anthropologists, for

example by Mauss (1936), Leroi-Gourhan, (1943) and Haudricourt (1968). In several cases anthropologists have noted that language seems to play a surprisingly small role in the transmission of knowledge. Borofsky (1987), for example, stresses this point in his analysis of knowledge transmission on the Polynesian atoll of Pukapuka. Whether one is learning specific techniques or generalized skills, knowledge transmission tends to occur in the context of everyday activities through observation and "hands-on" practice. There is a minimum of direct, verbal instruction. Similarly, Lave, in her study of Liberian tailors, notes that what she calls "apprenticeship learning," which relies on the "assumptions that knowing, thinking, and understanding are generated in practice" (Lave 1988, 1990:310), is more effective than formal teaching based on linguistic, Socratic forms.

The significance of such findings is much more important than we might at first suppose. This is because the fact that the transmission of knowledge for general Polynesian activities or for West African tailoring is largely nonlinguistic may have less to do with the culture of education in such places than with a general feature of the kind of knowledge that underlies the performance of complex practical tasks, which *requires* that it be nonlinguistic.

That this is so is suggested by various studies of learning in which, by contrast to the examples just mentioned, the original teaching is received through language, or at least in propositional form, but in which the process of becoming an expert seems to involve the transformation of the propositions of the teacher into fundamentally nonlinguistic knowledge (Dreyfus and Dreyfus 1986:chap. 1).[6] Thus J. R. Anderson (1983) points out how people who are taught driving through a series of propositions have to transform this knowledge into nonlinguistic, integrated procedures before the task can be effected rapidly, efficiently, and automatically—one might say properly. Only when they do not think about what they are doing in words are drivers truly experts. Probably some teaching needs to be done verbally, but there are also advantages in the nonlinguistic transmission of practical skills typical of nonindustrial societies since such transmission bypasses the double transformation from implicit to linguistically explicit knowledge made by the teacher and from linguistically explicit to implicit knowledge made by the learner.

Why should this be so? In order to begin to answer this question we need to turn to the process involved in becoming an expert. It is not surprising that practice in performing a complex task makes the practitioner more efficient, but studies of expertise show that the increase in efficiency is more puzzling than might at first appear. For example, when people are repeatedly asked to read a page of text upside down they gradually do this faster and faster, but the increase in speed is not continuous, nor does it go on forever. At first there is a rapid increase in efficiency which continues for a while, then it begins to slow down, until eventually there is no further increase. The shape of the curve of increased efficiency suggests (Johnson-Laird 1988:170, citing Newell and Rosenbloom 1981) that the process of learning involves the construction of a cognitive apparatus dedicated to cope with this sort of task. The establishment of that apparatus is slow, and while it is in construction there is significant improvement; however, once it has been set up no further improvement becomes possible. A chunk or apparatus concerned with a familiar activity has thus come into existence in the brain as a result of repeated practice (Simon 1979: 386ff.).

A more complex and much discussed example of what happens when someone becomes an expert comes from studies of master chess players. It has been convincingly argued that expert chess players do not differ from novices (who are not complete beginners) in knowing the rules of chess or in performing such motor tasks as moving one piece without knocking the others down. What seems to distinguish the expert from the novice is not so much an ability to handle complex strategic logico-mathematical rules, but rather the possession, in memory, of an amazingly comprehensive and organized store of total or partial chessboard configurations, which allows the expert to recognize the situation *in an instant* so as to know what should be done next (Dreyfus and Dreyfus 1986:32–35). However, bearing in mind the example of driving, what is surely happening is that the expert is not just remembering many games but has developed through long practice a specific apparatus which *enables her to remember* many games and configurations much more easily and quickly than the non-expert. She has learned how to learn this kind of information. This would explain how the expert can cope, not only with situations which she recognizes, but also with situations which are new, so long as they fall within the domain which she has learned to cope with efficiently.

Learning to become an expert would therefore be a matter not simply of remembering many instances, but of constructing a dedicated cognitive mechanism for dealing with instances of a particular kind. Such a mechanism, because it is concerned only with a specific domain of activity, can cope with information relating to that domain of activity remarkably quickly and efficiently, whether this be information about chess-piece configurations or motorway scenarios, and even though the specific cases of chess or motorway scenarios have not been previously encountered in exactly that way (Dreyfus and Dreyfus 1986: chap. 1).

If becoming an expert does involve the creation of apparatuses dedicated to handle families of related tasks, then this is surely something which an anthropologist must bear in mind. For what she studies is precisely people coping with familiar yet ever novel situations (Hutchins 1980). It seems reasonable to assume that the construction of dedicated apparatuses for dealing expertly with certain areas of activity is going on in the process of cultural learning of all common practical tasks. Indeed some recent work suggests that learning to become an expert in familiar areas is a necessary preliminary to other types of learning and to being able to cope with the less familiar and less predictable. The reason seems to be partly neurological.

In the case of car driving, it seems that as a person becomes an expert, not only does she drive better, not only does she transform what was once linguistic propositional information into something else, she also seems to employ much less neurological potential in doing the necessary tasks (Schneider and Shiffrin 1977), thereby freeing her for other mental tasks, such as talking on a car phone. Similarly, the extraordinary feats of memory of the chess master seem to be made possible by the efficient packing of information through the use of the expert apparatus for coping with novel situations of play.

There is therefore considerable evidence that learning is not just a matter of storing received knowledge, as most anthropologists implicitly assume when they equate cultural and individual representations, but that it is a matter of constructing apparatuses for the efficient handling and packing of specific domains of knowledge and practice. Furthermore, as suggested by the case of learning to drive, evidence shows that once these apparatuses are constructed, the operations connected with these specific domains not only are nonlinguistic but also must be nonlinguistic if they are to be efficient. It follows that much of the knowledge which anthropologists study necessarily exists in people's heads in a nonlinguistic form.

Before proceeding further, an ambiguity in what has been argued so far must be removed. To say that knowledge concerned with the familiar must be nonlinguistic could mean one of two things. It could mean simply that this knowledge is not formulated in natural language. On the other hand it could mean

something much stronger. It could mean that this knowledge is in no way language-like, that it is not governed by the characteristic sentential logic of natural and computer languages. Here I adopt the stronger of the two alternatives because I believe that the studies on expertise discussed above suggest that the knowledge organized for efficiency in day-to-day practice is not only nonlinguistic, but also not language-like in that it does not take a sentential logical form. To argue this and to make my argument less negative I now turn to the admittedly controversial assumptions of what has been called "connectionism."

CONNECTIONISM AND THE CHALLENGE TO SENTENTIAL LOGIC MODELS

What is particularly interesting for anthropology in connectionism is not so much connectionism itself but the reasons why a theory like it is necessary. Simply put, a theory such as connectionism is necessary because a sentential linear model of the mind-brain, sometimes called the sentence-logic model (Churchland & Sejnowski 1989), which is broadly similar in form to the semantics of natural language, cannot account for the speed and efficiency with which we perform daily tasks and cope with familiar situations.

Connectionism is an alternative theory of thought. It suggests that we go about the whole process of thought in a quite different way from what we had previously assumed. The problem with the folk way of describing thought procedures, for example of how a decision is reached, is that we tend to see the activity as a serial process of analysis carried on along a single line by a single processor. For complex yet familiar tasks such processing would be impossibly clumsy and lengthy. Instead, connectionism suggests that we access knowledge, either from memory or as it is conceptualized from perception of the external world, through a number of processing units which work in parallel and feed in information simultaneously. It suggests, too, that the information received from these multiple parallel processors is analyzed simultaneously through already existing networks connecting the processors. Only with this multiple parallel processing could complex understandings and operations be achieved as fast as they are. Otherwise, given the conduction velocities and synaptic delays in neurons, it is a physical-cum-biological impossibility for the number of steps required by a logical-sentential model of the mind-brain to be carried out in the time within which even the simplest mental tasks are ordinarily performed. A connectionist brain, on the other hand, could (at least hypothetically) work sufficiently fast (Feldman & Ballard 1982).

It is much too early to say whether connectionism will prove to be an accurate analysis of the working of the brain and, in any case, I am not in a position to be able to evaluate its neurological validity. What matters here, above all, is that the theory offers the kind of challenge to sentential logical models which anthropology requires, and it offers the kind of answers which would cope with the situations we seek to understand.

Since much of culture consists of the performance of these familiar procedures and understandings, connectionism may explain what a great deal of culture in the mind-brain is like. It also explains why this type of culture cannot be either linguistic or language-like. Making the culture efficient requires the construction of connected domain-relevant networks, which by their very nature cannot be stored or accessed through sentential logical forms such as govern natural language. Furthermore, as the discussion of apprenticeship learning shows, it is not even necessary for this type of knowledge ever to be put into words for it to be transmitted from one member of the community to another.

Putting Knowledge into Words

To claim that much of culture is neither linguistic nor language-like does not imply that language is unimportant. Nevertheless, contrary to what anthropologists tend to assume, we should see linguistic phenomena as a *part* of culture, most of which is nonlinguistic. Instead of taking language for granted, we should see its presence as requiring explanation.

The process of putting knowledge into words must require such a transformation in the nature of knowledge that the words will then have only a distant relationship to the knowledge referred to. But the process may also involve gains in different areas, as suggested by work, cited earlier in this article, on the transformation of prototype concepts into classical concepts (concepts which can be defined by a checklist of necessary and sufficient features).

IMPLICATIONS FOR ANTHROPOLOGY

Our discussion of the ways in which knowledge is organized has fundamental implications for anthropology. The first point is that culture is probably a different kind of phenomenon from what it has previously been thought to be, with the result that our understanding of culture has remained partial and superficial. Up to now, anthropology has tried to analyze culture through folk models of thought applicable only to sentential logical knowledge which, as noted, is but a small part of all knowledge.

Then there are methodological implications. If the anthropologist is often attempting to give an account of chunked and nonsentential knowledge in a linguistic medium (writing), and she has no alternative, she must be aware that in so doing she is not reproducing the organization of the knowledge of the people she studies but is transmuting it into an entirely different logical form. To effect such a transmutation is not impossible—after all we can describe things which are not linguistic. But in the attempt to evoke such knowledge we should avoid stylistic devices which turn attempts at description into quasi-theory, as was the case with structuralism.

Such conclusions raise the question of how we are ever going to get at this connected, chunked knowledge. But here I believe anthropologists have an advantage over other cognitive scientists in that they already do have a technique advocated by Malinowski: participant observation.

Because of its long-term character, involving continuous and intimate contact with those whom we study, participant observation makes us learn the procedures which these people have themselves learned and enables us to check up on whether we are learning properly by observing our improving ability to cope in the field with daily tasks, including social tasks, as fast as our informants.

One fact we always and rightly stress when explaining how our way of going about things contrasts with that of other social or cognitive scientists is the importance we attach to the everyday and how we believe that the most important aspects of culture are embedded in the basic mental premises of action. Anthropologists are particularly aware of this because many work in foreign cultures and so the exotic-in-the-everyday cannot but be prominent. We are also reminded of the importance of everyday practical culture because we do long-term fieldwork and participate for very long periods indeed. This learning about the practical is the best thing about anthropology. Dreyfus and Dreyfus are quite right to point out that, by failing to pay attention to the way real human experts operate, cognitive scientists have attempted to create artificial intelligences along lines that ignore the very charac-

teristics of human practice, but this is not a reason for arguing, as they do, for giving up the attempt altogether. It is a reason why, in the same way as anthropologists need other cognitive scientists, these other cognitive scientists would also benefit from cooperation with anthropologists having the experience of participant observation.

NOTES

1. This chapter is a reduced and slightly revised version of a 1991 article that appeared in *Man* (26:183-198), which, in turn, was a revision of my 1990 Frazer Lecture. Readers are encouraged to refer to the *Man* article for further elaboration of the themes developed here. They are based on research financed by The Spencer Foundation. I also benefitted greatly from the hospitality of the anthropology department of Bergen University where I was able to develop some of the ideas presented here. I would also like to thank F. Cannell, C. Fuller, D. Holland, N. Quinn, and C. Strauss for helpful comments on an earlier draft. Above all I would like to thank D. Sperber for introducing me to the subject and making many useful suggestions for the improvement on the text of the lecture as it was originally delivered.

2. I do not want to imply that all members of a community need possess all cultural knowledge. Discussions of "distributed cognition" by Cicourel and others suggest that this may not be so.

3. See Sperber (1985) to find this point fully argued.

4. Holland and Quinn (1987:19) draw attention to the significance of these for our understanding of culture.

5. Work on deaf and dumb children also seems to show that advanced conceptual thought does not require language (Petitto 1987; 1988). I am grateful to L. Hirschfeld for pointing out the significance of this work for my argument.

6. Although I am relying extensively on Dreyfus and Dreyfus's characterization of expertise (1986), I do this to reach quite different conclusions.

INTELLECTUAL ROOTS

Maurice Bloch is Professor of Anthropology at the London School of Economics and Political Science, University of London. His publications include *Placing the Dead: Tombs, Ancestral Villages, and Kinship Organization in Madagascar* (1971), *Marxism and Anthropology: The History of a Relationship* (1983), *From Blessing to Violence: History and Ideology in the Circumcision Ritual of the Merina of Madagascar* (1986), *Ritual, History and Power—Selected Papers in Anthropology* (1989), and *Prey into Hunter: The Politics of Religious Experience* (1992). He has also edited *Political Language, Oratory and Traditional Society* (1975), *Marxist Analyses and Social Anthropology* (1975), *Death and Regeneration of Life* (1982), and, with J. Parry, *Money and the Morality of Exchange* (1989).

During my early years I was brought up under the contradictory influences of French catholicism and French communism. Both of these I rejected but they left me with the conviction, which I still have, that the dominated are more interesting and valuable than the dominators. This, and the influence of a French children's book: *Deradji, Fils du Desert*, by an author whose name I forgot, about the humiliation of a Muslim boy in the colonial environment, made me decide that I wanted to study the culture of those who had been colonized.

This made me turn to anthropology. As a student, first at the London School of Economics and then at Cambridge, I was taught within the British anthropological tradition which then owed most to Radcliffe-Brown and Malinowski. I was particularly influenced by Firth, Mayer, Leach, Fortes, and Tambiah. I kept reading French anthropology and became swayed by the structuralists and French Marxists.

In reality, I have learnt much more from two other sources. The first are my friends and students (many of whom became my friends). Among my colleagues the ones who seem to have had the most effect on me are A. Strathern, J. Parry, D. Sperber, and E. Terray. Among my students I can see the influence of the following on my work: J. Kahn, D. Lan, J. Carsten, R. Astuti, and F. Cannell. The second major source of my ideas and opinions are several people in the Malagasy villages where I have worked; their names would mean nothing to readers of a book such as this, but I am well aware that they have taught me much of anthropology and much more.

20

A Cognitive/Cultural Anthropology

CLAUDIA STRAUSS AND NAOMI QUINN

Meet Paula. She was born shortly after the end of World War II and grew up in the suburb of a medium-sized U.S. city. Paula's life is a rebuke to current culture theory.[1]

On the one hand, her life has not duplicated those of her parents and others in previous generations of U.S. Americans. Paula's life has not even been exactly the same as the lives of other members of her own generation, her siblings and friends, who grew up in very similar conditions. Thus, she is hard to explain in terms of a theory of culture that would assume cultural understandings are unchanging and uniformly shared within a society's borders.

On the other hand, there is a certain consistency and predictability to Paula's actions. As an individual personality, she is somewhat predictable: Her friends will sometimes shake their heads and say, "Isn't that just like Paula?" As a representative of her historical cohort, she can be predictable as well: Her children have been known to roll their eyes and say in exasperation, "Mom, it's not the sixties anymore!" Finally, as a U.S. American she is also predictable to some degree: When she travels abroad, people who meet her sometimes say to one another afterward, "Americans!" Thus, Paula cannot be explained in terms of currently fashionable theories that see cultural-historical personalities as constantly in flux, depending on either the dominant discourses of the times or the actor's ever-changing strategic choices.

Paula is a fictional creation. We could have equally well have introduced you instead to Juan, Shefali, Rashid, or Chuko. The purpose of focusing on one person in a paper on culture is to make the point that current anthropological theory does a very bad job at explaining how individuals are created by their cultural environment and how they then not only recreate that cultural milieu but also change it.

Our Approach

In this paper we will outline an approach that we think works much better. It draws on a current theory of cognition called "connectionism." Ours, however, is not a model of "cold" cognition: One of the virtues of connectionism is that it suggests a model of mind that can be extended to include emotion and motivation. Finally, our approach also looks outside the person to the social forces that constantly shape and are shaped by persons. In locating culture in the minds of particular individuals, the social world individuals create, and the interaction between mind and world, our approach neither reifies culture nor falls prey to the alternative error of reducing it to an analytic abstraction we anthropologists ourselves have invented.

Our formulation might be considered a version of practice theory, especially as that is developed in Pierre Bourdieu's classic *Outline of a Theory of Practice* (1977a; also Bourdieu 1984 and 1990a). Like Bourdieu we think a theory of social facts and collective representations requires an understanding of the way individuals internalize these and recreate

284

them.[2] In both his model and ours it is highly significant that internalized representations are typically not precisely stated rules but are loose associative networks that enable flexible reactions to the particulars of any given event. Like Bourdieu, finally, we will stress the relative durability of these internalized representations.

Unlike Bourdieu,[3] however, we wish to state clearly that our theory of culture does not apply only or mainly to "traditional" societies. There are durable cultural understandings in the industrialized and postindustrialized societies too; that is one reason why we are using Paula for our fictional example.[4] Also, we do not intend to draw hard and fast lines between knowledge that is said and knowledge that is unsaid:[5] Our cognitive model eliminates the overly simplistic distinction Bourdieu draws between accessible knowledge "in the head" and inaccessible knowledge that is "embodied." Furthermore, in our model social actors not only acquire a sense of what is natural, they also acquire strongly motivating senses of what is desirable. They not only know, they also care. This caring, this motivation to enact some cultural understandings more than others, is critical to our formulation of social process and missing from Bourdieu's. Finally, unlike Bourdieu, we will show that our model accounts for the forces that lead to variation and change, along with the tendencies toward sharing and reproduction: that is, the "centrifugal" as well as the "centripetal" processes at work in culture (Bakhtin 1981a).

SCHEMA THEORY AND CONNECTIONISM

We have said that our focus will be cultural understandings. By "understandings" we mean what many cognitive scientists would call *schemas*;[6] cultural understandings are simply schemas that have come to be shared to a greater or lesser extent without being human

universals. The essence of schema theory[7] is that our thoughts and actions are not directly determined by features of the external world but are mediated by learned prototypes. These prototypes, or schemas, are the generic versions of experience that remain in memory. Such prototypes have an expectational force: When a present experience or a memory of past events has missing or ambiguous information, we may not be aware of this, because our schemas, if unmodified by new evidence to the contrary, will fill in these blank or "grey" areas. Schema theory in this sense is not new:[8] What current connectionist theories[9] give us is a new way of modeling schemas.

Before we describe connectionism, we should warn readers that the cognitive model we will present here departs from connectionist models they may have previously encountered. "Connectionism" is usually used to refer to the new computer models of mind that began to gain prominence in the mid-1980s (most notably, the models presented in Rumelhart, McClelland, and the PDP Research group 1986, McClelland, Rumelhart, and the PDP Research Group 1986, and McClelland and Rumelhart 1988). From the fact that computers can be programmed to mimic intelligent behavior in various respects, however, nothing can be concluded about the way human cognition really works. So we have drawn eclectically on neurobiology and psychology, as well as our observations as anthropologists, to create a fuller, more empirically grounded, model of cognition. We use connectionism as a heuristic—a way of drawing together and making sense out of otherwise scattered insights from different fields. The importance of connectionism is that it offers a very plausible alternative to a folk theory that we would guess most of our readers as well as most cognitive scientists have held about culture learning—a folk theory that we believe is incorrect.

In this widely shared folk model, knowledge is presumed to consist of stored propositions that are processed serially. Suppose, connectionists suggest, we think of knowledge not as sets of rulelike sentences stored in a central memory repository but rather as links among a widely distributed network of many little processing units that work like neurons. Some neurons are specialized ones activated by particular discrete features of the world (e.g., the sight of bright red or the taste of something bitter), some are activated by the combined excitatory and inhibitory messages of thousands of other neurons and thus come over time to represent more complex combinations of features, and some are connected to muscle cells, sending the messages that lead to behavior. Similarly, some units are thought of as receiving inputs from the world, others as sending outputs, and still others as mediating between input and output units. For our anthropological purposes there are several advantages to thinking of cultural schemas as consisting of collections of interconnected neuronlike units. Two primary advantages of this account are that learning can occur without explicit teaching and that such learning is compatible with flexible responses to new situations.

The Learning Process

Most of our expectations about the world are learned without explicit rules being taught us. Take Paula. When she was a child nobody had to teach her, as rules for her to memorize, the generalizations that her mother was more likely to be found in the kitchen than the basement workshop, that turkey appeared on the table at Thanksgiving, or that fairy tales often begin, "Once upon a time . . ." and end, "and they lived happily ever after." She just picked up these generalizations, incorporating them into schemas about motherhood, Thanksgiving, and fairy tales, by observing what goes with what in her world.

There is a well-established neural basis for learning what goes with what. When two neurons, A and B, are activated by cooccurrent features of experience and fire at the same

time, the connection between them is strengthened (Hebb 1949).[10] In the future, if A is activated, it will be more likely to activate B. While it takes many hundreds or thousands of neurons to represent mother, Thanksgiving, or fairy tales, we can, in the more hypothetical terms of a connectionist model, think of some small set of units as representing all the sights, sounds, smells, and so on that are part of our understanding of these things. Thus, the generalizations Paula has learned can be modeled as a strengthening of the connections between units that represent her mother and units that represent kitchen, between units for Thanksgiving and units for turkey, and so on. (The generalizations that constitute our separate understandings of mother, kitchen, Thanksgiving, and turkey could, in turn, be modeled as patterns of strong connections among units for the sights, sounds, smells, and so on that go together in our experience of each of these, on down to fine-grained features of experience.)

Learning of this sort is typically gradual. Usually it takes repeated exposure to a pattern of relations to build up the strongly interconnected, generally applicable associations that we identify as schemas. Every time Paula saw her mother and her friends' mothers in the kitchen, or read stories in which mother emerges from the kitchen, or saw mother in her apron on television shows like *Leave It to Beaver*, her "units" for mother and kitchen were activated and the connection between them strengthened. (Here and elsewhere, we mean that such learning can be simulated as a strengthening of connections between the units in connectionist models, but for brevity we may speak of these units and their connections as if they were actually what was in people's heads.) Eventually, given the historical period in which Paula grew up and the typical gender roles of that time, this link became a strong one, embedded in larger networks of other strong associations that make up the patterns of understandings Paula came to have about motherhood.

Yet, Paula's schemas are not rigid cognitive structures. She has not learned anything like a recipe or a computer program that spells out, sentence by sentence, what mothers are expected to do, how Thanksgiving goes, or the elements of European fairy tales. Instead, her schemas having to do with motherhood, Thanksgiving, and fairy tales are interacting sets of less or more strongly connected units, which are in turn connected to other such interacting sets in a seamless but far-flung web.

Flexible Responses

What happens when Paula brings her learned network of associations to a new experience? In connectionist models any experience activates the units that respond to the sensory features of that experience; these units, in turn, then activate the others to which they are strongly linked by learned associations from past experience, and so on. This spreading activation continues until some subjective reaction or behavior becomes more strongly activated than other possibilities. The combined influence of different units activated by the particular features of any given situation can lead to rather different outcomes from one situation to the next.

Consider, for example, Paula's tone of voice and posture when she converses. As she was growing up, she observed countless examples of conversations. In each, the identity, roles, and aims of the participants were associated with different tones of voice and postures. Over time, Paula learned certain typical associations: supplication usually went with soft tones, unassertive postures, and, often also, women, while orders and other forms of domination went with loud tones, assertive postures, and, often also, men. This generalization, however, underplays all the possibilities for variation. Paralinguistic features of voice can range from louder to softer tones, from breathy to steely voice quality, from hesitant to rapid speaking tempos, for example. Kines-

thetic features, such as direction and firmness of gaze, set of shoulders and spine, firm or fluttery hand gestures, have equally great possibilities for variation.

Thus our assumption is that Paula has not learned a small set of rules (for example, if you are a woman and if you want something, speak in a soft, hesitant, breathy voice) but rather a large number of connections of different strengths among units representing both features of the context (identity of the actors, purpose of their actions, content of their talk) and features of the paralinguistic and kinesthetic cues accompanying their talk. These multiple connections allow her to respond flexibly to new situations exhibiting combinations of features she may not have experienced together before. This is exactly what happened to Paula, for example, when she changed jobs and discovered that her new boss was a woman. The context of speaking to a woman activated one set of units for Paula, while the context of speaking to someone with power over her activated another, only partly overlapping, set. As these units simultaneously activated still further units, their combined influence eventually settled into one response more than others, suggesting a way of reacting that felt right to Paula: a vocal, postural, and gestural style that represented a compromise between the respectful manner she usually reserved for men in authority and the easy give-and-take that was her typical demeanor toward other women.[11]

In sum, schemas as construed in connectionist models are well-learned but do not dictate an unvarying pattern of behavior. They can adapt to new or ambiguous situations with "regulated improvisation" (to use Bourdieu's term for the social action enabled by the cognitive representations he terms "habitus," 1977a:11). The responses that are the output of connectionist networks are improvisational because they are created on the spot, but regulated because they are guided by previously learned patterns of associations; they are not improvised out of thin air.

IMPLICATIONS FOR A THEORY OF CULTURE

Cognition, Emotion, and Motivation

Paula's observations of her mother in the kitchen were not cool and detached. Certain feelings were part of that situation. When she was young the feelings were ones of comfort and security at being cared for, but as she grew older she became more aware that her mother did not like being so confined to the kitchen. Paula's unsympathetic reaction was to feel irritated with her mother for not insisting on a different division of labor in the household. As time went on, the mere sight of her mother in the kitchen could make Paula feel annoyed and could remind her, as well, how important it was to her to insist on a different domestic arrangement in her own future household.

Clearly, Paula learned more than associations between observable features of her childhood experiences; she also learned associations between these observable features and certain feelings. Those feelings, in turn, became connected to certain motivations for her: in this case, the determination not to be "stuck" in the kitchen herself. Connectionist modelers, most of whom have been concerned exclusively with the problem of getting computers to act intelligently, have not been much interested in how to explain emotion and motivation. On the other hand, connectionist models can readily be extended to include them.

To make this extension we need to assume that inner subjective states of wanting and feeling, like observation of properties of the outer, observable world, can also be simulated as the activation of units. This assumption is plausible in light of what we know about the psychology of emotion and motivation.[12] It follows from this assumption that Paula's associative network could come to represent mother as connected to kitchen, feelings of annoyance, and the aim of doing something different. Her memories of Thanksgiving at her grandparents', on the other hand, are

suffused with the warmth of a happy occasion free of the tension in her parents' house. So Paula associates Thanksgiving not only with turkey, cranberries, and stuffing, but also with warm, happy feelings, and, now, the intention of recreating that experience for her children.

As we might expect, Paula's reactions to her mother are not confined to reactions that arise when her mother is in the kitchen; they are part of a whole set of feelings that Paula associates with her mother. Experiences with her mother, in turn, are part of a larger set of experiences that have led Paula to build up strong associations between certain kinds of situations, the feelings they evoke, and her dispositions to respond to them in a certain way. In other words, the same process we have described by which Paula was shaped as a cultural and historical personality has also shaped her in all of her unique Paula-ness.[13]

The Said and Unsaid

Just as we envision no hard and fast lines between the realm of emotion[14] or motivation and the realm of cognition, we envision none between the realms of the said and the unsaid. If talk and other language are part of our experience, they will be represented in cognitive networks as one more feature of that experience; but unlabeled, undiscussed events can be represented as well. There need be no separate cognitive compartments for these different experiences, which can equally well be incorporated into associative networks, and there is certainly no reason to posit an internal translation program that converts raw experience into sentences in a brain language (*pace* Fodor 1975).

Centripetal Tendencies

In addition to their motivational force, which we have already discussed, cultural understandings have four further centripetal tendencies. First, cultural understandings can be relatively durable in individuals. Second, they can be relatively stable historically, being reproduced from generation to generation. Third, they can be relatively thematic, in the sense that certain understandings may be applied repeatedly in a wide variety of contexts. Finally, they can be more or less widely shared; in fact, we do not call an understanding "cultural" unless it is shared, to some extent, in a social group. The properties of mind we have described help explain all four of these centripetal tendencies.

Durable. Part of the reason why cultural understandings are durable is that these understandings—and all learning—result in changes in the strength of connections among neurons that are not easily undone. Patterns of neural connections can be overlain with other, stronger, patterns of connections, but they do not—barring brain trauma or pathology—completely disappear. (Note that this feature of our description does not follow from connectionist modeling, but reflects what is known about the brain itself.)

Paula, for example, can learn and enact new understandings: now that she is an adult, she and her husband, Michael, try to share cooking equally. But Paula still finds that if they do not make a conscious effort to do otherwise, she and Michael tend to drift into the gender roles they observed when they were growing up. When they are busy entertaining, for example, Paula tends to end up in the kitchen while Michael chats with the guests. Such strong cognitive patterns cannot simply be erased and replaced with alternative patterns. These well-learned understandings supply the interpretations and behaviors that come to Paula automatically; it takes deliberate thought and effort to set up new patterns of behavior.

Another part of the explanation of the durability of schemas is that they tend to be self-reinforcing. For the most part the schemas of babies are highly malleable. In the course of development, however, we assume that certain of these schemas become increasingly well

established, assimilating new experience to their pattern more than they accommodate themselves to new experience. This process can be understood connectionistically as follows: once a network of strongly interconnected units has been created, it fills in ambiguous and missing information by activating all the units in an interconnected network, even those not directly stimulated by current experience. Phenomenologically we should expect to find that we are sometimes led to think we have experienced all the features of the typical event when only some of its features are present (an outcome psychologists have demonstrated experimentally, e.g., Loftus 1979). This effect reinforces the expectations with which we started.

Paula has a colleague at work with whom she is on bad terms. In the past he has demeaned her in subtle and not so subtle ways, and Paula has come to build up the expectation that he will continue to do so. As a result, many of his comments, even those innocently intended, trigger her "there-he-goes-demeaning-me-again" schema, with the result that she reads noninnocent intentions into them. As far as she is concerned, her experience contains recurrent evidence that this colleague looks down on her, and each new such event only strengthens the associations with which she started.

Moreover, negative social schemas can lead to patterns of social interaction that do not allow disconfirming evidence to arise. Because she is white and grew up in a middle-class suburb, Paula has had little firsthand experience with inner-city African-Americans. Her stereotype, picked up from the media, is that poor inner-city African-American men are likely to be violent criminals. The last time she was in a large city she was approached by a shabbily dressed African-American man. Something about the way he looked at her triggered Paula's fear-laden associations, and she turned and ran. As it happens, he had thought she looked lost and had approached her to offer directions. For Paula, however, the experience reinforced the connection in her mind between poor African-American men and violence, and she has since told others about the incident as evidence that it is not safe to walk in the city anymore.

If Paula had stayed long enough to talk to this man, the positive experience might have been equally memorable: Schemas do not act as gatekeepers, preventing inputs from being sensed.[15] An incident that fails to fit one's existing schemas can be perceived as such and may even be long remembered because it was surprising. But fleeting, superficial encounters are likely to preclude any such surprises to existing interpretations. Such encounters typically result only in much missing and ambiguous information, which is then interpreted on the basis of previously learned expectations, reinforcing these expectations. We have worried, in fact, that by even introducing this brief fictional example we might be reinforcing, in some minds, the stereotype we described. If we have had that effect on any reader, then we have failed to make our cautionary point about the way in which negative stereotypes can persist and even strengthen in the absence of empirical support.

A further reason why some cultural schemas are durable is that emotional arousal during or after an experience strengthens the neural connections that result from that experience (W. J. Freeman 1991:81,82; Squire 1987:39-55). Thus, Paula's anger in interactions with her co-worker, and her fear in the inner-city incident, altered the neurochemical environment in which relations among features of those experiences were encoded to render the mental representations of those associations stronger than they would have been had she not cared so much about what she was observing. Each time she perceives her co-worker to be demeaning her, for example, her anger kicks in to heighten the strength of the associations she brings away from that incident, making these associations even more durable than they would be otherwise.

Up to this point we have discussed learning that happens without deliberate teaching. However, children and other novices do not learn everything unaided simply by observing the way their world is structured; they are often also taught—assiduously, in multiple ways, and in combination with powerful incentives and disincentives. Paula, for example, is typically American in believing in the importance of self-reliance (e.g., Bellah et al. 1985:55-65; Harkness, Super, and Keefer 1992). It is no accident that this is a durable value for her. Her parents not only lectured her and her brother, Daniel, on the importance of self-reliance, but also waited for them to tie their own shoelaces, left them to settle their own disputes, encouraged them to make their own decisions, and sent them to overnight camp so they would become accustomed to living away from home. They showed approval if she did something "all by yourself!" and discouraged her from asking for help too often. Her parents' efforts were reinforced by countless stories, speeches, and other messages she encountered, as she grew up, about the virtues of self-reliance. The result is that Paula not only finds it natural to be self-reliant, she also *wants* to be self-reliant in many situations.[16] As obvious as it is, this truism about how socialization works to establish enduring schemas and imbue these with motivation is missing from Bourdieu's (1977a) account and others that draw on his work (e.g., Ortner 1990; see Spiro 1987b and D'Andrade 1984 for a fuller discussion). In our connectionist terms, Paula has built up strong links between certain kinds of situations and associated feelings and motivations. New situations she encounters that are similar to previous ones in which self-reliance was learned arouse those feelings, which then create a neurochemical environment in which fresh successes or failures to be self-reliant are particularly memorable to her.

There is something more to the story. Paula's parents were as assiduous in teaching her and her brother good hygiene as they were in teaching them self-reliance, and the lessons about both have stuck. While they promoted hygiene on pragmatic grounds of health and social acceptance, however, her parents placed a particular significance on self-reliance that they did not put on cleanliness. Paula learned not only to want to be self-reliant, but also to think of herself as an exemplary person for being so (and a failure as a person for failing to be so). This association of self-reliance with an ideal of personhood makes Paula feel good about herself every time she is self-reliant, and this positive feeling about herself operates as a self-instigated reward, reinforcing every new experience of self-reliance and making her motivation to be self-reliant even more durable than it would have been otherwise (see Spiro 1987b for a similar argument).

Stable Historically. The durability of schemas for individuals has consequences for the stability of schemas historically, that is, their reproduction from one generation to another. First of all, when people enact the patterns they have learned, they recreate the public world of objects and events from which the next generation learns. For example, when Paula and Michael drift back into the gender roles they learned growing up, their behavior then becomes part of the observable world that shapes their children's schemas. Also, people act intentionally to pass on values that are important to them, including and especially those values they attach to being an exemplary person. Because Paula and Michael have been socialized to value self-reliance in themselves and others, they transmit that value to their children, often using child-rearing practices like the ones through which self-reliance was developed in them. By contrast, Paula is less diligent about teaching her children to be clean than her parents were; unassociated with ideas she has about being a good person, cleanliness seems less compelling to her, and she thinks that her mother over-emphasized it. Understandings like those Paula has about cleanliness are more subject to cross-generational lapse than ideas like those she has about self-reliance. Of course, the durability of cultural understandings depends as well on social forces such as the workings of power and the inertia of institutions, but the cognitive-motivational story we have outlined cannot be ignored as part of a theory of social reproduction.

Thematic. This point leads us to another aspect of cultural centripetality: the tendency of some schemas such as complexes of understandings about honor in the circum-Mediterranean area, about purity and pollution in India, or about self-reliance in the United States, to be evoked in a wide variety of contexts.

Since Paula and Michael say "please try to do it yourself" nearly every time their children ask for help (unless the obstacle is something that the children are felt to be incapable of overcoming), their children have come to associate obstacles of many different sorts with the expectation that they will overcome them on their own. That does not mean, however, that in the future this expectation will be triggered only by situations that are exactly the same as ones the children have encountered in the past. As conceptualized in connectionist models, we have said, schemas are not rigid structures with precisely stated rules of applicability but are loose patterns of associations. New experiences evoke an interpretation based on overall similarity of features of the current experience to repeated or particularly memorable combinations of features of previous experiences. So, in the future, any new obstacle that Paula and Michael's children experience will evoke their "do it on your own" expectation provided that it has the right sort of family resemblance to previous occasions when they learned to do it on their own.[17] Schemas like this one for self-reliance can generalize quite widely across a family of experiences, giving foundation to outside observers' descriptions of "national character" or the "ethos" of a people.

Furthermore, there is a complex interplay between properties of the culturally constructed world and properties of the mind. Because Paula, Michael, and their children have come to find it natural and desirable to be self-reliant, they will have an "elective affinity" (Weber 1946) to new products (e.g., microwavable meals for children), stories (e.g., the movie *Home Alone*), rhetoric (e.g., calls to reduce welfare "dependency") and the like that appeal to these understandings. If many people share understandings about self-reliance, these new public discourses, stories, products and so on will "sell" well. This popular response, in turn, will give messages to the powers-that-be about future policies and products to market and ways to market them, reshaping the landscape of public objects and events from which further cognitive associations are learned.

Shared. Interplay between the public world and private psyches also helps explain why certain schemas are so widely shared in a society. It is not necessary that two people have had exactly the same experiences (and no two people ever will) for them to arrive at some of the same schemas. According to connectionist models, the most frequently represented patterns of associations among features are internalized as strong connections, while random variations around the mode are represented by weaker connection weights that have much less effect on cognitive processing. (This leaves aside the effects of emotional modulation, which we will ignore for the moment.) Thus, in learning the cultural model that self-reliance is good, it does not matter that Paula acquired this understanding from parental homily A, personal experience B, and movie C, while Michael acquired it from a different assortment of experiences. Since both sets of inputs reveal the same general patterning of associated features, that pattern is represented by strongly interconnected units in each of their cognitive networks.

Much of the world is organized in exactly such a way as to ensure that people in the same social environment will indeed experience many of the same typical patterns. This modal patterning is broadly characteristic of human social life, a requirement of many of the practices by which people interact with each other, coordinate common activities, and collaborate in common ventures (D'Andrade 1987, 1989). To cite a mundane but not inconsequential example, Paula and her friends who have children and millions of other suburban mothers find themselves caught up in the common experience of incessant carpooling that is dictated by the structure of middle-class children's activities in combination with the system of suburban housing and reliance on automobiles that developed in the United States in the middle decades of this century. Another source of shared patterns are historical events and trends that affect cohorts of individuals. Paula's mother is hardly the only woman of her generation to have resented the gendered division of household labor, nor is Paula the only daughter of such a woman who determined she would organize her household differently.

The modal patterning of experience is also, we must not forget, a by-product not only of social movements like feminism but also of the exercise of power from above: Participation in certain institutions and allegiance to certain ideologies are enforced because this suits the interests of people in positions of power; hence not just any policy or product has a chance to be "elected" or "bought."[18] Our cognitive explanation of cultural sharing, like our explanations of other centripetal features of culture, does not exclude social forces; instead, we are arguing, cognitive and social forces interact to determine cultural dynamics.

Centrifugal Forces

The last section may have left the impression that our cognitive theory predicts uniformity of cultural understandings within a society, unchecked thematicity, and lack of change within individuals or over historical cohorts. It does not. The same cognitive model also helps to explain why Paula does not constantly enact a small, unaltering set of schemas, why her understandings are different from those of many other people raised under similar circumstances in the same period, and why her children are not doomed to acquire and enact schemas that are exactly the same as hers. Although it may take less space to convince a contemporary anthropological audience of these centrifugal tendencies, it is important for the unified theory of culture we are presenting that the same model can explain these forces as well.

The Impact of Experience. As we have indicated, cultural schemas differ not at all from other schemas except in being shared. Schemas unique to individuals are built up from idiosyncratic experience, while those shared by individuals are built up from various kinds of common experience. Some schemas are undoubtedly held in common by millions of people, shared by everyone growing up and living his or her adult life in a nation-state, with its hegemonic influence and its capability for broadcasting popular events to the far limits of its boundaries. Other schemas are shared by only some individuals—subgroups forming self-conscious subcultures, or individuals who happen to share similar experiences, or experts who have undergone the same esoteric training, for example. At what point in the continuum of sharedness we decide to call a given schema "cultural" is simply a matter of taste; we may, if we wish, speak of a family or workplace "culture," or "high culture," or a "subcultural theme." Cultural models are in people's heads, but a given cultural model need not be in everyone's head. Since subgroups such as households, genders, regions, ethnic minorities, and historical cohorts crosscut one another, an individual may share schemas with as many different groups of other individuals as he or she shares a history of membership—at the same time sharing all of his or her schemas

with no one else in any of these groups. This way of thinking about culture as differentially distributed cultural understandings, or schemas, seems to us to account for that cultural sharing which does occur without reifying culture as a bounded entity.

One of the most important consequences of connectionist models is that they raise the question of what, exactly, people experience. Both Paula and Michael learned the virtues of self-reliance as children, but there are differences in the specifics of the schemas they acquired. Michael, for example, did not learn to associate self-reliance with being able to mend his own clothes, while Paula did, and, as we shall see, Paula did not learn to associate self-reliance with being able to do home repairs, while Michael did. Thus, while it is true that Paula and Michael share a general understanding about the importance of self-reliance, there are many specific respects in which their schemas diverge.

Paula's and Michael's understandings diverge from their children's, as well, because the children have grown up observing still different patterns of behavior: not only the times when Paula and Michael drifted back into old gender roles but also the times when they shared housework more equally. Behaviors that require a deliberate effort for Paula and Michael will shape what their children come to take for granted. (However, the children's schemas are also shaped by the behaviors they learn about in other homes and in books, TV, movies, and so on. To the degree that these other behaviors tend to the mode or idealize the past, their children's understandings come closer to those that Paula and Michael consider traditional than they might expect; cf. Weisner 1990.) When this new generation reaches their thirties, forties, and fifties, their assumptions about what is natural and desirable will further reshape the public symbols and institutions from which still another generation acquires its schemas.

What is decisive is not the sheer quantity of representations of traditional versus nontraditional renditions of gender roles to which Paula's children are exposed. In the last section we focused on the overwhelming combined influence of different media presenting a similar message; here we need to add the caveat that people's mental representations do not always copy the most frequently presented associations in their environment (see Strauss and Quinn 1992 for examples). Due to the neurochemical processes we mentioned earlier, the learner's emotions and motivations make a difference in how those events are cognized. This can have centripetal effects, as we saw earlier in the example of self-reliance. It is just as possible, however, for emotions and motivations to play a centrifugal role in learning, because two individuals could be exposed to the same information but care differently about that information and so not internalize it the same way.[19] For example, Paula's brother Daniel had the same opportunities as his sister to observe their mother while they were growing up. Since the happiness of mothers in kitchens was not of especial interest to him, however, the mental associations he formed of her in this context were not as strong as Paula's and have since been overlain with different, more emotionally salient memories of their mother.

Paula is not only different from Michael and their children, but she is not always consistent herself in the schemas she enacts. Her self-reliance schema, for example, is not a rule that programs her to overcome all obstacles on her own. Instead, she has memory traces from the many situations in which she was expected to be on her own, as a result of which she finds it natural and desirable to be self-reliant in situations similar to those. However, she also learned, as she was growing up, that there were occasions when no one expected women to be self-reliant: when a car had a flat tire, for example, or a faucet was leaking. In fact, as far as she could see from both fictional and real-life examples, things seemed to work out well in those situations if the women involved acted helpless. Nowadays when Paula's car

gets a flat tire or the faucet is leaking or there is some other obstacle to overcome that relates to heavy, dirty, "male" activities, it seems natural to her to let Michael take care of it. To an observer Paula's behavior may seem inconsistent. Paula is unaware of the inconsistency, because her self-reliance understandings and her feminine helplessness understandings are represented in different parts of her vast neural network and are triggered in different sorts of contexts, so they rarely come into conflict in a given situation.[20] (See Strauss and Quinn 1992 and Strauss 1990 for other examples of such "encapsulation" or "containment.")

In addition, as we explained using the example of Paula's interaction with a boss who was a woman, even well-learned schemas do not dictate an unchanging response, because the response that is suggested depends on all the features of any given situation. As Paula's world changes, not only do some of her schemas change, but even her more resistant, durable associations adapt by combining in new ways with other associations to yield innovative responses.

Deliberate Effort. Nor are Paula's possibilities for innovation limited to new combinations of old associations. We noted early on in this paper that, by making a conscious, deliberate effort, Paula and Michael can enact patterns of behavior that are not the ones that come automatically to mind, given their childhood experiences. This deliberate effort is an example of what some cognitive psychologists call a "controlled" process, in contradistinction to "automatic" ones, which happen involuntarily (Schneider and Shiffrin 1977; Shiffrin and Schneider 1977). Well-learned, strong associations suggest automatic responses, but these responses can be overridden through conscious control.

Sometimes deliberate decisions of this sort lead to social change, depending on the larger social forces that determine the effectiveness of individual actions. Just as often, however, people apply deliberate effort toward the end of realizing socially valued, well-established goals. In any case, we would expect that deliberate cognitive effort is more likely to be fueled by well-learned schemas than by momentary enthusiasms. In another example we gave earlier, it is not sufficient to explain Paula's decision to share cooking equally with Michael as a product of the articles that she has recently read in *Ms.* magazine. Current feminist messages are not imprinted on a tabula rasa but appeal to Paula as a result of the learned, affectively and motivationally charged associations she brings from her past, like her early experience of her mother's unhappiness and ambivalence about kitchen chores. In other words, we do not have to choose between theories that acknowledge actors' agency and intentions and theories that acknowledge the role of durable, shared cultural schemas: Intentions depend on schemas. The cognitive theory we have outlined shows not just why, but how.

Culture as Public and Private

A cognitive theory alone is not sufficient to explain either cultural stability or cultural change. On the other hand, it is a necessary part of any such theory, and one that has been overlooked in the dominant anthropological discourse. This "overlooking"—indeed, more active "erasure"—results from the confluence of several historical streams. It falls naturally from the dualism dividing the collective from the individual that is part of our intellectual inheritance, and it is fixed in the modern disciplinary boundaries that define the turf that anthropologists and sociologists defend from incursion by psychologists and biologists. In the recent past of our discipline this territorial boundary marking was particularly evident in the symbolic anthropology of influential spokesmen like Schneider (1968) and Geertz (1973). "Though ideational," Geertz declared of culture, "it does not exist in someone's

head" (1973:10). The stream of thought that separates individual from society is sometimes also joined by another one, equally deep in Western philosophy and folk theory: suspicion of peculiar entities like another's thoughts and feelings that cannot be seen or poked with a stick. This behavioristic bias may be another factor that lay behind Geertz's preference for analyses of the "hard surfaces of life" (Geertz 1973:30) rather than something presumably softer, like ideas and feelings, that lie underneath the surface.[21]

Most recently a new generation of cultural anthropologists has critiqued symbolic anthropology soundly for its characterization of culture, and especially non-European cultures, as unchanging and monolithic. The new preoccupation is with the shifting and inconsistent forms that culture can take. The irony is that by not questioning symbolic anthropologists' rejection of the private, psychological side of culture, the new generation is left without a convincing theory of either stability or change. How can actors invent, negotiate, and contest their cultural worlds unless they have internalized motives for doing so? And motives do not change from moment to moment: at its most absurd, this view makes culture change seem no different than changing clothes.

It is time for us to confront the contradiction in the definition of culture we have inherited as meaningful, symbolic, signifying, conceptual, and ideational, but not to anyone in particular, that has distorted the analysis, and required circumlocutions in the analytic language, of so many anthropologists over the last two decades. It is time to question the idea of culture as invented, negotiated, and contested by human actors strangely lacking in any long-range purpose behind their creative and transformative efforts. It is time to say that culture is *both* public and private, both in the world and in people's minds.[22] By bringing the knowing subject back into social process we can better account for what we have learned about culture so far and begin to develop a deeper understanding of the problems that still elude us.

NOTES

1. An earlier draft of this paper was prepared for the invited session titled "Assessing Developments in Anthropology" and organized by Robert Borofsky for the 87th Annual Meeting of the American Anthropological Association in Washington, D.C., November 1989. We are grateful for Borofsky's comments on that earlier draft and his patience while we revised it for publication. The authors are also grateful for a careful reading and helpful comments on that draft made by Harriet Whitehead, comments on a longer version (Quinn and Strauss, in preparation) by Jane Hill, as well as fruitful discussions with Dorothy Holland on this and related topics.

2. Another Bourdieuian culture theorist, Sherry Ortner (1990), has wrestled with some of the same questions about culture that we address in this paper, and has proposed a solution that draws on the concept of "schemas," a term we will also introduce. Ortner's formulation differs from ours, however, in that her schemas are not grounded in cognitive theory. Because it is a thoughtful attempt that takes discussion as far as it can go within a noncognitive approach, Ortner's paper exposes clearly the impasse that noncognitive culture theory has reached.

3. Or, at least, unlike the Bourdieu of *Outline of a Theory of Practice* (1977a). His views are somewhat modified in *The Logic of Practice* (1990a).

4. See, for example, Quinn (1987, 1991) for detailed descriptions of a durable, widely shared U.S. American cultural model.

5. We are not the only ones to comment on this distinction. See, for example, Comaroff and Comaroff (1989).

6. In this paper we opt for an Anglicized ending rather than the original Greek one, using "schemas" as the plural rather than "schemata."

7. Casson (1983) provides a good review of schema theory and its applications in cultural anthropology, at least as it was envisioned in the cognitive science and cognitive anthropology of the 1970s and early 1980s.

8. Kant (1965 [1781]) used "schema" to refer to mental representations that guide the application of a priori categories to particular experiences. Piaget (1952) used the same term to refer to the learned, changing cognitive

structures that mediate children's (and adults') understandings of the world. See also Bartlett (1932).

9. These theories go under various names, such as "parallel distributed processing," "neural network theory," and "neural Darwinism." "Connectionism" is a generic term for all of these. Although the connectionist models proposed by various researchers differ, they share a core set of assumptions that are quite radical from the perspective of earlier work in the cognitive sciences. The description we will give has been most strongly influenced by one approach, parallel distributed processing (Rumelhart, McClelland, and the PDP Research Group 1986; McClelland, Rumelhart, and the PDP Research Group 1986; Smolensky 1988), but it is intended to cover the shared features of this whole class of models, with some modifications of our own.

10. This learning rule was proposed by Hebb and has since been confirmed experimentally (see discussion in Carlson 1986; Freeman 1991).

11. Other features of the situation emerged as important, too. For example, Paula found herself comparing her boss to her mother, who was roughly the same age, and her reactions to the former were affected by her well-learned reactions to the latter. We will discuss Paula's attitude toward her mother further below.

12. It may be that more goes on than the activation of neurons when we have a feeling—perhaps certain hormones are released by the neural triggers—but any such mechanism would be compatible with this model. This will be discussed at greater length in a forthcoming monograph, *Mind in Society / Society in Mind*, that Strauss is writing with Dorothy Holland.

13. Some psychodynamic processes can be incorporated into a connectionist model if we assume that early experiences tend to be linked to strong feelings related to survival and security and that strong inhibitions can develop at any age to prevent memories of traumatic events from coming to consciousness. The latter sort of knowledge would be unconscious because it is part of an associative network that has come to be linked to neural triggers of strong feelings of anxiety. See Kandel (1983) for a discussion of the neural mechanisms underlying learned anxiety and consequent avoidance of painful stimuli. Note that unconscious knowledge needs to be distinguished from knowledge that simply remains in the background of awareness because it is part of unproblematic behavioral routines. Bourdieu (1977a) tends to confuse the two forms of nonconscious knowledge.

14. "Emotion" is generally used, and we will use it here, to include not only subjective feelings of anger, joy, grief, and the like, but also the learned schemas that might come to be connected to such feelings (e.g., schemas for circumstances under which the feeling is usually evoked and proper ways of displaying it and managing it) as well as physiological correlates of those feelings (e.g., pounding heart and sweaty palms).

15. It is typical of anthropologists, in the tradition of a Whorfian-inspired linguistic determinism, to treat cultural concepts as gatekeepers. Contemporary anthropologists are likely to assimilate the schema idea to an extreme epistemological relativist position that cultural conceptions of things exclude alternative ways of perceiving them. Schemas do not act in this fashion, however (Alba and Hasher 1983).

16. See Lutz (1983, 1987) for a particularly clear example of this transmission process in another cultural context.

17. The Wittgensteinian terminology (1958:sec. 67) is deliberate: His family resemblance analysis of concepts fits the connectionist model nicely.

18. This, of course, is a standard criticism of Weber's otherwise insightful discussion.

19. The contrasting autobiographies of Clifton Taulbert (1989) and Anne Moody (1968) offer vivid examples of different associations held by two people growing up in similar circumstances in the same area at the same time. Taulbert (1989:144-146) and Moody (1968:129) attach very different connotations to the manners blacks were expected to show toward whites in Mississippi in the 1950s, for example, Taulbert exulting in his use of manners to get ahead, Moody raging at blacks like Taulbert who acceded to their use.

20. Such possibilities explain why attributions of personality types to individuals or cultures generally overstate the predictability and consistency of the individual or group of individuals so typed.

21. In fact, Geertz's influential essay, "Thick Description: Toward an Interpretive Theory of Culture," relies heavily on the virulently antimentalistic philosophy of Gilbert Ryle. See Strauss (1992) for a more detailed discussion of that essay.

22. We are not the only ones nor the first to say this. See, e.g., D'Andrade (1984); Bloch (1985a); Sperber (1985); Spiro (1987a); Shore (1991).

I N T E L L E C T U A L   R O O T S

Claudia R. Strauss is Assistant Professor of Cultural Anthropology at Duke University. Her primary research to date has been on the social and political attitudes of employees and neighbors of a controversial New England chemical plant; she has also conducted archival research in India on land tenure in the eighteenth century. Recipient of the 1983 Stirling Award in psychological anthropology, she is coeditor (with Roy D'Andrade) of *Human Motives and Cultural Models*, author of "Who Gets Ahead? Cognitive Responses to Heteroglossia in American Political Culture," and coauthor (with Dorothy Holland) of a forthcoming monograph, *Mind in Society/Society in Mind: A Critical Anthropology of Cognition.*

I chose to pursue a career in anthropology because of all the social sciences, it is the most holistic and the most receptive to diverse theories and methods.

As an undergraduate at the University of Rochester and at Brown University, I was a philosophy major, then became more interested in the factors that shape social outlooks—the problem that is still the focus of my research.

Bill Beeman and Marida Hollos in the Brown Anthropology Department gave me a background in psychological and linguistic anthropology and encouraged me. Because I was married to a Brown professor, I wanted to do my graduate work nearby. I chose Harvard in part because in its recent past it had a graduate program in Social Relations (combining sociology, psychology, and social anthropology). Although Social Relations had met its demise in the early 1970s, I thought its interdisciplinary spirit might still be alive.

It turns out I was wrong about that: When I arrived in 1976 about all that remained of Social Relations was the three departments' proximity in the William James building. Furthermore, the dominant ethos in social anthropology was decidedly antipsychologistic. John Whiting had become a minority voice in the department and, in any case, retired shortly after I started my graduate work. Our studies emphasized the British and French traditions, especially Lévi-Straussian structuralism; American anthropological approaches (not only psychological anthropology, but also linguistic anthropology and cultural ecology) were completely absent from the curriculum. The department was thus not particularly sympathetic to my interests.

In its areas of concentration, however, the graduate program was excellent. From David Maybury-Lewis, Nur Yalman, and Michael Fischer I acquired a strong grounding in the work of Marx, Weber, and Durkheim. This background still informs my research, which applies cognitive theory and linguistic methods to classic issues in Marx's and Weber's sociology of knowledge. Stanley Tambiah was a welcome addition to the department. Both the example of his work and the range of courses he taught (from Magic, Science, and Religion to Economic Anthropology) showed ways of combining idealist and materialist approaches. Finally, I was in the company of outstanding fellow students with whom I enjoyed discussing the issues raised in our classes. Ironically, several of us have gone on to do work in psychological and linguistic anthropology.

I made two short trips to India to study concepts of land tenure in the late eighteenth century—a topic that interested me following a Harvard Law School course on law and religion in India. However, contact with Indians working for social change made me question the usefulness of my research. In some ways, I was fairly typical of my generation (that is, those who were college-aged during the Viet Nam war) in having been politically active and concerned about the social relevance of my work. I wondered whether I could justify an academic career, and, even if I could, whether I shouldn't pursue a different topic of research.

Given my uncertainty about what to do next, I left my studies temporarily to take a full-time job doing public policy research. Luckily, the job I found was as a research assistant at the Van Leer Project at Harvard's Graduate School of Education. The project examined assumptions underlying educational practices in various societies; the results were to inform the Van Leer Foundation's future decisions regarding grants to educational programs around the world.

My participation in this project marked a turning point in my career plans. The anthropologist on the project was Bob LeVine. Bob eventually became my dissertation advisor, and I appreciated his wise, well-grounded anthropological judgments. More importantly, I saw that it was possible to do research that was both intellectually stimulating and useful in the real world. I determined to finish my dissertation; the only question was on what?

At this point I was fortunate to come across Naomi Quinn's 1982 *American Ethnologist* article analyzing American men and women's talk about commitment in marriage. Then I met Naomi at the 1983 A.A.A meetings and told her about my interest in applying her style of discourse analysis to interviews eliciting social and political attitudes in the United States. On both an intellectual and practical level she became a mentor for me. I'm glad to have this opportunity to pay tribute to her unselfish efforts on behalf of younger women academics because her support has been decisive in my career.

My present research connects problems that have interested me since I was an undergraduate to current intellectual issues. For example, the cognitive model outlined in the paper here can be used to critique some poststructuralists' tendency to decenter the human subject and construe everything as discourse. The aim of my work has instead been to understand the interaction between people and their cultural environment, an interaction in which neither side can be reduced to assemblages of discourses. These issues are developed further in a book I am writing with Dorothy Holland. Future projects include further investigations of what people's talk reveals about the ways in which cultural messages are internalized; a study of children's acquisition of culture that I am conducting with Naomi Quinn; a comparison of the methodological limitations of symbolic analysis, discourse analysis, and attitude survey research; and a study of attitudes about social welfare programs in the United States.

INTELLECTUAL ROOTS

Naomi Quinn is Associate Professor in the Department of Cultural Anthropology at Duke University and currently chairs that department. She is President-elect of the Society for Psychological Anthropology. Her most recent and most sustained research—focusing on U.S. Americans' cultural model of marriage and crystallizing her views on the nature of culture—is the subject of a book under preparation and of a series of articles including "The Cultural Basis of Metaphor" (1991) and "Convergent Evidence for a Cultural Model of American Marriage" (1987). The latter appeared in a volume she coedited with Dorothy Holland, *Cultural Models in Language and Thought.* She has, as well, an ongoing interest in anthropological research on gender, reflected in her early review article, "Anthropological Studies of Women's Status" (1977). Most recently, she and Claudia Strauss have begun research on culture acquisition, initial results of which appear in "Preliminaries to a Theory of Culture Acquisition" (1992).

Cultural anthropology, once I discovered it in college, was my calling. John Whiting, guest lecturing in my introductory anthropology course at Harvard, opened the possibility that cross-cultural research could be explanatory and not just descriptive. My undergraduate thesis advisor was Bea Whiting, who taught me to be both a close observer and a comparative thinker. Bea and Johnny and the interdisciplinary group of graduate students who worked with them at the research laboratory in Palfrey House gave me a taste of what it was like to work in a research environment; a commitment to evidence and to anthropology as science; and an abiding interest in the effects of childhood experience. After college, recovering from hepatitis, I worked at Palfrey House as a coder on the Six Cultures project.

By the time I completed graduate course work and went to Ghana to do my dissertation field research, I had already accumulated quite a bit of fieldwork experience. While still an undergraduate I had participated in a Harvard-Cornell-Columbia field school in highland Ecuador, where I later returned under a Fulbright Scholarship (and contracted the aforementioned hepatitis). A graduate student at Stanford, I attended another summer field school in Oaxaca, Mexico. While these experiences were more formative than full-fledged research, they confirmed my affinity for field research and made a thoroughgoing naturalist out of me.

In graduate school at Stanford, Roy D'Andrade (one of the then graduate students I had met at Palfrey House) became my advisor and my lifelong mentor. A fine teacher, he gave me a sure sense of research problems, an inventive, pragmatic approach to research design and methods, and a fascination with the unfolding history of our discipline. At Stanford my interest in the psychological was expanded to include cognition. I was engaged in the emerging ethnoscience tradition with its mentalist theory of culture, its effort to reconstruct people's cultural assumptions from careful analysis of what they said, and its respect for formal method. The first two of these themes shaped my anthropology directly; the third I reacted against. As did other students, I developed a critique of ethnoscience's overcommitment to formal methods and the limitations of the semantic theory underlying these formalisms. This paired theoretical and methodological dissatisfaction fueled our urgent search for something better in the way of cognitive theory, and, eventually also, our invention of new methods of discourse analysis more appropriate to our revised theoretical assumptions.

Intellectual genealogies focused on the individuals who influenced one may neglect the more diffuse but sometimes even more profound influence of broad intellectual movements. On me, as on other cognitive anthropologists of my generation, the most important of these intellectual influences, schema theory (fundamental to the paper in this volume), came from the new interdisciplinary field of cognitive science. A major setting for my education in cognitive science was the Social Science Research Council Committee on Cognitive Research, which I joined when Roy D'Andrade recommended me as his replacement, and on which I served in the seventies and eighties with psychologists like Eleanor Rosch and Amos Tversky and the linguist Charles Fillmore. During one of the conferences organized under the auspices of that committee, I got reacquainted with another linguist who happens also to be a distant cousin of mine, George Lakoff, and I became acquainted with George's work on metaphor. This work influenced me enormously, once again as much in the task of formulating a critique of it as in its direct influence on the way I thought about cultural understandings and their relation to discourse.

Genealogy as a metaphor could bias one to think only backward intergenerationally. But one of those most influential on my thinking has been my younger coauthor in this volume, Claudia Strauss. Collaborating with Claudia has pressed me to be more expansive in my theoretical ambitions and more logical in my argumentation. We laugh about my tendency to stress what we call in our paper "centripetal" properties of culture and overlook "centrifugal" ones, and her tendency to do just the reverse—as much as anything a reflection of our respective generations.

In my story not only intellectual continuity but intellectual fadism has had a place. I was hardly out of graduate school when the tradition in which I worked came under an attack motivated less by sound intellectual objections than by the latest struggle for disciplinary hegemony. As we describe in our paper, cognitive anthropology was erased, or nearly so. In my professional life I have tried to foster appreciation for the place of cognition in culture theory and for a more open, integrative theoretical stance than is typically tolerated in our fad- and faction-ridden discipline. Claudia's and my paper in this volume is offered as a concrete demonstration of the value of these principles.

21

Theories of Culture Revisited

ROGER M. KEESING

THE CULTURAL CONSTRUCTION OF THE "OTHER" AS DIFFERENT

If radical alterity did not exist, it would be anthropology's project to invent it.[1] Radical alterity—a culturally constructed Other radically different from Us—fills a need in European social thought: what Trouillot (1991) calls "the savage slot." I believe that in important senses, the radical otherness anthropologists have sought has not existed, at least for very many millennia. The tribal world in which we have situated that alterity—the world of Lévi-Strauss's "cold societies" of unchanging tradition—was our anthropological invention. We continue to invoke it; and some of us journey ever deeper into darkest New Guinea to find it, existing still.

The invention and evocation of this radical otherness which has been anthropology's project required a conceptual universe, a mode of discourse. Especially as the idea of "a culture" was developed in the Boasian tradition as a bounded universe of shared ideas and customs and as the idea of "a society" was developed in functionalist social anthropology as a bounded universe of self-reproducing structures, these concepts provided a framework for our creation and evocation of radical diversity. "A culture" had a history, but it was the kind of history coral reefs have: the cumulated accretion of minute deposits, essentially unknowable, and irrelevant to the shapes they form.

The world of timeless, endlessly self-reproducing structures, social and ideational, each representing a unique experiment in cultural possibility, has (we now know) been fashioned in terms of European philosophical quests and assumptions, superimposed on the peoples encountered and subjugated along colonial frontiers. The diversity and the uniqueness are, of course, partial "truths": the Tupinamba, the Aranda, the Baganda, the Vedda, the Dayak challenged comprehension and still do. But I believe we continue to overstate Difference, in search for the exotic and for the radical Otherness Western philosophy, and Western cravings for alternatives, demand.

I will touch again on this question of radical alterity, as it has been interpreted and created in anthropological discourse. My main concern here is to reexamine the concept of "culture," particularly our ways of talking and writing about "a culture." Hence I return to issues I addressed in a paper on "Theories of Culture" over fifteen years ago (Keesing 1974). I will begin by setting out a series of ironies and contradictions.

The Emphasis on Difference

A first irony is that the presently fashionable—in some quarters, at least, ascendant—symbolist/interpretive modes of anthropology require radical otherness more than ever, in a world where such boundaries as there ever were are dissolving by the day. To show that conceptions of personhood, of emotions, of agency, of gender, of the body are culturally constructed demands that Difference be demonstrated and celebrated, that "cultures" be put in separate compartments and characterized in essentialist terms. Yet the formerly tribal or peasant peoples whose lives we engage are caught up in a world system through which ideas flow freely. I have just come back from a Solomon Islands where dreadlocks in the style of Bob Harley and Kung Fu videos are the stuff of contemporary "culture." More than ever, the boundedness and the essentialism that motivate it must depart from observed "realities"; the gulf between what we see in the field and the ways we represent it widens by the minute.

In its current postmodernist mutations, cultural anthropology can effectively engage the complexities of the present as collages, juxtapositions of the old and the new, the endogenous and the exogenous; and can transcend our old preoccupations with "authenticity" and closed boundaries. In their general pronouncements, postmodernist anthropologists have often highlighted such complexities. Thus, Marcus and Fischer tell us (1986:78) that:

most local cultures worldwide are products of a history of appropriations, resistances, and accommodations. The [present] task . . . is . . . to revise ethnographic description away from [a] self-contained, homogeneous, and largely ahistorical framing of the cultural unit toward a view of cultural situations as always in flux, in a perpetual historically sensitive state of resistance and accommodation to broader processes of influence that are as much inside as outside the local context.

Amen. Yet in practice, American postmodernist anthropologists, with their roots in the interpretive/cultural constructionist tradition, often rhetorically invoke radical alterity in the same ways. Marcus and Fischer talk about "the most intimate experiences of personhood . . . distinctive of particular cultures" (1986:62) and of "Moroccan masculinity" as "superficially similar to masculinity in other cultures" (1986:62). "What if persons in

certain other cultures act from different conceptions of the individual?" (1986:45).

Poststructuralist thought, in its concern with texts as pervasive fictions (e.g. Derrida, Foucault, *écriture feminine*), has been caught in similar contradictions. Critically examining the takens-for-granted of Western thought, poststructuralism has undermined the old dualisms—civilized vs. primitive, rational vs. irrational, Occident vs. Orient—on which anthropology's exoticizations have implicitly rested. Yet at the same time, poststructuralist thought, too, urgently needs radical alterity, to show that our takens-for-granted represent European cultural constructions. To argue that our "logocentrism," our focus on reason, is a legacy of Greek philosophy, for example, requires a nonlogocentric alterity—*somewhere*—uncontaminated by Greeks. The various modes of feminism have always been caught in a dialectical tension between evoking tribal societies at least partly free from patriarchy and seeing the subordination of women as universal, but nonetheless historically contingent—hence preserving the theoretical and political possibility of a world not dominated by men or pervasively gendered by male-oriented, phallocentric thought. Either way, anthropology is drawn upon to provide the alterities to which envisioned ones are counterposed.

Reification and Essentialism

I will suggest that our conception of culture almost irresistibly leads us into reification and essentialism. How often, still, do I hear my colleagues and students talk as if "a culture" was an agent that could do things; or as if "a culture" was a collectivity of people. Of course, we profess that we don't really mean that "Balinese culture" does or believes anything, or that it lives on the island of Bali (it is all a kind of "shorthand"); but I fear that our common ways of talk channel our thought in these directions. Moreover, attributing to "Balinese culture" a systematic coherence, a pervasive sharedness, and an enduring quality—so that Bali remains Bali through the centuries, and from south to north, west to east (even nowadays, despite the tourists)—commits us to essentialism of an extreme kind. Balinese culture is the essence of Bali, the essence of Balineseness.

The essentialism of our discourse is not only inherent in our conceptualizations of "culture," but it reflects as well our vested disciplinary interests in characterizing exotic otherness. If we arrive in a New Guinea or Amazonian community and find people listening to transistor radios or watching videos, planting cash crops or working for wages, going to church and attending schools instead of conducting rituals in men's houses—and if what we came to study was their conception of Personhood or their cultural constructions of time and space—then we have to believe that their essential culturalness lives on despite the outward changes in their lives.

Everyday ways of contemporary talk have been heavily influenced by our anthropological concept of culture. In pervading popular thought, anthropology's concept of culture has been applied to complex, contemporary ways of life—"Greek culture," "French culture," "Chinese culture"—as well as to the exotic "primitive" ones in TV documentaries. Ironically, with our all-inclusive conception of "culture," as it has passed into popular discourse, have gone our habits of talk that reify, personify, and essentialize. I recently heard a radio announcer in Australia talk about "the different cultures living in our area."

Our essentialist, reified conception of "culture," having passed into everyday Western discourse, has been adopted by Third World elites in their cultural, nationalist rhetoric. If "a culture" is thinglike, if cultural essences endure, then "it" provides an ideal rhetorical instrument for claims to identity, phrased in opposition to modernity, Westernization, or neocolonialism. A crowning irony is that through this borrowing, our own conceptual diseases may strike us down from unexpected directions. "Culture," so essentialized and reified, can serve as an ideal symbol to deploy against foreign researchers, who can be pilloried for having stolen "it," having sold "it" for profit in the academic marketplace, or simply (as outsiders seeking to interpret someone else's mystical essence) having misunderstood and misrepresented "it."

The "Cultural" of Cultural Studies

At the same time that our anthropological concept of culture has been increasingly pervading popular thought and talk, social theorists of various persuasions have started to take "culture" much more seriously. "Cultural studies" has become a burgeoning field. Is this "culture" of cultural studies "culture" as we anthropologists have conceptualized it? In general, the answer is No. The "culture" of "cultural studies" (whether post-Marxist, post-modernist, or post-whatever) has been developed through a broadening and critical sharpening of the conception to which ours has for decades been counterposed: "culture" as the highest artistic and aesthetic refinements and achievements of a complex society. It is not that "cultural studies" are preoccupied only with paintings, statues and symphonies. An increasing engagement with language and semiotic theory[2] has led to a considerable broadening of the old concept of "culture" as high art—a broadening in an anthropological direction.

What distinguishes "their" culture from "our" culture most strikingly is the stress in cultural studies on the articulation of symbolic systems with class and power—the production and reproduction of cultural forms. I will suggest that instead of our traditional anthropological conception of culture being extended to complex contemporary "societies," we urgently need to draw on the conceptual refinements in contemporary social theory, including the "cultural" of "cultural studies," to interpret the production and reproduction of symbols among the peoples we have encountered along the colonial margins and in peasant communities.

We confront a deep irony, then, that our anthropological conception of culture has pervaded popular thought and has been applied willy-nilly to contemporary life; while, at the same time, some of us are beginning to question its utility and to look at alternative ways of thinking about collective symbols and meanings being explored outside our own discipline.

RETHINKING THE DEGREE OF CULTURAL DIVERSITY IN TODAY'S WORLD

Let me unpack some of these arguments. First, let me say something more about the invention of radical alterity, radical Otherness. Just how different the thought and experience of non-Western peoples are from our own is a moot point about which we could all argue ad nauseam. I recently spent some weeks immersed in conversation with a brilliant young Kwaio (Solomon Islands) man who still practices his ancestral religion and lives in a world where magic, ritual, and conversations with the dead are the stuff of everyday life. Maenaa'adi's cultural alterity is perhaps as radical as any in the world of the early 1990s (although he too lives in the collages of our time, riding buses and checking the time on his watch when he comes to town). He takes for granted that if his shadow were cast on a fissure where a leprosy victim's body had been thrown, he would die of leprosy. He takes for granted that every night, his shade encounters the shades of his ancestors, who give him messages of impending events. He recites magical spells a dozen times a day, with complete faith that they should work. Obviously, I am not claiming that Maenaa'adi's world of experience and mine are minor variants of one another: There is more to it than that. Yet I see no reason, in all the texts, to infer that the pragmatic way in which he finds his way

through his world is qualitatively different from the way in which I find my way through mine; or that his culturally constructed senses of individuation and agency (or personhood or causality or whatever) are strikingly different than mine.

We could argue endlessly about how radically diverse culturally constructed concepts of personhood and agency or experiences of emotion are. I believe that anthropologists have disciplinary vested interests in construing cultural diversity in more extreme terms than our ethnographic evidence justifies (Keesing 1989a). Moreover, we have ignored the implications of steadily mounting evidence that casts doubt on our extreme relativisms. Some of this evidence comes from the neurosciences and cognitive sciences, where the constraints of what can be learned and remembered by members of our species loom large, and logics of thought begin to look not at all exotic. Some comes from research on the neurobiology of mammalian emotional systems, including those of humans and other higher primates. Some comes from studies of language, both the formal structures of syntax and the logics of semantics and conceptualization. The burgeoning field of cognitive linguistics increasingly unites grammatical theory with other realms of cognition.[3]

Metaphor and Embodiedness

Languages, seen through this lens, look not at all exotic or radically diverse (even though particular languages obviously explore different logical and organizational possibilities in different ways). I don't want to go off on a tangent about this, but I want to note two lines of development I find particularly important with regard to anthropology's exaggerated relativisms. The first is the pervasive importance of *metaphor* in language: both (1) the way languages as conceptual systems are pervaded by conventional metaphor, as explicated (albeit imperfectly) by Lakoff and Johnson (1980), and (2) the way change in a language over time whereby lexical forms acquire grammatical functions—the process that has come to be called "grammaticalization"—follows metaphoric pathways (and in ways that reveal striking similarities from language family to language family as Bernd Heine and others have shown—see Heine and Reh 1984; Heine, Claudi, and Hünnemeyer 1992; Heine and Traugott 1992). I have suggested elsewhere that with our predilection to take the most exotic possible readings of cultural texts, in fieldwork languages we learn to quite limited degrees, ethnographers run the danger of elevating conventional metaphoric schemes into cosmological structures and religious philosophies (Keesing 1985, 1987, 1989a).

The second point, which has emerged partly through studies of language and conventional metaphor but has much wider implications is the degree to which the embodiedness of cultural experience is turning out to be critical. Studies of conventional metaphor and the linguistic encoding of relations of time, space, perception, and causality increasingly point to the centrality of embodied experience. Mark Johnson's *The Body in the Mind* (1987) powerfully argues the costs of Western philosophy's mind/body dualism and its focus on disembodied reason. Anthropology is now engaging embodiedness and the cultural construction of the body largely through "medical anthropology" (see e.g. Nancy Scheper-Hughes in this volume). But as Johnson's philosophical argument and feminist reflections on embodiedness (see e.g. Gatens 1983) illustrate, progress is being made on other fronts as well.

That all humans everywhere experience the world "out there" in and through their bodies, and that this embodiedness becomes the model for cultural conceptualization of spatial orientation, agency, perception, emotion, and thought, is not to say that the cultural elaborations of embodied experience all go in the same direction. Let me come back for a moment to my friend Maenaa'adi. In one sense, Maenaa'adi's experiences when he dreams and mine must be quite similar; yet he attributes a

reality status to the nocturnal wandering of his soul and its encounters with others, while I assume that it is all being fabricated in my dreaming imagination. To see one's shadow as a component of the body that may be damaged or polluted, to fear the possibility of soul loss, to attribute forms of illness to magically injected foreign objects, entails having conceptions of the boundaries and dynamics of one's body very different from mine.

Culturally constructed bodies and bodily images and experiences unquestionably vary in different times and places. Yet anthropology's theoretical predilections and disciplinary interests run in this direction and make us prone both to overstate the case and to miss or underestimate a reverse phenomenon. We know a good deal, through the writings of Foucault (e.g., 1973a, 1977) and recent anthropological explorations, about how the power of the body social is inscribed on the body physical. Yet we have not yet seen clearly enough, I think, the power of the body physical—as subjectively experienced by its "occupant"—to inscribe itself on cultural traditions and thus to constrain cultural diversity.

My point is not to argue endlessly what, I admit, is a partisan position with regard to radical cultural diversity. But I do want to register deep skepticism about much of what I read nowadays about the cultural construction of personhood, agency, and emotion. I believe that in a decade or two, when some of the biological/cognitive constraints on human thought, emotion, and learning have come more clearly into view, the extreme relativisms and cultural constructionist positions of our time will seem quaint in the extreme. That is what I mean by a radical alterity that does not exist.

HIDDEN AGENDAS IN CONVENTIONAL ANTHROPOLOGICAL CONCEPTIONS OF "CULTURE"

The second point I want to expand concerns the hidden agendas in conventional anthropological conceptions of "culture." I have suggested that our quest for radical alterity shapes and is shaped by our conceptualizations of "cultures" as discrete, self-contained, self-reproducing universes of shared customary practices and beliefs. For "a culture" to be a separate experiment in human possibility, it must not only be separate and internally coherent and homogeneous; the "experiment" must, as it were, be "natural" (in the sense that intentional agency and interest do not contribute to its cumulative coral reef-like form). There is a whole set of hidden agendas here. Indeed, anthropological theories of culture can be subjected to the same order of political critique as functionalist sociology in, say, its Parsonian variants—as stressing order, integration, and stasis, and hiding conflict, contradiction, and the ideological and hegemonic force of "shared" symbols and institutions. Marxists, feminists, and other critics of societies as-they-are have aptly pointed to all that is hidden by representations of "culture" and "society" as consensual, collective, coherent, integrated, and self-reproducing. The voices of subalternity (Guha 1983a, 1984a), contradictions and conflicts, the hegemonic force of dominant ideologies, cleavages of class and gender, are glossed over with a wave of the analytical brush.

Anthropological conceptualizations of "culture" have been—shall we say—innocent (in the sense of naivete, not culpability) in terms of the battle lines of social theory. Our ways of conceptualizing what used to be called the "primitive" world still embody a set of assumptions deriving from the nineteenth century about the collectiveness and sharedness of "custom." Counterposing Them to Us, nineteenth-century ethnology characterized "primitive" peoples subjugated along colonial frontiers in terms of the deep conservative force of tradition, the lack of individuation in the way they lived their lives, the unseen force of social convention. As anthropology refined "custom" into "culture," it preserved largely unexamined the assumptions

about collectivity and uniformity of culturally defined beliefs, norms, and experiences (although there were a few dissenting queries, notably those posed by Radin).[4] The coral reef conception of how cultures cumulate remained intact. Cleavages of gender and social inequality were unreflectively hidden. The production, ideological force, and hegemonic power of cultural meanings went substantially unexamined, in a discipline that grew up (especially in North America) in curious isolation from continental social theory.

What, then, of the present? Obviously things have changed, most notably through a serious input from Marxism in the 1960s and 1970s, the emergence of an anthropology of gender and the serious study of women's lives, and a much greater openness to issues of social theory. But have they changed enough in the needed directions?

Whereas the *lives* of those we now study are situated in the 1980-1990s world of global mass culture, consumerism, and capitalist labor relations and dependencies, their *cultures* still can be subjected to that analytical sleight of hand, that denial of "coevalness," so aptly characterized by Johannes Fabian in his powerful book *Time and the Other: How Anthropology Makes Its Object* (1983). Their *cultures* are hermetically sealed, beyond the reaches of time and the world system. I have recently written (Keesing and Jolly 1992) on the way anthropological characterizations of Melanesia, where I mainly work, persistently edit out Christianity, trade stores, labor migration, contemporary politics, and cash economy, exoticizing and essentializing "traditional culture" as it ostensibly survives in hinterland villages. This is not to say that contemporary anthropology is still unwaveringly committed to the portrayal of exotic cultural alterity, as a cursory reading of any recent American Anthropological Association annual meeting program will attest. Yet this pursuit of the exotic Other is still a persistent theme, and "culture" is a powerful device for its perpetuation (as a score of recent ethnographies of

New Guinea and eastern Indonesia would attest).

"Culture" in Third World Discourse

Let me return briefly to the way in which anthropological talk about "culture," with its irresistible temptations to reify, personify, and essentialize, has passed into the cultural nationalist discourse of Third World elites. For the latter, Westernized though they may be, to claim that "it" is "our culture" is to make claims of identity, authenticity, resistance, and resilience. Culture, so reified and essentialized, can be subjected to metonymic transformation, so that the cultural heritage of a people or a postcolonial nation can be represented by its fetishized material forms and performances: "traditional dress," dances, artifacts. So transformed, "it"—the cultural heritage, semiotically condensed (in the sense specified in footnote 2)—can be deployed in rituals of state, art festivals, tourist performances, and political appearances to reaffirm that "it" survives despite Westernization (and hence to deny the erosion, capitalist reorganization, and pauperization of rural life). It is worth observing that such a semiotic of cultural identity has its origin in nineteenth-century cultural nationalism in Europe, expressed in an intense search for ethnic roots and folk origins, for primordiality and cultural tradition. The museum and folkloric traditions so strong in eastern and northern Europe grew out of this romantic quest for origins and local folk tradition. The Third World has inherited these European semiotic systems, and institutions, in the colonial process, and they have been deployed in a parallel affirmation of cultural identity.

I have noted (1989a) the ironies that emerge when a conception of culture, indirectly borrowed from anthropology, is used to denounce foreign researchers, with anthropologists as the quintessential villains. They, as outsiders (it is argued), can never penetrate Our essence, never really understand Us. Once "a culture" has been reified and hypo-statized as a symbol, the outside researcher can also be accused of appropriating "it." "It" can be commoditized as well, depicted as having been alienated by an anthropologist and sold for profit in the academic marketplace. I take it as the crowning irony that our own conceptual diseases should be deployed against us.

LEARNING FROM DEVELOPMENTS IN "CULTURAL STUDIES"

Let me come back to the extreme cultural-constructionist and relativist positions, the postmodernist elevations of ethnography as the core of the discipline, and the indulgent subjectivism and narcissism of "experimental" ethnographic accounts, that have been so prominent in the practice and politics of recent American anthropology (see e.g. Clifford and Marcus 1986). I do not find it coincidental that these approaches have flourished during the conservative era of Thatcherism and Reaganism.[5]

There is no reason why the new modes of representation need be conservative, in ignoring contemporary state terror and taking for granted the political economy of global capitalism that continues to drain wealth out of Third World countries and hold them bonded in debt, pauperizes hinterland communities, and generates ecological devastation.[6] What remains unsaid in much of current anthropological writing speaks deafeningly, if we only step back to listen—as Edward Said has pointed out (Said 1989).

The not-so-hidden agendas in anthropological conceptions of culture take me to a further and final expansion of my argument. I have suggested that conceptions of culture narrower than those conventional in anthropology are being developed in the field of "cultural studies," as a burgeoning concern in social and critical theory. I have further suggested that the theoretical developments in this area could usefully illuminate anthropological understanding of the communities in which we work, "tribal," peasant, or urban.

Critical Theory

"Cultural studies" is very much contested ground, and it is being entered from a number of directions. One incursion comes from critical theory. Critical theory in its various forms has as its central concerns literature and "the arts." I would include here much of postmodernism, and much of continental poststructuralism, especially its American manifestations ("deconstruction" in literary criticism, etc.). The key intellectual sources for contemporary critical theory are extremely diverse in terms of "traditional" disciplinary compartments, and include not only literary critics, but also philosophers, psychoanalysts, anthropologists, linguists, and semioticians. "Cultural studies" in this mode takes as the "core" of the "cultural" the literary and artistic productions of complex contemporary "societies," hence builds from a conception of culture against which anthropology's encyclopedic conception has been opposed for decades. However, the concept of the cultural in "cultural studies" as envisioned by critical theorists has been broadened considerably, on the one hand by a pervasive concern with language in all its manifestations (the influence of semiotics and structuralism), and on the other, by postmodernism's refusal to persist with the "great divide" between "high" and "popular" culture (see Huyssen 1986).

"Post-Marxist" and Feminist Approaches

Other incursions into the realm of "cultural studies" have come from various forms of social theory. I will illustrate this with what I will (in the spirit of the time) call "post-Marxist" approaches. Here we can take as illustrative the work of Willis, Hall, Hebdige and the colleagues in England, the work of Ranajit Guha and his Subaltern Studies colleagues,[7] and the writings collected in the recent volume on *Marxism and the Interpretation of Culture* (Nelson and Grossberg 1988). The inspirations here in some cases come more directly from Gramsci than from Marx. But the ultimate origins lie in Marx's own insights regarding symbols and ideology.

For most post-Marxist theorists, too, the core of the "cultural" lies in publicly developed symbolic productions. However, there is a second and more anthropological reading of culture as concerned with the symbolic aspects of "everyday life" (notably in the work of Bourdieu, Guha and his colleagues, and Willis). As with the critical theorists, concerns with language and semiotics have led to a considerable broadening in conceptions of "the cultural." Grossberg and Nelson (1988:5-6) write that:

Cultural theory has now expanded the category of culture well beyond "the best that has been thought and said," beyond the general forms of art, language, and entertainment, beyond the leisure (that is, non-labor) activities of the general population. . . . A foregrounding of issues of language [has] promoted a broad concern with culture, symbolic forms, communication, and meaning. . . . Marxism began to [recognize] that cultural analysis needed to be concerned with all the structural and meaning-producing activities by which human life is created and maintained.

In this broadening, Gramsci's insights regarding hegemony and Foucault's insights regarding power and knowledge and critiques of ideology loom large.[8] A more subtle conception of the ideological process and the hegemonic power of meanings is emerging in recent post-Marxist writing. Ideologies, in this view, create not illusions per se, but idealized *subject positions* in terms of which (some elements of) the social and cultural worlds are portrayed: they define *perspectives* and hence *stances* and takens-for-granted, rather than simply veiling realities with deceptions. I quote from Stuart Hall (1988:44) to exemplify:

The circle of dominant ideas does accumulate the symbolic power to map or classify the world for others; its classifications do acquire not only the constraining power of dominance over other modes of thought but also the inertial authority of habit and instinct. It becomes the horizon of the taken-for-granted: what the world is and how it works . . . setting the limit to what will appear as rational, reasonable, credible, indeed sayable or thinkable, within the . . . vocabularies of motive and action available to us.

Feminist theory in its various forms has been another area where important theoretical clarity has been achieved. Feminists share with scholars in the Marxist tradition (and of course there is considerable overlap here) a theoretical starting point that questions and challenges any symbolically constructed status quo. No coral reefs here: Who produces the dominant symbolic systems of a society, what interests they serve and hide, what ideological force they carry, and how they operate hegemonically to shape the consciousness of those they subordinate are all rendered problematic from the outset.

Toward a Different View of the Cultural

If social theories in their various forms—poststructuralist, post-Marxist, feminist—have learned usefully from anthropology's broader conception of the cultural (albeit perhaps mainly indirectly via semiotics), I would argue that these alternative approaches to cultural theory being developed in "cultural studies" have much to teach anthropology. They are squarely concerned with precisely what anthropology's "culture" as coral reef hides: the historical situatedness, production, and hegemonic force of cultural meanings in terms of the internal structures and cleavages of "society."

Even in those tribal communities where we anthropologists have sought radical alterity, without cleavages of class, the production of cultural forms and their hegemonic force

demand interpretation. As we have sat in Amazonian or New Guinea men's houses recording cosmologies, rituals, pollution taboos, our coral reef conception of culture has deflected us away from such questions. Even when cleavages and inequalities beyond those of gender have been expressed all around us in daily life and talk, as in Bali or India, we have been prone to immerse ourselves in wondrous cultural richness, and not analyze the political economy of symbolic forms.

Let me try to be quite clear about what I am saying, and not saying. I am not arguing that we should adopt a concept of culture that takes paintings to be more cultural than cookbooks or umbrellas or pollution taboos, and try to force our comparative data into such compartments. I am saying that what anthropologists and other social theorists need is a concept of the cultural that adequately characterizes both complex modern ways of life and those of small-scale communities, past and present:

1. Such a view of the cultural (I avoid "culture" deliberately here, to avoid reification as best I can) would take the production and reproduction of cultural forms as problematic; that is, it would examine the way symbolic production is linked to power and interest (in terms of class, hierarchy, gender, etc.) and would hence probe what I have elsewhere called the "political economy of knowledge" (Keesing 1987).

2. Such a conception would assume that (many elements of) cultural traditions carry ideological force—again, not in a crude Marxist sense of distorting reality or creating false consciousness, but in Stuart Hall's (1988) reformulation of a Gramscian conception: that ideologies define the world in terms of idealized subject positions: "a brave warrior," "a virtuous woman," "a loyal subject," "a dutiful son."

3. Further, a critical conception of the cultural would begin with an assumption that in any "community"/"society," there will be multiple subdominant and partially submerged cultural traditions (again, in relation to power, rank, class, gender, age, etc.), as well as a hegemonic force of the dominant tradition. In these respects, feminist theory and post-Marxist theory in particular have opened to view and critically examined precisely what anthropological theory has been at pains to hide or deny.

4. Finally, a more critical cultural theory would make no assumptions about closed boundaries within which cultural meanings hold sway: "a culture" as bounded unit would give way to more complex conceptions of interpenetration, superimposition, and pastiche.

Revisiting theories of culture, then, I think in this realm we now have more to learn than to teach.

NOTES

1. The initial version of this paper was presented in a symposium on "Assessing Developments in Anthropology" organized by Rob Borofsky at the American Anthropological Association meetings in Washington, D.C., in November 1989. I am grateful to George Stocking for helpful comments in his role as discussant. An expanded version was presented as a lecture at the University of Manitoba in February, 1990; for comments and questions that led to further revisions, I am indebted to Rod Burchard, Jean-Luc Chodkiewicz, Yngve Georg Lithman, James Urry, and Raymond Wiest.

2. Editor's note: "The central idea in semiotics is a particular conception of the structure of the *sign* which is defined as a bond between a signifier and the signified: for example, the bond that exists between a series of sounds (signifier) and their meaning (signified) in a given language, or the social convention that the colour red stands for danger. Semiotic research involves . . . all the mechanisms which serve both to produce and obscure meanings, and to change meanings in sign systems" (Kuper and Kuper 1985:743).

3. Here I commend George Lakoff's book *Women, Fire and Dangerous Things* (1987); the new journal *Cognitive Linguistics* is also a valuable source.

4. Yngve George Lithman has usefully reminded me that the anthropological conception of culture was itself strongly influenced by wider intellectual developments (such as German romanticism, as it became expressed both in intellectual debates and in cultural nationalism); and George Stocking has commented in a similar vein on the transformations in social theoretic vision that separate the Boasian tradition and its invocations of "culture" from the Tylorian conception and project.

5. Cultural interpretations illuminate some questions, but they hide a host of others. If classical Orientalism, including its anthropological forms, was part and parcel of the imperialist process, the neo-Orientalism in which we are caught up is part and parcel of the global economy and political climate of our time.

6. See e.g. the recent writings of Michael Taussig on the culture of terror (Taussig 1987).

7. See Guha (1983b, 1984b, 1985, 1986, 1987).

8. Foucault demolished the classical Marxist theory of ideology as a class-interested disguise of underlying truth. To see ideologies as masking the truth assumes some privileged access to truth which is no longer philosophically admissible. Marx himself glimpsed in places much more subtle views of ideologies and their force, but it has remained for Gramsci and his contemporary successors to develop them coherently.

INTELLECTUAL ROOTS

Roger Keesing (1935-1993) was Professor of Anthropology at McGill University in Montreal. From 1974 to 1990 he was Professor of Anthropology in the Institute of Advanced Studies, The Australian National University. He studied the Kwaio of Malaita, Solomon Islands, for thirty years, and also did field research in the northwestern Indian Himalayas. His eleven books—including *Kin Groups and Social Structure* (1975), *Lightning Meets the West Wind: The Malaita Massacre* (1980), *Cultural Anthropology: A Contemporary*

Perspective (1981), *Kwaio Religion* (1982), *Kwaio Grammar* (1985), *Melanesian Pidgin and the Oceanic Substrate* (1988), and *Custom and Confrontation: The Kwaio Struggle for Cultural Autonomy* (1992)—and almost a hundred published papers cover a wide range of topics from cultural theory, social structure, religion, and symbolism, and cognition to colonial history and linguistics.

Growing up in an anthropological family, I had childhood experiences of fieldwork; but I discovered anthropology intellectually only as a Stanford undergraduate, after beginning in literature. George Spindler, Bernard Siegel, and my father Felix Keesing introduced me to the field; and I studied with Gregory Bateson, who remained a friend and strong intellectual influence in later years.

I began graduate study in the Harvard Department of Social Relations with Clyde Kluckhohn and Douglas Oliver in 1956-1957. When I returned in 1960 after three years as an Air Force officer in Turkey, Kluckhohn had just died, and the new excitement at Harvard centered around British kinship theory in the style of Needham and Leach (introduced by the newly arrived David Maybury-Lewis) and cognitive anthropology ("ethnoscience"), introduced there by Charles Frake and represented in the work of Goodenough and Conklin.

These two streams of influence channeled my thinking when I set off for Solomon Islands fieldwork in 1962. I had been interested in Central Asia after my experience in Turkey, but political difficulties of the Cold War era made fieldwork there unrealistic. The choice of the Solomons was inspired by Douglas Oliver: "You should find a culturally traditional Melanesian society, the way I did, and do really tough fieldwork while you're still young and resilient physically: you can study some comfortable place when you get older." (I think about that as I scale jungle cliffs and sleep on mud floors back in Kwaio country in my fifties.)

I intended a synthesis of cognitive and kinship perspectives in studying the cultural code whereby decisions were made regarding marriage, residence, and kinship—in a society where "non-unilineal descent groups" (a burning preoccupation of anthropologists in those days) seemed likely to be found. The Kwaio as I encountered them in the 1960s, strikingly conservative culturally, proved ideal for such study. (Although they were reputed to be wild and dangerous, the Kwaio have been enormously supportive and hospitable.) My Ph.D. dissertation and a number of papers written in the late 1960s and into the early 1970s explored these themes. By this time I was teaching at the new, experimental University of California at Santa Cruz, where undergraduate students I introduced to anthropology included a dozen who went on to get Ph.D.s.

By early 1970s I had become politicized by my students, and my interests shifted from cognition and social structure to more global and political interests, including a belated self-reeducation in Marxism and social theory.

My move to a chair in The Australian National University Research Institute in 1974 gave me an ideal opportunity to continue Solomons fieldwork (which increasingly went in these new directions) and to make several short fieldwork trips to Churah in the northwestern Indian Himalayas to look at the political economy of peasants and "development."

In the last twenty years, I have been examining questions I mainly ignored in my early research: class, gender, power, "development" and dependency, colonial discourse, cultural nationalism. I draw theoretical guidance from Marx, and more recently, from Gramsci, Foucault, Bourdieu, Hall, Said, Guha, and a range of feminist theorists (notably Rowbotham, Mitchell, Ehrenreich, English, Irigaray, and Wittig). These have been reflected in writing about the Solomons, in books and articles on struggles against colonial domination, life histories of Kwaio women, the political economy of "development," the politics of "custom," the structures of counterhegemonic discourse, and predation and violence of urban underclasses.

My interests in language (sustained in studies of the Kwaio language and the history of Melanesian pidgin English) and in the mind have been rekindled by the emergence of cognitive linguistics. The concerns with conventional metaphor, with the iconic, image-based character of language and thought, and an emphasis on embodied experience all point to underlying universals and provide antidotes to anthropology's excessive relativisms and exotica hunting. These interests have led me back to a renewed engagement with questions of

The Cultural in Motion

In the last section, we explored the cultural as an analytical concept. Here we take up the cultural's dynamic character. Anthropologists have commented on this aspect of the cultural for decades. But they have had trouble developing a coherent model of the complex dynamics involved. One can sense the difficulty by looking at a recent statement by Sanjek. Culture, he (1991:622) says, "is . . . under continuous creation—fluid, interconnected, diffusing, interpenetrating, homogenizing, diverging, hegemonizing, resisting, reformulating, creolizing, open rather than closed, partial rather than total, crossing its own boundaries, persisting where we don't expect it to, and changing where we do." What type of model does one use to conceptualize such a collection of traits?

This section focuses on three dimensions of the cultural: individual diversity, time, and space. The cultural, one might say, is not only moving along all these dimensions at once, but the dimensions are, at the same time, in motion—interacting with and adapting to one another. Little wonder, then, we have had trouble conceptualizing the dynamics involved.

One can, tentatively, categorize each contributor in this section as focusing on one of the above dimensions. I say tentatively, because it will be clear in reading the papers that they overflow labels, addressing issues that concern two or more dimensions. But if we accept various qualifications to the categorization, we might say that Vayda, myself, and Barth focus on the *dimension of individual diversity*. Vayda questions essentialist notions of the cultural, notions that emphasize a group's cultural essence or uniform character. I continue this theme, using differences in what people assert about certain topics to rethink what we mean by knowledge and knowing. Tying my analysis into current neurophysiological research on memory, I stress (like Vayda) the need for moving beyond old formulations and analyses. Barth (page 352) emphasizes the need "to recognize variability as a ubiquitous feature." He suggests reorienting the cultural concept to make it more open, contestable, fluid. Moore and Sahlins focus on the *dimension of time*. Moore discusses tools for analyzing the continuous and multiple reshapings of cultural meanings through time and how the past, present, and future merge into one another. Sahlins considers the subtle ways change overlaps with continuity as one group comes in contact with another. Kottak and Colson focus on the *dimension of space*. They explore the shifting interconnections that link local communities to large-scale regional and international systems. Looking a bit closer at these dimensions and how anthropologists have analyzed them in times past helps illuminate the contexts within which this section's contributors write.

313

THE DIMENSION
OF INDIVIDUAL DIVERSITY

Anthropologists have been aware of individual diversity within cultural groups for decades—perhaps even over a century if one includes Dorsey's 1884 *Omaha Sociology*. More than fifty years ago, Boas (1938:683) noted, "Most attempts to characterize the social life of peoples are hampered by the lack of uniform behavior of all individuals." And Sapir (1949: 570) commented, "Two Crows, a perfectly good and authoritative [informant] . . . could presume to rule out of court the very existence of a custom or attitude or belief vouched for by some other [informant] . . . equally good and authoritative."

What is perhaps most intriguing about the host of analyses that exist—and a little investigation will uncover scores of studies—is that research on the subject has proceeded somewhat akin to the "slash and burn" model touched on by Wolf and Wallace in the introduction (see page 12). Periodically people conduct intensive studies of the topic only to move on to something else after a few years. The topic then lies neglected for a period of time until it is "rediscovered" (again) by a new set of scholars.

A host of interesting insights have accumulated in the process as the following brief selection suggests. Sapir, for example, argues for a more sensitive accounting of the psychological factors behind individual variation. (The reference to Two Crows, just cited, comes from a paper entitled "Why Cultural Anthropology Needs the Psychiatrist.") "Only through an analysis of variation . . . [and] a minute and sympathetic study of individual behavior," Sapir (1949:576) states, will it "ultimately be possible to say things about society . . . and culture that are more than fairly convenient abstractions." Wallace (1970: 129) suggests that the cultural should be conceived less in terms of shared uniformity than in terms of what he calls the "organization of diversity": how "individually diverse organ-

isms work to maintain, increase, or restore [a] quantity of organization . . . within [heterogenous] sociocultural . . . systems." He notes (1970:32) that "cognitive sharing is not *necessary* for stable social interaction," only that we respond effectively to one another. Pelto and Pelto (1975:1) suggest, "Intragroup diversity . . . like genetic diversity within populations, is of great significance for ongoing processes of human adaptation." They compare cultural to biological evolution and consider the role diversity plays in each. Boster (1985) takes a different tack, noting commonalities underlying seemingly different assertions. "Deviations from the [Aguaruna] model" of manioc identification, he (1985:193) writes, "are patterned according [to] the sexual division of labor, membership in kin and residential groups, and individual expertise."

The problem has been in bringing these separate insights together into a unified framework. Anthropologists have been aware of their essentialist biases, their ignoring of cultural diversity, for some time. Kroeber (1948:574), some forty years ago, noted, "Any broad account of . . . [an] institution is bound to suppress as much as possible the highly variable roles of the actual individual men or women concerned." But we have not been able to successfully develop an effective model of the cultural that significantly moves us beyond the homogeneous image of old. The models suggested tend not to catch on. Following the "slash and burn" analogy, they are proposed and then quietly ignored. That is why Vayda's renewed call for "anti-essentialism" is so important.

Three significant issues remain to be addressed. First, we need to develop more effective empirical descriptions of individual diversity. On the one hand, we have Nadel's (in Tax et al. 1953:91) suggestion that we collect quantitative data "which enable . . . us to say of a particular mode of behavior that this is typical to such-and-such a degree and there is such-and-such a range of variability." On the other, it remains unclear, as Barth notes, to what extent complex subtleties can be reduced to statistical modeling. (The positivist/interpretivist debate casts its shadow here.)

Second, we need to be more precise about what is (and is not) shared within cultural groupings and, related to this, on what level (or levels) is sharing deemed to occur. Does sharing occur at the level of overt content—in terms of what people say and do in their everyday lives? And/or does it occur in terms of underlying principles, that while not directly observable, seem to shape people's interactions with one another? In considering the subtle relation between diversity and sharing, we need also keep in mind the possibility Vayda raises (especially in note 6)—of studying diversity in and of itself, without analyzing it in the context of cultural units, without committing ourselves to groups as the central focus of investigation.

Finally, we need to move from a content orientation—regarding which specific elements are (or are not) shared—toward a more processual one in which generation, perpetuation, and handling of diversity become central. This is the direction Wallace suggested thirty years ago and which Vayda, Barth and myself (as well as Bloch and Strauss and Quinn in the previous section) affirm. Barth's (1990: 640) recent Huxley lecture illustrates such a processual approach. Using examples from Southeast Asia and Melanesia, he indicates how different styles of knowledge transmission "generate deep differences in the form, scale and distribution of knowledge." Likewise, as Vayda notes (page 324), I (Borofsky 1987) emphasize a processual approach in examining a Polynesian atoll's traditions: "for Borofsky, as for Barth, how knowledge is acquired, retained, and transmitted contains the key to explaining variations."

THE DIMENSION OF TIME

There is no doubt anthropology once had an atemporal bias. A host of ethnographies merged the past and present into an "ethnographic present" that neither reflected the past nor the present but some theoretical combination of the two—expressing not an observed reality but an abstract sense of what might have been. Yet it is equally true anthropology has been concerned with issues of change and continuity for more than a century now. Expressing its centrifugal tendencies, anthropology has moved in two directions at once—both toward and away from a concern with the temporal.

Let me elaborate on anthropology's ongoing concern with the temporal since this is a key theme in the following contributions and also serves to balance out recent discussions regarding anthropology's atemporal orientation (e.g. Fabian 1983). Early anthropologists repeatedly expressed an interest in the temporal dimension. In 1896, Boas (in 1940:280) stressed the importance of studying "processes of growth" with, what he termed, the historical method. And in responding to a comment by his first graduate student (Kroeber), Boas (in 1940: 307) defensively replied in 1936: "I . . . have used years of my life . . . trying to unravel the historical development of social organization, secret societies, the spread of art forms, of folktales on the Northwest Coast of America." Sapir, another student of Boas, wrote in 1916 a classic monograph entitled *Time Perspective in Aboriginal American Culture*. It systematically surveyed methods for making cultural reconstructions—especially what inferences one might reasonably infer about which changes with what types of data. And Evans-Pritchard (1962:180), in advocating a renewed interest in history, emphasized that early anthropologists were concerned with the temporal: "In turning our backs on history we have turned them on the builders of our science who, up to as late as Hobhouse and Westermarck, had as their primary aim to discover the principles or developmental trends in social evolution, an aim which can only be attained if the facts of history are used." (Readers of Wolf's *Europe and the People Without History* might appreciate knowing that in 1908 Bernheim, as interpreted by Koppers in Thomas 1956:169, stressed: "Primitive peoples . . . should be a subject of history. There are no peoples without history.")

Anthropology's concern with the temporal dimension has taken a variety of forms. One can see it in the analyses of the early evolutionists such as Morgan, Tylor, and Frazer. Morgan's book *Ancient Society* (1963 [1877]), for example, was subtitled "Researches in the Lines of Human Progress from Savagery through Barbarism to Civilization." One can see it as well in the accounts of later evolutionists: in White's (1949) analysis of humans' increasing ability to harness sources of energy, in Childe's (1936) analysis of the transitions from food gathering to food production to urbanism, in Steward's (1963) concern with multilinear evolution and cultural ecology, and in Service's (1962) band-tribes-chiefdoms-state as well as Fried's (1967) egalitarian-rank-stratified-state schema. It also exists in a range of diffusion studies: in the age-area analyses of Wissler (1917), Kroeber (1939), and Kroeber and Driver (1932) as well as in the Kulturkreis analyses of Graebner (1911, see also Kluckhohn 1936). These authors viewed diffusion as the spatially spreading out over time of objects and ideas. And it occurs in a host of acculturation studies, for example: Mooney's (1965 [1896]) *The Ghost-Dance Religion and the Sioux Outbreak of 1890*, Linton's (1940) *Acculturation in Seven American Indian Tribes*, Wilson and Wilson's (1945) *The Analysis of Social Change, Based on Observations in Central Africa*, R. Redfield's (1953) *The Primitive World and Its Transformations*, and Spindler's (1955) *Sociocultural and Psychological Processes of Menomini Acculturation.*

Anthropologists, then, have conducted considerable research on the temporal. Let me provide a few illustrations of the breadth of studies involved. Kroeber (1957:20) observed that the "basic ideal pattern of Western women's dress . . . has gone through a thousand years of constant remodeling without any fundamental change." "The total silhouette shifts rather steadily for perhaps fifty years toward one extreme of proportion, such as a narrow skirt for women, and then for about fifty years toward the opposite, giving a wavelength of close to a century for the periodicity" (1948:333). (For further details of this analysis see Richardson and Kroeber 1940.)

Following the pattern Kottak and Colson discuss in their contribution, Firth returned to Tikopia, an isolated Polynesian outlier in the Solomon Islands. He systematically explored what had changed in the twenty-three years since his first research. Ostensibly, much was the same as in 1929 in terms of descent groupings, kinship and marriage, chieftainship, and religious beliefs (which included both pagan and Christian congregations). "Yet by 1952," (the time of his second visit) Firth (1959:342) noted, "something of fundamental importance had happened to Tikopia society. It had reached a condition from which one felt it would be difficult for it to retreat. . . . In the economic field [for example] there had been a great enlargement of the consumers' horizon." "The society seemed on the threshold of . . . radical change because of the implications of the ideas they had already accepted" (1959: 344). Among the most prominent was "the degree to which . . . [Tikopians had] surrendered the ultimate responsibility for their values . . . to authorities . . . in lands far afield." Firth caught Tikopian society, in other words, on the cusp of transformation. A host of small changes were finally adding up to a major one. Change was generating its own momentum.

Hallowell (1955) examined the psychological impact of change on the Ojibwa. Using Rorschach tests from three groups exhibiting varying degrees of acculturation, Hallowell explored how these acculturative differences affected Ojibwa personality patterns. He noted stresses in the most acculturated group due to "the lack of any positive substitute for . . . the aboriginal value system that had its core in [traditional] religious belief" (1955:357).

Women and men coped with this acculturative stress differently, Hallowell observed: while women made "an excellent social and psychological adjustment [to acculturation], the men, on the whole, were much less successful" (335).

Service's (1955) study of Indo-European relations explored a different aspect of the temporal. Service demonstrated a relationship between aboriginal social organization and the ethnic composition of present-day Latin American populations. The relationship centered on how colonial authorities instituted controls over indigenous populations after conquest. With indigenous state systems, which already had their own bureaucracies, administrative control was indirect and many people and cultural traditions survived. But where other forms of indigenous organization existed, which lacked full-fledged bureaucracies, the colonial powers imposed their own administrators. Here, cultural traditions (and indigenous population) were far more affected. "Rates and degrees of acculturation," Service (1955:423) asserted, "were most rapid and complete where [colonial administrative] control was most direct and personal."

Rethinking Old Conceptualizations

The temporal dimension has a new prominence in anthropological circles. Where before the temporal dimension was acknowledged as *relevant* (especially when one could move beyond conjectures about the past), it is fair to say today it is seen as *critical*. What factors have brought about this change?

First, there are now more historical materials to work with. We are harvesting the fruits of the Boasian and Malinowskian ethnographic revolution. We have a host of quality ethnographies—produced 50 or 60 years ago—which serve as baselines for modern studies of change. And we have data, as Kottak and Colson note, from a number of long-term projects. (Colson, for example, has worked among the African Tonga for over forty

years.) "In the process of long-term involvement, we not only accumulate a mass of data," she (1984:3) writes, "we also learn a good deal about limitations inherent in the collection of data." "Collection and data are both processes in time. . . . We are not the same when we return, nor can we return to the people who are the same." "It was Heraclitus who said," Colson continues, "we cannot step twice into the same river. I suspect that until recently few of us have been able to see how fast the river really flows."

Second, we have become more concerned with the histories of contact and colonialism. Today these are perceived as rich sources of ethnographic information, offering an important temporal dimension to fieldwork grounded in the present. "As part of the more general political enterprise in the early 1970s," Stoler (1989b:134) notes, anthropologists "reexamined how colonial politics affected . . . the histories of our subjects." There are subtleties here. "One of the ironies which marks the history of European relations with the rest of the world," Cohn (1981:233) remarks, "is that many of what we take to be authentic markers of the aboriginals of North America were created as a result of European contact." For example, the Ojibwa, just referred to in Hallowell's study, might well have coalesced into a tribe in the late 1600s as a result of the demands and dislocations of the fur trade (see Wolf 1982:170-172). The religious beliefs and practices Hallowell refers to as forming the basis for the "aboriginal value system" (including the Midewiwin) were probably at least partly shaped by American Indian-Western interactions. We are realizing, in other words, that not only has Western contact shaped indigenous organization through time, but, to some extent, historical records exist of these changes. This is generating considerable excitement in the discipline.

Third, anthropologists have been drawn into the "politics of culture." As Keesing notes, the cultural is now very much an object of contention—regarding who can speak for whom with what authority. Anthropologists are seeing the cultural being constructed (and reconstructed) before their very eyes. In both the rediscovery of old traditions and the formulation of new ones, we see the cultural in motion. It has become a tool of empowerment, a symbol for unifying one group against another. As today's headlines make clear, the cultural has become something to fight about.

Reaching for New Conceptualizations

It is these changing understandings that form the context for the papers that follow, especially Moore's and Sahlins's. In their reaching for new conceptualizations they focus on three issues that overlap with ones discussed in "Rethinking the Cultural." (Readers might wish to refer back to that section for elaboration of the themes involved.)

First, there is the question of how continuity and change tend to overlap with one another. The cultural, Cohn (1980:217) states, "is continually being invented or modified, without being totally transformed." This is why Moore (page 364) concerns herself with "the continuous and multiple shapings and reshapings" of meanings as well as with analyzing transformational sequences. As she implies, change and continuity are not always easy to separate out from one another. They are entwined in intricate ways.

Second, there is the question of how cultural units interact with one another over time—especially how one group seemingly dominates another culturally without the domination ever becoming complete. There is an "indigenization of modernity," as Sahlins stresses, in which the foreign is reinterpreted in local terms. And there is a curious hybridization of the cultural as various groups' beliefs seem to merge with those of the "world economic system" and yet remain distinct from them. Hannerz (1990:245) refers to transnational cultures as "bridgeheads . . . into other territorial cultures." The overlappings and differentiations involved in these interac-

tions may well be quite subtle (a point we saw made by Linton in his "One Hundred Percent American," quoted in the introduction to Section Four).

Finally, there is the "politics of culture" in which defining what is the cultural and who possesses it become highly politicized matters—open not only to intellectual debate but to violent conflict. We see the cultural not simply as something in motion, but as belonging to a set of larger political processes which help to define it.

THE DIMENSION OF SPACE

Anthropologists of earlier eras had an ambiguous appreciation for the cultural's spatial dimension. Some anthropologists portrayed the groups they studied as cultural isolates. From this perspective, cultural distinctiveness involved spatial separation—most noticeably from Westerners (but also perhaps from others). The obvious disruptions of Western contact buttressed such a perspective. External factors shaping a group's organization tended to be down-played. Colonial and missionary influences were set aside. So were a range of other factors. "One of the most admirable analyses of the detailed social structure . . . that has been published in recent years," Forde (in Tax et al. 1953:69) noted forty years ago, "is Professor Fortes's study of the Tallensi [1945] . . . But you will not find in Dr. Fortes's book any reference . . . [to the implications] of external slave-raiding from outside, which was endemic in the Tallensi area."

It is also true, however—again emphasizing anthropology's centrifugal tendencies—that various anthropologists have paid considerable attention to the spatial dimension. It was a key element, for example, in diffusion studies—such as those of the Kulturkreis and of the age-area variety—that used observed changes through space to infer changes through time. As in Spier's analysis of the Plains Indian Sun Dance (cited in Section Two), one traced out the spatial distribution of elements and, from these, inferred what diffused when and how. The spatial dimension also formed part of Kroeber's (1948:286) famous definition of peasants as "part-societies with part-cultures." Peasants "live[d] in relation to market towns," Kroeber noted, and "form[ed] a class segment of a larger population." To understand peasant groupings, one had to study the broader spatial whole of which they formed a part.

Today, few stress the isolated, pristine qualities of research locales. The spatial dimension—in terms of regional, national, and global influences on local communities—is repeatedly acknowledged. "One of the most important strengths of world-systems and [Marxist] mode of production approaches," Roseberry (1988:168) asserts, is "the placement of anthropological subjects within larger historical, political, and economic movements . . . the slave trade, the imposition of colonial regimes . . . [the] boom and bust cycles of international markets." And there is an acknowledgment of a need to "revise conventions of ethnographic description away from measuring change against self-contained, homogeneous [units] . . . toward," Marcus and Fischer (1986:78) state, "a view of cultural situations as . . . in a perpetual historically sensitive state of resistance and accommodation to broader processes of influence." Sahlins (1977:27) emphasizes indigenous groups can be actively involved in these interactions:

"The Hawaiians were not just the passive victims of [imperialism]. . . . On the contrary, the Hawaiian categorical order played a critical . . . role, shaping the organization of trade by . . . its own meaningful system of demand."

There is also growing appreciation for the fact that contact affects both parties involved in the interaction. Not only have European-Americans dramatically affected North American Indians over the past three centuries, for example, but, as Hallowell (1957 [1967:320]) notes, North American Indians have affected the European-American way of life: "Our contacts with the Indians have affected our speech, our economic life, our clothing, our sports and recreations, . . . folk and concert music, the novel, poetry, drama, even some of our basic psychological attitudes."

Two key issues need clarification regarding the spatial. First, we must think through the most effective unit (or units) for analysis. What is gained and what is lost, for instance, by focusing on a community versus a region versus a global network? The complex types of data Kottak and Colson collected raise questions regarding which types of frameworks most effectively handle what types of questions. And second, we must reassess (as Sahlins and Kottak and Colson indicate) how we might best represent relations between the West and the rest through time—how we might best trace the subtleties of interaction, accommodation, and resistance?

22

Actions, Variations, and Change: The Emerging Anti-Essentialist View in Anthropology[1]

ANDREW P. VAYDA

While positivists and interpretive anthropologists have been debating how patterns and order in sociocultural phenomena should be studied and what their determinants are, there has been increasing but still relatively little attention to the development on which I want to focus here, namely, the emergence of the view that patterns and order have been exaggerated or unduly emphasized and that variations and variability need to be studied more. In describing this development and making claims for its significance, I shall first use what I will call "anti-essentialist" illustrations and then essentialist ones. For the sake of greater clarity about programmatic issues in anthropology, my discussion will include some remarks about essentialism and anti-essentialism in relation to other debates among anthropologists.

ANTI-ESSENTIALISM

The intent in this section is to be illustrative rather than exhaustive about the emerging, variation-focused, anti-essentialist view.[2] A forceful statement of it was made in 1975 by Pelto and Pelto. They noted that since 1884, when Dorsey reported disagreements among Omaha Indians about their own culture, the observations of intracommunity heterogeneity reported by many other anthropologists have, for the most part, been quickly set aside in order to "get on with the job of describing 'social structure' and 'typical' cultural patterning" (Pelto and Pelto 1975:1). In line with this, a recent development among some anthropologists confronted with variations has been to seek to determine "cultural truth" by establishing on what, amidst variations, there is consensus among informants (Romney, Weller, and Batchelder 1986:315, Boster 1986: 429).

The Importance of Variation

By contrast, Pelto and Pelto see variations themselves as being fundamentally important—for example, as adaptations to microenvironments or to transitory contexts and as raw materials for eventually widespread social or cultural changes. Like anti-essentialist statements in some other fields (e.g., in biology and ecology, Gould 1982, Mayr 1982:46-47, and Simberloff 1980), the article by Pelto and Pelto is noteworthy for going beyond acknowledging variations to making them, rather than a type or pattern, the main objects of study. The anti-essentialist in anthropology, as in these other fields, sees variations as "fundamental reality" (Gould 1982:12) and not as mere accidents about norms. He rejects the

320

notion which Popper (1957:27-28) has made diagnostic of essentialism, namely, that whatever is shared or universal (e.g., "whiteness" as a property of many different things like snowflakes, tablecloths, and swans) has a reality of its own and is more deserving of scholarly or scientific attention than are single things or else sets or groups of single things.

In his research, the anti-essentialist is guided by questions about actual behavior and its consequences rather than by such questions as "what is the family?" or "what is the state?" or "what is revolution?" or "what is religion?" or "what is Pueblo Indian religion?" or "what is Javanese culture?" Unlike the essentialist, he does not make it his task to ferret out from the different things or events to which one or another of such terms is applied the "real" or "true" nature of some essence denoted by it (Popper 1957:29).[3] And when he himself makes use of such broad categories as "eating behavior" and "sexual behavior," it is with a view not to discovering norms for them or showing what they "really are" but rather to showing and explaining variations in, for example, what people eat (Vayda 1987a) and whether sexual partners are of the same or different sex and are married or not (Gould 1982, discussing the "radical anti-essentialism" of Alfred Kinsey's sex research).

Ethnographic expression of the anti-essentialist view in the 1970s and 1980s may be found in accounts in which variations are, in effect, the fundamental reality described and are not presented as deviance from putative norms or discounted as mere "noise" in the system. Thus, P. J. Wilson (1977:28) describes the Tsimihety people of Madagascar as flexibly, pragmatically, and unspectacularly going about their lives "without the constraints or esthetics of a systematic, ordering structure." Their actions and thoughts are said to vary according to personal situations:

Some villages irrigated their rice fields while others relied upon rain. Some organized cooperatives that exchanged labour; others worked on their own. Some men performed a certain ritual using a prayer; others omitted the prayer or used a different one.

There is, according to Wilson, no reason to suppose that such variation is the result of cultural disintegration. Although he found no distinctive Tsimihety way of doing things or, as he put it, no Tsimihety "ethnographic trademark," neither did he find the people to be living in chaos or anarchy.

Let me note just a few other accounts in which variation is similarly described. The Ibans of Sarawak are noteworthy because they have indeed seemed to some scholars to have an ethnographic trademark: expansive, forest-destroying, shifting cultivation (see the references in Padoch 1982:9-10, 117); they have been described as "the prototypical *mangeurs de bois*" (or eaters of forest) (Bronson 1972:193). However, in a 1982 monograph, Padoch shows them to act in various ways other than migrating to areas of primary forest when land or other resources available to them become limited. For example, they adopt more conservative cropping-fallow regimes and make their farming more labor-intensive; they also borrow more land for swiddens (i.e. slash-and-burn horticultural plots) and engage more in temporary wage labor. The Ibans emerging from the pages of Padoch's monograph are like the Tsimihety in pragmatically varying their behavior and responding to the different conditions in which they find themselves.

One of my own recent attacks on essentialist, typologizing, culture-as-norms tendencies in anthropology dealt with why people fought in the New Guinea highlands (Vayda 1989). Using data that I had collected in the 1960s on Maring warfare, I showed that an important feature which varied among Marings was fighting for land. Some Maring groups did it and others did not. Fear of enemy ancestor spirits deterred some Marings from taking enemy land and did not deter others. As has been argued by critics of my earlier publications on Maring warfare (e.g., Hallpike 1973:457-59, King 1976:313), not *all* Maring fighting was based on being short of land and fighting for it; however, contrary to the critics, *some* Maring fighting was. Indeed the variation was such as sometimes to be found between the main belligerents in a single war, one side fighting for land and the other for honor (which would be lost if its land, even if greatly exceeding its needs, were not to be defended). A result of inattention to such variation is the distortion of reality in typologies like Sillitoe's (1977), in which fighting for land is used to distinguish warfare as waged by members of a single large New Guinea ethnolinguistic unit, the Abelam, and is wrongly denied to members of other units, including the Maring.

Colson's contribution to the emerging view, as set forth in an important 1984 article, has special weight because it is based on studying a single people, the Gwembe Tonga of Zambia, since 1946. She found that each decade presented the Gwembe with "very different risks and possibilities" (for example, the trauma of forced resettlement, political struggles, guerrilla warfare, economic expansion, and economic decline) and that, as people experienced different challenges, they reordered their thinking and changed their goals (Colson 1984:5).

With respect to values in particular, she makes explicit that observations from long-term studies are not compatible with an essentialist view: "Values once thought to be fundamental for guiding the way particular people dealt with each other and their environment have turned out to be situational and time linked, rather than eternal verities that can be used to predict behavior over time, under all circumstances" (Colson 1984:7). Colson ends her article by referring to the pervasiveness of flux and sounding an anti-essentialist clarion call: "Anthropology advances as we look for diversity, for variability" (Colson 1984:12).[4]

Making Variations the Object of Analysis

Lest it be thought that the emerging view constitutes, as Harris (1987b:515) has suggested, a

revival of voluntarism and a doting on variations for the sake of disproving general theories and principles, it should be understood that the anti-essentialist view includes a concern with *explaining* variations and with using generalizations to explain them. Accordingly the programmatic issue is not the hoary one of generalization vs. particularism or of explanation vs. description (Harris 1968:chaps. 9-11; Magarey 1987) but rather the question of whether variations themselves, as much as, if not more than, any putative sociocultural patterns or norms, are to be made the objects of explanation and generalization. This latter question is, in effect, the one with which Colson (1984:12) was confronted when a colleague told her that "no one would think anthropology had anything to offer if it were said that values and institutions constantly change and that even between villages in the same region there are numerous differences." Appropriately enough, Colson reacted by thinking of Darwin and the Galapagos finches, that classic case of both seeing variations as significant and explaining them.

In a recent book, Barth (1987:8, 24) also turns to Darwin and his finches and, in accord with the "tradition of the wondering naturalist," expresses his commitment to identifying actual, empirically ascertainable but "generalizable" processes and mechanisms to account for variations. The variations with which he is specifically concerned occur in rituals and cosmological ideas among the Mountain Ok people of New Guinea. Pointing to the oscillation between public performance of rites every ten years or so in a community and the long periods of solitary, taboo-hedged safe-keeping of knowledge of the rites in the care of a small number of ritual experts, Barth notes that rites cannot be reproduced each time with complete fidelity and that the modifications which occur depend on such factors as the memories of the experts and their recourse to guesswork and improvisation, as well as to borrowing from neighboring groups (Barth 1987:chap. 4 and *passim*).

Incrementally these modifications can result in the variations which Barth observed among Mountain Ok communities, including such stark contrasts as associating the red body paint in certain initiation rituals with maleness and virility in some communities and with menstrual blood in others.[5] Barth makes clear that the objects of study for him are not "encompassing logical orders" (1987:8) or "structural wholes" (1987:83) or "internally homogeneous and shared, and externally bounded" cultures (1987:84) but rather variations themselves and the processes and mechanisms that produce them.

In my own recent work, I have similarly eschewed making cultures or other "wholes" the objects of study and have sought instead to explain actions or their consequences without regard to their cultural representativeness or typicality.[6] In the case of my study of why Marings fought, the focus was on fighting itself and on variations in its consequences and in the reasons for engaging in it. My explanation of these variations conforms to the so-called contextual mode which I have advocated in several recent publications (Vayda 1987a, 1987b, 1988; cf. Vayda 1983).

Explanation in the contextual mode consists of contextualizing actions or consequences by tracing the threads of influence upon them outward in space and backward in time.[7] The generalizations supporting explanations in particular cases are "generic assertions of intelligible connection" rather than the covering laws or universal generalizations once regarded by some positivists as indispensable for scientific explanation.[8] Thus, to support the explanations of actions in particular cases, connections may be asserted among certain *kinds* of actions, certain *kinds* of reasons for them, and certain *kinds* of contexts in which they take place. The connections are set forth as being intelligible and as occurring *sometimes* but not as being necessarily universal.

A simple example from my Maring study is the statement that people fight for what they do not have (Vayda 1989:169, 175). That such

generic assertions may be usefully made cross-culturally and transhistorically for the purpose of explaining actions was cogently argued by Martin in 1977 (Martin 1977:chap. 11) and, in effect, by Evans-Pritchard some years before then (Evans-Pritchard 1962:174-175; cf. Berlin 1960:19-21; Hart and Honoré 1959: 53). Having the good sense to pay less attention to theoretical professions than to how events are actually explained or rendered intelligible by anthropologists and sociological historians, Evans-Pritchard (1962:175) put it well by saying that "any event has the characters of uniqueness and generality" and that both have to be given consideration in an interpretation or explanation of it (cf. Gould 1988). Moreover, his examples, concerning currency-debasing actions and the struggles of kings with their barons, made it clear that the generality to which he referred extended beyond the boundaries of particular cultures or historical periods.

Another recent study which is focused on variations is Borofsky's monograph (1987) on tradition and change among the approximately 750 inhabitants of the Polynesian atoll of Pukapuka. Like Barth and unlike the main previous ethnographers of Pukapuka, Borofsky does not make it his objective to produce an account of a homogeneous culture or a coherent way of life with a unitary structure. Instead, he emphasizes that Pukapukan social alignments are fluid and flexible (Borofsky 1987:72) and sometimes assume forms which previous Pukapukan ethnographers, myself included, were not even aware of.[9] An example of such a form is what Pukapukans call the *Akatawa*, a bipartite division of the atoll's population and resources. From 1976 to 1980, this took the place of a tripartite village organization which had been in force for decades. The "Council of Important People" which instituted the 1976 *Akatawa* regarded it a traditional form of social organization which the island's younger people should know about. What was originally intended as a two-week revival was extended because "the people liked it" (Borofsky 1987:140). Borofsky (1987:35) notes that the *Akatawa* was not disruptive and that probably the most radical change it effected was in making him realize that Pukapukan social life was much more fluid and less structured than he had thought. But this realization is not the end point of Borofsky's analysis. Like Barth, he is concerned with making flux and variations intelligible by discovering mechanisms that produce them. In his search for mechanisms, Borofsky uses a naturalistic approach similar to Barth's and pays close attention to how Pukapukans acquire knowledge. He found that the main processes included informally observing and listening to others and that, because people differ in what they observe and hear, diversity develops not only in their ideas about how to perform such activities as lashing outriggers but also in their knowledge of possible ways of organizing people and allocating resources (Borofsky 1987:122 and *passim*). In the case of the *Akatawa*, evidence indicates that, before 1976, it probably was not well-known or else seen as having little traditional significance. How this changed beginning in 1976 is summarized by Borofsky (1987:141-142) as follows:

A few individuals' private (and probably vague) conceptions were drawn into the public realm and supported by both the "Council of Important People" and the populace at large. . . . Simply by working without major problems the Akatawa also gained a measure of authenticity. As people experienced the Akatawa from 1976 onward, as they publicly discussed it, as they reflected on its possible historical antecedents, marginal or vaguely formulated views regarding past Akatawa spread into the public domain and became crystallized, enunciated, and accepted. A meaningful new tradition developed.

It can be seen that for Borofsky, as for Barth, how knowledge is acquired, retained, and transmitted contains the key to explaining variations.

ESSENTIALISM

The contrast between the emerging view as exemplified by Borofsky and essentialist views can be highlighted by briefly considering earlier Pukapukan ethnography. In the case of Ernest and Pearl Beaglehole (1938), their emphasis on cultural uniformity, structure, and stasis at the expense of diversity, lability, and change may have been not so much the expression of a consistent philosophical view as a response to having to publish their Pukapukan data in a limited number of pages and within the format prescribed for the Bernice P. Bishop Museum's Polynesian surveys. Moreover, as Borofsky (1987:50-51) observes, although variations are recorded in the Beagleholes's field notes, they may have decided not to include them in their monograph because of their notions about the coherence that monographs must have.[10] On the other hand, in the case of the later ethnographer, Hecht, the discounting of variations does evince an essentialist bias, involving a quest for "congruence" and "unitary symbolic structuring" in Pukapukan symbols and behavior relating to such matters as gender, the landscape, and passage through the life cycle (Hecht 1976a, 1976b, 1977, cited in Borofsky 1987:61-63). Valid Pukapukan cultural patterns are, for her, constituted by data that fit together; other data need receive little notice (Hecht 1976a, 1976b, cited in Borofsky 1987:69-70). Consequently absent from Hecht's ethnography are the kinds of findings reported by Borofsky—for example, that the Pukapukans' own formulas about relations between matrilineal and patrilineal groupings were repeatedly contradicted in practice and that Pukapukans themselves acknowledged this (Borofsky 1987:71).

The Essentialist Bias

The kind of bias which Hecht's work expresses is an old one. Currently it is being challenged by chaos theory as a reaction to the centuries-old constrictions of a Newtonian worldview whereby data showing order and stability were valued much more than data showing their opposites (Pool 1989). But the bias goes back long before Newton, at least as far back as Plato and the other Greek philosophers who argued that true knowledge consists of discovering the hidden, persisting essential reality lying behind all that presents itself to our eyes as fugitive, variable, or accidental (Popper 1966:I, 31 and *passim*; cf. Popper 1957:26ff.). Glorified in Western thinking for more than two millennia, this bias is not limited to any particular present-day school of anthropology.[11]

Ecological anthropologists like Rappaport (1984:412) express it in programs for discovering the essential structure which all adaptive systems are presumed to have despite "specific and categorical differences" among them (see Vayda 1986:296-302 for a critique of Rappaport's program and its Greek metaphysics). Structural Marxists like Godelier (1977:46) extol Marx for his discovery of capitalist profit from unpaid labor as the hidden, essential pattern underlying observable economic relations. Cultural materialists like Harris (1979a: 219), although critical of both structural Marxists and Lévi-Straussian structuralists, speak approvingly of their seeking "to get away from surface appearances and to find the inner 'secret' of phenomena." Sahlins, as a structuralist and interpretive anthropologist, objects not only to Harris's use of "ecological cost accounting" for discovery of the inner secret (Sahlins 1978), but, more generally, to the explanatory practices of all functionalist anthropologists who regard the rich, symbolic complexity of cultural phenomena as mere appearance masking the essential function of the phenomena in meeting economic and biological needs (Sahlins 1976:chap. 2; for a nonstructuralist critique of Harris's cost/benefit explanations, see Vayda 1987a, 1987b). But then Sahlins himself (1976, 1978, 1979, 1981, 1985) claims that each society is ordered by a meaningful and essential cultural logic of which the society's members are more or less

unaware and that the criterion by which the events in which members participate are to be judged important and worthy of anthropological attention is whether we can discern this cultural logic or order (or changes therein) in the events (see especially Sahlins 1985:xiii, 108 on this criterion).

Consider, for example, Sahlins's structuralist analysis (1981, 1985) of Hawaiian history. He first presents Hawaiian culture as if, prior to Captain Cook's arrival, it were reproducing itself according to a set of binary oppositions (culture/nature : chiefs/commoners : *tabu/noa* : man/woman). Then, to justify his claim that "history is organized by structures of significance" (Sahlins 1981:8), he turns his attention to the period of early Hawaiian-European contact, a period during which, as one critic of Sahlins has noted, thousands of Hawaiians died in epidemics, the land was being deforested, venereal diseases spread, Hawaiians were being raped by American whalers and catechized by Calvinist missionaries, and food production declined and shortages developed as labor was diverted to sandalwood production (Gailey 1983:247; cf. Stannard 1989, who makes pre-contact population estimates whereby Hawaiian deaths in the period of early contact numbered in the *hundreds* of thousands). Amidst all this dislocation, the essential change which Sahlins finds is the restructuring of the binary oppositions, some being replaced and others realigned. If such change indeed illustrates, as Sahlins (1981:3) claims, structures in history as well as the history of structures, then plainly a problem with it is all the history that is left out (cf. N. Thomas 1989:chaps. 8, 9; for a comparable discounting of variations in the *archaeological* record in order to show "underlying" principles or structures, see Tilley 1989:189-90).

ANTI-ESSENTIALISM: NEITHER POSITIVISM NOR ANTI-SCIENCE

The main title of this article when it was read at an annual meeting of the American Anthropological Association (see note 1) was "Neither Positivism nor Anti-Science." In keeping with that original title, a point that I want to emphasize here is that essentialism vs. anti-essentialism is a very different issue from that of interpretive vs. positivist approaches in anthropology. With respect to positivism, I agree with Agger (1987:122) that "it is in Anglo-American social science primarily that positivism survives at all, more as a regulative idea used to exclude deviants (e.g., critical theorists, qualitative sociologists, hermeneuticists) than as a coherent theory of knowledge" (cf. Geertz 1985, C. Taylor 1980).[12]

Far from subscribing to the old positivist notion that the same, so-called materialist models of explanation used in classical physics and chemistry must be appropriate to all science, including social science, I have, in advocating the previously noted contextual mode of explanation, argued for including in the explanantia for human actions "not only features of the physical and institutional contexts but also the intentions, purposes, knowledge, and beliefs of the actors, all of which may themselves be made objects of explanation" (Vayda 1987a:500 and 1989:173). Not only positivism but also the Cartesian dualism which contributed to it have run their course (Rosenthal 1980, Searle 1984), and thus the point to be made clear here is that my objection to structuralist interpretations like those of Sahlins is not that they refer at all to mental events or mental states. My objection is rather that Sahlins and others fail to provide any adequate empirical or theoretical justification for assuming that certain mental phenomena or ways of thought are essential attributes of particular societies or cultures and that, because of this, they are the explanantia of choice for the actions of people who, by criteria of birth, upbringing, citizenship, and/or residence, might be regarded as belonging to those societies or cultures.

Certainly in the modern world, as Goody suggested more than twenty years ago, a person's various activities occur in different mental as well as material contexts so that he acts in one context "'as' a Muslim or Hindu, in another 'as' a trader, in another 'as' a member of a particular caste or patronymic group" (Goody 1968:9). Moreover, many of us today, far from "belonging" to a particular culture or living in the "culturally specific cognitive worlds" emphasized by some interpretive anthropologists (Holy 1987:7), have, as one humanist has put it, constructed our own nests of routine or identity with twigs and straws picked up from maybe a dozen "cultures" (Bryden 1989b; cf. Bryden 1989a; Barth 1989: 130; Clifford 1988:23). The beliefs and other mental phenomena that may be included in explanations of our behavior do not come from one culturally specific cognitive world, and such pronouncements as Sahlins's statement (1985:vii) that all events are contingent realizations of cultural patterns provide little help in making sense of the events in which we take part (cf. Greenwood 1987 on "social representations" vs. "agent representations").

A Matter for Empirical Determination

However, according to the anti-essentialist view, whether specific beliefs and meanings are shared widely and persist in a given society is, even in the premodern world, a matter for empirical determination rather than for a priori postulation on the basis of essentialist assumptions.[13] It is likewise an empirical question whether, even if they are widely shared and persistent, those beliefs and meanings rather than some more idiosyncratic or transient ones are the basis on which some particular actions are taken at particular times or in particular contexts.[14]

Anti-essentialism entails no opposition to using mental phenomena as explanantia for actions or events, but it does make an issue of *which* mental phenomena are so used and what the evidence for them is. No support for essentialism in these matters is provided by such studies of premodern situations as were cited in the previous section, including Barth's study of variations in rituals and cosmological ideas among New Guinea's Mountain Ok people and my own study of variations in what New Guinea's Maring people fought for and in whether or not their beliefs deterred them from taking enemy land.

The fact that mental phenomena figure (and figure importantly) in social science explanations does of course set them apart from most explanations in the natural sciences, and the special character of "intentionalistic" explanation as employed in the social sciences is increasingly a subject for philosophical inquiry (see, for example, Elster 1983:chap. 3; Searle 1984:chaps. 4, 5 and 1991). However, the license to use mental phenomena in explanations does not constitute a license for the anthropologist or other social scientist to attribute specific mental states or mental processes to his subjects without due regard for empirical evidence. As Barth (1987:8) has suggested, it remains appropriate for the anthropologist, like the natural scientist, to be committed to an ideal of naturalism whereby he ascribes to his objects of study only such properties and capabilities as he has reasonable empirical grounds to believe them to possess. Essentialists have often seemed only too ready to ignore this ideal.

And there is more than this ideal to be shared by social and natural scientists, despite differences in their subject matter. With the demise of positivism, the natural sciences too may be said to have become hermeneutic (Weinsheimer 1985:16ff.; cf. C. Taylor 1980). If explanation in both the social and natural sciences is recognized to consist of showing intelligible connections in the subject matter at hand, this bespeaks a unity worth stressing perhaps as much as any subject-matter differences. As anti-essentialists, we may then indeed claim to practice what is neither positivism nor anti-science.

NOTES

1. An earlier version of this article was published in *Canberra Anthropology*, vol. 13, no. 2, 1990:29-45. An Indonesian version is being published by the University of Indonesia Press in a collection of my essays concerning methodology and explanation in anthropology and human ecology. In an abridged version, the article was read for me in the symposium on "Assessing Developments in Anthropology" at the Annual Meeting of the American Anthropological Association, Washington, D.C., November 1989. I myself presented it in an anthropology seminar at The Australian National University in Canberra in April 1990.

2. See Borofsky 1987:165, note 7, for additional references.

3. On social science neglect of historical changes in what kinds of events such terms as "revolution" are applied to, see Farr 1982, 1989. For a concise statement of the different kinds of answers given in philosophy to questions about what all the things designated by a single term have in common, see Briskman 1982:305.

4. With regard to values, it may be noted also that essentialist assumptions about their clear-cut or heightened expression in dance and music in certain cultures have been punctured by studies showing diversity in these arts as well as in the values which they have been regarded as expressing. Examples are studies showing some Javanese dances and music to have (or have had) exuberance, irregularity, or suggestiveness far removed from the refined, courtly performances often thought to express the purportedly general Javanese values of grace, harmony, and emotional control (Hefner 1987, Pemberton 1987).

5. A hypothetical analogy which Barth puts forward to this contrast is having an image of Christ on the cross in the church of one English village and an image of the devil on the cross in the church of a neighboring village. Other variation among the Mountain Ok concerned such matters as whether (or to what extent) myths were told in the course of rites and whether sacred symbols were explicitly elaborated or not (Barth 1987:4-6).

6. It may be worth noting that not making cultures or other "wholes" the objects of study distinguishes Barth's and my concern with variations from the concern of those students of "cultural transmission" (e.g., Boyd and Richerson 1985, Cavalli-Sforza and Feldman 1981, Hewlett and Cavalli-Sforza 1986) who look at variations within a predefined, bounded unit (e.g., a culture or the culture of a predefined population like the Aka pygmies of central Africa) in order to develop or test quantitative models of change in such units with respect to their component traits. Anti-essentialists may study and explain particular variations without committing themselves to identifying the variations as traits of a culture or to somehow measuring their frequency within cultures

or other "wholes" or, indeed, to positing such bounded, continuant units as objects of investigation at all. Methodological problems arising from a bias in favor of studying bounded units or systems have been discussed by me elsewhere (Vayda 1986), and there are ontological problems as well (Barth 1987:84, Vayda 1986:296-300; see also Handler 1984 for arguments against regarding cultures or societies as bounded natural objects rather than as constructions whose reality is semiotic).

7. A complication which I have discussed at length elsewhere under the heading of "explanatory relativity" is the fact that "by having particular contrasts or alternatives in mind, we may in effect be regarding as the object of contextualization and explanation not simply an action or consequence but rather an action or consequence in contrast to some definite alternative" (Vayda 1989: 174). What may become the classic illustration of explanatory relativity has been provided by Garfinkel (1981:21ff.), who refers to the imprisoned Willie Sutton's answer when a reform-minded priest asked him why he robbed banks. "Because that's where the money is" makes sense as an explanation of why Sutton robbed banks instead of newsstands and candy stores but not as an answer to the priest's intended question of why Sutton robbed at all instead of living honestly.

8. The covering-law requirement is featured in the so-called deductive-nomological model of explanation. For more of an explication of the concept of intelligible connection than can be given here, see Martin 1976 (especially page 314 and note 7). Winch (1958:114-115, citing Wittgenstein 1956:pt. I, sec. 142-151) also discusses it, but, as noted by Bhaskar (1979:2), fails to recognize that its role in explanation is not peculiar to the social sciences.

9. I spent seven weeks on Pukapuka in 1957. The main ethnographers of Pukapuka prior to Borofsky were Ernest and Pearl Beaglehole, who were on the atoll for $7\frac{1}{2}$ months in 1934 and 1935, and Julia Hecht, who spent 13 months there in 1972–1974.

10. In addition to Borofsky, various anthropologists have suggested that notions of monographic coherence contribute to the playing down of variations or flux in what is published (Fardon 1988:15, Kay 1984, Vayda 1982, P. J. Wilson 1977).

11. Something like this has, in effect, been noted also by Geertz (1984:272), writing of sociobiologists, cognitive anthropologists, and others who share a "tendency to see diversity as surface and universality as depth." Geertz's claims for the importance of diversity are, however, more limited than mine insofar as he makes them for intercultural diversity in particular rather than for diversity more generally.

12. Agger (1987:122) goes on to say that "today the sciences of spirit aim at nomothetic understanding, where the sciences of nature have long ago given up that vision as unrealistic." According to him, most natural scientists "do not ape the presuppositionless stance of the Vienna Circle but recognize that natural science itself is historical and perspectival" (cf. Weinsheimer 1985:16).

13. For philosophers' arguments against essentialist assumptions concerning this, see Roth 1987, especially chapter 6. My emphasis on variations in this article, in reaction to essentialist neglect of them, is not intended to deny or obscure a point that has been made to me by Myron Cohen (1991b) with respect to numerous features of domestic enterprises and familial ethics which his research has shown to be common to villages in the "northern, southern, eastern, and western regions of agrarian China during late traditional times" despite marked differences in environment and spoken language (Cohen 1991a). The point is that sometimes the very fact that certain ideas and behavior are widely shared and long persistent surprises us and cries out for explanation. In the anti-essentialist view, such ideas and behavior may, like any ideas and behavior, be studied with respect to when, where, by whom, why, and with what effects are they held or performed, and we are not obliged to regard them as essential properties of some hypostatized entity like Chinese culture or Chinese society. (For a contrary, essentialist view, see Hallpike 1986:294-329 on "core principles" of Chinese society.)

14. Consider, for example, some conclusions emerging from studies which I and others have made concerning migration and land use by Indonesia's Bugis people (Vayda 1980, Vayda and Sahur 1985, Lineton 1975a, 1975b). Acknowledged as widely held and long persisting among Bugis are adventurousness and mobility as values and a belief in opportunities beyond one's village of residence. However, while some Bugis were roving the seas and setting up trading and cash-crop farming colonies throughout the Indonesian archipelago, most of the time of most Bugis was spent in leading peasant lives devoted to rice growing and fishing. However widespread and persisting the values and beliefs related to mobility may be, they are simply irrelevant to explaining a great deal of Bugis behavior. Moreover, even if our objects of explanation are present-day Bugis migrations or mobility, it can be argued that the Bugis trade, travel, adventuring, and pioneering that have been going on for centuries are significant less because of what they suggest about kinetophilia as a dynamic for Bugis behavior than because of their role in establishing and maintaining geographically extensive networks along which information about opportunities in other lands can flow back to whatever potential migrants there are, at particular times and for particular reasons, in Bugis settlements in the

South Sulawesi homelands or elsewhere (Vayda 1980:81; Vayda and Sahur 1985:107; cf. Kopytoff 1987:22-23 on mobility and adventurousness in Africa and also Gate-wood 1985:216 and passim on how actions may be "underlain by personal rather than collective representations").

INTELLECTUAL ROOTS

Andrew P. Vayda is a Professor of Anthropology and Ecology at Rutgers University. Formerly a professor at Columbia University, he has taught also at the University of Indonesia (most recently in 1990) and other Indonesian universities and has directed research projects in Indonesia and Papua New Guinea. The journal *Human Ecology* was founded by him, and he was its editor for five years. He has published several books and more than ninety articles. His current interests lie in the areas of concepts, methods, and explanations in anthropology and human ecology; tropical forest adaptations and land-use changes; and interrelations of cognitive and techno-environmental change. (Some of his articles reflecting these interests are cited in the bibliography of this volume.)

When I was a prelaw undergraduate student at Columbia University in the 1950s, what first attracted me to anthropology as a career was Elman Service's teaching, which presented a worldview integrating Julian Steward's ecological orientation with Leslie White's evolutionism and culturology. Service left Columbia just before I became a graduate student there, and so Morton Fried, who shared many of Service's ideas and interests, became my main teacher and advisor. Although I abandoned evolutionism and culturology many years ago, it is probably to Service and Fried that I owe my abiding interest in relations between people and their environments. My specific research, concerned mainly with the South Pacific and with maritime Southeast Asia, has included both extensive work with documentary materials and several periods of anthropological and ecological fieldwork.

The book *Maori Warfare* and the 1956 Ph.D. dissertation from which it derived were based on study in the libraries and archives of New Zealand during 1954 and 1955, and my interest in war in relation to environmental and demographic phenomena (the subject of my 1976 book *War in Ecological Perspective*) dates from this period. In 1956 and 1957, I did research on cultural change on three coral atolls of the Northern Cook Islands. From 1958 to 1960, I taught at the University of British Columbia and expanded my historical research to encompass warfare in Borneo as well as in New Zealand; I also began research with Wayne Suttles on the relation between fluctuations in food resources and the occurrence of ceremonial distributions of goods in Northwest Coast Indian and Melanesian societies. All of this research continued after I joined the faculty of Columbia University in 1960. Fifteen months during 1962 and 1963 and four months in 1966 were spent in New Guinea on a project which allowed me and my associates in a multidisciplinary team to test in the field some of the propositions that had emerged from the library research on war, economics, and ecology.

Collaborations with Anthony Leeds, Roy Rappaport, and the philosopher Paul Collins, and much of my own work during the 1960s, were concerned with cultural mechanisms regarded as contributing to balances between human populations and their resources. Then, in the 1970s, I became increasingly concerned with "unbalanced" relations between people and their environments. The move in 1972 from Columbia University, where I was then a full professor, to Cook College at Rutgers University was motivated partly by the desire to do research on such relations in contemporary settings and by the expectation that the college's interdisciplinary ecological programs would afford better opportunities for such research than I had had at Columbia. Founding and editing the interdisciplinary journal *Human Ecology* also contributed to changing the direction of my work and interests because of the increased contact with scholars in many disciplines and with a wide range of work on people-environment relationships in large modern societies as well as in the small, relatively isolated ones such as those I had previously studied. In accord with these reorientations, in 1974 I became associated with UNESCO's Man and Biosphere (MAB) Program, an international research and training program for developing an integrated social and ecological approach to problems and for providing information and methods for improved environmental policy making and management. In connection with this program, I participated in numerous international conferences and in feasibility studies concerned with forest conversion and conservation in Indonesia and Malaysia. Also, from 1979 to 1984, I directed two United States–Indonesian interdisciplinary research projects on interrelations of human actions and biotic change in the forests of the Indonesian province of East Kalimantan. The rapid changes occurring there, involving diverse movements of people, resources, and ideas across social, geographical, and ecosystemic boundaries, made me see more clearly the limitations of equilibrium approaches in ecological anthropology or human ecology and made me question more strongly the assumptions whereby such predefined wholes as cultures, societies, communities, and ecosystems are made the units of analysis in social and ecological science. Since completion of the East Kalimantan investigations, I have been much concerned with these and related methodological issues (including issues that philosophers and others have raised concerning contingency, human action, agency, and intentionality) and have been devoting much of my teaching and writing to them.

In thinking about such matters, I have received stimulation and insight from discussions with such anthropological colleagues as Bonnie McCay, George Bond, George Morren, Susan Lees, Fredrik Barth, Iwan Tjitradjaja, Myron Cohen, and James Anderson, and I have benefited from reading widely outside of anthropology. Among the authors to whom I feel especially indebted are the following: Karl Popper, for ideas about situational analysis and unintended consequences; Isaiah Berlin, for liberation from theoretical and methodological monism; philosophers like Donald Davidson and John Searle, for clarification of the critical role of intentionality in explaining human actions; Alan Garfinkel, for the concept of explanatory relativity; Jon Elster and Harold Kincaid, for bolstering my impatience with theories and clarifying alternatives to them in social science explanations; and Stephen Jay Gould, for ideas about the importance of chance and contingency in historical change and evolution.

My interests in both cognitive and ecological anthropology were brought together in my most recent Indonesian field experiences, which occurred in Java in 1990 and in East Kalimantan in 1992 and were focused on variation and change in the agro-ecological knowledge and practices of rice farmers. With my long-time ecological collaborators Timothy Jessup and Kuswata Kartawinata I am now making plans for new fieldwork in East Kalimantan on interrelations of cognitive, behavioral, and environmental phenomena.

23

On the Knowledge and Knowing of Cultural Activities[1]

ROBERT BOROFSKY

A seeming problem exists to the anthropological analysis of knowledge diversity. I say seeming because the problem lies less, I suggest, in what informants know than in our conceptions of what we assume this knowing to be. Still something seems not quite right.

As Goodenough (page 265) states in this volume, "We have traditionally thought of . . . a culture as being shared by a group's members." A sampling of introductory books on anthropology emphasizes this point. Kottak (1991:37-41), for example, describes culture as "all-encompassing . . . learned . . . symbolic . . . *shared* . . . patterned." Haviland (1990:30) defines it as "a set of rules or standards *shared* by members of a society" And Peacock (1986: 7) suggests it is "taken-for-granted but powerfully influential understandings and codes that are . . . *shared* by members of a group."[2] The assumption of sharing is based on an obvious point. People must share some degree of understanding if they are to effectively communicate with one another, if they are to participate in the same tasks, interact in the same group. To quote Goodenough (page 266) again: "People who interact with one another regularly . . . need to share sufficient understanding . . . so that they can work together to their satisfaction."

And yet the impression one gains from a host of anthropological studies is that considerable knowledge diversity exists in many cultural groups. A reasonable proportion of the diversity, moreover, seems to be in areas where we might expect a higher degree of shared understanding. Studies emphasize diversity in: family values (Swartz 1982), religious conceptions (Brunton 1980), bird classifications (Gardner 1976), plant knowledge (Hays 1976), hot-cold categorizations (Foster 1979), and views of the past (Borofsky 1987), to name a few. People living within the same community seem to espouse a range of beliefs, use a host of terms, that do not overlap in many cases.

Look as one will through all this literature on intracommunity diversity—and it is rather extensive—there is, however, little mention of people not interacting effectively with one another. How do we make sense of this? What knowledge is being shared in what ways?

To explore these questions I want to begin by considering a few ethnographic examples of diversity. The examples are taken from Pukapuka, a small Polynesian atoll in the South Pacific, where I conducted forty-one months of fieldwork between 1977 and 1981 (see Borofsky 1987). In discussing these examples from Pukapuka, I do not mean to imply other anthropologists have not also emphasized similar traits in other locales.[3] But I want to focus the discussion on a particular set of ethnographic examples so we can not only explore what people know within a specific context but also have a reference point

331

for the following discussion of knowledge and knowing.

Group Diversity in an Everyday Context: The Tale of Wutu

The Pukapukan tale of Wutu is described by the Beagleholes (ms. b:1021-1023) and myself (Borofsky 1987:118) and is generally viewed as well-known—by both adults and children, today as well as in the past. I asked ten individuals from each of the "a" through "h" cohorts listed in Table 1 to recite as much as they knew of the tale. (Details regarding this and other surveys noted in the paper are discussed in note 4).[4] Following Lévi-Strauss (1963:206-231), I then divided informants' accounts into constituent units to explore to what degree informants shared certain elements. The constituent units were:

(1) Wutu goes to an isolated spot, (1a) specification of location, (1b) specification of reason why he goes there, (2) Wutu falls asleep, (3) ghosts come to where Wutu is, (4) they make a plan to eat him, (5) they carry him away in a large wooden bowl (kumete), (6) they sing a chant (or chants): (6a) a chant centering around the phrase "ko wutu, ko wutu," (6b) a different chant centering around the phrase "tau laulau ma tau pala," (7) Wutu makes a plan of escape, (8) he defecates inside the wooden bowl (so the bowl will be heavy when he climbs out

of it), (9) Wutu climbs on to a tree reaching across the path, (10) the ghosts continue on to their selected spot, (10a) specification of location, (11) ghosts prepare to eat Wutu, (12) the ghosts throw down the wooden bowl, (13) the ghosts are covered with feces, (14) Wutu escapes from the ghosts, (15) Wutu runs away to another location, (15a) specification of location he runs to, (16) ghosts chase him, but (17) Wutu is saved, (17a) specification of reason why Wutu is saved.

Table 1 presents the degree to which these constituent units were shared by the sample of informants.

Clearly, there was only limited consensus regarding the story. People mainly agreed on the 6a chant. It reached a 67 percent level of consensus for six of the eight "a" to "h" cohorts, a 75 percent level for five of them. Other constituent units—such as 3, 4, 5, and 12—were shared to a lesser degree. And some units, such as 6b, were shared by only a few individuals. While the tale is reputed to be popular with children as well as adults, neither the 10- nor 20-year-old cohorts expressed any consensus regarding what transpired in the tale. Only those deemed by their peers to be experts on the subject—cohort h—were able to agree on anything near a coherent version of the tale. Clearly then, the tale of Wutu, though seemingly popular, was told in a range of ways.

Table 1   THE TALE OF WUTU

CATEGORY	67% CONSENSUS	75% CONSENSUS	100% CONSENSUS
a. 10-year-olds			
b. 20-year-olds			
c. 30-year-olds	3, 5, 6a	6a	
d. 40-year-olds	6a	6a	
e. 50-year-olds	6a	6a	
f. Elderly men	6a		
g. Elderly women	6a	6a	
h. Experts	3, 4, 5, 6a, 8, 9, 10, 12, 14, 15, 15a	3, 4, 5, 6a, 12	6a
All males	3, 6a	6a	
All females	6a		
Total: all groups	6a	6a	

Table 2   IDENTIFYING FISH IN PUKAPUKAN WATERS

CATEGORY	67% CONSENSUS		75% CONSENSUS		100% CONSENSUS	
30-year-olds	(119/141)	84%	(100/141)	71%	(48/141)	34%
40-year-olds	(119/141)	84%	(96/141)	68%	(44/141)	31%
50-year-olds	(115/141)	82%	(96/141)	68%	(39/141)	28%
Elderly	(102/141)	72%	(74/141)	52%	(14/141)	10%
Experts	(103/141)	73%	(77/141)	55%	(34/141)	24%
Experienced fishermen	(107/141)	76%	(78/141)	55%	(12/141)	9%

Group Diversity in a More Formal Context: Identifying Fish in Pukapukan Waters

In addition to the above data—whose collection reasonably paralleled how Pukapukans might discuss these matters (see Borofsky 1987:74–130)—I systematically surveyed informants regarding their recognition of Pukapukan fish. What made this second survey more formal than the previous one is that I used a set of pictures (from Fowler 1928), asking informants to decide which of the fish represented in the pictures existed in the waters around the atoll. For those fish identified as living in the atoll's waters, I inquired as to their names. While Pukapukans had little experience with tasks such as these, they seemed to readily grasp what was requested. And most appeared quite comfortable in making the identifications.

Table 2 summarizes data on the degree of informant consensus regarding fish pictured in Fowler (1928) that were (and were not) present in Pukapukan waters. Table 3 summarizes the data on informants' names for fish identi-

fied as present in these waters. (Readers who are interested in the subtleties of the computations in Table 3 are encouraged to examine note 5.)[5]

The percentages at the top of each table refer to levels of agreement. If one focuses on 67 percent as an appropriate level of consensus (i.e. two-thirds of the sample concur), then the 30-year-olds in Table 2 agreed on 119 out of 141 identifications, that is, they agreed regarding 84 percent of the pictures. If one focuses on a 100 percent level of consensus, the 30-year-olds concurred on only 48 out of 141, or 34 percent, of the pictures. The overall impression conveyed by the two tables is, if one accepts a somewhat lower level of agreement (i.e. 67 percent), then a reasonable degree of consensus existed (68 percent to 84 percent). If one stresses a higher level of agreement (i.e. 100 percent), there was a relatively low level of consensus (9 percent to 34 percent). In other words, while some knowledge was shared, a decent amount apparently was *not*, even though it involved one of the most basic and important activities male Pukapukans perform—fishing.

Table 3   NAMING FISH IN PUKAPUKAN WATERS

CATEGORY	67% CONSENSUS		75% CONSENSUS		100% CONSENSUS	
30-year-olds	(32/42)	76%	(26/42)	62%	(14/42)	33%
40-year-olds	(38/49)	78%	(28/49)	57%	(12/49)	24%
50-year-olds	(41/56)	73%	(33/56)	59%	(13/56)	23%
Elderly	(32/47)	68%	(25/47)	53%)	(4/47)	9%
Experts	(43/53)	81%	(30/53)	57%	(11/53)	21%
Experienced fishermen	(36/45)	80%	(25/45)	56%	(6/45)	13%

Individual Variability

I would note that not only did considerable diversity exist in different people's answers, but individual informants at times provided somewhat different statements regarding a particular topic. Table 4 indicates to what degree certain individuals told the tale of Wutu differently, on different occasions, over a three-year period (cf. Lowie 1942).[6]

A group session of experts—which Molingi, Petelo, Paani, and Kililua attended—generated the following version. It was narrated by Petelo with other participants contributing (and/or clarifying points) as they saw fit.

1, 1a (though some uncertainty existed on the exact location) 2, 3, 5, 6a, 6b (Petelo claimed this song was from a different tale but included it anyway), 7 (slightly different from norm in how phrased), 8, 9, 10, 12, 13, 14, 15, 15a (a little vague about exact location), 16, 17.

I want to stress that these informants presented clear, well-fashioned accounts each time they were questioned. And yet their accounts changed in different contexts and at different times.

We see variability not only in what people knew vis-à-vis others then but also in their own assertions. I want to suggest in this chapter that we need to do more than affirm the significance of intragroup diversity and individual variation. We need to also call into question our traditional conception of knowledge. Let me explain.

Table 4 REPEATED RENDITIONS OF WUTU BY SELECTED INFORMANTS

Three Renditions of the Tale

MOLINGI:
  Unchanged constituent units: 1, 4, 5, 6a, 8, 10, 12
  Slightly changed constituent units: 3, 9
  Changed constituent units: 1a, 2, 6b, 10a, 11, 13, 14, 15, 15a
PETELO:
  Unchanged constituent units: 1, 3, 5, 8, 9, 10, 12, 13, 14
  Changed constituent units: 1a, 2, 4, 6a, 7, 10, 15, 15a

Two Renditions of the Tale

PAANI:
  Unchanged constituent units: 1, 2, 3, 4, 5, 8, 9, 10, 12, 13, 14, 15, 16
  Changed constituent units: 1a, 6a, 7, 15a, 17, 17a
KILILUA:
  Unchanged constituent units: 4, 5, 6a, 6b, 7, 8, 9, 10, 10a, 12, 14, 15, 15a, 16
  Slightly changed constituent units: 1a, 1b
  Changed constituent units: 2, 3, 13, 17, 17a
VAILOA:
  Unchanged constituent units: 1, 2, 3, 4, 5, 7, 8, 9, 10, 11
  Slightly changed constituent units: 1a
  Changed constituent units: 6a, 11, 12, 13, 14, 15, 15a
PELEPELE:
  Unchanged constituent units: 1a, 5, 9, 10, 12, 13, 14, 15, 16
  Changed constituent units: 1, 3, 4, 6a, 8, 10a

KNOWLEDGE AND KNOWING

Within the literate, academic cultures in which anthropologists generally participate, it often seems appropriate to define an individual's knowledge as something definite, something concrete. After all, most anthropologists have gone through school systems emphasizing that knowledge can be written down in words, can be evaluated on tests. Certainly there is much knowledge that exists of this sort. But I want to emphasize there is also much knowledge that is not easily defined and described. And, furthermore, labeling such knowledge as diversity—because different informants give different answers regarding it—obscures key dynamics concerning the nature of knowing. Anthropologists help create a sense of diversity, I would suggest, by viewing some knowledge as structured or rigid when it is fluid and flexible.

A Continuum

To emphasize the flexible aspects of knowledge, we might conceive of a continuum between *knowledge* (i.e. understanding that is definite and delineated) and *knowing* (i.e. understanding that is more fluid and flexible in character). At the knowledge end of the continuum is the type of understanding, the type of cognizance, one tends to present in exams or record from informants as specific "facts" (e.g. the name for a common object, such as table, or the date for a specific event). This knowledge we tend to conceptualize as generally *not* changing from day to day, informant to informant, context to context. Moving along the continuum, toward knowing, are affirmations that tend to vary with varying contexts. As we saw with the tale of Wutu, individuals may present different accounts in different settings. Further along the continuum are assertions of knowing that seem relatively defined in some respects and relatively undefined in others. Wutu, for example, had a generally agreed-upon central core (i.e.

the 6a chant). But beyond this, the tale graded off, by degrees, into a host of divergent and uncertain assertions regarding what happened when. Here, knowing is not only diverse because it changes in different contexts but because there are parts of what is known which can be precisely delineated and parts which cannot. And finally, at the other end of the continuum, is knowing that generally tends to be fluid, that tends to be rather hard to pin down with precise parameters, with formal, set descriptions.

Much research suggests that varying degrees of structure exist in people's knowledge affirmations. Let me briefly draw readers' attention to some of this literature.

One of the abiding problems in the anthropology of knowledge is that once having separated out context from knowledge—so as to better describe key elements of what people know across a range of contexts—anthropologists face the problem of integrating context back into knowledge, placing what an informant knows back into the contexts within which it is known. Many scholars who focus on "situated learning" and "activity theory" try to avoid this problem by seeing knowledge as inherently embedded in contexts. Rogoff (1990:27), for example, states: "Rather than examining context as an influence on human behavior, I regard context as inseparable from human actions in cognitive . . . activities." Scribner (1984:39) suggests: "Skilled practical thinking is goal-directed and varies adaptively with the changing properties of problems and changing conditions in the task environment." Such practical thinking, she continues, "contrasts with the kind of academic thinking exemplified in the use of a single algorithm to solve all problems of a given type." Lave (1993:4–5) emphasizes: "Theories of situated everyday practice insist that persons acting and the social world of activity cannot be separated."

Though not necessarily emphasized in the literature, this perspective overlaps with a range of material beyond activity theory.

Colson (1984:7), cited by Vayda (page 322) in this volume, asserts for example: "Values once thought to be fundamental for guiding the way particular people dealt with each other and their environment have turned out to be situational and time linked." And Barth (page 356 in this volume) asserts that "all concepts are embedded in practice." The psychologist Mischel (1973:258–259) suggests certain research "findings remind us that what people do in any situation may be changed dramatically even by relatively trivial alterations in their prior experiences or by slight modifications in the particular features of the immediate situation" (also see Wright and Mischel 1988 and Shoda, Mischel, and Wright 1989).

One can perceive situational variability in informants' assertions regarding the previous Pukapukan data. Footnote 6 notes Paani willingly related the tale of Wutu to me *twice* but claimed, when interviewed by two high school students, not to really know it. And an analysis of Molingi's, Petelo's, and Paani's renditions of Wutu indicates their joint group account differed in definite ways from their individual accounts.

Contextual factors probably also helped shape Pukapukan responses in the fish identification survey. Though my method for collecting data paralleled that of many anthropologists, it did not parallel the way most Pukapukans utilize what they know about fish in everyday life. At least some of the diversity noted above probably stems from Pukapukans trying to frame responses to questions about which they had little collective experience—recognizing fish from photographs. D'Andrade (1992:51) makes an important point: "It is as if in looking for taxonomies the anthropologist . . . [is often] trying to find a format for holding knowledge which corresponds to a format used in the anthropologist's *scientific culture,* rather than discovering the form of *knowledge organization* used by the informant."

Pukapukans have names for a wide range of fish. But they do not analyze the identities of fish in most conversations. They tend to refer to them at a general level of discourse. In a conversation among friends, for example, a specific type of fish may be mentioned. But details regarding whether the fish is a malau loa, malau mania, malau moana, malau aniu, malau wangamea, malau kulu, or malau ngutu poto, if raised at all, usually tend to be of secondary importance.[7]

While Pukapukans readily completed the fish survey, I am saying, it was not a task they normally did in everyday life. One can understand then how variation might exist in their answers as they sought to apply knowledge, developed in one set of contexts, to a different, more formal, situation where somewhat unfamiliar expectations prevailed. Appropriately, informants deemed experts in such matters did not really show greater consensus in the survey than did other cohorts. All of them were "fishing" for answers in a sense—trying to provide knowledgeable responses, based on past experiences, to my somewhat unfamiliar, though understandable, questions.

Moving still further toward the knowing end of the continuum, considerable research has been undertaken in the area of prototypic judgments and fuzzy classifications—on the gradations and degrees of clarity and boundedness existing in cultural categories. Rosch's (see e.g. 1973a, 1973b, 1975, 1977, 1978a, 1978b, 1987) research, for example, indicates that categories often possess a general central core surrounded by more ambiguously classified peripheral elements. Rosch suggests: A category is defined "in terms of its clear cases rather than its boundaries" (Rosch 1978b:36); "categories are internally structured by gradients of representativeness . . . [with] category boundaries . . . not necessarily definite" (Mervis and Rosch 1981:109). Regarding categorization models aligned with Zadeh's research on fuzzy logic, Oden (1981:2897) suggests "fuzzy" models "are *not* based on essential features (there need be no properties that must definitely be present) . . . [rather] there . . . [are] degrees of membership in . . . [a] conceptual category."

In the story of Wutu, informants tended to agree that one constituent unit of the tale, the 6a ghost chant, was central to the story—though (as Table 1 indicates) there was not 100 percent consensus even on this. Moving out from the "core," a number of Pukapukans included constituent units 3 and 5 in their renditions of the tale, a bit fewer, units 4 and 12. Beyond that, ambiguities and uncertainties tended to exist regarding what was (or was not) a relevant part of the Wutu tale. In accord with psychological research on prototypes (see e.g. McCloskey and Glucksberg 1978, Niedenthal and Cantor 1984), it was in the less central areas that divergent and contradictory accounts tended to occur.

Perhaps the most difficult part of the knowledge-knowing continuum for some academics to accept is the far end portion of knowing—in which knowing seems to be generally fluid. "In any given instance," Keller and Keller (1993:127) suggest, "knowledge is continually being refined, enriched, or completely revised by experience." The psychologist Oden (1987:213) observes that concepts may not necessarily be "static structures with fixed referents and permanent linkages. . . . The intensional basis of concepts allows them to be constructed, amended, and tuned 'on the fly' as the needs of the concept-holder and the demands of the task require." "Individuals themselves . . . [may be] rarely consistent in the statements they make in elicitory contexts," the anthropologist Ellen (1979:354-355) suggests. "They may initially provide one name, or indeed several, reject them, and finally settle on something quite different. This is the identification which must normally be accepted as 'definitive,' although it is possible that further observation, consideration, or consultation may lead the informant to change his or her mind again." "The problem with work of this kind," he continues, "is that it requires definitive answers for analytical reasons, while it is known that the processes generating the answers are capricious." (Readers interested in arguing Ellen's point might familiarize

themselves with Mischel's personality research in psychology. Mischel 1973:255, for example, states: A range of research "results . . . are totally congruent with . . . conclusions . . . that emphasize the idiosyncratic organization of behavior within individuals.") Ellen (1979: 357) also states:

Variability is what we must expect, diversity is part of the system; homogeneity is not only not necessary, or even possible (Hays 1974:204, 305), but perhaps is also not always desirable. This is not only because people's knowledge, interests, and abilities in identification and classification vary, but also because people constantly use categories, without formally defining them, in ways which suggest different, even opposite, properties on different occasions (Bourdieu 1977a:110).

Brunton (1980) makes this point effectively in his article "Misconstrued Order in Melanesian Religion." Connerton (1989:70) refers to myths—including presumably tales such as Wutu—as "reservoirs of possibility." Ortutay (1959:207) states, "The decisive characteristic of . . . oral transmission is not simple preservation but a tendency towards embellishment and enrichment." And Harris (1970:1), in discussing Brazilian racial identity, emphasizes that "structurally adaptive consequences adhere to the maximization of noise and ambiguity" in certain categorizations.

We see elements of fluid, flexible knowing in Wutu. As noted, the 6a chant constitutes the central core of the tale—the one enduring element running through most renditions. Yet an analysis of the repeated renditions by Petelo, Paani, Vailoa, and Pelepele indicates they all changed this constituent unit in their repeated accounts of the tale—significant new words were added to the chant and/or seemingly important ones were left out.

Three Points

I would draw readers' attention to three points related to, and developing out of, this knowledge/knowing continuum. They emphasize the need to be sensitive to the processual dynamics surrounding both knowledge and knowing.

First, to focus solely on intellectual content—at the expense of social performance—is to miss an important aspect of what people know. At least one reason flexibility may be tolerated in various renditions of a tale such as Wutu, I suspect, is because such tales involve not only certain matters of content but also certain rhetorical styles of presentation. In story telling, the *act* of telling can be as critical as the *content* of the told (cf. R. Lakoff 1973, Grice 1975). The way Petelo and Molingi tell Wutu, for instance, conveys a sense of excitement. Independent of this or that detail, Petelo and Molingi know how to make the tale come alive. We need to move beyond focusing on the known as discrete content to grounding it in meaningful activity. We need to situate "learning in the trajectories of participation in which it takes on its meaning" to quote Lave and Wenger (1991:121).

This leads to my second point. Intragroup diversity is partly a matter of perception. If one views Wutu as a clear, delineated story, for example, then obvious differences exist in what people say. But if one views the story as more fluid in form, the variations are not as noticeable. The variations seem to fit within a vague, general framework of tendencies. We need to realize that diversity is partly in the eye of the beholder, partly in whether one deals with the subject matter as rigid or flexible in form. Lord (1960:27), in investigating Yugoslav tales, talked with an informant who claimed to have recited a song exactly as he had heard it previously. The informant emphasized his rendition was: "the same song, word for word, and line for line." In fact, Lord was able to demonstrate the two renditions were different. As Lord (1960:28) noted: To the bard, "'word for word and line for line' are simply an emphatic way for saying like." We need to understand *when a difference*

really makes a difference in what people assert and do if we are to understand diversity.

And third, we might reorient our analyses of the knowledge/knowing continuum. To date, cognitive analyses have tended to start with knowledge—with generally enduring patterns—and seek to determine how diversity and knowing develop out of them, that is to say, they analyze how certain generally stable schema take on different forms in different contexts. We might reverse the process, starting with knowing, and see how knowledge is constructed out of it.[8] We might focus, I am suggesting, on the conditions that *structure knowing into knowledge*.

Among the most prominent factors structuring knowing are the experiences of everyday life. People, in interacting with one another, come to share certain ways of communicating, of associating, with one another. Instead of emphasizing that people need to share certain knowledge in order to effectively interact, I would suggest that people share certain knowledge *because* they have learned how to interact with one another. What people share culturally is the *experience* of getting along with one another, of participating in meaningful activities together. This phrasing fits with the emphasis of several contributors in both Sections Four and Five of this volume regarding the cultural being embedded in shared activity. It also helps makes sense of Swartz's intriguing data on the Swahili. Regarding "a crucial dimension of culture, i.e. level of sharing as concerns family life and relations," Swartz (1982:321) notes, "Differences *within* a society [such as the Swahili] may be larger than differences *between* societies." He (1991: 294-295) goes on to observe "Status occupants [e.g. mothers] do not share more . . . understandings . . . [regarding] their statuses with fellow status members than . . . with nonmembers" (e.g. fathers). Where is sharing relatively high among the Swahili Swartz studied? It is high among family members and especially spouses (Swartz 1982: 333) because they constantly interact with one another. Similarly, Holland (1987:247) lists "face-to-face interaction" among group members and "achievement of stable, non-superficial relationships" as key determinants in respect to the distribution of cultural knowledge in a group (see also Boster 1985:193 in this regard).

Other factors structure knowing as well. I briefly touch on two here—power and objectification—though one might elaborate on other factors as well, especially ritual, if space permitted. Both Wolf and Keesing discuss power in their chapters; power is also central to Foucault's (e.g. 1973b, 1975, 1979, 1980a) analyses. Power can shape people's knowing in terms of what is and is not acceptable in interactions with others as well as, more generally, in terms of encouraging (or discouraging) certain beliefs and behaviors. In addition, it may, more subtly, frame the contexts within which knowledge exists, especially in terms of what Bourdieu (1977a:169) refers to as *doxa*—"that which is beyond question and which each agent tacitly accords by the mere fact of acting in accord with social convention." Focusing on power expands cognitive anthropology's purview, it draws cognitive anthropology into an arena where writers such as Marx, Durkheim, and Weber and issues such as politics, religion, and social change become central to one's analysis.

The anthropologist—as recent interpretivist and postmodern approaches emphasize—is also a key structuring agent of knowing. Bourdieu (1977a, 1990a) refers to this process, to give it a label, as objectification—the way the fluid knowing of everyday practice is formed into structured knowledge in anthropological writings (see e.g. 1990:36). In *Making History* (1987), I contrasted the way certain Pukapukans and anthropologists describe the Pukapukan past. Many Pukapukans continually change their traditions in the process of learning and validating them—so that their descriptions retain a knowing quality to them. And various anthropologists, in describing these same traditions, overstructure them, emphasizing uniformity at the expense of diversity and stasis at the expense of change—turning the fluid traditions, in other words, into knowledge.

Summarizing, I have stressed the need for broadening our conception of knowledge. By suggesting a continuum between knowledge and knowing, I have tried to bring together within one framework material relating to activity theory, prototypical judgments, "fuzzy" logic, and processual analysis. While noting the importance of structured, stable forms of knowledge, I have stressed the dynamic, fluid, and/or flexible aspects of knowing (since these tend to be downplayed in the literature). And without trying to denigrate the common approach in cognitive anthropology of starting with knowledge and seeing how knowing derives from it, I have suggested the time has come to also focus on an alternative approach. Seeing how knowing is structured into knowledge not only opens up new ways to think about the knowledge/knowing continuum, but builds bridges to anthropologists working beyond the traditional confines of cognitive anthropology on such concerns as power, hegemony, cultural materialism, ritual, politics of memory, postmodernism, and cultural studies. These concerns, relatively marginal to much research in cognitive anthropology today, need to be made more central to the field.

TWO TYPES OF MEMORY

In turning to recent neuroscientific work on memory, I want to continue the process of rethinking our conceptions of knowledge/knowing. Implicit in the following remarks is a recognition that we need to move beyond vague, suggestive possibilities about cognitive processing to a conversation with other disciplines, especially neuroscience, regarding the actual dynamics involved. Pulling new models out of a hat will no longer do in anthropology; neither will accepting one model over another based on which individuals of what status support it. We need to ground our analyses of knowledge and knowing in the overlapping understandings we can establish with other disciplines.

Implicit and Explicit Memory

Increasing evidence in neuroscience suggests that at least two types of memory exist in the human brain: one termed implicit (or nondeclarative or procedural) and the other explicit (or declarative or relational). According to Schacter (1992:559):

Implicit memory is an unintentional, nonconscious form of retention that can be contrasted with explicit memory, which involves conscious recollection of previous experiences. Explicit memory is typically assessed with recall and recognition tasks that require intentional retrieval of information from a specific prior study episode, whereas implicit memory is assessed with tasks that do not require conscious recollection of specific episodes.

Explicit or declarative memory, Squire (1992: 232) states, "provides the basis for conscious recollections of facts and events. . . . [It is] termed 'declarative' to signify that it can be brought to mind and that its content can be 'declared.'"

Nondeclarative memory includes information that is acquired during skill learning (motor skills, perceptual skills, cognitive skills), habit formation, . . . [and] other knowledge that is expressed through performance rather than recollection. Experience can cumulate in behavioral change but without affording conscious access to any previous learning episodes or to any memory content. (Squire 1992: 233)

While research on the biological basis of these memory distinctions is ongoing, current data suggest:

Declarative memories require the reciprocal anatomical connections that enable the neocortex to interact with the hippocampus and related structures, and the neocortex is thought to be the final repository of declarative memory. [The] skills and habits [of implicit memory] depend on corticostriatal projections. . . . One possibility is that the storage of information underlying skills and habits occurs at the synapses between cortical neurons and neurons in the neostriatum. (Squire, Knowlton, and Musen ms:55)

One can readily perceive the biological difference between the two types of memory in amnesia. Patients suffering from amnesia have lost their explicit memory. Amnesia patients retain their implicit memory.

In focusing on the differences between these two types of memory, I do not mean to imply that both may not be involved in various activities. In fact, certain activities may well require the two interacting with one another. Neither is a mutually exclusive system (see e.g. Harrington, Haaland, Yeo, and Marder 1990: 334; Squire, Knowlton, and Musen ms:12). But the two systems of memory do seem to possess different properties.

One intriguing line of research relates to the development of cultural patterns or rules in implicit memory. Knowlton, Ramus, and Squire (1992:172) explore the ability to classify items into categories—and, by implication, the ability to classify an array of cultural experiences into patterns—according to a set of abstract, implicit grammatical rules. Their (1992:177) results "argue for the participation of at least two independent memory systems in classification learning based on rules. One system stores in explicit memory the actual instances that are presented . . . the other . . . stores implicitly information that is abstracted about the stimuli . . . in the form of rules" (Squire 1992:234). "Memory for the specific items is not important in the second type of learning," Squire (1992:234) suggests. "Rather, the information that is invariant across many trials is important." While classification may rely on information stored in both implicit and explicit memory, Knowlton, Ramus, and Squire (1992:177) suggest that humans seem to rely mainly on implicit memory "when the categories are defined either by complex underlying rules or by features that are difficult to discover explicitly"—which is to say, implicit memory is used in dealing with many situations of everyday life.

I want to emphasize two points here. First, stored in implicit memory it appears are not detailed perceptions of what happened when as much as abstracted principles that organize an array of perceptions together into seemingly coherent patterns. The focus is on the repeated associations of experience rather than the variable ones—a perspective that nicely overlaps with Strauss and Quinn's elaboration of connectionist principles (in their chapter). And second, such patterns, because they are stored in implicit memory, are not readily verbalized or made conscious. These patterns can be best established in terms of performance rather than recall, social activity rather than intellectual explication.

In regard to Wutu, what informants such as Petelo, Molingi, and others hold in implicit memory, we might hypothesize, are a set of patterns regarding the story. These can be combined, as we saw, with a variety of specific points of content stored in explicit memory—which may vary from telling to telling—and still be described as the same general tale. What makes it the "same," I suggest, is not only a number of constituent units but the *skillful* way units are integrated together and presented as a social performance.

These data (and inferences drawn from them) nicely overlap with a wealth of anthropological materials. The implicit patterns, for example, are often referred to in anthropology today as schema—"simplified worlds" in D'Andrade's (1990:93) phrasing, "schematized interpretative framework[s]" in Holland's (1992:68). D'Andrade (1992b:54) suggests, in respect to cultural learning, that much "output behavior *looks* rule governed, but often the person cannot *state* the rule" (see also 1990:

99). The emphasis on habituated experiences as unconsciously embedded in the body fits well with Bourdieu's (1977a:214) concept of "habitus"—an "habitual [set of dispositions] . . . of the body" (see also Bourdieu 1977a:72-95, 1990a:52-65, and Mauss 1980:73). Likewise one might quote Giddens (1984:4) in this regard: "The vast bulk of the 'stocks of knowledge' . . . incorporated in encounters is not directly accessible to the consciousness of actors. Most such knowledge is practical in character: it is inherent in the capability to 'go on' within the routines of social life" (see also Connerton 1989, Johnson 1987). And in dealing with heteroglossia in American culture, Strauss (1990:314) states, "Rituals, nonsentential symbols, and daily routines are internalized . . . less as explicit theory than as implicit knowledge of what goes with what."

All this leads me to suggest that a considerable amount of what we might term the cultural is stored in implicit memory—which is to say, a considerable amount is primarily accessed through performance. From this point of view, the Geertz/Goodenough "debate" (discussed in the editorial introduction to Section Four) dissolves since implicit memory is certainly located in the brain (as Goodenough emphasizes) but it can best be observed in the public actions of people (in line with Geertz's perspective). We might reflect on a number of issues in this regard.

Trying to Make the Implicitly Known Explicit

We might query, for example, to what degree the implicit can be made explicit. Obviously, some of what we know implicitly can be described in overt linguistic form, can be verbally presented to others. Just as obviously, other parts of what we know cannot. The problem is delineating what parts of the implicitly known belong in which category. This is particularly important since, as D'Andrade (1990:68) has noted, "The relationship between culture and cognition has been investigated primarily in terms of the relationship between language and cognition." We need, as Bloch indicates in his chapter, to focus on less linguistically oriented perspectives as well.

Let me describe what is at issue through an example. Driving a car involves skilled, habituated knowledge/knowing. Asked by a friend how one drives a car, we might offer a thoughtful account of what is generally entailed. We might, if we wanted to be precise, formulate a set of rules (cf. Wallace 1965). And, if we wanted to be even more precise, we might formulate an additional set of rules to take care of the exceptions and the exceptions to exceptions. But all these rules would not reflect what we do mentally when we drive. Most people, that I know, tend to daydream or focus on other things while driving (such as listening to the radio). Try as we might, we cannot fully express in language the type of knowledge/knowing we use in driving. It is embodied in a variety of kinesthetic sensations which we cannot make fully explicit. As Dreyfus and Dreyfus (1986: 30) indicate: "We usually don't make conscious deliberative decisions when we walk, talk, drive, or carry on most social activities. . . . The expert driver becomes one with his car, and he experiences himself simply as driving."

This is not to say people cannot offer explicit, coherent statements about what they do and what they know. Obviously, they can. But the statements people tell others about their behavior may be quite different from the knowledge/knowing behind the behavior itself, as a host of social scientists have noted (see e.g. Bilmes 1986). "If the anthropologist is often attempting to give an account of chunked and nonsentential knowledge in a linguistic medium (writing)," Bloch (page 281 of his chapter) notes, "she must be aware that in so doing she is not reproducing the organization of the knowledge of the people she studies but is transmuting it into an entirely different logical form." The behavior, as Dreyfus and Dreyfus (1986:35ff.) point out, becomes transformed—generally into more rational, sentencelike, and/or decision-making terms. Trying to explicitly describe implicit knowledge/knowing is attempting to describe intellectually what we know experientially. We need to be careful not to overdescribe and underconceptualize the implicitly known.

It is interesting to note, in this regard, that informants often respond to questions about something they have implicitly experienced, but are consciously uncertain about, by reporting culturally explicit norms (see e.g. Bernard, Killworth, Kronenfeld, and Sailer 1984:508). The study by Kronenfeld et al. (cited in Bernard, Killworth, Kronenfeld, and Sailer 1984:509) is noteworthy in this respect: It involves "an experiment in which informants leaving restaurants were asked to report on what waiters and waitresses were wearing. Informants showed much higher agreement about what waiters were wearing than about what waitresses were wearing, despite the fact that none of the restaurants in question had waiters."

To what degree the implicitly known can be accurately transformed into the explicitly stated is a question of considerable importance. We come face to face with to what degree anthropologists can describe, without altering, important cultural principles and patterns known by informants. Interpretivism and neuroscience tend toward the same conclusion in this regard: There are serious problems in trying to objectively describe much of what other people know. We need be cautious in assuming the implicitly known can be made explicit and especially, as Bloch emphasizes, that nonlinguistic knowledge/knowing can be framed, without distortion, in linguistic terms.

Development of Implicit Patterns

Turning to a different issue, we need to consider how the coherent patterns formed in implicit knowledge/knowing develop. Based on research by Rosch (e.g. 1978b, Rosch and Mervis 1975), Gibson (e.g. 1979), Kosslyn (e.g. 1988, Kosslyn et al. 1989), Reber (e.g. 1992), and others, it seems likely that such patterns arise through the mental detection of seemingly invariant and/or covariant occurrences in a repeated number of closely related experiences. (I say seemingly because cultural perceptions obviously affect what is and is not perceived of as similar.) In other words, people appear to build up abstract conceptualizations of their experiences as a result of certain elements remaining the same or varying collectively together through a set of repeated activities. This is what Squire (1992:234) refers to when he suggests it is "the information that is invariant across many trials [that] is important." And this is what Hasher and Zacks (1984:1381) imply when they state, "Recent work demonstrates that conceptual knowledge depends directly on frequency information."

There is an obvious problem here. How does the brain take in the host of perceptual inputs it needs to establish what is and is not invariant, what is and is not associated with other elements? Apparently the human brain not only has this capacity but does it automatically. Quoting Hasher and Zacks (1984: 1379) again:

Information about frequency is recorded in memory without a person's intention to do so. . . . Unlike virtually every other cognitive skill examined in the history of the field, memory for frequency shows a developmental invariance from early childhood . . . to middle and old age. Similarly, there are no effects of differences among people in motivation, intelligence, and educational background.

This would help explain the fact that, as Dreyfus and Dreyfus (1986:22) note, the initial acquiring of a skill "requires so much concentration that . . . [one's] capacity to talk or listen to advice is severely limited." One is mentally focusing on establishing what is and

is not seemingly invariant and/or covariant. And it would help explain why, once these invariances and covariances are somewhat established, one can talk and daydream to a much greater extent while carrying out the same skill. Supporting this view are studies of positron emission tomography (PET) brain scans of certain habituated, skilled knowledge/knowing—such as playing the computer game Tetris (see Haier et al. 1992)—which indicate that once people have initially mastered a skill, they tend to consume less glucose from then on in processing inputs despite the fact that greater levels of skill may be demanded in subsequent performances (note Squire et al. 1992). It is important to stress that these invariants and covariations tend to be grounded in interactions with the environment, in solving the problems of everyday life. I would note that this focus on concrete activities reinforces a significant theme in the cognitive literature: "Problem solving in general," Lave (1990:322) suggests, "is dilemma-motivated." Or as Dreyfus and Dreyfus (1986:43) phrase it, "People are not very good at performing a task that is rarely relevant in the real world."

Research is continuing on several questions: How abstract are the abstractions that are built up regarding these invariances? To what degree are they rulelike? How do these conceptualizations develop, and transform themselves, over time? The answers to these questions are partly dependent, of course, on how we define such terms as "abstraction" and "rulelike." But, generally, it is safe to say they are still open questions at present—which means we should not presume one possibility is obviously more correct than another until further research is done.

The implication I draw from all this material is that we need to be careful in the formulation of cultural schema. As Burling (1964) noted many years ago, a particular set of categories may be conceptualized, in respect to its underlying schema, in a host of different ways. We might be tempted to emphasize the schema that explains the most behavior with the least number of qualifications. But such an approach ignores how humans seem to develop schema, how they come to conceptualize their own experiences. If we are to stick with Malinowski's dictum of understanding the "native's perspective," we need to focus more on the invariant and co-variant experiences of informants through time. And this suggests a somewhat different approach to the collection and conceptualization of field data than is now commonly used. Ethnographers need to pay greater attention to the frequency of events and especially the invariant and covariant experiences of their informants (cf. Oliver 1958, 1974:580, 583-584).

Anthropological Implications of Three Implicit Traits

In concluding this section, I want to briefly touch on a few implications regarding certain traits of the implicitly known. The first of these relates to Reber's (1992:123) suggestion that "the neurological structures that subserve the implicit cognitive system(s) are evolutionarily old and preceded the explicit and conscious system(s) by a considerable amount of time." (He, 1992:106, also suggests that "consciousness is an evolutionary late-comer that functions as a kind of executive system exerting control, to varying degrees, over the contents of the cognitive unconscious.") In regard to this evolutionary perspective, Reber (1992:123) notes that implicit cognitive processes are more resistant to "disruption of function by diseases and disorders"—a point we observed above in regard to amnesia. And, furthermore, implicit cognitive processes seem less affected by differentials in age and IQ. Reber (1992:118) hypothesizes, based on suggestive but not yet conclusive data, that "implicit functions . . . show little in the way of individual-to-individual variation compared with explicit functions." If this is so, we can see elements of the cultural in the implicitly known: abstract conceptualizations involving skills and per-

formances derived from overlapping experiences within a group that are generally shared by the group as a whole. I am not suggesting such implicit knowledge/knowing is all the cultural is. But I am suggesting it constitutes an important part of it.

Second, implicit cognitive patterns tend to be hyperspecific, that is, they have "limited access to response systems not involved in the original learning" (Squire 1992:237). "Knowledge embedded within one set of productions will not [readily] transfer to a task requiring different productions" (Willingham, Nissen, and Bullemer 1989:1059). Even slight differences—of an object's orientation or shading, the speaker's voice presenting the material, or a letter's type case—seem to influence implicit memory in experimental studies (see Squire, Knowlton, and Musen, ms:51).

This relates to two anthropological concerns. First, it concerns research on indigenous thought patterns, especially on to what degree "the thinking of people . . . is *embedded* in its contexts" to quote Levy (1973:269). Psychological and anthropological analyses have often phrased this issue as one of non-Western informants having a bias toward the concrete (with, perhaps, a less developed concern for the abstract). P. Boyer (1990:42), for example, suggests that "a notable feature of . . . [what he terms] traditional discourse is the emphasis on specific situations instead of theoretical inferences." But we can see the issue is less one of theoretical abstraction—since the implicit certainly involves abstract patterning—than it is of limited generalization beyond the contexts of initial learning or, as Cole (1990:106) phrases it, the "restricted transfer of problem-solving strategies" across contexts.

Second, though various scholars have repeatedly touched on the hyperspecific qualities of the implicitly known, anthropologists have, at times, downplayed this property in their descriptions of the cultural. The cultural is often defined in terms of broad, coherent patterns and processes that relate to a host of contexts and activities. Such a view of the cultural is not totally incorrect. Metaphoric cross-context associations are common in *explicit* knowledge/knowing. As Squire (1992:209) notes, "The hippocampus and the system to which it belongs, is essential for acquiring information about relationships, combinations, and conjunctions among stimuli, such that the resulting representation is flexible and accessible to multiple response systems." However, in conceptualizing the cultural we must take account not only of the cross-context/metaphoric, linguistically-oriented patterning of the *explicitly known* but also the context-based/activity-oriented patterning of the *implicitly known*. We need to examine, I am suggesting, in what ways and to what degree various aspects of the cultural seem—in indigenous terms—to cut across a range of activities and in what ways they seem to be restricted to a set of closely allied activities.

Finally, in accord with Reber's above remarks, I want to touch on the possibility that explicit memory is more affected by age than implicit memory (see e.g. Mitchell 1989, Musen and Treisman 1990, Mitchell, Brown, and Murphy 1990, Allen and Reber 1980, and Reber 1992). The existing data suggest that the organizing of information into conceptual patterns in implicit memory may be more enduring than the explicit recollection of particular experiences, particular points of information. That is to say, there is reason to believe that older informants may retain their authoritative styles of knowledge display long after they have lost, because of age, the specific details buttressing their assertions. What anthropologists may collect from "knowledgeable" elders in their interviews are sophisticated, authoritative social performances more than recollections of specific events and traditions. This was the essence of Petelo's situation. As noted in an earlier publication (Borofsky 1987:105), Petelo had definite "gaps in his knowledge [regarding a range of material] . . . [but] he [was] . . . a master at the art of appearing to know in front of others." The problem this raises is that anthropologists—because of their often uncertain understandings regarding the group being studied—may come to rely on elderly informants who act knowledgeable and authoritative. Such informants, however, may actually know less—in terms of specific details—about certain cultural phenomena than younger informants who present their information in less masterful ways. We need realize this in our data collecting.

CONCLUSION

This paper emphasizes that knowledge diversity is not simply a problem. It also represents an opportunity to rethink what we mean by cultural sharing and diversity, cultural knowledge and knowing, cultural processes in action. I have suggested the need to rethink and refocus our approaches to the cultural in at least four ways.

First, I have suggested reframing our conceptions of diversity and sharing. We have noted that people possess more than just formal, stable knowledge. They also possess fluid, dynamic knowing. In this regard, we might view diversity as existing partly in the eye of the beholder, in whether one views the subject under discussion as rigid or flexible in form. The question we need to ask regarding seeming diversity is: When does a difference actually make a difference? And this depends, as noted, on matters of performance and context. I also suggested we rethink the traditional paradigm that asserts people interact successfully because they share certain understandings. We might reverse the implied causal relation here. People share certain understandings *because* they have learned how to interact successfully—what they share are the experiences, built up over time, of successful interaction. From a developmental perspective, sharing follows from, rather than precedes, the interaction.

Second, we explored certain guidelines for conceptualizing the cultural. I particularly stressed the need to pay closer attention to the ordering processes that transform knowing into knowledge. And following from this, I indicated the importance of framing the structuring processes involved within the intellectual context of such major writers as Marx and Durkheim and such critical fields as political economy and cultural studies that lie beyond the traditional confines of cognitive anthropology.

Third, and developing out of this second theme, anthropologists have traditionally been concerned with trends in other disciplines. In this vein, I turned to neuroscience for help in understanding key processes at work regarding knowledge/knowing. We can be encouraged by how anthropological and neuroscientific perspectives tend to overlap. It provides a greater degree of confidence in our formulations than we might have otherwise. But there are also differences in their perspectives that encourage us to rethink certain positions and to explore alternative formulations. In respect to conceptualizing the cultural, I noted, for example, the tension between the activity-based patterning of the implicitly known and the cross-activity patterning of the explicitly known. And we touched on the fact that the implicitly known may be less subject to mental deterioration due to aging than the explicitly known. Such data open up new possibilities for investigation.

Finally, woven through these remarks are, I hope, suggestive signposts for conceptualizing the cultural in motion. I indicated that it is important to view the cultural not only in terms of knowledge but also in terms of knowing, and further that much of the implicitly known is embedded in cultural activities. During everyday activity, but especially during periods of cultural change, the implicit patterns behind various cultural activities tend to be both reaffirmed and remade. They are reaffirmed because these patterns constitute the basis upon which actions are conceived and taken. And they are remade because people alter their behavior as they adapt to new circumstances and contexts. Repeatedly

performing a set of new actions leads, over time, to a reshaping of the old patterns and/or the making of new ones. It is a perspective that not only overlaps with Sahlins's (1981, 1985, 1992) insightful analyses of continuity and change in Hawaii but also with current connectionist perspectives (see Straus and Quinn's chapter) and modern conditioning theory (see e.g. Rescorla 1988).

In conclusion, I would suggest we are making much progress toward understanding the cultural's dynamic nature. And one of the factors that encourages this progress is a recognition that we still have much to learn.

NOTES

1. I wish to express my appreciation to the following individuals who provided a number of comments and suggestions that proved quite helpful in revising this paper: Michael Cole, Elizabeth Colson, Virginia Dominguez, Janet Keller, Barbara Knowlton, Jean Lave, and Barbara Rogoff.

2. The emphasis of "shared," in each of the three quotes, is mine and does not appear in the original quotes.

3. See, for example: Barth (1975, 1987), Bilmes (1976), Boster (1985, 1987), Bricker (1975), Cavalli-Sforza, Feldman, Chen, and Dornbusch (1982), Fabrega and Silver (1973), Finnegan (1977), Furbee and Benfer (1983), Garro (1986), Harris (1970), Keesing (1982), Keesing and Tonkinson (1982), Lewis (1980), Lord (1960), Lowie (1942), Mathews (1983), Pelto and Pelto (1975), Rubinstein (1981), Sanjek (1977), Sankoff (1971), Sapir (1938), Scribner (1985), Stromberg (1981), Wallace (1961), Weller (1984), and Wexler and Romney (1972). For additional references, see Boster 1987:151.

4. For the surveys described in Tables 1, 2, and 3, I interviewed eighty individuals. The sample for the Wutu survey (Table 1) involved both males and females while the sample for the fish (Tables 2 and 3) involved only men. I focused on males in these latter surveys because they primarily do the fishing on the atoll and hence are more conversant with it. In the Wutu sample, there were five males and five females for each of the following approximate age cohorts: (a) 10-, (b) 20-, (c) 30- (d) 40-, and (e) 50-year-olds. In the fish identification survey there were ten males in each cohort.

In addition, I interviewed two other groups. One was a cohort of "experts" as deemed by a survey of their peers. For the Wutu sample, this group involved ten adults. Selection was based on a survey in which all men and women over fifty on the island—or 91 individuals—were questioned in regard to who they thought was knowledgeable about traditional matters. For the fish survey, the expert group involved fifteen adult males. Selection here was based on a survey in which all the men over fifty—or 57 individuals—were questioned in regard to people's knowledgeability on fishing matters. The other cohort interviewed involved elderly informants sixty-four years of age or older who were *not* part of the expert group. For the Wutu survey, this included ten elderly men and ten elderly women. For the fish survey, this included fifteen elderly men. Thus both the Wutu and fish surveys involved 80 informants.

The "experienced fishermen" cohort included all males in the sample 30 years of age and older—males who, on the basis of their age, should have had considerable experience with fishing. The younger age groups, while surveyed, are not included here since they were presumably less knowledgeable about fishing and hence would skew the results toward diversity. In the Wutu survey, these younger groups were included since the tale was reputed to be popular among them.

5. Deciding which fish to focus on in requesting names presented somewhat of a problem. Asking the Pukapukan name for fish few Pukapukans identified as living near the atoll seemed a bit absurd. One would be asking for the indigenous names of fish many Pukapukans claimed did not exist near the atoll and, presumably, they had not seen. For the Table 3 survey, I used the fish included at the 67 percent level of consensus in Table 2. This allowed consideration of a range of fish and provided a clear sense of to what extent various individuals' names for specific fish overlapped.

6. The eighty informants whose accounts are summarized in Table 1 were interviewed during the late spring of 1979. A group meeting of several "experts" (as assessed by their peers) was held in September 1980. Approximately two months later, I interviewed three of those who had attended the meeting—Molingi, Petelo, and Paani—to see if any changes had occurred in their versions of the tale subsequent to the meeting. Finally, in the late spring of 1982—about a year after I had left the atoll—two high school students again interviewed several informants from the original survey regarding the tale, including Kililua, Vailoa, and Pelepele. (Informants' accounts were taped on each occasion so a relatively precise rendering exists of what people said.)

Paani, who was ranked sixth (with Kililua) in terms of knowledgeability about traditional matters by his peers, claimed not to really know the tale when interviewed by the two high school students in the spring of 1982. He expressed no hesitation, however, in telling me the tale when I interviewed him on *two* previous occasions.

7. In the fish surveys, consensus was deemed to exist if informants concurred at the most generic level regarding a fish identification. For example, even though informants might identify a fish as malau ngutu poto, malau aniu, malau wangamea, or malau kulu, consensus was still viewed to exist because they all viewed the fish as a malau. Such scoring caused a bias toward consensus because some Pukapukans could clearly differentiate fish at a more precise, subcategory, level. My point is simply that, in general, most Pukapukans tended not to focus on such fine categorizations. I thought it unwise, as a result, to overemphasize such precision in tabulating the results of my survey.

8. This idea derives from a discussion with Jean Lave and owes much to a thoughtful suggestion by her.

INTELLECTUAL ROOTS

Robert Borofsky is Professor of Anthropology at Hawaii Pacific University and Book Review Forum editor of *Pacific Studies*. He has carried out research on Pukapuka, Cook Islands, from 1977 to 1981 resulting in the book *Making History: Pukapukan and Anthropological Constructions of Knowledge* (Cambridge 1987). Borofsky coedited (with Alan Howard) *Developments in Polynesian Ethnology* (Hawaii 1989), a volume exploring the current state and future direction of Polynesian studies. From 1988 to

1989, he was a Fellow at the Institute of Culture and Communication, East-West Center, where he first began developing this book. And in 1991-1992, he was Program Chair for the General Anthropology Division of the American Anthropological Association. Borofsky is currently at work on two books: *Pacific Histories,* an edited volume (with David Hanlon) regarding current issues in Pacific history, and a study of early Polynesian-Western contact, tentatively entitled *Of Guns and Gods.*

Having grown up in a family of psychologists, my interest in anthropology only developed gradually. My first encounter with the discipline came as a junior year abroad student at University College, London, where, partly by accident, I took courses in the anthropology department. Torn between social work and anthropology for graduate school, I got a master's degree in anthropology at Brandeis and then, because the experience proved unpleasant, went on to teach elementary school for some years and travel. It was only when I got to graduate school at Hawaii that I felt at home in anthropology.

I have had a number of distinguished teachers. In London, I took courses from Mary Douglas (who studied with Evans-Pritchard) and Daryll Forde (who, as head of the International African Institute, had strong ties with most of Britain's top anthropologists). In Hawaii, I worked particularly with Richard Lieban (a student of both Steward and Fried), Alan Howard (a student of Felix Keesing), and Douglas Oliver. Oliver, after being an undergraduate at Harvard (where Hooton and Cline influenced him), got his advanced degree from the University of Vienna. But he was most affected intellectually, he claims, by reading the ethnographies of British anthropologists such as Firth, Fortes, Evans-Pritchard, and Malinowski. Firth remains a hero for him (as he does for me) and he was personal friend of Fortes in later life.

These teachers conveyed two important things to me. They passed on to me a deep appreciation for ethnographies. At London and at Hawaii (particularly with Oliver), ethnographies were treated as something special, as skilled productions that persisted through time despite the frailties of theoretical fashions. (When I returned from my own fieldwork and began sketching out my dissertation, I reread Firth's *We the Tikopia* and Evans-Pritchard's *Witchcraft, Oracles and Magic among the Azande* for inspiration.) And they encouraged me to take pleasure in the crafting process of intellectual endeavors—to work slowly but well.

At Hawaii, I read widely—not just the major theorists cited by anthropologists today but also other perspectives in French, British, and American anthropology that, while less in vogue, I felt had much to offer. Still, I seemed to be repeatedly drawn back to the intersections among the works of Weber, Lévi-Strauss, and Marx. I was intrigued by how people constructed meanings about the world around them and how power, in interaction with a range of other variables, played a role in this process.

Other experiences were also important in my development. Coming of age intellectually in the 1960s, I find myself very much concerned with issues of social activism, power, and democracy. Forty-one months of fieldwork on a small Polynesian atoll had a critical impact. I kept finding new questions to explore, new mistakes to learn from, and new insights to reflect on. It was in the personal interactions with Pukapukans over time, in my seeking to understand how they perceived their traditions in relation to how I (and others) perceived them, that I found my love for the discipline. When I returned from fieldwork in 1981, Pacific history was "abuzz" with the recent publications of Sahlins (1981) and Dening (1980). Sahlins's *Historical Metaphors and Mythical Realities* influenced me; Dening's *Islands and Beaches* overwhelmed me. I dreamed then, and still dream now, of writing such a book. Greg Dening, through his example and encouragement, has had an important impact on my development.

Today, my interests remain eclectic. I am deeply committed to teaching as a part of the academic experience and am concerned about the state of undergraduate education in the United States. I continue to explore aspects of the anthropology of knowing discussed in this chapter. And I am intrigued by the history of cross-cultural encounters in the Pacific, particularly how they illuminate subtle dynamics of knowing and power. Pervading these interests and, to a degree, framing them is a continuing appreciation for the importance of ethnography in anthropology.

24

A Personal View of Present Tasks and Priorities in Cultural and Social Anthropology

FREDRIK BARTH

After the recent swift and turbulent changes of style and paradigms in cultural anthropology, it is hardly surprising that much of our work today takes its shape as a reaction to the onslaughts of postmodern, reflexive, and interpretive critiques.[1] There is a need for us to pick up the pieces and somehow resume the tasks of regular anthropology, not by rejecting or ignoring the critiques but by transforming and incorporating them as improved sensitivity and skills. The task may require a considerable restructuring of our most fundamental premises and concepts, and is still only spottily under way. Yet I sense a considerable convergence among many colleagues which I shall try to articulate in the following. But first, there is also a need to reconsider the priorities and the foci of attention which have preoccupied us lately, to make sure that we retrieve those traditional orientations which were valuable but may have become less salient during the debate of the last decade.

REFLECTIONS ON CULTURAL AND SOCIAL ANTHROPOLOGY TODAY

In other words, to assess past perspectives and future directions in (cultural and social) anthropology, it is important that we first reflect on what anthropology is being used

for, and what it could be used for. Our current purpose with it may only imperfectly reflect the discipline's potential. Our theoretical concerns may inadvertently come to focus on these particular interests, rather than the needs that arise from all the tasks of analyzing the broader object. I see a trend over recent years to let such particular interests direct theoretical attention in ways that have unnecessarily narrowed the scope of theoretical debate.

Anthropology started as a branch of natural history engaged in the study of primitive man, of savage cultures and societies, and grew into the comparative study of human life-ways—for a while even spoken of as "experiments in living"—with a view to gain broad insights into human potentials, and the foundations and forms of human life. For such themes, the study of cultures drastically different from our own has always been particularly relevant. And on the basis of such studies, the discipline proliferated into that very broad range of topics and orientations that has been its strength and weakness over the last two generations.

More recently, we have arrived in a position where American cultural anthropology's most salient focus seems to have changed and narrowed. It is true that cultural differences may attract more attention among intellectuals

349

today than ever before (as Keesing suggests, pp. 301ff). But observe the change in how it is used: less for exploring diversity and alternatives in the world, and more for supplying us with foils and parables for talking about ourselves. Alterity or "otherness" (e.g. other lifestyles) provides images that are good to think about for scholars who feel estranged, unauthentic, disoriented, and perhaps even embittered, and wish to ponder their condition. Reflexivity has served to bring out these orientations and concerns; but it is sobering to notice the attitudes that have been nurtured by our reflexivity. They include irony, elitism, aestheticism, and at best indignation over the conditions imposed on the less powerful. But why should love come across so weakly: love for people, for the problems, and wonder and love for the various forms of "otherness" with which we engage? I believe this reflects the narrowing of focus, and the limited uses to which cultural "otherness" (or alterity) is currently put in anthropological theorizing.

When the subfield of medical anthropology attracts so many young people today, it may be because it somehow escapes this stricture: it allows compassionate empathy and cultivates a concern for the other which is furthered, not hindered, by a sophisticated attention to her alterity.

Equally important, medical anthropology entails within its field of competence a kind of engagement with the practical world which most recent anthropological orientations have eschewed. Kuper (page 115) makes a similar point when he questions the extent of theoretical contributions made recently by metropolitan anthropology to the concerns of anthropologists in the Third World. A highly intellectual and internal critique has set priorities and focused interests so that we have lost much of our engagement with the real world and urgent issues. To illustrate with but a few absent themes: Anthropology has had pitifully little to say on the phenomenon of untranscendable poverty as it affects increasing hundreds of millions of people in all major cities

of the world. We have not been able to articulate a position, or even a noticeable interest, in the fact that human activity seems to be destroying humanity's own global habitat. And we are only marginally addressing the phenomena of increasing cultural pluralism and cultural blending in the world under present conditions of communication. I am not suggesting that our research agenda should be set by changing public policy issues. On the contrary, I am asking that our attention should be broadly directed to all major aspects of human life and be far *ahead* of governments and the public in our discussions; that our discipline should give us a much stronger voice in articulating issues in ways that would command the attention of scholars and public alike; and that we should recognize that the cutting edges of our theories can often be well tested by their relevance and power in practical matters.

If these are to be our standards by which we choose future directions in anthropology, where do we best start? The first step is to learn to make better and more constructive use of what has been achieved by colleagues and predecessors working from different premises. Only by the careful husbanding of productive insights can we enhance the power of our discipline. Theoretical creativity requires, of course, a freedom to criticize and reject, an independence of conventions, and a willingness to explore other and radical positions. But it also requires a well-trimmed resistance to embracing any such positions. One does not enhance one's creativity by frantically shopping for the latest fashion, and scuttling all previous established (and alternative) views. There is much pressure toward a stereotyped originality in American academia which easily produces individual narrowness and local dogmatism, schools and sects, and does not sufficiently favor skepticism, suspended judgment, and intellectual play. The postmodern rebellion against some of these constraints would be more fruitful if it were less concerned with style and stressed substance over form. We must be willing to be less dismissive, to suspend judgement and allow pluralism within our own positions and within our closest circle of significant others. One relevant exercise for any new perspective is to see what happens when one tries to re-describe the data and insights of old paradigms in its new terms—and then critique what is new for what it loses, not just celebrate it for what it wins.

The Relativist Perspective

One important anthropological perspective which particularly merits resuscitation is the weak version of relativity: the old ideal that "our" Western way of life should be reduced to the status of being only one among very many different and equally possible ways. This perspective has been nearly lost in the polarization of "we" and "they" which is an artifact of reflexivity: the egocentric position-ing of the ethnographic reporter in relation to "the" other. Such a rhetoric of reflexivity pro-vides a poor description of a whole world of cultural variations, different and of unjudged relative validity.

Yet anthropology needs to affirm this rela-tivist perspective for a number of reasons. It is counterintuitive to anyone embedded in a cultural tradition. From any one point of view, there will always appear to be "people like us" as against that pitifully inadequate merging of all the rest in one category of "strangers, others, people not like us." A rela-tivism that embraces a diversity of unposi-tioned cultural alternatives embodies a realism that must be learned, and learned anew by every generation. It has special importance since the awareness of it kindles a humility which improves interethnic relations, and is usually underrepresented in human discourse. No other discipline is better positioned to teach it than anthropology, and indeed most other disciplines are committed to its nega-tion. Within anthropology, it also provides a basic rule of thumb for theory and method:

Any existential human problem will have found diverse solutions, which must be worth knowing about, thinking about, and com-paring. And finally, its practice leads, pro-gressively, to the abandonment of "our" cul-ture as the self-evident measure of all others. It, thereby, furthers the project of turning anthropology into a common ground for humanity, a universe of discourse fitted to the discussion of all and every cultural form in a way that allows persons of differing cul-tural backgrounds to meet as equals: no discourse about "us" and "the other" can create such an arena. This does not deny the historical sources of anthropology but aids us in transcending them. Nor does it deny the hidden and not-so-hidden agendas which various positions within anthropol-ogy may contain. But it asks that they be revealed and frames such a debate most constructively within an anthropology which seeks to universalize the terms of its dis-course.

STUDYING HUMAN TRADITIONS OF KNOWLEDGE

The first premise for such a discourse is laid if we adopt the position formulated by Rappa-port (page 154) that our species is one that "lives, and can only live, in terms of meanings it itself must construct in a world devoid of intrinsic meaning but subject to natural law."[2] Serious divisions start over how best to model such a condition—how to come to grips with a global diversity of meanings and situate them in a world of physical constraints and biologi-cal processes. But even here, I sense a degree of convergence in contemporary practice toward procedures and concepts which also I favor, and which will be the focus of the rest of my comments. Our analyses will benefit if we privilege the interface where meaning and natural law articulate, i.e. the study of human traditions of knowledge. I would try to consti-tute my representation of what happens on this interface in processual terms, especially how people go about constructing meanings. And I would choose to approach it in its particular, where it can be observed and described from a vantage point as close to the events as possible.

In other words, I agree to the increasing warnings against essentializing (in Vayda's chapter, page 321ff). I suggest that we can best avoid its pitfalls by starting with the particular and observing relations over time, and in their variety. Problems will arise—those welcome, challenging, and enlightening problems—in the course of such a description. But then we have the advantage that they will largely be cast in a concrete form, such as: Do my descriptions capture what I see (i.e. how much of what is before me could be reconstructed from my description)? What might be relevant things that I am not noticing? And what do I see of which I am not able to give an account?

If our first goal is the apparently modest step of giving an adequate account of what is there before us, then we are less pressured to identify what is "essential" and feel less authorized to leave out other features which are also made visible by our recording concepts. We produce a fuller record of what seems to us to be there, and we allow ourselves time to reflect more deeply on its features. With any care at all, our descriptions will reveal variation, and force us to recognize variability as a ubiquitous feature of what we are observing. Such variation has been swept under the rug by our discipline so far—most summarily by those preset dogmas which assured us that what we see are instantiations of collective representations, norms, and structures. Perhaps such a stance can prove to be adequate in a number of cases. But the first salient feature of the data we collect will be that of diversity and variation. And these variations should stimulate our comparative consciousness and lead to further discovery as we search out patterned covariation, and thereby possible connections.

Exploring the Particular

The first rule of methodology entailed in this approach would be that we should apply or develop *discovery procedures* which enable us to explore the particular in its variability, rather than templates and schemas which entice us too swiftly to capture and characterize (the supposed essence of) the whole. That means developing a stronger consciousness of how we go about observing and less commitment to what it is we are supposed to find.

To avoid being submerged by the mere multifariousness of events, we do need provisional ideas of how to sort and connect them. Traditionally, anthropology has been heavily reliant on taxonomies and the accumulation of cases within a class—a procedure which rarely helps us to transcend our categories and discover the unexpected. Though I favor a return to a more persistently comparative perspective, there is little reason to return to the construction of typologies: more of our attention should be given to the contexts of the particulars, their embeddedness and linkages. That means learning from Bateson to "follow the loops" that link events together and that will give us leads in our search for connections and systems. It means working less swiftly toward constructing well-articulated theories and being more consciously concerned with alternative ways to order the investigation so that we will do a minimum of violence to what we observe by chopping it up. It puts pressure on us to adopt new categories as we go along, particularly from those we are living among, but also from our own accumulated experience. It allows us to entertain several sets of categories at once, tracing the loops that come into view in alternative refractions.

One contemporary position is to stress the importance of teamwork and a diversity of observers in fieldwork—to enhance both the investigation's compass and versatility. Personally I would rather give more emphasis to a research practice that attends more carefully to precision, in the sense of knowing what we are up to. Recent disquiet about the theoretical issues of objectivity, interpretation, and presentational style must now be carried into the field by every fieldworker, to enhance our sensitivity to what we can best think of as the existential status of events and accounts. Thus, for example, we should be conscious that the best firsthand account of events by a participant is just that—an account and not "what really happened." There is not only the possibility to consider that people wish to deceive us, or that we misunderstand them: theirs is in any case a *particular* cultural construction, and not what really happened. Our being there ourselves, and noting exactly what really happened, on the other hand, retrieves just that: exactly what we think really happened and not what the events meant (and thereby indeed *were*) to any of the participants. An awareness of the inescapable particularity of *every* interpretation must from now on be our constant companion.

If we are seriously concerned with traditions of knowledge—with the interface between the worlds of meaning and the natural world—we will have to be particularly precise: balancing our data on this razor's edge and building a description which constantly struggles to straddle the interface. To study knowledge, we want to study how acts designed in particular modulations of meaning engage the outside world. So we need to work both within the realm of the cultural, so that we can appreciate something of what acts and events mean, and we need to work outside of that cultural appreciation of the world, so we can form some kind of idea of how the causal connections of the outside world are refracted in the culturally constructed reality.

Two Enigmas

This formulation does not avoid—on the contrary, it induces a head-on confrontation with—the two basic enigmas that have engaged much recent theory: (1) how can we gain access to someone else's culturally constructed world, and remain faithful to its representation while at the same time reporting about it in *our* tradition of knowledge (see e.g. Borofsky 1987); and (2) how could we ever think to obtain a view of reality, of the events in the outside world which they are trying to grasp and address, and assume that our view of it would be anything but a particular cultural interpretation—namely, our own. These are precisely the enigmas which interpretive, reflexive, and postmodern theory have addressed. The postmodern account of ethnographic fieldwork has weakened our confidence in our ability to report about other worlds than our own. And the eloquent critique of positivist objectivity has made us increasingly wary of counterpoising a cultural account, and "the facts."

Such critical arguments have been compelling. But the result of how these arguments have been articulated has been to leave our tasks only ever more intractable. Today, I read a convergence among many anthropologists that we must find a way out of the impasse: from Marcus's call for the redesign of ethnography after the critique of its rhetoric to the more robust restatement of definitive research programs by others.

A first step is to criticize the way the problem was framed, thereby escaping the impasse and making the riddle dissolvable. One error was how the issue of cultural translation was distorted by a blanket and imprecise use of pronouns. Both "our" world and "their" world refer to gross fictions. Which is "our" world: That of shared Western conceptions? Of American middle-class conceptions? Those of a mediocre nuclear physicist? A sophisticated philosopher? A particular anthropologist? One who is a committed Marxist? A functionalist? A postmodern skeptic? Surely, the specification of any one of these alternatives as against any other would make a significant difference to the world we would name as ours. And how about "their" world, when we recognize the range of unspecified facts of positioning, variation, and orientation also among what we choose to call members of another "society"? Such diversity, indeed, can also be used in an internal critique.

Moreover, the very distinction between the dichotomized worlds of any "us" and "them" fades when I acknowledge the probable presence of a largely unexplored and certainly unspecified degree of overlapping between my range of conceptions and those of any particular other person—whatever her cultural background, positioning, experience. Dichotomized, homogenized, and unitary cultures are simply not adequate units in terms of which to critique, think about, and redesign a methodology for anthropology, once we have recognized the diversity of positioning and the range of conceptualizations in every population, as well as the present global eucumene of human communication (Barth 1989).

Thus, the question of how intersubjectivity and shared understandings are established cannot be represented as a special enigma of cross-cultural communication. We should acknowledge it as a key difficulty that has to be overcome, at least to some degree, in any incident of interaction and communication. The agonies of reflexivity and confusion reported in anthropological confessionals thus only mirror—or caricature—interpretive work that must be done by every participant in social relations. And anthropologists can learn much more if we are less engrossed in our own quest and give more attention to all the others and how they cope with these tasks in everyday life. This will be so, both because there is reason to distrust our own description of ourselves (it takes superb perspicacity and objectivity to give a faithful account of one's own confusion, and the thoughts and acts it precipitated), and because the situation of the anthropologist is somewhat special in that she combines high rank with high ignorance, and at the same time is guaranteed exit without cost. These are not the conditions under which most people labor.

Giving a Realistic Account

I therefore submit that we should use our presence, our privileged position, to observe and report on these processes as they take place between others. Indeed, the task of giving a realistic account, under varying cultural conditions, of how people achieve and reproduce a degree of conceptual accommodation and shared premises, I would see as the most important task of anthropology at the present. We must explore the bases on which such interpretive activity builds in a non-homogeneous and distributed culture; the collective and individual means people employ to establish shared footings; and the degree and configuration of convergence that is generated (cf. Wikan 1992). There is a complacent tendency in much current literature to minimize these complex issues by using the term "negotiated" about social encounters. But this expression is rarely accompanied by any attempt to describe the process to which it supposedly refers, or to explore its theoretical status and systemic implications. To me, "negotiation" seems to provide an infelicitous paradigm for what we should study, as it tends to take for granted a preestablished framework of shared premises, and suggests a purely verbal interchange in a clearly defined situation. Firstly, the struggle to converge on workable shared understandings is, I would think, more characteristically carried on in the context of action than by talking, and is embedded in the multiple purposes of humdrum life. Moreover, to further our understanding of the processes, it is not the strategically negotiated aspects that need emphasis, so much as our newly won awareness of the problematics of interpretation that should be tackled. The primary and most basic processes are those in which people must variously engage simply to make sense of their surroundings so as to be able to respond knowingly to them. We cannot fruitfully subsume those processes under the template of "negotiation," which is better suited to capture how they may, in a second-order process, also be trying to outmaneuver each other. The broader issues of how actors indeed interpret events will also, no doubt, be significantly clarified by further contributions from cognitive studies.

To replace the worn-out, fictitious, but familiarly simple template of distinct and internally homogeneous cultures, however, we should not at this point reach for the ultimate and true culture theory which will set things right once and for all. The pursuit of science in any discipline is, as we all know perfectly well, an unending quest. How much more realistic and intelligent we could be if we accepted that truism! Without at some point temporarily bracketing our self-critique, substantive progress becomes impossible. What we must try to develop is what seems at this moment the ontologically most plausible model of the phenomena we are studying, and then let that tentative model be our guide as we pursue problems and construct descriptions—which we in turn critique.

This returns us to the search for fruitful discovery procedures regarding the interface between culturally constructed meaning and natural events. On the issue of knowing something about events in the outside world, we can avoid making the analytical and epistemological problems fancier and more intractable than they need be. When, as happened to my wife and myself during recent fieldwork in Bali (Wikan 1990:131ff.)—you are present at a ceremony spoiled by a local rainstorm, and later hear it reported as an ideal, sunny occasion—you have learned something specific about how cultural meanings are constructed, and how they refract natural law. This does not mean that one arrogantly claims privileged knowledge of reality—indeed one may take the trouble to have one's meteorological observations confirmed by some others of the Balinese who were present. But the point is, the culturally refracted version is understandable and meaningful to them, as it will become to you, when you recognize that a bit of reality has been shaped and given meaning in conformity with an embracing construct of balance and harmony between cosmos, society, and morally excellent souls. Likewise, when Borofsky uses Fowler's *Fishes in Oceania* to study knowledge and consensus with respect to varieties of fish among a sample of Pukapukan males (see page 333), he is making no claim that Fowler is the key to the truth, only pursuing a discovery procedure to map out knowledge and its distribution in a population, in a case study of the interface between Pukapukan meanings and nature. In this way, we can get a grip on the empirically variable relationships between observed occurrence, and indigenous rendering and interpretation.

To make such judgments, we do not need to hold the ultimate and comprehensive keys to natural events. We only need to step gingerly and use the most instructive cases of discrepancy to discover, not what is really real, but what the processes are whereby meaning is constructed by others in *their* engagement with the world. This is all the more possible since the reorientation that I suggest also liberates us on another count: it no longer requires of us that we ascertain in one fell swoop the essential structure of that which we are studying—whether cultures, societies, or culture-in-nature. We will be working to identify the processes whereby people engage the world and each other; the understandings and meanings they thereby construct; and the connections between how they go about it and the shapes of the cognized worlds that are thus generated. This is no small order. But it can be done stepwise, one insight at a time: its parts do not stand and fall with our achieved success in grasping a whole structure. Processes are "parts" that can be studied and modeled separately with less loss of naturalism than can the "parts" of a structure or a pattern because they follow the loops of causal connection instead of chopping them over to produce the severed parts of the proverbial jigsaw puzzle.

THREE MODIFICATIONS TO THE TRADITIONAL CONCEPT OF CULTURE

To capitalize on what has been achieved during the recent critique of anthropology, we should take note of the features of culture which this critique has brought to the fore: multivocality (or possessing multiple meanings), multiplicity of possible interpretations, transcience. How does it affect our empirical findings if we try to give full due to such features and their entailments and consequences? Note that I am not suggesting that we adopt them either as a new set of premises on which we should base our analysis or as a set of hypotheses to be tested. It is rather a question of recognizing these descriptive features of the phenomena, and asking the twin questions: (1) how can we best model such disordered systems—patternings that place themselves somewhere significantly distant from both the totally regular and the totally chaotic pole? And (2) what would be the entailments for processes of social interaction, and the reproduction or change of present conditions, if these were indeed the salient features of culture and social life? In other words, we can tentatively adopt the description as plausibly "real," and then design and focus our discovery procedure accordingly. We still need to carry all our doubts with us and look for signs that our ideas may be wrong, and be alert to the opportunities any particular analysis may provide to falsify one or another of our suppositions. Meanwhile, we need to pursue the implications of the indeterminacy which the absence of a shared, homogeneous culture introduces. How can we model the processes of interaction, communication, and meaning construction in such a way that they both give a plausible account of social life as it unfolds *and* show how such processes reproduce their own preconditions? Because it is basic for the construction of any such model, a provisional and realistic assessment of how culture is indeed constituted and distributed is all the more significant for the analysis of social relations and culturally constructed meanings.

In this spirit, I would formulate three recent and particularly fruitful modifications of the more traditional concept of culture, which enhance its naturalism and should have consequences for our method. I choose to formulate them as assertions, for greater clarity:

1. All concepts are embedded in practice; and so their definition and thrust can only be determined in the context of that practice.

2. All views are singular and positioned; and anthropological accounts and generalizations about a cultural tradition will represent the anthropologist's own construction, based on her judgments and analyses.

3. All meanings remain contestable, within as well as between social circles and cultural traditions.

All Concepts Are Embedded in Practice

The first of these assertions says that culture is ideational; but that ideas and concepts cannot be modeled as if they were abstract, logical constructs linked together in an orderly universal science. On the contrary, they are images which are used when we engage the world—i.e. they are linked to contexts and purposes as well as to each other. Their definition inheres significantly in the rules of relevance that attach to them, the operations in which they are invoked. To grasp them, we should not sever them from these connections of practice and only consider them in the abstract, as thought. We must also observe them in their range of use, as knowledge.

This has immediate implications for how we should position ourselves, and proceed, during fieldwork. The optimal materials on cultural concepts are those which contextualize their evocation. This gives an enhanced importance to intimate participant observation, which alone gives access to unelicited, spontaneous materials on particular people speaking and acting in lived contexts.

But saying that we should attend to contexts seems to say that we should attend to everything: how do we get a grip on *which* contextual elements are salient and significant? I can offer no theoretically definitive answer based on a priori reasoning. But I have suggested that we should give special attention to *knowledge*, i.e. the meanings whereby people relate directly to an external world, which can then aid us as an object lesson when we try to capture their conceptions and concerns. We know indeed that our difficulty is one which is solvable in practice: every child is able to do so, presumably thanks to the way it is positioned. Through participation, it progressively learns its caretakers' ideas about the world, their concepts, language, and standards. In similar fashion, it facilitates our learning to locate it in a real-world context, with all the circumstances, incidentals, and coincidences that can help us to "become attuned to the attunement of others." Through participating in the experience we come to recognize the efforts of attention that are required in a practice—what seems in that context self-evident about a concept and its use, and what requires an effort of discrimination. Almost equally important, we also accumulate experience of all that is marginal to that which the concept discriminates, yet regularly associated with it. We thereby can come to share also some of the resonance of associational and connotational materials which the practice generates in those who live by it.

The other benefit of observing concepts in their practice context is the view it gives of the *social* processes in which concepts are embedded. Most concepts will be evoked and used in cooperative and interactive situations. In these contexts, the outcome—how a concept engages the world—will be determined in part by the sequential form of that interaction, as well as by the conceptual schemata

of the separate participants. In the structures analogous to life which people construct in games, we can recognize in chess, for example, that the "meaning" of checkmate comes about as the culmination of a series of moves, something which no manual can specify, and no single player can generate. Likewise, in the practice of life, the premises for what outcomes mean are delivered by our interactions with each other; the realizable resultant forms are conditioned by a social organization; and our thrills, disappointments, and understandings are the product of a sociology of interaction as well as a schematics of interpretation and classification.

Such a perspective holds the promise, or at least the hope, that it will empower us to move from the study of mere cultural representations to the fuller study of experience mediated by culture. If so, it would greatly enhance our capacity to model the extant diversity of meanings through which people engage the world, and the world-creating consequences of each particular concatenation of meanings.

All Views Are Singular and Positioned

The second assertion, that all views are positioned, may initially seem less subversive to traditional anthropological practice. It encourages us to attend more carefully to particular persons and interests, and to diversity in general. I judge the relevant data and their multiplicity of dimensions to be so great and varied that this can never be reduced to a question of statistical modeling. It will always require elaborate qualitative description, though quantitative data on particular features will be particularly valuable.

Such a conception of culture as ideational materials differentially distributed in a population entails a scenario where the differences between persons in knowledge, values, concepts, and perspectives animate a great deal of the action and interaction that takes place. Modeling these distributions and the ensuing transactions—and the processes whereby the differences, and the dynamics they generate, are themselves reproduced—provides the central problematics of social organization and the sociology of knowledge.

The multiplicity of voices which this view recognizes means, of course, that no voice is privileged and no one can give the definitive, essential version of "a culture." This does not mean a loss of precision in our descriptions; rather, it means a loss of distortion and an *enhanced* quality of descriptions in terms of their faithfulness. It does not reduce the importance of native models, and "letting their voice be heard," in our ethnographies. But it removes the aspect of abdication which may have tempted some ethnographers to this rhetoric. There is no way we can escape the full responsibility for our text as a representation, whether it is constructed as a collage of quotes, or is the result of a cooperation between ethnographer and informant, or is given the form of a tight model and analysis. It thus challenges us to develop better-argued frameworks for our choices and greater awareness of our theoretical assumptions. It puts the full task of constructing our analysis back on the shoulders of the discipline, where it belongs.

But what kind of modeling does it require? Perhaps we would do best if we stopped privileging the representation of "culture," and instead focused on the level of events, acts, people, and processes. But to the extent that cultural patterns remain salient as a level of description, we shall certainly have less use for structural models, since they inevitably lose something of their allure once we discontinue our search for the hidden essences of things. If our object of study is a diversity of positioned views and distributed cultural materials, from which ranges of events and acts are generated; and if our interest also embraces the processes whereby these events and acts may either reproduce or change their own preconditions, then we shall obviously need to construct systems models of a kind. But to represent phenomena as complex and varied as this, we must probably tackle the task of building models that represent disordered systems, systems in flux, forms which are at once both diffuse and emergent. There is still much theoretical discussion left to do before we know what this may entail and how it can be done. A premature espousal of chaos theory or other enticing new ideas will probably only produce new fads and new confusions. They should all be explored and played with. But above all we need to strain for a reasonable faithfulness in our accounts and see which concepts and models are needed to perform the task of description with enhanced naturalism and relevance, rather than formal and irrelevant elegance (cf. Sperber and Wilson 1986).

All Meanings Remain Contestable

This strategy seems all the more necessary when we consider the implications of the contestability of meanings. The implications of this apparently undismissable premise seem to make our materials even more evanescent. The diversity of positioning and multiplicity of views enlarge the field of contestation awesomely: We are faced not only with differences of interest, and the struggle and negotiation it generates; we must also acknowledge that such contenders are constructing different interpretations of the world and of each others' acts, and thus articulate oddly and often poorly with each other in their confrontations. Indeed, often their interactions seem to address each others' only vaguely conceived and perceived premises, or mystifying confusions, rather than be concerned with clearly embraced positions and interests.

Beyond that, persons living in such relatively disordered contexts cannot be expected to be coherent even in their own views and understandings within themselves as single actors—as indeed we know from experience, and from ourselves. That means that each actor will be prone to pursue inconsistent and incompatible ends simultaneously, indeed perhaps to hold value positions which are in practice or in principle diametrically at odds. Paine (1989) has recently provided an elegant and pointed discussion of one familiar scenario of this kind, involving love, gender, honor, and self-assertion, and illustrates the enigmas thereby generated.

But undermining even such foundations as may still seem intact after this, we must realize that not only is any interpretation, and thus the meaning of every event, contestable from a diversity of positions, but it also remains so through time. "What happened" continues to be eternally contestable. Any convergence of understanding achieved today may be invalidated tomorrow, as people revert to their memories of past events and reinterpret them, drawing the consequences of new understandings of old events and thus not only rewriting history, but literally changing the causes of the present. Anthropology's single-visit field tradition, but also our sometimes meticulous work to document extended cases as a verified record of events, claims, and counterclaims, for a long time blocked this shattering realization from view. Elizabeth Colson's longitudinal studies, and her perceptivity in acknowledging what the resulting materials contained, led her to recognize the continuing "reordering of experience" (Colson 1984) in a way which is bearing fruit in the most perceptive of current work and which can now also be derived theoretically.

At first flush, this realization may make it seem as if the very ground gives way under us: "what really happened" no longer stands still. Any attempt to construct a synthetic account of it comes to be of marginal interest since, to those who were parties to the events and live with their consequences, such an account would compose mainly a medley of unrecognized causes, rejected interpretations, and forgotten details. The significant data—how different persons using different bits of schemata construct passing interpretations during the course of their remittently innovative interaction—can never cohere as one verified account, because they do not exhibit that kind of order.

But again we should not despair. Field notes which inscribe the evanescent degrees of order and emergence to which this view sensitizes us will represent an *enhanced* account of what is taking place between people, and provide the *only* means by which we can capture the relevant processes and the precipitate of experience which is generated in persons and groups. Our task is not to reify illusory fact or structure, and incorporate them as specimens in our collection, but to record the flux which we can observe. Only from such data can we hope to produce valid models of how people act, communicate, and construct meanings together.

ENHANCING THE POWER OF OUR ANALYSES

If various positioned people bring different, probably highly inconsistently perceived, worlds with them to their meetings, and make their discrepant interpretations accordingly of what happens between them and around them—how can we ever expect them to converge in their ideas? Our field notes document a not inconsiderable degree of sharing—of concepts, ideas, outlines of cosmologies, and all the other cultural materials—in every community. Could this be produced and reproduced under the conditions of positioning, contestation, and transformation of memories that I have imputed to the interacting members of such communities?

Frankly, we have not designed the theories, models, and analyses which could tell us, but my own intuition is that, given the appropriate conceptual tools, we shall be able to show it to be so. A powerful force toward convergence is the ubiquitous expectation of mutual comprehension and shared reality which characterizes nearly all encounters between human beings.

To enhance the power of our analyses, I have long argued that we must turn from totalizing cultural models to generative models of processes (e.g. Barth 1966). I sense a welcome retreat in the newest currents within contemporary anthropology from an exaggerated focus on the abstraction of culture to a more versatile attention to the multiple levels of events, acts, experience, ranges of variation, contexts, and larger systems—all of them permeated by characteristically cultural processes, but not simply constitutive of a unitary culture.

I call specifically for the need to develop models of disordered systems. These must be models capable of representing large-scale social and cultural states-of-the-world without exaggerating and essentializing some salient or convenient apparent regularities into idealized representations of "the whole." This does not pose insuperable problems, but calls for innovative ways of modeling. Above all it calls for a shift in our tacit conceptual habits and a greater willingness to entertain complexity in our modeling of the world. The very irregularities, variations, and ranges of form that are disguised when we homogenize and essentialize may in fact hold the keys to the gross dynamics of our object. Likewise, on the micro level, we need to observe and model the diverse processes that produce opposed and divergent trends, to construct those parallelograms of forces which may profoundly shape aggregate forms.

No sleight of hand can substitute for the hard work of fitting together a complex representation of crossing and interfering partial connections. But unless we can give, however simplified, an account of how the larger configurations, and the processes that go on within them, are linked up and play out their various effects, we have not achieved the naturalistic robustness which is a first requirement of any kind of valid understanding. To the extent that we build such representations, we will also find that they engage the world more directly, both the diversity of constructed meanings which people project on it and the consequences of their acts in their surroundings. That will empower us to act with somewhat greater effect *on* the world, and thus achieve the enhanced relevance of our discipline for which the contemporary crisis calls.

NOTES

1. I wish to thank Bruce Knauft and members of the anthropology seminar at the University of Bergen for helpful criticisms of this manuscript.

2. This is not, of course, a universally shared premise in the worlds which people construct, but springs from a particular current within Western thought, and owes this articulation significantly to Max Weber. Yet it points to an orientation which is now increasingly embraced among people throughout the world (reflecting their shared hope to achieve a life of reduced suffering through greater control of their material circumstances) and so is a step in establishing the common discourse referred to in the preceding passage. Now is hardly the moment for anthropology, in an excess of zeal, to try to abandon it in favor of less materialist and less shared metaphysical positions, which we are also not honestly able to sustain in a life such as every one of my readers will be practicing. Moreover, while it should remain provisional as should all premises, it alone seems to allow us to frame within a set of shared constraints the efforts of people to act on their worlds—efforts which thereby become transitive and translatable in terms of each other. Without it, we cannot escape the hall of mirrors in which an extreme cultural relativity would reduce us to mere ironic commentators; also, the perspective of an anthropology of knowledge, toward which I argue in the following, would dissolve.

INTELLECTUAL ROOTS

Fredrik Barth is currently Research Fellow under the Norwegian Ministry of Culture and Professor of Anthropology at Emory University. He has previously taught at the universities of Oslo and Bergen, and as a visitor at various American departments of anthropology. He has carried out research in a number of areas, starting in the Middle East with a focus on tribal politics and ecology. His best-known works from this period are: *Political Leadership among Swat Pathans* (1959), *Nomads of South Persia* (1961), *Models of Social Organization* (1964), and the edited work *Ethnic Groups and Boundaries* (1969). He has also done fieldwork in New Guinea and Southeast Asia, and among his publications are *Ritual and Knowledge among the Baktaman of New Guinea* (1975) and *Cosmologies in the Making* (1987). A monograph entitled *Balinese Worlds* will appear in 1993.

After a wartime childhood in Norway, I started at the University of Chicago with an interest in paleontology and human evolution. But the active and rich teaching program of Fred Eggan, Sol Tax, Robert Redfield, and others broadened my intellectual horizon and led, after an interlude on a dig in Iraq with Bob Braidwood, to my choice of social anthropology as the focus of my work. My foundations derived indirectly from Radcliffe-Brown, who had taught my teachers during the 1930s.

Like many of my Chicago cohort, I went on to further studies in England. I chose the London School of Economics and developed a life-long association with Raymond Firth and, even more importantly, with Edmund Leach, whom I later followed to Cambridge for my Ph.D. In the structuralist ambience of the British school of social an-

thropology of the 1950s and the 1960s, this placed me in a somewhat oppositional role, aggravated by my admiration for Weber over Durkheim and Marx.

Through Firth and Leach, the influence of their teacher Malinowski strengthened my natural inclinations toward fieldwork. Indeed, my intellectual biography has probably been shaped more by the places I have been than by the books I have read or even the formative teachers I have known. Middle Eastern tribals taught me the turbulence and pragmatics of politics and the powerful constraints of ecology; the diversity of their modes of livelihood challenged me to think about comparative economics; and their situation as embattled minorities on an enormous continent forced me to face the problematics of ethnicity and boundaries. Likewise, the issues of Third World development were impressed on me through my trying to cope with them as a United Nations consultant in the Sudan and elsewhere. At the same time, the practical and intellectual tasks of building up national institutions for social anthropology in my native Norway also affected my perspective on our discipline and made it broader and more critical than it might otherwise have become.

A growing interest in religion, ritual, and the analysis of meaning took me to New Guinea, where my exposure to a singularly rich and evocative secret cult of fertility was formative in my understanding of how to analyze symbols. My ideas on cultural pluralism were changed by doing fieldwork in Oman. Lately, the challenges of Bali, where my wife and I started fieldwork in 1983, and most recently Bhutan, have provided the impetus again to rethink issues of culture and human action, and the ontology of the powerful continuities and contexts in which people everywhere in the world are embedded as actors and thinkers.

25

The Ethnography of the Present and the Analysis of Process

SALLY FALK MOORE

It has been reliably reported recently that history and ethnography have often been seen bedded together in the same text. That coupling and complementarity of two distinct forms of knowledge has enlivened and enriched both. But there is more to it than a happy marriage. Attention to the historical process has for some decades raised unsettling questions pertinent to all ethnographic projects, not just those that are bound together with archival investigations. The implication is surely that fieldwork is a witnessing of current history, history in the process of being produced. But how does that willing acknowledgment of the historical process affect fieldwork techniques? The definition of the "problem"? The frame of the analysis? Does a historical attitude toward the ethnography of the present imply that certain kinds of data are likely to be richer sources than others?

A PROCESSUAL APPROACH

This essay is intended to consider a few of the complex and by no means fully resolved questions that surround a processual approach.[1] There have been numerous and quite varied uses of the idea of "process," and many ethnographic attempts (with and without the label) to resolve the paradoxical task of describing a social scene as both being and becoming (notably Barth 1966; see Vincent

1986, summarizing the structure/process debate since 1974). The effort at analytic temporality in fieldwork is obviously not a simple matter. It amounts to trying to calculate the direction and significance of complex activities while they are in motion. To do fieldwork is to be witness to the active construction and challenging of relationships, meanings, categories, patterns, systems, orders, and, of course, their transformation and undoing as well. Fieldwork is simultaneously an attempt to comprehend the interlock between and among the repeated and the unique, the determined and the improvised, the propulsions of ongoing contests, the trajectories of ambition and submission, the dynamic factors in the organization of organizations. The fieldwork experience is in part solicited by the inquiries of the ethnographer, part proffered by the events that happen to occur (or be commented on) while he or she is in the field. Theory may inform the inquiry. It cannot control the happenings.

Anthropology's "Atemporality"

Fabian has alleged that anthropology's atemporality is "a scandal," that it has been our way of denying the "Other's" coexistence in the same world, our form of Orientalism or worse (Fabian 1983). His accusation, for all its energy and political indignation, comes a little late, and is heavily exaggerated. Without

362

covering the territory, but just considering a few prominent examples, one has only to think of the way history has figured in the work of Alfred Kroeber, Julian Steward, Eric Wolf, and Marshall Sahlins, or for that matter, in E. E. Evans-Pritchard, Georges Balandier, M. G. Smith, Stanley Tambiah, and in some of Clifford Geertz's work as well, to see that the totalism of Fabian's accusation is too sweeping by far (further see the compendium of definitions of culture published by Kroeber and Kluckhohn, 1963, and the large place given there to historical approaches).

The atemporality Fabian rails against once was real enough in some quarters, in the theoretical frameworks of Bronislaw Malinowski and A. R. Radcliffe-Brown, in some of the statistical comparisons of the enthusiasts of the Human Relations Area Files, and in many ethnographies. For a substantial time, and with the intention of making scientific comparisons, the societies of non-Western peoples were seen as types, variants within broad general categories that ranged from simplicity to complexity. There were two underlying assumptions of this approach. One was that "traditional" societies were so constructed that unless some external change of circumstances intervened, they replicated their social and cultural structures from one generation to the next. The second was that although these societies had in fact been variously interfered with by exogenous factors, conquest, the impact of colonization, slavery, missionizing and the world economy, and though they had changed substantially by the time they were observed, their previous state of affairs could be reconstructed. Both to salvage the "past" and to build models of it, the ethnographic project was strongly oriented toward just that "untimely" reconstruction. Given the definition of the exercise, the only processes that were of major interest were cyclical, the forms that were reproduced from generation to generation.

Stimulated by floods of new information, and by the hope of making scientific generalizations, anthropology took its comparative project seriously. But what it aimed to compare were social/cultural types and types of "institutions" and "customs," not sequences of transformations, and not an infinite overlapping and potentially shifting series of variants, and certainly not the transformed and transforming entity that had actually been observed in fieldwork (Needham 1983). The "explanatory" device was to show the connections among customs within a type, making manifest a total "logic" of the cultural and social order. The existence of the connections, the logic, and the order were postulated. What did not fit was deemed unimportant. "The subject matter of our enquiry is *standardized behaviour patterns*; their integrated totality is *culture*" (Nadel 1963:29). Thus the achievement of the period was to make the point that these were "systems" which had a social logic and were not a random, unorganized arbitrary aggregation of odd and exotic rules and practices.[2] Hence the project of contextualizing particular customs as conceived in a culturally logical matrix was almost inevitably a mode of total system building (Radcliffe-Brown 1952b: 181).

Malinowski, for example, contended that matters in the legal domain, such as the Trobriand concept of property, could only become comprehensible if described in full cultural context (1951:17-21). The abstract, but culturally loaded, Western idea of "ownership" had to be cast off, and the Trobriand realities exposed, with all the anatomical details showing. Malinowski was looking for a coherent normative order. The local ideas surrounding property were presumed to be a well-fitted part of a working whole. That integrated whole was "the culture." Behavior, of course, did not actually conform to the norms. Although Malinowski reported a considerable range of nonconformity and made certain theoretical uses of it, it did not suggest to him that the putative cultural order itself was full of contradictory meanings and transformational possibilities. He continued to see it as a synchronically coherent, self-reproducing system.

What would a postmodern anthropologist see instead? Clifford argues, "If 'culture' is not an object to be described, neither is it a unified corpus of symbols and meanings that can be definitely interpreted. Culture is contested, temporal, and emergent" (1986:19). The functional, totalizing cultural coherence that Malinowski took for granted theoretically no longer has much plausibility.[3] If there is no totally coherent "whole," no grand concept of "the culture" and "the society" as an integrated consistent unity, there is also no explanatory logical totality into which one can reliably fit any particular cultural item that comes along. Without a total "whole" the matter of necessary logical connections among lesser clusters of symbols and practices becomes a question rather than an answer. And if culture is "contested, temporal, and emergent," there also may be more than one answer.

Evidence of the Processual

For the ethnographer at work in the field today, where would one look to find visible evidence of the continuous and multiple shapings and reshapings of the idea of property? Indeed is the idea of "property" itself so Western-loaded that the terms of the question make open answers difficult to generate? Should inquiry proceed from the concrete, from the "social life of things" and thence to the people who deal with the "things" and from them to the conceptions invoked in their transactions (Appadurai 1986a:3-91)? Or should the ethnographic focus be on cultural categories and the changing uses to which they are put, the shifting meanings in what Sahlins calls the "symbolic dialogue of history"? In *Islands of History* he (Sahlins 1985: 145) says of the changing meanings:

The problem comes down to the relation of cultural concepts to human experience, or the problem of symbolic reference: of how cultural concepts are actively used to engage the world. . . . Brought to bear on a world which has its own reasons, . . . nothing guarantees . . . that intelligent and intentional subjects, with their several social interests and biographies, will use the existing categories in prescribed ways.

Used and changed at the same time, cultural categories can easily be infused with new meanings that attach to them in the practical situations that refer to them. While this conception of the matter has only recently seized the imagination of anthropologists along with Sahlins's captivating accounts of Captain Cook, this view is, in fact, the traditional self-description of the history of the common law. In common law theory, legal concepts acquire their meanings over time in the course of being "applied" to cases. Law is a domain in which the tension between forms of continuity and change is repeatedly manifested in the "application" of general categorical ideas to specific cases. Law used in practical situations is, therefore, an excellent locale for the study of the "symbolic dialogue of history." But there are many others. The process of categorical redefinition is ubiquitous. Nevertheless, one is obliged to question whether uncovering the shifting nuances of meaning that attach to particular cultural ideas should be the first objective of analysis. It is surely not the fortunes of cultural categories that occupy center stage in fieldwork, but the situations of the people who use them.

Ordinarily a fieldwork period is a forward-moving, fairly short time span, usually spent in one locality. That localism has its gains and its costs. What is to be done analytically with events in the local scene that link the small place of observation with longer-term, larger-scale entities? (See Barth 1978 on the implications of the large scale for anthropological analysis.) How is the large-scale connection to be handled? The political economy model of recent decades is one framework within which this question has been addressed. But there often is a lack of fit between the richness of the first-hand ethnographic material, and the well-worn second-hand model of the large scale. Shorthand phrases such as "the penetration of capitalism" are too summary to reveal much (though they seem to provide some writers with a lot of user satisfaction).

The Utility of Events as Data

I have argued that because events are seen to take place at a particular moment in the time stream, they have a different standing from forms of data that present themselves timelessly. This is not to discard any of the many other kinds of information or methods of investigation anthropologists have used in the past. Quite the contrary. They remain essential. Many kinds of nonevent information, from census figures to genealogies, from myths to discursive accounts to the doings of ancestral spirits, have great ethnographic value. They even have a time specificity that could be given emphasis. All fieldwork information is gathered at a particular moment and thus has at the very least a certain labeled, field-diary-entry temporality. But observed and recounted local events and reactions to events have another quality. Unlike many forms of dialogic interview material, the most significant events are not generated by, nor elicited by, the inquiries of the anthropologist. They consequently have a kind of purity as spontaneous local information. The action or reaction is locally constituted and locally produced. Equally important, events involving a number of persons often are the crossroads where many different interests and visions of things intersect. The study of the scrambled evidence at such intersections is a matter of no small interest. Events situate people in an unedited and "preanalyzed" context, before the cultural ideas they carry and the strategies they employ are extracted and subjected to the radical reorganization and hygienic order of the anthropologist's analytic purpose. They con-

tain the possibility of learning something unexpected.

If events are to have centrality as data, do all occurrences have equal standing as sources of information, or are some more likely to be revealing than others? Is a conversation an event? If so, what is not an event? I have suggested that within the frame of a particular line of inquiry certain events may be considered "diagnostic" (Moore:1987). For example in Moore (1991), I focused on major transfers of property occurring at different times in this century as diagnostic for the identification of economic and social change. Another paper (1977) proposed that there are "events of articulation" which show the situational articulation of different political interests. The instance used as illustration was a dispute in which alignments of kin, political party, and class were competitively involved in trying to control the outcome. It goes without saying that many other occurrences might serve as diagnostic. The question which events are diagnostic depends, of course, on what kinds of questions about culture and society and history one is trying to answer. The issue is one of relevance, not of attaching invariable significance to particular acts. An event *becomes* diagnostic in relation to a question.

Framing the Local Event in Time and Scale

Fieldwork is localized but the conceptual milieu of the anthropologist is much larger than the local scene. Fieldwork is time-specific but its moment is one episodic period in a longer stream. Methodologically what this implies is that a high degree of awareness of the limitations of a time-bound and locality-bound fieldwork project is central to effective inquiry. Transcending those limitations is the inner task of analysis. In what kind of fieldwork data are the implications of the larger dimensions and longer periods of time best captured? There are many possible answers to that question. However, the enormous useful-ness of events and commentaries on events as sources of "current history" can scarcely be overstated. It is not surprising that such a proposal should come from an anthropologist used to working with legal issues. After all, to the extent that legal anthropologists have concentrated on disputes and their settlement, their very subject matter has been to study *the institutional reprocessing of prior events.*

And what of local history? Only occasionally is there local historical material that compares in detail with the field notes being collected. By comparison, possible trajectories of the future often seem more visible. The potential direction of what may be a cumulative process sometimes can be quite clearly identified (though, of course, there can be no certainty). Is the life of the village of X becoming ever more tightly connected with the nearby town? Do the progressive exhaustion and erosion of the soil in parish Y portend an increasing out-migration?

Four technical issues face the time-minded ethnographer: (1) Can the time tempos of local "part societies" be fitted with the time frames of larger-scale transformations? (2) Can the "time of fieldwork" be analyzed as a seg-ment of a temporal flow if the specific past history of the locality is unknown? (3) Are there *types of data* that are especially suited to showing links between the small-scale and the large? (4) Are there types of data that are especially relevant to the connections between present and future? In short, how likely are significant issues of scale and time to present themselves in fieldwork, and in what sorts of activities and events are they embedded?

THE ANALYSIS OF AN EVENT

A peripheral incident "accidentally" presented in my own experience will illustrate some of the possibilities and limits of the technique of using events as key sources of information. It also provides an occasion for kicking hard at

the confines of the "tradition handed down from generation to generation" concept of culture. For example, see the recent, and not unconventional, textbook examples found in Kottak, "All humans grow up in the presence of a set of cultural rules transmitted over the generations. . . . These are the cultures or cultural traditions that anthropologists study" (1987:23); and Hatch, "Culture is the way of life of a people. It consists of conventional patterns of thought and behaviour . . . which are passed on from one generation to the next by learning" (1985:178). How much more ample, and not temporally restricted to "tradition," was Tylor's 1871 definition since it defined culture as "that complex whole acquired by man as a member of society" without confining culture to what was handed from one generation to the next (1958:1 [1871]). Surely to the extent that culture is "emergent" as Clifford appropriately asserts, it is also not always received from a previous generation and handed intact to the next. New ingredients, as well as evanescent ele-ments and qualities and transformational possi-bilities, are surely as "cultural" as old ones. A "current history" view of fieldwork must reject the durability test (and the exclusively "traditionalist" conception that has crept into some definitions of culture) or reject the cul-ture concept itself (which seems more drastic a move than necessary). Some radical modifica-tions of the meaning of "culture" through changing use would suffice, as for example in analyzing the following situation.

During one of my trips to rural Kilimanjaro I met a remarkable senior Mchagga man with whom I had not made contact on earlier visits. The reason our paths had not crossed was that he had been living in the capital city of Dar es Salaam, where he had been a high govern-ment official in Nyerere's Tanzania, while I had spent almost all of my African time on Kilimanjaro. I had heard of him, and it had occurred to me to approach him when I passed through Dar, but for a variety of rea-sons I had not done so. At the time that he appeared on Kilimanjaro he had just retired from government service and was about to resume living permanently in his house and gardens on the mountain. He was curious about my interests and the reason for my presence and approached me through intermediaries. We soon became friends and continued an intermittent correspondence until his death a few years ago.

I shall call him Danieli here, though that was not his name. Now it happened that Danieli's house, like those of many other Wachagga in the area of old settlement where I worked, was near to those of many of his patrilineal relatives. They all lived in contiguous garden compounds forming one of the many clusters of localized patrilineal kinsmen that characterize certain long settled banana belt parishes on the mountain. Danieli, like most Wachagga, was a Christian, and monogamous. He had, however, been married three times and divorced twice. At the time of marriage, each wife had been allocated one of the plots of his patrimonial holdings which he had been given by or inherited from his own father. He lived with his current wife but maintained regular friendly contact with the two previous wives. By the time Danieli returned to Kilimanjaro, most of the children of these marriages were adult. The married sons had local houses of their own constructed on plots in the patrilineal cluster that Danieli had provided, and the daughters had moved away on marriage. Some of the sons were also away from the mountain, scattered by their occupations, but some were there and others returned when they could.

Danieli's was an elite lineage. The prominence of some of its members could be traced to precolonial times. Of course, the particular bases of the power of lineage members shifted as colonial government, cash cropping, and major demographic changes swept over the mountain from the 1890s on. They changed their way of doing business, their religion, and they added a language. But what did not change for the successful (there were unsuccessful ones, too) members of this lineage was their position of relative advantage in comparison with other Wachagga families. Thus there was some degree of continuity of rank and high social position in certain families during a century of overwhelming change in many other matters.

Danieli looked forward to a cheerful old age, surrounded by grandchildren, and near to a variety of his many local economic and political interests over which he was determined to keep a close watch. He was prosperous and prominent, and took a rather dim view of many elements of the Tanzanian socialist experiment. When he first showed me around his compound, a man came out of one of the buildings adjacent to the main house and hurried to the garden. I asked Danieli who it was. "Oh," he said, "that is a servant. But now," he chuckled, "we pay them what the government tells us to pay, and we call them 'helpers'." He spoke English very well.

In a variety of ways it was evident that Danieli wanted to tell me what an important person he was and had been, and to be sure that I got the details right. He was a very worldly man and, indeed, was one of the few Wachagga who knew of anthropology. As a young man, he had met Malinowski whom he had received when he, Danieli, was a local official of importance on the mountain. Among other possessions, Danieli was keen to show me a file of his correspondence which included some letters he and Malinowski had exchanged.

On one of the afternoons we spent together, Danieli showed me photographs of himself on a number of public occasions in Dar es Salaam. Among these were some photos of parties held in his Dar house. Chuckling, he told me he still owned it and that it had been rented by a foreigner. That astonished me, since no sin was higher in the Nyerere list of possible improprieties by "leaders" than being a landlord.

In the early optimistic days after independence, President Nyerere and the other planners of African Socialism declared that they hoped to change the fundamental circumstances of economic life in Tanzania and thereby ultimately change the motivation of individuals. They also wanted to change the moral character of the citizenry. First they intended to do away with the opportunities for exploitation and for the accumulation of individual wealth. Then they would motivate—indeed impose frameworks for—an egalitarian, sharing mentality.

Necessarily underlying any such idealistic plan is a practical conception of what constitutes the priority list of evils that must be eradicated. Deeply embedded in Nyerere's publicly enunciated philosophy were convictions about the virtue of work and the wickedness of the idle and self-seeking. Not to work was to be a parasite. Not to share was to be an "individualist," an acquisitive accumulator, a competitor and exploiter instead of a cooperator. To be self-seeking was to desire and promote inequality (Nyerere 1966:Introduction).

In addition to these general values, there was implicit in Nyerere's rhetoric in the early days a kind of evolutionary idea. Africa must leap from a precapitalist to a socialist mode of production. It must therefore be diligent about avoiding and eradicating all "feudal" and capitalist tendencies. Among the forms that such wrongdoing might take "landlordism" was specifically identified. And the instrument for its eradication was legislation.

In the 1960s a series of Acts were passed to enfranchise tenants and to do away with landlords. In 1963, as a first step, the government abolished freehold titles. Various other Acts and policy statements followed. From a central government point of view, the preconceived target of this legislation was "landlordism." Nyerere (1966:166-167) made his ideas on the subject clear saying:

In rejecting the capitalist attitude of mind which colonialism brought to Africa, we must reject also the capitalist methods which go with it. One of these is *the individual ownership of land. . . . Landlords, in a society which recognizes individual ownership of land, can be, and usually are, in the same class as . . . loiterers . . . the class of parasites.*

The Arusha Declaration of 1967 was also explicit on the subject. Holding officials to a high standard in this matter, it said, "no TANU, or Government, leader should own houses which he rents to others" (the Arusha Declaration 1967:19). How did Danieli manage to keep his Dar house and rent it? And how did he get away with it?

Danieli had simply consulted a lawyer in Dar es Salaam and together they had worked out a type of transaction that would *look* legitimate. Nothing in the legislation in any way implied that land and houses could not be freely bought and sold. (A policy to prohibit such activities was enunciated much later, in 1983, but was not effectively implemented, at least not in the Kilimanjaro region.) Thus, once land titles were all appropriated by the state, what remained to be bought and sold was the right to *possession.* In the arrangement that Danieli made, he would "sell" the foreigner his house, but would hold a large mortgage on it. The foreigner would pay *x* shillings a month toward the "mortgage" during the years he was posted in Dar es Salaam. Then when it was time to leave, the house occupant would default on the mortgage and Danieli would foreclose and once again have his house. That is to say, what looked like a mortgage was, in fact, a rental agreement. If no one betrayed the game, all would be well, and, as long as I was able to follow the action, everything seemed to have worked out according to plan.

Thus did one event, Danieli's return to Kilimanjaro to his patrilineal kin, and to a "traditional" place in his community of birth as a hereditary leader, and as one of the senior elders of his lineage, also provide a glimpse of another event, the transfer of a major piece of property. The process to which this narrative was a clue was the way the elite of

Tanzania managed to maintain certain property interests despite legislation explicitly intended to restrict those very forms of property, and a government ideology that expressed a strong disapproval of those particular forms of wealth. Here are events on the large scale, the legislative installation of national policy by a government, linked to events on the microscale, the fortunes of an old fox.

Perceiving Broader Issues

What does this tell one about the Chagga conception of "property"? Surely the broad contextualization that Malinowski called for would be necessary for a full analysis, and this account has barely touched the complex of ideas that surrounds property on Kilimanjaro. But enough is apparent in Danieli's story to ask some questions about the usefulness of the classical idea of "a culture" in looking at this material. Was the new legislation not as much part of "the culture" of property then current among the Chagga as was the local practice of living in patrilineal clusters. And what about the fact that Danieli had to consult a lawyer to generate a scheme of evasion? The lawyer had a specialist's expertise in conceptions of property that were not shared, not part of the "common" culture. And only a very well-to-do Chagga would have had a city house and used a lawyer, so one could easily argue that there was an elite culture that included lawyers that was distinct from the culture of more ordinary folk. But all Chagga rural households were affected by the national legislation, by the imposition of new conceptual categories and restrictions on land-holding.

One swallow does not make a summer. The tactics of one elite individual who successfully circumvented the legislation suggest that there may have been more like him, but it does not demonstrate the flow of a process. However, it happened that during the intermittent periods of my fieldwork on Kilimanjaro, numbers of other shady transactions came to light involving other persons who were much less prominent and much less wealthy than Danieli. These indicated the strength of the "illegal" economy, and indeed the many holes in the official picture of Tanzanian reality. On the official side, there were some righteous confiscations of property and strategic exposures of violations. Occasionally officials enriched themselves in the process. Some property holders were heavily penalized, so there was reason for the evaders to be afraid. Everything depended on who was involved, what profit there might be in enforcement or nonenforcement for the local Party officials, and the like. The heavy dependence on relationships of trust, on networks, influential contacts, patrons, and the loyalty of kin and neighbors, was greatly intensified by an atmosphere in which economic illegality and its perils were normal. Almost anyone could betray someone if they chose. Almost everyone had some damaging knowledge of someone else, or even of many others. The interventions of the state and Party, and the counter-official activities that were under way (often perpetrated by officials themselves) were clearly interlinked parts of a long-term process. There are forms of law that almost inevitably give rise to twin forms of illegality. The invented socialist state had a hand in its own constant undoing. Like Penelope weaving by day and ripping by night, while she waited for Ulysses to return, the socialist state generated undoings of all its doings while it waited for the socialist dream to be realized.

In one tour of fieldwork it is not possible to be certain in which of several different directions the activities one sees and hears about will come out, which will have the greater cumulative momentum. But it may be possible to discern the factors that are in play in the situation. And there may well be subsequent visits. Obviously the character of the postcolonial state in Tanzania developed out of many elements, different for different regions, and the "totality" cannot be "imagined" or constructed out of such small fragments as the story of Danieli's "deal." But without such local and particular fragments on the state of the state, one knows even less. Can one speak of the "culture" of illegality where illegality is persistent and mundane? What can the anthropologist make of the web of relationships constructed around a state that is simultaneously building new bureaucratic institutions and new illegalities at virtually the same pace, and which glosses itself in an almost religious rhetoric of high political morality? What is to be done if a lot of the material is unpublishable lest it bring harm to trusting individuals or make subsequent research permission unobtainable?

The "legal" like the "economic" is a dimension of almost everything in social life. It is too little used as an entry point for ethnographers. Law cuts across all levels of scale, cannot be effective unless a good deal of it is public knowledge, provides ample numbers of occasions for noting cultural categories and moral posturings, concerns everything from marriage to the powers of the state, and often involves matters of sufficient importance so that those involved will pursue their interests despite the presence of the anthropologist. It is not legal rules abstracted from social life, but law embedded in the process of social life that is the object to be explored, law as referred to by implication in the substance of transactions, in allocations, in dispute management, in efforts at official control and legitimation, in ideas used in bargaining situations, in illegal activities. Law so approached may provide the ethnographer with a barely obstructed view of what goes on in the house, on the street, and even in some government offices.

FURTHER ISSUES IN THE ANALYSIS OF PROCESS

Sequences Unfolding in Time

The brief tale of crafty Danieli's retirement links local and large-scale matters, the individual and the state, hints at the wide networks and persistent advantage of an elite, and the importance of the division of knowledge. It shows how activities under way during the period of fieldwork were mounted with the idea of a planned and envisioned (but, of course, uncertain) future on both a local and a large scale. That *connection with the future* imbues the fieldwork data with a notional, forward-directed temporality that is quite distinct from a retrospective history of the past. Much of what is happening anywhere is visible as part of a sequence in time because the people involved are themselves acutely aware of the way they want to shape their future. By trying to "fix" the outcome, whether through legislation or through strategic transactions, whether through arrests and confiscations or through clever evasions, the various parties to the scene of action are contesting control over their today and tomorrow (note, in this context, Bourdieu on rules and strategies, 1977b:5–9). A processual perspective on such activities seems highly appropriate. Noting the process does not permit prediction, but it does strongly suggest possibilities. And it identifies both the locus of certain struggles over control of the future and the particular terms in which those are conceived.

And when does past history illumine current fieldwork? The answer is surely "always," whenever information about the past exists. It is always desirable for the ethnographer to know as much as possible how the present came into being, what sort of a sequence of transformations took place before the present acquired its shape. And sometimes present work can be turned to making existing archival materials intelligible. The particular form of the patrilineal cluster in which Danieli lived on the mountain in the 1970s was in many respects an artifact of recent decades, despite its historical connection with the patrilineal localism of the nineteenth century (Moore 1986). Without historical documentation to the contrary the lineage of the 1970s might have appeared utterly "traditional" to the outsider as it often does to the insiders. Knowing of the prominence of Danieli's family over the period of a century put his individual achievements in the perspective of antecedent, long-term asymmetrical relationships of advantage and disadvantage that affected the course of his life. His present was infused with past connections, but not wholly "determined" by them. His qualification for local, and later national, political positions depended on his ability to meet a combination of "traditional" and current criteria of eligibility, a not-unfamiliar situation in many postcolonial societies. Is Danieli's patrilineal connection and his idea of patrimonial property part of his "culture" but not the new state structure in which he performed and not the new national legislation and the ideas and practices it engendered?

Chopping up the social facts of fieldwork and putting them into two conceptual bins marked "old" and "new" is not the way to address the temporal problem. Such a sorting sounds as if it were saying something about sequence. But the effect of this classification is to remove the connections from view and to treat time simply as an exercise in a dualistic categorization (Comaroff 1984:571–583). From the point of view of the fieldwork material, such an approach dismantles a contemporaneous complex that is full of contradictory strategies, ideas, and activities and simplifies it into two crudely defined categories that are somehow preconceived as critical. Such a procedure destroys any evidence

there might be of an ongoing dynamic. The significant object of dynamic analysis is how a transformational sequence (or a sequence of repetitions) is generated over time. Too much attention to the old/new polarity can badly deform the way such a question is addressed.

That is all the more so where independent sources of local history are unavailable, and an appearance of the exotic is assumed to be a mark of cultural age. Since an absence of local history is not uncommon for the small social fields that anthropologists study, does that mean that a processual approach is thereby blocked? The answer is obviously "No." As has been made plain, a processual approach is not simply a prescription for a historical account in which the "fieldwork present" figures as the terminal point. A processual attitude toward the fieldwork problem not only imagines the present as an emerging moment, but conceives of the present as a time from which the next moment will emerge. The focus is on the unfolding of events and on inspecting closely the contents of the baggage that is brought to them and what is carried away afterward.

Reconceptualizing Culture: Composite Societies, Wholes and Parts, the Shared and Not-Shared

Anthropology has not only given itself an illusion of total explanation but has actually made considerable intellectual profits from its various house brands of "holism." The ideas of the shared "culture" as the unit of study, and the boundaries of "cultures" as the definers of the social units to be examined, are consequently still staples in many a theoretical kitchen. But just as the idea of generation to generation durability of culture must be problematized, so must the idea that culture is a kind of totality that is wholly "shared" as, for example, in Rabinow and Sullivan's summary definition, where culture is said to be "the shared meanings, practices, and symbols that constitute the human world" (1979:6). On first glance that seems unexceptionable. But what about the not-shared in "heterogeneous" or "complex" social entities? The cultural divisions and exclusivities of class and occupation within complex societies are well established (Bourdieu 1977b, 1984; A. Cohen 1981). "Ethnic" and religious cultural pluralism also would seem to be one of the hallmarks of most of the countries of the world. Migration has even repluralized those nation-states of Europe that once thought they were well on the way to cultural homogeneity. Does the question of "the shared" come down to a question of what size social unit is being discussed? What kind of social unit?[4]

Of course, the concept of cultural homogeneity is not just a heuristic one, used in analysis, but has current political implications. It is the epicenter of many forms of "ethnic" politics, local and national. Modern nationalist politicians would find comfort in the work of some anthropologists who identify organizational progress in government and technology with cultural uniformity. Gellner, for one, has argued that there is a necessary correspondence between the existence of cultural standardization and the achievement of a modern nation-state (1983). What are we to make of an argument that identifies modernity with homogeneity at a time when cultural pluralism within most states of the world is the norm rather than the exception? How does one put together the vigorous tendency toward transnational integration implied by exchange in the world economy, the enormous growth in recent times of transnational organizations, the increasing commonality produced by shared scientific knowledge and technology and systems of mass communication, and the simultaneous tendency toward extremes of disunity implied by the assertion, and the violent reassertion, of ethnic, religious, and political divisions? Cultural difference can be as much a political resource as a cultural commonality. And cultural commonality is no bar to the construction of deep social divisions.

The conjunctions of these many contradictory tendencies are of profound importance to almost any anthropological fieldwork today. Intense local studies carried out with an eye to these issues illumines the complex constitution of diverse large social "wholes." Ethnographic fieldwork can contribute to an understanding of how tightly or loosely the compound parts of the large-scale composites are glued together at this particular historical moment, and what the potential is for increasing coherence or for violent explosive fragmentation.

Some styles of anthropological work have retreated from these questions, settling for less, simply reporting the smallest-scale fieldwork data as local "experience" and leaving it at that. As Ulf Hannerz says, "Actor-centeredness . . . can become another means of avoiding the intellectual confrontation with problems of scale and complexity," and he grumbles about "genres of anthropological writing that select convenient ethnographic slices from an often vaguely conceived societal whole" (1986:365). "A cultural theory adequate to the task of understanding complex cultures must be able to deal with the fact that the division of labor is in large part a division of knowledge, making very problematic the notion that culture is by definition shared" (Hannerz 1986:363). Holy and Stuchlik (1983: 50) argue, along the same lines, that the social distribution of knowledge:

is articulated, not by being organized as an overall system (e.g. unified culture), but by the fact that, though the sharing is unevenly distributed there are continuous chains of overlapping shared knowledge among many different component groups (groups being characterized, among other things by a considerably higher degree of shared knowledge). The concept of sharing makes it possible to refer sets of notions to collectivities of individuals, while retaining the notion of the individuality of knowledge.

To what extent does this suggest a substitution of the concept of "social knowledge" for the concept of "culture"? For many the term "culture," because of its history, implies long-enduring group commonalities, while the idea of knowledge more easily problematizes the question of what is shared and what is not, and how recently acquired or ephemeral the "knowledge" might be. But "knowledge" does not fully capture all the nuances of "culture." Obviously, even if one wanted to, it would be impossible to trash the culture concept because it is so deeply rooted in the history of ideas and in the discipline of anthropology. But certainly it becomes more and more obvious that the totalizing use of the idea of "a culture," and the equating of one culture (passed on from generation to generation) with one society, can be an obstacle to seeing the importance of temporal factors, individual and categorical diversity, and local and large-scale juxtapositions.

Connections
to the Large-Scale "Whole"
beyond the Field Site

There has been a long history in anthropology of imagining the unseen large-scale "whole" beyond the field site. Three approaches have been especially important in shaping the discipline. One conceives the larger entity as a homogeneous cultural field, another imagines the "whole" as a regional or political unit, and the third thinks in terms of the world political economy. In each case the field site is connected with the larger scene in a different way.

Where the extent of the common culture is the criterion for defining the whole, it is not unusual to find the presumption that the culture of the field site can be generalized to a much larger geographical region and population. The fieldwork site is treated as typical, an example of like sites in the cultural area. In the more responsible instances, this expanded result is generated not just by imaginary multiplication but by sampling in a wider region.

Many areas are markedly heterogeneous and the diversity is recognized in the theoretical conception of the "whole." For example, there may be cities and towns as well as rural peasant areas, or a central government that rules over diverse ethnic groups. If that cultural pluralism enters the analysis, the polity that, actually "contains" the field site and its neighbors has often seemed the most obvious entity to use as the significant larger bounded "whole." The "culture" of the field site is then conceived of as existing juxtaposed to or interdigitated with different cultural systems. The "whole" is a complex composite with politically defined physical boundaries.

The third version of the whole, the political economy model, is much more of a theoretical abstraction, and treats the "world system" as the relevant totalization. Given that approach the description of the fieldwork scene is likely to give emphasis to obvious signs of connection with the world economy, such as cash cropping, migrant labor, long-distance trade and the like. Since the reach of the world economy is not only considerable but often controlling, the question of power is regularly embedded in the analysis. In fieldwork done in the political economy paradigm, the center of analytic attention is the penetration of the world economy into the fieldwork site. In most instances, the logic cannot go in the reverse direction. In the circumstances "What kind of a whole can it be that has this sort of subpart?" is a question that may appear useless to ask. The "whole" so conceived is too large to be susceptible of acquiring any significant part of its form from one field site. Besides in most hands the world system is not concrete enough to be a describable entity, and figures more as a grand postulate of long-term causality. Some enthusiasts hold out the hope of theoretical change in an ethnographic direction. Thus Marcus and Fischer argue that "one obvious course is for political economy to rebuild understandings of macro-level systems from the bottom up" (1986:80).

These three versions of the large-scale—the cultural, the political, and the economic—all have shortcomings. One major task for anthropology is to achieve a plausible combination of these perspectives. If this is not achieved the findings of local field studies will never have the reach and impact that they should. Fieldwork will be reduced to human-interest stories.

Some social theorists are preoccupied with similar small-scale/large-scale problems. So Habermas, for example, argues that "life-world" and "system" have become uncoupled in the modern world (1987:303). In his scheme of things money and power are the "steering systems" that reach into the life-world and distort its social integration. He contends that the uncoupling of the "systems" from the "life-world" have occurred both empirically and analytically, and that "the fundamental problem of social theory is how to connect in a satisfactory way the two conceptual strategies indicated by the notions of 'system' and 'life-world'" (1987:151). The totalizing models themselves may produce some of these problems of internal logic. The issues may be less formidable when addressed as limited, real-world, temporally specific, empirical questions.

All of the previous discussion has been carried on as if anthropology fully controlled the definition of its field of inquiry. But anthropology is itself caught in the historical moment. "None of the contents analyzed by the human sciences can remain stable in itself or escape the movement of History" (Foucault 1973b:310). Quite apart from the question whether there are unconscious conceptual constraints that are so naturalized they are not visible to us, there also are serious practical problems that are highly visible. It is well for anthropology to aspire to study all of the facets of the human condition, because that is a noble ambition. But not to ask whether anthropology is as much shaped by what anthropologists cannot study, as by what they can, is to choose to ignore the obvious. Today there are many violent locales where it is too dangerous to do fieldwork, yet what is going

on is of great analytic importance, other settings where access is refused, and many milieus where the nonspecialist observer, even if admitted, cannot fully understand what is going on for lack of specialized knowledge. There can be no illusions about the myriad practical constraints that currently surround the choice of ethnographic subject matter, and restrict what can be published even when contact has been achieved.

But despite the distortions of the discipline which these practical limitations impose, there should be no conceptual narrowing of the objectives of inquiry. Quite the contrary, the fewer the sites to which we have access, the more we must learn from them. The mining of events for their contents, close attention to the significance of conjunctions and sequences, and a broadly conceived processual approach can make fieldwork genuinely exploratory, and the present intelligible as current history.

NOTES

1. For earlier discussions of this topic by the same author see Moore 1978, 1986, 1987.

2. To the extent that they were trying to show coherence and order, the system builders had a conscious political agenda which was the opposite of that which later critics alleged was their unconscious objective. They thought they were showing how logical native peoples were. The critics have argued that the model of cultural coherence and stasis justified colonial domination and the accompanying policies of systemic intervention.

3. Malinowski the theorist is cast off, but Malinowski the ethnographer lives on. See Fardon (1990) for a lively discussion of the intellectual durability of ethnographic writing as opposed to the ephemerality of theory in anthropology. This volume of papers on regional factors in ethnographic writing is a welcome set of comments on current debates.

4. As the situation of women in "simple" societies becomes a more intensely inspected object of study, it becomes clear that cultural divisions also exist outside of "complex" societies.

INTELLECTUAL ROOTS

Sally Falk Moore is Professor of Anthropology at Harvard University, where she served as Dean of the Graduate School from 1985 to 1989. She also regularly teaches "Anthropological Approaches to Law" at Harvard Law School. Her books include *Power and Property in Inca Peru* (1938), *Law as Process* (1978), and *Social Facts and Fabrications: Customary Law on Kilimanjaro 1880-1980* (1986). She is a fellow of the American Academy of Arts and Sciences and is a past president of the American Ethnological Society and the Society for Political and Legal Anthropology.

My professional development had three major phases: an initial period as a lawyer, several subsequent years as a young anthropologist (and young mother) doing library research and publishing, but without professional employment, and the most recent twenty plus years as an Africanist, theorist, and teacher.

At Columbia Law School (1942-1945), I was profoundly influenced by Karl Llewellyn, not so much by his excursion into anthropology, but by his approach to American law. Two of his ideas were particularly important. One was his skepticism about legal rules and doctrines, his demonstrations that they all came in pairs (or multiples) that were to different effects. It followed that judges decided which rule to "use," that the judge, not the rule, determined the decision. His other pivotal conviction was that the social settings in which contracts were made were a part of their meaning, i.e. that the text alone could not indicate all the implied cultural and social understandings that lay between the contracting parties. Llewellyn's sociological imagination and his irreverence for the then-prevalent conception of legal reasoning were enormously liberating perspectives. My year on Wall Street continued my legal and sociological education. I learned much about the way the business world "worked." At the end of the first year I took a leave of absence to serve on the government legal staff at the Nuremberg trials. The experience shocked and fascinated me. Both the nature of the prosecution and the social history of the prosecuted deepened my already passionate interest in the political dimensions of collective social action.

It was after the Nuremberg experience that I turned to anthropology, originally without any intention of becoming an anthropologist, simply to engage in the comparative study of societies for a year. My goal was to enlarge my understanding of collective causality. At Columbia University I was exposed to the ideas of a distinguished faculty. Though none of my mentors was particularly focused on the problems that preoccupied me, the faculty was enthusiastically encouraging. I was particularly stimulated by contact with A. L. Kroeber, by the great breadth of his knowledge and his openness, even in old age, to new ideas. I learned a great deal from all of my Columbia teachers, and their interests certainly influenced me to write my dissertation on government, law, and property in Inca Peru. However, at the time it was my early encounter in the library with the writings of Claude Lévi-Strauss that had the most theoretical impact on my thinking. I found his analytic detachment from the world of practical action and from history unacceptable, but the way he analyzed patterns of thought tantalized and invited further exploration in the ideology and rhetoric of politics and law.

My first child was born in 1952 and my second in 1955, and I did not start teaching until the early 1960s, though I continued to write and publish. My husband's academic work took us to England in 1954 and we returned there at intervals over the next decades, ultimately for a total of seven years. As I result, I had a good deal of contact with the world of British social anthropology. These connections were strongly reinforced from the moment when, in the early 1960s, the family moved to Los Angeles. There my husband joined the history department at U.C.L.A. And there I met Hilda Kuper, a South African (who had studied with Malinowski) and M. G. Smith (a Jamaican, whose degree came from University College, London), and the three of us became fast friends. The African Studies Center at U.C.L.A. was at that time a place of considerable intellectual excitement and ferment. The end of colonial rule had led to a radical reassessment of anthropological theory and practice in Africa. Though I taught at U.S.C., I regularly attended the seminars run by the U.C.L.A. Center and deepened my ties with the many British anthropologists who came to participate in the Center's activities, several of whom I had met before. Hilda Kuper and Mike Smith and Max Gluckman, a frequent visitor to U.C.L.A., together encouraged me to embark on fieldwork in Africa. I started in 1968 on Kilimanjaro, and have returned intermittently ever since. The interest of those three—Kuper, Smith, and Gluckman—in politics, law, and theory, and, for that matter, in my own law-grounded, historically informed, nonstructural functional perspectives on these subjects, led to many long hours of productive argument and discussion. For me, from the British and Los Angeles phases on, anthropology ceased to be a solitary enterprise pursued in the library, and my professional life enlarged its scope, and its pleasures. As is obvious, my preoccupation with "the anthropology of the present" is not a new interest.

26

*Goodbye to Tristes Tropes: Ethnography in the Context of Modern World History**

MARSHALL SAHLINS

The reason an anthropologist studies history is that it is only in retrospect, after observing the structure and its transformations, that it is possible to know the nature of the structure.
Bernard S. Cohn, *An Anthropologist among the Historians and Other Essays*

Amidst all the hoopla about the new reflexive anthropology, with its celebration of the impossibility of systematically understanding the elusive Other, a different kind of ethnographic prose has been developing more quietly, almost without our knowing we were speaking it, and certainly without so much epistemological angst. I mean the numerous works of historical ethnography whose aim is to synthesize the field experience of a community with an investigation of its archival past. For decades now, students of American Indians, Indonesia and the Pacific Islands, South Asia and Africa, have been doing this kind of ethnohistory. But only a few—notably including Barney Cohn, Jean Comaroff, John Comaroff, and Terry Turner—have consciously raised the point that an ethnography with time and transformation built into it is a distinct way of knowing the anthropological object, with a possibility of changing the way culture is thought.

The present paper associates itself with this project of historical ethnography as a determinate anthropological genre. Especially I would like to offer some theoretical justification for a return to certain world areas such as North America and Polynesia, areas which have been too long slighted by ethnographers, or ever since it was discovered in the 1930s and 1940s that they were "acculturated." For these peoples have known how to defy their anthropological demotion by taking cultural responsibility for what was afflicting them. The very ways societies change have their own authenticity, so that global modernity is often reproduced as local diversity.

CULTURALISM: DEFIANCE OF THE MODERN "WORLD SYSTEM"

When I was a graduate student—back in the upper Paleolithic period—my teachers were already announcing the death of ethnography.

*Reprinted, in edited form, from *Journal of Modern History* 1993(65):1-25. ©1993, University of Chicago, Chicago, Ill.

It seemed that Marx's prophecy to the effect that Western hegemony is human destiny was at hand. By the rapid improvement of the instruments of production and communication, proclaimed the *Manifesto*, the bourgeoisie draws all nations, "even the most barbarian," into "civilization."

The cheap prices of its commodities are the heavy artillery with which it batters down all Chinese walls, with which it forces the barbarians' intensely obstinate hatred of foreigners to capitulate. It compels all nations, on pain of extinction, to adopt the bourgeois mode of production; it compels them to introduce what it calls civilization into their midst, i.e., to become bourgeois themselves. In one word, it creates a world after its own image.

The argument could well convey a sense of inevitability, since its conclusion was already contained in its ethnocentric premise. The effectiveness of this ultimate weapon of cheap commodities already presupposes a universal bourgeois subject, a self-interested creature of desire acting with an eye singular to the main chance. Yet the metaphor is even more ironic inasmuch as the Chinese wall proves not so vulnerable. On the contrary, as a mark of the limits of "civilization," hence a constraint on demand and the passage of goods, the wall succeeds in its time-honored function, which (according to Lattimore) has been rather to keep the Chinese in than the "barbarians" out. And even when foreign things or barbarian beings do conquer, their local reproduction and meanings are soon sinicized. Western capital and Western-made commodities do not easily make their way by demonstration effects. The idea that they will, this same refrain about China has been playing in Europe for three centuries now: all those hundreds of millions of customers just waiting for British woolens, then cotton textiles, steel cutlery, guns and ships, and lately jeeps, perfume, and TV sets. A modern bourgeois version of the quest for El Dorado, the dream of opening China to Western products, still

goes on, undiminished by the perennial failure to make it a reality. Except that now the attempt to discover a northwest passage to Cathay appears as an equally frustrating quest to convert Asian hearts and minds. Consider this recent notice in *The New York Times*:

"There used to be a missionary aspect to it, with a board of directors having a vision of an enormous consumer market—you know, two billion armpits in need of deodorant," said Matts Engstrom, chairman of California Sunshine Inc., a food company that does extensive business in China. "But since Tiananmen Square, they've realized that it is a long-term prospect, and even then unless you're in the right area you're not going to succeed."

Ironic too that Western social scientists should be elaborating theories of global integration just when this "new world order" is breaking down into so many small-scale separatist movements marching under the banners of cultural autonomy. Or are these claims of "ethnic identity"—to adopt Freud's characterization of the Balkans—merely the narcissism of marginal differences? Presumably the demands of cultural independence are only temporary. In the long run the hegemonic forces of the world-capitalist system must prevail. Still, as Durkheim said of an analogous forecast, a science that deals with the future has no subject matter.

The cultural self-consciousness developing among imperialism's erstwhile victims is one of the more remarkable phenomena of world history in the later twentieth century. "Culture"—the word itself, or some local equivalent—is on everyone's lips. Tibetans and Hawaiians, Ojibway, Kwakiutl and Eskimo, Kazakhs and Mongols, native Australians, Balinese, Kashmiris and New Zealand Maori: all now discover they have a "culture." For centuries they may have hardly noticed it. But today, as the New Guinean said to the anthropologist, "If we didn't have *kastom*, we would be just like white men."[1] Maurice Godelier tells of evolués among a

New Guinea people, the Baruya—policemen, teachers and other town dwellers—who twenty years earlier had shunned the tribal initiations, returning in 1979 to the villages to remedy this ritual deficit:

And it was one of them who . . . publicly explained to all the men of the tribe and young initiates that the initiations had to be continued because strength was needed to resist the life of the towns and the lack of work or money; people had to defend themselves. In my presence he shouted, "We must find strength in our customs; we must base ourselves on what the Whites call culture."

Reified notions of cultural differences, as indexed by distinctive customs and traditions, can and have existed apart from any European presence. What distinguishes the current "culturalism" (as it might be called) is the claim to one's own mode of existence as a superior value and a political right, precisely in opposition to a foreign-imperial presence. More than an expression of "ethnic identity"—a normal social science notion which manages to impoverish the sense of the movement—this cultural consciousness, as Turner remarks of Kayapo, entails the people's attempt to control their relationships with the dominant society, including control of the technical and political means that up to now have been used to victimize them. The empire strikes back. We are assisting at a spontaneous, worldwide movement of cultural defiance, whose full meanings and historic effects are yet to be determined.

Western intellectuals have been too often disposed to write off the meanings as trivial, on grounds that the claims to cultural continuity are spurious. In the going academic view the so-called revival is a typical "invention of tradition"—though no slight intended to Maori or Hawaiian folks, since all traditions are "invented" in and for the purposes of the present. (This functionalist disclaimer, incidentally, while meant to be nice to the peoples, has the effect of erasing

the logical and ontological continuities involved in the different ways that societies interpret and respond to the imperialist conjuncture. If culture must be conceived as always and only changing, lest one commit the mortal sin of essentialism, then there can be no such thing as identity, or even sanity, let alone continuity.) In any event, this Maori or Hawaiian "culture" is not historically authentic because it is a reified and interested value, a self-conscious ideology rather than a way of life, which moreover owes more in content to imperialist forces than to indigenous sources. All unwittingly, ideas of ancient custom are developed out of the colonial experience: an ethnic distinctiveness perceived from the vantage, if not also to the advantage, of the culture-of-dominance. At the Honolulu airport, visitors are welcomed by hula dancers in plastic "grass" skirts, swaying to slack-key Spanish guitars in an expression of the uniquely Hawaiian "aloha spirit." A culture of tourism, of the brand now widely marketed as aboriginal stock-in-trade. Moreover it was American Calvinist missionaries—"the mishes," Mark Twain called them—with their obsessions that made sexuality emblematic of Hawaiianness. So that now Hawaiians have nothing to do but recreate themselves in the image others have made of them.

Alternatively, the indigenous people are said to take their cultural distance only by evolving complementary or inverted forms of the colonial order. An historian (Nicholas Thomas) can thus find a ready audience for the assertion that Fijians have but recently, since the turn of the twentieth century, elaborated and objectified their well-known customs of generalized reciprocity called *kerekere*: in part by accepting the colonial definition of themselves as "communally organized" and more importantly, as a reaction-formation to the even more famous commercial instincts of White men. Reifying their easy give and take of goods, Fijians could represent themselves as generous, in contrast to the self-interest of the colonizers. Again, an anthropologist argues that the Javanese kingdom of Surakarta was able to survive under Dutch rule by displacing its demonstrations of power from fateful arenas of Realpolitik to innocuous rituals of marriage.

Yet even if these arguments were historically accurate they would still be culturally insufficient, since under similar colonial circumstances the Samoans did not *kerekere*, nor the Balinese merely marry. I return to this point again and again: "tradition" often appears in modern history as a culturally specific mode of change. Fijian exchange or *kerekere* also happens to be a good example of the facile historiography inspired by the principle that "there must be a White man behind every brown" (as Dorothy Shineberg put it)—an "elite historiography," in Guha's terms, unmindful of the culture and action of the subalterns. For the journals of missionaries and traders from the earlier nineteenth century not only provide abundant evidence that the *kerekere* custom was self-consciously practiced then in the same way it is described in modern ethnographies—Fijian "begging," as *kerekere* appears in the historical texts and is defined in a number of missionary dictionaries going back to 1839—not only that, but the documents indicate historically what one would expect logically: that the failure of White men to participate in *kerekere* led Fijians to construct them as selfish (by their insisting on buying and selling) rather than that the selfishness of White men led Fijians to construct themselves as generous (by developing a custom of *kerekere*). So when the mishes protest to the chief that they had come out of love for Fijians and to save them, the chief objects that it can't be so:

"You come here and you will only buy and sell, and we hate buying. When we ask you for a thing you say no. If a Feejeean said no, we sh^d kill him, don't you know that. We [of Bau] are a land of Chiefs. We have plenty of riches. . . . We have them without begging. We hate buying and we hate the lotu [Christianity]." He concluded by begging a

knife for one of his friends, which after such a conversation I thought it best to refuse, which I did as respectfully as possible. (Lyth 1851:74-76)

"Begging," an early American trader observed, "is the besetting sin of them all & both sexes do not hesitate to Cery Cery fuckabede as they call it." "Cery Cery fuckabede" was Warren Osburn's immortal 1835 transcription of the Fijian *kerekere vakaviti*, meaning "to ask for something in the Fijian manner," a phrase which also proves that Fijians objectified the practice some months before the first missionaries and some decades before the establishment of the colony, although not before centuries of contact and exchange with people from other island groups of the Pacific (Tonga, Rotuma, Uvea) (Osburn 1835:337-338).

There is a certain historiography that too often takes the "great game" of imperialism as the only game in town. It is prepared to assume that history is made by the colonial masters, and all that needs to be known about the people's own social dispositions, or even their "subjectivity," are the external disciplines imposed upon them: the colonial policies of classification, enumeration, taxation, education, and sanitation. The main historical activity remaining to the underlying people is to misconstrue the effects of such imperialism as their own cultural traditions. Worse yet, their cultural false consciousness is normalizing. In the name of ancestral practice, the people construct an essentialized culture: a supposedly unchanging inheritance, sheltered from the contestations of a true social existence. They thus repeat as tragedy the farcical errors about the coherence of symbolic systems supposed to have been committed by an earlier and more naive generation of anthropologists.

Wiser now, we trade in our naivety for melancholy. Ethnography in the wake of colonialism can only contemplate the sadness of the tropics ("tristes tropiques"). Like the rusting shantytowns in which the people live, here are bits and pieces of cultural structures, old and new, reassembled into corrupt forms of the Western imagination. How convenient for the theorists of the postmodern deconstruction of the "Other." Moreover, the new ethnographers can agree with the world systematists, as James Clifford with Eric Wolf, on the incoherence of the so-called cultures—and thus of the anthropologists' culture concept. Both are also critics of imperialism: the postmodernists blaming it for arrogant projects of ethnographic totalization, the world systematists for the empirical impossibility of realizing them. Yet all these tristes tropes of Western hegemony and local anarchy, of the contrast between a powerful world *system* and people's cultural incoherence, do they not mimic on an academic plane the same imperialism they would despise? As an attack on the cultural integrity and historical agency of the peripheral peoples, they do in theory just what imperialism attempts in practice.

Everyone hates the destruction rained upon the peoples by the planetary conquests of capitalism. But to indulge in what Stephen Greenblatt calls the "sentimental pessimism" of collapsing their lives within a global vision of domination, in subtle intellectual and ideological ways makes the conquest complete. Nor should it be forgotten that the West owes its own sense of cultural superiority to an invention of the past so flagrant it should make European natives blush to call other peoples culturally counterfeit.

THE INVENTION OF TRADITION IN EUROPE

In the fifteenth and sixteenth centuries, a bunch of indigenous intellectuals and artists in Europe got together and began inventing their traditions and themselves by attempting to revive the learning of an ancient culture which they claimed to be the achievement of their ancestors but which they did not fully understand, as for many centuries this culture had been lost and its languages corrupted or forgotten. For centuries also the Europeans

had been converted to Christianity; but this did not prevent them from now calling for the restoration of their pagan heritage. They would once again practice the classical virtues, even invoke the pagan gods. All the same, under the circumstances—the great distance of the acculturated intellectuals from a past that was effectively irrecoverable—nostalgia was not what it used to be. The texts and monuments they constructed were often bowdlerized facsimiles of classical models. They created a self-conscious tradition of fixed and essentialized canons. They wrote history in the style of Livy, verses in a mannered Latin, tragedy according to Seneca, and comedy in the mode of Terence; they decorated Christian churches with the facades of classical temples and generally followed the precepts of Roman architecture as set down by Vitruvius without realizing the precepts were Greek. All this came to be called the Renaissance in European history, because it gave birth to "modern civilization."

What else can one say about it, except that some people have all the historical luck? When Europeans invent their traditions—with the Turks at the gates—it is a genuine cultural rebirth, the beginnings of a progressive future. When other peoples do it, it is a sign of cultural decadence, a factitious recuperation, which can only bring forth the simulacra of a dead past.

On the other hand, the historical lesson could be that all is not lost.

THE HAWAIIAN HULA: ALL IS NOT LOST

Hula schools (*hālau hula*) have been flourishing in Hawaii since the early 1970s. Many function under the patronage of Laka, the ancient goddess of hula, are led by inspired teachers (*kumu*), and observe various rituals of training and performance. Hula schools are a significant element of what some participants are pleased to call "the Hawaiian renaissance."

Nothing essentialized here. All sorts of differences between schools in styles of music and movement, in rituals, in assertions about what is modern and what "Hawaiian." Many arguments turn on implications of opposition to the culture of the Haole (White man). Yet the hula as a sign of Hawaiianness, of the indigenous, was not born yesterday nor merely as the construction of the Hawaiian Tourist Board and prurient Haole interests. The hula has been functioning as a mode of cultural co-optation for more than 150 years—a significance, moreover, that was already inscribed in the meanings of hula performances before the first White men set foot in the Islands. For that matter, these first Haole visitors, Captain Cook & Co., were entertained by a great deal of lascivious-seeming hula.

"The young women spend most of their time singing and dancing, of which they are very fond," observed David Samwell, minor Welsh poet and surgeon of the Discovery, during Cook's stay at Hawai'i island in early 1779. Cook's stay coincided with the Makahiki, the festival of the annual return of the original god and deposed king Lono, come back at the New Year to renew the earth—or in another register, to repossess the wife and kingdom taken from him by an upstart rival. The visitation of Lono was ritually mediated and popularly celebrated by hula-dancing, especially the sexually arousing dances of young women. Of course not all Hawaiian hula was of this sort, but Samwell collected two hula chants in 1779 that were sufficiently amorous. The women would thus attract the god—if their performance did not actually signify a Frazerian sacred marriage. But then, toward the end of the Makahiki the reigning king sacrifices Lono, sending him back to Kahiki, the overseas homeland and ancestral source of life, a removal that captures the benefits of the god's passage for mankind.

Humanizing and appropriating Lono's seminal powers, the woman's hula expresses a general function of their sexuality, which is to mediate just such translations between god and man—or in Polynesian terms, between the states of tapu and noa (free). Hence the essential ambiguity of women from a certain theological point of view: their powers of defiling the god amounted to conditions of the possibility of human existence. Hence also, as the party of humanity, their powers of cultural subversion. Birth itself was a form of this same capacity to bring the divine into the human world, especially the bearing of a royal child. Accordingly, chiefly births were famous occasions for hula, as were the arrivals and entertainments of noble voyagers. And all these hula performances, including the annual seduction of Lono, would have the same broad finality, the domestication of the god. But note that within this frame the particular values varied from the restoration of an indigenous and beneficent king, the tragic figure of the dispossessed Lono, to the neutralization of the stranger-king, the classic figure of the usurper—the one who does Lono in.

Thus the historic function of the hula: its recurrent appearance through two centuries of Haole domination in defense of the ancien régime, and specifically of an Hawaiian kingship whose powers had been early on contested by a holy alliance of pious chiefly converts and puritanical American missionaries. Adapting the Protestant Ethic to Hawaiian projects of authority, the chiefs had learned to forward their commercial interests at the king's expense. Based on traditional conceptions of sacred power, on the establishment of links to Kahiki, this competition among ruling chiefs in the medium of commercial prowess greatly exacerbated the "impact" of the World System on Hawaiian culture.

The historic effects of capitalism were not directly proportional to its material force, a simple matter of physics. The huge debt amassed by the chiefs is rather a measure of the impetus given by the creative powers of mana to the destructive forces of capital. The comprador and foreign agents of the World System played the legendary part of the "sharks who travel inland," rapacious strangers from overseas, and they turned king into an historic version of Lono.

By the same cultural logic, the period of Lono's return, the Makahiki, was transposed by royal partisans into a festival of rebellion. For decades after it had ceased to be celebrated according to the customary rituals of world renewal, the Makahiki season became the occasion for improvised renewals of Hawaiian custom—expressed in and as the restoration of royal power.

Through all this the hula, together with complementary practices of jouissance, provided continuities of form and meaning. Indeed the hula uniquely represented the Makahiki in 1820-1821, the year following the famous "religious revolution" that had in principle abolished all such "idolatry" and ceremony. For many weeks between December and the end of February the disapproving missionaries were reporting people dancing in the courtyards of Honolulu "in honor of the king," Kamehameha II, and before the image of the hula god (probably Laka). The excitement proved to be the prelude to a series of libertine counterrevolutions in the later 1820s and early 1830s, all of them likewise breaking out at the time of the traditional Makahiki ceremony and enlisting its sentiments and practices in the political cause of the young king, Kamehameha III. Besides the hula, the old games and amusements of the New Year were revived, with effects enhanced by generous libations of Haole rum. The king dignified the first rebellion, in 1827, by sleeping with his paternal half-sister; in 1834 he finished off the last by fornicating with his full sister in front of the assembled Christian chiefs. At one time he abolished all the Calvinist interdictions on sexual relations and summoned the prostitutes of Honolulu to pay court to his current mistress.

Feminine sexuality was again enlisted in the cause of humanity: in rendering things noa, as Hawaiians conceived it, for in the context then existing the events meant the abolition of the Christian tabus as well as the return of the Hawaiian order. Nor was all this merely symbolic frolic. The king's sexual possession of the earth at times developed into the assertion of his sovereign rights over land, and more than once his carnival opposition to the Christian chiefs came near to armed conflict. But on each occasion the king was required to yield. In the denouement, as in other curious historical details, he lived out the destiny of the superseded god.

From 1830 or earlier the Christian chiefs periodically banned the hula, and from 1851 it was curbed by legislation. However, clandestine hula schools kept operating in the countryside, until they were again openly sanctioned—by kings. Excluding foreigners from attending the scene, Kamehameha V in 1866 allowed the people to mourn the death of his sister in the ancient fashion, which included hula dances. Especially was the hula favored with royal patronage during the revivalist reign of King Kalākaua (1871-1891). Kalākaua sponsored spectacular performances at his inauguration and fiftieth birthday celebration.

After Hawaii was annexed by the United States, the received functions of the hula were divided between the commercialized domestication of strangers in the tourist sector and the country schools less subject to modernizing innovations. The hula of the current Hawaiian Renaissance is an "invention" evolved particularly from the country schools. But it is not simply a colonial invention: a Western fabrication of Hawaiianness or else an Hawaiian fabrication in response to the West—which a certain colonial historiography, in some haste to make dupes of the ethnographers and victims of the indigenous people, or vice versa, is prematurely inclined to discover.

Not that the purpose of a historical ethnography is just to give salutary lessons in cultural continuity. More importantly, the purpose is to synthesize form and function, structure and variation, as a meaningful cultural process, sequitur to a specific cultural order rather than an eternal practical logic. The practical functions of institutions will appear as meaningful relations between constituted forms and historical contexts: the way the hula and the Makahiki festival, the hula by its translations of tapu to noa, the Makahiki by its reminiscences of sovereignty lost, were effectively counterposed to a Christianized ruling class. So would the local people integrate the World System in something even more inclusive: their own system of the world.

THE CULTURAL SCHEMES OF CAPITALISM

For its own part, the world system, as culture, is no less arbitrary. Only its familiarity allows us to maintain the delusion of a transparent and disenchanted order, singularly constructed by our material rationality, our human disposition to "rational choice."

However, material forces and circumstances always lead a double life in human societies; they are at once physical and meaningful. Without ceasing to be objectively compelling, they are endowed with the symbolic values of a certain cultural field. Reciprocally then, without ceasing to be symbolic, cultural categories and relationships are endowed with materiality. No chemist, Marx once said, has ever discovered the value of gold in its physical composition. Yet it is by this symbolic value that the objective characteristics of gold, such as its natural-geographic distribution in the earth, become powerful factors of world history.

It is sometimes necessary to remind ourselves that our pretended rationalist discourse is pronounced in a particular cultural dialect. Western capitalism in its totality is a truly exotic cultural scheme, as bizarre as any other, marked by the subsumption of material rationality in a vast order of symbolic relationships. We are too much misled by the apparent pragmatism of production and commerce. The whole cultural organization of our economy remains invisible, mystified as the pecuniary rationality by which its arbitrary values are realized. All the idiocies of modern life from Walkmans and Reeboks to mink coats and seven-million-dollar-a-year baseball players, and on to McDonald's and Madonnas and other weapons of mass destruction—this whole curious cultural scheme nonetheless appears to economists as the transparent effects of a universal practical wisdom. Yet even the producers who are perpetrating such tastes in the abstract interest of gain must be informed by the order of cultural values, that is, by what sells. Theirs is a classic fetishism of the commodity: the meaningful values are comprehended as pecuniary values. In the event, the invisible hand of the market economy functions like a perverse form of Hegel's cunning of reason; it is rather a cunning of culture which, by harnessing an absolute sense of rationality to a relative logic of signs, ushers in a (truly) golden age of symbolic freedom.

So it need not be surprising that when the advanced products of the West are successfully spread abroad, together with its higher attainments in economic rationality, all this practical reason is exposed to some cultural subversion.

As Bakhtin might say, Western commodities become the objects of alien words. Or not just words, of a whole alien discourse. In the planetary hinterlands, the powers of capital appear as forces of other universes. Although they may be at the margins of the world system, the people are not (to adopt Marx's image) solitary beings squatting outside the universe. They are social beings, conscious of themselves as persons of certain social sorts. They are fathers, cross-cousins, chiefs, Bear clansmen, elders, married women, Iroquois or Tibetans: persons functioning in determinate relations of kinship, gender, community, and authority; relations which thus entail specific rights and obligations, amities and enmities; conduct, then, which is materialized in definite modes of exchange and forms of wealth—hence social beings operating on cosmic notions of power, quotidian instincts of morality, selective skills of perception, relative ways of knowing and withal, large cultural resources of self-respect. We are not dealing with people who have nothing and are nothing.

To put it in the terms of Vološinov's semantics, the capitalist forms in these alien contexts acquire novel local accents. And here at least a synthesis with Saussure proves useful; the novel accents are also positional values whose differential relations to other categories of the indigenous scheme constitute logics of the possible effects of intrusive "forces." One might suggest an elementary subaltern principle of historiography: that no assertion of an imperialist discipline can be received as an event of colonial history without the ethnographic investigation of its practice. We cannot equate colonial history simply with the history of the colonizers. It remains to be known how the disciplines of the colonial state are culturally sabotaged.

THE INTERCULTURAL HISTORIC FIELD

However, to conceive of a simple opposition between the West and the Rest is in many ways an oversimplification. Colonial history is not well served either by its representation as a Manichean showdown between the indigenous people and the imperialist forces, to see which one will be able to culturally appropriate the other.

A number of anthropologists—among them Bruce Trigger, Ann Stoller, John Comaroff, Greg Dening—have taught us to reconfigure the usual binary opposition as a triadic historical field, including a complicated intercultural zone where the cultural differences are worked through in political and economic practice. "The beach," as Dening calls it—though it could as well be the plantation or the town—where "native" and "stranger" play out their working misunderstandings in creolized languages. Here are complex "structures of the conjuncture," such as the alliances that cross ethnic boundaries and correlate oppositions within the colonial society to political differences among the local people.

Think of how often the rivalry between Protestants and Catholics has been enlisted by Latin Americans or Pacific Islanders to the service of their own historic disputes. I have already mentioned something of the like in Hawaii. A recurrent conflict between the king and aristocratic chiefs, traditionally waged as the acquisition of foreign cum divine powers, was in the nineteenth century joined to the bitter jealousies in the Haole community between merchants and missionaries. Believing themselves the true heirs of the Protestant Ethic, the commercial men explicitly competed with the clergymen for leadership of the civilizing mission and the control of Hawaiians' devotion (which also entailed control of their labor). The praying chiefs standing with the missionaries and the drinking king with the merchants, the effect was an intercultural chiasmus, a structure that magnified the conflicts among Hawaiians by the differences in interest between Haole, and vice versa. The energies of one opposition were superimposed on the enmities of the other.

A powerful stimulus was given to the competition for grandeur among Hawaiian notables through the invidious accumulation of foreign luxuries, especially during the flush days of the trade in sandalwood for the Canton market. "Send out articles of a showy kind," an American trader wrote back to Boston in 1821, "everything new and elegant will sell at a profit; coarse articles are of no use." Pious as they had become, the ruling chiefs never learned to mortify their own flesh—the amount of which was continuing testimony to the favor of ancient divinities. The governors of the several islands weighed in at about 300 pounds apiece. Yet even if stretched to their organic limits, the chiefly persons could be metonymically extended to the foreign lands in the sky beyond the horizon, extended as far as China and England, by the importation of fancy clothing and swank domestic furnishings. China and England had replaced the old Kahiki, homeland of the gods, and now the flash of the foreign commodities evoked the celestial brilliance of ancient kings. Was this the origin of the aloha shirt?

Of course there are strictly functional demands to production for the market, adaptations that reach deeply into the indigenous society. And foreign meanings and economic dispositions come across the beach, along with the foreign goods. On the other hand, students of Pacific history are sometimes surprised at how easily the famous "penetration" of capitalism can be effected: with relatively little effort, violence, or threat.

CULTURES AND BOUNDARIES

Disease and destruction have too often followed, but they were not the means of access to the local people's desires or of the deployment of their labor to trade. Not that the islanders (any more than the Chinese) gave Westerners cause to congratulate themselves on the "demonstration effects" of their clearly superior goods, since the demands of the local peoples were soon enough selective rather than eclectic, and involved rather exotic senses of utility. Thus the flourishing nineteenth-century commerce in sperm whale teeth in Fiji, Hudson's Bay blankets in Northwest America, as well as Chinese silks and English broadcloths in Hawaii. Here was a period of indigenous "development," as I shall try to explain in a moment, during which all these foreign commodities were enriching native self-conceptions. It would thus be too easy to conclude from the people's receptivity that "Fijian culture" or "Kwakiutl culture" is an indeterminate concept, inasmuch as the so-called culture appears to lack any boundary, integrity, or totality.

A brief parenthesis only about cultural integrity or coherence, since we are here more concerned with boundaries. Anyhow we are not likely to soon hear an end to poststructuralist litanies about the contested and unstable character of cultural logics: about categories and perceptions that are different for women and men, chiefs and commoners, rich and poor, this village and that, yesterday and today. All the same, not everything in the contest is contested—which once more proves that we come here to paraphrase Durkheim, not to bury him. As polyphonic or heteroglossic as the monograph may be, one cannot legitimately insert a Japanese "voice" in a Sioux Indian ethnography.

In order for categories to be contested at all, there must be a common system of intelligibility, extending to the grounds, means, modes, and issues of disagreement. It would be difficult to understand how a society could function, let alone how any knowledge of it could be constituted, if there were not some meaningful order *in* the differences. If in regard to some given event or phenomenon, the women of a community say one thing and the men another, is it not because men and women have different positions in, and experience of, the same social universe of discourse? Are not the differences in what men and women say expressions of the social differences in the construction of gender? If so, there is a noncontradictory way—dare one say, a totalizing way?—of describing the contradictions, a system of and in the differences. End parenthesis: return to the boundary dispute.

I mean the currently fashionable idea that there is nothing usefully called "a culture," no such reified entity, since the limits of the supposed "cultures" are indeterminate and permeable, a lack of closure that again indicates a lack of system. Paradoxically, this argument misreads a cultural power of inclusion as the inability to maintain a boundary. It is based on an *underestimate* of the scope and systematicality of cultures, which are always universal in compass and thereby able to subsume alien objects and persons in logically coherent relationships. So far as Western imperialism is concerned—the one culture that has not been deconstructed by the changing of the avant garde, as it retains its essential and monolithic consistency as a system of power—for the local people the European is never altogether a stranger. As Marilyn Strathern says of Melanesia: "It has been something of a surprise for Europeans to realize that their advent was something less than a surprise."

Western peoples have no monopoly on practices of cultural encompassment, nor are they playing with amateurs in the game of "constructing the other." Every society known to history is a global society, every culture a cosmological order. And in thus including the universe within its own cultural scheme—as the Maori or native Australians include the order of nature in the order of kinship—the people accord beings and things beyond their immediate community a definite place in its reproduction.

Divinities or enemies, ancestors or affines, the "others" are in various ways the necessary conditions of a society's existence. Sources of power and cultural good things, though they may also be dangerous, these beings from the beyond represent a predicament of dependency in which all peoples find themselves. All must construct their own existence in relation to external conditions, natural and social, which they did not create or control yet cannot avoid. They are constrained in some way, if never the only possible way, by the passage of the seasons, the annual rainfall, the customs and actions of their neighbors. In such respects, no culture is sui generis. And a more or less self-conscious fabrication of culture in response to imperious outside "pressures" is a normal process—dialectic or schismogenic, perhaps, but not pathogenic. The diversity of human cultures, Lévi-Strauss remarks, "depends less on the isolation of the various groups than on the relations between them."

CULTURAL CONTINUITY AS A MODE OF CULTURAL CHANGE

Differences in the modes of cultural invention and reproduction appear with the advent of the colonial state. Interesting that from the perspective of many colonized peoples, it is this moment of domination, the assumption of subaltern status, that is most marked in historical consciousness rather than the first appearance of the White man or the earlier period of "contact." For Europeans, of course, the great rupture in the history of the rest of the world is initiated by their own appearance there—an epiphany that supposedly produces a change in the quality of historical time. In extreme (but not rare) formulations, nothing was happening before the European "discovery" (of places that had been known to mankind for millennia), merely a static reproduction of "traditional" forms; whereas, from the moment the first Western explorer or trader landed, the people's history became evenemential—and adulterated by the foreigners' culture. Still the Fijians, as many other colonized peoples, figure the historical break differently: "before the flag" and "after the flag," they say, referring to the establishment of British rule. This is the B.C. and A.D. of their world history, "Before Colonization" and "After Domination," and it entails a different sense of the cultural qualities of time and change.

"Before" was the time under their own cultural control. Western commodities and even persons could be encompassed within their own "development" projects. Foreign wealth subsidized native cultural schemes: the kingship in Hawaii, ceremonial feasting in Ponape and the New Guinea Highlands, hunting and warfare on the American Plains, potlatching on the Northwest Coast. This helps explain why certain things of European provenance—not only horses, tobacco, bush knives, or cloth but even Christianity—are still locally perceived as "traditional" culture. They refer to an epoch that might be called "develop-man." "Develop-man" was a word I overheard in a conversation between two New Guineans, when one of them inserted the English word "development" into a neo-Melanesian (pidgin) sentence. To me it came out sounding like "develop *man*," an error on my part that seemed to express truly the initial relation of many Pacific Islanders to the encroaching Western economy. The term captures an indigenous way of coping with capitalism, a passing moment that in some places has managed to survive for over a century.

The first commercial impulse of the people is not to become just like us but more like themselves. They turn foreign goods to the service of domestic ideas, to the objectification of their own relations and notions of the good life. Brought into the orbit of the capitalist world system, this global crusade of economic rationality, New Guinea Highlanders indeed prove themselves quick studies in commercial cunning—which they use to stage the most extravagant "traditional" ceremonies anyone could ever remember. More pigs have been eaten and more pearl shells exchanged in these recent festivals than ever was done in the good old days, not to mention the liberal consumption of such novelties as beer and tinned corned beef. Let the neocolonial bureaucrats or the development economists complain as they may, this is neither "waste" nor "backwardness." Precisely it is *development* from the perspective of the people concerned: their own culture on a bigger and better scale. "You know what *we* mean by development?" says a leader of the Kewa people to the ethnographer. "We mean building up the lineage, the men's house, killing pigs. That's what we have done."

Of course under a colonial state that relates to the underlying population by combined techniques of discipline, repression, and persuasion, the conditions of the people's cultural reproduction are radically altered for the worse. It is a period of humiliation, in which the political and economic prose of domi-

nation is often improved by a Christian poetry of human degradation. American missionaries used to complain endlessly that the problem with Hawaiians was that they lacked sufficient self-contempt. Eating, laughing, and copulating too much, while never working too long, the islanders simply could not understand how rotten they were. The whole Judeo-Christian cosmology of the human condition, of a human nature inherently corrupted by sin, of life as a punishment, this whole system of self-hatred had to be laid on them—"the furious, vindicative hatred of life," as Nietzsche called it, "life loathing itself." Only then, when they were sufficiently disgusted with themselves, would they be prepared to become like us, "civilized."

Around much of the world, however, the universalizing cultural project of the West does not so well succeed. The subaltern period is a "dominance without hegemony," as Guha puts it (for South Asia), marked by the compromises of the colonial state with the cultural particularism of the local people—who otherwise could not be ruled. In dominance without hegemony, Guha writes, "the life of civil society can never be fully absorbed in the activity of the state." The colonial regime is "doubly alienated" from the indigenous people, at once as foreign and as a state. It is an "absolute externality." The colonized adapt to its impositions by motivated permutations of their cultural traditions. Hence the sublimation of warfare in ceremonial exchange, or the so-called cargo cult that subsumes the colonial experience in a native theory of ancestral powers, to cite well known Oceanic examples. In the end, the people's humiliation is a double-edged sword, turned back against foreign dominance, as in the current "culturalism" or "the invention of tradition." "The expression of culture . . . is proof not only of *identity* but of dignity." These are the words of the martyred Amilcar Cabral.

And how else can the people respond to what has been inflicted on them except by devising on their own heritage, acting according to their own categories, logics, understandings? I say "devising" because the response may be totally improvised, something never seen or imagined before, not just a knee-jerk repetition of ancient custom. "Tradition" here functions as a yardstick by which the people measure the acceptability of change, as Lamont Lindstrom remarks of Tanna islanders. Cultural continuity thus appears in and as the mode of cultural change. The innovations follow logically—though not spontaneously, and in that sense not necessarily—from the people's own principles of existence. Traditionalism without archaism. Allan Hanson recounts a conversation with a "mammoth" old Tahitian who "has succeeded rather well in combining indigenous values with French influence." Sinking into a large chair after an excellent dinner and indicating the prominent place that a refrigerator occupied in his living room, he beamed contently at Hanson and said "Le ma'a [food] in the refrigerator—voila la vie tahitienne!"

A WORLD CULTURE OF CULTURES

Notice that for the people concerned, syncretism is not a contradiction of their culturalism—of the indigenous claims of authenticity and autonomy—but its systematic condition. The first thing of course is to survive. This is what the politics is decisively about. Yet the movement almost never envisions a utopian return to primordial days and ancestral ways. The traditional culture has its superior values, but refrigerators, outboard engines, and television sets are not among them. Modern culturalism includes the demand to have these things, or more precisely to domesticate them. Defenders of the indigenous order are prepared to make useful compromises with the dominant culture, even to deploy its techniques and ideals—in the course of distinguishing their own. Hawaiians, Amazonians, or native Australians stake claims to be the world's leading ecologists, the

original friends of the earth (Mother). But then, are they not just acting as proxy critics of Western society, deceiving and undoing themselves by mystifying Western values as native cultures? This seems not the correct interpretation, even granted that a peculiar ambiguity attends the modern culture movement—which from the left can be read as political resistance, if from the right as an ideological sellout. What I am trying to do here is get above the melee, as it seems to me that the local politics become means or expressions of a larger process of structural transformation: the formation of a world *system* of cultures, a Culture of cultures—with all the characteristics of a structure of differences.

In the upshot, in any local sector of the global system the transformation assumes the dual appearance of assimilation and differentiation. The local people articulate with the dominant cultural order even as they take their distance from it, jiving to the world beat while making their own music. Hence Michael Geyer's argument that similarity and difference develop together in modern world history, an observation that could be paired with Terry Turner's notices of the cultural dualism of Kayapo bodies, villages, and society as a whole—at each level externally Brazilian and internally Indian.

Interesting that earlier scholars of what is now perceived as "cultural inversion," this disposition of peoples in contact to elaborate the contrastive features of their respective traditions, that earlier scholars saw the cultural inversion as a structural equilibrium. Recall that Gregory Bateson originally defined "complementary schismogenesis" as a phenomenon of acculturation. And in *Naven* he argued that such processes of mutual differentiation are generally limited or counteracted, on pain of total separation and potential destruction. Of course this is the whole idea of how structures travel and are transformed in Lévi-Strauss's *Mythologiques*. Here again the oppositions between peoples in contact are balanced by resemblances as each strives to be as good as, and better than, thus the same as and different from, the other. "Everything happens as if, on the plane of beliefs and practices, the Mandan and Hidatsa had succeeded in organizing their differences into a system," he wrote in a well-known piece on the relations between myths and rites of neighboring peoples. The myths themselves speak of the wisdom of neighboring tribes staying far enough apart to be independent while remaining close enough together to be interdependent.

Of course, given the current theoretical and moral discourse of domination and subjection, the unearthing of such quaint relics as "structural equilibrium" or "structural complementarity" must appear feckless if not politically perverse. It might be better just to ignore the accumulated anthropological knowledge. This popular tactic is called "poststructuralism."

Alternatively, the old-timers remind us that a politics of culture is a process of structure. Rather than the overthrow of the world system, which is now an irreversible fact of their existence, the local peoples' inventions and inversions of tradition can be understood as attempts to create a differentiated cultural space within it. And actions that are at once indigenizing and modernizing appear as structural rather than just hypocritical.

Roger Keesing and others make the point that the leaders of modern movements of cultural revival are often the most acculturated people, and most successful in the commercial world whose values they ostensibly repudiate. Not long ago I spent the better part of a day with one in the mountains of south-central Taiwan, an artist of the Austronesian Paiwan people, the organizer of an aesthetic revival which is for him the means of an even larger project of cultural restoration. When I asked him why he wanted to return to Paiwan tradition, he answered with a criticism of modern materialism and individualism of a kind that can be heard in many Third World places: a life of money is inhuman by

comparison with Paiwan culture. This he said while eating a steak in a Western restaurant, in the Chinese town of Ping Dong, the restaurant being a sort of club to which he belonged, and to which he and his young Chinese wife escorted us from the mountains in the jeep he had recently purchased—from the proceeds of his two stores, where he sells his work and other ethnic products, including textiles from Indonesia and India. Yet there was nothing cynical about the man, on the contrary; and like everything else he did, his movement between cultures was graceful rather than incongruous. But then, who would be in a better position to mediate an intercultural relationship? And like the Polynesian ecologists or the Amazonian chief who turns a camcorder on the representative of the Brazilian Indian Service, does not the Paiwan artist make an assimilation of the dominant culture the means of sustaining a difference?

If all this makes any sense, if the world is becoming a Culture of cultures, then what needs to be studied ethnographically is the indigenization of modernity—through time and in all its dialectical ups and downs, from the earliest develop-man to the latest invention of tradition. Western capitalism is planetary in its scope, but it is not a universal logic of cultural change. In any event, we have been ourselves too dominated, historiographically and ethnographically, by its imperial claims. The agenda now is how it is worked out in other cultural manifolds.

FIJI: THE INDIGENIZATION OF MODERNITY

The first fifty years of capitalist develop-man in Fiji, roughly from 1800 to 1850, achieved unprecedented levels in outputs of cannibalism, thus confirming a certain totemic nightmare that has haunted the Western imagination at least since St. Augustine articulated it: that if human venality is unleashed, the big fish will eat the little fish. But modern academic hawkers of the World System have given too much credit to the trade in European muskets for local sandalwood and bêche-de-mer (sea cucumbers) as the reason for the interrelated developments in warfare, cannibalism, and state-formation in nineteenth-century Fiji.

The firepower of the musket and the labor requirements of the bêche-de-mer trade are said to have made the political fortunes of the kingdoms of Bau, Rewa, and their like. Yet these powerful states had already achieved their historic form and much of their dominion before any Europeans came, certainly well before the bêche-de-mer trade of the 1830s introduced an appreciable number of muskets into Fijian wars. Indeed, the control of Western trade by Bau and Rewa was due to their indigenous dominance, rather than vice versa, as neither of them enjoyed significant resources in sandalwood or bêche-de-mer within their own territories. Nor were the muskets then obtained by Fijians decisive in their wars. Notoriously subject to misfire in the humid tropics and quickly neutralized by changes in fortifications, muskets were in any event not employed by Fijians with great accuracy or efficiency. It was said by missionaries that Fijians loaded their muskets with powder in proportion to the size of the man they wished to kill—so that the bigger the target, the more likely the gun would blow itself up. Muskets were actually much more effective when they were many fewer, from about 1808 to 1825, as wielded then by renegade Botany Bay or Manila men in the service of Fijian ruling chiefs. For the mercenaries were careful to single out enemy paramounts and warrior champions ($q\bar{a}q\bar{a}$) as targets: leaders whose fall could put an entire army in disarray and open the way to a general massacre—by Fijians in the foreigners' train, using bows, spears, and clubs. Hence it was not European muskets that historically made Fijian chiefs powerful so much as the chiefs that made the muskets historically powerful. By virtue of the organization of Fijian society,

a little firepower went a long way, structurally. The effect came from Fijian principles of hierarchy, from a system in which the ruling chief was the condition of the possibility of his people's social existence. One good shot, then, and it was all over. Nor were the foreigners who did the shooting, flotsam and jetsam of Western imperialism, responsible for the political forms or ambitions of the nineteenth-century Fijian wars. Yet a certain trade did have some such significance: the trade in *whale teeth*, of the kind long acquired from Tongan islanders, and now obtained on easy terms from passing European merchants and whalers. Fijian intellectuals have long argued that the teeth of sperm whales were the true source of Bau's greatness.

Whale teeth were the highest Fijian valuables. In Radcliffe-Brown's terms, they were goods of supreme social value, with the power of constituting greater social relationships and totalities. Ritually presented in the appropriate way, as transactions of chiefs, they arranged wars, assassinations and noble marriages, made and unmade political alliances, saved villages and kingdoms from extermination, supplicated benefits from the god. In respect of their capacity to create society and to give life and death, whale teeth were like the god. Indeed the form of their presentation from the inferior to a superior was sacrificial: "May we live," says the inferior chief. "I take hold of the treasure," says the superior, "may you live; may your land endure." Thus Hocart's observation on the exchange value of whale teeth, to the effect that a few ounces of divinity are worth pounds of gross matter. Hence also the arguments of Fijians that have privileged whale teeth over muskets in the formation of the nineteenth-century states: the more whale teeth in circulation, the more power in existence in the Fiji Islands.

Proof? Lévi-Strauss talks about the chemist who, having carefully synthesized sodium chloride in the laboratory and confirmed its composition with the standard tests, just to make sure it's salt, tastes it. A good proof of the historic value of the whale teeth is that ethnographically, you can taste it. Not only because whale teeth continue to organize Fijian life—marriage alliances, respects to chiefs, or any "heavy" *kerekere* of goods or persons—and not only because the ritualized formulas of their exchange remain barely altered expressions of a transaction in divine benefits. There is also the extraordinarily high price of whale teeth in the pawnshops of Suva, the capital city. The power of the whale tooth appears in its historic transformations.

Not far from Suva, in the village of Cautatā, Poate Matairavula a few years ago showed me a small wooden chest, set in the furthest corner of the rear right-hand bedroom of his "European-style" house. The space was the modern equivalent of the most tabu part of the old Fijian house (the *loqi*), where the head of the family slept with his wife and reproductive forms of wealth were stored, including seed yams and the weapons that procured cannibal victims. The wooden chest, Matairavula explained, was the "basket of the clan" (*kato ni mataqali*), holding the collective treasure in whale teeth. Passing with the leadership of the clan, the chest was a palladium, a sacred safeguard of the group. So long as it is intact, Matairavula said, the *vanua*—the land, including the people—will be preserved. In 1984, Matairavula was showing me an example of an old "basket of state" (*kato ni tū*), the likes of which (so far as I know) have not been anthropologically noticed from this part of Fiji since Hocart's report in 1910 of the reminiscences of an old man from Namata, a village near Cautatā.

Matairavula's further explanations continued to echo these ancient memories. As chief of the clan himself, he could not go into the chest and take out whale teeth. That was for the herald, the "face of the land" (*matanivanua*), representative of the collectivity vis-à-vis the chief. A few days later, Matairavula and I and a few other men were on the ceremonial ground of Bau, together with the Cautatā herald who was carrying a

large whale tooth concealed in a worn black leather briefcase. We were a delegation from the village to the funeral of a high Bauan, of the ruling war-king clan, carrying the whale tooth as our "kissing" (*ai reguregu*) of the corpse. My own presence as a White man on the ceremonial ground of Bau was hardly a historic first. On the contrary, I could be moved beyond telling by the whole entangled history of Whites and Fijians in the nineteenth century that had been played out in this space.

History was also palpable in the ceremony. We were obliged to wear "traditional" Fijian costume on the Bau ground. Traditional costume was a cotton cloth sarong in floral print. Christian yes, but "before the flag." History was present too in all the villages that came contributing whale teeth to the store of the Bau war-kings' power. The Cautatā people were there because they are traditional border warriors of the Bau kingdom. It is a status they do not forget. A recent study indicates that of the villages in the Bau dominions, Cautatā has the highest rate of enlistment in the Fiji Military Forces.

As for the Fiji Military Forces, until the two *coups d'état* they effected in 1987 under Colonel Rabuka, this army was most famous as the mainstay of the United Nations peace-keeping corps in Lebanon and the Sinai. So after the second coup, when Fiji withdrew from the British Commonwealth and thereby abandoned the Queen's birthday celebrations, Colonel Rabuka, an admirer of the Israeli military, proclaimed as Fiji's National Day— Yom Kippur. I am told that in 1987, T-shirts could be seen in Suva with "Yom Kippur" printed in Hebrew on the front, and "Fiji National Day" in English on the back. In the same year Colonel Rabuka had himself installed as leader of the Fiji Military Forces— and *de facto* leader of the nation—in a "traditional" ceremony, the newspaper photos and descriptions of which resemble nothing so much as the installations of ancient warrior-kings. But then, "atonement" would be a fair translation for the appropriate ritual (*i soro*) begging forgiveness from traditional authorities for acts of usurpation—by the presentation of whale teeth.

KNOWING CULTURES IN TIME

In a genial argument of the *Essay Concerning Human Understanding*, John Locke says that we necessarily know things relationally, by their "dependences" on other things. However absolute and entire the objects of perception may seem to us, they "are but Retainers to other parts of Nature." Their observable qualities, actions, and powers "are owing to something without them; and there is not so complete and perfect a part, that we know, of Nature, that does not owe the Being it has, and the Excellancies of it, to its Neighbours." The observation has capital applications in anthropology—granted that philosophers have never been too happy with these "secondary qualities, mediately perceived."

Locke drew the fundamental implication that it is impossible to exhaust the empirical description of any object, since its properties can be known only through interaction with an indefinite number of other objects. It follows that the objectivity of objects is humanly constructed, that is, by an historically relative selection and symbolic valuation of some only of the possible concrete referents. Essentialized descriptions are not the platonic fantasies of anthropologists alone; they are general cultural conditions of human perception and communication.

More directly pertinent here, Locke is also saying that we know the attributes of things historically. We know things from the changes they make in, or receive from, other things. We know the sun by its powers of melting and bleaching wax even as we know wax as melting in the sun, hardening in the cold, divisible by a knife but unmarked by a feather, impervious to water, indigestible to people—one could wax on.

So it is with cultural orders. They reveal their properties by the way they respond to diverse circumstances, organizing those circumstances in specific forms and in the event changing their forms in specific ways. Here then, in a historical ethnography—an ethnography that extends, say, over a couple of centuries—here is a method for reconciling form and function in a logic of meaning, for discovering the relatively invariant and mutable dimensions of structures, for testing the historical potentialities and limits of different cultural schemes, for weighing and valuing conflicting contextual variations and thereby allowing a principled description of cultural orders as systems of difference. So far as all kinds of modern and postmodern anthropological problems are concerned, history will decide.

But then, the days are over for an ethnography that was the archaeology of the living, searching under the disturbed topsoil of modernity for the traces of a pristine and "primitive" existence. The cultures thus uncovered were indeed fossilized, but mainly by a way of knowing that abstracted them from life and history. It was a nostalgic calling, this kind of ethnography, inspired by theoretical conceits of progress that turned perceptions of others into glimpses of past time—provided the others were not "acculturated." Now history awakens us from these dogmatic slumbers. The old conceptual oppositions on which scientific ethnography was founded are dissolving: we discover continuity in change, tradition in modernity, even custom in commerce. Still, not all that was solid now melts into air, as a certain postmodernist has prematurely supposed. There remain the distinctive differences, the cultural differences.

NOTE

1. It may be true (as Pascal said) that three degrees of latitude make the difference between right and wrong, but with regard to the modern consciousness of "culture," nothing much changes over half the globe (in

longitude). Consider Terry Turner's observations in the South American tropical forest. In the late 1980s even monolingual speakers of Kayapo were using the Portuguese "cultura" in reference to traditional customs, including the performances of ceremony, that ought to be followed "in order to preserve the 'life,' 'strength' and 'happiness' of Kayapo social communities."

INTELLECTUAL ROOTS

Marshall Sahlins is Charles F. Grey Distinguished Service Professor of Anthropology at the University of Chicago. He is a member of the American Academy of Arts and Sciences and the National Academy of Science. His best known publications include: *Social Stratification in Polynesia* (1958), *Evolution and Culture* (coedited with Elman Service, 1960), *Moala: Culture and Nature on a Fijian Island* (1962), *Tribesmen* (1968), *Stone Age Economics* (1972), *The Use and Abuse of Biology* (1976), *Culture and Practical Reason* (1977), *Historical Metaphors and Mythical Realities* (1981), *Islands of History* (1985), and *Anahulu: The Anthropology of History in the Kingdom of Hawaii*, vol. 1, *Historical Ethnography* (1992).

The following statement is quoted from an article by Jocelyn Linnekin on Marshall Sahlins in Roland Turner (ed.), *Thinkers of the Twentieth Century*, 187:668-670.

The hallmark of . . . [Sahlins's] work is that he suggests creative and original solutions to difficult theoretical problems. A reviewer called him "one of the finest synthesizing minds in anthropology." Sahlins's analytic procedure is akin to rationalism rather than the "on-the-ground" empiricism that many anthropologists hold sacred. In a prose that is elegant and literary, if occasionally obscure, he freely discusses areas where anthropology and philosophy intersect, underscoring his points with citations from such diverse sources as Kant and Joseph Heller, Hobbes and Gilbert and Sullivan.

At the most general level, Sahlins's career has been dedicated to investigating the relationship between nature and culture, and specifically their order of determinacy: is culture constituted out of practical action, or is it arbitrary (in the linguistic sense) and logically prior to nature? In his early work, Sahlins presumed that nature came first in the equation, reflecting the tutelage of his mentor Leslie White. His dissertation investigated a Whitean hypothesis relating social stratification in Polynesian societies to differential energy-capture: "the degree of stratification varies directly with productivity." In this work, Sahlins adopted White's "layer-cake" model of culture, with the "technoenvironmental base" as prior and determinant, and social stratification relegated to the dependent "superstratum." An impressive piece of library research, *Social Stratification in Polynesia* is still an indispensable reference work for students of Polynesia, whether or not one agrees with its theoretical conclusions (which Sahlins himself has disavowed). Sahlins has since pointed out that stratification, far from being a dependent variable of energy-capture, is itself a spur to production, forcing the population to produce more than is needed to support the domestic group: "the political life is a stimulus to production."

After *Moala*, Sahlins broke decisively with the materialist paradigm, and has become one of its most articulate critics. The essays in *Stone Age Economics* stress the fundamental differences between modern and primitive societies, and warn against applying concepts such as scarcity, supply-and-demand, and maximization to non-Western economies: "Economic Man is a bourgeois construction." Influenced by the work of Karl Polanyi, Sahlins takes the "substantivist" position in opposition to economic "formalism," which holds that Western economic concepts are appropriate for the study of primitive societies. In an oft-quoted essay, Sahlins refutes anthropology's conventional understanding of hunters and gatherers as preoccupied with the food quest and living on the edge of starvation. Field studies have revealed that hunters and gatherers do have "leisure" as well as an adequate diet. Sahlins draws on this material to assert that hunters and gatherers are "the original affluent society."

Sahlins's current theoretical position has more in common with French structuralism and "semiotics," the theory of signs derived from the work of Ferdinand de Saussure, than with American symbolic anthropology. His association with Claude Lévi-Strauss is well-known. Sahlins is one of the few American anthropologists to work through the implications of Lévi-Strauss's concept of structure. *Culture and Practical Reason*, a brilliant and sweeping essay in intellectual history, documents Sahlins's passage from materialism to idealism (or his view of how anthropology really supersedes this opposition). Here he examines the work of major social theorists in light of two paradigms, the "cultural" and the "practical." . . . He asserts that the "practical" construction of culture reflects the ideology of Western society. As an alternative to a view of culture as Western society, Sahlins offers "some semiotic dimensions of our economy" to illustrate "Western Society as Culture." In this discussion he skillfully deciphers some of the "cultural codes" that order seemingly "practical" behavior in our own society.

Sahlins is at his best when exploring apparent dichotomies and paradoxes. In *Historical Metaphors and Mythical Realities* he attempts to resolve the "radical opposition" between structural anthropology and history by showing how history is ordered by prior categories and cultural precedents: "all structural transformation involves structural reproduction, if not the other way around." *Historical Metaphors* is a first installment in Sahlins's analysis of the encounter between Hawaiians and Europeans in the early contact period. Displaying an unusual enthusiasm for foreign goods and customs, the Hawaiian chiefs accelerated the destruction of their own culture. Sahlins explains that their behavior followed from certain well-established cultural precedents: "This apparently headlong rush to their own culture doom on the chiefs' part, this kind of 'acculturation,' can be shown to reflect basic Hawaiian principles, and, by virtue of these principles, to be selective rather than indiscriminate. For in realizing themselves as European chiefs, the Hawaiian nobility reproduced a customary distinction between themselves and the underlying population."

Against those who would subordinate culture to biological or material determinants, Sahlins asserts the uniqueness of humankind and the priority of the symbolic faculty. . . . In spite of his stature within the discipline, Sahlins eschews disciples, and has no interest in heading a "theoretical school." He is that rare scholar who is capable of challenging his own preconceptions. For this reason, one can learn from him, but not follow him. For this reason also, anthropologists eagerly await publication of his latest theoretical forays.

27

Multilevel Linkages: Londitudinal and Comparative Studies[1]

CONRAD KOTTAK AND ELIZABETH COLSON

Anthropology needs, and is developing, models of its subject matter that reflect the structure of today's world. Various recent multilevel, multisite, multitime research projects illustrate this development. Such projects are one indication of a shift toward the study of process, of an engagement with history, and of an anthropology that takes care to consider the role of political and economic power in forming what Meyer Fortes called "the field of social relations," by which he meant "the range of social relations, in time and space" (Fortes 1945:xi).

That range is now international. Probably no one alive today has not met someone from another country. Even in remote areas, local people now take their cues not just from immediate others but from a multitude of strangers who impinge on them, directly or via the mass media.

The . . . isolation of small communities . . . is in sharp decline because of the advance of urbanization, industrialization, and bureaucratization. Significantly, all these processes modify not only the objective relationships, but also the quality of the subjective relationships of those who live in little communities. These quantitative and qualitative dimensions of sociocultural change, and the rate at which they occur, have led to increased interest everywhere in social planning and in centralizing the allocation and distribution of resources. (Gallagher and Padfield 1980:4)

LINKAGES

Linkages is a convenient term to encompass the multistranded involvement in the world system that ethnographers must now consider in conceptualizing the influences affecting values, categories, institutional arrangements, and other symbolic systems. The linkages perspective is the antithesis of traditional anthropological "holism," which looked inward, assuming the existence of some entity—either a culture or a society—complete and autonomous. Linkages, crucial to social transformations, work to destabilize, rather than maintain, local systems over time.

A definition of linkages in relation to research methodology and content was the goal of a working group of anthropologists who first met in 1986.[2] All of us were concerned with the impact of international and national forces, including development projects, on our research locales. This concern inevitably raised questions about feedbacks between local, regional, and national-level institutions. Most members of the Linkages group had worked more than once in the same region. They knew the advantages of observing how people respond to different opportunities and perturbations at various stages of their lives. Our awareness that geographical mobility and modern communication systems make community boundaries very permeable led us to question old definitions of social units.

Seeking ways of dealing with mobility and tracking people across space and time, we recognized the value of research samples (communities and mobile individuals) that could be followed through time. What kinds of links did they have with others, including external agencies? This line of inquiry entailed a census approach (to provide information on demographic, occupational, and other changes), a network approach (to trace the far-flung relationships associated with geographical mobility and external interventions), plus survey and ethnographic techniques. Monitoring change also required dated inventories: of governmental and nongovernmental agencies, of transportation and other infrastructure, of the media, of goods available, household items, prices, and crucial events such as epidemics. Such inventories provide variables allowing us to differentiate communities and individuals.

One focus of linkages research is longitudinal study. Another is systematic intercommunity comparison, which requires several sample populations chosen because they vary with respect to key criteria. These samples can be from the same region, and the data collected part of the same study. They can also be from different regions (even different countries), if anthropologists can provide the minimum core data (T. S. Epstein 1978:220) to make comparison possible. Linkages research extends to the levels at which policies are worked out, examining archives and official records and interviewing planners, administrators, and others who impinge on the study population.

Such varied sources of data provide answers to specific questions about the results of interventions. We recognize that effects are not always immediate; time is necessary to register long-term consequences. People may react one way in an emergency, but their responses change as they live with and assess alterations in their environments. Linkages research is planned as an ongoing process requiring teamwork. Time and personnel are needed to follow a dispersing population, to study different sites, to interview at many organizational levels, to explore archives and records, and to do follow-up studies. Involvement of host country colleagues, including local assistants and other community residents, is a key to continuity. Research is wasted if it can't be communicated; teamwork helps make data usable for others. Thus linkages also refers to cooperation by people with common research interests in creating a community of data.

The studies being done by members of the Linkages group are explicitly comparative. Focusing on transformation and development, they blend ethnography and survey, synchrony and diachrony. Ideally, several anthropologists work together as an international team. Some Linkages projects are restudies that build on earlier ethnographic work. One example is a research project on the cultural context, meaning, and impact of Brazilian television, developed and directed by Conrad Kottak between 1983 and 1987.[3] That project emerged from Kottak's earlier work in Arembepe, Brazil (begun in 1962),[4] but it also included three other communities previously studied by anthropologists. Kottak and his colleagues (Brazilians and Americans) continue to monitor some of those communities, building longitudinal core data. An example of research in which the monitoring of change was part of the original design is the longitudinal study of social and economic processes in Gwembe District, Zambia. This study, planned in 1956 as a longitudinal project by Elizabeth Colson and Thayer Scudder, continues with Colson, Scudder, and Jonathan Habarad as primary researchers.[5]

Studies involving repeated visits also create linkages in the form of commitment to those studied and the claims they continue to make on anthropologists. Modern communication systems make continued involvement inevitable. We can hardly escape knowledge of the continuing history of those among whom we have worked.

Anthropology has become much more conscious of political and economic power, of hierarchy and inequity. As members of a world system, we can no longer take for granted the structuring of power relationships that advantage some and disadvantage others. Nor can we treat them in purely intellectual terms as symbolic structures or literary tropes. As Eric Wolf (1982) has pointed out, they have real consequences for real people. They are more than discourse.

FROM ISOLATE TO WORLD SYSTEM

Linkages researchers are obviously not alone in their concern with social change and development, their view of culture as a process rather than an entity, and their realization that communities consist of people who have variant opportunities and make different choices. We also join the many anthropologists who question the shibboleth of cultural relativism. Our world needs some agreement on basic human rights and ways of guaranteeing them. Anthropologists have seen local people fall victim to development projects, revolutionary violence, and warfare provoked by external interventions and the dictates of international markets. Unsurprisingly in today's world, many anthropologists now focus on violence and violation (Carmack 1988; Kapferer 1988; Loizos 1981; Parnell 1988; Tambiah 1986).

Many agents of multinational organizations have as their raison d'être interference in the lives of others to promote "development." We are not cultural relativists when we judge their activities. It is no accident that Cultural Survival emerged in the 1970s to offer an anthropological critique of intervention. Studies of development organizations and their policies are now common (e.g., Colson 1982; Hoben 1982; Justice 1986; Kottak 1985; Robertson 1982).

Ethnographers can no longer even hope to study people isolated from world markets or unaffected by centers of political and economic power. Archaeologists and historians familiar with records on Asia, Africa, and the Pacific have even questioned the historic existence of the ethnographic isolate. Eric Wolf (1982) has focused on the centuries-old interplay between state systems and "the people without history." More than 80 percent of the "cultures" in the World Ethnographic Sample are anything but pristine—having had a major encounter with a nation-state before any anthropologist ever reached them (Bradley, Moore, Burton, and White 1990). Most societies have been subject to colonialism or other political centralization. No matter what the subject or the research locale, we need to consider documents describing the interdependencies between local systems and larger economic and political networks (cf. Feirman 1985; Guyer 1987).

Anthropologists could believe in the static "ethnographic present" only when we were unaware of the extent to which local cultures are products of world history. In the 1930s, when little archaeology had been done, when dating techniques were rudimentary and imprecise, and when much archival information remained unexamined by historians, it was easier to think in terms of static societies, equilibria, and integrated systems. One recent example of the impact of archaeological and historical evidence on anthropological thinking is the challenge to the Kalahari San as representatives of early hunter-gatherers. We know now that for centuries the San have been intermittently pastoralists and agriculturalists and in touch with pastoralists and agriculturalists (Elphick 1977; Solway and Lee 1990).

Challenges also arise as a result of the accumulating ethnographic record. Anthropologists now do research where other anthropologists have worked. We have their publications, sometimes even their field notes. We must account for the differences between their findings and ours—not by adopting the stance of a dueling ethnographic individualist

(Freeman 1983), but by paying full attention to the forces of history and intracultural variation. Modern anthropological research is incomplete if we ignore the documents that chart decades of local and regional inter-relations. Historical events and responses are now routinely built into the ethnographic record—much to its enrichment.

Modern ethnographic records should be thought of as referring to different stages in the encounter of local populations with the world system. Ethnography should focus on the adjustments that occur continuously as people meet different challenges. Whether studying mental healing (Mullings 1984) or agriculture (Pottier 1988), today's ethnographers have access to data unavailable to their predecessors.

Geography also limits us less than in the past, when it could take months to reach a research site and return visits were rare. Once in the field, the ethnographer's social universe used to be the distance he or she could cover comfortably on foot, bicycle, boat, or horse. New systems of transportation that allow local people to move about also enable anthropologists to widen the catchment area of their research and to return repeatedly. Articles in the main journals now routinely include ethnographic data from two or more field stays. Continuity and change are built into the anthropologist's experience and field notes (Bond 1990). The perception of what change means for villagers becomes more poignant as our old friends ponder with us what is happening to them and what the world holds for all our children.

Restudies

Some of our richest ethnography comes from those who have gone back. Monica Wilson had known the Nyakyusa for more than 30 years when she wrote *For Men and Elders* (1977). Wendy James's study of "the flux and flow of indigenous and imported practices, and the waxing and waning of Christianity

and Islam" among the Uduk of Sudan (1988: vii) is based on more than three decades of observation. Roger Keesing has used his repeated visits to Guadalcanal to "situate Kwaio religion not on some abstract plane of formal structure, but in the minds and acts of individuals and in the social life of communities" (1982:3). Caroline Humphrey (1983) uses government documents, accounts by other ethnographers, and her own revisit to document the interplay between ideology and economy that influences how collective farmers in Siberia think about the Soviet system, and how this affects their productivity and relations with each other.

Restudies, whether by the original field-worker or another, are now common. They encourage the development of methods to deal with flux—even though they may not have been planned with that goal.[6] The conditions that encourage restudies have also made it possible for anthropologists to plan and carry out longitudinal fieldwork—in which time is part of the research design. Each such study must deal with economic fluctuations, migration, changing political influence, and changes in national and local ideologies. Anthropologists planning such studies would accept the dictate of John Bennett (1982:298), who initiated a decade of research on Saskatchewan family farms in the 1960s, that "the cultural typological approach" with "its built-in assumptions of homeostasis and unchanging ethos" must be rejected because it fails to account for the rapidity of change.

The theoretical assumptions underlying long-term studies clash with earlier formulations. We do not assume cultural integration, social equilibrium, harmony of values, or uniformity of response by individuals. Repeated visits show that people and communities respond differently to opportunities and hardships, depending on their resources, their social positions, their previous experiences, and the degree to which they have dealt with outsiders. There are multiple linkages between local residents and people and institutions throughout the world. The belief that community members share common values is a powerful myth, but experience can be shared only to a point. No matter how egalitarian or homogeneous communities may seem to a short-term visitor, their members have different values and interests. This is one source of change.

Engagement with Wider Systems

Local concerns—health, subsistence, self-respect, cognitive frameworks to make sense of experience—depend on engagement with wider systems. The inhabitants of distant cities provide reference groups on which local people base judgments. The speed with which styles spread confirms the interconnectedness that is now a part of the anthropologist's universe of study. The T-shirt flourishes everywhere. "Ethnic" clothing and jewelry inspire Western designers and are reexported to the world at large. People in South American barrios and African cities incur debt to finance Western-style weddings. Youngsters in small towns and rural areas dance "disco." Many communities maintain their local styles of dress, dance, and performance mainly to entertain jet-set tourists (Crick 1989; Kottak 1990; Graburn 1983; V. Smith 1977; Volkman 1990).

Linkages between rural and urban areas are ancient, although they first excited anthropological attention in the 1930s—for example in studies of African labor migration and settlement in the new towns of southern and central Africa (Schapera 1947; Hellman 1948; Richards 1940; Wilson 1941-1942). These studies were the forerunners of recent work on migration and resettlement (Eades 1986; Hansen and Oliver-Smith 1982; Morgan and Colson 1987; Talai 1989), including involuntary resettlement (see Practicing Anthropology 1990). In the 1940s and 1950s studies of adjustment to city life dominated the research on Africa. These studies led to "network" and "situational" analysis to confront the rapidity with which people changed their behavior in different settings (see J. C. Mitchell 1987). Since then, the Third World has witnessed an explosive growth of cities, which now provide the standards by which most people measure their well-being and success (Lloyd 1979).

Our species, with astonishing steadfastness, has viewed cities as filled with action, glamour, variety, opportunity, and the promise of an easier life, as can be seen dramatically when flying over any Third World capital, where shantytown suburbs are crammed with emigrants from outlying areas. Each new arrival is hopeful of making his fortune within the "lights of the city" and confident he will escape the backbreaking labor that has traditionally been his way of life. (Schwartz 1980:vii)

Communication systems radiating from the cities tell rural people what they lack and teach them that they must change if they want to share the wealth and pleasures of town. Government policies place rural interests below those of city dwellers—especially the bureaucratic elites—whose own reference groups are the international elites of the industrial world.

Exposure to external institutions and alternative ways of life comes through many channels, including the media. Seasonal, temporary, and permanent migration maintain social networks between rural people and their urban kin. Improved transportation transforms cities into market centers and information pools for a wide area. National and international agents invade the hinterland as tourists, development agents, conservationists, officials, and representatives of competing religious sects. Radio, television, and the videocassette recorder reach distant areas. The spread of literacy is a stated goal of all governments. The media, providing common fare, work toward a certain homogenization of standards. Audio and video recorders, however, have another potential. Local people use them to communicate with distant relatives, to preserve their traditions, and to record their interests. (See Michaels 1986 on the use of video-cameras in home-grown television in Walbiri, Central Australia.)

Any methodology that tries to extract the purely local from the wider system will miss much of what is going on and much that concerns the people being studied. For much that is significant anthropologists can rely neither on participant observation nor intensive interviews with selected informants regarded as the repositories of tradition. Local informants may be as mystified as we are with the exercise of power from regional, national, and international centers. The chain of intermediaries has many links; the knowledge that this is so can itself create a sense of alienation and dependency.

It is this larger context that we need to find ways of examining. These multiple linkages must be part of our research focus. The cities and towns visited by members of the sample population become a further extension of the study. Participation in a larger social universe is a goal held out to people in the hinterland. However, the terms on which incorporation takes place are usually to their disadvantage because their skills and resources prevent them from entering the system at what they regard as an honorable level. This was not true for a short period following the end of the colonial system in many parts of Africa, Asia, and Papua-New Guinea, when rapid promotion was the order of the day, and even primary education gave entry to the upper echelons of the civil service. Village children could aspire to become cabinet officers, United Nations employees, university professors, and high civil servants. Younger siblings could expect their help with education and jobs. Older kin benefited from the accomplishments of the young.

Three decades later, class differences are hardening. In much of the Third World, it is harder to use education to find secure employment. Nevertheless, we think that the desire of people in the hinterland to share in what they see as the advantages of the expanded world is fueling rapid change. A larger world appeals to human imagination and curiosity, the desire for information and experience, and the search for greater comfort and an easing of toil. People seize on the contacts offered them, or create their own linkages, because they hope to exploit the larger system.

We assume that certain constants of human motivation and response underwrite the patterns of incorporation reported from many parts of the world. Nevertheless, the interplay between national and regional centers and the people within their spheres of influence varies according to the degree to which communication is frequent, instantaneous, and pervasive; with the resources the centers can deploy to reward incorporation; and with the power exercised by the centers.

MULTISITE, MULTITIME RESEARCH IN BRAZIL

We offer some of our own applications of Linkages methodology to illustrate these points. For Brazil, where television is now pervasive, Kottak's research project on its cultural context and effects examines how TV has changed local life. The rationale for the research was the realization that television is one of the most powerful information disseminators, socializing agents, and public-opinion molders in the contemporary world. However, few social scientists had examined in depth what happens when communities become exposed to TV. Previous studies had been done mainly in English-speaking countries and had focused on a limited target group (usually children) or range of effects (usually psychological—e.g., violence). Other than in a few studies of Canadian Indian response to television (Granzberg and Steinbring 1980; Molohon 1984), anthropologists had paid little attention to television—perhaps reflecting the discipline's characteristic resistance to cultural homogenization, which TV's spread is usually seen as aiding. Kottak and his (mostly Brazilian) colleagues had to devise a methodology appropriate to the linkages created in Brazil by the new information sources. They had to combine in-depth ethnographic observation with survey research, the combing of media records, interviewing national figures, and doing content analysis of programs.

Brazil has the world's most watched commercial network (Rede Globo). Kottak became intrigued with the effects of television in Brazil in 1980 when he revisited Arembepe, Bahia state, which he had first studied in 1962. Compared with the 1960s, when Arembepeiros had been starved for information about the outside world, by 1980 their familiarity with nation and world was well advanced, and television seemed to be the main reason.

Richard Pace, an anthropologist who participated in Kottak's television project, reached similar conclusions for the Amazonian town of Gurupa,[7] which he studied between 1984 and 1986.

Before the spread of television, conversation often focussed on local events, local gossip, soccer, or an occasional diffuse comment on regional or national politics. A foreign anthropologist was often asked vague questions such as what kind of jungle grows in the United States, are all Americans rich, and what are cowboys like? With the spread of television, however, conversation took on a more cosmopolitan, more diverse nature. Events in North America, Europe, and the Middle East were discussed in detail. National politics were scrutinized. (It was the year [1985] that the military regime gave powers back to a civilian government.) I found myself discussing the goals of the American space program, the ideology of President Reagan, poverty in the United States, international terrorism, and the geophysical causes of earthquakes. (1987:20-21)

By 1980 Brazil had more TV sets than the rest of Latin America combined. The percent-

age of Brazilian households with television increased from 7 percent to 51 percent between 1964 and 1979, and the figure exceeds 75 percent in 1991. Through communications satellites, reception dishes, and retransmitting ground stations, people in remote villages now receive national programming. Reflecting Brazil's huge population (145 million) and its degree of economic development (the world's tenth largest economy), the middle class includes 40 to 50 million people, a tantalizing market (second in the Western Hemisphere) for television and the culture of consumption.

The Globo network, which blossomed under the aegis of an authoritarian centralized state and military dictatorship, moved quickly and efficiently to hook a product-and-information-hungry population. Today, Globo, which dominates Brazil's airwaves as no single network has ever done in North America, mainly shows its own productions and consistently attracts a nightly audience of 60 to 80 million people. All of Brazil's most popular TV programs are native productions. The most-watched are the national news and the telenovelas that Globo broadcasts nationally six nights per week. They consistently draw 60 percent to 95 percent audience shares.

The research project directed by Kottak from 1983 to 1987 was a multitiered study, investigating Brazilian television at national and local levels. The bulk of the national-level work was done between August 1983 and August 1984. Kottak interviewed television industry experts and personnel and did archival and statistical research in Brazil's established media-research organizations.[8] Concurrently, the project also included an initial, mainly qualitative, program content study.

The next stage was a local-level impact study involving systematic fieldwork by Brazilian and American researchers. This began in January 1985 in four communities in different regions. The aim was to gather qualitative and quantitative data (using standard protocols) to permit systematic comparison of communities and people with different degrees of exposure to television. In-depth fieldwork was done in those four communities, located in the south (Ibirama), south-central (Cunha), northeast (Arembepe), and Amazonian (Gurupa) regions.

Each site fitted another aspect of the research design—longitudinal study—building on prior research. Each community had been previously studied, providing information on what life had been like before television. However, one weakness with the original project design was that all four communities were rural and poor. As the researchers tried to compare those sites with information from urban sources, they realized that a link was missing. They needed to extend their field procedures, including ethnographic observation and structured interviewing, to the urban, socioeconomically contrasting settings in which most Brazilians now live. Thus, two wealthier and more urban settings in the states of Rio de Janeiro (Niteroi) and São Paulo (Americana) were selected for study in 1986. These studies were necessarily briefer than the first four.

With fieldwork continuing through 1987, the project has examined the varied cultural, social, economic, and psychological effects associated with the introduction of television to the study populations.[9] It has also considered many other sources of exposure to external situations and currents of change.[10] Systematic comparison incorporating a time dimension showed that television's most profound effects on people, society, and culture take place gradually. Effects may well be imperceptible (both to natives and researchers) at a given time. However, the research design (studying a gamut of communities and people exposed to television for different lengths of time) did reveal many areas of influence.

The project confirmed that TV impact occurs in stages. There is an initial stage (Stage I—in progress in Gurupa) of strangeness and novelty. The medium (the set) rather than the message (content) is the mesmerizer. Stage II (Cunha, Arembepe) is a ten- to fifteen-year

period of maximum receptivity. People accept, reject, interpret, and rework TV messages. Because TV saturation is still only partial, many statistical correlations between viewing and other factors are obvious. Televiewing produced the strongest correlations in the stage II communities of Arembepe and Cunha.

Ibirama is entering, and Americana and Niteroi are fully in, Stage III. Once TV has reached most homes in a community, measures of its impact there become less obvious. This is because as an innovation pervades a population, its presence differentiates less and less. However, this third stage—during which TV impact appears to be least—has a subtle but powerful legacy. Stage IV, exemplified by Americans of the baby-boom generation and younger, encompasses the cumulative effects of TV on full-grown natives who have spent their lives in a society pervaded by television and the behavior patterns and mass culture it spawns. During this fourth phase the more profound and long-term sociocultural effects of television become obvious (Kottak 1990).

TV's role in promoting or hindering social interaction depends both on the culture it enters and the stage of community saturation. An initial effect (Stages I and II) is to promote social contact, by bringing people from different households together to watch. In Stages I and II, set ownership and hours of operation correlate very strongly with number of household visitors. However, in Stage III, with set ownership widespread, people stay home to watch their own sets.

The project also offered support for the researchers' prior assumption that cultural, political, and economic variation within towns, regions, and nations is vital in understanding the effects of technology on human behavior. TV impact is not a matter of simple, automatic, programmed responses to irresistible, omnipotent stimuli. Viewing, interpretation, and impact all take place in the context of the prior culture(s) and experiences of members of the audience. Viewers are not the purportedly passive "couch potatoes" who populate American commentary. Instead, they are human beings who make discriminations and choices about television in ways that make sense to them. They watch to validate beliefs, develop fantasies, and find answers to questions that the local setting discourages or condemns. People use TV to relieve frustrations, build or enhance images of self, chart social courses, and formulate daring life plans. Sometimes the interaction between viewer and set leads to unrealistic plans, false hopes, disappointment, and frustration. However, the process of TV impact is not one in which an all-powerful Big Brother zaps a defenseless zombie.

Program choices and preferences reflect pre-existing social categories and contrasts, power differentials, and variant predispositions within the local culture. Audiences use television in varied ways. They go on watching because they find meaning in its images and content. In Ibirama, for instance, Alberto Costa (n.d.) concluded that women and young adults of both sexes were particularly attracted to telenovelas. These relatively powerless social groups used Globo's telenovelas to challenge conservative local norms.

Building on experience with the TV project, Kottak and his associates are doing new research in Brazil—on environmental risks and their perception. Again the work is proceeding at national and local levels—across a range of sites differently exposed to risks (Costa, Kottak, Prado, and Stiles, 1991). Two of the sites (Ibirama and Arembepe) were also included in the television study, so that longitudinal monitoring continues. The project has three basic assumptions:

1. Technological innovation, risk perception, and environmental awareness are cultural phenomena.

2. These are generated through processes of social and cultural change at the national and the local level in response to the economic and political position that a group occupies in the world system.

3. These changes also depend on the internal dynamic of the cultural models existing in any society both at macroscopic (national) and microscopic (local) levels.

Such research foci as TV impact and environmental risk perception illustrate the kinds of issues that are likely to be explored when long-term association with a research community exposes researchers to the consequences of various interventions.

SOCIAL TRANSFORMATION IN GWEMBE DISTRICT

Another multilevel, multitime, multisite comparative study, of Gwembe District, Zambia, also illustrates Linkages methodology. Gwembe District has multistranded links with overlapping larger systems—provincial, national, and international. Transportation and communication networks, labor markets, marketing boards for cash crops, international agencies, and political mobilization interpenetrate the local systems of relationships and evaluation. The people of Gwembe are aware of this, from their experience on the ground and the mass media (to which, however, they are much less exposed than Brazilians are).

In the 1950s most Gwembe men worked as labor migrants in what is now Zimbabwe or South Africa, yet people still puzzled over scraps of information about the rest of the world. They asked: Is England a city as large as Bulawayo? Is it to the south or the north? Is America another city?

The people of Gwembe no longer ask these questions. Although television and telephone reach only three townships, people travel to the cities to visit kin and seek work, and thus have media exposure. In the 1980s, fewer newspapers reached the villages than in the 1960s and 1970s. This is one sign of the decline of the national economy, which has resulted in a shortage of newsprint and deterioration of roads. Nevertheless, people rely on radios (one or two in most villages since the early 1960s) for world news, weather forecasts, and word of the death of kin settled elsewhere in Zambia. The postal service, largely nonexistent in the 1950s, is not always efficient, but mail does arrive. Jets fly overhead and link the capital of Zambia to other African capitals and to London, Paris, and New York. Everyone knows some Gwembe man or woman who has been to Europe, America, India, or Japan.

In the early 1950s, strangers—even from nearby regions of Zambia—rarely visited Gwembe. Since then a multitude have arrived. Some stay a few hours; others, months or years. Foreigners come as tourists, anthropologists, prospectors, missionaries, international consultants, employees of mining and agricultural corporations, and workers for the voluntary organizations active in the district since the 1970s.

Local people know something about international relations. They are keenly aware of how the decline in copper prices has affected the Zambian economy and of what it means to be subject to South African raids. Every village has an urban diaspora to remind it of fluctuations in the economy. Those who remain in the village use deteriorating buses and cars to move between village and town. They think of themselves as citizens of Zambia, a larger entity created over the past thirty years.

The longitudinal study of Gwembe District, like other such studies—such as that of Tzintzuntzan, Mexico, begun in 1945 (Foster 1978; Kemper 1978)—has had to develop a research methodology adapted to geographical and social mobility and changing degrees of international embeddedness. It has also had to find ways of dealing with the fact that communities have different resources, access to roads and other amenities, and levels of administrative overview.

Gwembe District covers 12,611 square kilometers. Its population grew from about 55,000 in 1956 to 96,879 in 1980 (Serpell and Munachonga 1986:4, 8). For decades about 45 percent of the able-bodied men have been absent as labor migrants at any time. The 1980 census (the most recent one available) gives a sex ratio of 88.5; the district continues to lose many men. Most Gwembe people live in villages with 100 to 800 inhabitants. Of the small towns that emerged in the 1960s, one has a coal mine, and three are administrative centers. The Gwembe population exploits a much larger pool of resources than the District offers. They have access to the towns and industries of Zambia. (Until 1965 they also had easy access to Zimbabwe.)

The Zambia-Zimbabwe border forms one boundary of the District; this offers both opportunity and danger. During the Zimbabwe War of Independence in the 1970s, Gwembe was a theater of guerrilla warfare, which damaged its infrastructure and killed some villagers. However, the border also encourages a trade in smuggled goods, including gemstones illicitly mined in the Gwembe hills, and gives poachers access to the game reserves of Zimbabwe.

The Gwembe research project is multisite, because no single village or neighborhood could adequately represent Gwembe's diversity (Colson and Scudder 1975; Scudder and Colson 1978). Four villages and their surrounding neighborhoods, in different localities, form the research core. They and their inhabitants have been followed for four decades. Periodic village censuses (1956-57, 1962-63, 1965, 1972-73, 1981-82, and 1987-88) provide basic data on demography, economy, and other variables chosen to monitor changes in kinship and ritual behavior. Censused people who have moved are traced and interviewed (if possible) to see how their careers compare with those of people who have stayed in the village. Information on labor migration, visits between town and country, remittances, and other linkages illuminate the extent to which rural and urban belong to a single system. Besides the village samples, Colson, Scudder, and their associates have constructed other samples as needed to pursue particular questions. One example is a snowball sample of Gwembe men and women who attended secondary school before 1972. In that crucial year for understanding elite formation, the number of secondary school leavers surpassed the supply of jobs requiring secondary education.

Zambian assistants have kept records of local events and daily diaries of food bought and eaten. From field notes it is possible to reconstruct prices for different periods. Shifts in village preferences are documented by shopping lists provided by villagers wishing goods from urban shops. Field notes also contain observations based on attendance at moots, local courts, village and district meetings, church services, funerals, and rituals associated with households and neighborhoods.

Such information is supplemented by interviews with traders and officials, technical workers, political leaders, and expatriates employed by missions and international voluntary agencies. It has also been possible to obtain access to government and other records, both published and unpublished, including those of special missions. Zambian social scientists who have worked in the district also provide insights into the changes taking place.

Successively different questions have come to the fore, while basic data on communities and individuals continue to be collected. The first focus of study was the impact of a large hydroelectric dam, which flooded much of the Zambezi River plain and subjected the Gwembe people to forced resettlement. However, the dam also spurred road building and other activities that brought the people of Gwembe more closely in touch with the rest of Zambia (Colson 1971; Scudder 1982; Scudder and Habarad 1991).

When the dam was built, primary education was poorly developed, and very few men had attended secondary school. By the late 1960s education had become a major concern at Gwembe and was playing an important role in major changes then taking place. Accordingly, Scudder and Colson (1980) designed research to examine the role of the system of national education in providing access to new opportunities and in increasing social differentiation within the district and nation. At the same time, it was evident that drinking was a growing problem. A third major study therefore examined the interplay of markets, transportation, and exposure to town values implicated in the transformation of domestic brewing and a radical change in drinking patterns (Colson and Scudder 1988).

Using the data recorded over years of revisits, it has also been possible to examine the role of markets, extension services, development agencies, and mining, all of which have transformed local agriculture. These linkages have made Gwembe (and the rest of Zambia) more vulnerable to international price structures, the directives of the World Bank and the International Monetary Fund, and the pressures of other international agencies. In the 1980s, Gwembe villagers, like other Zambians, talk of the desirability of forex (foreign exchange). They are aware of the legal and black market rates of exchange. In the mid-1980s, economic vulnerability led to the expropriation of village land to the advantage of transnational agribusinesses financed from Germany, the United States, Ireland, and Hong Kong (Scudder 1985; Scudder and Habarad, 1991).

The wealth of data gathered through longitudinal study of Gwembe has made it possible to examine many other aspects of change. One example is the transformation of local courts, which have come under closer supervision from the center and are held to standardized procedures laid down by the Zambian lawyers (trained in Europe and America) in the Ministry of Justice (Colson 1976). Longitudinal data on political action and local governance underlie the recent study of villagers' innovative use of the lower echelons of the political party organization to supplement local institutions that no longer function effectively (Habarad n.d.).

From the beginning the Gwembe study was planned to be more than an ethnographic account of a single time segment. It was designed to examine the impact of large-scale development projects and national development strategies. Along with other longitudinal studies it has shown the limitations of synchronic studies and the pitfalls of the once-standard one-year study.

The findings from Gwembe apply to experiences of incorporation and transformation in much of the Third World (see Bodley 1988). During the last 100 years Gwembe has been incorporated into a colonial system, has had its men forced into distant labor markets, has been subject to alien political rule and then the politics of independence, and has been missionized by Christian churches. More recently Gwembe has been subject to foreign development missions, has had its environmental base profoundly altered by one of the world's largest man-made lakes, has suffered the forced resettlement of most of its population, and has shifted to a cash economy dominated by commercial agriculture. Gwembe is now increasingly losing land to highly capitalized foreign enterprises. Mining activities and pesticides used in commercial agriculture are endangering water supplies and lake fisheries.

Immunization of children and other health measures have lowered death rates, but diseases from the world pool periodically make life hazardous. Droughts and high food prices increase malnutrition. Since the early 1980s, like the rest of Zambia and much of central and eastern Africa, Gwembe has been menaced by the spread of AIDS, for which its population is trying to find an explanation. The frequency of recent droughts, often back to back, may be an indication that Gwembe is also now affected by the climatic shifts associated with the buildup of pollutants in the atmosphere (largely due to activities in the northern hemisphere) and the destruction of the tropical rain forests, again mainly a reflex of international markets.

Gwembe is no remote and exotic enclave, unique in its experience. It is an epitome of situations endemic to the contemporary world. This is what makes this longitudinal study a good barometer for examining the linkages between changes at the local level and the shifting policies and demands of the international system.

METHODOLOGICAL QUESTIONS

Neither the Kottak projects nor the Gwembe study fit the category of community study. Nor do they rely on random samples of people chosen to represent some larger universe. Each study seeks to capitalize on the advantages associated with earlier methods of intensive ethnography. In each project, the design calls for the creation of several sample populations in different locales, chosen because they contrast with one another in significant fashion. This variation forms the focus for research. The intention is to illuminate processes of change rather than make statements about cultural cohesion.

Such large and complex research arenas yield overwhelming masses of data. It becomes difficult to keep a perspective and to use all the information effectively. This is one of the unsolved problems created when research integrates data collected over time, studies interactions at many levels, and compares sample populations and individual careers using many variables. To permit other researchers to use and build on our work, the data must be made intelligible. Because our longitudinal and comparative studies are meant to provide known samples that can be used when new questions arise, appropriate data preparation and storage are essential. This poses a challenge to traditional anthropological funding agencies, which are accustomed to financing small-scale studies by lone fieldworkers, often providing no funds for analysis. Linkages projects produce masses of data, and grant budgets (like those in the other social sciences) must recognize the need for coding and analysis.

The Linkages group has been using the Gwembe data base as a testing ground for creating computer programs appropriate for longitudinal research in anthropology. Douglas White, of the University of California at Irvine; James Lee, of the California Institute of Technology; and their students are constructing time series rates on mortality, fertility, marital unions, labor migration, household and homestead size, and many other variables. These time series can be used to test various hypotheses about the effects of environmental factors, government policies, economic fluctuations, and other external interventions.

Success here will provide tools for others who do, or plan to do, similar research. Success will also mean that the Gwembe data base can be used as a research tool by other anthropologists. Several such data bases will help anthropologists make more effective arguments when they critique or participate in planning interventions.

CONCLUSION

The theoretical underpinnings and the methodologies associated with multitime, multisite, multilevel studies, which we call the Linkages approach, build on earlier work in anthropology, as we stated earlier. Julian Steward's large-scale and comparative projects (Steward et al. 1956, Steward 1967) designed to examine cultural transformations have influenced our ideas about embeddedness and multistranded linkages. The pioneering work carried out on urbanization and the rural-urban continuum by Max Gluckman, Clyde Mitchell, and others at the Rhodes-Livingstone Institute provides other sources of influence. More recently the regional analysis of Carol Smith (1984a, 1987) and the world

systems approaches of Mintz (1985), Wallerstein (1974, 1980), and Wolf (1982) have reinforced our recognition that local societies are never isolates, but must be understood in much larger contexts. Tools for comparative analysis have been developed by survey researchers, by anthropologists working with the Human Relations Area File and the World Ethnographic Sample, and by others interested in systematic comparison.

Although what we are doing and advocating is increasingly common in anthropology, the Linkages approach contributes especially by combining the strengths of the long-term study and the possibilities for systematic comparison, ordering, and analysis provided by computer technology. Our methodology permits fine-grained synchronic and diachronic comparisons to test intuitions and hypotheses about the meanings of the shifting interconnections linking local people to large-scale systems.

Anthropologists have provided basic ethnographic information for much of the world. However, good ethnography now depends on recognizing that the world system supplies much of what informs local action and that we must pay attention to the past and the future as well as to the present. Television, radio, newspapers, travel, education, proselytizing religions, multinational organizations, military machines, and international markets are institutions that affect us all. These modern linkages belong in the anthropological record.

NOTES

1. Thayer Scudder read and commented on an earlier draft. We have also benefitted from the comments of our fellow members of the Panel on Social Transformations in Preindustrial and Industrializing Societies.

2. The original group included Lilyan Brudner-White, Michael Burton, Elizabeth Colson, Scarlet Epstein, Nancy Gonzalez, David Gregory, Conrad Kottak, Thayer Scudder, and Douglas White. Later it was joined by Robert Van Kemper and Chad McDaniel.

3. Kottak's television research has been supported by three agencies, in addition to the University of Michigan (through a sabbatical leave): (1) the Wenner-Gren Foundation for Anthropological Research, for a grant to study "The Electronic Mass Media and Social Change in Brazil" (1983-84); (2) the National Science Foundation for a research grant (NSF-G-BNS 8317856-Kottak) to study "The Social Impact of Television in Rural Brazil" in the states of Bahia, Para, Santa Catarina, and São Paulo (6/84-11/86); and (3) the National Institute of Mental Health for a research grant (DHHS-PHS-G-5-R0 1-MH388 15-03-Kottak) to investigate "Television's Behavioral Effects in Brazil," supporting field team research and data analysis in six Brazilian rural communities (1/1/85-12/31/88).

4. Along with Isabel (Betty) Wagley Kottak, Conrad Kottak has been studying Arembepe, Bahia state, a coastal town whose population now numbers about 2,000 people, since 1962 (Kottak 1983). Youngest of our TV project research sites, Arembepe was settled late in the nineteenth century by freed slaves from sugar plantations in Bahia's Reconcavo region. In 1985, for the TV project, two other researchers joined the Kottaks. Irani Escolano, a Brazilian, was at that time a graduate student in survey methods at Hunter College of the City University of New York. Pennie Magee, an anthropology graduate student at the University of Florida, had previously spent many years in Brazil.

5. Elizabeth Colson first visited Gwembe District in 1949. In 1956 she and Thayer Scudder began a long-term study initially tied to research on the impact of a large hydroelectric dam and the resettlement of the population of the area to be flooded. Scudder and Colson have revisited the District frequently, in 1956-1957, 1960, 1961-1962, 1965, 1967, 1968, 1972-1973, 1975, 1978, 1981-1982, 1983, 1987, 1989. Jonathan Habarad joined the study in 1987 and spent eighteen months in Gwembe. Douglas White, James Lee, and their students have been involved in the analysis of the village census data since 1987. The research has been supported by the Rhodes-Livingstone Institute (now the Institute for African Studies in the University of

Zambia), FAO, the Joint Committee on Africa of the Social Science Research Council and the American Council of Learned Societies, the John Guggenheim Foundation, and the National Science Foundation through grants in 1972-1973, 1981-1982, 1987, and 1987-1988.

6. This became apparent at the first conference on long-term field studies in social anthropology held in 1975 (Foster et al., eds. 1979).

7. Gurupa or Ita is another longitudinal site, originally studied by Charles Wagley in 1949 (Wagley 1953), subsequently by Darrell Miller and Richard Pace (1987).

8. Later, to round out the national-level component of the research, in summer 1986 Dr. Joseph Straubhaar of Michigan State University's Department of Telecommunication, whose previous research had also focused on Brazilian television, worked with Rio-based project consultant Lucia Ferreira Reis, gathering additional information in Rio and São Paulo. They obtained data from the major Brazilian public-opinion and media-research organizations. These data were obtained for the cities transmitting the television signals received in each project community, for the period during which research was going on in the communities, to be compared with the community data to provide a regional- and national-level perspective on television diffusion and impact, and to permit rural-urban contrast.

9. In addition to Kottak's book (1990), which provides an overview of the main research findings, articles are being prepared on such topics as TV and race, TV and family planning, and TV and economic development.

10. We also investigated various links with the external world, including telephone use, frequency, destination, and purpose of travel outside, military service, and prior urban residence. Our questionnaires contained several queries concerning information sources other than television, including newspapers, magazines, books, radio, and movies.

INTELLECTUAL ROOTS

Conrad Phillip Kottak is Professor of Anthropology at the University of Michigan, where he has taught since 1968. Kottak is the current (1990-1992) chair of the General Anthropology Division of the American Anthropological Association. A cultural anthropolo-

gist, he has done fieldwork in Brazil (since 1962), Madagascar (since 1966), and the United States. Kottak's books include *Assault on Paradise: Social Change in a Brazilian Village* (2nd ed., 1992), *Prime-Time Society: An Anthropological Analysis of Television and Culture*

(1990), *The Past in the Present: History, Ecology and Cultural Variation in Highland Madagascar* (1980), and his texts *Anthropology: The Exploration of Human Diversity* (5th ed., 1991) and *Cultural Anthropology* (5th ed., 1991). His edited books include *Researching American Culture* (1982) and *Madagascar: Society and History* (1986).

I received my A.B. (1963) and my Ph.D. degrees (1966) from Columbia University. There I worked closely with Marvin Harris, my dissertation committee chair, and Robert Murphy. Through my own reading and my professors and colleagues at Columbia University and the University of Michigan, I have been influenced by Leslie White and particularly Julian Steward. White, for many years a dominant figure in the Michigan anthropology department, championed a revival of interest in cultural evolution. Like White I was frustrated by the Boasian preoccupation with the particular and the Boasian unwillingness to say that some elements of culture play a more important role in social change than others. I admired White's willingness to generalize, synthesize, and grapple with the causes of major social transformations. I met Leslie White when I came to Michigan in 1968, but he was near retirement, and we never knew each other well. Still, some of White's key views lived on in his former Michigan students and colleagues, Marshall Sahlins and Elman Service (both of whom studied at Columbia where they were also influenced by Steward).

More important than White in my intellectual genealogy is Julian Steward, whom I never met. Long before I got to Columbia, Steward had moved to the University of Illinois, but his influence lived on at Columbia, especially in my professors Harris, Murphy, and Morton Fried. It is to Steward (through Harris—and, later, my colleague Roy Rappaport at Michigan) that I trace my interest in cultural ecology. In his book *Theory of Cultural Change* (1963), Steward urged anthropologists to investigate the causal relationships between environmental features and aspects of culture. From Steward and his students I learned that ecology could mold cultures in particular directions; this influence shows up when we compare cultures across space, or study them through time. I liked Steward's "multilinear evolutionism" (the notion that cultures develop differently, depending

on their environments and economies, but may still be compared). I used some of Steward's evolutionary models in my study of cultural adaptive radiation in Madagascar (*The Past in the Present: History, Ecology, and Cultural Variation in Highland Madagascar*, 1980). Steward's work on state formation ("Cultural Causality and Law: A Trial Formulation of the Development of Early Civilization") inspired me as I researched state formation in Uganda and Madagascar. (My professors Morton Fried and Elliott Skinner also helped guide my interest in African state formation.) Steward's interests in cultural ecology and evolution strongly influenced the cultural materialism of Marvin Harris, my major professor. Finally, Steward influenced me through the research project he directed in Puerto Rico (published as *The People of Puerto Rico* in 1956). From this project I learned that anthropologists should pay attention to international, national, and regional forces, as well as the local setting. Steward's Puerto Rico project demonstrated the value of team research, systematic comparison, and a broad historical perspective. I also trace my intellectual genealogy to Steward through his student and Puerto Rico collaborator Eric Wolf (a former colleague at Michigan). My recent work in particular has been influenced by Eric Wolf's world-system approach (as elaborated in his *Europe and the People without History*, 1982). I can even trace part of my interest in the integrative role of the media in national culture to Steward's Puerto Rico project. Since the mid-1980s my work on the mass media, popular culture, and national cultures has converged with that of the Brazilian anthropologist Roberto DaMatta, and thus links up with his intellectual genealogy.

Sometimes intellectual genealogy becomes actual genealogy. My father-in-law was Charles Wagley, a former Columbia anthropology professor and well-known Brazilianist. Along with Marvin Harris (also Wagley's student), Wagley honed my interest in Brazil, in team research, and in systematic comparison (through the research project described in Wagley's *Race and Class in Rural Brazil*, 1952). Finally, my research in Madagascar was suggested and nurtured by the French social anthropologist George Condominas with whom I studied at Columbia and briefly in Paris. Condominas spurred my interest in state formation in Madagascar.

My general interests are in the processes by which local cultures join larger systems. This interest links my early work on ecology and state formation in Africa and Madagascar to recent and current research on the human dimension of global environmental change, economic development, national and international culture, and the mass media. My work on American and Brazilian popular culture, especially in Brazil from 1983 to 1987, led to *Prime-Time Society*, a comparative study of the nature and impact of television. My current research (which is both theoretical and applied)

focuses on environmental issues and people's reactions to them. I believe that environmental conservation is an appropriate goal—from global, national, long-run, and even local perspectives. However, if traditional resources are to be placed off limits they must be replaced with culturally appropriate alternatives. As my article with Colson indicates, I am quite interested in the media, ecology, social change, and comparative and longitudinal studies.

INTELLECTUAL ROOTS

Elizabeth Colson is an Emeritus Professor of Anthropology at the University of California—Berkeley. She has carried out research among a number of different groups including Native Americans, Japanese Americans, and Australians. Her most well-known fieldwork is among the Plateau Tonga and Gwembe Tonga of Zambia and covers a forty-year period—from 1946 to 1989. Her research has resulted in numerous publications, among them *The Makah* (1953), *Marriage and the Family among the Plateau Tonga* (1958), *Social Organization of the Gwembe Tonga* (1960), *The Social Consequences of Resettlement* (1971), *Tradition and Contract* (1975), *Planned Change* (1982), and with Thayer Scudder, *Secondary Education and the Formation of an Elite* (1980) and *For Prayer and Profit* (1988). She is a member of the National Academy of Science, the American Academy of Arts and Sciences, and an Honorary Fellow of the Royal Anthropological Institute.

Initially, at the University of Minnesota, I studied under Wilson Wallis, who in turn had studied at Oxford University under Robert Marett who was a student of Edward Tylor. Wallis had also attended seminars by Franz Boas. Wallis encouraged a view that anthropology was about humanity at all times and all places (not simply a study of "primitive" groupings). As a graduate student at Minnesota, I also studied with David Mandelbaum, who had been a student of Edward Sapir and earlier of Melville Herskovits, and had been

influenced by Clark Wissler. At Radcliffe, where I took my Ph.D., I worked with Clyde Kluckhohn. He had been a Rhodes Scholar at Oxford, under Robert Marett, but had gone on to Vienna where he had worked with Father Schmidt and others involved in the Kulturkreise School. On his return to the United States he moved closer to Edward Sapir as he developed his concern for the interplay between personality and culture and his interest in values. Kluckhohn fostered a recognition for the importance of long-term field studies. Kluckhohn also expected his students to read rather generally—including the work of psychologists, sociologists, and those who became known as "British social anthropologists." (He was then discussing with Talcott Parsons and Gordon Alport the formation of a department of social relations, to bring together cultural anthropology, sociology, and psychology.)

As a member of the New York University Field Laboratory in the Social Sciences for three summers, I received field training from Burt and Ethel Aginsky. They were both students of Boas and of Ruth Benedict, and at that time were participating in the Kardener-Linton seminar at Columbia, where the interplay between personality and culture was being explored. Through the Laboratory's focus on present-day concerns, the Aginskys encouraged me to think of anthropology as a study of action. Another member of the Kardiner-Linton seminar was Alexander Leighton, under whom I worked as an assistant social science analyst at the Colorado War Relocation Camp, better known as Poston. By that time, however, I was moving away from the study of personality and culture to explore more carefully work on social structure, encouraged by Edward Spicer who had also worked with Leighton. Spicer had been a student of Radcliffe-Brown at Chicago and was then at the height of his interest in social structure and functionalism. Spicer gave me a strong impetus toward analyzing activities that people engage in, together with how they phrase these activities, as means of understanding the people themselves.

In 1946 I joined the Rhodes-Livingstone Institute, where Max Gluckman was then director. Gluckman was initially trained in anthropology by Winifred Hoernle (who herself was trained at Cambridge under Rivers) and had gone as a Rhodes Scholar to Oxford where Marett was still the dominant figure in anthropology. Like all of his generation studying in Britain at that time, Gluckman attended the Malinowski seminar at the London School of Economics, but when Radcliffe-Brown arrived at Oxford, Gluckman found him more intellectually congenial than Marett or Malinowski. Gluckman was interested in conflict resolution, especially the maintenance of some form of community in potentially disruptive situations. He also stressed, as Kluckhohn did, the importance of collecting good demographic data. Revulsion against the situation in South Africa and Nazi activity in Germany and against the general misery of the Great Depression had led him, like many others of his generation, to read rather extensively in Marxist literature. The migration of German intellectuals also meant that the German sociological traditions, including the work of Max Weber, became part of the intellectual ferment of the time, although Durkheim and his school continued to have more influence on most English anthropologists.

I spent the year 1947-1948 at Oxford University, along with fellow research officers of the Institute (John Barnes and Clyde Mitchell), where Max Gluckman had just become Senior Lecturer, Meyer Fortes was reader, and Edward Evans-Pritchard had replaced Radcliffe-Brown as Professor. It was the high noon of interest in social structure as the dominant concern of ethnography. Students at Oxford during that year included Paul Bohannan, Laura Bohannan, Mary Douglas, and John Middleton. Once a week, I went to London for the big joint seminar run by Raymond Firth of the London School of Economics and Daryll Forde of University College, London. This was considered the continuation of the old Malinowski seminar and was run in much the same fashion. Audrey Richards, Siegfried Nadel, Edmund Leach, John Persitiany, and Kenneth Little were regular and active participants.

My teaching covered a range of topics, from political anthropology and comparative social organization to comparative religion, migration studies, and the history of anthropological theory. My research has likewise been many-faceted, both geographically and in terms of theoretical concerns. But much of it has focused on the consequences of dislocation or the threat of dislocation. I have argued for the importance of longitudinal field studies that can provide a better basis for the anthropological study of process of change and continuity. I am currently at work on several articles examining responses to forced relocation and, with Thayer Scudder, am preparing a book on religious responses among Tonga-speakers of Southern Zambia through a century of change.

Applying Anthropological Perspectives

F or those who care about anthropology's role as an agent of positive change—its role as a reformer's science (in Edward Tylor's phrasing)—there is much to feel uneasy about today. Instead of mostly development, democracy, and ethnic tolerance in the world—goals that surrounded the formation of the United Nations, Western aid programs, and a host of newly independent nations after World War II—we often now find poverty, repressive dictatorships, and ethnic conflict. It is not altogether clear why, despite much concerted effort to the contrary, this has occurred.

Anthropology's Vision

As suggested in the volume's introduction, a significant gap exists between the hopes of anthropology's moral vision and the reality of its practical accomplishments. Anthropology weaves three themes together.

First, it emphasizes people's shared humanity. It stresses what unites, rather than what separates, various ethnic and racial groups. It enlarges people's sense of moral community. It provides, as Kluckhohn (1949:1) asserts, "a scientific basis for dealing with the crucial dilemma of the world today: how can peoples of different appearance, mutually unintelligible languages, and dissimilar ways of life get along peaceably together?"

Second, it values cultural difference. Anthropologists feel, quoting Kluckhohn (1949:270) again, "the world must be kept safe for differences. Knowledge of the problems of others and of alien ways of life must become sufficiently general so that positive toleration becomes possible." Herskovits (1963:544-545) suggests: "If a world society is to emerge from the conflict of ethnocentrisms we call nationalisms, it can only be on a basis of live and let live, a willingness to recognize the values that are to be found in the most diverse ways of life." From an anthropological perspective, cultural difference is an asset, a resource, to draw on. Lévi-Strauss, in his contribution, observes, "It is differences between cultures that makes their meetings fruitful" (page 422) not cultural sameness. Intriguingly he notes the West has been predicting the disappearance of "traditional" societies for over a century now. And yet, despite numerous changes in these societies, they have not subordinated their cultural identities to some "world culture" or "modern order." The societies still retain a sense of cultural distinctiveness.

Third, anthropology uses cultural difference as a way of critiquing Western society. Making known alternative ways of behaving, alternative forms of belief, anthropology encourages us to reflect on our own lifestyles. It leads us to perceive new possibilities. "We

413

have been comparing . . . our civilization and . . . Samoa, in order to illuminate our own methods of education," Mead (1928:234) writes in her famous book, *Coming of Age in Samoa*. "If now we turn from the Samoan picture and take away . . . the main lesson . . . that adolescence is not necessarily a time of stress and strain, but that cultural conditions make it so, can we draw any conclusions which might bear fruit in the training of adolescents?" She answered yes. What she suggested helped change American sexual mores. Anthropology, to quote Carrithers (1992: 199), "challenge[s] people and encourage[s] them to consider new possibilities in the conduct of . . . [human] relations."

APPLYING ANTHROPOLOGY'S VISION

Anthropology's Accomplishments

Anthropology has had a degree of success in asserting its vision. It has done quite well as a recorder of cultural differences, as a witness to other ways of life. Its ethnographies describe how people live in diverse locales—from the arctic to the tropics, from the slums to the savannahs. And through modern technology—using books, movies, and television programs—it conveys a rich understanding of these people and their ways of life to the general public. The !Kung bushmen of South Africa, the Samoans of Polynesia, the Yanomamo of South America, are now part of many people's "cultural consciousness." They are cited on a host of occasions by a range of people. They now play a role in defining who we, as Americans (or Canadians, Russians, or Brazilians), are and what we might still yet become. In the process of acting as witnesses to other ways of life, anthropologists have also been able, at times, to convey a sense of social injustice that has ignited indignation beyond the affected communities. They have given a greater voice to the dis-

empowered and marginal groups than they might otherwise have. Scheper-Hughes does this in her recent book *Death without Weeping: The Violence of Everyday Life in Brazil*. Mooney (1965 [1893]) did the same in his *Ghost-Dance Religion*, which described the massacre of between 200 and 300 Sioux Indians at Wounded Knee in 1890. And Cultural Survival (described below) continues this tradition through its reports detailing the suffering of many "Fourth World" ethnic minorities.

The anthropological message of cultural relativism has been acknowledged by a wide range of people. "Acceptance of relativity of morals and values," Kroeber (1953:375) writes, "invests our conceptualizations of each culture with a certain degree of autonomy." Many appreciate the need for understanding the contexts of others' values before judging them.

Anthropology's Problems

While one might take hope from what anthropology has sought to accomplish, it has had difficulty in achieving much of its noble vision. First, anthropologists have not been able to escape their own cultural contexts. Anthropology, as a discipline, Hymes (1969b: 50) notes, "developed along side and within the growth of the colonial and imperial powers. By what they have studied (and what they have not studied) anthropologists have assisted in, or at least acquiesced to, the goals of imperialist policy." Though the relation of anthropology to colonialism has become generally accepted, one should be careful about overgeneralizing. A close look at who was involved with what programs suggests many anthropologists opposed colonial domination and spoke out (though not always loudly) for more indigenous understanding and representation (cf. Lévi-Strauss 1966b:123). Anthropologists did not always conform to their contexts. Yet it is fair to say they did not necessarily escape them either. In the phrasing of Clifford (1983:142): "Cultural dominance was a given context for their work, and they adopted a range of liberal positions within it. Seldom 'colonialists' in any direct, instrumental sense, ethnographers accepted certain constraints while, in varying degrees, questioning them."

Another problem for anthropology concerns an ambiguity regarding cultural relativism. The perspective stresses we need appreciate others in their own terms. But if others do not accord us the same tolerance we accord them, what then? "The anthropological outlook demands toleration of other ways of life," Kluckhohn (1949:268) writes, "so long as they do not threaten the hope for world order." But what does "hope for world order" refer to? Who defines it? For what purposes?

A third problem has been anthropology's inability to enunciate an effective vision for social change that brings major results without major bloodshed. Implicit in anthropology's vision is the notion (derived from the Enlightenment) that others are reasonable (as we define it) and that truth and understanding (as we define them) will prevail when known. "I hope to demonstrate that a clear understanding of the principles of anthropology," Boas (1928:11) writes, "illuminates the social practices of our times and may show us, if we are ready to listen to its teachings, what to do and what to avoid." Or as Malinowski (1938:xi) phrased it, anthropologists seek to "show the way in which sound knowledge can be translated into useful practice." Yet experience teaches us that change is not a simple process. The dynamics of power—not just knowledge—play a critical role in it. And anthropologists frequently lack real political power. "The anthropologist is himself a victim, and his power of decision is a fiction," writes Diamond (1969:401). Few anthropologists achieve high political positions. (Perhaps the most prominent one was Jomo Kenyatta, who led Kenya to independence and was its first postindependence president.) Ultimately, the very power of anthropology's vision—its ennobling, almost sacred, quality—one might

hypothesize results from its separation from the practical, political realities of everyday life. Clearly, more is needed than ideals to change the world. And anthropology has not been able to effectively enunciate what this "more" really is or how it would operate.

We might take two projects as illustrative of the ambiguities that surround anthropology's attempts at applying knowledge from the study of humans to the service of humans (to paraphrase Tax 1964:254). The Cornell-Peru Project attempted to bring change to Hacienda Vicos, a manor located in a high Andean valley of Peru. Formally lasting from 1952 to 1966, it sought, in the words of Holmberg (1955:23), one of the project's founders, to assist a peasant "community to shift . . . itself from a position of relative dependence and submission in a highly restricted and provincial world to a position of relative independence and freedom within the larger framework of Peruvian national life." Cornell University took over the hacienda's lease and through a range of programs and personnel, often funded by outside agencies (and assisted by outside power brokers at key moments), brought about significant change. Did it succeed over the long term? Paige (1975:175) asserts: "The Vicos experiment . . . illustrates the limits of effective land reform in the absence of radical political change. . . . The Vicosinos were constrained not by the culture of poverty, but by repression . . . [and] massive national social forces." Mangin (1979:83) cryptically suggests, "It is hard . . . to see that the community is worse off for it." But Doughty (1987:458-459) is positive: "As a contribution to applied anthropology and to Peru, the Vicos project should be remembered for what it accomplished: the successful completion of the first holistically designed, community development and land reform program, which upheld and enhanced the dignity, conditions of life, and citizen rights of impoverished Indian serfs against the weight of colonial tradition and the ultimate wishes of the elites." In the final analysis, one's assessment of the Vicos project depends on what one deems is possible within a political-economic setting where an entrenched elite enforces its dominance over a rural peasantry, sometimes brutally, with tacit governmental support.

The other anthropological program is Cultural Survival, founded by David and Pia Maybury-Lewis. "Since 1972, Cultural Survival has supported projects designed to help indigenous peoples survive, both physically and culturally, the rapid changes which contact with expanding industrial society brings" (*Cultural Survival Quarterly* 1984:81). "Survival, as individuals and as cultures, means [for indigenous peoples] the possibility of adapting to change in their own way and on their own terms" (*Action for Cultural Survival* 1992:6). In contrast to the Vicos project, such efforts are broad-based, involving work with a range of indigenous peoples in a range of settings. And, expressive of the increased globalization of communicative, political, and economic networks today, Cultural Survival focuses not only on indigenous self-help projects but on linking these to public awareness programs beyond the affected communities as support for them. Thus, it not only assists building "markets for products that native communities can harvest in a sustainable manner" but also, at the same time, maintains "briefings . . . for schools, community groups, and the media" (*Cultural Survival Quarterly* 1992:2) about issues related to indigenous peoples. The hope is to keep at bay, through international pressure, political and economic forces which are disempowering, if not destroying, indigenous communities. To date, Cultural Survival has received much positive publicity. There is little doubt that it has made significant changes in many people's lives. (Several of these are documented in the organization's annual reports.) However, despite a host of successes, many wonder if such work can be more than a holding action. The political-economic elites and forces that cause so many abuses in Third World settings may be restrained by Cultural

Survival's efforts, but they are not transformed by them. It is hard bringing significant change to local communities by trying to change a whole country, the whole world. The goal is too expansive, too broad, to realistically succeed. But it is also hard to help local communities without trying to change a country or the world because, especially today, outside forces impact on local communities in so many ways. In these two programs—Vicos and Cultural Survival—one perceives anthropology's hopes for change. And one sees some of the problems anthropologists encounter in trying to bring it about.

ETHNIC CONFLICT AND THE CULTURAL ORGANIZATION OF POLITIES IN THE MODERN WORLD

As much as any social force today, ethnic conflict bring's anthropology's vision into question. Hobsbawm (1992:8) suggests xenophobia (i.e. the hatred of that which is foreign) "looks like becoming the mass ideology of the [end of the] twentieth century." "What holds humanity together today," he states, "is the denial of what the human race has in common." Citing Tagil, Tambiah (page 434) raises a critical question: Why do ethnic differences become the basis for intense political conflict in certain modernizing societies? This ties into Tishkov's question: Why have the grievances toward the old communist system been channeled into ethnic conflict and *ethnonationalism* (i.e. the seeking of political sovereignty by each ethnic group)? One can see both authors reaching for answers. We are grappling here with problems at the edge of our understanding. Readers might reflect on the interactions among several factors.

First, with the decline of direct colonial rule in Third World countries, Western powers have turned to more subtle forms of political control. The domination is still there. But it is now phrased in terms of world trade or International Monetary Fund and World Bank loans—encouraging modernization while increasing debt. Third World desires for a higher standard of living and more consumer goods—what one might call an ideology of consumerism—have also encouraged this subtle form of domination. While there is no doubt living conditions have significantly improved in a host of countries, every person in every nation is not going to reach the West's level of consumerism. The earlier hope that this could possibly occur over time, most now perceive as unrealistic. It is increasingly a world of consumer "limited good" (in anthropological terms)—in which one group's success restricts the success of others. Thus, particularly within a nation (where the struggle for control over resources can be carried on more effectively than on a global scale), one group is pitted against another for largesse and the benefits of a consumer-oriented lifestyle.

Ethnicity not only constitutes a way of mobilizing groups to compete for consumer benefits. It also acts as a way of tempering consumerism's worst excesses. Individual consumer wants are placed within traditional and/or religious frameworks where they are shaped (and reshaped) by broader principles of sharing. Intense ethnic affirmations, from this perspective, thus constitute a response to both the pleasures and the problems of consumerism in the Third World.

Second is the issue of popular sovereignty. Popular sovereignty—the power of the many to rule from below rather than the few from on top—became a powerful political force toward the end of the eighteenth century. It formed the basis not only for the American and French revolutions but for the dismemberment of European colonial empires. In this century, Woodrow Wilson and Vladimir Lenin have been two leading advocates for using ethno-nationalism as the basis for nation-states. But what is a nation? Quoting Hobsbawm (1990:5-6):

Attempts to establish objective criteria for nationhood, or to explain why certain groups have become "nations" . . . have often been made based on a single criteria such as language or ethnicity or a combination of criteria such as language, common territory, common history, cultural traits or whatever else. . . . All such objective definitions have failed, for the obvious reason that . . . the criteria used . . . [are] fuzzy, shifting, and ambiguous.

"National identity" often becomes, as P. Sahlins (1989:271) notes, "a socially constructed and continuous process of defining 'friend' and 'enemy.'" Simmel (in Hobsbawm 1990: 167-168) makes a similar point: "Within certain groups, it may . . . be a piece of political wisdom to see to it that there be some enemies in order for the unity of the members to be effective and for the group to remain conscious of this unity as a vital interest." One might wonder, I am suggesting, to what degree conflict—or at least opposition—constitutes an inherent part of ethno-nationalism.

And where does popular sovereignty end in relation to ethno-nationalism? How small can an ethno-nation be? A million people, a thousand, a hundred? As Connor (1973:1) states: "In a world consisting of thousands of distinct ethnic groups and only some one hundred and thirty-five states, the revolutionary potential inherent in [ethnic] self-determination is quite apparent." Despite rhetoric to the contrary, ethnicity has not generally proved an effective basis for defining nation-states. To quote Connor (1973: 11): Ethno-nationalism's "lack of successful application must be one of its most astonishing characteristics . . . less than ten percent of all states are essentially homogeneous."

Governments, especially those based on popular sovereignty, face a tremendous political problem with ethno-nationalism. "Governmental responses to the threat of ethno-nationalism have been quite varied," Connor (1973:18-19) observes. "Despite the great variety in approaches and techniques, however, it does not appear that any government has found a workable solution, other than the morally unacceptable ones of genocide and expulsion." We are led to ask: Why are most states multiethnic in character? And under what conditions can popular sovereignty coexist with ethno-nationalism in multiethnic states?

Third, what many states lack today is a tie that binds its diverse people together. Many of the Third World nation-states formed from colonial empires after World War II were accidents of colonial history. They lacked any internal coherence in and of themselves. Unfortunately many of the indigenous elites that replaced the colonial regimes in governing these new states never really established a sense of cultural coherence within their nations. They tended to focus on their own self-advancement. To quote the Algerian psychiatrist Frantz Fanon (1963:128-129), from his famous book *The Wretched of the Earth*:

Everywhere . . . [the] national bourgeoisie has shown itself incapable of extending its vision of the world sufficiently, we observe a falling back towards old tribal attitudes. . . . The national bourgeoisie, since it is strung up to defend its immediate interests, and sees no further than the end of its nose, reveals itself incapable of . . . bringing national unity into being, or of building up the nation on a stable and productive basis.

Fanon's remark leads to at least two important questions: What keeps a polity together if not raw power? How are the "have-nots"—those with less power and/or wealth—given a meaningful stake in the social order?

One of the more intriguing aspects of ethno-nationalist rhetoric in the twentieth century is the way it obscures asymmetrical power relations through an affirmation of common cultural identity. Why do people seemingly assume the elites of the new order—*their* cultural elites—will prove to be less dominating and abusive than the elites of the old order? To quote Toland (1993:2): "The idea of a 'pure' nation state with one monolithic voice has never been and probably never will be a reality." Conflicts over power

go on as before. We might ponder whether the politically volatile rhetoric of ethno-nationalism, like democratic elections and military coup d'etat, should be viewed as a way to disrupt the "applecart" of the established order. In states where violence and political repression limit effective opposition, ethno-nationalism can be a powerful coalescing force, an important rallying point, of resistance against the status quo. In relatively weak states—and this now includes many states given the modern global economy—ethno-nationalism can significantly disrupt, if not overwhelm for a time, established political structures.

Ethno-nationalism, which seemed so promising at the beginning of this century in the speeches of Woodrow Wilson and Vladimir Lenin (and which helped form the basis for various European states in the last century), now seems to be more a symbol of pain than of promise. Ultimately, it reflects the failure of various states to effectively handle the political issue of representation since, as Cohen (1993: 235) notes, "Statehood is correlated with multi-culturalism . . . uniethnic states are the exception not the rule." In the hatred, violence, and genocide of recent ethno-nationalism, we see our hopes for social inclusiveness and political tolerance shattered. It is not a nice image, for it strikes close to home. It emphasizes ambiguities within our own democratic system. And the cultural, as something with delineable boundaries, seems tarnished by how various people have applied it in recent times. In constituting an intellectual framework for ethnic identity (and through it ethno-nationalism), it has, sadly, become a vehicle for much intolerance.

WHAT VALUE CAN ANTHROPOLOGY HAVE IN THE MODERN WORLD?

Anthropology has not enunciated an effective theory of change without bloodshed. But it has enunciated a moral vision of how different people of different cultural perspectives might live together through mutual understanding. It emphasizes a needed moral framework that joins, rather than separates, people. This is the issue Geertz addresses: How are we to get along as different people with different interests? We must be able, he emphasizes, to grasp other people's perspectives without assimilating them to our own. "Comprehending that which is, in some manner of form, alien to us and likely to remain so, without either smoothing it over with vacant murmurs of common humanity . . . or dismissing it as charming," Geertz (page 465) writes, "is a skill we have arduously to learn, and having learnt it, always very imperfectly, to work continuously to keep alive."

There is little dramatic change in this. But there is a sense of morality that may offer an affirming flame in difficult times.

28

*Anthropology, Race, and Politics: A Conversation with Didier Eribon**

CLAUDE LÉVI-STRAUSS

ANTHROPOLOGY'S FUTURE DIRECTION

D.E. (Didier Eribon): In your first course at the Collège de France, you asked questions about the future of anthropology. What would your answers be today?

C.L.-S. (Claude Lévi Strauss): I would have to make several alterations, because there has been some evolution during this quarter of a century, and things are not completely the same, particularly concerning the societies that anthropology studies.

D.E.: Because the societies that interest the anthropologist are traditional societies, and they are vanishing one after another. . . .

C.L.-S.: Did you know that they were saying that back in the eighteenth century? The first scholarly societies founded to study man justified their mission by proclaiming, "We must hurry, they won't last much longer." When Frazer, the year I was born, taught his first course at the University of Liverpool, he said the same thing. It is a leitmotif of anthropological research. I admit that the processes have speeded up and that we can reasonably foresee the end. However, there are still so many things that have been little or poorly studied in the dozens or hundreds of societies that still exist and will continue to exist for a good number of years, that I see a need to intensify our efforts instead of abandoning them. And then, even if we imagine a time when all these cultures have disappeared. . . . Greece and Rome have been gone for a long time, but we continue to study them and offer new views about them.

D.E.: But for these cultures we have documents, monuments.

C.L.-S.: These monuments . . . we are the ones, because of the attention we have paid to them, who have made them so!

D.E.: Do you believe it would be as easy to constitute documents or monuments for a small population in Brazil?

C.L.-S.: For a population that has been little or poorly studied, or studied over a very short period of time, you are right. The loss will be complete. But—confining myself to America, which I know the best—the collections of the Library of Congress, of the American Philosophical Society, and others abound with manuscripts, many of which have not yet been studied or even catalogued.

D.E.: These are forgotten treasures?

C.L.-S.: Yes, and they probably represent by their volume as much as Greece and Rome have left us.

---

*Reprinted, in edited form, from Claude Lévi-Strauss and Didier Eribon, *Conversations with Lévi-Strauss*, Chicago: University of Chicago Press, Chicago, Ill., 1991. ©1991, the University of Chicago.

Anthropology's Changing Character

D.E.: So anthropology is not an endangered science?

C.L.-S.: It will change its character. If there is no longer an object to fieldwork, we will become philologists, historians of ideas, specialists in civilizations now accessible only through documents gathered by earlier observers. And who knows whether new differences will not appear among a humanity that is in great danger of losing its diversity?

D.E.: Do you have the feeling that humanity is heading toward total uniformity?

C.L.-S.: Total is too strong a word. But never has it been possible to speak so convincingly of global civilization as it is today.

D.E.: Might not anthropology continue to function by taking an interest in contemporary societies closer to us, such as the French countryside?

C.L.-S.: Such projects are neither a survival tactic nor a retreat. They have their own intrinsic value. If they are a later development, it is because we had the impression that we knew more about our own societies than we did about exotic cultures; there was a sense of urgency propelling us to study the others. Furthermore, the older stages of our own societies are revealed to us first of all through archives—using the term broadly—that reach back over several centuries. For the societies of central Brazil or Melanesia, 5 to 10 percent of the material we have is historical. The rest of it is the work of ethnographers. In the case of our societies, the proportion is reversed. Here the role of the anthropologist is confined to completing and enriching work that is first of all the task of the historian.

D.E.: The future of anthropology is likewise related to institutional matters. Do you think that the situation of the discipline is more satisfactory today than when you first became interested in it?

C.L.-S.: When I started out in my career as an anthropologist, there was no such thing as an anthropology chair in any of the French universities. I believe the first person to hold such a position was Marcel Griaule, just before or during the Second World War—I no longer remember. Today anthropology has become a discipline in its own right, taught in the universities. With respect to the urgency of the work remaining to be done, the number of jobs and chairs is still insufficient.

D.E.: Like other disciplines, anthropological research must run up against a lack of money—you have to have a budget!

C.L.-S.: Except that in the case of physicists or biologists, it is easy to see that they need money to operate their laboratories because that is where they perform their experiments and verify those of their colleagues. It is less readily seen that the laboratories of anthropologists are found thousands of miles away and that they require means to go and live there.

RACE, CULTURAL DIVERSITY, AND POLITICS

Race and History, Race and Culture

D.E.: In 1952, with the pamphlet *Race and History*, you departed from a purely anthropological viewpoint to take what could be called a "political" view, a view that dealt with contemporary problems, at any rate.

C.L.-S.: I was asked to write it. I don't think I would have written it on my own.

D.E.: How did the request come about?

C.L.-S.: UNESCO asked several authors to write a series of booklets on the racial question. Leiris was asked, myself.

D.E.: There you assert the idea of the diversity of cultures, question the idea of progress, and proclaim the need for a "coalition" of cultures.

C.L.-S.: Overall, I was looking for a way to reconcile the notion of progress with cultural relativism. The notion of progress implies the idea that certain cultures, in specific times or places, are superior to others because they have produced works that the others have shown themselves incapable of producing. And cultural relativism, one of the foundations of anthropological thought, at least in my generation and the one before it (some are contesting it today), states that there is no criterion that enables one to make an absolute judgment as to how one culture is superior to another. If, at certain times and certain places, some cultures "move" while others "stand still," it is not, I said, because of the superiority of the first, but from the fact that historic or geographical circumstances have brought about a collaboration among cultures, which are not unequal (nothing makes it possible for us to decree them as such), but different. These cultures begin to move as they borrow from others or seek to oppose them. In other periods or in other places, cultures that remain isolated as closed worlds lead a stationary life.

D.E.: This has become a classic antiracist document; it is even read in the lycees (or French secondary schools). Did you write the second article, "Race and Culture," in 1971, as a reaction against this gospel?

C.L.-S.: It too was the result of a request from UNESCO, for a conference to open an international year to combat racism.

D.E.: Later you said, "This piece caused an uproar, and that was my intent."

C.L.-S.: That's perhaps a bit strong. One thing is certain—it did cause an uproar, at least at UNESCO. Twenty years after *Race and History* they asked me to speak again about racism, probably expecting me to repeat what I had already said. I don't like to repeat myself; and above all, much had happened during these twenty years, including my own grow-

ing irritation with periodic displays of fine feelings, as if that could suffice. It seemed to me that on the one hand racial conflicts were only getting worse, and on the other there was a confusion about notions such as those of racism and antiracism; because of this carelessness, racism was being fueled instead of weakening.

D.E.: This time you spoke of the differences that separate and distinguish cultures from one another. This went against your earlier statements.

C.L.-S.: Not at all. When people read the first piece, they read every other line. One critic, I think he was from *L'Humanité,* wanted to prove that I had changed tactics, and quoted a long passage from "Race and Culture" as proof. This passage was in *Race and History.* Since I found it apropos, I had used it again, word for word.

A Paradox Regarding Cultural Diversity

D.E.: Perhaps the most shocking thing about "Race and Culture" was the idea that cultures want to be opposed to one another.

C.L.-S.: At the end of *Race and History* I was stressing a paradox. It is differences between cultures that makes their meetings fruitful. Now, this exchange leads to progressive uniformity: the benefits cultures reap from these contacts are largely the result of their qualitative differences, but during these exchanges these differences diminish to the point of disappearing. Isn't that what we are seeing today? . . .

What can we conclude from all this, except that it is desirable for cultures to retain their diversity or for them to find renewal in diversity? Only—and this is what my second piece was saying—one has to agree to pay the price: to know that cultures, each of which is attached to a lifestyle and value system of its own, foster their own peculiarities, and that this tendency is healthy and not—as people would like to have us think—pathological.

Each culture develops as a result of its exchanges with other cultures. But each must put up some resistance. If not, very shortly there won't be anything unique to exchange. Both an absence and an excess of communication have their dangers.

D.E.: How do you explain that your first piece was so successful and the second was not?

C.L.-S.: The first was published as a little book. The second was the text of a talk and never appeared on its own. And if in comparison to the second the first has been well received, I can't do anything about it; they form a whole. I will add that the second, in which I attempted to include results of work on population genetics, is more difficult to read. And even with *Race and History*, not a year goes by without lycee students coming to see me or telephoning and saying, "We have a report to do and we don't understand a thing!"

D.E.: What would you do if today UNESCO asked you to give another talk on the same topic?

C.L.-S.: There's no chance of that!

The Notion of Racism

D.E.: But newspapers and radio stations often ask your opinion on the question of racism, and in general you refuse to answer.

C.L.-S.: I have no wish to answer because in this area confusion reigns, and, no matter what I say, I know beforehand that it will be misinterpreted. As an anthropologist, I am convinced that racist theories are both monstrous and absurd. But by trivializing the notion of racism, applying it this way and that, we empty it of its meaning and run the risk of producing a result counter to the one we seek. For what is racism? A specific doctrine, which can be summed up in four points. One, there is a correlation between genetic heritage on the one hand and intellectual aptitudes and

moral inclinations on the other. Two, this heritage, on which these aptitudes and inclinations depend, is shared by all members of certain human groups. Three, these groups, called "races," can be evaluated as a function of the quality of their genetic heritage. Four, these differences authorize the so-called superior "races" to command and exploit the others, and eventually destroy them. Both the theory and practice are indefensible for a number of reasons that I laid out in "Race and Culture" after or at the same time as other writers did, and with as much vigor as in *Race and History*. The problem of the relationships between cultures is on another level.

D.E.: And so, for you, the hostility of one culture toward another is not racism?

C.L.-S.: Active hostility, yes. Nothing gives one culture the right to destroy or even oppress another. This negation of the other inevitably takes its support from transcendent reasons: either racism or its equivalent. But that cultures, all the while respecting each other, can feel greater or less affinity with certain others, is a factual situation that has always existed. It is the normal course of human conduct. By condemning it as racist, one runs the risk of playing into the enemy's hand, for many naive people will say, if that's racism, then I'm racist.

You know of my attraction for Japan. When I'm in the metro in Paris and I see a couple that looks Japanese, I look at them with interest and sympathy, ready to give them a hand. Is that racism?

D.E.: If you look at them with kindness, no; but if you had said, "I look at them with hatred," I would have said yes.

C.L.-S.: And nevertheless, I am basing my feelings on physical appearance, behavior, the sounds of the language. In everyday life, everyone does the same in order to "place" a stranger. It would take a lot of hypocrisy to attempt to forbid this type of approximation.

D.E.: Are there certain physical appearances that arouse your antipathy?

C.L.-S.: Do you mean ethnic types? No, of course not. All of them include subtypes, some of which we find attractive, some not. In some Indian communities in Brazil I felt surrounded by handsome people; I found others presented a sorry sight. Generally the Nambikwara women seemed more attractive than the men; it was the opposite among the Bororo. When we make such judgments we are applying the aesthetic canons of our culture. Under the circumstances the only rules worth paying attention to are those of the parties involved.

Similarly, I belong to a culture that has a distinctive lifestyle and value system, so cultures that are extremely different don't automatically appeal to me.

D.E.: You don't like them?

C.L.-S.: That's going too far. If I study them as an anthropologist I work with all the objectivity and even all the empathy I am capable of. That doesn't keep some cultures from fitting in more easily with my own. . . . Robert Lowie was a great anthropologist who honored me with his friendship. His works on the Crow and the Hopi are authoritative. However, he confided to me that he got along perfectly with the first, while he could hardly stand the second.

"Multicultural Society"

D.E.: Indeed, when people ask you about racism, it is less about relations among different cultures on different continents than in French society of today and in what is called a "multicultural society." There was even a rumor last year that the government was thinking of asking you to lead a commission entrusted with the task of reforming the laws on nationality, but it abandoned the idea because it might have seemed shocking to ask an anthropologist.

C.L.-S.: If what you are saying is true, that's very interesting—the government *is* afraid to shock the immigrants by comparing them to the peoples studied by anthropologists, as if there were an implicit hierarchy among cultures.

D.E.: If I am to understand your definition of the term, you judge that in France today there is no racism.

C.L.-S.: There are some disquieting phenomena, but except in the case of killing an Arab because he is Arab, an act that should be swiftly and mercilessly punished, they are not a reflection of racism in the true sense of the word. There are and always will be communities inclined to like others whose values and lifestyles do not go against their own and who will find others less easy to accept. This does not mean that, even in the second case, relations cannot and should not remain calm. If my work requires silence, and an ethnic community is comfortable with noise or even likes it, I won't blame the community and make accusations about its genetic heritage. Still, I'll prefer not to live too close and will be little appreciative if, on such a spiteful pretext, I am to be found guilty.

D.E.: In 1988, can a society be monocultural, given the melting pots of populations, migrations, immigration?

C.L.-S.: The term is meaningless, because there never has been such a society. All cultures are the result of a mishmash, borrowings, mixtures that have occurred, though at different rates, ever since the beginning of time. Because of the way it is formed, each society is multicultural and over the centuries has arrived at its own original synthesis. Each will hold more or less rigidly to this mixture that forms its culture at a given moment. Who can deny that, even taking internal differences into account, there is a Japanese culture, an American culture? There is no country more the product of a mixture than the United States, and nonetheless there exists an "American way of life" that all inhabitants of the country are attached to, no matter what their ethnic origin.

Since you are asking me about France, I will answer that in the eighteenth and nineteenth centuries its value system represented something attractive for Europe and beyond. The assimilation of immigrants didn't cause any problems. There would be none today if, from primary school onward, our value system appeared as solid and alive to all as it did in the past.

D.E.: All Western societies are clearly encountering this problem of impossible assimilation: England, Germany. . . . The coexistence of cultures in those countries seems as difficult as it is in France.

C.L.-S.: If Western societies aren't capable of sustaining or generating intellectual and moral values powerful enough to attract people from outside, people they wish to have adopt these values, then, undoubtedly there is something to be alarmed about.

Colonialism and Decolonization

D.E.: Your work, especially the two texts we have just mentioned, has often been seen as parallel to anticolonial movements. What do you think about that?

C.L.-S.: I read that from time to time. I even read recently that the success of *Tristes Tropiques* was linked to the rise of the idea of the Third World. That is a misinterpretation. The societies I was defending or for which I was endeavoring to witness are even more threatened by the new setup than they were by colonization. The governments of countries that have won their independence since the Second World War have no sympathy for the "backward" cultures that still exist among them.

There is a second reason, which may sound cynical to you: I'm not interested in people as much as beliefs, customs, and institutions. So I defend the small populations who wish to

remain faithful to their traditional way of life, away from the conflicts that are dividing the modern world. Those who leave this state and take part in our conflicts cause political and even geopolitical problems; everyone knows that, in this matter, cases of conscience are rarely all on one side.

D.E.: Do you distrust the notion of the Third World more than that of decolonization? Colonialism was the major sin of the West. However, with respect to the vitality and plurality of cultures, I don't see that we have made a great leap forward since its disappearance.

D.E.: Anthropology has been accused of being in collusion with colonialism. Does this view seem well founded to you?

C.L.-S.: It is an historical fact that anthropology was born and developed in the shadow of colonialism. However, contrary to the colonial enterprise, anthropologists have sought to protect beliefs and ways of life that cultures were forgetting at an increasing rate.

D.E.: Some people have gone so far as to say that anthropology perpetuated colonial domination after the fact. . . .

C.L.-S.: When native peoples, after undergoing nearly total destruction, wish to reestablish links with their past, it often happens that they rely on books by anthropologists for help. I know quite a few examples of this.

The Observer
and the Observed

D.E.: According to the critics, the Westerner nonetheless maintains his supremacy over the culture he is observing.

C.L.-S.: It's not a question of the supremacy of the observer, but of the supremacy of observation. In order to observe, one must be outside. One can—it is an ethical choice—prefer (but is it possible?) to melt into the community whose existence one shares and to identify with it. Knowledge lies on the outside.

D.E.: So knowledge only comes from the separation between subject and object?

C.L.-S.: It is one aspect. The second time around, one attempts to reconnect them. No knowledge would be possible without a distinction between the two moments; but the originality of ethnographic inquiry consists of this endless switching back and forth.

D.E.: In his book on the logic of writing, Jack Goody raises in a fascinating way the problem of relations between the observer and the society under observation; when one studies oral traditions, civilizations that have no writing, the simple fact of transcribing these traditions changes them and imposes the observer's categories of perception and, with them, those of his own culture. Do you have something to say about that?

C.L.-S.: The remark seems right, but trivial. This is true of all observation, even in the most advanced sciences. Of course one must remain aware that while transcribing an observation, whatever it is, one is not preserving the facts in their original authenticity; they are being translated into another language, and something is lost in the process. But what can we conclude from it? That one can neither translate nor observe?

INTELLECTUAL ROOTS *

Claude Lévi-Strauss is a French "ethnologist . . . famous as an exponent of structuralism. . . . After studying both law (*licence*) and philosophy (*licence* and *agrégation*), Lévi-Strauss chose ethnology as his area of specialization. Attracted by the possibility of doing fieldwork, he accepted a position at the University of São Paulo in Brazil from 1935 to 1937. During school vacations and again in 1938 to 1939, Lévi-Strauss organized expeditions into the Brazilian interior to study the Bororo, Nambikwara, and other Indian groups. Mobilized during 1939 and 1940, Lévi-Strauss was spirited out of France following the [French] defeat by a Rockerfeller Program to save prominent Jewish intellectuals. In New York from 1941 to 1945, he taught in the New School for Social Research, and on a second stay in 1946-1947 served as French cultural officer. During the war Lévi-Strauss joined a community in exile in the United States dominated by leading surrealists and became close friends with André Breton and Max Ernst. After holding positions at the National Center for Scientific Research, the Musée de l'Homme and the Ecole Pratique des Hautes Études, Lévi-Strauss was elected to the Collège de France in 1959 where he directed a laboratory of social anthropology until his retirement in 1982. The Académie Française elected him to membership in 1973."

His major works include (with English translation titles and dates, French dates are in brackets): *La Vie Familiale et Sociale des Indiens Nambikwara* [1948], *The Elementary Structures of Kinship* (1969) [1949], *Race et Histoire* [1952], *Tristes Tropiques* (1973) [1955], *Structural Anthropology*, two volumes (1963-1976) [1958-73], *Totemism* (1963) [1962], *The Savage Mind* (1966) [1962], *Introduction to the Science of Mythology*: vol. 1, *The Raw and the Cooked*, vol. 2, *From Honey to Ashes*, vol. 3, *The Origin of Table Manners,* vol. 4, *The Naked Man* (1969-1981) [1964-1971], *The Scope of Anthropology* (1968), *The Way of the Masks* (1982) [1975], *Myth and Meaning: Five Talks for Radio* (1978), *The View from Afar* (1985) [1983], *The*

*The general biographical information given here is quoted from A. Douglas (1992). For a list of Lévi-Strauss's numerous awards and honorary degrees see Redfield (1987:455).

Jealous Potter (1988) [1985], and *Histoire de Lynx* [1991]. In addition, readers might refer to *Conversations with Claude Lévi-Strauss* (1969) [1961] edited by Charbonnier and *Conversations with Claude Lévi-Strauss* (1991) [1988] by Lévi-Strauss and Didier Eribon.

This dialogue is reprinted, in edited form, from Claude Lévi-Strauss and Didier Eribon, *Conversations with Lévi-Strauss,* Chicago: University of Chicago Press, Chicago, Ill., 1991.

D.E.: Why had you decided to become an anthropologist?

C.L.-S.: Let's say that it was a combination of circumstances. Since childhood I had a passion for exotic curios. . . . In addition, toward 1930 it began to be known among the young philosophers that a disciple called anthropology existed and that it aspired to obtain official recognition. . . . Moreover, I read a couple of works by English and American anthropologists, particularly Robert Lowie's *Primitive Society,* that won me over because the theoretician and the fieldworker were combined. I was envisaging a way of reconciling my professional education with my taste for adventure. . . . Finally, Paul Nizan, whom I had met two or three times at family gatherings . . . told me that he himself had been drawn to anthropology. That encouraged me. (1991:16–17)

D.E.: Did . . . [Boas's] work mean a great deal to you?

C.L.S.: It was essential. . . . Boas was . . . one of the first—somewhere I wrote that it was Saussure, but in fact Saussure never expressed himself on the subject, it flows indirectly from his work—to insist on an essential fact in the human sciences: the laws of language function on an unconscious level, beyond the control of speaking subjects; thus they can be studied as objective phenomena, representative for this reason of other social facts. (1991:38–39)

D.E.: [Was the] meeting [with the linguist Roman Jakobson] . . . a decisive one for you?

C.L.-S.: It was enormously important. At the time I was a kind of naive structuralist, a structuralist without knowing it. Jakobson revealed to me the existence of a body of doctrine that had already been formed within a discipline, linguistics, with which I was unacquainted. For me it was a revelation. . . .

D.E.: . . . And right away you were able to apply his methods to your work on kinship.

C.L.-S.: Things didn't happen that way. I didn't apply his ideas; I became aware that what he was saying about language corresponded to what I was glimpsing in a confused way about kinship systems, marriage rules, and more generally, life in society. (1991:41, 99)

C.L.-S.: The nature and importance of my borrowings from linguistics have been misunderstood. Besides being a general inspiration, which, I admit, is enormous, they boil down to the role of unconscious mental activity in the production of logical structures, which was emphasized by Boas, who was an anthropologist as much as a linguist. Second, there is this basic principle that component parts have no intrinsic meaning; it arises from their position. This is true of language, and it is also true for other social facts. I don't believe I have asked anything else from linguistics, and Jakobson, during our conversations, was the first to recognize that I was making an original use of these notions in another area. (1991:112–13)

D.E.: The idea of transformation has a key place in your analyses. . . . Where did you find it, in logic?

C.L.-S.: Neither in logic nor linguistics. I found it in a work that played a decisive role for me and that I read during the war while I was in the United States: *On Growth and Form,* in two volumes, by D'Arcy Wentworth Thompson, which was first published in 1917. The author, a Scottish naturalist . . . interpreted the visible differences between species or between animal or vegetable organs within the same genera, as transformations. This was an illumination for me, particularly since I was soon to notice that this way of seeing was part of a long tradition: behind Thompson was Goethe's botany, and behind Goethe, Albrecht Dürer and his *Treatise on the Proportions of the Human Body.* Now the notion of transformation is inherent in structural analysis. I would even say that all the errors, all the abuses committed through the notion of structure are a result of the fact that their authors have not understood that it is impossible to conceive of structure separate from the notion of transformation. Structure is not reducible to a system: a group composed of elements and the relations that unite them. In order to be able to speak of structure, it is necessary for there to be invariant relationships between elements and relations among several sets, so that one can move from one set to another by means of a transformation. (1991:113)

D.E.: . . . One of the objections often made against you [is that] you have read a great deal but have done little fieldwork.

C.L.-S.: That was the result of circumstances. If I had gotten a visa for Brazil in 1940, I would have gone back to my initial field sites and done more work. If the war hadn't broken out, I would probably have gone on another mission. Fate led me to the United States, where due to a lack of means and the international situation I was not in a position to launch any expeditions but where, on the other hand, I was entirely free to work on theoretical issues. . . . I also became aware that in the previous twenty or thirty years a considerable quantity of material had been accumulated; but it was in such disarray that one didn't know where to begin or how to utilize it. It seemed urgent to sort out what this mass of documents had brought us. Finally, why not admit it? I realized early on that I was a library man, not a fieldworker. . . . I did more fieldwork than my critics would admit. In any case, I did enough to learn and to understand what fieldwork is, which is an essential prerequisite for making a sound evaluation and use of the work done by others. (1991: 43–45)

D.E.: . . . What led you to write such a book [as *Tristes Tropiques*]?

C.L.-S.: It all began with a request on the part of Jean Malaurie. . . . It had never dawned on me to write about my travels. However, in the period I was going through, I was convinced that I had no future in the university system, so the idea of just writing what came to me was tempting. Also, as time went on, I had gained a certain distance. It was no longer a matter of transcribing a journal of my expedition. I had to rethink my old adventures, reflect upon them, and draw some kind of conclusions. (1991:58)

D.E.: . . . You told me the other day that your entire career had been outside the traditional university environment.

C.L.-S.: . . . I had taught in Brazil, in the United States, then in France at the Ecole des Hautes Études. But never in the university.

D.E.: What were the advantages of working outside of the traditional university system?

C.L.-S.: More freedom and, in a sense, tolerance for a less regimented spirit. (1991:75)

C.L.-S.: . . . Freud played a major role in my intellectual development, equal to the role of Marx. He taught me that even phenomena of the most illogical appearance can be subjected to rational analysis. I found Marx's work comparable as it relates to ideologies (which are collective instead of individual phenomena, also essentially irrational): it is possible to reach beyond appearances to find a logically consistent foundation, regardless of the moral judgements one might have with respect to it. . . . (1991:107–108)

C.L.-S.: Marx was the first in the social sciences to use systematically the methodology of models. All of *Capital*, for example, is a model constructed in the laboratory and set in motion by the author so he could view the results in conjunction with observed events. Also, in Marx I found the fundamental idea that one cannot understand what is going on inside people's heads without connecting it to the conditions of their practical existence, something I have tried to do throughout the Mythology books. . . . Only a few lessons from Marx's teaching have stayed with me—above all, that consciousness lies to itself. And then, as I've already said, it is through Marx that I first glimpsed Hegel, and behind him, Kant. You were asking me about the influences on my work: fundamentally, I'm a commonsense Kantian, and at the same time, perhaps, a born structuralist. . . . Even [in my early childhood] I was looking for invariants! (1991:107–108)

D.E.: What have you retained from Kant?

C.L.-S.: That the mind has its constraints, which it imposes on an ever-impenetrable reality, and it reaches this reality only through them. (1991:108)

D.E.: Basically, your researach method in the Mythology series is rather close to that of Dumézil: to define a geographical area and try to find the same mental structures within it. However, there is a fundamental difference; he had an important historical sequence at his disposal, while you, when you analyze the American myths, cannot find their historical depth.

C.L.-S.: I don't need to tell you how much I owe to the work of Dumézil. I learned a great deal and found much encouragement there. But the difference you mentioned is not the only one. Dumézil and I have different goals. He wished to prove that a system of representations, whose presence had been noted in several parts of Asia and Europe, had a common source. For me, on the contrary, the historical and geographical unity was there from the first: America, peopled by successive waves of immigrants who generally all had the same origin and whose entry into the New World took place, according to different authorities, between 70,000 and 5,000 B.P. [i.e. Before Present]. So I was looking for something else: first of all, to account for the differences between the mythologies whose unity was given by history; and second, starting with an individual case, to understand the mechanisms of mythic thought. (1991:131–32)

C.L.-S.: Wagner played a capital role in my intellectual development and in my taste for myths. . . . Not only did Wagner build his operas on myths, but he proposed a way of analyzing them that can be clearly seen in the use of the leitmotiv. The leitmotiv prefigures the mytheme. Moreover, the counterpoint of leitmotivs and poetry achieves a kind of structural analysis, since it works by shifts or displacements to superimpose moments of the plot that otherwise would follow each other in a linear sequence. Sometimes the leitmotiv, which is musical, coincides with the poem, which is literary; sometimes the leitmotiv recalls an episode that has a structural relationship to the happening at the time, either by analogy or contrast. I only understood that later on, well after I began my analysis of myths, and at a time when I believed myself completely cut off from the spell of Wagnerism. Let's say that I was brooding on Wagner for several decades. (1991:176)

D.E.: At the end of the *Jealous Potter* you write that myth is a "magnifying mirror" of the way we habitually think. Is that the issue that guided you through this long series of books?

C.L.-S.: The issue is the same as the one in *Elementary Structures of Kinship*, except that instead of treating sociological facts it deals with religious facts. But the question doesn't change; in the presence of chaos of social practices or religious representations, will we continue to seek partial explanations, different for each case? Or will we try to discover an underlying order, a deep structure whose effect will permit us to account for this apparent diversity and, in a word, to overcome this incoherence? (1991:141)

29

The Politics of Ethnicity[*]

STANLEY J. TAMBIAH

A somber reality and disillusionment of our epoch, which emerged from the ashes of the Second World War, is that although there have been successes in the push toward development and modernization, eradication of disease and the spread of literacy, economic and political development programs have generated and stimulated, whether by collusion or in reaction, in good faith and poor anticipation, massive civil war and gruesome interracial and interethnic bloodshed. The same epoch has witnessed the rise of repressive authoritarianism in both military and democratic guises, fortified by Western weaponry, and inflamed by populist slogans and fundamentalist doctrines, and assisted by a flagrant manipulation of mass media which have vastly expanded their reach.

The optimism of sociologists, political scientists, and anthropologists who naively foretold the impending onset of the "integrative revolution" and inevitable decline of "primordial loyalties" such as kinship, caste, and ethnicity in third world countries has by now waned and dimmed with disenchantment. The introduction of constitutions and democratic institutions, enshrining human rights, universal franchise, the party system, elected legislature, majority rule, and so on, has often resulted in strange malformations that are far removed from the goals of liberty, justice, tolerance, and freedom that were the ideological supports of Western European and North American "liberal-democratic" syntheses. Something has gone gravely awry with the center-periphery relations throughout the world, and a manifestation of this malaise is the occurrence of widespread ethnic conflict accompanied in many instances by collective violence amongst people who are not aliens but enemies intimately known.[1]

ETHNICITY AND ETHNIC IDENTITY

Ethnic identity above all is a collective identity: we are self-proclaimed Sinhalese, Malays, Ibos, Thais, and so on. It is a self-conscious and vocalized identity that substantializes and naturalizes one or more attributes—the usual ones being skin color, language, religion, territorial occupation—and attaches them to collectivities as their innate possession and their mytho-historical legacy. The central components in this description of identity are ideas of inheritance, ancestry and descent, place or territory of origin, and the sharing of kinship, any one or combination of which may be invoked as a claim according to context and calculation of advantages. These ethnic collectivities are believed to be bounded and to be self-producing and enduring through time.

Although the actors themselves, invoking these claims, speak as if ethnic boundaries are

---

[*]Reprinted, in edited form, from *American Ethnologist*, 1989, 16(2):335–349, by permission of the American Anthropological Society.

clear-cut and defined for all time, and think of ethnic collectivities as self-reproducing bounded groups, it is also clear that from a dynamic and processual perspective there are many precedents for "passing" and the change of identity, for incorporations and assimilations of new members, and for changing the scale and criteria of collective identity. Ethnic labels are in application porous.

Ethnic groups, especially in contemporary times of widespread ethnic conflict, seem to be intermediate between local kinship groupings (such as lineages, clans, kindreds, and so on) and the nation as a maximal collectivity. Moreover, especially marked in the modern context, and within that context conspicuous in many third world societies, is the mounting awareness that ethnic affiliation and ethnic identity are overriding other social cleavages and superseding other bases of differentiation to become the master principle and the major identity for purposes of sociopolitical action. This state of affairs therefore raises the possibility that ethnicity (projected upon the old bases of identity in terms of language, "race," religion, place of origin) as a basis for mobilization for political action has challenged and is challenging the primacy for such mobilization of social class on the one hand and nation-state on the other. Therefore, in a general analysis two relevant issues that need to be addressed are: to what extent and in what way ethnicity modifies, incorporates, or even replaces class conflict as a major paradigm for interpreting social conflict and change; and also in what manner ethnicity has impacted on the aims and activities of nation-making and national integration, which were taken to be the principal tasks of the newly founded third world nation-states. I cannot in this essay take up the matter of class, but will have something to say on the second issue.

The Ubiquity of Ethnic Conflict

There is no denying of course that linguistic, national, religious, tribal, racial (and other)

divisions and identifications, and competitions and conflicts based on them, are old phenomena, yet the recent salience of the term ethnicity "reflects a new reality and a new usage reflects a change in that reality" (Glazer and Moynihan 1975:5) on a global scale in the latter half of the twentieth century, both in the industrialized first world and the "developing" third world.

It seems that the sudden resurgence of the term ethnicity in the social science literature of the 1960s and early 1970s took place not only to describe certain manifestations in the third world, but also in reaction to the emergence of ethnic movements in the industrialized and affluent world, especially in the United States, in Canada, and in Western Europe. (See, for example, Connor 1972, 1973; Esman 1977.)

The late-twentieth-century reality is evidenced by the fact that ethnic groups, rather than being mostly minority or marginal subgroups at the edges of society, expected in due course to assimilate or weaken, have figured as major "political" elements and major political collective actors in several societies. Moreover, if in the past we typically viewed an ethnic group as a subgroup of a larger society, today we are also faced with instances of majority ethnic groups within a polity or nation exercising preferential or "affirmative" policies on the basis of that majority status.

The first consideration that confirms ethnic conflict as a major reality of our time is not simply its ubiquity alone, but also its cumulative increase in frequency and intensity of occurrence. Consider these conflicts, by no means an exhaustive listing, that have occurred since the sixties (some of them have a longer history, of course):[2] conflicts between anglophone and francophone in Canada; Catholic and Protestant in Northern Ireland; Walloon and Fleming in Belgium; Chinese and Malay in Malaysia; Greek and Turk in Cyprus; Jews and other minorities on the one hand and Great Russians on the other in the Soviet Union; and Ibo and Hausa and Yoruba in Nigeria; the East Indians and Creoles in Guyana. Add, to these instances, upheavals that became climactic in recent years: the Sinhala-Tamil war in Sri Lanka, the Sikh-Hindu, and Muslim-Hindu, confrontations in India, the Chackma-Muslim turmoil in Bangladesh, the actions of the Fijians against Indians in Fiji, the Pathan-Bihari clashes in Pakistan, and last, but not least, the inferno in Lebanon, and the serious erosion of human rights currently manifest in Israeli actions in Gaza and the West Bank. That there is possibly no end to these eruptions, and that they are worldwide has been forcibly brought to our attention by a century-old difference that exploded in March 1988 between Christian Armenians and Muslim Azerbaijanis in the former U.S.S.R.

Most of these conflicts have involved force and violence, homicide, arson, and destruction of property. Civilian riots have evoked action by security forces: sometimes as counteraction to quell them, sometimes in collusion with the civilian aggressors, sometimes both kinds of action in sequence. Events of this nature have happened in Sri Lanka, Malaysia, India, Zaire, Guyana, and Nigeria. Mass killings of civilians by armed forces have occurred in Uganda and in Guatemala, and large losses of civilian lives have been recorded in Indonesia, Pakistan, India, and Sri Lanka.[3]

The escalation of ethnic conflicts has been considerably aided by the amoral business of gunrunning and free trade in the technology of violence, which enable not only dissident groups to successfully resist the armed forces of the state, but also civilians to battle with each other with lethal weapons. The classical definition of the state as the authority invested with the monopoly of force has become a sick joke. After so many successful liberations and resistance movements in many parts of the globe, the techniques of guerrilla resistance now constitute a systematized and exportable knowledge. Furthermore, the easy access to the technology of warfare by groups in countries that are otherwise deemed low in

literacy and in economic development—we have seen what Afghan resistance can do with American guns—is paralleled by another kind of international fraternization among resistance groups who have little in common save their resistance to the status quo in their own countries, and who exchange knowledge of guerrilla tactics and the art of resistance. Militant groups in Japan, Germany, Lebanon, Libya, Sri Lanka, and India have international networks of collaboration, not unlike—perhaps more solidary than—the diplomatic channels that exist between mutually wary sovereign countries and the great powers. The end result is that professionalized killing is no longer the monopoly of state armies and police forces. The internationalization of the technology of destruction, evidenced in the form of terrorism and counterterrorism, has shown a face of free-market capitalism in action unsuspected by Adam Smith and by Immanuel Wallerstein.

The revolution in the media, their instant transmission of visual images and auditory messages, linking metropolitan centers and distant places, and their wide coverage of events, such that news broadcasts (whether by NBC, CBS, or ABC) present diverse events occurring at diverse places as a single synchronic and simultaneously occurring reality. These communication processes bind us in a synchronicity of fellow witnesses of world events. We come to feel that the worldwide incidents of ethnic conflict are of the same order and are mutually implicated: the strife in Northern Ireland; the kidnappings in Lebanon; the beatings on the West Bank of Israel; the bombings in Germany; the killing of civilians in Sri Lanka; the riot against the Sikhs in Delhi; the massing of Korean youth against a rightist government; the attacks on the "bush negroes" by the townsmen of Suriname; the sniping by the Contras in Nicaragua; the explosive tensions between Armenians and Azerbaijanis—all belong to a contemporary world suffused by violence. The internationalization of violence and the simultaneity of its occurrences viewed on our TV screens make us all vicarious spectators and participants responding with our sympathies and our prejudices.

ETHNIC DISTRIBUTIONS IN CONTEMPORARY PLURAL SOCIETIES

A distributional chart indicating the number of ethnic groups and their demographic proportions in various contemporary countries will be useful for appreciating the ubiquity of ethnic conflicts. Among other things, these distributions crucially affect not only the processes that produce conflict but also the strategies and efficacy of coalitions that are made in plural societies, coalitions ranging from constructive and relatively long-lasting alliances and bargains to temporary and fragile pacts of convenience and opportunism.

The following list constitutes a crude chart that indicates some of the demographic combinations that affect the course of ethnic politics.

1. Countries that are virtually homogeneous in ethnic composition (with 90 to 100 percent being ethnically the same): Japan, Korea, Bangladesh.

2. Countries that have a single overwhelmingly dominant ethnic majority that constitutes 75 to 89 percent of the population: Bhutan, Burma, Cambodia, Taiwan, Vietnam, Turkey.

3. Countries where the largest ethnic group makes up 50 to 75 percent of the population and where there are several "minority" groups: Thailand, Sri Lanka, Laos, Iran, Afghanistan, Pakistan, Singapore, and (probably) Nepal.

4. Countries where there are two large dominant groups of roughly the same size (with or without small minority enclaves in their midst): Malaysia (where the Malays make up about 44 percent and the Chinese about 36 percent); Guyana (East Indians, the larger group, making up 50 percent, and the Creoles); Fiji (Fijians and Indians are nearly of the same size); Guatemala (where the Ladinos and Indians are about equal size).

5. Our last category consists of the truly pluralistic countries composed of many ethnic groups where no one or two of them are dominant, and where not all groups may be actively implicated in ethnic politics. Examples here are Nigeria (with Ibo, Yoruba, Hausa, and Fulani being the major entities) and countries such as Indonesia, the Philippines, and India, whose populations are more varied. However, within these complex societies, internal ethnic politics may take dualistic form within regions, as in the case of Sikhs versus Hindus in Punjab, and indigenous "hill tribes" versus Bengalis in Mizoram (India), and Christians versus Moros in the Philippines.

We may include the former U.S.S.R. in the last category. The former U.S.S.R. had more than 100 distinct nationalities and ethnic groups living in 15 republics, and ethnic tensions in these republics today are best viewed in regional terms.

Horowitz (1985:30-35) has underscored an important distinction that affects the nature and dynamics of ethnic conflict, namely whether the groups in question are ranked (in some sort of hierarchy or stratified scheme informed by asymmetrical valuations) or unranked or parallel groups divided by vertical cleavages.

Some examples of ranked ethnic groups within societies are Rwanda (especially in 1959), Zanzibar (in 1966), and, more debatably, Ethiopia and Liberia. However, by far the most salient category for a comparative study is the countries containing by and large unranked ethnic groups, such as Malays and Chinese in Malaysia; Sinhalese and Tamils in Sri Lanka; East Indians and Creoles in Guyana;

lbo, Hausa, Fulani, and Yoruba in Nigeria; Christian Filipino and Moro in the Philippines; and the Thais and Muslims in Thailand.[4]

As Tagil has put it, the main problem to be explained is "why ethnicity becomes more easily politicizable in modern society and in those societies on the threshold of modernization, as compared with earlier phases of history" (Tagil 1984:36). The present context of politicized ethnicity is distinctly a marked phase in the political and economic history of newly independent countries. If we take the colonial legacy as our point of departure it is possible to identify roughly three sequential and overlapping phases.

THE COLONIAL LEGACY

Let us begin with the colonial experience itself, the British raj in India, Sri Lanka, Burma, Malaya, the Dutch rule in the Dutch East Indies, the French in Algeria, Indochina, and so on. The colonial experience was of course many-faceted and complex, but for our theme of ethnic conflict the following features of the colonial legacy are relevant.

The colonial powers more often than not aggregated people and territory into larger polities than existed before, sometimes arbitrarily so, at other times by attempting to follow social and demographic constellations on the ground. The whole process was further compounded by geopolitical competition between imperial powers in laying claim to their own territories. India, despite Emperor Asoka and the Mughal Empire, reached its maximal aggregation under British rule; so did Sri Lanka, Malaya, Burma, Nigeria, Kenya, and so on. The Dutch control of Java and Sumatra and the other islands was likewise a unification never known before.

The internal policies of the colonial powers in complex ways both consolidated existing differences and stimulated bodies of people, primarily socially separated, to interact in common areas. While colonial powers, like the British, codified "regional," "tribal," "caste," or "communal" bodies of customs relating to marriage, inheritance, religious practices, and so on, for the most part not interfering with these sociocultural differences, they also introduced and standardized colony-wide commercial and criminal law codes and regulations. This standardizing and homogenizing process went hand in hand with imperial economic policies and ventures, which brought the colonies in their own dependent manner into the orbit of world capitalism. The policies related to taxation and preferential trade, and the ventures took the form of plantations, or business firms (agency houses), which in turn stimulated occupations such as those practiced by lawyers, engineers, doctors (in Western medicine), accountants, and so on.

These particularizing and standardizing policies were a double-edged sword, used in the interest both of development and progress and of divide and rule. They produced in diverse tropical colonial contexts from the Netherland Indies to Jamaica varieties of "plural societies" that became the subject of analysis from J. S. Furnivall to M. G. Smith.[5] Of the process of the enlargement of territorial horizons and subgroup amalgamations that took place in Asia and Africa in the colonial period, Donald Horowitz has remarked in his recent comprehensive and impressive work, *Ethnic Groups in Conflict:*

The colonists often created territories out of clusters of loosely linked villages and regions. . . . Out of the welding together of local environments a great many new groups appeared, among them the Malays in Malaysia, the Ibo in Nigeria, the Kikuyu in Kenya, the Bangala in Zaire, and the Moro in the Philippines. Some such groups were "artificial" creations of colonial authorities and missionaries, who catalyzed the slow merger of related peoples into coherent entities. (1985:66-67)

It is interesting that the Malays for example, who vociferously claim to be *bhumiputra*, "the sons of the soil," are the outcome of a coalescence not only of a major component from Malaya but also of various groups from as far afield as Sumatra, the Celebes, Borneo, and Java. The claim itself is a highly emotive and embracing identity developed vis-à-vis the large numbers of Chinese immigrants who found their way into their midst (see also Nagata 1979).

THE THREE PHASES OF THE ERA OF INDEPENDENCE

I would like to delineate three phases in the political history of a number of third world countries like India, Sri Lanka, Malaysia, Guyana, and Nigeria, which received their independence soon after the end of the Second World War. The characteristic issues of each phase are stated in terms of the ideological rhetoric and distinctive labels used by politicians and academic commentators alike. (I do not intend these phases to be taken as discontinuous shifts but merely as showing different emphases.)

1. The first stage is the actual "decolonization" process itself, when Western imperial powers, following the Second World War, "transferred power" to local elite groups. While the whole colonial period created certain dislocations, decolonization itself was preceded and accompanied by violence when, as was the case with Algeria, the colony fought a "war of liberation." In other colonies, such as Sri Lanka and Burma, the transfer of power was more peaceful though not entirely without the staging of civil disobedience movements and other forms of resistance, as, for example, those mounted in India by the Indian National Congress or in Malaya by the Chinese communist guerrillas.

2. The second phase, spanning the late 1950s and gathering momentum in the 1960s, was characterized by optimistic and even strident claims made in these newly independent countries concerning their objectives of "nation making," strengthening "national sovereignty," creating "national culture" and "national identity," and achieving "national integration." The slogans of the time accented "national" dimensions, and in doing so played down and wished away internal diversity and social cleavages in favor of the primacy of nation-states as the accredited units of the United Nations and the modern world system.

This phase of optimistic nation building was enacted as the work of "national coalition governments," examples of which were Nehru presiding over a monolithic Congress Party; Cheddi Jagan, an East Asian, and L. F. S. Burnham, a Creole, in the early 1950s heading the People's Progressive party in Guyana; Tengku Abdul Rahman presiding over the Malaysian Alliance, again in the 1950s, and D. S. Senanayake at the same time over the United National Party in Ceylon. Political parties seemed willing to collaborate rather than emphasize their separate interests and their special constituencies.

This phase was also marked by confident expectations of expanding economic horizons, instanced by faith in economic planning and growth, and the spawning of "five-year plans" funded by foreign aid, whose smooth flow it was hoped would make the world safe for capitalism and democracy.

3. In a dislocating and sometimes disconcerting manner this hopeful expansive phase of nation building has been put to the test, seriously questioned, imperiled, and even reversed in the third phase, from the 1960s onward, by the eruption of ethnic conflict. The divisiveness has revolved around issues of language, race, religion, and territory. Accordingly, there has been a shift again in slogans and concepts. "Ethnic groups" and "ethnic conflict" are the salient labels for talking about these events. The terms "plural society," "devolution of powers," "traditional homelands," "self-determination"—old words

given new force and urgency—have begun to frame the political debate and academic analyses. The central political authority, the state, which in the previous phase of nation building and economic growth was designated as the prime actor and central intelligence in initiating, directing, and controlling the country's future and historical trajectory, is now, after years of escalating ethnic divisiveness and pluralistic awareness, counseled to be a "referee" adjudicating differences and enabling regional cultures and societies to attain their "authentic" identities and interests.

THE POLITICS OF ETHNICITY

A part of the answer to the story of the politicization of ethnicity lies in our tracking of the manner in which large numbers of people in the new polities have become, or been made to become, conscious of ethnic identity, and how in turn they have been energized as collectivities to engage in political action. The awareness that collective ethnic identity can be used and manipulated in political action is of course related to the increasing possibilities of contact through the improvement of transport, of the quick adoption and deployment of modern media, and of the raised levels of education and literacy and the spread of what Benedict Anderson (1983) has called "print capitalism." Another explanation lies in the proliferation and popularization of street theaters and public arenas, occasions for collective massing of people, ranging from political rallies and elections and referendums to strikes, demonstrations, sit-ins, and mass protests. All these capabilities for large-scale political action have occurred in tandem with population explosions in third world countries, with the migration of vast numbers of rural peoples to cities and metropolitan centers and to locations where industries or where peasant resettlement schemes have been established. Another significant factor is the proliferation of schools, colleges, and universities,

which have provided sites, just as factories had done in the history of industrial development, for the mobilization and massing of activists for engaging in political action.

One of the settings for the politicization of ethnicity is the evolution of the welfare state in the more advanced industrial economies of the world, and the advent of the socialist state, or states committed to welfare policies, in the "developing" third world. In both contexts the state has become "a crucial and direct arbiter of economic well being, as well as of political status and whatever flows from that" (Glazer and Moynihan 1975:8).

The welfare and socialist states appear to be especially responsive to ethnic claims. Within democratic governmental systems there are many occasions at municipal, regional, and central levels for like-minded ethnic members to mobilize and make claims on behalf of groups, both small enough and conspicuous enough to experience real gain from concessions made.

This "strategic efficacy" (as Glazer and Moynihan put it, 1975:10) of ethnicity in making claims on the resources of the modern state inevitably in turn reinforces and maintains ethnic political machinery—patron/client networks, bossism, and patronage structures— through which affirmative actions or pork-barrel distributions are dispensed. As much or more of the monies earmarked for social services and welfare may end up in the hands of those who dispense them as those who receive them.

While these considerations apply generally, there is a special chain of circumstances that has led third world democracies in particular to enact their politics on the basis of ethnicity. At the time of decolonization in the Caribbean, in many parts of Africa, and in South and Southeast Asia, the grant of independence and the transfer of power were packaged with constitutions that were framed in terms of Western principles of "natural rights," and civil liberties and Western procedures and institutions of "representative government."

These charters from the Western point of view, framed in the secular political language of universal rights and government by representation, conferred on the rural masses and the migrants to fast-forming cities a massive dose of rights, and the opportunity for involvement in the political process (to a degree not previously experienced). Quickly transformed from a "passive" existence into political actors and voting banks, with the power to elect politicians and vote parties to power, they discovered that they could even demand or extort rewards, reforms, and privileges from their elected parties who constituted for a while the "central" political authority.

Ethnic Groups As Key Political Actors

But increasingly it became clear that the alleged secular constitution and institutions of representative government predicated on the individual rights of citizens, and the willingness of "one-man-one-vote" citizens to form parties on the basis of competitive interests, did not generate the expected outcomes. Instead, collectivities, which we may call ethnic groups, have become the political actors, seeking affirmative action for the achievement or restoration of privileges and life chances in the name of ethnic (or racial) equalization. Ethnic equalization rather than freedom and equality of the individual is the principal charter of participatory democracy in many of the plural and multiethnic societies of our time. It has been the experience in India, Sri Lanka, and Malaysia that once political demands are made on the basis of ethnic affiliation for the distribution of economic rewards, occupational positions, and educational privileges, the norm of "equality of opportunity" is progressively and irreversibly displaced by the norm of "equality of result."[6] It is commonly the case that affirmative action and quota allocations on the basis of depressed or backward status do not speedily produce results through the ladder of equality of opportunity and increased access to schools and educational institutions. Thus, in time disadvantaged groups push toward equality of results, by fiat if necessary, and for direct redistributive policies in order to equalize income, living conditions, and such on a group basis. But equality of result, or redistributive politics, are essentially "zero-sum" games, in which there are distinct losers and winners. And inevitably these invidious outcomes lead to more open political competition and conflict. Finally, as a result of the revolution in rising expectations, the more successful constituencies are in achieving their political rights to vote, to elect parliaments, to wield the stick of accountability, the more assiduously will they advocate the enjoyment of social rights—such as the right to a job, adequate health care, unemployment insurance, and so on—as entitlements from the state.

The equalization on a group basis of opportunities and rewards in the expanding universe of redistributive politics may equally be the slogans of majorities or minorities in a plural society. The language of claims is best described as that of ethnic group entitlements on the basis of relative comparison and relative deprivation. The entitlement claims of rewards equalization are contentiously sought through a privileged use of one language, or the additional use of a language so far excluded, or the imposition of special quotas providing privileged access to higher education, job opportunities, and business entrepreneurship. The "zero-sum" atmosphere of these quintessential entitlement claims reflects a restrictive worldview that has surfaced with a vehemence precisely at a time when certain expansionary and massive movements of people to urban places and to peasant resettlement schemes have and are taking place, and when mass educational and literacy programs are being implemented. The futuristic exhortation that a national effort of productive expansion, which increases the opportunities and rewards for all, will obviate or mitigate the need for ethnic quotas falls on deaf ears, partly because employment and income levels rise only slowly, and income distribution disparities continue to persist, and because distributive equality on ethnic lines is a politically rousing demand that promises rapid material results.

For purposes of systematic discussion the different scenarios and trajectories pertaining to ethnic conflict should be brought within the ambit of an interpretive framework[7] that addresses questions of how ethnic groups in an arena see themselves as acquiring, maintaining, and protecting their claimed-to-be-legitimate group entitlements (1) to capacities and "symbolic capital" such as education and occupation, (2) to material rewards such as incomes and commodities, and sumptuary privileges that enable distinct styles of life, and (3) to "honors" such as titles and offices, markers of ethnic or national pride, and religious and linguistic precedence and esteem. These honors are accorded by the state and/or other authorities who are the principal arbiters of rank. The quests for group worth, group honor, group equivalization, and so on are central foci in the politics of ethnicity, and are a critical ingredient in the spirals of intense sentiments and explosive violence that ensue.

Three Overlapping Scenarios

I can envisage three overlapping scenarios which, although they are parts of a larger mural, can be presented as posing different issues and different outcomes. They cover a fair range of major ethnic conflicts occurring in recent times:

1. Especially applicable to the political economies of colonial countries under British or Dutch rule in West Africa, East Africa, the Caribbean, Indonesia, and so on is the picture of a plural society that Furnivall and Boeke among others sought to characterize. In these societies certain ethnic groups may occupy special economic and social niches as merchants and traders (Lebanese and Syrians in West Africa, Indians in Uganda, Chinese in Malaya and Indonesia, Indians in Fiji), as

plantation labor (indentured Indian labor in Guyana or Sri Lanka), or as "bankers" and financiers (Nattukottai Chettiars in Burma and Ceylon). Again, especially in colonial capitals, there could be more complex mosaics: certain trades, certain crafts, certain local "banking" and credit activities being the monopoly of both indigenous and foreign communities. The occupation of niches and specialization in certain activities tend to create a segmented labor market, and militate against social class solidarities that cut across ethnic lines. Ethnic division of labor stunts working-class action and middle-class associational links.

Such a colonial heritage tends to crystallize expectations of "entitlements" as collective ethnic privileges. The colonial rulers helped to create these political maps when they distributed status honors, according to their calculations of which groups should be rewarded, protected, or encouraged. But these ethnic specializations and expectations, having persisted into the era of independence, have tended to generate ethnic conflicts when certain strains develop to imperil the maintenance of boundaries. One such strain occurs when the importation of a category of manufactured goods from the industrial West threatens a local craft or makes a local service group redundant and dispensable. A fall in fortunes may threaten the group's ability to have access to the basic consumption goods of everyday life, and it may therefore face famine in a market of plenty and a depression in status in a political climate of expanding "development." But the most severe erosion of niche equilibrium has come from those governments of the new states that have tried to open up what they consider to be the privileged monopolies of ethnic enclaves, which are accused of restrictive practices as regards recruitment and provision of services. The dispossession of Natukkottai Chettiars in Rangoon, and the expulsions of Indian merchants from Uganda, are examples of the new civilian authorities invading what they consider to be rich preserves to enrich themselves and their civilian supporters. Foreign specialized minorities are thus vulnerable to the policies of forcible ejection and/or dispossession by governments promoting the interests of "indigenous" majorities.

2. The second scenario relates not so much to the declining fortunes of well-placed communities, but to the rising expectations and capacities of satellite minorities on the periphery who find themselves under the domination of majorities entrenched at the center, and sometimes are in addition faced with the majority advancing into their frontier "homelands." In Burma, Thailand, Laos, and northeast India, a shorthand phrasing of this collision is "hills people" or "hill tribes" versus the "valley people." This bifurcation carries other contrasts in agricultural styles (sedentary versus slash-and-burn), in written versus oral languages, espousal of Hinduism or Buddhism versus the religion of spirit cults. Sometimes these satellite communities have sought advance through the ministrations of Christian missionaries, and in any case, in the new post-independence polities, they have requested "affirmative action," proportionate to their demographic numbers, with regard to their participation in the task of nation-state making and in the education programs of the dominant centers. These satellite ethnic/tribal minorities tend to be potential secessionists, and as Horowitz puts it, "The largest number of secessionists can be characterized as backward groups in backward regions" (Horowitz 1985: 36). Examples are Karens and Shans in Northern Burma, Muslims (Moros) in the Philippines, the Nagas and Mizos in India, and the Kurds in Iraq.

3. The third scenario represents the kind of ethnic conflict and tensions with which I am especially concerned in this essay. I have adapted some concepts coined by M. G. Smith (1969a, 1969b) in order to characterize them. Smith has discussed how processes of "differential incorporation" lead to the outcome of "structural pluralism." Plural societies manifest differential incorporation within the larger polity when certain collectivities within it are subject to sectionally unequal distributions of legal, political, educational, and occupational rights and are thus reduced to a subordinate status.

The "second-class citizenship" of a social category identified by common disabilities and disqualifications, whether racial, religious, economic, or other grounds is merely one common mode of differential incorporation. Communal rolls, restrictive property franchises, and similar arrangements also express and maintain the differential incorporation of specific collectivities within a wider society. Such mechanisms are generally developed to enhance the power of the ruling section. (Smith 1969a:430)

South Africa and Guatemala are extreme and notorious cases of asymmetrical incorporation, but there are more benign forms; the Malays, the Sinhalese in Sri Lanka, are current examples of the majoritarian claims to "affirmative action" defended on demographic strength and legitimated by mytho-historical sons-of-the-soil claims. These claims lead inevitably to structural asymmetrical pluralism and are inevitably resisted by the minorities. An instructive example of this special pleading on behalf of a majority in place is Prime Minister Mahathir bin Mohamad's political tract, *The Malay Dilemma* (1970).

Such attempts to subordinate previously unranked and equal groups who wield considerable capacities and skills, and to incorporate them unequally in the polity as inferior citizens, invite retaliations and counteractions. Alert to the threats of discrimination and subordination, and in the first instance fighting for inclusion within the polity on equal terms, they may gradually as their situation worsens—as has happened in Sri Lanka—gravitate toward the politics of devolution, and even secession. Horowitz aptly phrases the options thus: "Unlike ranked groups, which form part of a single society, unranked groups constitute incipient whole societies" (1985:31).

Ethnic conflicts manifest and constitute a dialectic. On the one hand there is a universalizing and homogenizing trend that is making people in contemporary societies and countries more and more alike (whatever the actual fact of differential access to capacities, commodities, and honors) in wanting the same material and social benefits of modernization, whether they be income, material goods, housing, literacy and schooling, jobs, recreation, and social prestige. On the other hand these same people also claim to be different, and not necessarily equal, on the basis of their ascriptive identity, linguistic difference, ethnic membership, and rights to the soil. In this latter incarnation, they claim that these differences, and not those of technical competence or achievement, should be the basis for the distribution of modern benefits and rewards. These compose the particularizing and separating trend among the populations of modern polities.

Moreover, in modern political arenas the appeal to old affiliations and distinctions enables a mobilization of people on a scale never known or possible before, partly by the use of modern media of communication and propaganda, by the transmission through printed textbooks of tendentious ideas in proliferating schools, and by the release of energies, both creative and destructive, at levels never before achieved, for deployment in elections and in mass activities. These developments are not merely old wine in new bottles, or new wine in old bottles, for there are more potent transformative processes at work by which old categories and definitions of ethnic identity and interests are revalued and given new dimensions and contours. For example, for all their appeal to old labels and historical claims, the Sinhalese, the Malays, the Fijians in their present manifestations, are collectivities formed in the late colonial and postcolonial epochs. Their ethnic labels and boundaries are porous and flexible indeed. At the same time we witness the new values of modernization and progress—industrial employment, profes-

sional skills, or the practice of Western medicine—being *recategorized* as entitlements and sumptuary privileges indexed as quotas assignable to preexisting ethnic or racial or indigenous groupings. The time of becoming the same is also the time of claiming to be different. The time of modernizing is also the time of inventing tradition as well as traditionalizing innovations; of revaluing old categories and recategorizing new values; of bureaucratic benevolence and bureaucratic resort to force; of participatory democracy and dissident civil war. The time is not simply one of order, or disorder, or antiorder: it is compounded of all three. Ubiquitous and violent ethnic conflict is one of the marks of these intense times through which we are living and which we can see only darkly through the looking glass. These violent and ubiquitous explosions challenge and strain our conventional social science explanations of order, disorder, and conflict. However inadequately, we must cope with the phenomenon of destructive violence that accompanies ethnic conflict today.

NOTES

1. My book *Sri Lanka: Ethnic Fratricide and the Dismantling of Democracy* (1986) attempted to grapple with this problem in my own country. In this essay I hope to address some general issues.

2. These instances occurring in Europe have a longer history, and they continue today; the protests of Basques in Spain, the Croats in Yugoslavia; other ethnic minority struggles in Eastern Europe; the rivalries between Flemings and Walloons in Belgium; and the increasingly bitter conflict in Northern Ireland. Some scholars would include the struggles of the blacks against the white discrimination in the United States and in South Africa as falling within the ambit of ethnic conflict.

3. There are many listings of ethnic conflict as a worldwide phenomenon. For example, see Tagil 1984 and Horowitz 1985.

4. There are in some of these countries, hill tribe or "aboriginal" minorities in Thailand, Malaysia, Philippines which are considered "inferior" in status to the

dominant communities that try to inflict on them certain policies detrimental to their survival.

5. In his *Colonial Policy and Practice* (1948:304-305), Furnival defined plural society as consisting of "different sections of the community living side by side, but separately, within the same political unit. . . . Each group holds by its own religion, its own culture and language, its own ideas and ways. As individuals they meet, but only in the market place, in buying and selling. Even in the economic sphere there is division of labour along racial lines. Natives, Chinese, Indians and Europeans have all different functions, and within each group, subsections have particular occupations." For a sample of Furnival and Smith's views see Furnival 1939,1948; Smith 1969a, 1969b.

6. These expressions are from Bell 1975:146-147.

7. This proposal combines concepts taken from the writings of Amartya Sen, Pierre Bourdieu, and Donald L. Horowitz.

INTELLECTUAL ROOTS

Stanley J. Tambiah is Professor of Anthropology at Harvard University, where he has taught since 1976. He began his fieldwork in Sri Lanka (1956-1959), the island of his birth, and then since 1960 has concentrated on Thailand, about which country he has written three monographs. Recently, since 1983, he has revived his interest in Sri Lanka, whose disastrous ethnic conflict has engaged him. He is the author of the following books: *Buddhism and the Spirit Cults in Northeast Thailand* (1970), *World Conqueror and World Renouncer: A Study of Religion and Polity in Thailand against a Historical Background* (1976), *The Buddhist Saints of the Forest and the Cults of Amulets: A Study of Charisma, Hagiography, Sectarianism and Millennial Buddhism* (1984), *Culture, Thought and Social Action* (1985), *Sri Lanka: Ethnic Fratricide and the Dismantling of Democracy* (1986), and *Magic, Science, Religion and the Scope of Rationality* (1990). A book entitled *Buddhism Betrayed? Religion, Politics and Violence in Sri Lanka* appeared in the spring of 1992. He served as the president of the Association for Asian Studies (1989-1990), and is a fellow of the American Academy of Arts and Sciences.

My research and writing has in areal terms primarily related to South and Southeast Asia, and, in substantive and theoretical terms, touched on: (1) kinship and marriage transactions, (2) schemes of classification and their social uses, (3) communicative and performative features of ritual, and (4) the interrelations among religion, politics, and society both historically and in recent times. My current work on ethnic identity, ethnic conflict, and collective violence, though primarily focused on South Asia, necessarily takes into account the momentous developments taking place in Eastern Europe and the former U.S.S.R.

My graduate studies were conducted at Cornell University (1952-1954) in what was then a joint department of sociology and anthropology. Especially under the tutelage of Robin Williams, Jr., who was himself a student of Talcott Parsons at Harvard, I was introduced to the writings of major social theorists, especially Max Weber, whose comparativist studies and theorizing on the major "world religions," systems of authority including charisma and the routinization of charisma, forms of rationality, and processes of historical change have had a major and enduring bearing on my own formulations. A close study of Durkheim's major writings was also an absorbing pursuit. On the anthropological side, aside from reading extensively ethnographic texts on South and Southeast Asia, I became familiar with the work of Robert Redfield, whose discussions of peasant societies, the folk-urban continuum, and primary and secondary civilizations were relevant to my own concern with processes of change in a variety of Sri Lankan rural communities. Morris Opler, Bryce Ryan, Lauriston Sharp, and Peter Blau were some of my other instructors at Cornell.

After completing my graduate studies I returned to Sri Lanka to teach for a few years, and then in 1960 I went to Thailand to engage in teaching and research under the auspices of UNESCO. In 1963, I went to Cambridge University in England, and became closely associated with Meyer Fortes, Edmund Leach, and Jack Goody. At Cambridge I acquired a detailed knowledge of their theoretical cum ethnographic contributions to the study of kinship, politics and social organizations and became familiar with a range of studies subsumed under the gross label "British structural-functionalism," for example, the work of Malinowski, Radcliffe-Brown, Evans-Pritchard, Audrey Richards, Max Gluckman, and Victor Turner. But my most important colleague, friend, and "mentor" at Cambridge was Edmund Leach, whose developing interests in "structuralism," structural linguistics, semiotics, and classification, and whose adaptation of the contributions of Roman Jakobson and Claude Lévi-Strauss, positively stimulated me. My first monograph on Thailand and many of my essays in *Culture, Thought and Social Action* bear witness to Leach's influence, though at the same time I was discovering on my own the possibilities of Austinian linguistic philosophy for a performative theory of ritual.

While at Cambridge I had also begun a new phase of fieldwork in Thailand, complemented by library study, on the relation between Theravada Buddhism, kingship, and polity—both historically and in contemporary times. I left England in 1973 for the United States to join the Department of Anthropology at the University of Chicago. There my many-stranded interests in comparative and historical studies, in the dialectical relation between religions, politics, and society, and in the branches of semiotics (including the theories of Charles Peirce) were further clarified and extended by association with Marshall Sahlins, Michael Silverstein, Frank Reynolds (of the Divinity School), and several other colleagues.

In 1976 I moved to Harvard, and have continued to pursue and enlarge these interests in both ethnographic texts and theoretical writings. But a new concern gripped me when the ethnic conflict in Sri Lanka between the Sinhalese and Tamils reached a crisis stage in 1983. I felt a strong personal need and an intellectual urge to try and grasp that conflict in the full knowledge that I was both a Sri Lankan, by birth a member of the Tamil minority, and an anthropologist. A sustained interest in the ongoing Sri Lankan conflict and the knowledge that similar conflicts were raging in the neighboring countries of India, Pakistan, Bangladesh (and many other parts of the world, including most recently in Eastern Europe) have prompted me to undertake a comparative study of collective violence and civilian riots in South Asia. While all my previous theoretical and substantive interests and knowledge are relevant to the study of ethnic conflict and collective violence, I have the nervous as well as expectant sense that I am entering a domain which is difficult to map and demands a stretching of capacities to conceptualize and interpret.

30

Inventions and Manifestations of Ethno-Nationalism in Soviet Academic and Public Discourse

VALERY A. TISHKOV

People are returning back to a process of self-awareness, to a search for their own roots. And every people—large and small—is God's creation. Nobody should deprive these peoples, especially the smaller ones, of the right to study and understand themselves.
Mikhail Gorbachev (1991)

In this paper, I address certain issues regarding nationalism, using examples from the former Soviet Union—or today what might be termed Soviet (Dis)union—to draw out some larger implications. My concern is with the interrelationships among ethnic nationalism, intellectual discourse, and politics during this century. The paper offers reflections about a still-changing situation. They are not complete. But, hopefully, they will help foster further dialogue between Soviet and Western scholars after what, for many, has been a long and painful hiatus. My comments consider what has recently become a critical problem in many countries throughout the world and has elicited much anthropological discussion. I also ask what steps intellectuals, especially anthropologists, might take in helping to temper some of the worst excesses that have arisen and, in the process, bring forth a better understanding of the complexities involved.

THE INVOLVEMENT OF POLITICS IN THE STUDY OF ETHNO-NATIONALISM

What is striking about the academic study of ethno-nationalism—the entwining of nation-alism with ethnic identity—for Eastern European scholars in recent decades is the degree to which the topic has been wrapped up in political rather than intellectual considerations (if I may make that distinction). Scholars have generally supported the communist regimes which saw fit to proclaim ethnic groupings as "socialist nations." This has especially occurred in the former U.S.S.R (where many major ethnic groupings were granted nation status), Yugoslavia, Czechoslovakia, and in eastern Germany (where "the German socialist nation" was treated as a ethnic entity separate from the rest of Germany). Ethno-nationalism constituted a political category in which Stalin's conception of the ethno-nation—as a group sharing common territory, economic ties, language, and a culturally constituted collective mentality—dominated all conceptions of the subject, inside and outside anthropology.

In spite of recent ideological liberalization, no serious reevaluation or theoretical breakthrough has taken place in post-Soviet social sciences regarding the nationality issue, and the ethnic unrest behind it, even though such tensions helped break up the former Soviet

443

Union. The Soviet concept of ethnicity is still heavily primordialistic. It is based on an academic theory of "ethnos" which overlaps with Marxist-Leninist theory.[1] For decades social scientists in the Soviet Union studied ethnic groups as "ethno-social organisms" (defined by attributes of common territory, language, culture, and identity). An enormous amount of intellectual energy went into the study of ethnogenesis and ethnic history of the Soviet Union's peoples in this regard. Anthropological and historical writings provided dominant groups in particular regions with their own cultural heroes, roots (reaching back even into upper paleolithic times), and sense of pride as "indigenous nations."

This vision of ethnicity was closely tied into the official ideology of ethno-nationalism dominating the Soviet state—a politics in which ethnic groups legitimated their borders and statuses forming administrative units or republics. The scholarly taxonomic classification of "types of ethnic entities" (tribe, "narodnost," and nation)—involving such conceptual categorizations as "ESO" (ethno-social organization) and "ETHNIKOS" (people of the same nationality living outside of their "own" state territories)—justified the administrative statehood granted to what I call titular nationalities (i.e. those which gave titles to republics).[2]

Ethno-nationalism, both as a theoretical paradigm and as political practice, dominated Soviet academic studies. These studies shaped the definitions and arguments of politicians, intellectuals, and the "common man" regarding ethnicity. To a very considerable extent, this Soviet theory constructed certain social realities and enforced particular definitions on political activists as well as on mass public movements.

The complex dialogue between science and praxis was not part of the anthropological research agenda in this country. There was little space, for example, for arguments and explanations regarding less positivistic methodologies one might use in studying ethnic phenomena. Unexpected by most Soviet and Western specialists, the outburst of nationalist sentiments and ethnic conflicts in the Soviet Union put them in a difficult situation. The contemporary situation demonstrated the inadequacy of much of what had been previously published on ethnic issues. These specialists needed to reevaluate previous postulates. What kind of responses were given to these challenges?

Recent academic writings in the West on the ethnic situation in the former Soviet Union seem to possess features related to the political engagements of the scholars involved. For Western writers, most of whom are political scientists, the prevailing approaches are often motivated by a reflex to fight communism and totalitarianism and by a euphoria of liberal victory over the Soviet system. Nationalism, ethnic unrest, and dismembering the Soviet Union are seen as a logical outcome of a long-agonizing, illegitimate empire. They are a manifestation of democratization and the right to self-determination.[3] The main point of dispute within this group is over their own status concerns—who in the past was the first to say this or who was lucky enough to predict the recent course of events. As a result, real ethnographic research is still rather scarce—partly because of existing political limitations and partly because of the apparent lack of interest in it. Ethnographic research on the problem has only dealt with a few groups and these usually are not the most vocal and conflict-ridden cases.[4]

As for the Soviet specialists the major watershed among them runs along two lines which are not theoretical or methodological but, following my point above, political and ethnic. For "periphery" scholars in the republics, ethnocentric interpretations are dominant. These are indirectly controlled by nationalistic forces and power institutions. Any approaches and opinions differing from the publicly accepted unilateral position may be proclaimed as "subversive," expressed by "enemies of the nation" and "agents of the Kremlin.[5] The prevailing themes of their writings are: elaborating lists of grievances against others; justifications for state, territorial, political, and cultural rights of titular nationalities; and a search for external enemies (mainly in Moscow or in neighboring republics) as responsible for ethnic conflicts.[6] Historic-ethnographic in-group descriptions without serious interest in the significance of ethnic interactions, within and outside the region, were and still are the most striking features of this former Soviet "peripheral" anthropology.

Scholarship of the "center" (mainly Moscow and St. Petersburg) is more academically oriented. It is less influenced by personal ethnic sentiments though there are cases of openly expressed pro-Russian concerns or sympathies for the minority and underprivileged groups studied.[7] There are at least two major subgroups within this group which stand methodologically together on the same side of the positivistic, scientific barricades of primordial interpretation of ethnicity. They offer mainly politically motivated explanations for questions of nationality, problems of ethnic conflict, and prospects for the future. One group shares the views of the radical democrats that criticize the policy of the previous regime regarding nationalities. Blame is also focused on conservative communist plots that seek to obstruct the "historically unavoidable move" of each ethnic group to acquire its own statehood as a basis for keeping its culture and identity and for bettering socioeconomic conditions.[8] The other group has a more pro-center, antinationalistic orientation. It questions the ethnic principles of state organization, especially the sudden and uncontrolled process of devolution of power in favor of ethnic elites in the republics. They assert that this has led to violations of individual rights and suppression of minorities which, in turn, have stimulated violent ethnic confrontations.[9]

Both groups explain events in terms of materialistic, economic, and social class analyses; a simplistic, culturally based, "we-they" dichotomy; or particular theories of conflict. Promising new developments in the West remain unexplored by students of Soviet ethnicity—such as postmodernist interpretations of ethnicity as a constructed phenomenon and recent approaches to the origins of ethnic conflicts in terms of social psychology and group behavior. Such approaches are quite often seen as sophisticated masquerades for chauvinistic, undemocratic, empire-saving, and whitewashing approaches to the subject of ethnicity. But the most evident weakness of contemporary Soviet ethnography is its lack of strong empirical research regarding the current "on the ground" situation. Quite often all we have are old-fashioned sociological surveys or enlightened journalism.

THE HISTORICAL CONTEXTS OF ETHNO-NATIONALISM

If we explore the contexts within which ethno-nationalism developed in Europe, especially Eastern Europe, we perceive a pattern. The collapse of absolutist monarchies and colonial empires in Eastern Europe gave people an idea of enormous myth-making and political potential: the nation as a kind of mediating substance through which a civil society acquires the right to sovereignty and delegates political power. This idea encouraged those who aspired to build democratic civil societies to create national movements and sovereign states based on certain culturally dominant elements. These movements became the basis for ethnic (or ethno-) nationalism which treats nations as a form of ethnic grouping. There is a tendency for the national state to become an ethnic state, in this regard, and to accept its ethnicity as the legitimate basis for the functioning of the state, its economy, and cultural institutions.

Ethno-nationalism was extremely popular among European social democrats in the nineteenth and early twentieth centuries. It helped in dismembering the Ottoman and Austro-Hungarian empires as well as in forming a new political map of Eastern Europe after the First World War. Ironically, once Eastern European nationalists had acquired independence for their own nations, they discovered that it was impossible to realize the idea of ethno-nationalism in relation to the nation-state (one ethnic group-one state). The boundaries between new states included minorities who felt endangered by the new dominating groups and their political elites. New national leaders started pursuing toward minorities the same policy of intolerance as they had suffered from the old imperial rulers. Weakened by internal and interstate conflicts, these political entities became an easy prey for the bloody designs of Hitler and Stalin that precipitated World War II.[10]

In the vast multiethnic entity known as the Russian Empire, in place of the unifying idea of the nation, the feudal, eclectic formula of "orthodoxy, autocracy, and rootedness" prevailed until the beginning of the twentieth century. The term *Rossian*, meaning "all-Russian," is derived from the title of the state, and denoted a citizen of the Empire irrespective of ethnic origin.[11] Imperial laws were based on a notion of one nation which included ethnic Russians, Ukrainians, and Byelorussians as well as such peoples as those belonging to the Volga-Urals region (included within the Empire since the sixteenth century). All these subjects acted according to one set of laws and regulations. The peoples of the more recently acquired periphery were treated as *inorodzi* ("aliens") for whom there were special regulations.

The dichotomy between the concepts of "Rossian" and "Russian" emphasizes an important distinction—between imperial state and ethnic group—which has been in existence for a long time in intellectual discourse, including famous prerevolutionary writers and political figures. Outstanding thinkers such as Piotr Struve (1990:247-248)

understood the nation as "a spiritual unity, constructed and supported by a common culture and by a common national identity." The complex, contradictory process of Russian nation building before the Revolution of 1917 included, at the same time, powerful and rapidly growing national identity movements among non-Russian groups of the Empire. By the last decade of the nineteenth century, Georgia's intellectuals, for example, had had considerable input into the making of the Georgian nation and establishing an independent republic in 1918 (see Suny 1988b). The same path was followed by some other major groups on the ethnic periphery of the Russian Empire.

During the Revolution of 1917, in contrast to their political opponents who stood for a "one and undivided" Russia, Lenin and the Bolsheviks used the slogan of the right to self-determination as a tremendously effective political weapon in winning the non-Russian regions to their side. This slogan was not simply a hypocritic political ploy. Rather it involved both a tactical response to existing political realities and a utopian belief in building a new world based on "proletarian and class solidarity." Supported by this assertion, the peoples of Poland, Finland, and the Baltic region successfully established separate states in the early liberal years of Soviet power. (In other locations, however, such as the Caucasus, the Red army resisted such territorial changes.) During the civil war, the policy of the Soviet state on nationalities was often a decisive factor in winning territories under new authorities by granting autonomous status to major non-Russian regions of the Russian republic.

This was done in spite of the fact that nationalism was still little more than an elite credo. It was shared by a set of relatively isolated urban intellectuals and hardly touched the bulk of the ethnic populations of the Russian Empire, made up mostly of peasants who continued to identify either with their region or religion (Suny 1988a). In some regions, such as Central Asia, ethnic identities were so weak and so overshadowed by clan or regional loyalties that it was impossible to give any referent ethnic marker to a new republic or autonomous formation (for example, Turkestan in the Russian Federation, and the Bukharan and Horesmian Republics). In some cases the ethnic mosaic was so complex that the self-determining unit described itself in nonethnic terms (such as the Republic of Mountainous Peoples, or Dagestan, in the Caucasus).

Nonetheless, ethno-nationalism became the basis on which socialist federalism was constructed. The principle of national (read: ethnic) statehood was enshrined as the basis for Soviet federalism. A socialist federated state was considered to be composed of ethno-political administrative units, in which each "indigenous socialist nation" had its own "statehood," as opposed to "bourgeois federalism" where the constituent parts were held to be primarily regional economic formations.[12]

All Soviet constitutions embodied the principle of a right to self-determination for ethno-nations, up to and including the right of secession. But it should be stressed that this "brave" social experiment arose within the context of one-party, totalitarian rule and strict centralization enforced from Moscow, beginning with the first years of industrialization. The formal declaration of this principle did not involve actual procedures for its realization.

Even at the formal level, the principle applied only to certain categories of ethnic groups—those with union republic status. The others were arranged along a hierarchical ladder of relative autonomy, down to a level that made no provision for any administrative structure whatsoever. Additionally, among the peoples of the Soviet Union, there were those who were deprived of territories once occupied as well as those who suffered border "adjustments" and/or changes in administrative organization.

EXPLAINING THE MODERN TURN TO ETHNO-NATIONALISM

Given the devastations brought by the Soviet regime to practically all ethnic groups of the country, it might seem easy to explain the cause of the contemporary explosion of ethno-nationalism by noting a long list of grievances. I also contributed to this widely accepted explanation in previous publications (Tishkov 1991). But exploring the issue further leads to a more subtle dynamic. Of concern is not only how a few years of perestroika revealed deep dissatisfactions and discontent among Soviet citizens with the existing social order. Also of concern is why this dissatisfaction became channeled into ethno-nationalism. R. Suny (1989:306) is right in saying:

[The] process of nation-building under Soviet rule was facilitated considerably by early Bolshevik policies. In particular, the party's commitment to Lenin's notion of national self-determination and its establishment of a pseudo-federal administrative system, the first in the world with territorial units based on ethnicity, to consolidate, rather than erode, ethnic and national cohesion.

This insight could be supplemented by Zbigniew Brzezinski's observation that in spite of proclaiming itself as an international doctrine, communism in fact intensified popular nationalist passions and fused with and even reinforced intolerant nationalism: "It produced a political culture imbued with intolerance, self-righteousness, rejection of social compromise and a massive inclination toward self-glorifying oversimplification. . . . Nationalism was thereby nurtured, rather than diluted, in the communist experience" (1989-1990:2).

Beginning with the policy of "nativization" in the 1920s an immense effort was put into training native cadres of professionals and educators, into developing local languages and schooling, and into establishing professional high culture institutions (literature, theater, science, cinema, books and printing, etc.). Prestigious manifestations of "the flourishing socialist nations" were sponsored and encouraged by the political center (in Moscow) even in times of political repression. After fifty years of "nativization" policy, the proportion of national intelligentsia and specialists with university diplomas was roughly equivalent for Russian and non-Russian groups. For a few groups (e.g. Armenians and Georgians) the proportion with diplomas was a few times higher compared with Russians.

This officially generated ethno-nationalism produced local elites in the republics who were quite vocal and inclined to wasteful status displays in support of themselves. In the weakly modernized republics of the U.S.S.R., such elites, especially its bureaucratic *nomenklatura,* frequently degenerated into feudal/clan or mafia-type structures, neither of which tolerated any kind of opposition. Their energies tended to be directed toward establishing the priority claims of their group against those of neighboring peoples for territory, heroes, and/or cultural legacies. And they displayed definite signs of local chauvinism—pretensions not only of inflated status but aspirations to assimilate the small, sparsely populated enclaves of ethnically different peoples living in the republic. In some former union and autonomous republics, indigenous elites felt that the most disturbing challenge to their authority came from Russian-speaking populations,[13] who comprise a majority of the country especially in urban centers. That kind of historical background cannot be ignored by specialists looking for answers to the rise of ethno-nationalism.

The Soviet situation is complex. It cannot be explained merely as a reflection of the worldwide trend toward ethnic revival and the growth of modern postindustrial nationalism, although these factors have undoubtedly had some influence. Nor can it be explained as the cumulative, long-suppressed discontent with historical injustices or with the low level of social and cultural conditions. (In the final analysis, the strongest and most highly organized national movements have not arisen in the most backward regions of the country nor among the most socially downtrodden ethnic groups.) It can also not be explained as resulting from "errors" in the implementation of Soviet policy toward nationalities and "deviations" from Leninist principles—a simplistic suggestion offered by many authors and politicians.

I suggest—and this has implications beyond Eastern Europe—that we must focus on the inability of the political order to create even the most rudimentary civil institutions that would allow for effective local self-government or the creation of political and social structures through which citizens and groups, including ethnic groups, could defend and realize their diverse and particular interests and rights. As soon as the once omnipotent and all-encompassing power of the party apparatus weakened and official ideology collapsed, the fatal inability of the hierarchy of state structures to regulate and govern social affairs became obvious. For millions of Soviet citizens, aroused to political activism, facing a lack of truly effective forms for realizing their demands, the appeal of ethnic group loyalty and of the nationalist idea became the sole and most understandable basis for collective action and the expression of protest regarding conditions of social despair and profound political disillusionment. Ethno-nationalism became prominent as an alternative to a strong, centralized state with ineffective representation at the local level. It called on romantic, emotional images for a new form of solidarity without necessarily resolving the problems of democratic representation at the local level. If and how these are to be resolved under ethno-nationalism remains to be seen.

THE POWER OF ETHNO-NATIONALISM

Many Western anthropologists share the vision of nations as "imagined communities," as cultural artifacts constructed by intellectuals (writers, historians, anthropologists, etc.). But none of these postmodern interpretations have been applied to the Soviet context.[14] My modest attempts to write about the nation as a constructed idea, rather than as an obvious reality, met with full misunderstanding and repugnance despite the fact that past and current Soviet realities tend to confirm the thesis.[15]

After decades of literary and practical nation-building, ethno-nationalism has become entwined in a wide spectrum of public ideologies and political mentalities. It has won considerable social support. And perestroika greatly facilitated the process. Activists of more than a dozen ethnic groups—beginning with strong cultural minorities and native groups of the north—also started to speak about their own "nations." Demands to be recognized as separate "ethnos" and "nations" have been formulated by Gagauz in Moldavia, by Karpato-Russians in Ukraine, by Siberian Tatars, and by those native groups of the North where local authorities proclaimed their own autonomous republics. Elsewhere leaders are still fighting to gain state status for their groups (such as the Far Eastern groups of the Amur River).[16]

Large ethnic elites—used to living under uncompetitive and dependent conditions assigned to them by the center—challenged their subordinate status by demanding full sovereignty (or independence) for the purpose of a "national revival" and the building of a "national state." The new political climate allowed intellectuals to push aside relatively easily the old party and state apparatus, thereby gaining political power in most regions of the country. A vacuum of professional politicians, among reformers and nationalists, allowed a number of the intelligentsia with Ph.D.s and strong academic credentials—mainly in social sciences and humanities—to take prominent leadership positions.

Taking advantage of the populace's high literacy rate, the new political leaders within the nationalities movement used the print media to further a sense of exclusive collective loyalty. They used the considerable data accumulated in local academies on language and literature as well as historical and archaeological reconstructions of traditional culture, as "a source for inventing ethnic (national) myths" (Gittelman 1991:34). The shamanistic effects and emotional appeal of the new leaders' presentations, first in mass public meetings and then through TV broadcasting of parliamentary debates, became a great mobilizing force.

The physical and emotional distance between academic debates, public discourse, and political and militant actions practically disappeared. An article in a newspaper or in a scholarly journal could become the reason for a public meeting or a protest demonstration. A speech in parliament and a letter by Gamsakhurdia (Georgia's then president) about ancient Georgian stone inscriptions at Sukhumi bridge, for example, caused bloody clashes between Georgians and Abkhazians at that locale. In turn, the opposition to Gamsakhurdia, which was led by university professors and prominent cultural figures, using the Georgian Academy of Sciences building as a military headquarters, was able to mobilize armed public support to overthrow the Georgian leader, who had been elected, almost unanimously, by the same people no more than six months before.

Seen from this perspective, the modern ideology of ethno-nationalism is not so much a reflection of social praxis. Rather, the social praxis of ethno-nationalism was shaped by ideological discourse and academic postulates. Soviet ethno-nationalism was and still is both a result of and a reaction to "etatization" (i.e. the making of state socialism) and the hierarchical structuring of ethnicity from above when citizens of the country were classified and divided into "nations," "*narodnosts*," and "national groups" depending on voluntaristically and arbitrarily formed borders of administrative units.

It is not easy to write this in today's highly politicized academic climate. But the above analysis suggests that interethnic strife and conflicts, not to mention the disintegration of the U.S.S.R., derives not only from a failed communist social experiment, but equally from the "progress" achieved in developing the Soviet "socialist nations" as republics. Contemporary political folklore and even many academics are not yet ready to accept this conclusion. Hence, it should be viewed as a subject for additional research and testing.

We need to explore ethno-nationalism in public Soviet and post-Soviet discourse as a form of poetic therapy, as a form of healing for the deep trauma experienced by the Soviet people on individual and collective levels. Ethno-nationalism represents a means for regaining lost pride and "personal worth" (using D. Horowitz's 1985 phrasing). Quite often this poetization breaks with reality. It appeals to a memory of ethos for this or that community and calls on people to act accordingly. Under some social and political conditions, poetization can mobilize immense constructive, creative potentials of ethnicity. It can also cause the emergence of a world-spreading "Kalashnikov's culture"—a culture of intolerance and destruction in which men with machine guns constitute the force behind what are stipulated to be "nationalist goals." Both perspectives are evident in the modern politics of the Soviet (Dis)union. Their joint future remains to be written, especially regarding the ongoing tensions between nationalist ideologies and multiethnic polities now dominating post-Soviet politics. On a larger scale, the size and economic/political viability of political units—how big or how small they can be and still act effectively in Europe or Asia today—is also at issue, as is the degree to which people at a local level can be seemingly represented within large modern polities.

THE ROLE OF INTELLECTUALS IN THE PRESENT HISTORICAL DRAMA

What kind of role can intellectuals play in this historical drama full of militant realities? An answer was given by M. Foucault (1980b: 62):

The intellectual no longer has to play the role of an advisor. The project, tactics and goals to be adopted are a matter for those who do the fighting. What the intellectual can do is to provide instruments of analysis, and at present this is the historian's essential role. What's effectively needed is a ramified, penetrative perception of the present, one that makes it possible to locate lines of weakness, strong points, positions where the instances of power have secured and implanted themselves by a system of organization dating back 150 years. In other words, a topological and geological survey of the battlefield—that is the intellectual's role. But as for saying, "Here is what you must do!", certainly not.

But this has not happened in the Soviet case. Generated by primordialistic visions of ethnicity and by a historical materialistic mentality of social engineering involving the "realization of historical law," Soviet political and academic rhetoric did not change much after the collapse of the Union and its ideology. The use of Leninist principles as the reference point for authority was easily replaced by the "sacral and providential character of nationhood" as the reference point.

Demoralized by his ouster from the process he personally had initiated, M. Gorbachev (1991) started to speak about ethnic groups in a different manner: "People are returning back to a process of self-awareness, to a search for their own roots. And every people—large and small—is God's creation. Nobody should deprive these peoples, especially the smaller ones, of the right to study and understand themselves." This thesis was echoed in the emotional statements by various writers and scholars elevated to top political positions. Byelorussian writer Basil Bykov (1991), a member of the former all-Union Parliament, wrote on "the sacred and God's right of nation to self-determination." Ukrainian writer Boris Oleinyk (1990), also a member of the Presidium of the former all-Union Parliament, called nations "the eternal categories like the Sun and the Moon." The historian Elena Guskova (1991), in discussing the Yugoslavian case, drew a conclusion about the universal historical trend for groups of people "first to disintegrate and to define themselves and only then to integrate." And the ethnographer Galina Starovoitova (1989)—in the course of a spectacular political career during which she was, among other things, a member of two parliaments and an advisor to President Yeltsin on nationality issues—frequently wrote and spoke publicly about the "growing interest among people to such eternal values as family and nation." The "ethno-nation" was presented, by her, as "a basis for civil society." The former academic and nationalist leader and now President of Armenia, Levon Ter-Petrosyan (1991), postulated the principle in a most explicit form: "The right of a nation to self-determination is absolute. And once the people decide to take their fate in their own hands, nothing, including violence, can reverse the process."

Post-Soviet social science still is, as it was in the past, strongly political, and emerging postcommunist politics is heavily over-loaded with legacies of the past respecting scholarly rhetorics and popular myths. The "ethno-nation" as a definer of identity is a very real belief today. But what is even more real are the practices and mass actions of its adherents, who, in the name of ethno-national principles, have created millions of refugees and killed thousands among the rank and file.

NOTES

1. For the most comprehensive text on this subject, see Connor (1984). For critical analyses of Soviet academic writings on ethnicity, see Skalnik (1986) and (1988). Note as well John L. Comaroff (1991) and Shanin (1989).

2. For the past two decades, this vocabulary dominated Soviet analyses in the treatment of so-called "ethnic processes." In English translation, see Bromley (1988), Kozlov (1988), and Bromley and Kozlov (1989).

3. Since 1986 at least a dozen books and over a hundred scholarly articles were published by Western anthropologists and political scientists on Soviet nationalities issues. See, for example, Nahaylo and Swoboda (1990), Graham Smith (1990), Motyl (1990), and Hajda and Beissinger (1990).

4. We can mention here only four of many books: Caroline Humphrey (1983) on the Buryats, Marjorie Balzer (forthcoming) on the Khanty, Tamara Dragadze (1988) on the Georgians, and Martha Olcott (1987) on the Kazakhs.

5. There have been many stories of moral and even physical persecutions of a number of intellectuals in the Baltic republics, Moldova, Ukraine, Armenia, Georgia, and Kazakhstan widely described in the local and even central press over the last two or three years.

6. Most of this literature is in local languages. But many brochures and articles were written in Russian, for example, on Transcaucasian issues: Miminoshvili and Pandjikidze (1990), Barsegyan (1989), Arutyunyan (1990), The Truth about Nagorno-Karabakh (1989), and Nagorno-Karabakh (1988).

7. See Kozlov (1990 and 1991). As to statements that are pro-minorities, see a number of articles in the journal *Soviet Ethnography*, especially a discussion on the status of the Pamir peoples of Tadjikistan, 1989, no. 5.

8. Koroteeva, Perepelkin, and Shkaratan (1988), Perepelkin and Shkaratan (1989), Krupnik (1990), Pain and Popov (1990). These are all in Russian.

9. See Cheshko (1989), Bromley (1989a), Yamskov (1991), Guboglo (1989).

10. The best anthropological and historical analyses of this period for the transformation and the apogee of nationalism were done by Gellner (1983) and Hobsbawm (1990).

11. On the concepts of "Russia" and "all-Russian," see such an early writer as N. N. Karamzin (1980).

12. See Constitution of the U.S.S.R.: Political-Legal Commentary (1982:207-2088).

13. The widely used and politicized category "Russian-speaking population" is actually misleading for several reasons. Firstly, a substantial number of people among titular groups are also Russian-speaking. Secondly, some nontitular minorities in the republics do have less command of the Russian language than titular groups. Finally, small indigenous groups of the North and Siberia and demographically dispersed minorities are predominantly Russian-speaking but retain their strong cultural characteristics and ethnic identities.

14. For some of these attempts to broaden the theoretical scope in explanations of Soviet ethno-nationalism see: Dutter (1990:311- 334), Social Science Theory and Soviet Nationalities (1990), Hough (1990:1-65), and Comaroff (1991).

15. See Bromley (1989b); for political debate, see XXVIIIth Congress of the Communist Party of the Soviet Union (1990).

16. As a Minister of Nationalities and a Director of the Institute of Ethnology and Anthropology, I have received over the last three years at least a dozen such requests or petitions, including the most recent one from the Cossacks—an example of emerging identity based on historical and political tradition more than on cultural characteristics.

INTELLECTUAL ROOTS

Valery A. Tishkov is Director of the Institute of Ethnography and Anthropology of the Russian Academy of Sciences and former Minister of Nationalities in the present Yeltsin Russian government. Born in 1941, he was educated at Moscow State University (M.A. 1964) and the Moscow Pedagogical Institute (Ph.D., 1969). He has been an Assistant and Associate Professor at the Magadan Pedagogical Institute (1964-1966, 1969-1972), a researcher in the Institute of General History of the U.S.S.R. Academy of Sciences (1972-1976), and General Secretary of the Academy's Division of History (1976-1982). Before assuming his present position in the Institute in 1989, he was both Head of the American Ethnic Studies and Deputy Director. His publications include many books and articles on Canadian history and historiography and contemporary politics, on the native peoples of North America, on United States and Canadian ethnology, and on current events. A series of his articles have been published in the West in *Third World Quarterly, Theory and Society, Journal of Soviet Nationalities, New Times,* and *Soviet Anthropology and Archeology.* He is presently completing a monograph concerning ethnic issues during and after the breakup of the Soviet Union.

In the early 1960s, I became a student of history at Moscow State University, majoring in modern Western history. This decision was a response to the younger generation's growing awareness of Western values during the post-Stalin thaw. Marxism-Leninism was the dominant doctrine for students and professors at that time and for a few decades thereafter—that is, until the time of real political liberalization in the mid-1980s. History was taught as a deterministic unilineal process and human evolution was mainly viewed in terms of socioeconomic formations relating to categories of class and to class struggle. Ethnography—the Soviet term for social and cultural anthropology—was not a separate social science discipline and, together with archaeology, was considered as a subdiscipline of history. Both subdisciplines were required for all students in the History Department.

Many outstanding scholars were among my professors. We used textbooks written by older generations of Soviet historians (e.g. M. D. Kosven on the history of material culture, S. A. Tokarev on Russian ethnography, Propp and Meletinski on spiritual and cultural values, M. Bahktin on the history of literary thought, and so forth).

My M.A. thesis was on contemporary Western history, particularly the United States position at the Potsdam Conference. For it, I relied primarily on Anglo-American primary sources and scholarly publications. Because of the existing ban on Soviet archives, political and diplomatic history was not an interesting challenge for my more advanced research. Following two years of teaching at the

Pedagogical Institute in Magadan (the capital of the Gulag Archipelago), I therefore moved into the field of early North American history for my Ph.D. dissertation.

For more than ten years, ethnohistory, especially French-English relations in British North America, became the primary focus of my research. Most of my publications, including my dissertation and a monograph, were devoted to pre-Confederation Canadian history. During this period in Russia many academic exchanges existed, and I had a chance to make several research trips to Canada where I worked in various archives. At the same time, I established numerous contacts with outstanding Canadian historians such as Ramsay Cook and Fernand Ouellet.

In 1982, I was invited by the late academician Y. Bromley to become head of American Studies at the Institute of Ethnography of the U.S.S.R. Academy of Sciences. This recent date makes me consider myself a newcomer to the field of anthropology which, at the time, involved a rather isolated community of Soviet ethnographers with very strong historical approaches which especially emphasized ethno-genesis and interpretations of ethnicity. Nonetheless, this Institute had, and still keeps, rather high professional standards of empirical field research. It was one of the few Soviet academic institutions, for example, where the social sciences were not markedly degraded by ideology and politics by the Soviet regime or by Communist Party control. Strange as it may sound

to my Western colleagues, when I look through all my publications, I can find no more than two or three references to Karl Marx's works and not a single reference to the works of Lenin. In fact, there was never a serious need to use their works for my research and I never experienced any serious external demands to include them in published writings from the Academy's publishing house.

It has been only for the past few years, since I assumed the position of Deputy Director of the Institute, that I have become more seriously interested in the theoretical horizons of world anthropology. Among major influences on my work, I should mention Western authors on ethnicity and nationalism—such as Gellner, Hobsbawm, Smith, Wolf, Connor, and Anderson. These thinkers helped me overcome a simplistic and narrow vision of ethnic issues both before and after the demise of the Soviet Union. What is most striking in my recent readings on postmodernism in philosophical anthropology is the discovery of strong "Russian roots" for many of the theoretical innovations relating to contemporary epistemological analysis. Bygotski, Bakhtin, Chayanov, Propp, and a few other forgotten or neglected names from Stalin's time were actually among the major predecessors of Western anthropological structuralism and postmodernism. Such works testify to our strong past intellectual tradition and hold out promise for the future modernization of Russian anthropology.

31

*The Uses of Diversity**

CLIFFORD GEERTZ

Anthropology has been fatally involved over the whole course of its history (a long one, if you start it with Herodotus; rather short, if you start it with Tylor) with the vast variety of ways in which men and women have tried to live their lives. At some points, it has sought to deal with that variety by capturing it in some universalizing net of theory: evolutionary stages, pan-human ideas or practices, or transcendental forms (structures, archetypes, subterranean grammars). At others, it has stressed particularity, idiosyncrasy, incommensurability—cabbages and kings. But recently it has found itself faced with something new: the possibility that the variety is rapidly softening into a paler, and narrower, spectrum. We may be faced with a world in which there simply aren't any more headhunters, matrilinealists, or people who predict the weather from the entrails of a pig. Difference will doubtless remain—the French will never eat salted butter. But the good old days of widow burning and cannibalism are gone forever.

In itself, as a professional issue, this process of the softening of cultural contrast (assuming it is real) is perhaps not so disturbing. Anthropologists will simply have to learn to make something of subtler differences, and their writings may grow more shrewd if less spectacular. But it raises a broader issue, moral, aesthetic, and cognitive at once, that is much more troubling, and that lies at the center of much current discussion about how it is that values are to be justified: what I will call, just

to have something that sticks in the mind, The Future of Ethnocentrism.

I shall come back to some of those more general discussions after a bit, for it is toward them that my overall concern is directed; but as a way into the problem I want to begin with the presentation of an argument, unusual I think and more than a little disconcerting, which the French anthropologist Claude Lévi-Strauss (1985) develops at the beginning of his recent collection of essays, contentiously entitled (contentiously, at least, for an anthropologist) *The View from Afar—Le regard éloigné*.

LÉVI-STRAUSS ON ETHNOCENTRISM

Lévi-Strauss's argument arose in the first place in response to a UNESCO invitation to deliver a public lecture to open the International Year to Combat Racism and Racial Discrimination, which, in case you missed it, was 1971. "I was chosen," he (1985:xi) writes,

---

*Reprinted, in edited form (the headings have been added and a few other minor editing changes have been made), from Sterling McMurrin (ed.), *The Tanner Lectures on Human Values*, vol. 7, Salt Lake City and Cambridge: University of Utah Press and Cambridge University Press, 1986, by permission of the trustees of the Tanner Lecture Series.

454

because twenty years earlier I had written [a pamphlet called] "Race and History" for UNESCO [in which] I had stated a few basic truths. . . . [In] 1971, I soon realized that UNESCO expected me [simply] to repeat them. But twenty years earlier, in order to serve the international institutions, which I felt I had to support more than I do today, I had somewhat overstated my point in the conclusion to "Race and History." Because of my age perhaps, and certainly because of reflections inspired by the present state of the world, I was now disgusted by this obligingness and was convinced that, if I was to be useful to UNESCO and fulfill my commitment honestly, I should have to speak in complete frankness.

As usual, that turned out not to be altogether a good idea, and something of a farce followed. Members of the UNESCO staff were dismayed that "I had challenged a catechism (the acceptance of which) had allowed them to move from modest jobs in developing countries to sanctified positions as executives in an international institution" (1985:xi). The then Director General of UNESCO, another determined Frenchman, unexpectedly took the floor so as to reduce Lévi-Strauss's time to speak and thus force him to make the improving excisions that had been suggested to him. Lévi-Strauss, incorrigible, read his entire text, apparently at high speed, in the time left.

All that aside, a normal day at the U.N., the problem with Lévi-Strauss's talk was that in it "I rebelled against the abuse of language by which people tend more and more to confuse racism . . . with attitudes that are normal, even legitimate, and in any case, unavoidable" (1985:xii)—that is, though he does not call it that, ethnocentrism.

Ethnocentrism's Positive Aspects

Ethnocentrism, Lévi-Strauss argues in that piece, "Race and Culture," and, somewhat more technically in another, "The Anthropologist and the Human Condition," written about a decade further on, is not only not in

itself a bad thing, but, at least so long as it does not get out of hand, rather a good one. Loyalty to a certain set of values inevitably makes people "partially or totally insensitive to other values" (1985:xii) to which other people, equally parochial, are equally loyal. "It is not at all invidious to place one way of life or thought above all others or to feel little drawn to other values." Such "relative incommunicability" does not authorize anyone to oppress or destroy the values rejected or those who carry them. But, absent that, "it is not at all repugnant":

It may even be the price to be paid so that the systems of values of each spiritual family or each community are preserved and find within themselves the resources necessary for their renewal. If . . . human societies exhibit a certain optimal diversity beyond which they cannot go, but below which they can no longer descend without danger, we must recognize that, to a large extent, this diversity results from the desire of each culture to resist the cultures surrounding it, to distinguish itself from them—in short to be itself. Cultures are not unaware of one another, they even borrow from one another on occasion; but, in order not to perish, they must in other connections remain somewhat impermeable toward one another. (1985:xiii)

It is thus not only an illusion that humanity can wholly free itself from ethnocentrism, "or even that it will care to do so" (1985:xiii); it would not be a good thing if it did do so. Such a "freedom" would lead to a world "whose cultures, all passionately fond of one another, would aspire only to celebrate one another, in such confusion that each would lose any attraction it could have for the others and its own reason for existing" (1985:xiii).

Distance lends, if not enchantment, anyway indifference, and thus integrity. In the past, when so-called primitive cultures were only very marginally involved with one another—referring to themselves as "The True Ones," "The Good Ones," or just "The Human Beings," and dismissing those across the river or over the ridge as "earth monkeys" or "louse eggs," that is, not, or not fully, human—cultural integrity was readily maintained. A "profound indifference to other cultures . . . a guarantee that they could exist in their own manner and on their own terms" (1985:7). Now, when such a situation clearly no longer obtains, and everyone, increasingly crowded on a small planet, is deeply interested in everyone else, and in everyone else's business, the possibility of the loss of such integrity, because of the loss of such indifference, looms. Ethnocentrism can perhaps never entirely disappear, being "consubstantial with our species" (1985:xiii), but it can grow dangerously weak, leaving us prey to a sort of moral entropy:

We are doubtless deluding ourselves with a dream when we think that equality and fraternity will some day reign among human beings without compromising their diversity. However, if humanity is not resigned to becoming the sterile consumer of values that it managed to create in the past . . . capable only of giving birth to bastard works, to gross and puerile inventions, [then] it must learn once again that all true creation implies a certain deafness to the appeal of other values, even going so far as to reject them if not denying them altogether. For one cannot fully enjoy the other, identify with him, and yet at the same time remain different. When integral communication with the other is achieved completely, it sooner or later spells doom for both his and my creativity. The great creative eras were those in which communication had become adequate for mutual stimulation by remote partners, yet was not so frequent or so rapid as to endanger the indispensable obstacles between individuals and groups or to reduce them to the point where overly facile exchanges might equalize and nullify their diversity. (1985:23)

Whatever one thinks of all this, or however surprised one is to hear it coming from an anthropologist, it certainly strikes a contemporary chord. The attractions of "deafness to the appeal of other values" and of a relax-and-enjoy-it approach to one's imprisonment in one's own cultural tradition are increasingly celebrated in recent social thought. Unable to embrace either relativism or absolutism—the first because it disables judgment, the second because it removes it from history—our philosophers, historians, and social scientists turn toward the sort of we-are-we and they-are-they *imperméabilité* Lévi-Strauss recommends.

Whether one regards this as arrogance made easy, prejudice justified, or as the splendid, here-stand-I honesty of Flannery O'Connor's "when in Rome do as you done in Milledgeville," it clearly puts the question of The Future of Ethnocentrism—and of cultural diversity—in rather a new light. Is drawing back, distancing elsewhere, The View from Afar, really the way to escape the desperate tolerance of UNESCO cosmopolitanism? Is the alternative to moral entropy moral narcissism?

RORTY'S CULTURAL SELF-CENTEREDNESS

The forces making for a warmer view of cultural self-centeredness over the last twenty-five or thirty years are multiple. There are those "state of the world" matters to which Lévi-Strauss alludes, and most especially the failure of most Third World countries to live up to the thousand-flowers hopes for them current just before and just after their independence struggles. Amin, Bokassa, Pol Pot, Khomeini at the extremes, Marcos, Mobuto, Sukarno, and Mrs. Gandhi less extravagantly, have put something of a chill on the notion that there are worlds elsewhere to which our own compares clearly ill. There is the successive unmasking of the Marxist utopias—the Soviet Union, China, Cuba, Vietnam. And there is the weakening of the Decline of the West pessimism induced by world war, world depression, and the loss of empire. But there is also, and I think not least important, the rise in awareness that universal consensus—transnational, transcultural, even transclass—on normative matters is not in the offing. Everyone—Sikhs, Socialists, Positivists, Irishmen—is not going to come around to a common opinion concerning what is decent and what is not, what is just and what is not, what is beautiful and what is not, what is reasonable and what is not; not soon, perhaps not ever.

If one abandons (and of course not everyone, perhaps not even most everyone, has) the idea that the world is moving toward essential agreement on fundamental matters, or even, as with Lévi-Strauss, that it should, then the appeal of relax-and-enjoy it ethnocentrism naturally grows. If our values cannot be disentangled from our history and our institutions and nobody else's can be disentangled from theirs, then there would seem to be nothing for it but to follow Emerson and stand on our own feet and speak with our own voice. "I hope to suggest," Richard Rorty writes in a recent piece (marvelously entitled "Postmodernist Bourgeois Liberalism"), "how [we postmodernist bourgeois liberals] might convince our society that loyalty to itself is loyalty enough . . . that it need be responsible only to its own traditions" (1983:585). What an anthropologist in search of "the consistent laws underlying the observable diversity of beliefs and institutions" (Lévi-Strauss 1985:35) arrives at from the side of rationalism and high science, a philosopher, persuaded that "there is no 'ground' for [our] loyalties and convictions save the fact that the beliefs and desires and emotions which buttress them overlap those of lots of other members of the group with which we identify for purposes of moral and political deliberation" arrives at from the side of pragmatism and prudential ethics (Rorty 1983:586).

The similarity is even greater despite the very different starting points from which these two savants depart (Kantianism without a transcendental subject, Hegelianism without an absolute spirit), and the even more different ends toward which they tend (a trim world of transposable forms, a disheveled one of coincident discourses), because Rorty, too, regards invidious distinctions between groups as not only natural but essential to moral reasoning:

[The] naturalized Hegelian analogue of [Kantian] "intrinsic human dignity" is the comparative dignity of a group with which a person identifies herself. Nations or churches or movements are, on this view, shining historical examples not because they reflect rays emanating from a higher source, but because of contrast-effects—comparison with worse communities. Persons have dignity not as an interior luminescence, but because they share in such contrast-effects. It is a corollary of this view that the moral justification of the institutions and practices of one's group—e.g., of the contemporary bourgeoisie—is mostly a matter of historical narratives (including scenarios about what is likely to happen in certain future contingencies), rather than of philosophical meta-narratives. The principal backup for historiography is not philosophy but the arts, which serve to develop and modify a group's self-image by, for example, apotheosizing its heroes, diabolizing its enemies, mounting dialogues among its members, and refocusing its attention. (Rorty 1983:586-87)

A Personal View

Now, as a member of both these intellectual traditions myself, of the scientific study of cultural diversity by profession and of postmodern bourgeois liberalism by general persuasion, my own view, to get round now to that, is that an easy surrender to the comforts of merely being ourselves, cultivating deafness and maximizing gratitude for not having been born a Vandal or an Ik, will be fatal to both. An anthropology so afraid of destroying cultural integrity and creativity, our own and everyone else's, by drawing near to other people, engaging them, seeking to grasp them in their immediacy and their difference, is destined to perish of an inanition for which no manipulations of objectivized data sets can compensate. Any moral philosophy so afraid of becoming entangled in witless relativism or transcendental dogmatism that it can think of nothing better to do with other ways of going at life than to make them look worse than our own is destined merely to conduce (as someone has said of the writings of V. S. Naipaul, perhaps our leading adept at constructing such "contrast-effects") toward making the world safe for condescension. Trying to save two disciplines from themselves at once may seem like hubris. But when one has double citizenships one has double obligations.

ALTERNATIVES *TO* US AS OPPOSED TO ALTERNATIVES *FOR* US

Their different demeanors and their different hobby-horses notwithstanding (and I confess myself very much closer to Rorty's messy populism than to Lévi-Strauss's fastidious mandarinism—in itself, perhaps, but a cultural bias of my own), these two versions of to-each-his-own morality rest, in part anyway, on a common view of cultural diversity: namely, that its main importance is that it provides us with, to use a formula of Bernard Williams's, alternatives *to* us as opposed to alternatives *for* us. Other beliefs, values, ways of going on, are seen as beliefs we would have believed, values we would have held, ways we would have gone on, had we been born in some other place or some other time than that in which we actually were.

So, indeed, we would have. But such a view seems to make both rather more and rather less of the fact of cultural diversity than it should. Rather more, because it suggests that to have had a different life than one has in fact had is a practical option one has somehow to make one's mind up about (Should I have been a Bororo? Am I not fortunate not to have been a Hittite?); rather less, because it obscures the power of such diversity, when personally addressed, to transform our sense of what it is for a human being, Bororo, Hittite,

Structuralist, or Postmodern Bourgeois Liberal, to believe, to value, or to go on: what it is like, as Arthur Danto has remarked (1984: 646-647), echoing Thomas Nagel's famous question about the bat,[1] "to think the world is flat, that I look irresistible in my Poiret frocks, that the Reverend Jim Jones would have saved me through his love, that animals have no feeling or that flowers do—or that punk is where it's at." The trouble with ethnocentrism is not that it commits us to our own commitments. We are, by definition, so committed, as we are to having our own headaches. The trouble with ethnocentrism is that it impedes us from discovering at what sort of angle, like Forster's Cavafy, we stand to the world; what sort of bat we really are.

This view—that the puzzles raised by the fact of cultural diversity have more to do with our capacity to feel our way into alien sensibilities, modes of thought (punk rock and Poiret frocks) we do not possess, and are not likely to, than they do with whether we can escape preferring our own preferences—has a number of implications which bode ill for a we-are-we and they-are-they approach to things cultural. The first of these, and possibly the most important, is that those puzzles arise not merely at the boundaries of our society, where we would expect them under such an approach, but, so to speak, at the boundaries of ourselves. Foreignness does not start at the water's edge but at the skin's. The sort of idea that both anthropologists since Malinowski and philosophers since Wittgenstein are likely to entertain that, say, Shi'is, being other, present a problem, but, say, soccer fans, being part of us, do not, or at least not of the same sort, is merely wrong. The social world does not divide at its joints into perspicuous we's with whom we can empathize, however much we differ *with* them, and enigmatical they's, with whom we cannot, however much we defend to the death their right to differ *from* us. The wogs begin long before Calais.

Increasing the Reach of Our Minds

Both recent anthropology of the From the Native's Point of View sort (which I practice) and recent philosophy of the Forms of Life sort (to which I adhere) have been made to conspire, or to seem to conspire, in obscuring this fact by a chronic misapplication of their most powerful and most important idea: the idea that meaning is socially constructed.

The perception that meaning, in the form of interpretable signs—sounds, images, feelings, artifacts, gestures—comes to exist only within language games, communities of discourse, intersubjective systems of reference, ways of worldmaking; that it arises within the frame of concrete social interaction in which something is a something for a you and a me, and not in some secret grotto in the head; and that it is through and through historical, hammered out in the flow of events, is read to imply (as, in my opinion, neither Malinowski nor Wittgenstein—nor for that matter Kuhn or Foucault) meant it to imply—that human communities are, or should be, semantic monads, nearly windowless. We are, says Lévi-Strauss, passengers in the trains which are our cultures, each moving on its own track, at its own speed, and in its own direction. The trains rolling alongside, going in similar directions and at speeds not too different from our own are at least reasonably visible to us as we look out from our compartments. But trains on an oblique or parallel track which are going in an opposed direction are not. "[We] perceive only a vague, fleeting, barely identifiable image, usually just a momentary blur in our visual field, supplying no information about itself and merely irritating us because it interrupts our placid contemplation of the landscape which serves as the backdrop to our daydreaming"(1985:10). Rorty is more cautious and less poetic, and I sense less interested in other people's trains, so concerned is he where his own is going, but he speaks of a more or less accidental "overlap" of belief systems between "rich North American

bourgeois" communities and others that "[we] need to talk with" as enabling "whatever conversation between nations may still be possible" (1983:588). The grounding of feeling, thought, and judgment in a form of life—which indeed is the only place, in my view, as it is in Rorty's, that they can be grounded—is taken to mean that the limits of my world are the limits of my language, which is not exactly what the man said.

What he said, of course, was that the limits of my language are the limits of my world, which implies not that the reach of our minds, of what we can say, think, appreciate, and judge, is trapped within the borders of our society, our country, our class, or our time, but that the reach of our minds, the range of signs we can manage somehow to interpret, is what defines the intellectual, emotional, and moral space within which we live. The greater that is, the greater we can make it become by trying to understand what flat earthers or the Reverend Jim Jones (or Iks or Vandals) are all about, what it is like to be them, the clearer we become to ourselves, both in terms of what we see in others that seems remote and what we see that seems reminiscent, what attractive and what repellent, what sensible and what quite mad; oppositions that do not align in any simple way, for there are some things quite appealing about bats, some quite repugnant about ethnographers.

It is, Danto (1984:647) says in that same article I quoted a moment ago, "the gaps between me and those who think differently than I—which is to say everyone, and not simply those segregated by differences in generations, sex, nationality, sect, and even race— [that] define the real boundaries of the self." It is the asymmetries, as he also says, or nearly, between what we believe or feel and what others do, that make it possible to locate where we now are in the world, how it feels to be there, and where we might or might not want to go. To obscure those gaps and those asymmetries by relegating them to a realm of repressible or ignorable difference, mere unlikeness, which is what ethnocentrism does and is designed to do (UNESCO universalism obscures them—Lévi-Strauss is quite right about that—by denying their reality altogether), is to cut us off from such knowledge and such possibility: the possibility of quite literally, and quite thoroughly, changing our minds.

CLASHING SENSIBILITIES IN A POSTMODERN WORLD

The history of any people separately and all peoples together, and indeed of each person individually, has been a history of such a changing of minds, usually slowly, sometimes more rapidly; or if the idealist sound of that disturbs you (it ought not, it is not idealist, and it denies neither the natural pressures of fact nor the material limits of will), of sign systems, symbolic forms, cultural traditions. Such changes have not necessarily been for the better, perhaps not even normally. Nor have they led to a convergence of views, but rather to a mingling of them. What, back in his blessed Neolithic, was indeed once something at least rather like Lévi-Strauss's world of integral societies in distant communication has turned into something rather more like Danto's postmodern one of clashing sensibilities in inevadable contact. Like nostalgia, diversity is not what it used to be; and the sealing of lives into separate railway carriages to produce cultural renewal or the spacing of them out with contrast-effects to free up moral energies are romantical dreams, not undangerous.

Moral Reasoning in this Context

The general tendency that I remarked in opening for the cultural spectrum to become paler and more continuous without becoming less discriminate (indeed, it is probably becoming more discriminate as symbolic forms split and proliferate) alters not just its

bearing on moral argument but the character of such argument itself. We have become used to the idea that scientific concepts change with changes in the sorts of concerns to which scientists address themselves—that one does not need the calculus to determine the velocity of a chariot or quantal energies to explain the swing of a pendulum. But we are rather less aware that the same thing is true of the speculative instruments (to borrow an old term of I. A. Richards's—who got it from Coleridge—which deserves to be resuscitated) of moral reasoning. Ideas which suffice for Lévi-Strauss's magnificent differences do not for Danto's troubling asymmetries; and it is the latter with which we find ourselves increasingly faced.

More concretely, moral issues stemming from cultural diversity (which are, of course, far from being all the moral issues there are) that used to arise, when they arose at all, mainly between societies—the "customs contrary to reason and morals" sort of thing on which imperialism fed—now increasingly arise within them. Social and cultural boundaries coincide less and less closely—there are Japanese in Brazil, Turks on the Main, and West Indian meets East in the streets of Birmingham—a shuffling process which has of course been going on for quite some time (Belgium, Canada, Lebanon, South Africa—and the Caesars' Rome was not all that homogeneous), but which is, by now, approaching extreme and near universal proportions. The day when the American city was the main model of cultural fragmentation and ethnic tumbling is quite gone; the Paris of *nos ancestres les gaulois* is getting to be about as polyglot, and as polychrome, as Manhattan, and may yet have an Asian mayor (or so, anyway, many of *les gaulois* fear) before New York has an Hispanic one.

This rising within the body of a society, inside the boundaries of a "we," of wrenching moral issues centered around cultural diversity, and the implications it has for our general problem, "the future of ethnocentrism," can perhaps be made rather more vivid with an example; not a made-up, science fiction one about water on anti-worlds or people whose memories interchange while they are asleep, of which philosophers have recently grown rather too fond, in my opinion, but a real one, or at least one represented to me as real by the anthropologist who told it to me: The Case of the Drunken Indian and the Kidney Machine.

The Drunken Indian and the Kidney Machine

The case is simple, however knotted its resolution. The extreme shortage, due to their great expense, of artificial kidney machines led, naturally enough, to the establishment a few years ago of a queuing process for access to them by patients needing dialysis in a government medical program in the southwestern United States directed, also naturally enough, by young, idealistic doctors from major medical schools, largely northeastern. For the treatment to be effective, at least over an extended period of time, strict discipline as to diet and other matters is necessary on the part of the patients. As a public enterprise, governed by antidiscrimination codes, and anyway, as I say, morally motivated, queuing was organized not in terms of the power to pay but simply severity of need and order of application, a policy which led, with the usual twists of practical logic, to the problem of the drunken Indian.

The Indian, after gaining access to the scarce machine, refused, to the great consternation of the doctors, to stop, or even control, his drinking, which was prodigious. His position, under some sort of principle like that of Flannery O'Connor's I mentioned earlier of remaining oneself whatever others might wish to make of you, was: I am indeed a drunken Indian, I have been one for quite some time, and I intend to go on being one for as long as you can keep me alive by hooking me up to this damn machine of yours. The doctors, whose values were rather different, regarded

the Indian as blocking access to the machine by others on the queue, in no less desperate straits, who could, as they saw it, make better use of its benefits—a young, middle-class type, say, rather like themselves, destined for college and, who knows, medical school. As the Indian was already on the machine by the time the problem became visible they could not quite bring themselves (nor, I suppose, would they have been permitted) to take him off it. But they were very deeply upset—at least as upset as the Indian, who was disciplined enough to show up promptly for all his appointments, was resolute—and surely would have devised some reason, ostensibly medical, to displace him from his position in the queue had they seen in time what was coming. He continued on the machine, and they continued distraught, for several years until, proud, as I imagine him, grateful (though not to the doctors) to have had a somewhat extended life in which to drink, and quite unapologetic, he died.

Now, the point of this little fable in real time is not to show how insensitive doctors can be (they were not insensitive, and they had a case), or how adrift Indians have become (he was not adrift, he knew exactly where he was); nor to suggest that either the doctors' values (that is, approximately, ours), the Indian's (that is, approximately, not-ours), or some trans-parte judgment drawn from philosophy or anthropology and issued forth by one of Ronald Dworkin's herculean judges, should have prevailed. It was a hard case and it ended in a hard way; but I cannot see that either more ethnocentrism, more relativism, or more neutrality would have made things any better (though more imagination might have). The point of the fable—I'm not sure it properly has a moral—is that it is this sort of thing, not the distant tribe, enfolded upon itself in coherent difference (the Azande or the Ik that fascinate philosophers only slightly less than science fiction fantasies do, perhaps because they can be made into sublunary Martians and regarded accordingly), that best represents, if somewhat melodramatically, the general form that value conflict rising out of cultural diversity takes nowadays.

The antagonists here, if that's what they were, were not representatives of turned-in social totalities meeting haphazardly along the edges of their beliefs. Indians holding fate at bay with alcohol are as much a part of contemporary America as are doctors correcting it with machines. (If you want to see just how, at least so far as the Indians are concerned—I assume you know about doctors—you can read James Welch's shaking novel, *Winter in the Blood*, where the contrast effects come out rather oddly.) If there was any failure here, and, to be fair, it is difficult at a distance to tell precisely how much there was, it was a failure to grasp, on either side, what it was to be on the other, and thus what it was to be on one's own. No one, at least so it seems, learned very much in this episode about either themselves or about anyone else, and nothing at all, beyond the banalities of disgust and bitterness, about the character of their encounter. It is not the inability of those involved to abandon their convictions and adopt the views of others that makes this little tale seem so utterly depressing. Nor is it their lack of a disincorporated moral rule—The Greatest Good or The Difference Principle (which would seem, as a matter of fact, to give different results here)—to which to appeal. It is their inability even to conceive, amid the mystery of difference, how one might get round an all-too-genuine moral asymmetry. The whole thing took place in the dark.

KNOWING ONE ANOTHER

What tends to take place in the dark—the only things of which "a certain deafness to the appeal of other values" or a "comparison with worse communities" conception of human dignity would seem to allow—is either the application of force to secure conformity to the values of those who possess the force; a

vacuous tolerance that, engaging nothing, changes nothing; or, as here, where the force is unavailable and the tolerance unnecessary, a dribbling out to an ambiguous end.

Grasping an Alien Turn of Mind

It is surely the case that there are instances where these are, in fact, practical alternatives. There doesn't seem much to do about the Reverend Jones, once he is in full cry, but physically to stop him before he hands out the Kool-Aid. If people think punk rock is where it's at, then, at least so long as they don't play it in the subway, it's their ears and their funeral. And it is difficult (some bats are battier than others) to know just how one ought to proceed with someone who holds that flowers have feelings and that animals do not. Paternalism, indifference, even superciliousness, are not always unuseful attitudes to take to value differences, even to ones more consequential than these. The problem is to know when they are useful and diversity can safely be left to its connoisseurs, and when, as I think is more often the case, and increasingly so, they are not and it cannot, and something more is needed: an imaginative entry into (and admittance of) an alien turn of mind.

In our society, the connoisseur *par excellence* of alien turns of mind has been the ethnographer (the historian too, to a degree, and in a different way the novelist, but I want to get back on my own reservation), dramatizing oddness, extolling diversity, and breathing broad-mindedness. Whatever differences in method or theory have separated us, we have been alike in that: professionally obsessed with worlds elsewhere and with making them comprehensible first to ourselves and then, through conceptual devices not so different from those of historians and literary ones not so different from those of novelists, to our readers. And so long as those worlds really were elsewhere, where Malinowski found them and Lévi-Strauss remembers them, this was, though difficult enough as a practical task, relatively unproblematical as an analytical one. We could think about "primitives" ("savages," "natives," . . .) as we thought about Martians—as possible ways of feeling, reasoning, judging and behaving, of going on, discontinuous with our own, alternatives to us. Now that those worlds and those alien turns of mind are mostly not really elsewhere, but alternatives for us, hard nearby, instant "gaps between me and those who think differently than I," a certain readjustment in both our rhetorical habits and our sense of mission would seem to be called for.

The uses of cultural diversity, of its study, its description, its analysis, and its comprehension, lie less along the lines of sorting ourselves out from others and others from ourselves so as to defend group integrity and sustain group loyalty than along the lines of defining the terrain reason must cross if its modest rewards are to be reached and realized. This terrain is uneven, full of sudden faults and dangerous passages where accidents can and do happen, and crossing it, or trying to, does little or nothing to smooth it out to a level, safe, unbroken plain, but simply makes visible its clefts and contours. If our peremptory doctors and our intransigent Indian (or Rorty's "rich North American[s]" and "[those we] need to talk with") are to confront one another in a less destructive way (and it is far from certain—the clefts are real—that they actually can) they must explore the character of the space between them.

The Job of Ethnography

It is they themselves who must finally do this; there is no substitute for local knowledge here, nor for courage either. But maps and charts may still be useful, and tables, tales, pictures, and descriptions, even theories, if they attend to the actual, as well. The uses of ethnography are mainly ancillary, but they are nonetheless real; like the compiling of dictionaries or the grinding of lenses, it is, or would be, an enabling discipline. And what it en-

ables, when it does so, is a working contact with a variant subjectivity. It places particular we's among particular they's, and they's among we's; where all, as I have been saying, already are, however uneasily. It is the great enemy of ethnocentrism, of confining people to cultural planets where the only ideas they need to conjure with are "those around here," not because it assumes people are all alike, but because it knows how profoundly they are not and how unable yet to disregard one another. Whatever once was possible and whatever may now be longed for, the sovereignty of the familiar impoverishes everyone; to the degree it has a future, ours is dark. It is not that we must love one another or die (if that is the case—Blacks and Afrikaners, Arabs and Jews, Tamils and Singhalese—we are I think doomed). It is that we must know one another, and live with that knowledge, or end marooned in a Beckett-world of colliding soliloquy.

The job of ethnography, or one of them anyway, is indeed to provide, like the arts and history, narratives and scenarios to refocus our attention; not, however, ones that render us acceptable to ourselves by representing others as gathered into worlds we don't want and can't arrive at, but ones which make us visible to ourselves by representing us and everyone else as cast into the midst of a world full of irremovable strangenesses we can't keep clear of.

Until fairly recently (the matter now is changing, in part at least because of ethnography's impact, but mostly because the world is changing) ethnography was fairly well alone in this, for history did in fact spend much of its time comforting our self-esteem and supporting our sense that we were getting somewhere by apotheosizing our heroes and diabolizing our enemies, or with keening over vanished greatness; the social comment of novelists was for the most part internal—one part of Western consciousness holding a mirror, Trollope-flat or Dostoyevsky-curved, up to another; and even travel writing, which at least attended to exotic surfaces (jungles, camels, bazaars, temples) mostly employed them to demonstrate the resilience of received virtues in trying circumstances—the Englishman remaining calm, the Frenchman rational, the American innocent. Now, when it is not so alone and the strangenesses it has to deal with are growing more oblique and more shaded, less easily set off as wild anomalies—men who think themselves descended from wallabies or who are convinced they can be murdered with a sidelong glance—its task, locating those strangenesses and describing their shapes, may be in some ways more difficult; but it is hardly less necessary. Imagining difference (which of course does not mean making it up, but making it evident) remains a science of which we all have need.

KEEPING AN IMPORTANT SKILL ALIVE

But my purpose here is not to defend the prerogatives of a homespun science whose patent on the study of cultural diversity, if it ever had one, has long since expired. My purpose is to suggest that we have come to such a point in the moral history of the world (a history itself of course anything but moral) that we are obliged to think about such diversity rather differently than we have been used to thinking about it. If it is in fact getting to be the case that rather than being sorted into framed units, social spaces with definite edges to them, seriously disparate approaches to life are becoming scrambled together in ill-defined expanses, social spaces whose edges are unfixed, irregular, and difficult to locate, the question of how to deal with the puzzles of judgment to which such disparities give rise takes on a rather different aspect. Confronting landscapes and still lifes is one thing; panoramas and collages quite another.

Living in a Cultural Collage

That it is the latter we these days confront, that we are living more and more in the midst of an enormous collage, seems everywhere apparent. It is not just the evening news where assassinations in India, bombings in Lebanon, coups in Africa, and shootings in central America are set amid local disasters hardly more legible and followed on by grave discussions of Japanese ways of business, Persian forms of passion, or Arab styles of negotiation. It is also an enormous explosion of translation, good, bad, and indifferent, from and to languages—Tamil, Indonesian, Hebrew, and Urdu—previously regarded as marginal and recondite; the migration of cuisines, costumes, furnishings, and decor (caftans in San Francisco, Colonel Sanders in Jogjakarta, barstools in Kyoto); the appearance of gamelan themes in *avant garde* jazz, Indio myths in Latino novels, magazine images in African painting. But most of all, it is that the person we encounter in the greengrocery is as likely, or nearly, to come from Korea as from Iowa, in the post office from Algeria as from the Auvergne, in the bank from Bombay as from Liverpool. Even rural settings, where alikeness is likely to be more entrenched, are not immune: Mexican farmers in the Southwest, Vietnamese fishermen along the Gulf Coast, Iranian physicians in the Midwest.

I need not go on multiplying examples. You can all think of ones of your own out of your own traffickings with your own surroundings. Not all this diversity is equally consequential (Jogja cooking will survive finger-lickin'-good); equally immediate (you don't need to grasp the religious beliefs of the man who sells you postage stamps); nor does it all stem from cultural contrast of a clear-cut sort. But that the world is coming at each of its local points to look more like a Kuwaiti bazaar than like an English gentlemen's club (to instance what, to my mind—perhaps because I have never been in either one of them—are the polar cases) seems shatteringly clear. Ethnocentrism of either the louse eggs or of the there-but-for-the-grace-of-culture sort may or may not be coincident with the human species; but it is now quite difficult for most of us to know just where, in the grand assemblage of juxtaposed difference, to center it.

Being Able to Understand What Is Alien to Us

Our response to this, so it seems to me, commanding fact, is, so it also seems to me, one of the major moral challenges we these days face, ingredient in virtually all the others we face, from nuclear disarmament to the equitable distribution of the world's resources, and in facing it counsels of indiscriminate tolerance, which are anyway not genuinely meant, and, my target here, of surrender, proud, cheerful, defensive, or resigned, to the pleasures of invidious comparison serve us equally badly; though the latter is perhaps the more dangerous because the more likely to be followed. The image of a world full of people so passionately fond of each other's cultures that they aspire only to celebrate one another does not seem to me a clear and present danger; the image of one full of people happily apotheosizing their heroes and diabolizing their enemies alas does. It is not necessary to choose, indeed it is necessary not to choose, between cosmopolitanism without content and parochialism without tears. Neither are of use for living in a collage.

To live in a collage one must in the first place render oneself capable of sorting out its elements, determining what they are (which usually involves determining where they come from and what they amounted to when they were there) and how, practically, they relate to one another, without at the same time blurring one's own sense of one's own location and one's own identity within it. Less figuratively, "understanding" in the sense of comprehension, perception, and insight needs to

be distinguished from "understanding" in the sense of agreement of opinion, union of sentiment, or commonality of commitment. We must learn to grasp what we cannot embrace.

The difficulty in this is enormous, as it has always been. Comprehending that which is, in some manner of form, alien to us and likely to remain so, without either smoothing it over with vacant murmurs of common humanity, disarming it with to-each-his-own indifferentism, or dismissing it as charming, lovely even, but inconsequent, is a skill we have arduously to learn, and having learnt it, always very imperfectly, to work continuously to keep alive; it is not a connatural capacity, like depth perception or the sense of balance, upon which we can complacently rely.

It is in this, strengthening the power of our imaginations to grasp what is in front of us, that the uses of diversity, and of the study of diversity, lie. If we have (as I admit I have) more than a sentimental sympathy with that refractory American Indian, it is not because we hold his views. Alcoholism is indeed an evil, and kidney machines are ill-applied to its victims. Our sympathy derives from our knowledge of the degree to which he has earned his views and the bitter sense that is therefore in them, our comprehension of the terrible road over which he has had to travel to arrive at them and of what it is—ethnocentrism and the crimes it legitimates—that has made it so terrible. If we wish to be able capaciously to judge, as of course we must, we need to make ourselves able capaciously to see. And for that, what we have already seen—the insides of our railway compartments; the shining historical examples of our nations, our churches, and our movements—is, as engrossing as the one may be and as dazzling as the other, simply not enough.

NOTE

1. Editor's note: The reference is to Thomas Nagel, "What Is It Like to Be a Bat?" *Philosophical Review*, vol. 83, October 1974.

INTELLECTUAL ROOTS

Clifford Geertz is Harold F. Linder Professor of Social Science at the Institute for Advanced Study, Princeton. He has carried out extensive field research over a forty-year period in Indonesia and in Morocco and is the author (or coauthor) of thirteen books and the editor of two others. Among his more prominent works are *The Religion of Java* (1960), *Agricultural Involution* (1963), *Islam Observed* (1968), *The Interpretation of Cultures* (1973), *Negara* (1980), *Local Knowledge* (1983), and *Works and Lives* (1988). He is a member of the National Academy of Sciences, the American Academy of Arts and Sciences, and the American Philosophical Society, and is a Corresponding Member of the British Academy.

I had no anthropological training whatsoever as an undergraduate (it was not even taught at Antioch College when I attended it just after World War II), and, economics aside, very little social science of any kind. A philosophy and literature major, the field was suggested to me by my advisor, a Deweyian philosopher. He knew Clyde Kluckhohn, who was just then getting the Social Relations Department at Harvard under way with the cooperation of the sociologist Talcott Parsons, the clinical psychologist Henry Murray, and the social psychologist Gordon Allport, and thought I might flourish there. I applied and did indeed flourish, studying not only with such anthropologists as Kluckhohn, Benjamin Paul, Evon Vogt, Douglas Oliver, David Schneider, and later on Cora DuBois (who became my thesis advisor), but with various sociologists and psychologists as well. The Social Relations Department was an experiment in interdisciplinary study which was, at least for a decade or two, quite successful.

My then wife, Hildred Geertz, who was also a student in the Department, and I were offered the opportunity to participate in a group research project in Java, which we did from 1952 to 1954, along with our colleagues Alice Dewey, Donald Fagg, Rufus Hendon, Robert Jay, and Edward Ryan. There was a general division of ethnographic labor in which I concentrated mainly on religion, but pursued a wide variety of other concerns as well. My main orientation at that time, due as much to Parsons as to Kluckhohn, was Weberian, and I was concerned to see whether his "Protestant Ethic" argument could be adapted for reformist Indonesian Muslims, the conclusion being, rather unsurprisingly, that it could and it couldn't.

In any case, after a couple years back in Cambridge, during which I worked with some development economists at M.I.T and wrote an analytical history of the "involutional" development of Javanese agriculture, my wife and I returned to Indonesia, this time to Bali, where my main concerns were social organization and the development of the indigenous state.

Upon returning from this second field trip, I spent the year at the Center for Advanced Study in the Behavioral Sciences in Palo Alto. It was an "anthropological year" there, with perhaps the largest collection of anthropologists, all of them older and more eminent than I, ever in attendance at one time: Fred Eggan, Meyer Fortes, George Peter Murdock, Cora DuBois, Joseph Greenberg, Melford Spiro, Lloyd Fallers. I spent the following year teaching at Berkeley, but while I was at the Center a number of people from the University of Chicago invited me to join them in founding the Committee for the Comparative Study of New Nations there, and in 1960, I did so.

The Chicago department, where I spent ten years, was an extraordinarily lively one, with in addition to Eggan, Sol Tax, Milton Singer, Robert Braidwood, Norman McQuown, and other senior figures, a number of junior ones such as myself—Robert Adams, McKim Marriott, Melford Spiro, Manning Nash, David Schneider, Lloyd Fallers, Clark Howell—who banded together to revise the core curriculum. What later came to be known as "symbolic anthropology" perhaps first emerged there in full form, and the period was in any case an extremely vital one, critically important to me. While at Chicago I also began fieldwork in Morocco, making three or four trips there, and introducing a number of graduate students into field research.

In 1970 I was invited to be the first professor of social science at the Institute for Advanced Study, where I have been ever since, the only anthropologist on the faculty, though I have been able to invite a large number of anthropologists and other social scientists to come there for a year's research. I am presently in the process of trying to write a book recapitulating not only this rather unstandard career (I have spent, all told, perhaps only two or three years wholly involved in an anthropology department as such, and though I have taught a fair amount, as much of it has been outside the confines of anthropology in the strict sense as within them), but what I think I have learned from pursuing it.

This has turned out to be a daunting task. Sorting out the "influences" upon one's work, trying to determine retrospectively its general direction, deciding what parts of it seem central, which less so is an invitation to self-deception. I have always been interested in "philosophical" issues, from my undergraduate days forward, but have always wished to pursue them not abstractly but in terms of concrete material, about Java, about Bali, about Morocco, or wherever. The present paper, though in the nature of the case more generally cast, is in that tradition: an attempt to look at critically important intellectual issues from the angle of a working anthropologist.

Assessing the Field

A host of distinguished anthropologists have presented a range of thoughtful analyses regarding the present state and future direction of cultural anthropology. In drawing their various themes together in this chapter, a caution is in order. A concluding chapter such as this can only be a personal assessment. Readers will also have their own views if the volume has achieved its aim—to encourage critical reflection on the present state of the discipline. The volume constitutes a resource we can all share, ponder over, and use in developing our visions of anthropology. It draws us into discussing—as a community—where cultural anthropology is and where it might go.

If, as Wolf (1980:20) suggests, "a discipline draws its energy from the questions it asks," then I perceive three concerns presently energizing the field—relating to matters of process, continuity, and significance. The contributions discuss process in a double sense. There is a sensitivity to the processes by which we conceptualize the cultural. What are the limitations to our present conceptualizations? How might they be improved? And there is a concern for analyzing the cultural's complex, processual dynamics. How do continuity and change overlap with one another through time in a locale? And how are regional and global forces reshaped in the process of shaping communities? There is also a concern with continuity—with tying the discipline's past productions into present ones. Some contributors query if, in the momentum of our "fads and fashions," the discipline is being rein-

vented each generation. In what sense, they ask, are we (and are we not) building an intellectual discipline? And, finally, there is a question regarding anthropology's relevance in the modern world. What value does it have as an intellectual discipline? What solutions does anthropology offer to our present dilemmas? Let me take each of these in turn, elaborating on some of their implications.

THE SHIFT TOWARD PROCESS

The shift toward process has been more evolutionary than revolutionary—involving subtle, incremental changes rather than a single, dramatic one. We can find precursors of it in the work of anthropologists one, two, or even three generations back. (Some—such as Morgan, Boas, Sapir, and Kroeber—are mentioned in the contributions and editorial introductions; others, readers will recall from separate readings.) That is why it is best to refer to what has occurred as a shift in emphasis. The "new" is also partly "old."

What brought about this shift toward process? One factor encouraging the change in emphasis is the present wealth of ethnographic data. Combining information from early ethnographies with present ones, we see cultural groups in clearer perspective and in greater temporal depth. "Anthropologists now do research where other anthropologists have worked," Kottak and Colson (pages 398-399) note. "We have their publications, sometimes even their field notes. We must account for the differences between their findings and ours . . . by paying full attention to the forces of history and intracultural variation." Along with our ever-increasing ethnographic documentation has come an increasing appreciation for historical data. History is now very much "in" in anthropology. Using long frames of time—rather than the "ethnographic present"—allows us to move beyond abstract assertions of cultural persistence to detailed analyses of what does (and does not), in fact, endure. "In what sense," Goody (page 253), for example, asks, is "the culture of contemporary New England . . . the same as that of the beginning of the nineteenth century, [or] of the early period dominated by the Puritans, [or] of Stuart England which they had left, [or] of the earlier Chaucerian England to which their ancestors belonged."

The other key factor—besides our present wealth of data—bringing about a perspectival shift is a changing world. "The context of anthropology has changed since its birth," Godelier (page 108) notes. Tishkov discusses the dramatic changes of this past decade in Eastern Europe. And Tambiah (page 435) comments on three important changes within the Third World:

The first stage is the . . . "decolonization" process itself, when Western imperial powers, following the Second World War, "transferred power" to local elite groups. . . . The second . . . spanning the late 1950s and gathering momentum in the 1960s, was characterized by optimistic and even strident claims made in these newly independent countries concerning their objectives of "nation making," strengthening "national sovereignty," creating "national culture" and "national identity," and achieving "national integration." . . . In a dislocating and sometimes disconcerting manner this hopeful expansive phase of nation building has been put to the test, seriously questioned, imperiled and even reversed in the third phase, from the 1960s onward.

The shift toward process is manifested in a number of ways within this volume. But I would especially highlight three relating to:

(1) conceptions of the cultural, (2) broadening the foci of analysis, and (3) the dynamics of change.

Ambiguities and Limitations in Earlier Conceptions of the Cultural's Dimensions

Today interpretivists and positivists alike acknowledge that serious problems exist with earlier formulations of the cultural. Interpretivist-oriented anthropologists, for example, emphasize that concepts such as the cultural are social constructions, are impositions of order on the dynamic flux of human behavior. And more positivist-oriented anthropologists, basing their assessments on detailed, empirical observation, stress that the cultural concept overly structures (and hence misrepresents) the subtle dynamics, the fluid complexities, of everyday life.

"One of anthropology's central achievements," Levy (page 180) notes, "has been the isolation of 'culture' as a coherent way of understanding aspects of human behavior and experience." But as Levy (page 180) goes on to stress, the cultural concept "split[s] the world up in ways that have generated new conceptual problems while managing to perpetuate some old ones in a new language." Various contributors discuss this point. Vayda (page 324) criticizes the "quest for 'congruence' and 'unitary symbolic structuring'" implicit in the cultural concept. Keesing (page 301) refers to anthropology's "invention and evocation of . . . radical otherness." Bloch (page 281) emphasizes that "our understanding of culture has remained partial and superficial." And Moore (page 373) observes: "It becomes more and more obvious that the totalizing use of the idea of 'a culture,' and the equating of one culture (passed on from generation to generation) with one society, can be an obstacle to seeing the importance of temporal factors, individual and categorical diversity, and local and large-scale juxtapositions."

That is why, following Keesing (page 309), I refer to "the cultural" rather than "culture." It de-emphasizes the reified, objectified nature of culture, conveying a sense of the concept's adjectival, descriptive qualities (cf. D'Andrade 1992a:229). It stresses we are exploring something in motion—something we catch in process and label so we have a way of referring to it.

Strathern develops a related theme concerning the anthropological concept of "society." "Society was a vehicle for a kind of Western holism," she (page 205) notes, "a totalizing concept through which modern people could think the holisms of others." In a footnote she (page 216, note 1) adds, summarizing Thornton's (1988) argument, "much of the significance of 'society' lay in its power as a rhetorical trope for the organization of anthropological data. Positing analytical components capable of theoretical integration presumed an entirety to the object of study as a whole made up of parts, so that society emerged as a holistic precipitate of analysis." In working through the problem, she (page 206) raises important questions for us to ponder:

First, how to conceptualize a society that was not composed of groups; and second, the relationship of parts to wholes. If groups were the vehicles through which societies presented themselves to their members, then without group membership what was a person a part of?

The Cultural as a Historically Situated Concept. Several contributors emphasize that the cultural concept has historical roots and that this shapes the concept's use today. Keesing (page 307) observes our present sense of "cultural identity has its origin in nineteenth-century cultural nationalism in Europe, expressed in an intense search for ethnic roots and folk origins, for primordiality and cultural tradition." It is for this reason, as Goody (page 254) suggests, "the concept of 'a culture' tends to have a highly nationalistic flavor about it, certainly highly political." Visualizing a cul-

ture as homogeneous, he notes, is "a way of covering up the cracks in the fabric of society." The concern for political empowerment comes out in Sahlins's (page 379) discussion of what he terms the current "culturalism":

What distinguishes the current "culturalism" (as it might be called) is the claim to one's own mode of existence as a superior value and a political right, precisely in opposition to a foreign-imperial presence. More than an expression of "ethnic identity" . . . [it] entails the people's attempt to control their relationships with the dominant society, including control of the technical and political means that up to now have been used to victimize them.

Anthropologists, in describing indigenous cultural forms, he (page 379) adds, "are assisting at a spontaneous, worldwide movement of cultural defiance, whose full meanings and historic effects are yet to be determined."

We need to explore, in greater detail, how different groups' conceptions of the cultural interact with one another—how, for example, Western colonial powers used cultural traditions to order and pacify subjugated populations (see e.g. Anderson 1991:181) and how these populations, in turn, used cultural traditions to resist colonial domination. Das points out how Dumont appropriated Brahman conceptualizations of Indian society in hope of explaining not only India to the West but the West to itself. And Tishkov describes the Soviet case. He (pages 446-447) notes that "Lenin and the Bolsheviks used the slogan of the right to [ethnic] self-determination as a tremendously effective political weapon in winning the non-Russian regions to their side" during the Russian revolution. As a result, "ethno-nationalism became the basis on which socialist federalism was constructed." Cultural units became the basis for political units. But the cultural politics that facilitated the formation of the Soviet Union in time became a key factor in the Soviet Union's collapse. The political rhetoric of a totalitarian state involving "self-determination for ethno-nations, up to and including the right of secession" (page 447), became taken seriously as the state's totalitarian powers lessened under Gorbachev and *perestroika*. Quoting Tishkov (pages 448-449):

For millions of Soviet citizens, aroused to political activism, facing a lack of truly effective forms for realizing their demands, the appeal of ethnic group loyalty and of the nationalist idea became the sole and most understandable basis for collective action and the expression of protest regarding conditions of social despair and profound political disillusionment. Ethno-nationalism became prominent as an alternative to a strong, centralized state with ineffective representation at the local level. It called on romantic, emotional images for a new form of solidarity without necessarily resolving the problems of democratic representation at the local level.

We see, in Tishkov's analysis, the cultural not only as a historically situated concept but as a historical force in and of itself—shaping and being shaped by diverse groups in search of power.

Coherence and Sharing. Several contributors question the degree to which coherence and sharing occur within social groupings. Nader (page 87) suggests "culture is not homogenous, nor always consensual." Vayda (page 320) emphasizes the emerging anti-essentialist view which "sees variation as 'fundamental reality.'" I (page 338) note diversity is "partly in the eye of the beholder, partly in whether one deals with the subject matter as rigid or flexible in form." And Harris (page 63) affirms the cultural materialist "definition of culture stands opposed to the fixed, 'essentialist' notions that inspire those who define culture as a realm of pure and uniform ideas hovering over the hubbub of the daily life of specific individuals."

Related to this questioning is an increased concern for empirically delineating (rather than philosophically postulating) the degree to which cultural coherence and sharing actually occur in particular settings. As Moore (page 364) nicely phrases it, "the matter of necessary logical connections among . . . clusters of symbols and practices . . . [is] a question rather than an answer." "Whether specific beliefs and meanings are shared widely and persist in a given society," Vayda (page 326) asserts, is "a matter for empirical determination rather than . . . a priori postulation."

From this common point, contributors suggest moving in one of two directions. First, there are efforts to rethink the nature of sharing. What do people, in fact, share with one another in a group? What might be shared, I suggest in my contribution, is not simply facts but the ways facts are handled, are woven together, to solve problems in everyday experiences. This fits with Bloch's (page 280) assertion that expertise involves not only "received knowledge" but also "apparatuses for the efficient handling . . . of specific domains of knowledge and practice." And it relates to Strauss and Quinn's concern with shared experiences: "people in the same social environment," they (page 292) observe, "will . . . experience many of the same typical patterns." What is perhaps shared then are processes for dealing with cultural content as much, if not more than, the content itself. Our ethnographies need to emphasize this fact more.

Second, and related to this rethinking effort, is a concern for understanding the processes by which sharing comes about. "I have long argued," Barth (page 360) notes, "that we must turn from totalizing cultural models to generative models of processes." "The task of giving a realistic account . . . of how people achieve and reproduce a degree of conceptual accommodation and shared premises . . . [is] the most important task of anthropology at the present" he (page 354) asserts. Goodenough (page 266) notes, "A theory of . . . culture must account for . . . the processes that work toward an appearance of consensus in what people know." And Wolf (page 226) suggests, "Power is implicated in meaning through its role in upholding one version of significance as true, fruitful, or beautiful, against other possibilities." There are two sets of processes here: (1) the production (and reproduction) of knowledge diversity (and/or consensus) from one generation to another and (2) the organization of diversity (or enforcement of conformity) as a political process at one period in time. Barth (1975, 1987), in his recent work, leans toward the former, Wolf (in his contribution) toward the latter. We need to see how both processes operate, especially in relation to one another.

Sahlins raises an important caution in regard to the issue of sharing. Sahlins (page 393), readers will remember, asserts, "Essentialized descriptions are not the platonic fantasies of anthropologists alone; they are general cultural conditions of human perception and communication." And, "In order for categories to be contested at all, there must be a common system of intelligibility, extending to the grounds, means, modes, and issues of disagreement" (page 386). What he is getting at is that we must see beyond the obvious fact that differences exist in a group. We must ask ourselves whether the differences are systematic—whether different types of people (in terms of status, gender, or what have you) express systematic differences, with, for example, men asserting one thing and women another. He is querying whether there can be a system of differences, whether, in his words, there is "some meaningful order *in* the differences" (page 386).

We are drawn back then to two key questions raised above: To what degree and in what ways does sharing exist within a community? And, equally important, how does the sharing that does exist come about?

Seeming Distinctions.   One can find questioning of traditional anthropological distinctions in earlier works. But reading this volume's contributions, one senses that the questioning has become more intense. First, there is a questioning of the institutional categories commonly used in ethnographies—such as kinship, economy, politics, and religion. How effective are these distinctions today, contributors ask? Although "in Western societies separate functions are carried out by separate institutions," Godelier (page 101) notes that this is not necessarily the case in other cultures. Yanagisako and Collier (page 192) write, "It is impossible to understand interactions within 'domestic spheres' without simultaneously understanding the organization of political and economic arenas." And Goody (page 251) comments, "It is hard to see any advantage that has accrued from treating the ideational level . . . as a distinct domain."

Related to this questioning of traditional ethnographic categories, contributors stress the need to understand the processes by which people—anthropologists and informants alike—construct cultural categories regarding the world around them. Yanagisako and Collier (page 195) propose, "Rather than take for granted that societies are constituted of functionally based institutional domains, . . . [we should] investigate the social and symbolic processes by which human actions . . . [come to be organized] into seemingly 'natural' social domains." And Strathern (page 215) cautions that "'our' project [i.e. our anthropologically constructed categories] should not be mistaken for 'theirs'" (i.e. for the categories of our informants).

Second, continuing the problem of analytical distinctions, is the need to rethink what we mean by "the cultural." "We often speak of culture as if it were an attribute of distinct social groups in a bounded fashion," Goody (page 256) notes, "but that may not be at all the case when one looks at specific elements of behavior." We need to rethink to what degree we want to stay with the more current conception of the cultural—as the property of a delimitable group (with somewhat formalized borders)—versus return to an older concept of the cultural as an exemplary or elitist ideal. Goody (pages 254-255) touches on an elitist notion of the cultural in his discussion of

T. S. Eliot. And Tambiah's (1985:280) notion of the Galactic polity ("with its rhetoric and ritual display of the exemplary center") ties nicely into an exemplary perspective. There are strong historical roots for such a conception of the cultural. Anderson (1991:19) observes, "Older imagining of states . . . [were] defined by centers, . . . [with] porous and indistinct" borders. They were defined by displays at the center rather than by boundaries at the periphery. We need to consider, I am suggesting, the conceptual value of focusing on the cultural as being *of* a group versus *for* a group—a shared property versus an exemplary ideal.

Related to this issue is a questioning of the old opposition between "indigenous" and "foreign." "Culture," Goody (page 259) notes, "is no longer encapsulated in local communities" if indeed it ever was. What is critical here is not demarcating a boundary—between the domestic and the foreign (however one might define these)—but exploring the dynamic tensions between the two. "In any local sector of the global system the transformation assumes the dual appearance of assimilation and differentiation," Sahlins (page 389) notes. "The local people articulate with the dominant cultural order even as they take their distance from it, jiving to the world beat while making their own music."

Finally, traditional efforts at conceptualizing the temporal are questioned. Vayda challenges the essentialist notion of the "past" as a storer of enduring values. He (page 322) quotes Colson: "Values once thought to be fundamental . . . have turned out to be situational and time linked, rather than eternal verities." "Chopping up the social facts of fieldwork and putting them into two conceptual bins marked 'old' and 'new' is not the way to address the temporal problem," Moore (page 371) stresses. "Such a sorting sounds as if it were saying something about sequence. But the effect of this classification is to remove the connections from view and to treat time simply as an exercise in a dualistic categorization." We need to explore the connections, the interactions, the processes by which, quoting Yanagisako and Collier (page 199), "social systems change and, at the same time . . . remain relatively stable." The whole way by which the reproduction of cultural patterns produces change, and change seems to follow certain patterns, needs further analysis—a point Sahlins (1981, 1985) repeatedly emphasizes in his work, and, I might add, Vogt (1960) stressed thirty years ago in an article entitled "Structure and Process."

The Cultural As Centered in Activities. A traditional anthropological concern is, to quote Service (1985:259), whether the cultural "is to be explained on its own terms, or whether it is only . . . an aspect of mind. . . . Does [it] . . . consist of real things and events . . . or is it an 'abstraction' from behavior with its real locus in the minds of the people being studied?" Many contributors concur that the cultural is profitably analyzed in terms of on-going activities. "I have found it theoretically helpful," Goodenough (page 266) asserts, "to think of both culture and language as rooted in human activities." "Most important aspects of culture," Bloch (page 282) suggests, "are embedded in the basic mental premises of action." Barth (pages 356-357) emphasizes, "All concepts are embedded in practice. . . . Most concepts will be evoked and used in cooperative and interactive situations." "It is not legal rules abstracted from social life," Moore (page 370) states, "but law embedded in the process of social life that is the object to be explored." And Sahlins (page 393), citing Locke, affirms that "properties can be known only through interaction . . . we know things from the changes they make in, or receive from, other things." Goodenough (page 270) notes that this perspective fits with Malinowski's analysis of institutions. Richards (1957:24-25) points out that in describing an institution, Malinowski focused on "the functioning of the particular activity considered"—on an institution as a set of ongoing activities rather than as an abstract set of social rules or knowledge categories. Even an item of material culture, such as the canoe, was discussed "in relation to the groups of men who built it, and used it, the technique of its construction, [and] the magic used over it."

There are two debates that emerge out of this general consensus. First, we see in Goodenough's and Strauss and Quinn's contributions a continuation of the Goodenough/Geertz debate described in Section Four. As Ortner (1984:129) notes, Geertz argues "that culture is not something locked inside people's heads, but rather is embodied in public symbols, symbols through which members of a society communicate their worldview." In contrast, Goodenough (page 267) asserts that "a theory of culture gets into trouble if it sees a culture as having an existence apart from the individual people whose interactions give rise to" it. Strauss and Quinn (page 295) query: "How can actors invent, negotiate, and contest their cultural worlds unless they have internalized motives for doing so?" (Levy, pages 181-182, points out this latter position has deep Boasian roots.) At stake, in the analysis of cultural activities, is a dispute over the strengths (and significance) of symbolic, social approaches versus cognitive, psychological ones. Both Strauss and Quinn and I explore ways for bringing these two perspectives together. Drawing on recent research on implicit memory in neuroscience, I suggest, for example:

A considerable amount of what we might term the cultural is stored in implicit memory—which is to say, a considerable amount is primarily accessed through performance. From this point of view, the Geertz/Goodenough "debate" . . . dissolves since implicit memory is certainly located in the brain (as Goodenough emphasizes) but it can best be observed in the public actions of people (in line with Geertz's perspective). (page 341)

Second, we see a dispute regarding the applicability of linguistic models to cognitive processes. Goodenough (page 265) emphasizes

that "what we refer to as languages and cultures are the same order of phenomena. . . . What we learn about language can be useful in helping to think about culture." But Bloch (page 250) challenges this view—that "culture is inseparably linked to language . . . or that culture is . . . 'language like,' consisting of linked linear propositions." Bloch stresses the importance of nonsentential forms of knowing derived from experiential activities. "Much of the knowledge which anthropologists study," he (page 280) emphasizes, "exists in people's heads in a nonlinguistic form."

The issues discussed here are important. Up to now we have been able to get along reasonably well without delving deeply into the complex dynamics surrounding knowing, especially the knowing of public symbols. We have been able to get by making tentative assumptions about what seemed reasonable to us. But as our ethnographic data and methods become increasingly refined, we will have to be more precise in our formulations—assessing them, refining them—so we can better understand in what ways and to what degree the cultural is embedded in action, or, following Levy's analogy, dancers dance dances.

This is why, as Bloch, Strauss and Quinn, and I emphasize, there is a need to be sensitive to developments in cognitive science. "Some of the theories emerging in cognitive science," Bloch (page 276) stresses, "are *central* to the concerns of anthropology . . . and should lead anthropologists to re-examine many of the premises of their work."

Broadening the Foci of Analysis

Local-Global Relations. There is a clear trend in the volume toward broadening the processes and topics deemed relevant to ethnographic analysis. Where ethnographies once primarily focused on local communities, they now often include significant material on regional, national, and/or international matters. Marcus (page 44) discusses "opening up, to contemporary processes of apparent global homogenization, the local knowledge classically represented and described by ethnographers." He (page 46) suggests, "The identity of . . . any group is produced simultaneously in many different locales of activity, by many different agents." Nader (page 90) discusses gender perceptions *between* societies, emphasizing that gender arrangements at the local level "are related to macro-level distinctions between 'us and them.'" Wolf (page 223) stresses the importance of analyzing "processes operating on a macroscale, as well as in microsettings." And Kottak and Colson (page 408) state, "Good ethnography now depends on recognizing that the world system supplies much of what informs local action." "Linkages is a convenient term," they (page 396) note, "to encompass the multistranded involvement in the world system that ethnographers must now consider in conceptualizing the influences affecting [local] values, categories, [and] institutional arrangements."

This broadening of perspective has enriched our understanding of the anthropological project. We now consider our research within a framework of global, center-periphery relations. R. Rosaldo (1989:217) states the point well: "All of us," he notes, "inhabit an interdependent late twentieth-century world marked by borrowing and lending across porous national and cultural boundaries that are saturated with inequality, power, and domination." "The essentialism of our discourse," Keesing (page 303) suggests, reflects "our vested disciplinary interests in characterizing exotic otherness." And "the identity of the anthropologist and his world," Marcus (page 50) states, "is likely to be profoundly related to that of the particular 'world' he is studying. . . . [Recognizing] the chain of pre-existing historic or contemporary connection between the ethnographer and her subjects . . . remain[s] a defining feature of the current experimental sensibility in ethnography."

A thought-provoking example of this orientation is Mintz's (1985) *Sweetness and Power*, relating to sugar's developing importance in British society. Quoting him (1985:158, 180):

The profound changes in dietary and consumption patterns in eighteenth- and nineteenth-century Europe were not random or fortuitous, but the direct consequences of the same momentum that created a world economy, shaping the asymmetrical relationships between the metropolitan centers and their colonies and satellites. . . . (158)

Whereas the plantations [in the European colonies] were long viewed as sources of profit through direct capital transfer for reinvestment at home, or through the absorption of finished goods from home, the hypothesis offered here is that sugar and other drug foods, by provisioning, sating—and, indeed, drugging—farm and factory workers, sharply reduced the overall cost of creating and reproducing the metropolitan proletariat. (180)

The Colonial Periphery. As Mintz's study implies, a widening of ethnographic perspectives has an enriching effect on the understanding of ourselves over time in relation to others. It has opened up new topics for anthropological analysis—including, notably, the behavior of Westerners in contact and colonial situations. Not only are "exotic others"—!Kung, Samoans, Inuit Eskimos—intellectual foils for understanding ourselves now but so are our Western relatives who traveled abroad in times past. Interactions on the colonial periphery are now perceived as lenses for interpreting the metropole. "As we attempt broader ethnographies," Stoler (1989a:652) writes, "we may begin to capture how European culture and class politics resonated in colonial settings [and] how class and gender discriminations . . . reverberated in the metropole" (cf. Comaroff and Comaroff 1992). Dening (1986) and Borofsky and Howard (1989) emphasize that the contact period in Polynesia contains a treasure trove of information regarding European cultural dynamics. In the way "the British possessed Tahiti," Dening (1986:112) observes, "they displayed [it] . . . as a mirror for themselves."

Gender. As Lamphere (in di Leonardo 1991: viii) notes, "bringing the issue of gender to the fore allows us to sharpen, refine, and reorient traditional anthropological problems." Like the above topics, gender constitutes an important perspective from which to rethink significant social dynamics—for understanding (as di Leonardo 1991:25 observed) "the mutual interpenetrations of gender, sexuality, kinship, and political economy at home and abroad." This is Yanagisako and Collier's (page 190) point: "Our goal is at once to revitalize the study of kinship and to situate the study of gender at the theoretical core of anthropology by calling into question the boundary between these two fields." Also, using gender, Nader and Yanagisako and Collier open up new ways to examine human inequalities. They lead us to consider the same question Godelier asks but from a different angle: How are inequalities perpetuated as well as disguised in human communities?

Broadening our sense of relevant foci for analysis—to include local-global relations, the colonial periphery, and gender—means more than simply adding new topics of study, I am suggesting. It means using such perspectives to rethink a host of anthropological problems.

The Subtle Complexities of Change through Time

A key part of the shift toward process has been an absorption—or more precisely reabsorption—in the processual dynamics of change. Harris (page 63) emphasizes that "culture is at bottom an unfolding material process." Wolf (page 224) considers the question of how to move "from viewing organization as product or outcome to understanding organization as process." And Barth (page 360) stresses the importance of generative, processual models in enhancing the power of anthropological analysis.

Interactional Analyses. A significant concern, within this shift, is the increasing prominence of complex, interactional analyses. Rather than A affecting B (or B, A), it is now more of A and B mutually affecting one another. This is clear regarding the generation of cultural meaning. "If people act . . . in terms of meanings they or their ancestors have conceived," Rappaport (page 156) states, "they are as much in the service of those conceptions as those conceptions are parts of their adaptations." Behavior, Murphy (page 58) notes, "occurs within *histories* in which the actor is both producer and product, creator and victim, warden and prisoner." Yanagisako and Collier (page 200) argue for "models specifying the dialectical relationship between practice and ideas." And Moore (page 364) refers to the "continuous and multiple shapings and reshapings" of ideas. The fact that this shift toward process overlaps with Ortner's earlier development of practice theory emphasizes that this shift is more a developing momentum than a radical break with the past. "What a practice theory seeks to explain," Ortner (1984:149, 152, 154) wrote in 1984, "is the genesis, reproduction, and change of form and meaning . . . how does the system shape practice . . . [and] how does practice shape the system." (Intriguingly, while her idea continues, her label for the perspective apparently has not. None of the contributors directly refer to practice theory.)

The complexities of the interactions are still being assessed, as one can see from the diverse perspectives enunciated here (and in the anthropological literature at large). Both Harris and Godelier directly address this issue. They ask: Are some factors more prominent than others in shaping change and, if so, what are they? How do they operate? These are critical questions to answer as we seek to understand the subtle dynamics of change.

One key element in the dynamics of change is power, a topic discussed by several contributors. Scheper-Hughes and Moore illustrate some of the complexities involved. At the same time power is being asserted as a voice for change, they note, the phrasing of such assertions may help undermine the possibility for real change. Resistance *to* domination may, at times, help perpetuate the status quo *of* domination. "Illness and illness metaphors are coded messages . . . by the suffering and the aggrieved," Scheper-Hughes (page 238) suggests. "The rub is, however, that whenever defiance and protest are expressed in the bodily language of symptoms, there is . . . the danger of an individualized, medicalized response. . . . The possibility of using bodily distress to generate a radical critique of the social order is lost." And Moore (page 369) adds: "Like Penelope weaving by day and ripping by night . . . the socialist state [of Tanzania] generated undoings of all its doings while it waited for the socialist dream to be realized." We need to look behind the rhetoric of change to see how and why change actually tends to come about in certain contexts.

Integrating Local and Global Histories. A good way to sense the complexities involved here is to analyze, through time, the interactions between local communities and larger regional or international networks. While the "world system's" influences are observed to be widespread—Hannerz (1990) refers to a "world culture"—local cultural differences continue to exist. Tambiah (page 440) describes the problem:

On the one hand there is a universalizing and homogenizing trend that is making people in contemporary societies and countries more and more alike (whatever the actual fact of differential access to capacities, commodities, and honors) in wanting the same material and social benefits of modernization, whether they be income, material goods, housing, literacy and schooling, jobs, recreation, and social
prestige. On the other hand these same people also claim to be different, and not necessarily equal, on the basis of their ascriptive identity, linguistic difference, ethnic membership, and rights to the soil.

At issue, as Marcus (page 44ff) points out, is understanding the subtle, complex ways resistance and accommodation co-occur.

Clearly, international networks impact on local settings. To quote Kottak and Colson (page 400): Today, "local concerns—health, subsistence, self-respect . . . —depend on engagement with wider systems." But it is also true that there are local resistances to these wider networks. Indigenous people participate in their destinies by ordering the global "reality" in their own terms. "The local people," Sahlins (page 384) observes, "integrate the World System . . . [into] their own system of the world." It is ironic, he (page 378) comments, "that Western social scientists should be elaborating theories of global integration just when this 'new world order' is breaking down into so many small-scale separatist movements marching under the banners of cultural autonomy." Tambiah (page 431) adds: "The late-twentieth-century reality is evidenced by the fact that ethnic groups . . . expected in due course to assimilate or weaken, have figured as major 'political' elements and major political collective actors in several societies." Tishkov, in his discussion of the former Soviet Union, illustrates just how strong such forces can be.

An essential problem is how to integrate the West and "the rest" into a unified framework where we can see the complex, interactive processes involved at close hand—"the global interconnections of human aggregates," in Wolf's (1982:385) phrasing. "The West and the rest, long locked in historical embrace," Comaroff and Comaroff (1992:45) note, "cannot but be interrogated together." Where once we framed West-rest integration in terms of evolutionary, hierarchical stages—in which the West stood above the rest—the challenge today is to frame this integration in terms of world history. Wolf's (1982) book *Europe and the People without History* has become a classic in this respect. Smith (1984b:196) illustrates the direction the discipline seems headed:

What I hope to do in this brief sketch of Guatemalan history is to capture some of the tensions and dialectic of social life in a situation where people who had non-capitalist values and institutions confronted expanding capitalism to produce a unique historical outcome. . . . I want to show not only how capitalist expansion affected one small local system, but also how local institutions interacted with externally imposed forces to create a particular dynamic that affected capitalist expansion itself.

What we need to continue studying—in a host of locales from a range of perspectives—are the processes of give-and-take occurring in West-rest interactions. Western groups often try to define the contexts within which accommodation and resistance develop—asserting a subtle (or not so subtle) form of political hegemony. They seek to regulate trade, define the valuation of goods and statuses, assert what forms of opposition are (and are not) acceptable. Indigenous groups seek to do the same as they interpret outside forces within their own indigenous frameworks. Such interactions are often facilitated by a set of overlapping understandings that allow for both accommodation *and* resistance. There is truth in more than one sense, I would suggest, in observing that culture is on everybody's lips today (see Sahlins, page 378). Culture represents a shared symbol for talking about issues of domination, development, homogenization, identity, accommodation, and resistance. As anthropologists know, cultural meanings are being shaped and reshaped across a complex, international terrain today.

The "Invention" of Tradition. One of the more intriguing problems arising out of this dynamic concerns what has been termed "the invention of tradition," after a book of that title edited by Hobsbawm and Ranger (1983).

Both Tambiah and Tishkov touch on the theme in reference to the construction of ethnic identity. "'Traditions' which appear or claim to be old," Hobsbawm (1983:1) asserts, "are often quite recent in origin and sometimes invented." "Plenty of political institutions, ideological movements and groups [of the past two centuries] were so unprecedented," he (1983:7) adds, that "historic continuity had to be invented . . . by creating an ancient past beyond effective historical continuity either by semi-fiction . . . or by forgery." Some of the invented traditions may surprise Western readers. The authors discuss Scottish kilts, Wales' Celtic ties, and aspects of royal British pageantry. While the book has proven an academic and public success in the West, efforts by anthropologists to carry this same theme over into other regions—such as Linnekin's (1983) account of Hawaiian traditions and Hanson's (1989) account of New Zealand Maori ones—have met with mixed reviews. They have resulted in some positive academic recognition and some rather hostile criticism by indigenous activists. Apparently, it is one thing to call your own traditions invented; it is quite another to call other people's that. Three interacting elements seem at work.

First, there is the just-noted politics of domination and resistance that pervades current discussions of the cultural. "Cultural consciousness," Sahlins (page 379) remarks (citing T. Turner), "entails the people's attempt to control their relationships with the dominant society." Keesing (page 307) observes, for "Third World elites . . . Westernized though they may be, to claim that 'it' is 'our culture' is to make claims of identity, authenticity, resistance and resilience." From this perspective, accepting anthropological views of their traditions as invented only helps, in Sahlins' (page 381) phrasing, to make the conquest, to make others' subordination, complete (cf. Carter 1987:160-161). From an indigenous perspective, Das (page 136) concurs: "The condition for participation in the making of the sociological [and anthropological] discourse for the non-Western anthropologist is an active renunciation of contemporary possibilities in her own culture."

Second, the cultural (as repeatedly stressed) has a fluid, dynamic, character which anthropologists must continually be sensitive to. As implied in my paper and Borofsky (1987), cultural "invention" may be more the norm than the exception among most groups. Sahlins (page 389) suggests that tradition "functions as a yardstick by which the people measure the acceptability of change." And Moore (page 371) notes: "A processual attitude toward . . . fieldwork . . . imagines the present as an emerging moment."

The problem regarding anthropological pronouncements on the subject lies in the fact that, and this is the third element, anthropologists have often been less sensitive than they might be to the above conditions. Anthropologists traditionally have downplayed the cultural's dynamic elements for what Keesing (page 306) refers to as a "coral reef conception" involving "timeless, endlessly self-reproducing structures" (page 301). Nor are anthropologists always aware of (and/or concerned by) the "cultural politics" that surround their labeling of other people's traditions as "invented." We see, in this, support for DaMatta's (page 127) assertion that important debates in North America and England often tend "to be viewed as 'theoretical,' 'technical,' and frankly 'academic'"—anthropologists seem to downplay the broader political implications of their work. Das (page 134) suggests much the same thing: "While for the Western reader, the identification of the fundamental unity of India in the caste system is a question of apprehending other values *intellectually,* at least some Indian readers are likely to use this sociological proposition as a *political* weapon."

Anthropologists, I am saying, have misperceived *our* invention of cultural stasis as *others'* invention of process. (Their traditions have not followed our ahistorical conception of tra-

dition and so we label them "invented.") And others have taken our historically situated cultural concept, that was used in the nationalist struggles of Europe, as a tool of resistance and empowerment in their struggles against us. This is what Keesing (page 307) refers to in asserting that "our own conceptual diseases . . . [have been] deployed against us." Shifting through both the subtle complexities and social conflicts involved here, we find much to reflect on. Listening carefully to others' responses to our application of anthropological concepts, we have an opportunity to grow as a discipline.

Agency. Four contributors (Das, Keesing, Sahlins, and Strauss and Quinn) refer to the notion of agency. While the concept has deep roots in political philosophy, it has been introduced into anthropology comparatively recently. "The central problem for practice theory" regarding agency and actors, Ortner (1989:14) states, is "the question of how actors who are so much products of their own social and cultural context can ever come to transform the conditions of their own existence, except by accident." Levy (page 183), in his contribution, phrases it as the need to "examine the person as an active center of history and context."

Giddens, citing what has become a classic in the discipline by Willis, *Learning to Labor: How Working Class Kids Get Working Class Jobs* (1981), raises an important issue regarding agency. Willis shows, Giddens (1984:289) states, "how the rebellious attitudes which the boys take towards the authority system of the school have definite unintended consequences that affect their fate." Or to use Aronowitz's description in the introduction to Willis's (1981:xi) American edition:

By stressing the importance of a counterculture among those who are the objects of educational manipulation, . . . [Willis] shows how kids, through their own activity and ideological development, reproduce themselves as a working class. The mechanism is their opposition to authority, their refusal to submit to the imperatives of a curriculum that encourages social mobility through acquisition of credentials.

Capitalist-industrial constraint, Giddens (1984: 289) states, "is shown to operate through the active involvement of the agents concerned, not as some force of which they are passive recipients."

Victor Turner comes at the issue of agency from another perspective. In *Dramas, Fields, and Metaphors*, for example, Turner (1974:13) explores "the ways in which social actions of various kinds acquire form through the metaphors and paradigms in their actors' heads . . . and, in certain intensive circumstances, generate unprecedented forms that bequeath history new metaphors and paradigms." The case of Thomas Becket's murder and subsequent canonization is a case in point. Turner explores the personalities and cultural paradigms that encouraged Becket's death. And he discusses how Becket's murder became the focal point for a further cultural paradigm which, in turn, helped precipitate other historical events. We see cultural paradigms, broad historical forces, and individual personalities interacting with one another in socially critical ways and with major historical import. Turner (1974: 60) writes: "The tale and myth of Becket have survived eight centuries and can still arouse fierce partisanship . . . [due to their being] caught up into an accelerating cleavage between church and state . . . [that] was compounded by the first serious stirrings of nationalist sentiment in England." Turner's social drama/root paradigm view of cultural dynamics could add much to current debates about historical process, I believe. It represents an important perspective, presently on the margins, waiting to be rediscovered by the profession.

The question of agency raises important issues—regarding how individuals do (or do not) bring about change, do (or do not) unintentionally support the status quo in rebelling against it, and do (or do not) become key figures who motivate others in significant social causes. As anthropology encompasses broader time spans, as questions of power take on more significance, there is much in these analyses to ponder regarding social change and the role individuals play in it.

Reaffirming Empirical Concerns. A final aspect of this processual shift is a movement away from postulating processes of change toward observing them. (A similar shift occurred in the 1930s—see Herskovits 1965:412.) "Whether specific beliefs and meanings . . . persist in a given society is," Vayda (page 326) asserts, "a matter for empirical determination rather than for a priori postulation." "Our task is not to reify illusory fact or structure," Barth (page 359) states, "but to record the flux which we can observe." Affirming both Moore's "centrality of events" and Kottak and Colson's "multilevel, multitime, multisite comparative" studies, Barth (page 358) suggests, "perhaps we would do best if we stopped privileging the representation of 'culture', and instead focused on the level of events, acts, people, and processes"—a theme Harris (pages 66-67) indicates is the premise behind the etic/behavioral emphasis of cultural materialism.

A CONCERN FOR DISCIPLINARY CONTINUITY

Reading the contributions, one perceives a clear concern for disciplinary continuity—for placing our present explanations within the context of the field's past understandings. Explicitly or implicitly, the same questions repeatedly come up: How do we draw on the past as we move into the future? Are we making progress as an intellectual discipline? Wolf (page 220) believes "that the search for explanation in anthropology can be cumulative; that knowledge and insights gained in the past can generate new questions, and that new departures can incorporate the accomplishments of the past." Barth (page 349) suggests that "there is also a need . . . [to] retrieve those traditional orientations which were valuable but may have become less salient during the debate of the last decade." Kuper (page 117) observes, a "source of intellectual vitality in anthropology may lie in the rediscovery of our shared theoretical interests."

Anthropology's Progress

If we reflect on what has been accomplished to date in anthropology, there is much we can take pride in. Two achievements seem particularly noteworthy.

Two Key Successes. One is the development of a comprehensive ethnographic data base regarding diverse ways of life. We need only look at the Human Relations Area Files or at a range of introductory texts to perceive the massive amounts of ethnographic data anthropologists have collected during this century. To be competent in a region, Kuper (page 116) observes, anthropologists today "must master a library of secondary sources." Such classics as Firth's *We the Tikopia,* Evans-Pritchard's *The Nuer,* Fortes's *The Web of Kinship among the Tallensi,* Malinowski's *Argonauts of the Western Pacific,* Lowie's *The Crow Indians,* and Radin's *Crashing Thunder* offer generation after generation of anthropologists not only a rich source of information to analyze but also a high set of standards to emulate. And, as Lévi-Strauss (page 425) observes, when indigenous "peoples, after undergoing nearly total destruction, wish to reestablish links with their past, it often happens that they rely on books by anthropologists for help."

Second, while many of the problems intriguing earlier anthropologists still remain unsolved (as Service, 1985, points out), we nonetheless have become more sophisticated in the phrasing of our research questions, the collection of our data, and the analysis of our results. What Firth (1975:7) stated eighteen

years ago holds even more so today—as a careful analysis of earlier ethnographies with current ones makes clear: "As compared with the work of a quarter of a century ago . . . that of today seems to me to be much more sophisticated and much more sensitive in many respects. The analysis of social interaction is more complex, taking more variables into account and relating them more systematically to produce more soundly based generalizations" (cf. Colson 1992:51).

Anthropological Biases. Where the discipline's progress has been most called into question, perhaps, is in the listing of intellectual biases reputedly held by past and/or present generations of anthropologists. The list is unsettling. Nader (page 84) notes, "Much has been written about the reasons for doing anthropology that implies that the very existence of a disciplinary anthropology was due to colonialism or more generally to imperialism." Marcus (page 43) refers to the "sophisticated and historically informed discussion [that has gone on over the past two decades regarding] . . . anthropology as a situated intellectual formation in the history of Western colonialism." DaMatta (pages 127-128) observes, "The more compartmentalized a university system becomes—as is the case in North America and England—the more it has an 'academic' . . . life . . . [involving] empiricist traditions . . . . [and a] purely programmatic and methodological approach." And Keesing (page 301) states: "The world of timeless, endlessly self-reproducing structures . . . [has] been fashioned in terms of European philosophical quests and assumptions, superimposed on the peoples encountered and subjugated along colonial frontiers."

From one perspective, such statements are a strong indictment of the discipline's objectivity. They imply our impressive ethnographic data base is clearly biased in a rather definite set of ways. But, from another perspective, such statements represent a positive affirmation of anthropology. "No one I've ever known in the social sciences has seriously thought that humans could become . . . completely objective field researchers," Bernard (page 172) states. "Objectivity means becoming aware of one's biases, and transcending them, not the lack of any biases."

We have done reasonably well in uncovering various ethnographic biases in our debates as an intellectual community. We have come to view the history of anthropology, to paraphrase Hallowell (1965), as an anthropological problem. The discipline's progress seems clear then, not in the ability to avoid biases—something Bernard implies is part of the human condition—but in our ability to become aware of them through time. "What is unique about anthropology as a discipline," Das (page 133) notes, "is its use of the 'Other'—of societies and cultures radically different— to overcome the limits of anthropology's origin and location" (cf. Carrithers 1992:177-199).

One important step in becoming sensitive to our biases has been the ongoing enlargement of anthropology's intellectual community. Not only do indigenous informants offer feedback on anthropological productions today, but anthropology has become a more global profession with an increasingly more global dialogue among its practitioners. "Ethnographers from the West," Kuper (page 115) observes, "who go out to work in . . . [other] countries are now . . . joining up with . . . local communities of scholars, engaging in common debates, and finding themselves liable to stinging criticism for failures in empathy, political sensitivity, and local knowledge."

Issues Needing to Be Addressed

Taking a positive tack, I have described anthropology's progress to date as a half-filled glass. One might also view it as a half-empty one. "Anthropology," Eggan (1977:11) observes, "has achieved a position in the scholarly world but it is a position of promise rather than achieved accomplishments." Firth (1975:17) notes: "Few generalizations of a truly explanatory order have yet emerged in modern social anthropology." The tension between what Rappaport has termed anthropology's two traditions—its positivist and interpretive perspectives—proved useful in the early development of the discipline. Each moderated the enthusiasms of the other. Interpretivists surrounded positivists' assertions of "objectivity" with notes of caution. And positivism emphasized the pragmatic limits of personalized, interpretive accounts for the discipline's development. In their bickering and opposition, they helped lay a discipline's foundation. It is through their opposition to one another, in a way, that several earlier noted biases were uncovered. But one wonders if what was a beneficial tension in the discipline's early days has now become a disempowering one—limiting rather than encouraging the discipline's further development.

Much in the volume should give readers pause for reflection in this regard. "A well known . . . problem," Salzman (page 34) states, "is the fact that the vast multitude of anthropological conferences, congresses, articles, monographs, and collections, while adding up to mountains of paper . . . do not seem to add up to a substantial, integrated, coherent body of knowledge that could provide a base for the further advancement of the discipline." "The credibility of our field reports," he (page 35) continues, "rests mainly on their uniqueness, that is, on the absence of any other reports that might present contrary 'findings,' that is, test their reliability." This ties in to what DaMatta (page 124) refers to as DeVoto's "law": "The more anthropologists write about the United States, the less I believe what they say about Samoa."

The basing of promising theoretical possibilities on uneven ethnographic records has given anthropology a particular intellectual style. Salzman (page 35) refers to "the theoretical fads and fashions that come and go in anthropology with a dazzling speed." Wolf (page 220) notes that "we are continuously slaying paradigms, only to see them return to life, as if discovered for the first time. . . . As each successive approach carries the axe to its predecessors, anthropology comes to resemble a project in intellectual deforestation." And Barth (page 350) makes reference to "frantically shopping for the latest fashion, and scuttling all previous established (and alternative) views." "The shrewd career strategy," Salzman (page 36) suggests, "is not to do sound and sensitive ethnography, but to come up with a sexy new approach or slogan that will make you a hero of a new anthropological 'ism.'"

Building on the Past. It is because of this trend that several contributors express concern about losing touch with valuable aspects of the discipline's past. Nader (page 86), for example, worries about the costs incurred when comparative consciousness is downplayed as a form of analysis. Kuper (page 117), Barth (page 351), and Kottak and Colson (page 399) note the benefit in reanalyzing earlier ethnographic materials. And Bernard (page 178) appreciatively talks of past attempts to combine quantitative and qualitative research.

Having a sense of intellectual continuity is important for a discipline. Statements by contributors regarding their intellectual roots emphasize time and time again the relation of present perspectives to past ones. Anthropology is not simply a progression of separate "-isms," one after another. It involves a process of mentoring, of scholars influencing one another, of individuals exchanging and testing each other's ideas. From several contributors' statements—Bernard, Harris, Kottak, Murphy, Rappaport, Vayda, and Wolf—we perceive Steward's importance in this regard. Collier, Colson, Geertz, and Nader describe Kluckhohn's significance; Keesing, Levy, Nader, Rappaport, and Scheper-Hughes, Bateson's; and DaMatta, Godelier, Kuper, Moore, Murphy, Sahlins, Strathern, and I,

Lévi-Strauss's. Benedict is touched on by Colson, Wolf, and Yanagisako; Mead by Harris, Levy, Rappaport, and Scheper-Hughes; Leach by Barth, Bloch, Colson, Strathern, and Tambiah; Kroeber by Bernard, Harris, Moore, and Nader; Powdermaker by Bernard, Scheper-Hughes, and Wolf; Murdock by Bernard and Goodenough; and Gluckman by Colson, Moore, and Nader. In the contributors' statements regarding their intellectual roots, we see important threads of continuity through time.

We might ponder, in this respect, how future generations will view Marx, given the recent collapse of communist regimes in Eastern Europe. As Godelier points out, many of Marx's ideas are still quite relevant. Do we shoot the messenger because part of his message did not work out as intended? It is a rather strict standard to hold any scholar to and especially one, such as Marx, who has had a tremendous impact on Western thought.

A Sense of Common Standards. One important step to overcoming the problem of faddism is moving beyond the current interpretivist/ positivist debate to alternative means of quality control for our analyses. We need to develop a sense of standards beyond our own coteries, beyond our own specialties, that encompasses the discipline as a whole. In terms of such standards, contributors focus on two themes: (1) being able to distinguish relatively valid from relatively invalid assertions and (2) being sensitive to the strengths and weaknesses of current methods.

In regard to the first theme a few contributors offer suggestive leads. Harris (page 64), for example, emphasizes assertions should be: "(1) predictive (or retrodictive), (2) testable (or falsifiable), (3) parsimonious, (4) of broad scope, and (5) integratable or cumulative within a coherent and expanding corpus" of data. And Goodenough (page 263) indicates the assertions should be replicable (within limitations), rich (in the sense of accounting for more data), and if possible parsimonious.

Yet, as a review of the contributions as a whole suggests, few agreed-upon standards exist in the discipline. All we can say is that different contributors hold different positions. The fact that we still remain somewhat uncertain concerning the validity of statements in the ethnographic accounts by Mead and Freeman relating to Samoa and by Redfield and Lewis relating to Tepoztlan suggests some of the hurdles needing to be overcome.

The solution to this problem of validity lies, I would suggest, in the long-term, multi-participant projects that Kottak and Colson and others in this volume espouse (cf. Foster et al. 1979). Kottak and Colson make clear the rich, "thick" data one acquires through these projects. Only through time, only through a set of overlapping ethnographies are we able to distinguish valid from less valid accounts. This is the point I (Borofsky 1987:155) stress in *Making History:* "Understanding develops not from a single ethnography but over time. Through a dialogue with others possessing different constructions and perspectives, we move beyond the complacency of our own constructions toward increased knowledge."

In regard to the second theme, Bernard discusses the limitations of participant observation and the need for overcoming them. He (page 174) stresses (as do Salzman and Levy) that "training in methods should be a key part of both the undergraduate and the graduate curriculum in anthropology." "Controlling many different methods for collecting and analyzing qualitative and quantitative data," he (page 176) notes, "liberates us to investigate whatever theoretical questions attract us."

Experimentation's Value. With a move toward a more consensual set of disciplinary standards and a better sensitivity to our methodological limitations, experimentation—a long-standing tradition within anthropology—should be more readily acknowledged for the positive force it is within the discipline. Lacking a means to evaluate new intellectual perspectives, various contributors look askance at recent innovations such as postmodernism. They see them as transient fads undermining disciplinary progress.

But with a more consensual set of evaluative standards, experimentation can constitute an important vehicle for disciplinary development. It has certainly proved so in the past. "Early works now known by the dubiously flattering label of 'classics,'" Firth (1975:5) observes, "were experimental: in trying to provide more systematic and more relevant ethnography; in pointing to a range of theoretical problems calling for further exploration; and in testing, less successfully, the market for serious unglamorized information on basic social issues in communities with ways of life alien to the Western world." Experimentation, Marcus (page 41) suggests, provides "the opportunity . . . to formulate new questions, to materialize new objects of study, and to explore new discursive spaces through experiments with form." One sees this in Scheper-Hughes's (page 231) innovative approach to medical anthropology—integrating "the representational *body social;* the controlling, biopower forces of the *body politic;* and the . . . attribution of meanings to the individual and existential *body personal.*" One similarly sees it in Yanagisako and Collier's (page 198) focus on marriage transactions; in Nader's (page 90ff) use of contrastive comparisons to understand gender relations; and in a host of other contributions throughout the volume.

The point is that for productive disciplinary development, for a moving beyond our past but retaining a continuity with it, we need to *find some common ground* between the polarizing perspectives of positivism and interpretivism. Choosing only one or the other ignores important issues. Rappaport (page 154) makes this point well:

Our two traditions have not always lived very easily together. . . . But any radical separation of the two is misguided . . . because . . . the relationship between them, in all its difficulty, tension, and ambiguity, expresses the condition of a species that lives, and can only live, in terms of meanings it itself must construct in a world devoid of intrinsic meaning but subject to natural law. Any adequate anthropology must attempt to comprehend the fullness of its subject matter's condition.

Finding common ground between the poles of these perspectives, bringing them together within a common framework, means we can move, as a discipline, toward both shared standards and innovative experiments that mutually reinforce one another. Without some common ground, we spin our wheels and make little progress. We talk past one another across a high wall.

I do not mean to cover over the differences that separate interpretive from positivistic perspectives. But, without diminishing each's significance, we need find a way to bring them into a common framework. We need see them as complementary, as overlapping approaches for building a discipline and, as Rappaport points out, for studying the human condition. We need to have both within our community, both within a common harness pulling us forward. This is what I take Nader (page 84) to imply in her concern with "the idea accompanying each successive criticism . . . [that its] approach was supreme and exclusive." And it is what Godelier (page 109) supports in his call for a "critical vigilance that never stops learning. . . . We must build on what we have taken from . . . [our predecessors] in order to continue on our common and contentious way."

Other Voices. In our increasingly interconnected world—in which informants critique ethnographies and anthropologists come from a host of countries—Western anthropologists must not presume to dominate the intellectual conversation. Other voices, other perspectives, constitute a critical part of our intellectual community.

Das (page 134) raises an important issue regarding "the double bind in which the Indian anthropologist finds herself" as both ethnographer of and participant in Indian society. She (page 134) observes:

The danger for the Indian anthropologist is that she is vulnerable to the charge of being either "defensive" or "chauvinistic." The educated Hindu cannot speak with an authentic voice on matters pertaining to caste or religion since she is condemned [according to the French sociologist Dumont] to seeing the institutions of her society "from a Western point of view." . . . If, however, she speaks from a point of view that may be characterized as "Indian" or "Hindu" or "Islamic" she will be accused of being "backward looking."

Das (pages 134-135) continues:

The spatial distance between India and the West allows Western scholars to study "caste" and its values at the level of the intellect. But these "obsolete" values provide neither political opportunities nor political challenges to the Western reader. To the Indian anthropologist who lives in societies imbued with these values, according to Dumont, the challenge is to overcome these traditional institutions and values in order to build a modern nation-state. The only attitude that the modern Indian can take to her own traditions is to place them in the past. In no case can these traditions offer an intellectual resource to contemporary societies. The functions of spatial distance (for Westerners) are performed by temporal distance (for Indians) so that her own past appears as the "other" for the Indian anthropologist.

We are left with an important question: In what ways and on whose terms are non-Western *scholars* and non-Western *informants* integrated into the anthropological community? The question very much needs addressing (see Fahim 1982). It is implicit in our past; it overwhelms our present. It defines in what sense the "anthropological community" is an inclusive, rather than exclusive, one. And it emphasizes that the role of Western anthropologists is not simply to talk and teach but to listen and learn.

Questions of Power. Wolf (page 218) argues that "we actually know a lot about power, but have been timid in building upon what we know." (Some years ago, 1969:258, he termed anthropologists "babes in the woods" regarding our ability to deal with the subject.) "This has implications," he (page 218) continues, "for assessing the insights of the past and for raising new questions."

Various contributors refer to power (though one should be cautious about assuming all contributors mean the same thing by it). They raise several important issues. Some query the role of power in stimulating change and/or maintaining the status quo. Harris (page 72), for example, discusses the role of "power holders"; Nader (page 91) considers "male attempts to maintain authority in societies increasingly threatened by . . . international power relations"; and Godelier (page 105) discusses the role of "violence and consent . . . in the genesis and the perpetuation of social inequalities." Others are concerned with how power is entwined with structures of beliefs. Keesing (page 309), for instance, is interested in "the way symbolic production is linked to power and interest"; Rappaport (pages 160-161) discusses the tension between sanctity and power in supporting authority; and Wolf (page 226) asserts it is power that "guarantees . . . the structures of significance." Others explore the dynamics of political resistance. Scheper-Hughes (page 233) refers to the medical weapons of the weak and observes (page 239): "The presence of suffering, especially when . . . expressed in the language of symptoms, exposes the gap between bodies that refuse the demand to suffer quietly and the requirements of antagonistic economic and social orders."

While one must be careful not to treat power as a new anthropological buzzword—as a term with more rhetorical than conceptual significance—one cannot help but see important issues needing to be explored. In the past, anthropologists often downplayed the political dynamics within and/or beyond the local communities they studied. *We now must address such issues of power head-on.*

ANTHROPOLOGY'S SIGNIFICANCE IN THE MODERN WORLD

In the gap between the high ideals of anthropology's moral vision and the realities of its practical accomplishments lie important questions: What value does anthropology have as an intellectual discipline? What problems should anthropology address in today's world? What might it realistically achieve?

As various contributors have suggested, anthropology's record in addressing modern social problems is somewhat spotty. "What remains unsaid in much of current anthropological writing speaks deafeningly, if we only step back to listen," Keesing (page 307) observes. Anthropology, he notes, has ignored "contemporary state terror and . . . [taken] for granted the political economy of global capitalism that continues to drain wealth out of Third World countries and hold them bonded in debt." Barth (page 350) notes:

Anthropology has had pitifully little to say on the phenomenon of untranscendable poverty as it affects increasing hundreds of millions of people in all major cities of the world. We have not been able to articulate a position, or even noticeable interest, in the fact that human activity seems to be destroying humanity's own global habitat. And we are only marginally addressing the phenomena of increasing cultural pluralism.

Salzman (page 31) suggests, "our work remains marginal to . . . [our informants'] lives." Godelier (page 97) queries: "Are the social sciences capable only of tagging along behind events, of analyzing societies without noticing that they are already in the process of vanishing? Are they never able to predict new developments?" And remembering his training at Harvard, DaMatta (page 120) recalls "lively discussions among vociferous students and nice professors, but they stayed off political questions which were not considered part of . . . [an] anthropologist's training."

A Moral Framework

What anthropology can do best perhaps—given the realities of modern problems and politics—is provide a moral framework in a post-Enlightenment world where secular rationality has questioned, if not replaced, religious values as the standard for guiding human relations. It is the problem Durkheim faced in his role as an educational change agent in the Third French Republic (which he directly addressed in *The Division of Labor in Society* and indirectly in *The Elementary Forms of Religious Life*).

From the days when the Jacobins had destroyed Catholicism in France and then attempted to fill the ensuing moral void by inventing a synthetic Religion of Reason, to Saint-Simon's New Christianity and Comte's Religion of Humanity, French secular thinkers had grappled with the modern problem of how public and private morality could be maintained without religious sanctions: They had asked, just like Ivan Karamasov [in Dostoyevsky's novel The Brothers Karamasov*]: "Once God is dead, does not everything become permissible?"* (Coser 1971:137)

"We face a terrible contradiction," Rappaport (page 162) notes:

The reordering of knowledge that has liberated humans to discover the laws of the physical world is antagonistic not only to superstition, dogmatism and irrationality, but hostile to the very processes by which the peculiarly human components of the world are constructed and ordered. The epistemology of modern science threatens to destroy the onto-logical ground of meaning. To put it a little differently, in discovering the physical aspects of the world we undermine its conventional founda-tions.

Related to this theme, Lévi-Strauss (page 425) queries whether Western societies are today "capable of sustaining . . . intellectual and moral values powerful enough to attract people from outside." And Das (page 141) discusses "remoralizing areas of life denuded of moral meaning by the growth of a bureau-cratic, impersonal rationality." Citing Saran, she continues: "For him the articulation of tradition is not so much a return to a glorious past, as the development of a different notion of 'normality' that may challenge . . . the pathologies of modern society." It is in this sense that Bellah, Madsen, Sullivan, Swidler, and Tipton (1991:86), in assessing the possi-bilities for *The Good Society* in America, cite Lewis Mumford. "The great gift of civilization . . . is twofold [he says]: a cultural tradition to locate ourselves in and a vision of renewal that lures us forward."

Anthropology emphasizes three elements necessary for a moral framework in the modern world. First, as I have repeatedly noted, anthropology enlarges our sense of moral community. "Ethnography should make available to humanity as a whole what it discovers . . . in individual societies," Rappa-port (1986:347) states, "so that humanity as a whole . . . can construct larger conceptions of itself and its place in nature." Instead of Lockean individualism (where individuals, pursuing their separate goals, bring about a common good through economic "laws"), anthropology emphasizes our interconnected-ness with one another, our shared humanity, that reaches beyond individualism to a sense of community.

It is important to recognize this vision faces a critical issue: What moral standards does one apply within this broad community? Con-tributors sketch out various options. Barth (page 351) emphasizes the need for a weak version of relativism that "furthers the project of turning anthropology into a common ground for humanity, a universe of discourse fitted to the discussion of all and every cultural form in a way that allows persons of differing

cultural backgrounds to meet as equals."
Kottak and Colson (page 398) stress the need
to "join the many . . . who question the
shibboleth of cultural relativism. Our world
needs some agreement on basic human rights
and ways of guaranteeing them." Geertz
suggests a framework within which our
discussions on this topic might take place:

*The uses of cultural diversity . . . lie less along the
lines of sorting ourselves out from others and others
from ourselves so as to defend group integrity . . .
than along the lines of defining the terrain reason
must cross if its modest rewards are to be reached
and realized. . . .* (page 463)

*"Understanding" in the sense of comprehension,
perception, and insight needs to be distinguished
from "understanding" in the sense of agreement of
opinion, union of sentiment, or commonality of
commitment. We must learn to grasp what we
cannot embrace.* (page 465)

Second, growing out of this sense of
community, is anthropology's concern with
holism—a sense of interconnectedness not
only with one another but with our environment. We must come to understand how
people survive in difficult settings beyond our
own comfortableness—in squatter settlements,
in refugee camps, in the "untranscendable
poverty" that encompasses "hundreds of millions of people" (to adopt Barth's phrasing).
How do people persist under such conditions—in what ways with what impacts on
themselves and others? (One is reminded of
Sandburg's poem "The People Will Live
On": "The people so peculiar in renewal and
comeback, You cannot laugh off their capacity to take it.") Anthropology's emphasis on
participant observation allows us to come to
know the people living under such conditions
as individuals. We are brought close up to the
problems they face. And we can describe them
in personal ways others will understand.

As Rappaport stresses, we do not simply live
in an environment; we are *part* of one. Both
our present and our future are shaped by the
interconnections that bind us together. "Given

humanity's powers to construct and destroy,
and its position of dominance in ecosystems it
itself destabilizes, its responsibility can no
longer be to itself alone but must be to the
world as a whole," Rappaport (page 165)
stresses. "If evolution, human and otherwise,
is to continue humanity must think not
merely *of* the world but on *behalf* of the
world."

And third, anthropology helps us to find
value in (and an understanding of) the cultural
diversity that pervades our globe. "Whatever
once was possible and whatever may now be
longed for, the sovereignty of the familiar
impoverishes everyone," Geertz (page 463)
states: "It is not that we must love one another
or die (if that is the case—Blacks and
Afrikaners, Arabs and Jews, Tamils and
Singhalese—we are I think doomed). It is that
we must know one another, and live with that
knowledge, or end marooned in a Beckett-
world of colliding soliloquy." He (page 465)
continues:

*Comprehending that which is, in some manner of
form, alien to us and likely to remain so, without
either smoothing it over with vacant murmurs of
common humanity, disarming it with to-each-his-
own indifferentism, or dismissing it as charming,
lovely even, but inconsequent, is a skill we have
arduously to learn, and having learnt it, always
very imperfectly, to work continuously to keep alive;
it is not a connatural capacity, like depth perception
or the sense of balance, upon which we can
complacently rely.*

Anthropology's Limited Tools

Anthropology's powers of persuasion are
limited. "Anthropology is itself," Moore (page
374) notes, "caught in . . . [a] historical moment." But the discipline can do at least three
things to encourage the realization of its
vision.

First, it can act as a public witness and
recorder of our times—bringing to others an
understanding of what life is like in the

marginal corners of the world, making known the suffering and joys that exist in the shadows away from our own awareness. When local writers, poets, and artists take up this role, ethnographers can add a powerful supplement to what they say—enriching our understanding by multiplying the perspectives involved. "One cannot forget," DaMatta (page 123) notes, "that bearing witness is a critical part of our practice as scholars." Ethnography, Nader (1969:285) suggests, makes "victimization visible." This is what Scheper-Hughes does in her description of living conditions in northeastern Brazil. "The act of witnessing is what lends our work its moral (at times its almost theological) character" she (1992:xii) suggests in her book *Death without Weeping*. "These are not ordinary lives that I am about to describe," she (1992:xii-xiii) states. "They are short, violent, and hungry lives. I am offering here a glimpse . . . through a glass darkly." "Without ethnography," Marcus and Fischer (1986:82) observe, "one can only imagine what is happening to real social actors caught up in complex macroprocesses. Ethnography is . . . a sensitive register of change at the level of experience."

Anthropology has done much in this regard and has much to be proud of. But there are also some noticeable gaps in what anthropology is witnessing. For a discipline that repeatedly berates itself for its past ties to colonialism, anthropology's lack of description of modern terror in Third World settings is quite noticeable. And yet the horrors of the Khmer Rouge (in Cambodia), Renamo (in Mozambique), the "Generals" (in Argentina and Chile), Mobotu (in Zaire), ethnic conflict (in Yugoslavia), and starvation (in Somalia) cry out for description if we have the courage to study them. Exemplary are anthropological studies such as Taussig's (1987) and those in Nordstrom and Martin (1992) (cf. Timmerman 1981). Nordstrom (1992:261) conveys a sense of what political terror can mean.

Both state . . . and guerrilla forces [in Mozambique and Sri Lanka] use the construction of terror . . . as a mechanism for gaining and maintaining sociopolitical control over a population. . . . Dirty wars seek victory, not through military and battlefield strategies, but through horror. Civilians, rather than soldiers, are the tactical targets, and fear, brutality, and murder are the foundation on which control is constructed.

Taussig (1987:8) emphasizes this point as well: Repressive regimes use "the cultural elaboration of fear" to "control massive populations, entire social classes, and even nations." "Cultures of terror are nourished by the intermingling of silence and myth." In addition, we need to also describe the symbiotic relationship that has developed between indigenous elites and external aid—how, supported by outside funds, indigenous elites have often severed moral ties with their own masses, brutalizing and ignoring them as they see fit (see e.g. K. E. Friedman 1994).

Second, besides acting as a witness, anthropology can help in conceptualizing the dynamics behind modern social problems. Understanding them is not necessarily easy. There is often an overabundance of information and a limited amount of synthesis. ("Everybody gets so much information all day long that they lose their common sense," Gertrude Stein, 1973:61, once suggested.) We need to understand how the different aspects of today's problems fit together—what is critically related to what—in order to come to terms with them effectively. Anthropology is ideally placed to help in this process. The discipline takes pride in drawing on a range of disciplines, a host of perspectives, in solving problems. This is what Rappaport (page 164) refers to when he suggests: the "qualities, which . . . sometimes lead others to regard anthropology as the most 'backward' . . . of the modern social sciences are the very factors which suit it for leadership in the emergence of the postmodern science." "The more [economists, sociologists, and psychologists]

. . . are enticed into the narrow corridors of mechanistic predication," Tambiah (1985:357) asserts, "the greater the obligation of anthropology to hold fast to its totalizing aspirations." (Related to this, Kuper, page 116, predicts that "most theoretical innovations in the next generation [for anthropology] will be interdisciplinary.")

One can see contributors framing important dynamics. Godelier (page 105), for example, addresses the question of how domination works in a host of contexts: "What roles do violence and consent, respectively, play in the genesis and the perpetuation of social inequalities?" Lest we be too quick to provide a simple answer, he (page 105) reminds us, following Marx, of the complexities involved: "Order depends not only on repression, but on silence and disguise as well"—a theme that Willis also develops in his book *Learning to Labor.* Nader (pages 92-93) offers working hypotheses regarding the worsening condition of women in certain modern settings. Tambiah (page 434) struggles with the question (raised by Tagil) of "why ethnicity becomes more easily politicizable in modern society and in those societies on the threshold of modernization." And Tishkov (page 447) queries why grievances toward the old communist system were channeled into ethnonationalism. While contributors do not deal with other questions—such as development— recent anthropological books on the subject do help frame some of the issues involved. J. Ferguson's (1990:256) *The Anti-Politics Machine* is one example:

By uncompromisingly reducing poverty to a technical problem, and by promising technical solutions to the sufferings of powerless and oppressed people, the hegemonic problematic of "development" is the principal means through which the question of poverty is de-politicized in the world today. At the same time, by making the intentional blueprints for "development" so highly visible, a "development" project can end up performing extremely sensitive political operations involving the entrenchment and *expansion of institutional state power almost invisibly under cover of a neutral, technical mission to which no one can object. The . . . [effect] is twofold: alongside the institutional effect of expanding bureaucratic state power is the conceptual or ideological effect of depoliticizing poverty and the state.*

Ritchie's (1992) *Becoming Bicultural* and Weiner's (1992) "Anthropology's Lessons for Cultural Diversity" are part of a related effort to conceptualize the complex subtleties involved in multiculturalism.

Finally, given the discipline's current fashionableness in the social sciences, anthropology has an important persuasive role to play in our society. Anthropology has had limited success in this role to date. And as Das (page 143) notes, the problems to be overcome are not easy:

Unlike . . . [earlier] social scientists who came into the world of knowledge as part of the anticolonial, nationalist enterprise, the modern generation of social scientists in India have to live with a destruction of certainty as the condition under which they engage in the production of knowledge about Indian society. . . . They can only insert their voices within a plurality of voices in which all kinds of statements—prescriptive, normative, descriptive, indicative—are waging a virtual battle about the nature of Indian society and the legitimate space for social sciences in this society.

Still, the potential exists for persuasion and, through it, the possibility for change. Anthropology can have considerable impact (as its involvement in Cultural Survival illustrates). But it must draw itself further into the public arena. And it must speak out more with the power it has established—becoming an important voice in public discussions and projects of change.

There is much truth in Rappaport's (page 164) implication that anthropology needs to be judged not only by its ideas but by its social accomplishments: "What Toulmin calls 'postmodern science' is an order of knowledge *and* action in which both those who seek to discover natural law and those who seek to understand the nature of the world's constructed meanings are reunited with a world which they do not merely observe but in which they participate for better or for worse." Barth (page 350) addresses a similar point: "Our discipline should . . . [present] a much stronger voice in articulating issues in ways that would command the attention of scholars and public alike. . . . We should recognize that the cutting edges of our theories can often be well tested by their relevance and power in practical matters." It is a difficult standard to be held to. But it is one we need aim for. It challenges anthropology to be more than it has been in the past while, at the same time, it draws encouragement from that past. The challenge now facing anthropology is nothing less than improving human relations on a global scale—a critical task in our increasingly global age.

Having the contributors' perspectives brought together in one volume has allowed us to gain a better sense of cultural anthropology's intellectual dynamics. We have perceived much about the discipline's present state and something about where the discipline might go in the future. But the volume, I would stress, does not stand by itself. It is part of a larger discussion. Its value lies not only in what it says but in what it encourages others to say. It continues a conversation begun more than a century ago regarding the anthropological project. And it offers suggestive perspectives for developing this conversation in the years ahead. It represents both an affirmation, and a questioning, of our shared traditions, our shared hopes, as an intellectual community.

References

Abelson, R.
1981 Psychological Status of the Script Concept. American Psychologist 36:715-729.

Aberle, David
1957 The Influence of Linguistics on Early Culture and Personality Theory. In Gertrude Dole and Robert Carneiro, eds. *Essays in the Science of Culture*, pp. 1-29. New York: Thomas Crowell.

Abrams, Michael, and Arthur Reber
1988 Implicit Learning: Robustness in the Face of Psychiatric Disorders. Journal of Psycholinguistic Research 17(5):425-439.

Abruzzi, W.
1982 Ecological Theory and Ethnic Differentiation among Human Populations. Current Anthropology 23:13-32.
1988 *Ecological Succession and Mormon Colonization in the Little Colorado River Basin.* Salt Lake City: University of Utah Press.

Action for Cultural Survival
1992 July/August Bulletin.

Adams, Richard N.
1966 Power and Power Domains. America Latina 9(2):3-5, 8-11.
1970 *Crucifixion by Power: Essays on Guatemalan Social Structure, 1944-1966.* Austin: University of Texas Press.
1975 *Energy and Structure: A Theory of Social Power.* Austin: University of Texas Press.
1977 Power in Human Societies: A Synthesis. In Raymond Fogelson and Richard Adams, eds. *The Anthropology of Power*, pp. 387-410. New York: Academic.

Agger, B.
1987 Review of Norman Stockman's *Antipositivist Theories of the Sciences*. Philosophy of the Social Sciences 17:121-123.

Alba, Joseph, and Lynn Hasher
1983 Is Memory Schematic? Psychological Bulletin 93:203-231.

Albers, Patricia, and Seymour Parker
1971 The Plains Vision Experience: A Study of Power and Privilege. Southwestern Journal of Anthropology 27(3):203-233.

Alexander, Jack
1978 The Cultural Domain of Marriage. American Ethnologist 5:5-14.

Alexander, Jeffrey
1985 Positivism. In Adam Kuper and Jessica Kuper, eds. *The Social Science Encyclopedia*, pp. 631-633. London: Routledge & Kegan Paul.

Allen, Rhianon, and Arthur Reber
1980 Very Long Term Memory for Tacit Knowledge. Cognition 8:175-185.

Altorki, S., and C. Fawzi El-Solh, eds.
1988 *Arab Women in the Field: Studying Your Own Society.* Syracuse, N.Y.: Syracuse University Press.

American Psychiatric Association
1987 *Diagnostic and Statistical Manual of Mental Disorders*, 3rd ed., revised (DSM-111-R). Washington, D.C.: American Psychiatric Association.

Anderson, Benedict
1983 *Imagined Communities: Reflections on the Origin and Spread of Nationalism.* London: Verso.
1991 *Imagined Communities: Reflections on the Origin and Spread of Nationalism*, rev. ed. New York: Verso.

Anderson, J. R.
1983. *The Architecture of Cognition.* Cambridge, Mass.: Harvard University Press.

Appadurai, Arjun
1986a Introduction: Commodities and the Politics

of Value. In Arjun Appadurai, ed. *The Social Life of Things*, pp. 3-63. New York: Cambridge University Press.
1986b Theory in Anthropology: Center and Periphery. Comparative Studies in Society and History 28:356-361.

Ardener, Shirley
1975 *Perceiving Women.* New York: Wiley.
1978 [ed.] *Defining Females: The Nature of Women in Society.* New York: Wiley.

Arensberg, Conrad
1972 Culture as Behavior: Structure and Emergence. Annual Review of Anthropology 1:1-26. Palo Alto: Annual Reviews.

Arkusch, R. D., and L. O. Lee, trans. and eds.
1989 *Land without Ghosts: Chinese Impressions of America from the Mid-Nineteenth Century to the Present.* Berkeley: University of California Press.

Arusha Declaration
1967 Dar es Salaam: Publicity Section, TANU.

Arutyunyan, V. B.
1990 *Events in Nagorno-Karabakh.* Yerevan, Armenia: Academy of Sciences.

Asad, Talal
1973 [ed.] *Anthropology and the Colonial Encounter.* New York: Humanities Press.

Austin, J. H.
1962 *How to Do Things with Words.* New York: Oxford University Press.

Babcock, Barbara, ed.
1978 *The Reversible World.* Ithaca, N.Y.: Cornell University Press.

Bakhtin, Mikhail.
1981a Discourse in the Novel. In Michael Holquist, ed., Caryl Emerson and Michael Holquist, trans. *The Dialogic Imagination: Four Essays by M. M. Bakhtin*, pp. 259-422. Austin: University of Texas Press.
1981b *Problemas da Poética de Dostoiévski.* Rio de Janeiro: Forense-Universitaria.
1984 *Rabelais and His World.* Translated by

Helene Iswolsky. Bloomington: Indiana University Press.

Balandier, Georges
1970 [1967] *Political Anthropology.* New York: Random House.

Balee, W.
1984 The Ecology of Ancient Tupi Warfare. In B. Ferguson, ed. *Warfare, Culture and Environment*, pp. 241-265. Orlando, Fla.: Academic.

Balzer, Marjorie
n.d. The Tenacity of Ethnicity: Khanty and Russian Interactions in West Siberia. (In preparation)

Barnes, Andrew, and Peter Stearns
1989 Social History and Issues in Human Consciousness. New York: New York University Press.

Barnett, H. G.
1940 Culture Process. American Anthropologist 42:21-48.

Barsegyan, Hikar
1989 *The Truth Is Precious . . . To the Problem of Nagorno Karabakh.* Yerevan, Armenia: Znanie.

Barth, Fredrik
1966 Models of Social Organization. Royal Anthropological Institute, Occasional Papers, No. 23.
1975 *Ritual and Knowledge among the Baktaman of New Guinea.* New Haven, Conn.: Yale University Press.
1978 [ed.] *Scale and Social Organization.* Oslo, Universitetsforlaget. New York: Columbia University Press.
1987 *Cosmologies in the Making: A Generative Approach to Cultural Variation in Inner New Guinea.* New York: Cambridge University Press.
1989 The Analysis of Culture in Complex Societies. Ethnos 54:120-142.
1990 The Guru and the Conjurer: Transactions in Knowledge and the Shaping of Culture in Southeast Asia and Melanesia. Man 25:640-653.
1992 Social/Cultural Anthropology. In *Wenner-Gren Foundation Report for 1990 and 1991*, pp. 62-70. New York: Wenner-Gren Foundation.

Bartlett, Frederic C.
1932 *Remembering: A Study in Experimental and Social Psychology.* New York: Macmillan.

Bates, Daniel, and Fred Plog
1990 *Cultural Anthropology*, 3rd ed. New York: McGraw-Hill.

Bateson, Gregory
1958 *Naven.* Stanford, Calif.: Stanford University Press.
1972 The Role of Somatic Change in Evolution. In *Steps to an Ecology of Mind*, pp. 346-363. New York: Ballantine.
1979 *Mind and Nature: A Necessary Unity.* New York: Dutton.

Battaglia, D.
1990 *On the Bones of the Serpent: Person, Memory and Mortality in Sabarl Island Society.* Chicago: University of Chicago Press.

Beaglehole, E., and P. Beaglehole
1938 Ethnology of Pukapuka. Bernice P. Bishop Museum Bulletin 150. Honolulu: Bernice P. Bishop Museum.
n.d. Myths, Stories and Chants from Pukapuka (manuscript). Honolulu, Hawaii: Bernice P. Bishop Museum Library.

Beal, Samuel
1957-1958 [1885] *Chinese Accounts of India*, vols. 1 and 2. Translated from the Chinese of Hiuen Tsiang. Calcutta: Susil Gupta (India) Limited.

Beattie, J. H. M.
1955 Contemporary Trends in British Social Anthropology. Sociologus 5(1):1-14.

Beauvoir, de Simone
1974 [1949] *The Second Sex.* New York: Vintage.

Bell, Daniel
1975 Ethnicity and Social Change. In N. Glazer and D. Moynihan, eds. *Ethnicity, Theory and Experience.* Cambridge, Mass.: Harvard University Press.

Bellah, Robert N., Richard Madsen, William M. Sullivan, Ann Swidler, and Steven M. Tipton
1985 *Habits of the Heart: Individualism and Commitment in American Life.* New York: Harper & Row.
1991 *The Good Society.* New York: Knopf.

Benedict, Ruth
1934 *Patterns of Culture.* Boston: Houghton Mifflin.

1943 Franz Boas as an Ethnologist. American Anthropologist 45(3, 2): 27–34.

Bennett, John W.
1982 *Of Time and the Enterprise: North American Family Farm Management in a Context of Resource Marginality.* Minneapolis: University of Minnesota Press.

Berg, Gerald M.
1986 Royal Authority and the Protector System in Nineteenth-Century Imerina. In Conrad P. Kottak, et al., eds. *Madagascar: Society and History*, pp. 175-192. Durham, N.C.: Carolina Academic.

Berkhofer, R. F.
1973 Clio and the Culture Concept: Some Impressions of a Changing Relationship in American Historiography. In L. Schneider and C. M. Bonjean, eds. *The Idea of Culture in the Social Sciences.* Cambridge, England: Cambridge University Press.

Berlin, Isaiah
1960 History and Theory: The Concept of Scientific History. History and Theory 1:1-31.
1966 *The Hedgehog and the Fox: An Essay on Tolstoy's View of History.* New York: Simon and Schuster.
1980 *Against the Current: Essays in the History of Ideas.* New York: Viking.

Bernard, H. R.
1992 Preserving Language Diversity. Human Organization 51:113-119.

Bernard, H. R., and P. D. Killworth
1977 Informant Accuracy in Social Network Data II Human Communications Research 4:3-18.

Bernard, H. R., P. D. Killworth, D. Kronenfeld, and L. Sailer
1984 The Problem of Informant Accuracy: The Validity of Retrospective Data. Annual Review of Anthropology 13:495-517.

Bernard, H. R., and J. Salinas
1989 *Native Ethnography: A Mexican Indian Describes His Culture.* Newbury Park, Calif.: Sage.

Berreman, G. D.
1962 *Behind Many Masks.* Ithaca, N.Y.: Society for Applied Anthropology.

Bhaskar, R.
1979 *The Possibility of Naturalism: A Philosophical Critique of the Contemporary Human Sciences.* Atlantic Highlands, N.J.: Humanities Press.

Biersack, A.
1984 Parela "Women-Men": The Reflexive Foundations of Gender Ideology. American Ethnologist 11(1):118-138.
1991 Introduction: History and Theory in Anthropology. In Aletta Biersack, ed. *Clio in Oceania: Toward a Historical Anthropology,* pp. 1-36. Washington, D.C.: Smithsonian Press.

Biglan, Anthony
1988 Behavior Analysis and the Larger Context. Behavior Analysis 23:25-32.

Bilmes, Jack
1976 Rules and Rhetoric: Negotiating the Social Order in a Thai Village. Journal of Anthropological Research 32:44-57.
1986 *Discourse and Behavior.* New York: Plenum.

Birdwhistell, Raymond L.
1953 *Introduction to Kinesics.* Louisville, Ky.: University of Louisville Press.

Bloch, M.
1985a From Cognition to Ideology. In Richard Fardon, ed. *Power and Knowledge: Anthropological and Sociological Approaches,* pp. 21-48. Edinburgh: Scottish Academic.
1985b *Marxism and Anthropology.* New York: Cambridge University Press.
1986 *From Blessing to Violence: History and Ideology in the Circumcision Ritual of the Merina of Madagascar.* New York: Cambridge University Press.

Blumer, H.
1969 *Symbolic Interactionism.* Englewood Cliffs, N.J.: Prentice Hall.

Boas, F.
1904 The History of Anthropology. Science 20: 513-524.
1908 *Anthropology.* New York: Columbia University Press.
1911a Handbook of American Indian Languages. Part I. Bureau of American Ethnology Bulletin 40.
1911b *The Mind of Primitive Man.* New York: Macmillan.
1928 *Anthropology and Modern Life.* New York: Norton.
1938 [ed.] *General Anthropology.* Boston: D. C. Heath.
1940 *Race, Language and Culture.* New York: Macmillan.
1966 *Kwakiutl Ethnography.* Helen Codere, ed. Chicago: University of Chicago Press.

Bodley, John H., ed.
1988 *Tribal Peoples and Development Issues: A Global Overview.* Mountain View, Calif.: Mayfield.

Bohannan, Paul
1992 *We, The Alien: An Introduction to Cultural Anthropology.* Prospect Heights, Ill.: Waveland.

Bohannan, Paul, and Mark Glazer, eds.
1988 *High Points in Anthropology,* 2nd ed. New York: Knopf.

Boltanski, Luc
1984 *As Classes Sociais e o Corpo.* Rio de Janeiro: Graal.

Bolton, Ralph
1992 Mapping Terra Incognita: Sex Research for AIDS Prevention: An Urgent Agenda for the 1990s. In Gilbert Herdt and Shirley Lindenbaum, eds. *The Time of AIDS,* pp. 124-158. Newbury Park, Calif.: Sage.

Bond, George
1990 Fieldnotes: Research in Past Occurrences. In Roger Sanjek, ed. *Fieldnotes: The Makings of Anthropology,* pp. 273-289. Ithaca, N.Y.: Cornell University Press.

Boon, James
1982 *Other Tribes; Other Scribes: Symbolic Anthropology in the Comparative Study of Cultures, Histories, Religions, and Texts.* Cambridge, England: Cambridge University Press.

Borkenau, Franz
1981 *End and Beginning: On the Generations of Cultures and the Origins of the West.* Edited with an Introduction by Richard Lowenthal. New York: Columbia University Press.

Borofsky, Robert
1987 *Making History: Pukapukan and Anthropological*

Constructions of Knowledge. Cambridge, England: Cambridge University Press.

Borofsky, Robert, and Alan Howard
1989 The Early Contact Period. In Alan Howard and Robert Borofsky, eds. *Developments in Polynesian Ethnology,* pp. 241-275. Honolulu: University of Hawaii Press.

Boster, James
1985 "Requiem for the Omniscient Informant": There's Life in the Old Girl Yet. In Janet Dougherty, ed. *Directions in Cognitive Anthropology,* pp. 177-197. Urbana: University of Illinois Press.
1986 Exchange of Varieties and Information between Aguaruna Manioc Cultivators. American Anthropologist 88:428-436.
1987 [ed.] Intracultural Variation. American Behavioral Scientist 31(2).

Bourdieu, Pierre
1977a *Outline of a Theory of Practice.* Cambridge, England: Cambridge University Press.
1977b *Reproduction.* Beverly Hills, Calif.: Sage.
1984 *Distinction: A Social Critique of the Judgement of Taste.* Cambridge, Mass.: Harvard University Press.
1990a *The Logic of Practice.* Stanford, Calif.: Stanford University Press.
1990b *In Other Words: Essays toward a Reflexive Sociology.* Stanford, Calif.: Stanford University Press.

Bowerman, M.
1977 The Acquisition of Word Meaning: An Investigation in Some Current Concepts. In P. Johnson-Laird and P. Wason, eds. *Thinking: Readings in Cognitive Science.* Cambridge, England: Cambridge University Press.

Boyd, R., and P. J. Richerson
1985 *Culture and the Evolutionary Process.* Chicago: University of Chicago Press.

Boyer, Ernest
1987 *College: The Undergraduate Experience in America.* New York: Harper and Row.

Boyer, Pascal
1990 *Tradition as Truth and Communication: A Cognitive Description of Traditional Discourse.* New York: Cambridge University Press.

Bradley, Candace, Camella Moore, Michael Burton, and Douglas White
1990 A Cross-Cultural Historical Analysis of Subsistence Change. American Anthropologist 92(2): 447-457.

Braroe, Niels Winther, and George L. Hicks
1967 Observations on the Mystique of Anthropology. The Sociological Quarterly 8(2):173-186.

Brezinski, Zbigniew
1989-1990 Post-Communist Nationalism. Foreign Affairs 68(5).

Bricker, Victoria, ed.
1975 Intra-Cultural Variation. American Ethnologist 2(1).

Bright, Charles, and Susan Harding, eds.
1984 *Statemaking and Social Movements: Essays in History and Theory.* Ann Arbor: University of Michigan Press.

Briskman, L.
1982 Essentialism without Inner Natures? Philosophy of the Social Sciences 12:303-309.

Brislin, R. W., W. J. Lonner, and R. M. Thorndike
1973 *Cross-Cultural Research Methods.* New York: Wiley.

Bromley, Yulian V.
1988 *Theoretical Ethnography.* Moscow: Nauka.
1989a National Problems under Conditions of Perestroyka. Problems of History 1. [in Russian]
1989b On the Terminological Aspects of Problems of Nationalities. Soviet Ethnography 6. [in Russian]

Bromley, Yulian V., and Viktor Kozlov
1989 The Theory of Ethnos and Ethnic Processes in Soviet Social Sciences. Comparative Studies in Society and History 31(3).

Bronson, B.
1972 Farm Labor and the Evolution of Food Production. In B. Spooner, ed. *Population Growth: Anthropological Implications.* Cambridge, Mass.: M.I.T. Press.

Brown, Paula
1992 Review of Marilyn Strathern *The Gender of the Gift.* Pacific Studies 15(1):123-129.

Brown, Richard
1973 Anthropology and Colonial Rule: Godfrey Wilson and the Rhodes-Livingstone Institute, Northern Rhodesia. In Talal Asad, ed. *Anthropology and the Colonial Encounter*, pp. 173-197. London: Ithaca Press.

Brown, Roger
1973 *A First Language: The Early Stages.* Cambridge, Mass.: Harvard University Press.

Bruner, Edward, ed.
1983 *Test, Play and Story: The Construction and Reconstruction of Self and Society.* Washington, D.C.: American Ethnological Society.

Brunton, Ron
1980 Misconstrued Order in Melanesian Religion. Man 15:112-128.

Bryden, R.
1989a Review of Mavis Gallant *In Transit.* New York Times Book Review, May 28, p. 3.
1989b Personal Communication (Letter to A. P. Vayda, June 13, 1989).

Buber, Martin
1953 *Good and Evil: Two Interpretations.* New York: Scribner's.

Bultmann, R.
1964 The Greek and Hellenistic Use of Alethia. In I. G. Kittel, ed. *The Theological Dictionary of the New Testament*, vol. I. Grand Rapids, Mich.: Eerdmans.

Burghart, Richard
1990 Ethnographers and Their Local Counterparts in India. In R. Fardon, ed. *Localizing Strategies*, pp. 260-278. Washington. D.C.: Smithsonian Press.

Burke, P.
1978 *Popular Culture in Early Modern Europe.* Cambridge, England: Cambridge University Press.

Burling, R.
1964 Cognition and Componential Analysis: God's Truth or Hocus-Pocus? American Anthropologist 66:20-28.

Bykov, Basil
1991 Komsomolskay Pravda. 19 June, 1991.

Cachia, Pierr
1973 A 19th Century Arab's Observations on European Music. Ethnomusicology 17(1):41-51.

Cafagna, A. C.
1960 A Formal Analysis of Definitions of "Culture." In G. E. Dole and R. L. Carneiro, eds. *Essays in the Science of Culture.* New York: Cromwell.

Cancian, F.
1963 Informant Error and Native Prestige Ranking in Zinacantan. American Anthropologist 65: 1068-1075.

Cardoso de Oliveira, Roberto
1960 *O Processo de Assimilação dos Terena.* Rio de Janeiro: Museu Nacional.

Carlson, Neil
1986 *Physiology of Behavior*, 3rd ed. Boston: Allyn and Bacon.

Carmack, Robert M., ed.
1988 *Harvest of Violence: The Maya Indians and the Guatemalan Crisis.* Norman, Okla: University of Oklahoma Press.

Carrier, James
n.d. Cultural Content and Practical Meaning: The Construction of Symbols in Formal American Culture. Manuscript. Port Moresby, Papua New Guinea.

Carrithers, Michael
1990 Is Anthropology Art or Science? Current Anthropology 31(3):263-282.
1992 *Why Humans Have Culture.* New York: Oxford University Press.

Carter, Paul
1987 *The Road to Botany Bay: An Exploration of Landscape and History.* New York: Knopf.

Cassell, J., and S. E. Jacobs
1987 *Handbook on Ethical Issues in Anthropology.*

Washington, D.C.: American Anthropological Association.

Casson, Ronald
1983 Schemata in Cognitive Anthropology. Annual Review of Anthropology, 12:429–462.

Cavalli-Sforza, L. L., and M. W. Feldman
1981 *Cultural Transmission and Evolution: A Quantitative Approach.* Princeton, N.J.: Princeton University Press.

Cavalli-Sforza, L., M. Feldman, K. Chen, and S. Dornbusch
1982 Theory and Observation in Cultural Transmission. Science 218:19–27.

Chaiklin, Seth, and Jean Lave
1993 *Understanding Practice: Perspectives on Activity and Context.* New York: Cambridge University Press.

Chall, Jeane, and Sue Conrad
1991 *Should Textbooks Challenge Students.* New York: Teachers College Press.

Chapple, Eliot Dismore, and Carelton Stevens Coon
1942 *Principles of Anthropology.* New York: Henry Holt.

Chartier, R.
1984 Culture as Appropriation: Popular Cultural Uses in Early Modern France. In S. L. Kaplan, ed. *Understanding Popular Culture: Europe from the Middle Ages to the Nineteenth Century.* Berlin: Mouton.

Cheshko, S. V.
1989 Economic Sovereignty and National Question. Kommunist No. 2. [in Russian]

Childe, V. G.
1936 *Man Makes Himself.* London: Watts.

Chock, Phyllis P.
1974 Time, Nature and Spirit: A Symbolic Analysis of Greek-American Spiritual Kinship. American Ethnologist 1:33–46.

Chomsky, N.
1985 The Bounds of Thinkable Thought. The Progressive, October.

Chowning, Ann
1989 Death and Kinship in Molima. In F. Damon and R. Wagner, eds. *Death Rituals and Life in the Societies of the Kula Ring.* De Kalb: Northern Illinois University Press.

Churchland, P. S., and T. Sejnowski
1989 Neural Representation and Neural Computation. In L. Nadel et al., eds. *Neural Connections, Mental Computations.* Cambridge, Mass.: M.I.T. Press.

Clifford, James
1983 Power and Dialogue in Ethnography: Marcel Griaule's Initiation. In George Stocking, ed. *Observers Observed: Essays on Ethnographic Fieldwork,* pp. 121–156. Madison: University of Wisconsin Press.
1986 Introduction. In James Clifford and George E. Marcus, eds. *Writing Culture,* pp. 1–26. Berkeley: University of California Press.
1988 *The Predicament of Culture: Twentieth Century Ethnography, Literature, and Art.* Cambridge: Harvard University Press.

Clifford, James, and George Marcus, eds.
1986 *Writing Culture: The Poetics and Politics of Ethnography.* Berkeley: University of California Press.

Cohen, Abner
1981 *The Politics of Elite Culture.* Berkeley: University of California Press.

Cohen, M. L.
1991a Being Chinese: The Peripheralization of Traditional Identity. Daedalus 120(2):113–134.
1991b Personal Communication. January 6.

Cohen, Ronald
1993 Conclusion: Ethnicity, the State, and Moral Order. In Judith Toland, ed. *Ethnicity and the State,* pp. 231–258. New Brunswick, N.J.: Transaction Publishers.

Cohn, Bernard
1980 History and Anthropology: The State of Play. Comparative Studies in Society and History 22(2):198–221.
1981 Anthropology and History in the 1980s. Journal of Interdisciplinary History 12(2):227–252.

Cole, Michael
1990 Cognitive Development and Formal Schooling: The Evidence from Cross-Cultural Research.
In Luis Moll, ed. *Vygotsky and Education*, pp. 89–
110. New York: Cambridge University Press.

Collier, Jane F.
1984 Two Models of Social Control in Simple
Societies. In Donald Black, ed. *Toward a General
Theory of Social Control*, vol. 2, *Selected Problems*, pp.
105–140. New York: Academic.
1986 From Mary to Modern Woman: The Material Basis of Marianismo and Its Transformation in
a Spanish Village. American Ethnologist 13(1):100–
107.
1987 Rank and Marriage: Or, Why High-Rank-
ing Brides Cost More. In Jane Fishburne Collier
and Sylvia Junko Yanagisako, eds. *Gender and Kinship: Essays toward a Unified Analysis*, pp. 197–220.
Stanford, Calif.: Stanford University Press.
1988 *Marriage and Inequality in Classless Societies*.
Stanford, Calif.: Stanford University Press.

Collier, Jane, and Michelle Z. Rosaldo
1981 Politics and Gender in Simple Societies. In
Sherry B. Ortner and Harriet Whitehead, eds.
Sexual Meanings, pp. 275–329. New York: Cambridge University Press.

Collier, J., and J. Yanagisako, eds.
1987 *Gender and Kinship: Essays toward a Unified
Analysis*. Stanford, Calif.: Stanford University Press.

Colson, Elizabeth
1971 *The Social Consequences of Resettlement: The
Impact of the Kariba Resettlement upon the Gwembe
Tonga*. Manchester: Manchester University Press.
1976 From Chief's Court to Local Court. In
Myron J. Aronoff, ed. *Freedom and Constraint*, pp.
15–19. Assen/Amsterdam, The Netherlands: Van
Gorcum.
1982 *Planned Change: The Creation of a New Community*. Berkeley: University of California, Institute
of International Studies.
1984 The Reordering of Experience: Anthropological Involvement with Time. Journal of Anthropological Research 40:1–13.
1985 Defining American Ethnology. In June
Helm, ed. *Social Contexts of American Ethnology,
1840-1984. 1984 Proceedings of the American Ethnological Society*, pp. 177–184. Washington, D.C.:
American Anthropological Association.

1989 Overview. Annual Review of Anthropology
18:1–16.
1992 Social/Cultural Anthropology. In *Wenner-
Gren Foundation Report for 1990 and 1991*, pp. 49–
61. New York: Wenner-Gren Foundation.

Colson, Elizabeth, and Thayer Scudder
1975 New Economic Relationships between the
Gwembe Valley and the Line of Rail. In David
Parkin, ed. *Town and Country in Central and Eastern
Africa*, pp. 190–210. London: Oxford University
Press.
1988 *For Prayer and Profit: The Ritual, Economic,
and Social Importance of Beer in Gwembe District,
Zambia, 1950-1982*. Stanford, Calif.: Stanford
University Press.

Comaroff, Jean
1982 Medicine: Symbol and Ideology. In Peter
Wright and Andrew Treacher, eds. *The Problem of
Medical Knowledge: Examining the Social Construction
of Medicine*, pp. 49–69. Edinburgh: Edinburgh University Press.
1985 *Body of Power. Spirit of Resistance*. Chicago:
Chicago University Press.

Comaroff, Jean, and John Comaroff
1986 Christianity and Colonialism in South
Africa. American Ethnologist 13(1):1–22.
1989 Anthropology and the Nature of Consciousness. Paper delivered at an invited session, "The
Categories of Modernity," 88th Annual Meeting of
the American Anthropological Association, Washington, D.C.

Comaroff, John
1984 The Closed Society and Its Critics: Historical Transformations in African Ethnography.
American Ethnologist 11(3):571–583.
1989 Images of Empire, Contests of Conscience:
Models of Colonial Domination in South Africa.
American Ethnologist 16(4):661–685.
1991 Humanity, Ethnicity, Nationality: Conceptual and Comparative Perspectives on the USSR.
Theory and Society 20 (special issue on "Ethnicity
in the USSR").

Comaroff, John, and Jean Comaroff
1992 *Ethnography and the Historical Imagination*.
Boulder, Colo.: Westview.

Conklin, Harold C.
1957 *Hanunoo Agriculture.* Rome: Food and Agricultural Organization of the United Nations.
1980 *Ethnographic Atlas of Ifuago.* New Haven, Conn.: Yale University Press.

Connerton, Paul
1989 *How Societies Remember.* New York: Cambridge University Press.

Connor, Walter
1972 Nation-Building or Nation Destroying. World Politics 24(3):319–355.
1973 The Politics of Ethnonationalism. Journal of International Affairs 27(1):1–21.
1984 *The National Question in Marxist-Leninist Theory and Strategy.* Princeton, N.J.: Princeton University Press.

Constitution of the USSR: Political-Legal Commentary
1982. Moscow: Politizdat. [in Russian]

Coon, C.
1948 *A Reader in General Anthropology.* New York: Henry Holt.

Coppet, D. de
1981 The Life-Giving Death. In S. C. Humphreys and H. King, eds. *Mortality and Immortality: The Anthropology and Archaeology of Death.* London: Academic.
1985 Land Owns People. In R. H. Barnes, D. de Coppet, and R. J. Parkin, eds. *Contexts and Levels: Anthropological Essays on Hierarchy.* Oxford: JASO.

Coser, Lewis
1971 *Masters of Sociological Thought: Ideas in Historical and Social Context.* New York: Harcourt, Brace, Jovanovich.

Costa, Alberto
n.d A Voice for the Silence: Television, Culture, and Change in Ibirama. Unpublished paper. To appear in Conrad Phillip Kottak, ed. Television's Social Impact in Brazil. In preparation.

Costa, Alberto, Conrad Kottak, Rosane Prado, and John Stiles
1991 Ecological Awareness and Risk Perception in Brazil. In Pam Puntenney, ed. *Special Issue of Bulletin of the National Association of Practicing Anthropologists.* Washington, D.C.: American Anthropological Association.

Crapanzano, Vincent
1985 *Waiting: The Whites of South Africa.* New York: Random House.

Crick, Malcolm
1982 Anthropology of Knowledge. Annual Review of Anthropology 11:287–313.
1989 Representations of International Tourism in the Social Sciences: Sun, Sex, Sights, Savings, and Servility. Annual Review of Anthropology 18:307–400.

Cultural Survival Quarterly
1984 Women in a Changing World 8(2).
1992 At the Threshold 16(2).

Cunha, Celso
1975 *Gramática do Português Contemporâneo.* Belo Horizonte, Brazil: Editora Bernardo Alvares S.A.

DaMatta, Roberto
1976a *Um Mundo Dividido: A Estrutura Social dos Indios Apinayé.* Coleção Antropologia 10. Petropolis: Editora Vozes Ltda. (English edition: *A Divided World: Apinayé Social Structure.* Translated by Alan Campbell. Cambridge, Mass.: Harvard University Press, 1982.)
1976b Quanto Custa ser Indio no Brasil? Considerações sôbre o Problema da Identidade Etnica. DADOS 13.
1979 *Carnavais. Malandros e Heróis: Para uma Socioloaia do Dilema Brasileiro,* 5 ed. Rio de Janeiro: Guanabara. (English edition: *Carnivals, Rogues and Heroes: An Interpretation of the Brazilian Dilemma.* Translated by John Drury. London and Notre Dame: University of Notre Dame Press. 1991.)
1983 An Interpretation of Carnaval. Sub/stance nos. 37/38: 162–170.
1987a A Originalidade de Gilberto Freyre, ANPOCS: Boletim Informativo e Bibliográfico de Ciências Sociais 24:1–72, Rio de Janeiro.
1987b *Mulher: A Mulher e o Feminino na Pintura Brasileira.* Rio de Janeiro: Acervo Galeria de Arte.

Damon, F.
1989 The Muyuw *Lo'un* and the End of Marriage. In F. Damon and R. Wagner, eds. *Death Rituals*

and Life in the Societies of the Kula Ring. De Kalb: Northern Illinois University Press.

D'Andrade, Roy
1974 Memory and the Assessment of Behavior. In H. M. Blalock, Jr., ed. *Measurement in the Social Sciences*. Chicago: Aldine.
1984 Cultural Meaning Systems. In R. A. Shweder and R. A. LeVine, eds. *Culture Theory: Essays on Mind, Self, and Emotion*, pp. 88–119. Cambridge, England: Cambridge University Press.
1987 Modal Responses and Cultural Expertise. American Behavioral Scientist 31(2):194–202.
1989 Cultural Sharing and Diversity. In R. Bolton, ed. *The Content of Culture: Constants and Variants: Studies in Honor of John M. Roberts*, pp. 349–361. New Haven, Conn.: HRAF Press.
1990 Some Propositions about the Relations between Culture and Cognition. In J. Stigler, Richard Shweder, and Gilbert Herdt, eds. *Cultural Psychology*, pp. 65–129. New York: Cambridge University Press.
1992a Afterword. In Roy D'Andrade and Claudia Strauss, eds. *Human Motives and Cultural Models*, pp. 225–232. New York: Cambridge University Press.
1992b Cognitive Anthropology. In Theodore Schwartz, Geoffrey White, and Catherine Lutz, eds. *New Directions in Psychological Anthropology*, pp. 47–58. New York: Cambridge University Press.

D'Andrade, Roy, and Claudia Strauss, eds.
1992 *Human Motives and Cultural Models*. New York: Cambridge University Press.

Danto, Arthur
1984 Mind as Feeling; Form as Presence; Langer as Philosopher. Journal of Philosophy 81:641–647.

Darnell, R.
1984 Comment on Shankman. Current Anthropology 25:271–272.

Das, Veena
1977 *Structure and Cognition: Aspects of Hindu Caste and Ritual*. Delhi: Oxford University Press.

Davis, Natalie Zemon
1975 *Society and Culture in Early Modern France*. Stanford, Calif.: Stanford University Press.

Debrunner, A.
1967 Logos. In G. Kittel, ed. *The Theological*

Dictionary of the New Testament, vol. IV, pp. 69–77. Grand Rapids, Mich.: Eerdmans.

de Certeau, Michel
1984 *The Practice of Everyday Life*. Berkeley: University of California Press.

DeHavenon, A. L.
1990 Charles Dickens Meets Franz Kafka: The Maladministration of New York City's Public Assistance Program. New York University's Review of Law and Change 17:231–254.

Dening, Greg
1986 Possessing Tahiti. Archaeology in Oceania 21(1):103–118.

Despres, L.
1975 Ethnicity and Resource Competition in Guyanese Society. In L. Despres, ed. *Ethnicity and Resource Competition in Plural Societies*, pp. 87–117. The Hague: Mouton.

Deutsch, Karl W.
1959 Comments on "American Intellectuals." Daedalus: Journal of the American Academy of Arts and Sciences 88:488–491.

Deutscher, I.
1972 *What We Say/What We Do*. Glenview, Ill.: Scott Foresman.

Diamond, Stanley
1969 Anthropology in Question. In Dell Hymes, ed. *Reinventing Anthropology*, pp. 401–429. New York: Random House.

Diener, P., D. Nonini, and E. Robkin
1978 The Dialectics of the Sacred Cow: Ecological Adaptation versus Political Appropriation in the Origins of India's Sacred Cattle Complex. Dialectical Anthropology 3:221–241.

Di Leonardo, Micaela, ed.
1991 *Gender at the Crossroads of Knowledge: Feminist Anthropology in the Postmodern Era*. Berkeley: University of California Press.

Dionne, Joseph
1992 *Publishing for the Individual*. New York: McGraw-Hill.

Divale, W., and M. Harris
1976 Population, Warfare and the Male Supremacist Complex. American Anthropologist 78:521-538.

Dominguez, Virginia
1989 *People as Subject, People as Object: Selfhood and Peoplehood in Contemporary Israel.* Madison: University of Wisconsin Press.

Dorsey, J. O.
1884 Omaha Sociology. Annual Report, Bureau of Ethnology, Smithsonian Institution 3:211-370.

Doughty, Paul
1987 Vicos: Success, Rejection, and Rediscovery of a Classic Program. In Elizabeth Eddy and William Partridge, eds. *Applied Anthropology in America*, pp. 433-459. New York: Columbia University Press.

Douglas, A.
1992 Lévi-Strauss, Claude. In Wayne Northcutt, ed. *Historical Dictionary of the French Fourth and Fifth Republics, 1946-1991*, pp. 266-267. New York: Greenwood.

Douglas, Mary
1966 *Purity and Danger: An Analysis of Concepts of Pollution and Taboo.* London: Routledge & Kegan Paul.
1970 *Natural Symbols: Explorations in Cosmology.* New York: Pantheon.
1975 Louis Dumont's Structural Analysis. In *Implicit Meanings: Essays in Anthropology*, pp. 181-192. London and Boston: Routledge & Kegan Paul.

Dragadze, Tamara
1988 *Rural Families in Soviet Georgia.* London: Routledge.

Dreyfus, H., and S. Dreyfus
1986 *Mind over Machine: The Power of Intuition and Expertise in the Era of the Computer.* New York: The Free Press.

Dreyfus, Hubert, and Paul Rabinow
1982 *Michel Foucault: Beyond Structuralism and Hermeneutics*, 2nd ed. Chicago: University of Chicago Press.

Dumont, Louis
1957 For a Sociology of India. Contributions to Indian Sociology I:7-22.
1960 The First Step. Contributions to Indian Sociology IV:7-12.
1966 A Fundamental Problem in the Sociology of Caste. Contributions to Indian Sociology 9:17-33.
1971 [1966] *Homo Hierarchicus: The Caste System and Its Implications.* London: University of Chicago Press. (Original French edition published 1966.)
1986 *Essays on Individualism: Modern Ideology in Anthropological Perspective.* Chicago: University of Chicago Press.

Durkheim, Emile
1915 *The Elementary Forms of the Religious Life.* New York: The Free Press.
1933 *The Division of Labor in Society.* New York: The Free Press.
1938 *The Rules of Sociological Method.* New York: The Free Press.
1951 *Suicide: A Study in Sociology.* Glencoe, Ill.: The Free Press.

Durkheim, Emile, and Marcel Mauss
1963 *Primitive Classification.* Chicago: University of Chicago Press.

Dutter, Lee E.
1990 Theoretical Perspectives on Ethnic Political Behavior in the Soviet Union. Journal of Conflict Resolution 34(2):311-334.

Eades, Jeremy, ed.
1986 *Migrants, Workers, and the Social Order.* London: Tavistock.

Earle, Timothy K.
1978 Economic and Social Organization of a Complex Chiefdom: The Halelea district, Kauai, Hawaii. Museum of Anthropology, University of Michigan, Anthropological Papers No. 63.
1987 Chiefdoms in Archaeological and Ethnohistorical Perspective. Annual Review of Anthropology 16:279-308. Palo Alto: Annual Reviews.
1989 The Evolution of Chiefdoms. Current Anthropology 30(1):84-88.

Eggan, Fred
1954 Social Anthropology and the Method of Controlled Comparison. American Anthropologist 56:743-763.
1955 [ed.] *Social Anthropology of North American Tribes*, enlarged ed. Chicago: University of Chicago Press.
1965 Some Reflections on Comparative Method in Anthropology. In Melford Spiro, ed. *Context and Meaning in Cultural Anthropology*, pp. 357-372. New York: The Free Press.
1968 Kinship. In David Sills, ed. *International Encyclopedia of the Social Sciences*, vol. 8, pp. 390-401. New York: Macmillan.
1977 The History of Social/Cultural Anthropology. In Anthony F. C. Wallace et al., eds. *Perspectives on Anthropology, 1976*, pp. 1-13. American Anthropological Association Special Publication 10. Washington, D.C.: American Anthropological Association.

Eisenberg, Leon
1977 Illness and Disease. Culture, Medicine, and Psychiatry 1(1):9-23.

Eliot, T. S.
1948 *Notes towards the Definition of Culture*. London: Faber and Faber.

Ellen, Roy
1979 Omniscience and Ignorance: Variation in Nuaulu Knowledge, Identification and Classification of Animals. Language in Society 8(3):337-364.

Elphick, Richard
1977 *Kraal and Castle: Khoikhoi and the Founding of White South Africa*. New Haven, Conn.: Yale University Press.

Elster, J.
1983 *Explaining Technical Change*. Cambridge, England: Cambridge University Press.

Ember, Carol, and Melvin Ember
1985 *Anthropology*, 4th ed. Englewood Cliffs, N.J.: Prentice-Hall.

Epstein, A. L.
1958 *Politics in an Urban African Community*. Manchester, England: Manchester University Press.

Epstein, T. Scarlett
1978 Mysore Villages Revisited. In George Foster et al., eds. *Long-Term Field Research in Social Anthropology*, pp. 209-226. New York: Academic.

Erikson, Erik
1963 [1950] *Childhood and Society*. New York: Norton.

Esman, Milton J., ed.
1977 *Ethnic Conflict in the Western World*. Ithaca, N.Y.: Cornell University Press.

Estroff, Sue
1981 *Making It Crazy: An Ethnography of Psychiatric Clients in an American Community*. Berkeley: University of California Press.

Etienne, Mona, and Eleanor Leacock, eds.
1980 *Women and Colonization: Anthropological Perspectives*. New York: Praeger.

Evans-Pritchard, E. E.
1937 *Witchcraft, Oracles and Magic among the Azande*. Oxford, England: Clarendon.
1956 *Nuer Religion*. Oxford, England: Clarendon.
1962 *Social Anthropology and Other Essays*. New York: The Free Press of Glencoe.
1983 The Position of Women in Primitive Societies and Our Own. In *The Position of Women in Primitive Societies and Other Essays in Social Anthropology*. New York: The Free Press.

Fabian, Johannes
1983 *Time and the Other: How Anthropology Makes Its Object*. New York: Columbia University Press.

Fabrega, Horacio, and Daniel Silver
1973 *Illness and Shamanistic Curing in Zinacantan*. Stanford, Calif.: Stanford University Press.

Fahim, Hussein
1982 *Indigenous Anthropology in Non-Western Countries*. Durham, N.C.: Carolina Academic.

Fanon, Frantz
1963 *The Wretched of the Earth*. New York: Grove.

Fardon, R.
1988 *Raiders and Refugees: Trends in Chamba Political Development 1750 to 1950*. Washington, D.C.:

Smithsonian Institution Press.
1990 [ed.] *Localizing Strategies: Regional Traditions of Ethnographic Writing.* Washington, D.C.: Smithsonian Institution Press.

Farr, J.
1982 Historical Concepts in Political Science: The Case of "Revolution." American Journal of Political Science 26:688-708.
1989 Understanding Conceptual Change Politically. In T. Ball, J. Farr, and R. L. Hanson, eds. *Political Innovation and Conceptual Change*, pp. 24-49. Cambridge, England: Cambridge University Press.

Favret-Saada, Jeanne
1977 *Deadly Words: Witchcraft in the Bocage.* New York: Cambridge University Press.
1989 Unbewitching as Therapy. American Ethnologist 16(1):40-56.

Feher, Michel, Ramona Naddaff, and Nadia Tazi, eds.
1989 *Fragments for a History of the Human Body.* New York: Zone.

Feinman, Gary M., and Jill Neitzel
1984 Too Many Types: An Overview of Sedentary Prestate Societies in the Americas. *Advances in Archaeological Method and Theory* 7:39-102. Michael B. Schiffer, ed. New York: Academic.

Feirman, Steven
1985 Struggle for Control: The Social Roots of Health and Healing in Modern Africa. African Studies 28(2, 3):73-147.

Feldman, J., and D. Ballard
1982 Connectionist Models and Their Properties. Cognitive Science 6:205-54.

Ferguson, B.
1984 Introduction: Studying War. In B. Ferguson, ed. *Warfare, Culture and Environment*, pp. 1-61. Orlando, Fla.: Academic.
1989 Game Wars? Ecology and Conflict in Amazonia. Journal of Anthropological Research 45: 179-206.

Ferguson, James
1990 *The Anti-Politics Machine: "Development," Depoliticization, and Bureaucratic Power in Lesotho.* Cambridge, England: Cambridge University Press.

Fernandez, James
1975 On Reading the Sacred and the Profane. Journal for the Scientific Study of Religion 14: 191-197.

Fillmore, C.
1975 An Alternative to Checklist Theories of Meaning. Proceedings of the First Annual Meeting of the Berkeley Linguistic Society, pp. 123-131.

Finnegan, Ruth
1977 *Oral Poetry.* Cambridge, England: Cambridge University Press.

Firth, Raymond
1936 *We the Tikopia.* London: George Allen & Unwin.
1951 *Elements of Social Organization.* London: Watts.
1959 *Social Change in Tikopia: Re-Study of a Polynesian Community after a Generation.* London: George Allen & Unwin.
1968 Anthropology: Social Anthropology. In David Sills, ed. *International Encyclopedia of the Social Sciences*, pp. A:320-324. New York: Macmillan.
1975 An Appraisal of Modern Social Anthropology. Annual Review of Anthropology 4:1-25.

Firth, R., J. Hubert, and A. Forge
1969 *Families and Their Relatives: Kinship in a Middle-Class Sector of London.* London: Routledge & Kegan Paul.

Fischer, Michael
1986 Ethnicity and the Post-Modern Art of Memory. In James Clifford and George Marcus, eds. *Writing Culture*, pp. 194-233. Berkeley: University of California Press.

Fischer, Michael, and Mehdi Abedi
1990 *Debating Muslims: Cultural Dialogues in Postmodernity and Tradition.* Madison: University of Wisconsin Press.

Fodor, Jerry A.
1975 *The Language of Thought.* Cambridge, Mass.: Harvard University Press.

Fortes, Meyer
1945 *The Dynamics of Clanship among the Tallensi.* London: Oxford University Press.
1949 *The Web of Kinship among the Tallensi.*

London: Oxford University Press.
1953 Social Anthropology at Cambridge since 1900: An Inaugural Lecture. Cambridge, England: Cambridge University Press.
1958 Introduction. In Jack Goody, ed. *The Developmental Cycle in Domestic Groups*, pp. 1–14. Cambridge, England: Cambridge University Press.
1969 *Kinship and the Social Order*. Chicago: Aldine.
1970 *Time and Social Structure and Other Essays*. London: Athlone Press.
1978 An Anthropologist's Apprenticeship. Annual Review of Anthropology 7:1–30.
1984 Foreword. In Peter Lawrence, *The Garia*. Melbourne: University of Melbourne Press.
1987 *Religion, Morality and the Person*. Cambridge, England: Cambridge University Press.

Fortes, M., and E. E. Evans-Pritchard, eds.
1940 *African Political Systems*. New York: Oxford University Press.

Foster, George
1978 Fieldwork in Tzintzuntzan: The First Thirty Years. In George Foster et al., eds. *Long-Term Field Research in Social Anthropology*, pp. 165–184. New York: Academic.
1979 Methodological Problems in the Study of Intracultural Variation: The Hot/Cold Dichotomy in Tzintzuntzan. Human Organization 38:179–183.

Foster, George, Thayer Scudder, Elizabeth Colson, and Robert Kemper
1979 *Long-Term Field Research in Social Anthropology*. New York: Academic.

Foucault, M.
1973a *The Birth of the Clinic*. Translated by Alan Sheridan. London: Tavistock. (First published, 1963, as *Naissance de la Clinique*, Presses Universitaires de France.)
1973b *The Order of Things*. New York: Random House.
1975 *The Birth of the Clinic*. New York: Vintage.
1977 *Discipline and Punish: The Birth of the Prison*. Translated by Alan Sheridan. London: Allen Lane. (First published, 1975, as *Surveiller et Punir: Naissance de la Prison*. Paris: Gallimard.)
1979 *Discipline and Punish*. New York: Vintage.
1980a *The History of Sexuality*. New York: Vintage.
1980b *Power/Knowledge: Selected Interviews and Other Writings 1972-1977*. Colin Gordon, ed. New York: Pantheon.
1984 The Subject and Power. In Brian Wallis, ed. *Art after Modernism: Rethinking Representation*, pp. 417–432. New York: The New Museum of Contemporary Art.

Fowler, H. W.
1928 *Fishes in Oceania*. Bernice P. Bishop Museum Memoir 10. Honolulu: Bishop Museum Press.

Fox, Richard G., ed.
1991 *Recapturing Anthropology: Working in the Present*. Santa Fe, N.M.: School of American Research Press.

Fox, Robin
1967 *Kinship and Marriage*. Middlesex, England: Penguin.

Frankenberg, Ronald
1988a "Your Time or Mine?" An Anthropological View of the Tragic Temporal Contradictions of Biomedical Practice. International Journal of Health Service 18(1):11–34.
1988b Gramsci, Culture and Medical Anthropology. Medical Anthropology Quarterly 2:324–37.

Freeman, Derek
1961 On the Concept of the Kindred. Journal of the Royal Anthropological Institute 91:192–220.
1983 *Margaret Mead and Samoa: The Making and Unmaking of an Anthropological Myth*. Cambridge, Mass.: Harvard University Press.

Freeman, L. C., and A. K. Romney
1987 Words, Deeds and Social Structure: A Preliminary Study of the Reliability of Informants. Human Organization 46:330–334.

Freeman, L. C., A. K. Romney, and S. Freeman.
1987 Cognitive Structure and Informant Accuracy. American Anthropologist 89:310–325.

Freeman, Walter J.
1991 The Physiology of Perception. Scientific American, February:78–85.

Freyre, Gilberto
1933 *Casa Grande e Senzala*. Rio de Janeiro: José Olympio Editor.

Fried, Morton
1967 *The Evolution of Political Society: An Essay in Political Anthropology.* New York: Random House.

Friedl, Ernestine
1975 *Women and Men: An Anthropologist's View.* New York: Holt, Rinehart and Winston.

Friedman, Jonathan
1974 Marxism, Structuralism, and Vulgar Materialism. Man 9:444–469.
1992a Narcissism, Roots, and Post-Modernity: The Constitution of Selfhood in the Global Crisis. In Scott Lash and Jonathan Friedman, eds. *Modernity and Identity*, pp. 331–366. Oxford, England: Blackwell.
1992b The Past in the Future: History and the Politics of Identity. American Anthropologist 94(4):837–859.

Friedman, K. Ekholm
1994 *An African Tragedy: Liberation of the State from the Masses in Central Africa.* Stockholm: Bonnier Alba.

Furbee, Louanna, and Robert Benfer
1983 Cognitive and Geographical Maps: Study of Individual Variation among Tojolabal Mayans. American Anthropologist 85:305–334.

Furnival, J. S.
1939 *Netherlands India.* Cambridge, England: Cambridge University Press.
1948 *Colonial Policy and Practice: A Comparative Study of Burma and Netherlands India.* Cambridge, England: Cambridge University Press.

Gailey, Christine Ward
1983 Categories without Culture: Structuralism, Ethnohistory and Ethnocide. Dialectical Anthropology 8:241–250.
1987 *Kinship to Kingship: Gender Hierarchy and State Formation in the Tongan Islands.* Austin: University of Texas Press.

Gallagher, Art, Jr., and Harland Padfield
1980 Theory of the Dying Community. In Art Gallagher, Jr. and Harland Padfield, eds. *The Dying Community*, pp. 1–22. Albuquerque: University of New Mexico Press.

Gandhi, M. K.
1922 *Indian Home Rule.* Madras, India: Ganesh & Co.

Gardner, Peter
1976 Birds, Words, and a Requiem for the Omniscient Informant. American Ethnologist 3:446–468.

Garfinkel, A.
1981 *Forms of Explanation: Rethinking the Questions in Social Theory.* New Haven, Conn.: Yale University Press.

Garro, Linda
1986 Intracultural Variation in Folk Medical Knowledge: A Comparison between Curers and Noncurers. American Anthropologist 88:351–370.

Gatens, H.
1983 A Critique of the Sex/Gender Distinction. In Beyond Marxism. Intervention, special issue: 143–160.

Gatewood, J. B.
1985 Actions Speak Louder Than Words. In J. W. D. Dougherty, ed. *Directions in Cognitive Anthropology*, pp. 199–219. Urbana: University of Illinois Press.

Geertz, Clifford
1957 Ritual and Social Change: A Javanese Example. American Anthropologist 59:32–54.
1965 The Impact of the Concept of Culture on the Concept of Man. In J. R. Platt, ed. *New Views on the Nature of Man.* Chicago: University of Chicago Press.
1966 Religion as a Cultural System. In Michael Banton, ed. *Anthropological Approaches to the Study of Religion*, pp. 1–46. New York: Praeger.
1968 *Islam Observed: Religious Developments in Morocco and Indonesia.* Chicago: University of Chicago Press.
1973 *The Interpretation of Cultures.* New York: Basic Books.
1974 *Myth, Symbol, and Culture.* New York: W. W. Norton.
1983 *Local Knowledge: Further Essays in Interpretive Anthropology.* New York: Basic Books.
1984 Distinguished Lecture: Anti Anti-Relativism. American Anthropologist 86:263–278.
1985 Waddling In. Times Literary Supplement

4288(June 7):623–624.
1988 *Works and Lives: The Anthropologist as Author.*
Stanford, Calif.: University of Stanford Press.
1990 Comment. Current Anthropology 31(3):
274–275.
1991 An Interview with Clifford Geertz by
Richard Handler. Current Anthropology 32(5):
603–613.

Gellner, Ernest
1983 *Nations and Nationalism.* Ithaca, N.Y.:
Cornell University Press.
1988 The Stakes in Anthropology. The American
Scholar. Winter:17–30.

Gibson, James
1979 *The Ecological Approach to Visual Perception.*
Boston: Houghton Mifflin.

Giddens, Anthony
1984 *The Constitution of Society: Outline of a Theory
of Structuration.* Berkeley: University of California
Press.

Gillison, G.
1991 The Flute Myth and the Law of Equivalence: Origins of a Principle of Exchange. In M.
Godelier and M. Strathern, eds. *Big Men and Great
Men: Personifications of Power in Melanesia.* Cambridge, England: Cambridge University Press.

Ginsburg, Faye
1989 *Contested Lives: The Abortion Debate in an
American Community.* Berkeley: University of California Press.

Ginsburg, Faye, and Rayna Rapp
1991 The Politics of Reproduction. Annual Review of Anthropology 20:311–343.

Gittelman, Zvi
1991 Formation of Jewish Culture and Identity in
the USSR: The State as a Social Engineer. Soviet
Ethnography 1. [in Russian]

Givens, David, and Susan Skomal
1992 The Four Fields: Myth or Reality? Anthropology Newsletter 33(7):1, 17.

**Glazer, Nathan, and Daniel P. Moynihan,
eds.**
1975 *Ethnicity, Theory and Experience.* Cambridge,
Mass.: Harvard University Press.

Glenn, Sigrid
1988 Contingencies and Metacontingencies:
Towards a Synthesis of Behavior Analysis and Cultural Materialism. The Behavior Analyst 11:161–
179.

Gluckman, Max
1955 *Rituals of Rebellion in South-East Africa.*
Manchester, England: Manchester University Press.
1957 Introduction. In Ronald Frankenberg,
Village on the Border, pp. 1–8. Manchester, England:
Manchester University Press.

Godelier, Maurice
1972 [1966] *Rationality and Irrationality in Economics.* New York: Monthly Review Press.
1977 [1972] Perspectives in Marxist Anthropology. Cambridge Studies in Social Anthropology
18. Cambridge, England: Cambridge University
Press.
1986a [1982] *The Making of Great Men.* Cambridge, England: Cambridge University Press.
1986b [1984] *The Mental and the Material.*
London: Verso.
1991 [ed.] *Transitions et Subordinations au Capitalisme.* Paris: Maison des Sciences de l'Homme.

**Godelier, Maurice, and Marilyn Strathern,
eds.**
1991 *Big Men and Great Men: Personifications of
Power in Melanesia.* New York: Cambridge University Press.

Goffman, Irving
1956 *Asylums.* Garden City, N.Y.: Doubleday.

Golde, P., ed.
1970 *Women in the Field.* Chicago: Aldine.

Goldman, Irving
1975 *The Mouth of Heaven: An Introduction to
Kwakiutl Religious Thought.* New York: Wiley.

Goldschmidt, Walter
1985 The Cultural Paradigm in the Post-War
World. In June Helm, ed. *Social Contexts of American Ethnology, 1840-1984,* pp. 164–176. Washington, D.C.: American Ethnological Society.

Goldstein, Leon
1957 On Defining Culture. American Anthropologist 59:1075–1079.

González, N. S.
1986 The Anthropologist as Female Head of Household. In T. L. Whitehead and M. E. Conaway, eds. *Self, Sex and Gender in Cross-Cultural Fieldwork*, pp. 84–102. Urbana: University of Illinois Press.

Good, K.
1987 Limiting Factors in Amazonian Ecology. In M. Harris and E. Ross, eds. *Food and Evolution: Toward a Theory of Human Food Habits*, pp. 407–426. Philadelphia: Temple University Press.

Goodenough, Ward H.
1951 Property, Kin, and Community on Truk. Yale University Publications in Anthropology 46.
1957 Cultural Anthropology and Linguistics. In P. Garvin, ed. *Report of the Seventh Annual Round Table Meeting on Linguistics and Language Study*. Washington, D.C.: Georgetown University Press.
1963 *Cooperation in Change*. New York: Russell Sage Foundation.
1970 *Description and Comparison in Cultural Anthropology*. Chicago: Aldine.
1981 *Culture, Language, and Society*, 2nd ed. Menlo Park, Calif.: Benjamin-Cummings.
1989 Cultural Anthropology: Science and Humanity. Crosscurrents 3:78–82.
1990 Evolution of the Human Capacity for Beliefs. American Anthropologist 92:597–612.

Goody, Jack
1968 Introduction. In Jack Goody, ed. *Literacy in Traditional Societies*, pp. 1–26. Cambridge, England: Cambridge University Press.
1973 Bridewealth and Dowry in Africa and Eurasia. In Jack Goody and S. J. Tambiah, eds. *Bridewealth and Dowry*, pp. 1–58. Cambridge, England: Cambridge University Press.
1976 *Production and Reproduction: A Comparative Study of the Domestic Domain*. New York: Cambridge University Press.
1983 *The Development of the Family and Marriage in Europe*. New York: Cambridge University Press.
1991 Towards a Room With a View: A Personal Account of Contributions to Local Knowledge, Theory and Research in Fieldwork and Comparative Studies. Annual Review of Anthropology 20:1–23.
1993 *The Culture of Flowers*. New York: Cambridge University Press.

Gopal, Sarvepalli
1991 Introduction. In S. Gopal, ed. *Anatomy of a Confrontation: The Babri Masjid-Ramjanmabhumi Issue*, pp. 11–21. Delhi: Viking.

Gorbachev, Mikhail
1991 Interview. Literary Gazette. December 4, 1991.

Gould, S.J.
1982 Of Wasps and WASPS. Natural History, December, pp. 8–13.
1988 Mighty Manchester. New York Review of Books, October 27, pp. 32–35.

Graburn, Nelson, ed.
1983 *The Anthropology of Tourism*. New York: Pergamon.

Graebner, Fritz
1911 *Methode der Ethnologie*. Heidelberg: C. Winter.

Gramsci, Antonio
1971 *Selections from the Prison Notebooks of Antonio Gramsci*. New York: International Publishers.

Granzberg, G., and T. Steinbring
1980 *Television and the Canadian Indian*. Winnipeg, Manitoba: University of Winnipeg Press.

Greenhouse, C.
1986 *Praying for Justice: Faith, Order and Community in an American Town*. Ithaca, N.Y.: Cornell University Press.

Greenwood, J. D.
1987 Scientific Psychology and Hermeneutical Psychology: Causal Explanation and the Meaning of Human Action. Human Studies 10:171–204.

Griaule, Marcel
1965 Conversations with Ogotemmêli: An Introduction to Dogon Religious Ideas. London: Oxford University Press.

Grice, H. P.
1975 Logic and Conversation. In Peter Cole and Jerry Morgan, eds. *Syntax and Semantics*, vol. 3, *Speech Acts*, pp. 41–58. New York: Academic.

Gross, D.
1975 Protein Capture and Cultural Development in Amazonia. American Anthropologist 77:526–549.

Grossberg, L., and G. Nelson
1988 Introduction. In G. Nelson and L. Grossberg, eds. *Marxism and the Interpretation of Culture.* Urbana: University of Illinois Press.

Guboglo, M. N.
1989 National Groups and Minorities in a System of Interethnic Relations in the USSR. Soviet Ethnography 1. [in Russian]

Guha, Ranajit
1983a *Elementary Aspects of Peasant Insurgency in Colonial India.* New Delhi: Oxford University Press.
1983b *Subaltern Studies I.* Delhi: Oxford University Press.
1984a The Prose of Counter-Insurgency. In R. Guha, ed. *Subaltern Studies II: Writings on South Asian History and Society.* Delhi: Oxford University Press.
1984b *Subaltern Studies II.* Delhi: Oxford University Press.
1985 *Subaltern Studies III.* Delhi: Oxford University Press.
1986 *Subaltern Studies IV.* Delhi: Oxford University Press.
1987 *Subaltern Studies V.* Delhi: Oxford University Press.
1989 Dominance versus Hegemony: Notes on British Historiography of India. In R. Guha, ed. *Subaltern Studies VI*, pp. 210–309. Delhi: Oxford University Press.

Guskova, Elena
1991 Moscow News. September 17.

Guyer, Jane
1987 Feeding African Cities. In Jane Guyer, ed. *Feeding African Cities*, pp. 1–54. Bloomington: Indiana University Press.

Haas, J.
1982 *The Evolution of the Prehistoric State.* New York: Columbia University Press.

Habarad, Jonathan
n.d. Neighborhood and Nation in Gwembe District, Zambia.

Habermas, Jurgen
1987 *The Theory of Communicative Action*, vol. 2. Boston: Beacon Press.

Haier, R. J., B. V. Siegel, A. MacLachlan, E. Soderling, S. Lottenberg, and M. S. Buchsbaum
1992 Regional Glucose Metabolic Changes after Learning a Complex Visuospatial/Motor Task: A Positron Emission Tomographic Study. Brain Research 570(1, 2):134–143.

Hajda, Lubomyr, and Mark Beissinger, eds.
1990 *The Nationalities Factor in Soviet Politics and Society.* Boulder, Colo.: Westview.

Hall, D.
1984 Introduction. In S. L. Kaplan, ed. *Understanding Popular Culture: Europe from the Middle Ages to the Nineteenth Century.* Berlin: Mouton.

Hall, S.
1988 The Toad in the Garden: Thatcherism among the Theorists. In G. Nelson and L. Grossberg, eds. *Marxism and the Interpretation of Culture.* Urbana and Chicago: University of Illinois Press.

Hallowell, A. Irving
1955 *Culture and Experience.* Philadelphia: University of Pennsylvania Press.
1957 The Backwash of the Frontier: The Impact of the Indian on American Culture. In Walker Wyman and Clifton Kroeber, eds. *The Frontier in Perspective*, pp. 229–258. Madison: University of Wisconsin Press. (Reprinted in Paul Bohannan and Fred Plog, eds. *Beyond the Frontier*, pp. 319–345. Garden City, N.Y.: Natural History Press, 1967.)
1965 The History of Anthropology as an Anthropological Problem. Journal of the History of the Behavioral Sciences 1:24–38.

Hallpike, C. R.
1973 Functionalist Interpretations of Primitive Warfare. Man 8:451–470.
1986 *The Principles of Social Evolution.* Oxford, England: Clarendon Press.

Hammond, Peter
1964 *Cultural and Social Anthropology: Selected Readings.* New York: Macmillan.

Handler, R.
1984 On Sociocultural Discontinuity: Nationalism and Cultural Objectification in Quebec. Current Anthropology 25:55-71.

Hannerz, Ulf
1986 Theory in Anthropology. Small is Beautiful: The Problem of Complex Cultures. Comparative Studies in Society and History 28:362-367.
1990 Cosmopolitans and Locals in World Culture. In Mike Featherstone, ed. *Global Culture: Nationalism, Globalization and Modernity*, pp. 237-251. Newbury Park, Calif.: Sage.

Hansen, Art, and Anthony Oliver-Smith, eds.
1982 *Involuntary Migration and Resettlement: The Problems and Responses of Dislocated People.* Boulder, Colo.: Westview.

Hanson, Allan
1989 The Making of the Maori: Culture Invention and Its Logic. American Anthropologist 91: 890-902.

Harkness, Sara, Charles H. Super, and Constance M. Keefer
1992 Learning to Be an American Parent: How Cultural Models Gain Directive Force. In R.G. D'Andrade and C. Strauss, eds. *Human Motives and Cultural Models*, pp. 163-178. New York: Cambridge University Press.

Harner, M.
1977 The Ecological Basis for Aztec Sacrifice. American Ethnologist 4:117-135.

Harrington, Deborah, Kathleen Haaland, Ronald Yeo, and Ellen Marder
1990 Procedural Memory in Parkinson's Disease: Impaired Motor but Not Visuoperceptual Learning. Journal of Clinical and Experimental Neuropsychology 12(2):323-339.

Harris, Marvin
1958 *Portugal's African Wards.* New York: American Committee on Africa.
1964a *The Nature of Cultural Things.* New York: Random House.
1964b Racial Identity in Brazil. Luso-Brazilian Review 1:21.
1964c *Patterns of Race in America.* New York: Walker.

1967 Reply to John Bennet. Current Anthropology 9:252-253.
1968 *The Rise of Anthropological Theory: A History of Theories of Culture.* New York: Thomas Crowell.
1970 Referential Ambiguity in the Calculus of Brazilian Racial Identity. Southwestern Journal of Anthropology 26:1-14.
1974 *Cows, Pigs, Wars, and Witches: The Riddles of Culture.* New York: Random House.
1977 *Cannibals and Kings: The Origins of Cultures.* New York: Random House.
1978 No End of Messiahs. The New York Times, November 26, Sec. IV:21.
1979a *Cultural Materialism.* New York: Random House.
1979b Reply to Sahlins. New York Review of Books, June 28, pp. 52-53.
1980 History and Ideological Significance of the Separation of Social and Cultural Anthropology. In Eric Ross, ed. *Beyond the Myths of Culture: Essays in Cultural Materialism*, pp. 391-407. New York: Academic.
1981a *America Now: The Anthropology of a Changing Culture.* New York: Simon and Schuster.
1981b Comment on Freed and Freed. Current Anthropology 22:492-494.
1984 Animal Capture and Yanomano Warfare: Retrospective and New Evidence. Journal of Anthropological Research 40:183-201.
1985 *Good to Eat.* New York: Simon and Schuster.
1987 Foodways: Historical Overview and Theoretical Prolegomenon. In M. Harris and E. Ross, eds. *Food and Evolution toward a Theory of Human Food Habits*, pp. 57-90. Philadelphia: Temple University Press.
1987b Reply to Vayda. Human Ecology 15:512-518.
1988a *Culture, People, Nature: An Introduction to General Anthropology.* New York: Harper and Row.
1989 *Our Kind.* New York: Harper and Row.
1990 *Cultural Anthropology*, 3rd ed. New York: Harper and Row.
1991 Anthropology: Ships That Crash in the Night. In R. Jessor, ed. *Perspectives in Social Science: The Colorado Lectures.* Boulder, Colo.: Westview.
1992 *Culture, People, Nature*, 6th ed. New York: Harper and Row.

Harris, M., and E. Ross
1987 *Death, Sex, and Fertility: Population Regulation*

in Pre-Industrial and Developing Societies. New York: Columbia University Press.

Harris, O.
1978 Complementarity and Conflict: An Andean View of Women and Men. In J. S. LaFontaine, ed. *Sex and Age as Principles of Social Differentiation.* New York: Academic.

Hart, H. L. A., and A. M. Honoré
1959 *Causation in the Law.* Oxford, England: Clarendon Press.

Hasher, L., and R. T. Zacks
1984 Automatic Processing of Fundamental Information: The Case of Frequency of Occurrence. American Psychologist 39(12):1372-1388.

Hatch, Elvin
1973 *Theories of Man and Culture.* New York: Columbia University Press.
1985 Culture. In Adam Kuper and Jessica Kuper, eds. *The Social Science Encyclopedia,* pp. 178-180. London: Routledge & Kegan Paul.

Haudricourt, A.-G.
1968 La Technologie Culturelle: Essai de Methodologie. In J. Poirier, ed. *Ethnologie Generale.* Paris: Pleiade.

Haviland, William
1990 *Cultural Anthropology,* 6th ed. Fort Worth, Tex.: Holt, Rinehart and Winston College Division.

Hayden, Brian
1986. The Influence of Basic Resource Characteristics on Reproductive Behavior. In W.P. Handwerker, ed. *Culture and Reproduction,* pp. 176-195. Boulder, Colo.: Westview.
1990 Nimrods, Piscators, Pluckers, and Planters: The Emergence of Food Production. Journal of Anthropological Archaeology 9:31-69.

Hayden, Brian, et al.
1986 Ecological Determinants of Women's Status among Hunter/Gatherers. Human Evolution 1: 449-474.

Hays, Terence
1974 Mauna: Explorations in Ndumba Ethnobotany. Ph.D. dissertation. Seattle: University of Washington.

1976 An Empirical Method for the Identification of Covert Categories in Ethnobiology. American Ethnologist 3:489-507.

Headland, Thomas, K. Pike, and M. Harris, eds.
1990 *Emics and Etics.* Newbury Park, Calif.: Sage.

Hebb, Donald O.
1949 *The Organization of Behavior: A Neuropsychological Theory.* New York: Wiley.

Hecht, J.
1976a "Double Descent" and Cultural Symbolism in Pukapuka, Northern Cook Islands. Ph.D. dissertation. Chicago: University of Chicago.
1976b "Double Descent" and Cultural Symbolism in Pukapuka, Northern Cook Islands. Dissertation abstract submitted to the National Science Foundation.
1977 The Culture of Gender in Pukapuka: Male, Female and the *Mayakitanga* "Sacred Maid." Journal of the Polynesian Society 86:183-206.

Hefner, R. W.
1987 The Politics of Popular Art: *Tayuban* Dance and Culture Change in East Java. Indonesia 43:75-94.

Heidegger, Martin
1959 *Introduction to Metaphysics.* New Haven, Conn.: Yale University Press.

Heine, B., U. Claudi, and F. Hünnemeyer
1992 *Grammaticalization: A Conceptual Framework.* Chicago: University of Chicago Press.

Heine, B., and M. Reh
1984 *Grammaticalization and Reanalysis in African Languages.* Hamburg: Helmut Buske.

Heine, B., and E. Traugott, eds.
1992 *Grammaticalization,* 2 vols. Amsterdam: John Benjamins.

Hellman, Ellen
1948 *Rooiyard: A Sociological Study of an Urban Slum.* Rhodes-Livingstone Paper 13. Manchester, England: Manchester University Press.

Herbert, Christopher
1991 *Culture and Anomie: Ethnographic Imagination*

in the Nineteenth Century. Chicago: University of Chicago Press.

Herskovits, Melville
1963 *Cultural Anthropology.* New York: Knopf.
1965 A Genealogy of Ethnological Theory. In Melford Spiro, ed. *Context and Meaning in Cultural Anthropology,* pp. 403-415. New York: The Free Press.

Hertz, Robert
1960 *Death and the Right Hand.* London: Cohen and West.

Herzfeld, Michael
1987 *Anthropology through the Looking Glass: Critical Ethnography in the Margins of Europe.* New York: Cambridge University Press.

Hewlett, B. S., and L. L. Cavalli-Sforza
1986 Cultural Transmission among Aka Pygmies. American Anthropologist 88:922-934.

Hoben, Alan
1982 Anthropologists and Development. Annual Review of Anthropology 11:349-375. Palo Alto, Calif.: Annual Reviews Inc.

Hobsbawm, Eric
1965 *Primitive Rebels: Studies in Archaic Forms of Social Movement in the 19th and 20th Centuries.* New York: W. W. Norton.
1983 Introduction: Inventing Traditions. In Eric Hobsbawm and Terence Ranger, eds. *The Invention of Tradition,* pp. 1-14. New York: Cambridge University Press.
1990 *Nations and Nationalism Since 1780: Programme, Myth, Reality.* New York: Cambridge University Press.
1992 Ethnicity and Nationalism in Europe Today. Anthropology Today 8(1):3-8.

Hobsbawm, Eric, and Terence Ranger, eds.
1983 *The Invention of Tradition.* New York: Cambridge University Press.

Holland, Dorothy
1987 Cultural Sharing across Gender Lines: An Interactionist Corrective to the Status-Centered Model. American Behavioral Scientist 31:234-249.
1992 The Woman Who Climbed Up the House: Some Limitations of Schema Theory. In Theodore

Schwartz, Geoffrey White, and Catherine Lutz, eds. *New Directions in Psychological Anthropology.* New York: Cambridge University Press.

Holland, Dorothy, and Margaret Eisenhart
1990 *Educated in Romance: Women, Achievement, and College Culture.* Chicago: University of Chicago Press.

Holland, D., and N. Quinn, eds.
1987 *Cultural Models in Language and Thought.* New York: Cambridge University Press.

Holmberg, Allan
1955 Participant Intervention in the Field. Human Organization 14:23-26.

Holy, Ladislav
1987 Introduction. Description, Generalization and Comparison: Two Paradigms. In L. Holy, ed. *Comparative Anthropology,* pp. 1-21. Oxford, England: Basil Blackwell.

Holy, Ladislav, and Milan Stuchlik
1983 *Actions, Norms and Representations.* New York: Cambridge University Press.

Honigman, John, ed.
1973 *Handbook of Social and Cultural Anthropology.* Chicago: Rand McNally.

Horowitz, Donald L.
1985 *Ethnic Groups in Conflict.* Berkeley: University of California Press.

Hough, Jerry F.
1990 The Logic of Collective Action and the Pattern of Revolutionary Behavior. Journal of Soviet Nationalities 1(2).

Hoy, David
1986 Power, Repression, Progress: Foucault, Lukes, and the Frankfurt School. In David Hoy, ed. *Foucault, A Critical Reader,* pp. 123-147. Cambridge, Mass.: Basil Blackwell.

Hsu, Francis
1983 *Rugged Individualism Reconsidered: Essays in Psychological Anthropology.* Knoxville: University of Tennessee Press.

Humphrey, Caroline
1983 *Karl Marx Collective: Economy, Society and*

Religion in a Siberian Collective Farm. Cambridge, England: Cambridge University Press.
versity of California Press.

Hutchins, E.
1980 *Culture and Inference: A Trobriand Case Study.* Cambridge, Mass.: Harvard University Press.

Huyssen, A.
1986 *After the Great Divide: Modernism, Mass Culture, Postmodernism.* Bloomington and Indianapolis: Indiana University Press.

Hymes, Dell
1969a [ed.] *Reinventing Anthropology.* New York: Random House.
1969b The Uses of Anthropology: Critical, Political, Personal. In Dell Hymes, ed. *Reinventing Anthropology*, pp. 3–79. New York: Random House.

Illich, Ivan
1982 *Gender.* New York: Pantheon.

Inden, R.
1986 Orientalist Constructions of India. Modern Asian Studies 20:401–446.
1990 *Imagining India.* Oxford, England: Basil Blackwell.

Ishihara, Shintaro
1991 *The Japan That Can Say No.* New York: Simon and Schuster.

James, Alice
1964 *The Diary of Alice James.* New York: Dodd, Mead.

James, Wendy
1988 *The Listening Ebony: Moral Knowledge, Religion, and Power among the Uduk of Sudan.* Oxford, England: Clarendon Press.

Jameson, Fredric
1987 Regarding Postmodernism—A Conversation with Fredric Jameson. Social Text 17:29–54

Johnson, Allen, and Timothy Earle
1987 *The Evolution of Human Society: From Foraging Group to Agrarian State.* Stanford, Calif.: Stanford University Press.

Johnson, Jeffrey
1990 *Selecting Ethnographic Informants.* Newbury Park, Calif.: Sage.

Johnson, Mark
1987 *The Body in the Mind: The Bodily Basis of Meaning, Imagination, and Reason.* Chicago: University of Chicago Press.

Johnson-Laird, P.
1988 *The Computer and The Mind: An Introduction to Cognitive Science.* London: Fontana.

Justice, Judith
1986 *Policies, Plans, and People: Culture and Health Development in Nepal.* Berkeley: University of California Press.

Kaberry, Phyllis
1939 *Aboriginal Women: Sacred and Profane.* London: Routledge.
1952 *Women of the Grassfields: A Study of the Economic Position of Women in Bamenda, British Cameroons.* London: H. M. Stationery Office.

Kahn, Charles H.
1979 *The Art and Thought of Heraclitus.* Cambridge, England: Cambridge University Press.

Kandel, Eric
1983 From Metapsychology to Molecular Biology: Explorations into the Nature of Anxiety. American Journal of Psychiatry 140:1277–1293.

Kant, Immanuel
1965 [1781] *Critique of Pure Reason.* New York: St. Martin's.

Kapferer, Bruce
1988 *Legends of People, Myths of State: Violence, Intolerance, and Political Culture in Sri Lanka and Australia.* Washington, D.C.: Smithsonian Institution.

Kaplan, Abraham
1968 Positivism. In David Sills, ed. *International Encyclopedia of the Social Sciences*, vol. 12, pp. 389–394. New York: Macmillan.

Karamzin, N. N.
1980 Speech Delivered at the Grand Meeting of the Imperial All-Russian Academy. *Literary Criti-*

cism from 1800 to the 1820s, pp. 36–47. Moscow: Nauka. [in Russian]

Kaufmann, Walter
1968 *Nietzsche: Philosopher, Psychologist, Antichrist.* Princeton, N.J.: Princeton University Press.

Kay, P.
1984 Cultural Integration: Fact or Fiction. In R. A. Shweder and R. A. LeVine, eds. *Culture Theory,* pp. 17–18. Cambridge, England: Cambridge University Press.

Keeley, Lawrence
1988 Hunter-Gatherer Economic Complexity and "Population Pressure": A Cross-Cultural Analysis. Journal of Anthropological Archaeology 7:373–411.

Keesing, Felix M.
1958 *Cultural Anthropology: The Science of Custom.* New York: Rinehart.

Keesing, Roger M.
1972 Paradigms Lost: The New Ethnography and the New Linguistics. Southwestern Journal of Anthropology 28:299–332.
1974 Theories of Culture. Annual Reviews of Anthropology 3:73–97.
1976 *Cultural Anthropology: A Contemporary Perspective.* New York: Holt, Rinehart and Winston.
1981 *Cultural Anthropology: A Contemporary Perspective,* 2nd ed. New York: Holt, Rinehart and Winston.
1982 *Kwaio Religion: The Living and the Dead in a Solomon Island Society.* New York: Columbia University Press.
1985 Conventional Metaphor and Anthropological Metaphysics: The Problematic of Cultural Translation. Journal of Anthropological Research 41:201–218.
1987 Anthropology as Interpretive Quest. Current Anthropology 28:161–176.
1989a Exotic Readings of Cultural Texts. Current Anthropology 30(43):1–42.
1989b Anthropology in Oceania: Problems and Prospects. Oceania 60:55–59.

Keesing, R. M., and M. Jolly
1992 Epilogue. In J. Carrier, ed. *History and Tradition in Melanesian Anthropology,* pp. 224–247. Berkeley: University of California Press.

Keesing, Roger, and Robert Tonkinson
1982 Reinventing Traditional Culture. Mankind 13(4).

Keil, F. C., and N. Batterman
1984 A Characteristic-to-Defining Shift in the Development of Word Meaning. Verbal Learning and Verbal Behavior 23:221–236.

Keller, Charles, and Janet Dixon Keller
1993 Thinking and Acting with Iron. In Seth Chaiklin and Jean Lave, eds. *Understanding Practice: Perspectives on Activity and Context,* pp. 125–143. New York: Cambridge University Press.

Kelly, Raymond
1977 *Etoro Social Structure.* Ann Arbor: University of Michigan Press.

Kemper, Robert Van
1978 Fieldwork among Tzintzuntzan Migrants in Mexico City: Retrospect and Prospect. In George Foster et al,, eds. *Long-Term Field Research in Social Anthropology,* pp. 189–207. New York: Academic.

King, V. T.
1976 Migration, Warfare, and Culture Contact in Borneo: A Critique of Ecological Analysis. Oceania 46:306–327.

Kirch, Patrick V.
1985 *Feathered Gods and Fishhooks: An Introduction to Hawaiian Archaeology and Prehistory.* Honolulu: University of Hawaii Press.

Kirk, G. S.
1954 *Heraclitus: The Cosmic Fragments.* Cambridge, England: Cambridge University Press.

Kleinknecht, H.
1967 The Logos in the Greek and Hellenistic World. In G. Kittel, ed. *The Theological Dictionary of the New Testament,* vol. IV, pp. 77–91. Grand Rapids, Mich.: Eerdmans.

Kleinman, Arthur
1980 *Patients and Healers in the Context of Culture.* Berkeley: University of California Press.
1986 *Social Origins of Distress and Disease.* New Haven, Conn.: Yale University Press.
1988 *The Illness Narratives.* New York: Basic Books.

Kligman, Gail
1988 *The Wedding of the Dead: Ritual, Poetics and Popular Culture in Transylvania.* Berkeley: University of California Press.

Kluckhohn, Clyde
1936 Some Reflections on the Method and Theory of the Kulturkreislehre. American Anthropologist 38(2):157-196.
1942 Myths and Rituals: A General Theory. Harvard Theological Review 25:45-79.
1949 *Mirror for Man: The Relation of Anthropology to Modern Life.* New York: McGraw-Hill.

Knauss, P. K.
1987 *The Persistence of Patriarchy: Class, Gender and Ideology in Twentieth-Century Algeria.* New York: Praeger.

Knowlton, Barbara, Seth Ramus, and Larry Squire
1992 Intact Artificial Grammar Learning in Amnesia: Dissociation of Classification Learning and Explicit Memory for Specific Instances. Psychological Science 3(3):172-179.

Kobben, A. J. F.
1956 The Comparative Functional Method in Anthropology. Sociologus (Berlin) 6:1-18.

Kopytoff, I.
1987 The Internal African Frontier: The Making of African Political Culture. In I. Kopytoff, ed. *The African Frontier*, pp. 3-84. Bloomington: Indiana University Press.

Koroteeva, V. V., L. S. Perepelkin, and O. I. Shkaratan
1988 From Bureaucratic Centralism to Economic Integration of Sovereign Republics. Kommunist 15. [in Russian]

Kosslyn, Stephen
1988 Aspects of a Cognitive Neuroscience of Mental Imagery. Science 240:1621-1626.

Kosslyn, Stephen, Olivier Koenig, Anna Barrett, Carolyn Backer Cave, Joyce Tang, and John Gabrieli
1989 Evidence for Two Types of Spatial Representations: Hemispheric Specialization for Categorical and Coordinate Relations. Journal of Experimental Psychology: Human Perception and Performance 15:723-735.

Kottak, Conrad Philip
1967 Race Relations in a Bahian Fishing Village. Luso-Brazilian Review 4:35-52.
1972 Ecological Variables in the Origin and Evolution of African States: The Buganda Example. Comparative Studies in Society and History 14: 351-380.
1983 *Assault on Paradise: Social Change in a Brazilian Village.* New York: McGraw-Hill.
1985 When People Don't Come First: Some Lessons from Completed Projects. In Michael Cernea, ed. *Putting People First: Sociological Variables in Rural Development*, pp. 325-356. New York: Oxford University Press.
1987 *Cultural Anthropology*, 4th ed. New York: Random House.
1990 *Prime-Time Society: An Anthropological Analysis of Television and Culture.* Belmont, Calif.: Wadsworth.
1991 *Anthropology: The Exploration of Human Diversity*, 5th ed. New York: McGraw-Hill.

Kozlov, Viktor
1988 *The Peoples of the Soviet Union.* Bloomington: Indiana University Press.
1990 National Question: Paradigms, Theory and Practice. Istoria SSSR 1. [in Russian]
1991 "Imperial Nation" or Unprivileged Nationality. Moscow 1. [in Russian]

Krieger, L.
1986 Negotiating Gender Role Expectations in Cairo. In T. L. Whitehead and M. E. Conaway, eds. *Self, Sex and Gender in Cross-Cultural Fieldwork*, pp. 84-102. Urbana: University of Illinois Press.

Kroeber, Alfred
1939 Cultural and Natural Areas of Native North America. University of California Publications in American Archaeology and Ethnology 38. Berkeley: University of California Press.
1943 [ed.] Franz Boas: The Man. American Anthropologist 45(3, 2):5-26.
1948 *Anthropology.* New York: Harcourt, Brace and World.
1952 *The Nature of Culture.* Chicago: University of Chicago Press.
1953 Concluding Review. In Sol Tax, Loren

Eiseley, Irving Rouse, and Carl Voegelin, eds. *An Appraisal of Anthropology Today*, pp. 357-376. Chicago: University of Chicago Press.
1957 *Style and Civilizations*. Ithaca, N.Y.: Cornell University Press.

Kroeber, Alfred, and Harold Driver
1932 Quantitative Expression of Cultural Relationships. University of California Publications in American Archaeology and Ethnology 29:253-423. Berkeley: University of California Press.

Kroeber, Alfred L., and Clyde Kluckhohn
1963 *Culture: A Critical Review of Concepts and Definitions*. New York: Random House.

Kroeber, Alfred L., et al.
1953 *Anthropology Today: An Encyclopedic Inventory*. Chicago: University of Chicago Press.

Krupnik, I. I.
1990 National Question in the USSR: In Search of Explanations. Soviet Ethnography 4. [in Russian]

Kuhn, T.
1970 *The Structure of Scientific Revolutions*, 2nd ed. Chicago: University of Chicago Press.
1977 Second Thoughts on Paradigms. In F. Suppe, ed. *The Structure of Scientific Theories*, 2nd ed., pp. 459-481. Urbana: University of Illinois Press.

Kung, Hans
1980 *Does God Exist?* Garden City, N.Y.: Doubleday.

Kuper, Adam
1982 Lineage Theory: A Critical Retrospect. Annual Reviews of Anthropology 11:71-95.
1983 *Anthropology and Anthropologists: The Modern British School*. London: Routledge & Kegan Paul.
1988 *The Invention of Primitive Society: Transformations of an Illusion*. London: Routledge.
1989 Coming of Age in Anthropology? Nature 338:453-455.
1991 Anthropologists and the History of Anthropology. Critique of Anthropology 11(2):125-142.
1992 [ed.] *Conceptualizing Society*. London: Routledge.

Kuper, Adam, and Jessica Kuper, eds.
1985 *The Social Science Encyclopedia*. Boston: Routledge & Kegan Paul.

Ladurie, LeRoy Emmanuel
1979 *Carnival in Romans*. New York: George Brazillar.

Lakatos, I.
1970 Falsification and the Methodology of Scientific Research Programmes. In I. Lakatos and A. Musgrave, eds. *Criticism and the Growth of Knowledge*, pp. 91-195. Cambridge, England: Cambridge University Press.

Lakoff, G.
1987 *Women, Fire and Dangerous Things: What Categories Reveal about the Mind*. Chicago: University of Chicago Press.

Lakoff, G., and H. Johnson
1980 *Metaphors We Live By*. Chicago: University of Chicago Press.

Lakoff, Robin
1973 The Logic of Politeness; or, Minding Your P's and Q's. In Claudia Corum, T. Cedric Smith-Stark, and Ann Weiser, eds. *Papers from the Ninth Regional Meeting, Chicago Linguistic Society, April 13-15, 1973*, pp. 292-305. Chicago: Chicago Linguistic Society.

Lan, David
1985 *Guns and Rain: Guerrillas and Spirit Mediums in Zimbabwe*. London: James Currey; Berkeley and Los Angeles: University of California Press.

Lancaster, Nelson Roger
1988 *Thanks to God and the Revolution*. New York: Columbia University Press.

La Pierre, R. T.
1934 Attitudes vs. Actions. Social Forces 13:230-237.

Latour, Bruno
1987 *Science in Action: How to Follow Scientists and Engineers through Society*. Milton Keynes: Open University Press.
1989 *The Pasteurization of France*. Cambridge, Mass.: Harvard University Press.

Lave, J.
1988 *Cognition in Practice*. Cambridge, England: Cambridge University Press.
1990 The Culture of Acquisition and the Practice of Understanding. In J. Stigler, Richard Shweder, and Gilbert Herdt, eds. *Cultural Psychology*, pp. 309–327. Cambridge, England: Cambridge University Press.
1993 The Practice of Learning. In Seth Chaiklin and Jean Lave, eds. *Understanding Practice: Perspectives on Activity and Context*, pp. 3–32. New York: Cambridge University Press.

Lave, Jean, and Etienne Wenger
1991 *Situated Learning*. New York: Cambridge University Press.

Lawrence, Peter
1969 The State versus Stateless Societies in Papua New Guinea. In B. J. Brown, ed. *Fashion of Law in Papua New Guinea*. Sydney: Butterworth.
1971 The Garia of the Madang District. In R. M. Berndt and P. Lawrence, eds. *Politics in New Guinea*. Nedlands: University of Western Australia Press.
1984 *The Garia: An Ethnography of a Traditional Cosmic System in Papua New Guinea*. Melbourne: University of Melbourne Press.

Leach, Edmund
1954 *Political Systems of Highland Burma*. Boston: Beacon.
1961 *Rethinking Anthropology*. London: Althone.

Leacock, Eleanor Burke
1981 *The Myth of Male Dominance*. New York: Monthly Review Press.

Leaf, Murray
1979 *Man, Mind, and Science: A History of Science*. New York: Columbia University Press.

Leavitt, Gregory
1986 Ideology and the Materialist Model of General Evolution. Social Forces 65:525–553.
1989 The Disappearance of the Incest Taboo. American Anthropologist 91:116–131.
1991 Misconceptions of "Culture and Personality." Paper Presented at the 1991 American Anthropological Association Meeting.

Lehman, David
1988 Deconstructing DeMan's Life: An Academic Idol Falls into Disgrace. Newsweek, February 15, p. 62.

Leroi-Gourhan, A.
1943 *Evolution et Techniques*. Paris: A. Michel.

LeVine, Robert
1973 *Culture, Behavior, and Personality*. Chicago: Aldine.
1991 Misconceptions of "Culture and Personality." Paper presented at the American Anthropological Association Meeting.

Lévi-Strauss, Claude
1955 *Tristes Tropiques*. Paris: Plon.
1957 *Tristes Trópicos*. São Paulo: Anhembi.
1963 *Structural Anthropology*. New York: Basic Books.
1966a *The Savage Mind*. Chicago: University of Chicago Press.
1966b The Scope of Anthropology. Current Anthropology 7(2): 112–123.
1967a The Effectiveness of Symbols. In *Structuralism*, chap. 10. New York: Anchor Books.
1967b The Story of Asdiwal. In Edmund Leach, ed. *The Structural Study of Myth and Totemism*, pp. 1–47. London: Tavistock.
1969 [1949] *The Elementary Structures of Kinship*. Boston: Beacon.
1985 *The View from Afar*. New York: Basic Books.

Lévi-Strauss, Claude, and Didier Eribon
1991 *Conversations with Claude Lévi-Strauss*. Chicago: University of Chicago Press.

Levy, Robert I.
1973 *Tahitians: Mind and Experience in the Society Islands*. Chicago: University of Chicago Press.
1989 The Quest for Mind in Different Times and Different Places. In Andrew Barnes and Peter Stearns, eds. *Social History and Issues in Human Consciousness*. New York: New York University Press.
1990 *Mesocosm. Hinduism and the Organization of a Traditional Newar City in Nepal*. Berkeley: University of California Press.

Lewis, Gilbert
1980 *Day of Shining Red*. New York: Cambridge University Press.
1986 The Look of Magic. Man 21:414–437.

Lewis, Ian
1971 *Ecstatic Religion: An Anthropological Study of Spirit Possession and Shamanism.* Harmondsworth, England: Penguin.

Lewis, Lionel
1992 Review of Ernest Pascarella and Patrick Terenzini, *How College Affects Students: Findings and Insights from Twenty Years of Research.* Academe July-August: 44–47

Lewis, Oscar
1953 Controls and Experiments in Field Work. In A. L. Kroeber, ed. *Anthropology Today*, pp. 452–475. Chicago: University of Chicago Press.
1956 Comparisons in Cultural Anthropology. In William Thomas, ed. *Current Anthropology, A Supplement to Anthropology Today*, pp. 259–292. Chicago: University of Chicago Press.

Lima, Rocha
1975 *Gramatica Normativa da Lingua Portuguesa.* Rio de Janeiro: Livraria José Olympio Editora.

Limon, Jose
1989 Carne, Carnales, and the Carnavalesque: Bakhtinian *Batos*, Disorder and Narrative Discourses. American Ethnologist 16(3):471–486.

Lindesmith, Alfred, and Anselm Strauss
1950 A Critique of Culture-Personality Writings. American Sociological Review 15:587–600.

Lineton, J.
1975a An Indonesian Society and Its Universe: A Study of the Bugis of South Sulawesi (Celebes) and Their Role within a Wider Social and Economic System. Ph.D. Dissertation. School of Oriental and African Studies, University of London.
1975b Pasompe' Ugi': Bugis Migrants and Wanderers. Archipel 10:173–201.

Linke, Uli
1990 Folklore, Anthropology, and the Government of Social Life. Comparative Studies in Society and History 32(1):117–148.

Linnekin, Jocelyn
1983 Defining Tradition: Variation on the Hawaiian Identity. American Ethnologist 10:241–252.

Linton, Ralph
1937 One Hundred Per-Cent American. The American Mercury 40:427–429. (Reprinted in James Spradley James and Michael Rynkiewich, eds. *The Nacerima: Readings in American Culture*, pp. 405–406. Boston: Little, Brown. 1975.)
1940 [ed.] *Acculturation in Seven American Indian Tribes.* New York: Appleton.

Lipset, Martin S.
1959 American Intellectuals: Their Politics and Status. Daedalus: Journal of the American Academy of Arts and Sciences 88:460–486.

Llewelyn, K. N., and E. A. Hoebel
1941 *The Cheyenne Way: Conflict and Case Law in Primitive Jurisprudence.* Norman: University of Oklahoma Press.

Lloyd, Peter
1979 *Slums of Hope: Shanty Towns of the Third World.* London: Penguin.

Lock, Margaret
1986 Plea for Acceptance: School Refusal Syndrome in Japan. Social Science and Medicine 22(2):99–112.
1988a Introduction. In M. Lock and D. Gordan, eds. *Biomedicine Examined.* Dordrecht, the Netherlands: Kluwer Academic Publishers.
1988b New Japanese Mythologies: Faltering Discipline and the Ailing Housewife. American Ethnologist 15:43–61.

Lock, Margaret, and Nancy Scheper-Hughes
1990 A Critical-Interpretive Approach in Medical Anthropology: Routines and Rituals of Discipline and Dissent. In Thomas Johnson and Carolyn Sargent, eds. *Medical Anthropology: Contemporary Theory and Method*, pp. 47–72. New York: Praeger.

Loftus, E. F.
1979 *Eyewitness Testimony.* Cambridge, Mass.: Harvard University Press.

Loizos, Peter
1981 *The Heart Grown Bitter: A Chronicle of Cypriot War Refugees.* Cambridge, England: Cambridge University Press.

Lord, Albert
1960 *The Singer of Tales.* Cambridge, Mass.: Harvard University Press.

Lowie, Robert
1920 *Primitive Society.* New York: Boni and Liveright.
1937 *The History of Ethnological Theory.* New York: Holt, Rinehart and Winston.
1942 *Studies in Plains Indian Folklore.* University of California Publications in American Archaeology and Ethnology, vol. 40. Berkeley: University of California Press.
1953 Ethnography, Cultural and Social Anthropology. American Anthropologist 55:527-534.

Lukács, Georg
1965 *Ensaios sôbre Literatura.* Rio de Janeiro: Editora Civilizacao Brasileira S.A.

Lutz, Catherine
1983 Parental Goals, Ethnopsychology, and the Development of Emotional Meaning. Ethos 11: 246-262.
1987 Goals, Events, and Understanding in Ifaluk Emotion Theory. In D. Holland and N. Quinn, eds. *Cultural Models in Language and Thought,* pp. 290-312. Cambridge, England: Cambridge University Press.

Lyth, R. B.
1851 Tongan and Fijian Reminiscences. (Original in Mitchell Library, ML/B549, Sydney, Australia.)

Maalouf, A.
1984 *The Crusader through Arab Eyes.* Translated by J. Rothschild. New York: Schocken.

MacCormack, Carol, and Marilyn Strathern, eds.
1980 *Nature, Culture and Gender.* New York: Cambridge University Press.

Maclachlan, Morgan
1983 *Why They Did Not Starve: Biocultural Adaptation in a South Indian Village.* Lanham, Md.: University Press of America (Institute for the Study of Human Issues).

Madan, T. N.
1978 On Living Intimately with Strangers. In Andre Beteille and T. N. Madan, eds. *Encounter and Experience,* pp. 35-51. Delhi: Vikas Publications.

Magarey, S.
1987 That Hoary Old Chestnut, Free Will and Determinism: Culture vs. Structure, or History vs. Theory in Britain. A Review Article. Comparative Studies in Society and History 27:626-639.

Magnarella, P.
1982 Cultural Materialism and the Problem of Probabilities. American Anthropologist 84:138-145.

Maine, Sir Henry
1861 *Ancient Law.* London: Murray.

Mair, Lucy
1969 *Anthropology and Social Change.* London School of Economics Monographs on Social Anthropology 38. London: Athlone.

Malagodi, Edward
1986 On Radicalizing Behaviorism: A Call for Cultural Analysis. The Behavior Analyst 9:1-18.

Malinowski, Bronislaw
1938 Introductory Essay on The Anthropology of Changing African Cultures. International African Institute Memorandum 15:vii-xxxviii.
1944 *A Scientific Theory of Culture.* Chapel Hill: University of North Carolina Press.
1948 *Magic, Science and Religion.* New York: Doubleday.
1951 [1926] *Crime and Custom in Savage Society.* New York: Humanities.
1961 [1922] *Argonauts of the Western Pacific.* New York: Dutton & Company.

Mandelbaum, David
1968 Anthropology: Cultural Anthropology. In David Sills, ed. *International Encyclopedia of the Social Sciences,* vol. 1, pp. 313-319. New York: Macmillan.

Mangin, William
1979 Thoughts on Twenty-Four Years of Work in Peru: The Vicos Project and Me. In George Foster et al., eds. *Long Term Field Research in Social Anthropology,* pp. 65-84. New York: Academic.

Manners, Robert, and David Kaplan, eds.
1968 *Theory in Anthropology.* Chicago: Aldine.

Manolescu, Kathleen M.
1987 An Approach to the Ethnography of Farming as a Culturally Structured Technological System. Ph.D. Dissertation, University of Pennsylvania. Ann Arbor: University Microfilms International.

Marano, L.
1982 Windigo Psychosis: The Anatomy of an Emic-Etic Confusion. Current Anthropology 23: 385-412.

Marcus, George E.
1989 The Problem of the Unseen World of Wealth for the Rich: Toward an Ethnography of Complex Connections. Ethos 17(1):114-123.

Marcus, George, and Michael M. J. Fischer
1986 *Anthropology as Cultural Critique.* Chicago: University of Chicago Press.

Marcus, George, with Peter Hall
1992 *Lives in Trust: The Fortunes of Dynastic Families in Late Twentieth-Century America.* Boulder, Colo.: Westview.

Margolis, M.
1984 *Mothers and Such.* Berkeley: University of California Press.

Marriot, McKim
1966 The Feast of Love. In *Krishna: Myths, Rights, and Attitudes.* Honolulu: East-West Center Press.

Martin, Emily
1987 *The Woman in the Body: A Cultural Analysis of Reproduction.* Boston: Beacon.

Martin, M. Kay, and Barbara Voorhies
1975 *Female of the Species.* New York: Columbia University Press.

Martin, R.
1976 Explanation and Understanding in History. In J. Manninen and R. Tuomela, eds. *Essays on Explanation and Understanding,* pp. 305-334. Dordrecht, the Netherlands: Reidel.
1977 *Historical Explanation: Re-enactment and Practical Inference.* Ithaca, N.Y.: Cornell University Press.

Marx, Karl
1906 [1867-1894] *Capital: A Critique of Political Economy.* New York: Modern Library.
1956 *Selected Writings in Sociology and Social Philosophy.* Edited and translated by T. B. Bottomore. New York: McGraw-Hill.

Mascia-Leeds, F., P. Sharpe, and C. Cohen
1989 The Postmodernist Turn in Anthropology: Cautions from a Feminist Perspective. Signs 15: 7-33.

Mathews, Holly
1983 Context-Specific Variation in Humoral Classification. American Anthropologist 85:826-847.

Mauss, M.
1936 Les Techniques du Corps. Journal of Psychology 32(3-4).
1967 *The Gift: Forms and Functions of Exchange in Archaic Societies.* New York: Norton & Company.
1979 Body Techniques. In M. Mauss, *Sociology and Psychology,* pp. 97-123. London: Routledge & Kegan Paul.
1980 Techniques of the Body. Economy and Society 2(1):70-88.

Maybury-Lewis, David
1965 *The Savage and the Innocent.* Boston: Beacon.
1967 *Akwe-Shavante Society.* Oxford, England: Clarendon Press.

Mayr, E.
1982 *The Growth of Biological Thought.* Cambridge, Mass.: Belknap.

McClelland, James L., and David E. Rumelhart
1988 *Explorations in Parallel Distributed Processing: A Handbook of Models, Programs, and Exercises.* Cambridge, Mass.: M.I.T. Press.

McClelland, James L., David E. Rumelhart, and the PDP Research Group
1986 *Parallel Distributed Processing: Explorations in the Microstructure of Cognition,* vol. 2. Cambridge, Mass.: M.I.T. Press.

McCloskey, Michael, and Sam Glucksberg
1978 Natural Categories: Well Defined or Fuzzy Sets? Memory and Cognition 6(4):462-472.

McDonogh, Gary
1986 *Good Families of Barcelona: A Social History of*

Power in the Industrial Era. Princeton, N.J.: Princeton University Press.

McNabb, S. L.
1990 The Uses of "Inaccurate" Data: A Methodological Critique and Applications of Alaska Native Data. American Anthropologist 92:116-129.

Mead, Margaret
1928 *Coming of Age in Samoa.* New York: William Morrow.

Meillassoux, Claude
1981 *Maidens, Meal, and Money: Capitalism and the Domestic Community.* New York: Cambridge University Press.

Mencher, J.
1980 On Being an Untouchable in India. In E. Ross, ed. *Beyond the Myths of Culture: Essays in Cultural Materialism,* pp. 261-294. New York: Academic.

Merleau-Ponty, Maurice
1962 *Sinais.* Lisboa: Editorial Minotauro Lda.

Mervis, Carolyn, and Eleanor Rosch
1981 Categorization of Natural Objects. Annual Review of Psychology 32:89-115.

Messerschmidt, D. A., ed.
1981 *Anthropologists at Home in North America: Methods and Issues in the Study of One's Own Society.* New York: Cambridge University Press.

Michaels, Eric
1986 *The Aboriginal Invention of Television in Central Australia, 1982-1986.* Canberra: Australian Institute of Aboriginal Studies.

Mill, J. S.
1866 *Auguste Comte and Positivism.* Philadelphia, Pa.: Lippincott.
1956 [1859] *On Liberty.* New York: Liberal Arts Press.

Miller, Barbara
1981 *The Endangered Sex.* Ithaca, N.Y.: Cornell University Press.

Mills, C. W.
1940 Methodological Consequences of the Sociology of Knowledge. American Journal of Sociology 46:316-330.

Miminoshvili, Roman, and Guram Pandjikidze
1990 *The Truth about Abkhazia.* Tbilisi: Merani.

Miner, Horace
1956 Body Ritual among the Nacirema. American Anthropologist 58:503-507.

Mintz, Sidney
1985 *Sweetness and Power: The Place of Sugar in Modern History.* New York: Viking Penguin.

Mischel, Walter
1973 Toward a Cognitive Social Learning Reconceptualization of Personality. Psychological Review 80(4):252-283.

Mitchell, David
1989 How Many Memory Systems? Evidence from Aging. Journal of Experimental Psychology: Learning, Memory, and Cognition 15(1):31-49.

Mitchell, David, Alan Brown, and Dana Murphy
1990 Dissociations between Procedural and Episodic Memory: Effects of Time and Aging. Psychology and Aging 5(2):264-276.

Mitchell, J. Clyde
1957 The Kalela Dance. Aspects of Social Relationships among Urban Africans in Northern Rhodesia. Rhodes-Livingstone Paper No. 27. Manchester: Manchester University Press for Rhodes-Livingstone Institute.
1987 *Cities, Society, and Social Perception: A Central African Perspective.* Oxford, England: Clarendon Press.

Mohamad, Mahathir bin
1970 *The Malay Dilemma.* Singapore: Time Books International.

Molohon, Kathryn
1984 Response to Television in Two Swampy Creek Cree Communities on the West Coast of James Bay. Kroeber Anthropological Society Papers 63 and 64:95-103.

Moody, Anne
1968 *Coming of Age in Mississippi.* New York: Dell.

Mooney, James
1965 *The Ghost-Dance Religion and the Sioux Outbreak of 1890.* Chicago: University of Chicago Press. (Originally published in 1896 as Part 2 of the Fourteenth Annual Report of the Bureau of Ethnology to the Secretary of the Smithsonian Institution, 1892-93. Washington, D.C.: U.S. Government Printing Office.)

Moore, O. K.
1952 Nominal Definitions of "Culture." Philosophy of Science 19:245-256.

Moore, Sally Falk
1977 Individual Interests and Organization Structures: Dispute Settlements as "Events of Articulation." In Ian Hamnett, ed. *Social Anthropology and Law,* A.S.A. Monograph No. 14, pp. 159-188. London: Academic.
1978 *Law as Process.* London: Routledge & Kegan Paul.
1986 *Social Facts and Fabrications.* Cambridge, England: Cambridge University Press.
1987 Explaining the Present: Theoretical Dilemmas in Processual Ethnography. American Ethnologist 14(4):727-736.
1991 From Giving and Lending to Selling: Property Transactions Reflecting Historical Changes on Kilimanjaro. In Richard Roberts and Kristin Mann, eds. *Law in Colonial Africa.* Portsmouth, N.H.: Heinemann and Currey.

Moreno, Albrecht
1982 Bossa Nova: Novo Brasil. The Significance of Bossa Nova as a Brazilian Popular Music. Latin American Research Review 17(2):129-141.

Morgan, Lewis Henry
1870 *Systems of Consanguinity and Affinity of the Human Family.* Washington, D.C.: Smithsonian Institution.
1963 [1877] *Ancient Society or Researches in the Lines of Human Progress from Savagery through Barbarism to Civilization.* E. Leacock, ed. New York: World Publishing.

Morgan, Scott, and Elizabeth Colson, eds.
1987 *People in Upheaval.* Staten Island, N.Y.: Center for Migration Studies.

Morren, G.
1984 Warfare in the Highland Fringe of New Guinea: The Case of the Mountain Ok. In B. Ferguson, ed. *Warfare, Culture, and Environment,* pp. 169-208. Orlando, Fla.: Academic.

Morsy, S.
1991 Safeguarding Women's Bodies: The White Man's Burden Medicalized. Medical Anthropology Quarterly 5(1):19-23.

Mosko, M.
1985 *Quadripartite Structure: Categories, Relationships and Homologies in Bush Mekeo Culture.* Cambridge, England: Cambridge University Press.
1989 The Developmental Cycle among Public Groups. Man 24:470-484.

Motyl, Alexander J.
1990 *Sovietology, Rationality, Nationality Coming to Grips with Nationalism in the USSR.* New York: Columbia University Press.

Mullings, Leith
1984 *Therapy, Ideology, and Social Change.* Berkeley: University of California Press.

Munn, Nancy
1986 *The Fame of Gawa: A Symbolic Study of Value Transformation in a Massim (Papua New Guinea) Society.* Cambridge, England: Cambridge University Press.

Murdock, George Peter
1949 *Social Structure.* New York: The Free Press.
1965 *Culture and Society: Twenty-Four Essays.* Pittsburgh: University of Pittsburgh Press.

Murphy, Robert F.
1970 Basin Ethnography and Ecological Theory. In Earl H. Swanson, ed. *Languages and Cultures of Western North America: Essays in Honor of Sven S. Liljeblad,* pp. 152-171. Pocatello: Idaho State University Press.
1971 *The Dialectics of Social Life: Alarms and Excursions in Anthropological Theory.* New York: Basic Books.
1972 *Robert Lowie.* New York: Columbia University Press.
1976 Introduction: A Quarter Century of American Anthropology. In Robert Murphy, ed. *Selected Papers from the American Anthropologist, 1946-1970,*

pp. 1–22. Washington, D.C.: American Anthropological Association.
1977 Man's Culture and Woman's Nature. Annals of the New York Academy of Sciences 293:15–24.
1987 *The Body Silent.* New York: Henry Holt.

Murray, Gerald F.
1980 Population Pressure, Land Tenure, and Voodoo: The Economics of Haitian Peasant Ritual. In Eric Ross, ed. *Beyond the Myths of Culture*, pp. 295–322. New York: Academic.

Musen, Hail, and Anne Treisman
1990 Implicit and Explicit Memory for Visual Patterns. Journal of Experimental Psychology: Learning, Memory, and Cognition 16(1):127–137.

Naddaf, S.
1986 Mirrored Images: Rifa'ah al-Tahtawi and the West: Introduction and Translation. Alif, Journal of Comparative Poetics 6:Spring.

Nadel, S. F.
1947 *The Nuba.* London: Oxford University Press.
1951 *The Foundations of Social Anthropology.* London: Cohen and West.
1952 Witchcraft in Four African Societies. American Anthropologist 54:18–29.
1963 *The Foundations of Social Anthropology,* 4th ed. London: Cohen and West.

Nader, Laura
1969 Up the Anthropologist—Perspectives Gained from Studying Up. In Dell Hymes, ed. *Reinventing Anthropology*, pp. 285–311. New York: Random House.
1989a The ADR Explosion: The Implications of Rhetoric in Legal Reform. In *Windsor Yearbook of Access to Justice*, Spring.
1989b Occidentalism, Orientalism and the Control of Women. Cultural Dynamics, pp. 1–33.
1989c Post-Interpretive Anthropology. Anthropological Quarterly, Fall.
1990 *Harmony Ideology: Justice and Control in a Mountain Zapotec Village.* Stanford, Calif.: Stanford University Press.

Nagata, Judith
1979 *Malaysian Mosaic: Perspectives from a Poly-Ethnic Society.* Vancouver: University of British Columbia Press.

Nagorno-Karabakh
1988 *An Historical Essay.* Yerevan, Armenia: Academy of Sciences.

Nahaylo, Bohdan, and Victor Swoboda
1990 *Soviet Disunion: A History of Nationalities Problem in the USSR.* London: Hamish Hamilton.

Naroll, Raoul
1962 *Data Quality Control.* Glencoe, Ill.: The Free Press.

Nash, J.
1979 *We Eat the Mines and the Mines Eat Us: Dependency and Exploration in Bolivian Tin Mines.* New York: Columbia University Press.

Needham, Rodney
1971 Remarks on the Analysis of Kinship and Marriage. In Rodney Needham, ed. *Rethinking Kinship and Marriage*, pp. 1–34. London: Tavistock.
1983 *Against the Tranquility of Axioms.* Berkeley: University of California Press.

Nelson, C., and V. Olesen
1977 Veil of Illusion: A Critique of the Concept of Equality in Western Thought. Catalyst 10–11:8–36.

Nelson, G., and L. Grossberg, eds.
1988 *Marxism and the Interpretation of Culture.* Urbana and Chicago: University of Illinois Press.

Netting, Robert McC.
1968 *Hill Farmers of Nigeria.* Seattle: University of Washington Press.

Neumann, Klaus
1992 *Not the Way It Really Was: Constructing the Tolai Past.* Honolulu: University of Hawaii Press.

Newell, A., and P. S. Rosenbloom
1981 Mechanisms of Social Acquisition and the Law of Practice. In J. R. Anderson, ed. *Cognitive Skills and Their Acquisition.* Hillsdale, N.J.: Erlbaum.

Niedenthal, Paul, and Nancy Cantor
1984 Making Use of Social Prototypes: From Fuzzy Concepts to Firm Decisions. Fuzzy Sets and Systems 14:5–27.

Nimuendajú, Curt
1939 The Apinayé. Washington, D.C.: The Catholic University of America.
1946 The Eastern Timbira. University of California Publications in American Archaeology and Ethnology 14.

Nordstrom, Carolyn
1992 The Backyard Front. In Carolyn Nordstrom and JoAnn Martin, ed. *The Paths to Domination, Resistance, and Terror.* Berkeley: University of California Press.

Nordstrom, Carolyn, and JoAnn Martin, eds.
1992 *The Paths to Domination, Resistance, and Terror.* Berkeley: University of California Press.

Nyerere, Julius
1966 *Freedom and Unity.* Dar es Salaam: Oxford University Press.

Obeyesekere, Ganarath
1981 *Medusa's Hair: An Essay on Personal Symbols and Religious Experience.* Chicago: University of Chicago Press.

Oden, Gregg
1981 A Fuzzy Propositional Model of Concept Structure and Use: A Case Study in Object Formation. In G. E. Lasker, ed. *Applied Systems Research and Cybernetics,* vol.VI, pp. 2890-2897. Elmsford, N.Y.: Pergamon.
1987 Concept, Knowledge, and Thought. Annual Review of Psychology 38:203-227.

Ohnuki-Tierney, Emiko
1990 *Culture through Time: Anthropological Approaches.* Stanford, Calif.: Stanford University Press.

O'Laughlin, M. Bridget
1977 Production and Reproduction: Meillassoux's Femmes, Greniers, et Capitaux. Critique of Anthropology 8:3-32.

Olcott, Martha
1987 *The Kazakhs.* Stanford, Calif.: Stanford University Press.

Oleinyk, Boris
1990 XXVIIIth Congress of CPSU. C.97.

Oliver, Douglas
1958 An Ethnographer's Method for Formulating Descriptions of "Social Structure." American Anthropologist 60:801-826
1974 *Ancient Tahitian Society.* Honolulu: University of Hawaii Press.

O'Neill, John
1985 *The Five Bodies: The Human Shape of Modern Society.* Ithaca, N.Y.: Cornell University Press.

Ong, Aihwa
1987 *Spirits of Resistance and Capitalist Discipline.* Albany: State University of New York Press.
1988 The Production of Possession. American Ethnologist 15:28-42.

Ortner, Sherry
1974 Is Female to Male as Nature Is to Culture? In Michelle Z. Rosaldo and Louise Lamphere, eds. *Woman, Culture, and Society,* pp. 67-87. Stanford, Calif.: Stanford University Press.
1984 Theory in Anthropology since the Sixties. Comparative Studies in Society and History 26:126-166.
1989 *High Religion: A Cultural and Political History of Sherpa Buddhism.* Princeton, N.J.: Princeton University Press.
1990 Patterns of History: Cultural Schemas in the Foundings of Sherpa Religious Institutions. In E. Ohnuki-Tierney, ed. *Culture through Time: Anthropological Approaches,* pp. 57-93. Stanford, Calif.: Stanford University Press.

Ortner, Sherry, and Harriet Whitehead
1981 Introduction: Accounting for Sexual Meanings. In Sherry B. Ortner and Harriet Whitehead, eds. *Sexual Meanings,* pp. 1-27. New York: Cambridge University Press.

Ortutay, Gyula
1959 Principles of Oral Transmission in Folk Culture. Acta Ethnographica 8:175-221.

Osburn, Joseph Warren
1835 Journal of a Voyage in the Ship Emerald. Pacific Manuscripts Bureau, Microfilm 203. Hamilton Library, University of Hawaii.

Otto, Rudolph
1923 *The Idea of the Holy.* Translated by J. W. Harvey. London: Oxford University Press.

Pace, Richard B.
1987 Economic and Political Change in the Amazonian Community of Ita, Brazil. Doctoral Dissertation, University of Florida, Department of Anthropology. Ann Arbor: University of Michigan.

Padoch, C.
1982 Migration and Its Alternatives among the Iban of Sarawak. Verhandelingen van het Koninklijk Instituut voor Taal-, Land- en Volkenkunde 98. The Hague: Martinus Nijhoff.

Paige, Jeffrey
1975 *Agrarian Revolution*. New York: The Free Press.

Pain, E. A., and A. A. Popov
1990 Interethnic Conflicts in the USSR. (Some Approaches to the Study and to Practical Solution). Soviet Ethnography 1. [in Russian]

Paine, R.
1989 High-Wire Culture: Comparing Two Agonistic Systems of Self-Esteem. Man 24(4):657-672.

Pandey, G.
1990 *The Construction of Communalism in Colonial North India*. Delhi: Oxford University Press.

Parker, Richard
1990 *Bodies, Pleasures and Passions: Sexual Culture in Contemporary Brazil*. Boston: Beacon.

Parnell, Philip C.
1988 *Escalating Disputes: Social Participation and Change in the Oaxacan Highlands*. Tucson: University of Arizona Press.

Parsons, Elsie
1991 [1915-1924] *Pueblo Mothers and Children*. Santa Fe, N.M.: Ancient City Press.

Parsons, Talcott
1972 Definitions of Health and Illness in Light of American Values and Social Structure. In E. G. Jaco, ed. *Patients. Physicians and Illness*, pp. 107-127. New York: The Free Press.
1973 Culture and the Social System Revisited. In L. Schneider and C. M. Bonjean, eds. *The Idea of Culture in the Social Sciences*. Cambridge, England: Cambridge University Press.

Pascarella, Ernest, and Patrick Terenzini
1991 *How College Affects Students: Findings and Insights from Twenty Years of Research*. San Francisco: Jossey-Bass.

Passmore, John
1967 Logical Positivism. In Paul Edwards, ed. *The Encyclopedia of Philosophy*, vol. 5, pp. 52-57. New York: Macmillan.

Paulsen, A.
1981 The Archaeology of the Absurd: Comments on Cultural Materialism, Split Inheritance, and the Expansion of Ancient Peruvian Empires. American Antiquity 46:31-47.

Pausewang, S.
1973 *Methods and Concepts of Social Research in a Rural and Developing Society*. Munich: Weltforum Verlag.

Peacock, James
1986 *The Anthropological Lens: Harsh Light, Soft Focus*. New York: Cambridge University Press.

Peirce, Charles Sanders
1960 *The Collected Papers of Charles Sanders Peirce*. Charles Hartshorne and Paul Weiss, eds. Cambridge, Mass.: Harvard University Press.

Pelto, Perti, and Gretel Pelto
1975 Intra-Cultural Diversity: Some Theoretical Issues. American Ethnologist 2(1):1-18.

Pemberton, J.
1987 Musical Politics in Central Java (or How Not to Listen to a Javanese Gamelan). Indonesia 44:17-29.

Perepelkin, L. S., and O. I. Shkaratan
1989 Economic Sovereignty and Ways for Development of the Peoples. Soviet Ethnography 4. [in Russian]

Petersen, Glenn
1989 Pohnpei Ethnicity and Micronesian Nation-Building. In Michael Howard, ed. *Ethnicity and Nation-Building in the Pacific*, pp. 285-308. Tokyo: The United Nations University.

Petitto, L. A.
1987 On the Autonomy of Language and Gesture: Evidence from the Acquisition of Personal Pro-

nouns in American Sign Language. Cognition 27: 1-52.
1988 Language and the Prelinguistic Child. In F. S. Kessel, ed. *The Development of Language and Language Researchers: Essays in Honor of Roger Brown.* Hillsdale, N.J.: Erlbaum.

Piaget, Jean
1952 *The Origins of Intelligence in Children.* New York: W. W. Norton.

Pike, Kenneth L.
1954 *Language in Relation to a Unified Theory of the Structure of Human Behavior,* Part 1, Summer Institute of Linguistics, 2nd rev. ed. The Hague: Mouton, 1967.

Pilcher, William
1972 *The Portland Longshoremen: A Dispersed Urban Community.* New York: Holt, Rinehart and Winston.

Plattner, S.
1989 Ethnographic Method. Anthropology Newsletter, January.

Pocock, John G. A.
1971 *Politics, Language and Time: Essays in Political Thought and History.* New York: Atheneum.

Pool, R.
1989 Chaos Theory: How Big an Advance? Science 245:26-28.

Popper, K. R.
1957 *The Poverty of Historicism.* Boston: Beacon.
1966 *The Open Society and Its Enemies,* 5th ed. Princeton, N.J.: Princeton University Press.
1965 *Conjectures and Refutations: The Growth of Scientific Knowledge.* New York: Basic Books.

Pospisil, Leopold
1963 Kapauku Papuan Economy. Yale University Publications in Anthropology 61.

Pottier, Johan
1988 *Migrants No More: Settlement and Survival in Mambwe Villages, Zambia.* Bloomington: Indiana University Press.

Powdermaker, Hortense
1939 *After Freedom: A Cultural Study in the Deep South.* New York: Viking.
1943 The Channelling of Negro Aggression by the Cultural Process. American Journal of Sociology 48:122-300.
1962 *Copper Town: Changing Africa.* New York: Harper and Row.

Practicing Anthropology
1990 Involuntary Resettlement and Development Anthropology. Practicing Anthropology 12(3).

Price, B.
1984 Competition, Productive Intensification, and Ranked Society: Speculations from Evolutionary Theory. In B. Ferguson, ed. *Warfare, Culture, and Environment,* pp. 209-240. New York: Academic.

Quinn, Naomi
1987 Convergent Evidence for a Cultural Model of American Marriage. In D. Holland and N. Quinn, eds. *Cultural Models in Language and Thought,* pp. 173-192. Cambridge, England: Cambridge University Press.
1991 The Cultural Basis of Metaphor. In J. Fernandez, ed. *Beyond Metaphor: Trope Theory in Anthropology,* pp. 56-93. Stanford, Calif.: Stanford University Press.

Quinn, Naomi, and Claudia Strauss
n.d. A Cognitive Framework for a Unified Theory of Culture. (In preparation)

Rabinow, Paul, and William M. Sullivan, eds.
1979 *Interpretive Social Science, A Reader.* Berkeley: University of California Press.
1987 *Interpretive Social Science: A Second Look.* Berkeley: University of California Press.

Radcliffe-Brown, A. R.
1922 *The Andaman Islanders.* Cambridge: Cambridge University Press.
1950 Introduction. In A. R. Radcliffe-Brown and Daryll Forde, eds. *African Systems of Kinship and Marriage,* pp. 1-85. London: Oxford University Press.
1952a The Comparative Method in Social Anthropology. Journal of the Royal Anthropological Institute 81:15-22.
1952b *Structure and Function in Primitive Society.* Glencoe, Ill.: The Free Press.

Radin, P.
1933 *The Method and Theory of Ethnology*. New York: McGraw-Hill.
1983 [1926, ed.] *Crashing Thunder: The Autobiography of a Winnebago Indian*. Lincoln: University of Nebraska Press.

Ranger, Terence O.
1970 *The African Voice in Southern Rhodesia 1898-1930*. London: Heinemann.
1975 *Dance and Society in Eastern Africa 1890-1970: The Beni Ngoma*. Berkeley and Los Angeles: University of California Press.

Rappaport, Roy A.
1971 The Sacred in Human Evolution. Annual Review of Ecology and Systematics 2:23-44.
1979a Adaptive Structure and its Disorders. In *Ecology, Meaning, and Religion*, pp. 145-172. Berkeley, Calif.: Atlantic Books.
1979b *Ecology, Meaning, and Religion*. Richmond, Calif.: North Atlantic Books.
1979c The Obvious Aspects of Ritual. In *Ecology, Meaning, and Religion*, pp. 173-222. Berkeley: North Atlantic Books.
1979d Sanctity and Lies in Evolution. In *Ecology, Meaning, and Religion*, pp. 222-246. Berkeley: North Atlantic Books.
1984 *Pigs for the Ancestors*, enlarged ed. New Haven, Conn.: Yale University Press.
1986 Desecrating the Holy Woman. The American Scholar, Summer: 313-347.
1989 Humanity's Evolution and Anthropology's Future. Paper presented at "Assessing Developments in Anthropology," 1989 annual meeting of the American Anthropological Association, Washington, D.C.

Reber, Arthur
1992 The Cognitive Unconscious: An Evolutionary Perspective. Consciousness and Cognition 1:92-133.

Reber, Arthur, Faye Walkenfeld, and Ruth Hernstadt
1991 Implicit and Explicit Learning: Individual Differences and IQ. Journal of Experimental Psychology: Learning, Memory, and Cognition 17(5):888-896.

Redfield, James
1987 Lévi-Strauss, Claude. In Ronald Turner, ed.

Thinkers of the Twentieth Century, pp. 454-457. Chicago: St. James Press.

Redfield, Robert
1953 *The Primitive World and Its Transformations*. Ithaca, N.Y.: Cornell University Press.

Reiter, Rayna
1975a Introduction. In Rayna Reiter, ed. *Toward an Anthropology of Women*, pp. 11-19. New York: Monthly Review Press.
1975b [ed.] *Toward an Anthropology of Women*. New York: Monthly Review Press.

Rescorla, R. A.
1988 Pavlovian Conditioning: It's Not What You Think It Is. American Psychologist 43:151-160.

Revel, J.
1984 Forms of Expertise; Intellectuals and "Popular" Culture in France (1650-1800). In S. L. Kaplan, ed. *Understanding Popular Culture: Europe from the Middle Ages to the Nineteenth Century*. Berlin: Mouton.

Ribeiro, Darcy
1974 *Uirá sai à Procura de Deus: Ensaios de Etnologia e Indigenismo*. Rio de Janeiro: Paz e Terra.

Rice, K. A.
1980 *Geertz and Culture*. Ann Arbor, Mich.

Richards, Audrey
1939 *Land, Labour, and Diet in Northern Rhodesia*. New York: Oxford University Press.
1940 Bemba Marriage and Present Economic Conditions. Rhodes-Livingstone Paper 4. Livingstone: Rhodes-Livingstone Institute.
1956 *Chisungu: A Girl's Initiation Ceremony Among the Bemba of Northern Rhodesia*. New York: Grove.
1957 The Concept of Culture in Malinowski's Work. In Raymond Firth, ed. *Man and Culture: An Evaluation of the Work of Bronislaw Malinowski*, pp. 15-31. London: Routledge & Kegan Paul.

Richardson, J., and A. L. Kroeber
1940 *Three Centuries of Women's Dress Fashions: A Quantitative Analysis*. Berkeley: University of California Press.

Ricoeur, Paul
1971 The Model of the Text: Meaningful Action

Considered as a Text. Social Research 38:529-562.

Riesman, David
1952 *Faces in the Crowd.* New Haven, Conn.: Yale University Press.

Ritchie, James
1992 *Becoming Bicultural.* Wellington, New Zealand: Huia and Daphne Brasell Associates.

Robertson, A. L.
1982 *The People and the State.* Cambridge, England: Cambridge University Press.

Rogoff, Barbara
1990 *Apprenticeship in Thinking: Cognitive Development in Social Context.* New York: Oxford University Press.

Rogoff, Barbara, and Jean Lave, eds.
1984 *Everyday Cognition: Its Development in Social Context.* Cambridge, Mass.: Harvard University Press.

Romney, A. K., S. C. Weller, and W. H. Batchelder
1986 Culture as Consensus: A Theory of Culture and Informant Accuracy. American Anthropologist 88:313-338.

Rorty, Richard
1983 Postmodernist Bourgeois Liberalism. Journal of Philosophy 80:583-589.
1989 *On Ethnocentrism: A Reply to Clifford Geertz.* Michigan Quarterly Review (Summer).

Rosaldo, Michelle Z.
1974 Woman, Culture, and Society: A Theoretical Overview. In Michelle Z. Rosaldo and Louise Lamphere, eds. *Woman, Culture, and Society*, pp. 17-42. Stanford, Calif.: Stanford University Press.
1980 The Use and Abuse of Anthropology: Reflections on Feminism and Cross-Cultural Understanding. Signs: Journal of Woman in Culture and Society 5(3):389-417.

Rosaldo, M. Z., and L. Lamphere, eds.
1974 *Woman, Culture and Society.* Stanford, Calif.: Stanford University Press.

Rosaldo, Renato
1980 *Ilongot Headhunting, 1883-1974: A Study in Society and History.* Stanford, Calif.: Stanford University Press.
1989 *Culture and Truth: The Remaking of Social Analysis.* Boston: Beacon.

Rosch, Eleanor
1973a Natural Categories. Cognitive Psychology 4:328-350.
1973b On the Internal Structure of Perceptual and Semantic Categories. In Timothy Moore, ed. *Cognitive Development and the Acquisition of Language*, pp. 111-144. New York: Academic.
1975 Cognitive Representations of Semantic Categories. Journal of Experimental Psychology: General 104(3):192-233.
1977 Classification of Real World Objects: Origins and Representations in Cognition. In P. Johnson-Laird and P. Wason, eds. *Thinking: Readings in Cognitive Science.* Cambridge, England: Cambridge University Press.
1978a Cognitive Representations of Semantic Categories. Journal of Experimental Psychology 104:192-223.
1978b Principles of Categorization. In Eleanor Rosch and Barbara Lloyd, eds. *Cognition and Categorization*, pp. 27-48. Hillsdale, N.J.: Lawrence Erlbaum.
1987 Wittgenstein and Categorization Research in Cognitive Psychology. In Michael Chapman and Roger Dixon, eds. *Meaning and the Growth of Understanding*, pp. 151-166. New York: Springer-Verlag.

Rosch, Eleanor, and Carolyn Mervis
1975 Family Resemblances: Studies in the Internal Structure of Categories. Cognitive Psychology 7:573-605.

Roseberry, William
1988 Political Economy. Annual Review of Anthropology 17:161-185.

Rosenthal, D.
1980 Philosophy of Mind. Social Research 47:789-802.

Ross, E.
1978a The Evolution of the Amazon Peasantry. Journal of Latin American Studies 10:193-218.
1978b Food Taboos, Diet and Hunting Strategy: The Adaptation to Animals in Amazonian Ecology. Current Anthropology 19:1-36.

1980a Introduction. In E. Ross, ed. *Beyond the Myths of Culture*, pp. xix-xxix. New York: Academic.

1980b Patterns of Diet and Forces of Production: An Economic and Ecological History of the Ascendancy of Beef in the United States Diet. In Eric Ross, ed. *Beyond the Myths of Culture: Essays in Cultural Materialism*, pp. 181-225. New York: Academic.

1983 The Riddle of the Scottish Pig. Bioscience 33:99-106.

1987 An Overview of Trends in Dietary Variation from Hunter-Gatherer to Modern Capitalist Societies. In M. Harris and E. Ross, eds. *Food and Evolution: Toward a Theory of Human Food Habits*, pp. 7-56. Philadelphia: Temple University Press.

Ross, J.
1984 Effects of Contact on Revenge Hostilities among Achuara Jivaro. In B. Ferguson, ed. *Warfare, Culture, and Environment*, pp. 83-109. Orlando, Fla.: Academic.

Roth, P. A.
1987 *Meaning and Method in the Social Sciences.* Ithaca, N.Y.: Cornell University Press.

Rubinstein, Robert
1981 Knowledge and Political Process on Malo. In Michael Allen, ed. *Vanuatu*, pp. 135-172. New York: Academic.

Rumelhart, David E., James L. McClelland, and the PDP Research Group
1986 *Parallel Distributed Processing: Exploration in the Microstructure of Cognition*, vol. 1. Cambridge, Mass.: M.I.T Press.

Sacks, Karen
1976 State Bias and Women's Status. American Anthropologist 78:565-569.

Sacks, Oliver
1984 *A Leg to Stand On.* New York: Summit Books.

Sahlins, Marshall
1976 *Culture and Practical Reason.* Chicago: University of Chicago Press.

1977 The State of the Art in Social/Cultural Anthropology: Search for an Object. In Anthony F. C. Wallace, J. Lawrence Angel, Richard Fox, Sally McLendon, Rachel Sady, and Robert Sharer, eds. *Perspectives on Anthropology, 1976*, pp. 14-32. American Anthropological Association Special Publication 10. Washington, D.C.: American Anthropological Association.

1978 Culture as Protein and Profit. New York Review of Books, November 23, pp. 45-53.

1979 Reply to Harris. New York Review of Books, June 28, pp. 51-53.

1981 *Historical Metaphors and Mythical Realities: Structure in the Early History of the Sandwich Islands Kingdom.* Ann Arbor: University of Michigan Press.

1985 *Islands of History.* Chicago: University of Chicago Press.

1988 Cosmologies of Capitalism: The Trans-Pacific Sector of "The World System." Proceedings of the British Academy 74:1-51.

1992 *Anahulu: The Anthropology of History in the Kingdom of Hawaii*, vol. 1, *Historical Ethnography.* Chicago: University of Chicago Press.

Sahlins, Peter
1989 *Boundaries. The Making of France and Spain in the Pyrenees.* Berkeley: University of California Press.

Said, Edward
1978 *Orientalism.* New York: Pantheon.
1989 Representing the Colonized: Anthropology's Interlocutors. Critical Inquiry 15:205-225.

Sanday, Peggy
1981 *Female Power and Male Dominance: On the Origins of Sexual Inequality.* Cambridge, England: Cambridge University Press.

Sanders, W. T., and B. Price
1968 *Mesoamerica: The Evolution of a Civilization.* New York: Random House.

Sanders, W. T., R. Santley, and J. Parsons
1979 *The Basin of Mexico: Ecological Processes in the Evolution of a Civilization.* New York: Academic.

Sanderson, Stephen
1990 *Social Evolutionism: A Critical History.* Oxford, England: Basil Blackwell.

Sangren, Steven
1988 Rhetoric and the Authority of Ethnography:

"Postmodernism" and the Social Reproduction of Texts. Current Anthropology 29:405-435.

Sanjek, Roger
1977 Cognitive Maps of the Ethnic Domain in Urban Ghana Reflections on Variability and Change. American Ethnologist 5:603-622.
1991 The Ethnographic Present. Man 26(4):607-628.

Sankoff, Gillian
1971 Quantitative Analysis of Sharing and Variability in a Cognitive Model. Ethnology 10(4): 389-408.

Sapir, Edward
1916 Time Perspective in Aboriginal American Culture: A Study in Method. Geological Survey Memoir 90, Anthropological Series No. 13. Ottawa: Canada Department of Mines. (Reprinted in Selected Writings of Edward Sapir in *Language, Culture and Personality*, pp. 389-462. Berkeley: University of California Press, 1949.)
1924 Culture, Genuine and Spurious. American Journal of Sociology 29:401-429.
1925 Sound Patterns in Language. Language 1:37-51.
1938 Why Cultural Anthropology Needs the Psychiatrist. Psychiatry 1:7-12.
1949 *Selected Writings of Edward Sapir in Language, Culture and Personality*. David Mandelbaum, ed. Berkeley, Calif.: University of California Press.

Saran, A. K.
1962 A Review of Contributions to Indian Sociology, No. IV. Eastern Anthropologist 15:25-31.
1989 Gandhian Concept of Politics: Towards a Normal Society. Gandhi Marg. 1:675-727.

Schacter, Daniel
1992 Understanding Implicit Memory: A Cognitive Neuroscience Approach. American Psychologist 47(4):559-569.

Schaden, Egon
1965 Aculturaco Indigena: Ensaio sôbre os Fatôres e Tendências da Mudança Cultural de Tribos Indias em Contacto com o Mundo dos Brancos. Revista de Antropologia 13(1, 2).

Schama, S.
1987 *The Embarrassment of Riches: An Interpretation of Dutch Culture in the Golden Age*. London: Collins.

Schapera, I.
1947 *Migrant Labour and Tribal Life: A Study of Conditions in the Bechuanaland Protectorate*. Oxford, England: Oxford University Press.
1953 Some Comments on Comparative Method in Social Anthropology. American Anthropologist 55:353-362.

Scheffler, Harold
1985 Filiation and Affiliation. Man 20:1-21.

Scheper-Hughes, Nancy
1979 *Saints, Scholars and Schizophrenics: Mental Illness in Rural Ireland*. Berkeley: University of California Press.
1981 Dilemmas in Deinstitutionalization: A View from Inner City Boston. Journal of Operational Psychiatry 12(2):90-99.
1983a Benevolent Anarchy: Workable Model or Utopian Vision? Medical Anthropology Quarterly 14(2):3, 11-15.
1983b Introduction. The Problem of Bias in Androcentric and Feminist Anthropology. Women's Studies 10:109-116.
1984 Infant Mortality and Infant Care: Cultural and Economic Constraints on Nurturing in Northeast Brazil. Social Science and Medicine 19(5): 535-546.
1987a Mental in Southie. Culture, Medicine and Psychiatry 11(1):1-25.
1987b *Child Survival: Anthropological Approaches to the Treatment and Maltreatment of Children*. Dordrecht, the Netherlands: Reidel.
1988a Carnaval Marginal: A Topsy-Turvey View of the Brazilian Festival. Paper and videotape presented at the American Anthropological Association Meetings, 1988 Annual Meetings.
1988b The Madness of Hunger: Sickness, Delirium and Human Needs. Culture, Medicine and Psychiatry 12:429-458.
1990 Three Propositions for a Critically Applied Medical Anthropology. Social Science and Medicine 30:189-197.
1991 Hortense Powdermaker: The Berkeley Years (1967-1970)—A Personal Reflection. Journal of Anthropological Research 47:457-471.
1992 *Death without Weeping: The Violence of Everyday Life in Brazil*. Berkeley: University of California Press.
1993 The Way of an Anthropologist Companheira. In Brian Schwimmer and D. Michael Warren, eds. *Anthropology in the Peace Corps*, pp. 100-113. Ames: Iowa State University Press.

Scheper-Hughes, Nancy, and Margaret Lock
1986 Speaking Truth to Illness. Medical Anthropology Quarterly 17(5):137–140.
1987 The Mindful Body: A Prolegomenon to Future Work in Medical Anthropology. Medical Anthropology Quarterly. n.s., 1(1): 6–41.

Scheper-Hughes, Nancy, and A. M. Lovell, eds.
1987 *Psychiatry Inside Out.* New York: Columbia University Press.

Schiffer, M.
1983 Review of Cultural Materialism. American Antiquity 48:190–194.

Schlegel, Alice
1977 Toward a Theory of Sexual Stratification. In Alice Schlegel, ed. *Sexual Stratification*, pp. 1–40. New York: Columbia University Press.

Schneider, David M.
1964 The Nature of Kinship. Man 64:180–181.
1968 *American Kinship: A Cultural Account.* Englewood Cliffs, N.J.: Prentice-Hall.
1972 What Is Kinship All About? In Priscilla Reining, ed. *Kinship Studies in the Morgan Centennial Year*, pp. 32–63. Washington, D.C.: Anthropological Society of Washington.
1976 Notes toward a Theory of Culture. In Keith H. Basso and Henry A. Selby, eds. *Meaning in Anthropology*, pp. 197–220. Albuquerque: University of New Mexico Press.
1984 *A Critique of the Study of Kinship.* Ann Arbor: University of Michigan Press.

Schneider, David M., and Raymond T. Smith
1973 *Class Differences and Sex Roles in American Kinship and Family Structure.* Englewood Cliffs, N.J.: Prentice-Hall.

Schneider, L., and C. M. Bonjean, eds.
1973 *The Idea of Culture in the Social Sciences.* Cambridge, England: Cambridge University Press.

Schneider, W., and R. M. Shiffrin
1977 Controlled and Automatic Human Information Processing: I. Detection, Search, and Attention. Psychological Review 84:1–66.

Scholte, Bob
1969 Toward a Reflexive and Critical Anthropology. In Dell Hymes, ed. *Reinventing Anthropology*, pp. 430–457. New York: Random House.

Schwartz, Douglas
1980 Foreword. In Art Gallagher Jr. and Harland Padfield, eds. *The Dying Community*, pp. vii–ix. Albuquerque: University of New Mexico Press.

Scott, James
1985 *Weapons of the Weak: Everyday Forms of Peasant Resistance.* New Haven, Conn.: Yale University Press.

Scribner, Sylvia
1977 Modes of Thinking and Ways of Speaking: Culture and Logic Reconsidered. In P. Johnson-Laird and P. Wason, eds. *Thinking*, pp. 483–500. New York: Cambridge University Press.
1984 Studying Working Intelligence. In Barbara Rogoff and Jean Lave, eds. *Everyday Cognition: Its Development in Social Context*, pp. 9–40. Cambridge. Mass.: Harvard University Press.
1985 Knowledge at Work. Anthropology and Education Quarterly 16:199–206.

Scudder, Thayer
1982 The Impact of Big Dam-building on the Zambezi River Basin. In M. T. Farvar and J. P. Milton, eds. *The Careless Technology: Ecology and International Development*, pp. 206–235. New York: Natural History Press.
1985 A History of Development in the Twentieth Century: The Zambian Portion of the Middle Zambezi Valley and the Lake Kariba Basin. Working Paper 22. Binghamton, N.Y.: Institute for Development Anthropology.

Scudder, Thayer, and Elizabeth Colson
1978 Long-Term Field Research in Gwembe Valley, Zambia. In G. Foster, et al., eds. *Long-Term Field Research in Social Anthropology*, pp. 227–254. New York: Academic.
1980 *Secondary Education and the Formation of an Elite: The Impact of Education on Gwembe District, Zambia.* London: Academic.

Scudder, Thayer, and Jonathan Habarad
1991 Local Responses to Involuntary Relocation and Development in the Zambian Portion of the Middle Zambezi Valley. In J. A. Mollet, ed. *Migrants in Agricultural Development*, pp. 178–205. Oxford, England: Oxford University Press.

Searle, J.
1984 *Minds, Brains and Science.* Cambridge, Mass.: Harvard University Press.

Serpell, Namposya, and Monica Munachonga
1986 Needs Assessment Survey of Rural Women in the Gwembe and Namwala Districts of Southern Province, Zambia. Report No. 1 Gwembe District. Prepared for the Department of Agriculture, Ministry of Agriculture and Water Development, Home Economics Section, Lusaka, Zambia.

Service, Elman
1955 Indian-European Relations in Colonial Latin America. American Anthropologist 25:411–423.
1962 *Primitive Social Organization: An Evolutionary Perspective.* New York: Random House.
1985 *A Century of Controversy: Ethnological Issues from 1860 to 1960.* New York: Academic.

Shanin, Theodor
1989 Ethnicity in the Soviet Union: Analytical Perceptions and Political Strategies. Comparative Studies in Society and History 31(3).

Shanks, M., and C. Tilley
1987 *Reconstructing Archaeology.* Cambridge, England: Cambridge University Press.

Shapiro, Judith
1981 Anthropology and the Study of Gender. Soundings: An Interdisciplinary Journal 64(4): 446–465.

Shiffrin, R. M., and W. Schneider
1977 Controlled and Automatic Human Information Processing: II. Perceptual Learning, Automatic Attending, and a General Theory. Psychological Review 84:127–190.

Shoda, Y., W. Mischel, and J. C. Wright
1989 Intuitive Interactionism in Person Perception: Effects of Situation-Behavior Relations on Dispositional Judgments. Journal of Personality and Social Psychology 56(1):41–53.

Shore, Bradd
1991 Twice-Born, Once Conceived: Meaning Construction and Cultural Cognition. American Anthropologist 93:9–27.

Shweder, Richard
1991 *Thinking through Cultures: Expeditions in Cultural Psychology.* Cambridge, Mass.: Harvard University Press.

Shweder, R., and R. D'Andrade
1980 The Systematic Distortion Hypothesis. In R. Shweder, ed. *Fallible Judgment in Behavioral Research,* pp. 37–58. San Francisco: Jossey-Bass.

Sichone, Owen B.
1989 The Development of an Urban Working-Class Culture on the Rhodesian Copperbelt. In Daniel Miller, Michael Rowlands, and Christopher Tilley, eds. *Domination and Resistance,* pp. 290–298. London: Unwin Hyman.

Sillitoe, P.
1977 Land Shortage and War in New Guinea. Ethnology 16:71–81.

Simberloff, D.
1980 A Succession of Paradigms in Ecology: Essentialism to Materialism and Probabilism. Synthese 43:3–39.

Simon, H.
1979 *Models of Thought.* New Haven, Conn.: Yale University Press.

Singer, Merrill
1989 The Coming of Age of Critical Medical Anthropology. Social Science and Medicine 28(11): 193–1203.

Singer, Merrill, Lani Davidson, and Gina Gerdes
1988 Culture, Critical Theory and Reproductive Illness Behavior in Haiti. Medical Anthropology Quarterly 4:370–385.

Singer, Milton
1968 Culture: The Concept of Culture. In David Sills, ed. *International Encyclopedia of the Social Sciences,* vol. 3, pp. 527–543. New York: Macmillan.

Skalnik, Peter
1986 Towards an Understanding of Soviet Ethos Theory. South African Journal of Ethnology 9:157–166.
1988 Union Sovietique-Afrique du Sud: Les "Theories" de l'Etnos. Cahiers d'Etudes Africaines 27(2):157–176.

Skinner, B. F.
1984 Selection by Consequences. Behavioral and Brain Sciences 7:477-510.

Smith, Carol A.
1984a Local History in Global Context: Social and Economic Transitions in Western Guatemala. Comparative Studies in Society and History 26:109-133.
1984b Local History in Global Context: Social and Economic Transitions in Western Guatemala. Comparative Studies in Society and History 26(2): 193-228.
1987 Regional Analysis in World-System Perspective: A Critique of Three Structural Theories of Uneven Development. Review 10(4):597-648.

Smith, E. E.
1988 Concepts and Thought. In R. J. Sternberg and E. E. Smith, eds. *The Psychology of Human Thought*. Cambridge, England: Cambridge University Press.

Smith, Graham, ed.
1990 *The Nationalities Question in the Soviet Union*. London: Longman.

Smith, L., M. Sera, and B. Gattuso
1988 The Development of Thinking. In R. J. Sternberg and E. E. Smith, eds. *The Psychology of Human Thought*. Cambridge, England: Cambridge University Press.

Smith, M. G.
1969a Some Developments in the Analytical Framework of Pluralism. In L. Kuper and M. G. Smith, eds. *Pluralism in Africa*, pp. 415-458. Berkeley: University of California Press.
1969b Institutional and Political Conditions of Pluralism. In L. Kuper and M. G. Smith, eds. *Pluralism in Africa*, pp. 27-65. Berkeley: University of California Press.

Smith, Valene, ed.
1977 *Hosts and Guests: The Anthropology of Tourism*. Philadelphia: University of Pennsylvania Press. (2nd edition 1989).

Smolensky, Paul
1988 On the Proper Treatment of Connectionism. Behavioral and Brain Sciences 11: 1-74.

Social Science Theory and Soviet Nationalities
1990 Journal of Soviet Nationalities 1(2).

Solway, Jacqueline, and Richard Lee
1990 Foragers, Genuine and Spurious: Situating the Kalahari San in History (with CA treatment). Current Anthropology 31(2):109-146.

Sperber, Dan
1985 Anthropology and Psychology: Towards an Epidemiology of Representations. Man 20:73-87.

Sperber, D., and B. Wilson
1986 *Relevance: Communication and Cognition*. Cambridge, Mass.: Harvard University Press.

Spier, Leslie
1921 The Sun Dance of the Plains Indians: Its Development and Diffusion. American Museum of Natural History Anthropological Papers, vol. 16, part 7, pp. 451-527.

Spindler, George
1955 *Sociocultural and Psychological Processes in Menomini Acculturation*. University of California Publications in Culture and Society, vol. 5. Berkeley: University of California Press.

Spiro, Melford E.
1987a Collective Representations and Mental Representations in Religious Symbol Systems. In B. Kilborne and L. L. Langness, eds. *Culture and Human Nature: Theoretical Papers of Melford E. Spiro*, pp. 161-184. Chicago: University of Chicago Press.
1987b Social Systems, Personality, and Functional Analysis. In B. Kilborne and L. L. Langness, eds. *Culture and Human Nature: Theoretical Papers of Melford E. Spiro*, pp. 109-144. Chicago: University of Chicago Press.

Spradley, James
1970 *You Owe Yourself a Drunk: An Ethnography of Urban Nomads*. Boston: Little, Brown.

Spriggs, Mathew
1988 The Hawaiian Transformation of Ancestral Polynesian Society: Conceptualizing Chiefly States. In John Gledhill, Barbara Bender, and Mogens Trolle-Larsen, eds. *State and Society: The Emergence*

and Development of Social Hierarchy and Political Centralization, pp. 57-73. London: Unwin Hyman.

Squire, Larry
1987 *Memory and Brain*. New York: Oxford University Press.
1992 Declarative and Nondeclarative Memory: Multiple Brain Systems Supporting Learning and Memory. Journal of Cognitive Neuroscience 4(3):232-243.

Squire, L., B. Knowlton, and G. Musen
n.d. The Structure and Organization of Memory. (In preparation for the Annual Review of Psychology)

Squire, L. R., J. G. Ojemann, F. M. Miezin, S. E. Petersen, T. O. Videen, and M. E. Raichle
1992 Activation of the Hippocampus in Normal Humans: A Functional Anatomical Study of Memory. Proceedings of the National Academy of Sciences of the United States of America 89(5): 1837-1841.

Srinivas, M. N.
1977 *A Village Remembered*. Delhi: Oxford University Press.
1966 *Social Change in Modern India*. Berkeley: University of California Press.

Stannard, D. E.
1989 *Before the Horror: The Population of Hawai'i on the Eve of Western Contact*. Honolulu: Social Science Research Institute, University of Hawaii.

Starovoitova, Galina
1989 We Live in Expectation of a Right Decision. Soviet Karabakh, 22 August.

Steedman, Carolyn Kay
1987 *Landscape for a Good Woman: A Story of Two Lives*. New Brunswick, N.J.: Rutgers University Press.

Stein, Gertrude
1973 *Reflection on the Atomic Bomb*. Robert B. Haas, ed. Los Angeles: Black Sparrow Press.

Steward, Julian
1950 Area Research: Theory and Practice. Social Science Research Council Bulletin 63. New York:

Social Science Research Council.
1963 *Theory of Culture Change: The Methodology of Multilinear Evolution*. Urbana: University of Illinois Press.
1967 [ed.] *Contemporary Change in Traditional Societies*, 3 vols. Urbana: University of Illinois Press.
1973 *Alfred Kroeber*. New York: Columbia University Press.

Steward, Julian, et al.
1956 *The People of Puerto Rico: A Study in Social Anthropology*. Urbana: University of Illinois Press.

Stocking, George
1968 *Race, Culture, and Evolution: Essays in the History of Anthropology*. New York: The Free Press.
1976 Ideas and Institutions in American Anthropology: Thoughts toward a History of the Interwar Years. In *Selected Papers from the American Anthropologist, 1921-1945*, pp. 1-50. Washington, D.C.: American Anthropological Association.

Stokes, Martin
1992 *The Arabesk Debate: Music and Musicians in Modern Turkey*. Oxford, England: Clarendon Press.

Stoler, Ann
1989a Making Empire Respectable: The Politics of Race and Sexual Morality in 20th-Century Colonial Cultures. American Ethnologist 16(4): 634-660.
1989b Rethinking Colonial Categories: European Communities and the Boundaries of Rule. Comparative Studies in Society and History 31(1):134-161.

Stowasser, B., ed.
1987 *The Islamic Impulse*. London: Croom Helm. (Also published by the Center for Contemporary Arab Studies, Washington, D.C.)

Strathern, Marilyn
1980 No Nature, No Culture: The Hagen Case. In Carol MacCormack and Marilyn Strathern, eds. *Nature, Culture, and Gender*, pp. 174-222. Cambridge, England: Cambridge University Press.
1981a Culture in a Netbag: The Manufacture of a Subdiscipline in Anthropology. Man 16:665-688.
1981b Self-Interest and the Social Good: Some Implications of Hagen Gender Imagery. In Sherry B. Ortner and Harriet Whitehead, eds. *Sexual*

Meanings, pp. 166-191. New York: Cambridge University Press.
1987 [ed.] *Dealing with Inequality: Analyzing Gender Relations in Melanesia and Beyond.* New York: Cambridge University Press.
1988 *The Gender of the Gift: Problems with Women and Problems with Society in Melanesia.* Berkeley: University of California Press.
1992 Response. Pacific Studies 15(1):149-159.

Strauss, Claudia
1990 Who Gets Ahead? Cognitive Responses to Heteroglossia in American Political Culture. American Ethnologist 17(2):312-328.
1992 Models and Motives. In R. D'Andrade and C. Strauss, eds. *Human Motives and Cultural Models*, pp. 1-20. Cambridge, England: Cambridge University Press.

Strauss, Claudia, and Naomi Quinn
1992 Preliminaries to a Theory of Culture Acquisition. In H. L Pick, P. van den Broek, and D. C. Knill, eds. *Cognition: Conceptual and Methodological Issues*, pp. 267-294. Washington, D.C.: American Psychological Association.

Stromberg, Peter
1981 Consensus and Variation in the Interpretation of Religious Symbolism: A Swedish Example. American Ethnologist 8:544-559.

Struve, Piotr
1990 Historical Essence of the Russian Revolution and National Goals. In *Essays on Russian Revolution*, pp. 247-248. Moscow.

Suny, Ronald Grigor
1988a Nationalism and Class as Factors in the Revolution of 1917. CSST Working Paper 9, October. Ann Arbor: The University of Michigan.
1988b *The Making of the Georgian Nation.* Bloomington: Indiana University Press.
1989 Nationalist and Ethnic Unrest in the Soviet Union. World Policy Journal. Summer.

Swanson, Guy
1960 *The Birth of the Gods: The Origin of Primitive Beliefs.* Ann Arbor: University of Michigan Press.

Swartz, Marc
1982 Cultural Sharing and Cultural Theory: Some

Findings of a Five-Society Study. American Anthropologist 84:314-338.
1991 *The Way the World Is: Cultural Processes and Social Relations among the Mombasa Swahili.* Berkeley: University of California Press.

Tagil, Sven, ed.
1984 *Regions in Upheaval.* Stockholm: Esselte Stadium.

Talai, Vered Amit
1989 *Armenians in London: The Management of Social Boundaries.* Manchester, England: Manchester University Press.

Tambiah, Stanley Jeyaraja
1985 *Culture, Thought, and Social Action: An Anthropological Perspective.* Cambridge, Mass.: Harvard University Press.
1986 *Sri Lanka: Ethnic Fratricide and the Dismantling of Democracy.* Chicago: University of Chicago Press.
1988 Foreword. In Remo Guidieri, Francesco Pellizzi, and Stanley Tambiah, eds. *Ethnicities and Nations: Processes of Interethnic Relations in Latin America, Southeast Asia, and the Pacific*, pp. 1-6. Austin: University of Texas Press (for Rothko Chapel).
1990 *Magic, Science, Religion, and the Scope of Rationality.* New York: Cambridge University Press.

Taulbert, Clifton
1989 *Once Upon a Time When We Were Colored.* Tulsa, Okla.: Council Oak Books.

Taussig, Michael
1980 *The Devil and Commodity Fetishism in South America.* Chapel Hill: University of North Carolina Press.
1987 *Shamanism, Colonialism and the Wild Man: A Study in Terror and Healing.* Chicago: University of Chicago Press.
1990 Terror as Usual. Social Text. Fall/Winter: 3-20.
1992 *The Nervous System.* New York: Routledge.

Tax, Sol
1956 The Integration of Anthropology. In William Thomas, ed. *Current Anthropology: A Supplement to Anthropology Today*, pp. 313-326. Chicago: University of Chicago Press.
1964 The Uses of Anthropology. In Sol Tax, ed. *Horizons of Anthropology*, pp. 248-258. Chicago: Aldine.

1977 Anthropology for the World of the Future: Thirteen Professions and Three Proposals. Human Organization 36(3):225–234.
1988 Pride and Puzzlement: A Retrospective Record of 60 Years in Anthropology. Annual Review of Anthropology 17:1-21.

Tax, Sol, Loren Eiseley, Irving Rouse, and Carl Voegelin, eds.
1953 *An Appraisal of Anthropology Today.* Chicago: University of Chicago Press.

Taylor, C.
1980 Understanding in Human Science. Review of Metaphysics 34:3-23.

Taylor, Julie
1979 *Eva Peron: The Myths of a Woman.* Chicago: University of Chicago Press.

Tedlock, Dennis
1989 *Days from a Dream Almanac.* Urbana: University of Illinois Press.

Ter-Petrosyan, Levon
1991 Interview. Komsomolskaya Pravda. July 6, 1991.

Terray, Emmanuel
1972 *Marxism and "Primitive" Societies.* New York: Monthly Review Press.

Thapar, Romila
1989 Imagined Religious Communities? Ancient History and the Modern Search for a Hindu Identity. Modern Asian Studies, May, pp. 209–231.

Theirs, Jean Baptiste
1697-1704 *Traité des Superstitions selon l'Écriture Sainte.* Paris: A. Dezallier.

Thomas, D. H.
1989 *Archaeology.* 2nd ed. Fort Worth, Tex.: Holt, Rinehart and Winston.

Thomas, K. V.
1971 *Religion and the Decline of Magic.* London: Weidenfeld and Nicholson.

Thomas, Nicholas
1989 *Out of Time: History and Evolution in Anthropological Discourse.* Cambridge, England: Cambridge University Press.

Thomas, William, ed.
1956 *Current Anthropology: A Supplement to Anthropology Today.* Chicago: University of Chicago Press.

Thompson, E. P.
1966 *The Making of the English Working Class.* New York: Vintage.

Thornton, Robert
1988 The Rhetoric of Ethnographic Holism. Cultural Anthropology 3:285-303.

Tilley, C.
1989 Interpreting Material Culture. In I. Hodder, ed. *The Meanings of Things: Material Culture and Symbolic Expression,* pp. 185-194. London: Unwin Hyman.

Tillich, Paul
1957 *Dynamics of Faith.* New York: Harper and Row.

Timerman, Jacobo
1981 *Prisoner without a Name, Cell without a Number.* New York: Knopf.

Tishkov, Valery
1991 The Soviet Empire before and after Perestroyka. Theory and Society, Fall.

Toland, Judith
1993 Introduction: Dialogue of Self and Other: Ethnicity and the Statehood Building Process. In Judith Toland, ed. *Ethnicity and the State,* pp. 1-20. New Brunswick, N.J.: Transaction Publishers.

Tonnies, F.
1957 *Community and Society (Gesellschaft und Gemeinschaft).* East Lansing: Michigan State University Press.

Toulmin, Stephen
1982 *The Return to Cosmology. Post-modern Science and the Theology of Nature.* Berkeley: University of California Press.

Trajano Filho, Wilson
1988 Que Barulho é esse, o dos Pós-Modernos? Anuário Antropológico 86:133-152.

Trotter, R.
1988 Research Methods Training Requirements in Anthropology. Anthropology Newsletter 29(7): 28, 26.

Trouillot, M.-R.
1991 Anthropology and the Savage Slot: The Poetics and Politics of Otherness. In R. Fox, ed. *Recapturing Anthropology: Working in the Present*, pp. 17-44. Santa Fe, N.M.: School of American Research Press.

The Truth about Nagorno-Karabakh
1989 Documents and materials. Yerevan, Armenia: Yerevan University, 1989.

Turnbull, C.
1986 Sex and Gender: The Role of Subjectivity in Field Research. In T. L. Whitehead and M. E. Conaway, eds. *Self, Sex and Gender in Cross-Cultural Fieldwork*, pp. 17-27. Urbana: University of Illinois Press.

Turner, Bryan
1984 *The Body and Society: Explorations in Social Theory*. Oxford, England: Basil Blackwell.

Turner, Terrence
1980 The Social Skin. In J. Cherfas and R. Lewin, eds. *Not Work Alone*, pp. 112-140. London: Temple Smith.

Turner, Victor
1969 *The Ritual Process: Structure and Anti-Structure*. Chicago: Aldine.
1974 *Dramas, Fields, and Metaphors: Symbolic Action in Human Society*. Ithaca, N.Y.: Cornell University Press.

Twain, Mark
1962 *Letters from the Earth*. New York: Harper & Row.

XXVIIIth Congress of the Communist Party of the Soviet Union
1990 Session on "National Politics of CPSU." Bulletin for Delegates of the Congress. Moscow. [in Russian]

Tyler, Stephen
1969 [ed.] *Cognitive Anthropology*. New York: Holt, Rinehart and Winston.

1986 Post-Modern Ethnography: From Document of the Occult to Occult Document. In J. Clifford and G. Marcus, eds. *Writing Culture: The Poetics and Politics of Ethnography*, pp. 122-140. Berkeley: University of California Press.

Tylor, Edward Burnett
1889 On a Method of Investigating the Development of Institutions; Applied to Laws of Marriage and Descent. Journal of the Royal Anthropological Institute 18:245-272.

1958 [1871] *Primitive Culture*. New York: Harper and Row.

Underhill, Ruth
1936 *The Autobiography of a Papago Woman*. Menasha, Wisc.: American Anthropological Association.

Unger, Roberto Mangabeira
1975 *Knowledge and Politics*. New York: The Free Press.

Vaidyanathan, A., K. N. Nair, and M. Harris
1982 Bovine Sex and Species Ratios in India. Current Anthropology 23:365-383.

Valeri, Valerio
1985 *Kingship and Sacrifice: Ritual and Society in Ancient Hawaii*. Chicago: University of Chicago Press.

Valery, Paul
1989 Some Simple Reflections on the Body. In M. Feher, R. Naddaff, and N. Tazi, eds. *Fragments for a History of the Human Body*, pp. 394-405. New York: Zone.

Van Gennep, Arnold
1960 *The Rites of Passage*. Chicago: University of Chicago Press.

Van Binsbergen, Wim M. J., and Matthew Schofeleers, eds.
1985 *Theoretical Explorations in African Religion*. London: Kegan Paul International.

Varenne, Hervé
1989 Collective Representation in American

Anthropological Conversations: Individual and Culture. Current Anthropology 25(3):281-300.

Vargas, Ernest
1985 Cultural Contingencies. Review of Marvin Harris *Cannibals and Kings*. Journal of the Experimental Analysis of Behavior 43:419-428.

Vayda, A. P.
1980 Buginese Colonization of Sumatra's Coastal Swamplands and Its Significance for Development Planning. In E. C. F. Bird and A. Soegiarto, eds. *Proceedings of the Jakarta Workshop on Coastal Resources Management*, pp. 80-87. Tokyo: United Nations University.
1982 Foreword. In Christine Padoch, *Migration and Its Alternatives*. Verhandelingen van het Koninklijk Instituut voor Taal-, Land- en Volkenkunde 98. The Hague: Martinus Nijhoff.
1983 Progressive Contextualization: Methods for Research in Human Ecology. Human Ecology 11:265-281.
1986 Holism and Individualism in Ecological Anthropology. Reviews in Anthropology 13:295-313.
1987a Explaining What People Eat: A Review Article. Human Ecology 15:493-510.
1987b Reply to Harris. Human Ecology 15:519-521.
1988 Actions and Consequences as Objects of Explanation in Human Ecology. Environment, Technology, and Society 51:2-7 (Also in R. J. Borden, et al., eds. *Human Ecology: Research and Applications*, pp. 9-18. College Park. Md.: Society for Human Ecology.)
1989 Explaining Why Marings Fought. Journal of Anthropological Research 45:159-177.

Vayda, A. P., and A. Sahur
1985 Forest Clearing and Pepper Farming by Bugis Migrants in East Kalimantan: Antecedents and Impact. Indonesia 39:93-110.

Verdon, Michel
1983 *The Abutia Ewe of West Africa: A Chiefdom that Never Was*. Studies in the Social Sciences No. 38. Berlin and New York: Mouton.

Vincent, Joan
1986 System and Process, 1974-1985. Annual Review of Anthropology 15:99-119.

Voget, Fred
1975 *A History of Ethnology*. New York: Holt, Rinehart and Winston.

Vogt, Evon
1960 On the Concepts of Structure and Process in Cultural Anthropology. American Anthropologist 62: 18-33.

Volkman, Toby Alice
1990 Vision and Revisions: Toraja Culture and the Tourist Age. American Ethnologist 17(l):91-110.

Wagley, Charles
1953 *Amazon Town: A Study of Man in the Tropics*. New York: Macmillan.

Wagner, Roy
1986 *Asiwinarong: Ethos, Image, and Social Power among the Usen Barok of New Ireland*. Princeton, N.J.: Princeton University Press.

Wallace, Anthony F. C.
1961 *Culture and Personality*. New York: Random House.
1965 Driving to Work. In Melford Spiro, ed. *Context and Meaning in Anthropology*, pp. 277-292. New York: The Free Press.
1966a *Religion: An Anthropological View*. New York: Random House.
1966b Review of I. C. Jarvie's *The Revolution in Anthropology*. American Anthropologist 68:1254-1255.
1970 *Culture and Personality*, 2nd ed. New York: Random House.

Wallerstein, I.
1974 *The Modern World-Systems: Capitalist Agriculture and the Origins of the European World-Economy in the Sixteenth Century*. New York: Academic.
1980 *The Modern World System II: Mercantilism and the Consolidation of the European World-Economy, 1600-1750*. New York: Academic.

Warner, Richard
1985 *Recovery from Schizophrenia: Psychiatry and Schizophrenia*. Boston: Routledge & Kegan Paul.

Warner, W. Lloyd, and Paul Lunt
1941 *The Social Life of a Modern Community*. New Haven, Conn.: Yale University Press.
1942 *The Status System of a Modern Community*. New Haven, Conn.: Yale University Press.

Wax, R.
1986 Gender and Age in Fieldwork and Field-

work Education: "Not Any Good Thing Is Done by Man Alone." In T. L. Whitehead and M. E. Conway, eds. *Self, Sex and Gender in Cross-Cultural Fieldwork*, pp. 129-150. Urbana: University of Illinois Press.

Weber, Max
1946 [1915] The Social Psychology of the World Religions. In H. Gerth and C. Wright Mills, eds. *From Max Weber: Essays in Sociology*, pp. 267-301. New York: Oxford University Press.

Webster, D.
1985 Surplus, Labor, and Stress in Late Classic Maya Society. Journal of Anthropological Research 41:375-399.

Webster, Steven
1982 Dialogue and Fiction in Ethnography. Dialectical Anthropology 7:91-102.

Webster's Ninth New Collegiate Dictionary
1984 Springfield, Mass.: Merriam-Webster.

Weiner, Annette
1976 *Women of Value, Men of Renown: New Perspectives on Trobriand Exchange*. Austin: University of Texas Press.
1979 Trobriand Kinship from Another View: The Reproductive Power of Women and Men. Man 14:328-348.
1983 "A World of Made is Not a World of Born: Doing Kula in Kiriwina." In J. W. Leach and E. R. Leach, eds. *The Kula: New Perspectives on Massim Exchange*, Cambridge, England: Cambridge University Press.
1992 Anthropology's Lessons for Cultural Diversity. The Chronicle of Higher Education Section 2:B1-B2.

Weinsheimer, J. C.
1985 *Gadamer's Hermeneutics: A Reading of Truth and Method*. New Haven, Conn.: Yale University Press.

Weisberg, R. W.
1980 *Memory, Thought and Behavior*. New York: Oxford University Press.

Weisner, Thomas S.
1990 Nonconventional Family Lifestyles and Sex Typing in Six-Year-Olds. Child Development 61:1915-1933.

Weller, Susan
1984 Consistency and Consensus among Informants: Disease Concepts in a Rural Mexican Village. American Anthropologist 86:966-975.

Werbner, Richard P.
1989 *Ritual Passage, Sacred Journey: The Form, Process and Organization of Religious Movement*. Washington, D.C.: Smithsonian Institution Press; Manchester, England: Manchester University Press.

Wexler, Kenneth, and Kimball Romney
1972 Individual Variations in Cognitive Structures. In Kimball Romney, Roger Shepard, and Sara Nerlove, eds. *Multidimensional Scaling*, pp. 73-92. New York: Seminar Press.

White, Geoffrey, and John Kirkpatrick
1985 *Person, Self, and Experience: Exploring Pacific Ethnopsychologies*. Berkeley: University of California Press.

White, Leslie
1949 *The Science of Culture: A Study of Man and Civilization*. New York: Grove.

Whitehead, T. L., and M. E. Conaway, eds.
1986 *Self, Sex and Gender in Cross-Cultural Fieldwork*, pp. 17-27. Urbana: University of Illinois Press.

Whiting, Beatrice
1950 *Paiute Sorcery*. Viking Fund Publications in Anthropology 15. New York: Viking Fund.

Wikan, Unni
1990 *Managing Turbulent Hearts: A Balinese Formula for Living*. Chicago: University of Chicago Press.
1992 Beyond the Words: The Power of Resonance. American Ethnologist 19(3):460-482.

Williams, Raymond
1977 *Marxism and Literature*. London: Oxford University Press.
1983 *Culture and Society, 1970-1950*. New York: Columbia University Press.

Willingham, Daniel, Mary Jo Nissen, and Peter Bullemer
1989 On the Development of Procedural Knowledge. Journal of Experimental Psychology: Learning, Memory, and Cognition 15(6):1047-1060.

Willis, Paul
1981 *Learning to Labor: How Working Class Kids Get Working Class Jobs.* New York: Columbia University Press.

Wilson, Godfrey
1941-1942 An Essay on the Economics of Detribalization in Northern Rhodesia. Rhodes-Livingstone Institute Papers 5, 6.

Wilson, Godfrey, and Monica Wilson
1945 *The Analysis of Social Change, Based on Observations in Central Africa.* Cambridge, England: Cambridge University Press.

Wilson, Monica
1977 *For Men and Elders.* New York: Africana.

Wilson, P. J.
1977 The Problem with Simple Folk. Natural History, December, pp. 26-32.

Winch, P.
1958 *The Idea of a Social Science and Its Relation to Philosophy.* London: Routledge & Kegan Paul.

Wissler, C.
1917 *The American Indian: An Introduction to the Anthropology of the New World.* New York: McMurtrie. (Republished 1922. London: Oxford University Press.)

Wittgenstein, Ludwig
1956 *Remarks on the Foundations of Mathematics.* Oxford, England: Blackwell.
1958 *Philosophical Investigations*, 3rd ed. Translated by G.E.M. Anscombe. New York: Macmillan.
1969 *On Certainty.* New York: Harper and Row.

Wolf, Eric
1957 Closed Corporate Peasant Communities in Mesoamerica and Central Java. Southwestern Journal of Anthropology 13:1-18.
1964 *Anthropology.* Englewood Cliffs, N.J.: Prentice-Hall.
1969 American Anthropologists and American Society. In Dell Hymes, ed. *Reinventing Anthropology*, pp. 251-263. New York: Random House.
1980 They Divide and Subdivide and Call It Anthropology. New York Times, December 14, sec. IV, p. 20.

1982 *Europe and the People without History.* Berkeley: University of California Press.

Wright, J. C., and W. Mischel
1988 Conditional Hedges and the Intuitive Psychology of Traits. Journal of Personality and Social Psychology 55(3):454-469.

Wrong, Dennis
1993 The Present Condition of American Sociology. A Review Article. Comparative Studies in Society and History 35(1):183-196.

Yamskov, A. N.
1991 Interethnic Conflicts in Transcaucus: Causes and Tendencies. Polis 2. [in Russian]

Yanagisako, Sylvia Junko
1978 Variance in American Kinship: Implications for Cultural Analysis. American Ethnologist 5:15-29.
1979 Family and Household: The Analysis of Domestic Groups. Annual Review of Anthropology 8:161-205.
1985 *Transforming the Past: Tradition and Kinship among Japanese Americans.* Stanford, Calif.: Stanford University Press.
1987 Mixed Metaphors: Native and Anthropological Models of Gender and Kinship Domains. In Jane Fishburne Collier and Sylvia Junko Yanagisako, eds. *Gender and Kinship: Essays toward a Unified Analysis*, pp. 86-118. Stanford, Calif.: Stanford University Press.

Yengoyan, Aram A.
1986 Theory in Anthropology: On the Demise of the Concept of Culture. Comparative Studies in Society and History 28:368-374.

Young, Allen
1980 The Discourse on Stress and the Reproduction of Conventional Knowledge. Social Science and Medicine 14B:133-146.
1982 The Anthropologies of Illness and Sickness. Annual Review of Anthropology 11:257-285.
1988 Unpacking the Demoralization Thesis. Medical Anthropology Quarterly 2(1):3-16.
1989 The Moral Order of a Psychiatric Unit Treating War Related Post-Traumatic Stress Disorder. Paper presented at the 1989 Annual Meeting of the American Anthropological Association.

Name Index*

---

*Note: Page numbers in **bold face** indicate contributions to this volume; page numbers in *italic* indicate Intellectual Roots.

Subject Index